THE MENORAH TREASURY

Frontispiece of John Selden's *De Jure Naturali*, Strasburg, 1665 • *Noah Teaching the Nations His Commandments*

THE

MENORAH TREASURY

Harvest of Half a Century

EDITED BY

LEO W. SCHWARZ

The Jewish Publication Society of America

5733–1973 : PHILADELPHIA

THE
JACOB R. SCHIFF
★ LIBRARY ★
OF JEWISH
CONTRIBUTIONS TO
AMERICAN DEMOCRACY

Number 23 in The Series

Copyright © 1964 by
The Jewish Publication Society of America
First edition, second printing, 1973
ISBN 0–8276–0021–6
Library of Congress Catalog Card Number 64-16760
Manufactured in the United States of America
by The Haddon Craftsmen

Designed by Sidney Feinberg

TO

HENRY HURWITZ

EDITOR OF THE MENORAH JOURNAL
1915-1961

and

The Menorah Writers

This volume was made possible by the Jacob R. Schiff Fund and the generosity of a number of individuals and foundations who valued and admired the work of the Menorah movement and the late Henry Hurwitz.

Foreword

THE MENORAH JOURNAL was an outgrowth of the Menorah movement which originated at Harvard University in 1906 and rapidly spread to over eighty colleges and universities in the United States and Canada. The object of the movement was to advance Jewish culture and ideals through study and creative expression and to enrich and clarify the life of Jewry as an integral part of the life of mankind. Apart from the influence of the movement upon several generations of students and through them upon the Jewish American community, its enduring contribution was the publication of *The Menorah Journal* for almost half a century. No other literary or scholarly Jewish journal published during that period (1915-1962) equalled *The Menorah Journal* in scope and distinction.

The first issue of *The Menorah Journal*, published in January 1915, announced its policy in these words:

Conceived as it is and nurtured as it must continue to be in the spirit that gave birth to the Menorah idea, *The Menorah Journal* is under compulsion to be absolutely non-partisan, an expression of all that is best in Judaism and not merely of some particular sect or school or locality or group of special interests; fearless in telling the truth; promoting constructive thought rather than aimless controversy; animated with the vitality and enthusiasm of youth; harking back to the past that we may deal more wisely with the present and the future; recording and appreciating Jewish achievement, not to brag, but to bestir ourselves to emulation and to deepen the consciousness of *noblesse oblige*; striving always to be sane and level-headed; offering no opinions of its own, but providing an orderly platform for the discussion of mooted questions that really matter; dedicated first and foremost to the fostering of the Jewish "humanities" and the furthering of their influence as a spur to human service.

The pages of *The Menorah Journal* are an expression of that spirit and policy. The editors won the collaboration of established scholars and writers and public-spirited men and women in the community. Nor was this all. Their notable achievement was the continual fostering of fresh talent in art, music and letters. One could call a roll of almost two hundred such young artists, essayists, journalists, poets and storytellers, many of whom have since won international repute.

Moreover, *The Menorah Journal* was not only an organ of creative expression; it became the fomenter and forum of original thought among Jews both here and abroad. The fostering of a cultural humanism set into motion an intellectual ferment that broke the trammels of the prevailing formalism and brought about the examination of Jewish life and issues from the standpoint of modern intelligence and scientific criticism. The ideal of humanism challenged the best Jewish minds to produce a future worthy of the past. Fresh insights and interpretations by historians, philosophers and social thinkers adorned issue after issue, and their writings were discussed in the general journals. In *The New Republic* of December 23, 1925, for example, Waldo Frank spoke of the *Menorah* as "the most promising Jewish activity in the United States. It corroborates the feeling that America is indeed coming of age. For it is very close to the self-critical and creative temper of the American youth everywhere, confronted as we all are with an inherited chaos of deformed and misapplied ideals from which we must make order and on which we must ineluctably build our future." Three years later, in an issue inaugurating *The Menorah Journal* as a monthly magazine, an editorial stated: "It is for us to reassert the Jewish conception of the wholeness of human life. The whole is religious and must be sanctified. It cannot be divided up into sacred and profane. And the whole life of ours must be humanistic, seeking the good of man in this world, in the free but disciplined cultivation of all of our human faculties and quests."

The application of this policy had splendid results. For fifteen years *The Menorah Journal* flourished. But by 1930 the Great Depression had taken its toll. Both the Menorah movement and *The Journal* received a body blow from which they never recovered. Publication continued but without the regularity that is essential to growth. That *The Journal* was published at all was due to the devotion, skill and ingenuity of Henry Hurwitz. His friends and admirers joined to make possible a Valedictory Issue in 1962 in honor of his memory.

The idea of a Menorah anthology is not new. As early as 1923 a tentative table of contents for a volume of Menorah essays was drawn up, but attempts to interest a publisher came to nothing. During the thirties and forties a small fraction of the material was incorporated in anthologies and textbooks. Then, in the Spring-Summer issue, 1952, an announcement appeared of a plan—to mark the fortieth year of publication—of bringing out the first volume of *The Menorah Treasury*, "eventually to consist of ten or twelve volumes. . . . Each volume will be devoted to one *genre* of writing—essays (social, historical, religious, philosophical), drama, poetry, short stories and sketches, letters from abroad, and discussion of books. A volume or two will be given to art—critiques and reproductions." This ambitious plan, like other imaginative Menorah projects, for instance the Menorah College and the Menorah Collegium, did not reach fruition. After the termination of the Menorah Association and *The Menorah Journal* by the Board of Trustees in 1963, the Jewish Publication Society of America agreed to publish the present one-volume Menorah anthology.

This *Menorah Treasury* is designed to present selections of prose and verse that represent the spirit of *The Menorah Journal*. They have been chosen for their combination of intrinsic merit and cultural relevance. Hence the arrangement of the contents is thematic, bringing into focus the dominant ideas and ideals of the Jewish heritage and the perennial issues of contemporary Jewish life. The book clearly shows that by maintaining a high level of thought and literary excellence, *The Menorah Journal* both expressed what is best in Judaism and made a contribution to American culture.

Much excellent material had to be omitted because it did not fit into the structure of the book. One may disagree with the plan to issue a dozen volumes; yet few will disagree that it would require another volume or two to make available things memorable and significant that otherwise will collect dust in issues of *The Menorah Journal* that are either rare or unobtainable.

It was Henry Hurwitz who conceived and nurtured *The Menorah Journal* and served as its Editor from beginning to end. It is a pity that he could not have survived another three years to celebrate the jubilee of the publication. I came to know him when I was an undergraduate and collaborated with him in many Menorah undertakings since the late twenties. He possessed a cultivated mind and above all he was a man of taste and imagination. By matchless skill and boundless devotion, he made *The Menorah Journal* what he intended it to be—a magazine of intellectual distinction and superior craftsmanship. His influence will

abide in the one hundred and fifty-seven issues of *The Journal* he bequeathed as the cultural inheritance of American Jewry, and perhaps
even more so in the periodicals for which it serves as a model and in
the men and women who felt and thought with *The Menorah Journal*
for two generations.

To help readers place the selections in the perspective of times in
which they were written, the date of publication has been placed at the
end of each selection. The issues of *The Journal* in which the selections
appeared are fully identified in the Biographical Notes.

I wish to thank the Jewish Publication Society of America and its
Editor, Dr. Solomon Grayzel, for their interest in the undertaking and
their courage in publishing the book.

LEO W. SCHWARZ

Contents

❦

CHRONICLES

THE SPIRIT OF IRONY

POETS' LEGACY

MAN THE CREATOR

THE PROMISE OF AMERICA

Illustrations

✥

(xvii)

PROLOGUE

Menorah

⌘

WILLIAM ELLERY LEONARD

We've read in legends of the books of old
How deft Bezalel, wisest in his trade,
At the command of veilèd Moses made
The seven-branched candlestick of beaten gold—
The base, the shaft, the cups, the knops, the flowers,
Like almond blossoms—and the lamps were seven.

We know at least that on the templed rock
Of Zion hill, with earth's revolving hours
Under the changing centuries of heaven,
It stood upon the solemn altar block,
By every Gentile who had heard abhorred—
The holy light of Israel of the Lord;
Until that Titus and the legions came
And battered the walls with catapult and fire,
And bore the priests and candlestick away,
And, as memorial of fulfilled desire,
Bade carve upon the arch that bears his name
The stone procession ye may see today
Beyond the Forum on the Sacred Way,
Lifting the golden candlestick of fame.

The city fell, the temple was a heap;
And little children, who had else grown strong
And in their manhood venged the Roman wrong,
Strewed step and chamber in eternal sleep.
But the great vision of the sevenfold flames
Outlasted the cups wherein at first it sprung.
The Greeks might teach the arts, the Romans law;

The heathen hordes might shout for bread and games;
Still Israel, exalted in the realms of awe,
Guarded the Light in many an alien air,
Along the borders of the midland sea
In hostile cities, spending praise and prayer
And pondering on the larger things to be—
Down through the ages, when the Cross uprose
Among the northern Gentiles to oppose:
Then huddled in the ghettos, barred at night,
In lands of unknown trees and fiercer snows,
They watched forevermore the Light, the Light.

The main seas opened to the west. The Nations
Covered new continents with generations
That had their work to do, their thought to say;
And Israel's hosts from bloody towns afar
In the dominions of the ermined Czar,
Seared with the iron, scarred with many a stroke,
Crowded the hollow ships but yesterday
And came to us who are tomorrow's folk.
And the pure Light, however some might doubt
Who mocked their dirt and rags, had not gone out.

The holy Light of Israel hath unfurled
Its tongues of mystic flame around the world.
Empires and Kings and Parliaments have passed;
Rivers and mountain chains from age to age
Become new boundaries for man's politics.
The navies run new ensigns up the mast,
The temples try new creeds, new equipage;
The schools new sciences beyond the six.
And through the lands where many a song hath rung
The people speak no more their fathers' tongue.
Yet in the shifting energies of man
The Light of Israel remains her Light.
And gathered to a splendid caravan
From the four corners of the day and night,
The chosen people—so the prophets hold—
Shall yet return unto the homes of old

Under the hills of Judah. Be it so.
Only the stars and moon and sun can show
A permanence of light to hers akin.

What is that Light? Who is there that shall tell
The purport of the tribe of Israel?—
In the wild welter of races on that earth
Which spins in space where thousand other spin
The casual offspring of the Cosmic Mirth
Perhaps—what is there any man can win,
Or any nation? Ultimates aside,
Men have their aims, and Israel her pride.
She stands among the rest, austere, aloof,
Still the peculiar people, armed in proof
Of Selfhood, whilst the others merge or die.
She stands among the rest and answers: "I,
Above ye all, must ever gauge success
By ideal types, and know the more and less
Of things as being in the end defined,
For this our human life by righteousness.
And if I base this in Eternal Mind—
Our fathers' God in victory or distress—
I cannot argue for my hardihood,
Save that the thought is in my flesh and blood,
And made me what I was in olden time,
And keeps me what I am today in every clime."

(—1915)

THE HERITAGE

The Twilight of Hebraic Culture

❧〰❧

MAX L. MARGOLIS

So LONG as Jewish psalms are sung in the cathedrals of Christendom and Jewish visions are rehearsed by Christian catechumens, the Synagogue will continue to hold in veneration the chest where reposes its chiefest glory. Surely a book which thrills the religious emotions of civilized mankind cannot but be an object of pride to the people that produced it. Stupendous as the literary output of the Jewish people has been in post-biblical times, the Scriptures stand on a footing of their own. Throughout the era of the dispersion they have held their unique position and have exercised a most potent influence on the Jewish soul. And the modern man taught by Lowth and Herder, and the modern Jew under the spell of Mendelssohn and the Haskalah, have their minds open to the aesthetic side of the "Bible as literature."

To the Jew, however, the Scriptures are possessed of an interest beyond the religious and literary. They are the record of his achievements in the past when his foot rested firm and steady on native soil, of a long history full of vicissitudes from the time when the invaders battled against the kings of Canaan to the days when the last visionary steeled the nation's endurance in its struggle with the heathen. They are the charter of Jewish nobility, linking those of the present to the wanderer from Ur of the Chaldees.

As a finished product the Hebrew Scriptures came after the period of national independence. When canon-making was in its last stage, Jerusalem was a heap of ruins. The canon was the supreme effort of Judaea—throttled by the legions of Rome—withdrawing to its inner defences. The sword was sheathed and deliverance was looked for from the clouds. The Scriptures were to teach the Jew conduct and prayer, and the chidings of the prophets were listened to in a penitential mood, but also joyfully because of the consolations to which they led. The canon-makers had an eye to the steadying of a vanquished people

(9)

against the enemy without and the foe within. For there arose teachers who proclaimed that the mission of the Jew was fulfilled: free from the fetters of a narrow nationalism, of a religion bound up with the soil, he was now ready to merge his individuality with the large world when once it accepted that measure of his teaching suited to a wider humanity. The temple that was made with hands was destroyed, and another made without hands was building where men might worship in spirit and truth. The dream was fascinating, the danger of absorption was acute, because it was dressed up with the trappings of an ideal to which many believed the Scriptures themselves pointed.

There was a much larger range of writings in Palestine and a still larger in Egypt. The list included historical works carrying on the story of the people's fortunes beyond Alexander the Great; novelistic tales like that of the heroic Judith luring the enemy of her people to destruction, or that exquisite tale of Jewish family life as exemplified by the pious Israelite captive Tobit; books like the wise sayings of Jesus, son of Sirach, the Wisdom of Solomon, or the Psalms of Solomon, all modelled after patterns in the canon; midrashic expositions of the law, like the Little Genesis; apocalyptic visions going by the name of Enoch and the Twelve Patriarchs and Moses and Isaiah and Esdras, whose prototype may be sought in the canonical Daniel. Over and above the three parts which the Synagogue accepted there were a fourth and fifth; but by an act of exclusion the canon was concentrated upon the three and the others were cast overboard. The canon was the creation of the Pharisaic doctors, who drew a line at a point of their own choosing, and decreed that writings "from that time onward" did not defile the hands.

THE MAKING OF THE CANON BY THE PHARISEES

The Pharisees held the ground when the nation had politically abdicated. The war with Rome had been brought on by the intransigent hotspurs of Galilee and the commune of Jerusalem. John, son of Zakkai, parleyed with the enemy that Jamnia with its House of Study might go unscathed. There the process began which culminated in the gigantic storehouse of legal lore which was to dominate Jewish life and Jewish literature for centuries, commentary being piled upon commentary and code upon code. For in the sum total of Scriptures the Torah was admittedly to be the chief cornerstone, albeit prophecy and wisdom had not lost their appeal; and in moments of relaxation or when addressing their congregations worn out with the strife of the present, the scholars of the wise brought out of the ancient stock many a legend and quaint saying and even apocalyptic vision, transporting the mourners for Zion into the ecstasies of the future redemption. While official Judaism was committed to the dialectics of the Halakah, in the unofficial Haggadah mysticism exercised a potent influence by underground channels, as it were, issuing in later days in Kabbalah and offsetting the rational philosophies borrowed from Hellas. For the time being, however, the dominant note was legistic, Pharisean.

The Pharisees had been lifted by the national catastrophe into the leading position. They had previously been a party among many parties, and their Judaism one of the many varieties. The Sadducees, their chief opponents, had a literature of their own: the day upon which their "Book of Decrees" was consigned to destruction was made a legal holiday upon which fasting was prohibited. But even writings which were lightly touched by the Sadducee spirit were frowned upon: the Siracide was barely tolerated on the outside because he made light of individual immortality, and believed in the eternity of Israel and the Zadokite priesthood. The Pharisees had been on the opposition during the latter period of the Maccabeans: so with partisan ruthlessness they excluded from the canon the writings commemorative of the valorous deeds of those priest-warriors who freed the people from foreign overlordship and restored the Davidic boundaries of the realm. Because the apocalyptic visions inclined to teachings not acceptable to the dominant opinion, they were declared not only heterodox, heretical, but worthy of destruction. Had the stricter view prevailed, the sceptical Preacher—now, to quote Renan, lost in the canon like a volume of Voltaire among the folios of a theological library— would have shared the fate of Sirach and Wisdom and the other writings which Egypt cherished after Palestine had discarded them. And there were mutterings heard even against the Song, that beautiful remnant of the Anacreontic muse of Judea. It was then that Akiba stepped into the breach and by bold allegory saved that precious piece of what may be called the secular literature of the ancient Hebrews.

The process concluded by the Pharisees had begun long before. The Pharisee consummated what the scribe before him had commenced, and the scribe in turn had carried to fruition the work inaugurated by the prophet. Just as the Pharisee decreed what limits were to be imposed upon the third part of the Scriptures, the scribe in his day gave sanction to the second, and at a still earlier period the prophet to the wide range of literature current in his days. Sobered by national disaster, the scribe addressed himself to the task of safeguarding the remnant of Judea in the land of the fathers. There were schisms in the ranks, and all kinds of heresies, chief among which stood the Samaritan. The nation's history was recast in a spirit showing how through the entire past faithful adherence to Mosaism brought in its wake national stability, and conversely a swaying from legitimacy and law was responsible for disaster. With the Torah as a guide, prophecy was forced into the channels of orthodoxy. Heterodox prophets, the "false prophets," were consigned to oblivion. Their opponents alone were given a hearing. Secular history there was to be none; there was room only for the sacred. We may take it for granted that the "prophets of Baal," as their adversaries triumphantly nicknamed them, had their disciples who collected their writings and recorded the deeds of *their* spirit. But they were one and all suppressed. The political achievements of mighty dynasts had been recorded by annalists; the pious narrators in the so-called historical books of the canon brush them aside, gloss over them with a scant hint or reference; what is of absorbing interest to them is the activity of an Elijah or an Elisha, or the particular pattern of the altar in the Jerusalem sanctuary. In their iconoclastic warfare upon the abomination of Samaria, the prophets gave a partisanly distorted view of conditions in the North which for a long time had been the scene of Hebrew tradition and Hebrew life.

THE DEATH-BLOW TO THE OLD HEBRAIC CULTURE

What these upheavals meant in the history of Hebrew literature and culture can only approximately be gauged. One thing is certain: they all and one dealt the death-blow to the old Hebraic culture. When the excavator sinks his spade beneath the ground of a sleepy Palestinian village, he lays bare to view from under the overlaid strata, Roman and Greek and Jewish and Israelitish, the Canaanite foundation with its mighty walls and marvelous tunnels, its stelae and statuettes, its entombed infants sacrificed to the abominable Moloch. Similarly if we dig below the surface of the Scriptures, we uncover glimpses of

the civilization of the Amorite strong and mighty, which generations
of prophets and lawmakers succeeded in destroying root and branch.
On the ruins of the Canaanite-Amorite culture rose in the latter days
Judaism triumphant; the struggle—prolonged and of varying success—
marked the ascendancy of the Hebraic culture which was a midway
station between the indigenous Canaanite civilization on the one hand
and that mighty spiritual leaven, Mosaism in its beginnings and
Judaism in its consummation, on the other. The Hebraic culture was
a compromise. It began by absorbing the native civilization. The
danger of succumbing to it was there, but it was averted by those
whom their adversaries called the disturbers of Israel. And even to the
last, when the sway of Judaism was undisputed, the Hebraic culture
could not be severed from the soil in which it was rooted. It was part
of a world-culture just as it contributed itself thereto.

Whether living in amity or in warfare, nations influence each other
to a marked degree. They exchange the products of their soils and their
industry—they also give and take spiritual possessions. Culture is a
compound product. The factors that are contributory to its make-up
are the soil and the racial endowment recoiling against the domination from without which, though now wholly overcome, is resisted
with might and main. Cultures are national amidst an international
culture. They express themselves in a variety of ways, chiefly in
language and literature. For while blood is thicker than water, the
pen is mightier than the sword. Out of a mass of myth and legend
and worldly wisdom the Hebrews constructed, in accordance with
their own bent of mind, their cosmogonies and ballads and collections
of proverbs. At every shrine the priests narrated to the throngs of
worshippers the marvelous stories of local or national interest.

THE DIFFERENCE BETWEEN HEBRAIC CULTURE AND JUDAISM

The chief feature of the Hebraic culture was that it was joyous. The
somber seriousness of latter day Judaism had not yet penetrated it.
Israel rejoiced like the nations. The young men and maidens danced
and wooed in the precincts of the sanctuaries which dotted the country
from Dan to Beersheba. The festivals were seasons of joy, the festivals of the harvest and of the vintage. The prophets called them
carousals and dubbed the gentlemen of Samaria drunkards. Prob-

ably there were excesses. But life was enjoyed so long as the
heavens withdrew not the moisture which the husbandman was in
need of. The wars which the kings waged were the wars of the
Lord, and the exploits of the warriors were rehearsed throughout
the land—they were spoken of as the Lord's righteous acts. National victories strengthened the national consciousness. Taunt songs
were scattered on broadsides. The enemy was lampooned. At the
height of national prosperity, when Israel dwelt in safety in a land of
corn and wine moistened with the dew of the heavens, the pride of
the nation expressed itself in the paean, "Happy art thou, O Israel:
who is like unto thee, a people victorious through the Lord, the shield
of thy help, and that is the Sword of thy excellency!" Excellency then
meant national independence and welfare. It was the period of the
Omrides whose exploits are merely hinted at in our sources, whose
sway marked the nascent struggle between Hebraism and Judaism.
For the time being, Hebraic culture was on the ascendant, successor
to the indigenous Canaanite civilization which it had absorbed, re-
modelled, developed.

The chief difference between the Hebraic culture and Judaism
which supplanted it consists in the fact that, whereas the latter was
bookish, transforming its votaries into the "people of the book," the
former was the sum total of all that goes to make up the concern of a
nation living upon its own soil. Bookishness, literature, has a place in
the affairs of a nation, but it contributes only a side in its manifold
activities. The spoken word precedes the written. The writer has an
eye to aftertimes. He lives in the future. The speaking voice addresses
itself to the present and its varied needs. Saints are canonized after
death. The act of canonization means the verdict of the survivors who
from a distance are able to gauge the merits of past deeds. When a
literature is pronounced canonical or classical, it is no more. In its
dying moments it is reduced to rule, and its range becomes norm. But
normalization is an act of choosing, of accepting and excising. A living
literature is far from being normalized. Much that is written serves a
temporary purpose, but is none the less effective while it has vogue.
However, it is only a part of the national activities, mirroring them
and commenting upon them. So is religion another part of the national
life. Government policy and legal procedure and the arts and the
crafts occupy a nation's living interests. It speaks to us from beneath
the Hebrew Scriptures by which it is overlaid, themselves the remnant

of what in times gone by stirred the nation's spirit. A revival of that culture may come, but when it comes it will be tempered by Judaism. And the Hebrew Scriptures which constitute the bridge between them both will act as the peacemaker.

(—*1915*)

The Idea of Torah in Judaism

GEORGE FOOT MOORE

T HE WORD and idea most characteristic of Judaism in all its history is "Torah," and when your committee did me the honor to invite me to deliver the Leopold Zunz Lecture,* casting about me for a subject fitting the occasion and the purpose of the foundation, I could think of none more appropriate than just this central and, so to speak, constitutive idea.

I have used the Hebrew "Torah," not out of any predilection for foreign phrase but because I have no English for it. It is a common observation that terms in different languages do not cover one another in extension. There is, for example, no one English word that corresponds to the French *droit*, as we should find it used in a treatise on law. The case is much worse with Torah. For Judaism is implicit in that word. It means what it means because it belongs to a group, or system, of religious concepts which as such are peculiar to Judaism; it arouses feelings that come out of the peculiar history and religious experience of the Jewish people. The words by which we may try to represent it in another language—whether it be the Greek *nomos*, the Latin *lex*, the German *Gesetz*, or the English "law"—are not equivalent because they lack these implications and bring with them other and quite different associations. Even for the external aspect of Torah, *nomos*, *lex*, *Gesetz*, "law" are inadequate: they convey the idea of normative authority derived from the custom of the community, the edict of a ruler, or the statute of a legislative body; none of them suggest the divine origin and authority which is inseparable from Torah. Moreover, the word Torah itself does not mean "law," in the juristic sense, but something more like "instruction, direction"; nor is the Torah exclusively or even predominantly legal. The instructions or responses of the priests are Torah; the message of the prophets is Torah; the

* Delivered under the auspices of the Intercollegiate Menorah Association at the University of Cincinnati on December 10, 1921.

(16)

counsel of the wise is Torah; a Psalmist introduces his review of the great deeds of God, "Give ear, my people, to my Torah"; in the Pentateuch, Genesis is as truly Torah as Leviticus, the story of the Exodus and the wandering, the exhortations of Moses in Deuteronomy, as truly as the strictly legislative parts of the books.

Still less do these various terms for "law" express the content of Torah, which may be concisely defined as revealed religion, with the further weighty implications, first, that the whole Torah is a revelation of religion; second, that all religion is explicitly or implicitly contained in the revelation; and finally, that revealed religion embraces the whole life of the individual and the nation; there is no partition between secular and religious; righteousness and holiness are the principles of civil and social life as well as of that which we set off as specifically religious, of morals as well as of piety, of ceremonial purity as well as moral integrity.

Scripture was a written deposit of Torah the authenticity of which was guaranteed by the fact that the writers had the holy spirit of prophecy. The fact was universally assumed, but there was no theory of the mode of inspiration; the Platonic conception which Philo adopted has no parallel in rabbinical sources.

The Rabbinical Attitude Toward the Scriptures

Where a religion possesses Scriptures to which divine authority is attributed, it sooner or later becomes necessary to determine what these Scriptures are, or to put it in the way in which the necessity actually arises, to exclude the writings to which this character is erroneously attributed. This process is commonly called the formation of a canon (list) of Sacred Scripture. This stage was reached in Judaism in the generation before the destruction of the Temple. By that time the custom had long prevailed of reading lessons in the synagogues from the Pentateuch and the Prophets, and their right, thus protected by liturgical use, was undisputed. Serious difference of opinion seems to have existed only concerning Ecclesiastes and the Song of Solomon, upon which about the turn of the century an authoritative decision was pronounced favorable to both. In the next generation a similar decision was reached to the effect that the book of Sirach was not Sacred Scripture, nor did this quality attach to the Gospel and other writings of the heretics (*minim*).

The Scriptures were conceived not only to be as a whole a revelation from God, but to be such in every single word and phrase, and to be everywhere pregnant with religious meaning; for religion, by precept or example, is the sole content of revelation. This led, as it has done wherever similar opinions have been entertained, to a fractional method of interpretation which found regulation, instruction, and edification in words and phrases isolated from their context and combined by analogy with similar words and phrases in wholly different contexts, and to subtle deductions from peculiarities of expression. To a student indoctrinated in modern philological methods, the exegesis of the rabbis and the hermeneutic principles formulated from their practice and as a regulative for it often seem ingeniously perverse; but we must do them the justice to remember that not only their premises but their end was entirely different from ours. We propose to ourselves to find out what the author meant, and what those whom he addressed understood from what he said; and to this end we not only interpret his words in their relation to the whole context and tenor of the writing in which they stand, but endeavor to reconstruct the historical context—the time, place, circumstance, and occasion of the utterance, its position in the religious development, and whatever else is necessary to put ourselves, so far as possible, in the situation of contemporaries. The aim of the rabbis, on the contrary, was to find out what God, the sole author of revelation, meant by these particular words, not in a particular moment and for particular persons, but for all men and all time. What they actually did was, speaking broadly, to interpret everything in the Scriptures in the sense of their own highest religious conceptions, derived from the Scriptures or developed beyond them in the progress of the intervening centuries. Thus they not only deduced piles of *halakhot* from every tittle of the Torah, like Akiba, with a subtlety that was quite beyond Moses' comprehension and almost made him faint, but found everywhere the enlightening truths and edifying lessons which they put into the text to take out again. But that has always been the method of religious exegesis as distinguished from historical.

The Written and the Unwritten Torah

The Scripture was for them a revelation of God, complete, and wholly consistent in all its parts and in every utterance. That it contains an imperfect record of the historical development of a religion, or in theological phrase, the record of a progressive revelation for the education of the human race—such modern ideas, if they could have understood them at all, would have seemed a plain denial that the Torah is from Heaven.

Torah was not coterminous with Scripture. Only the smaller part of God's revelation had ever been written down; the unwritten Torah handed on from generation to generation by tradition was much more voluminous. That the written Torah was from the beginning and all through accompanied by a living tradition is unquestionable. A large part of what we call the legislation in the Pentateuch could never have been carried out in practice, or even understood, apart from domestic and social tradition, the ritual tradition of the priests, and the juristic tradition of the elders and the judges. Indeed the lapidary conciseness of the formulation in the written law itself presumes such a concomitant. We are not here concerned with the history either of the written or the unwritten Torah as modern scholars endeavor to construct it, but only with the consistent doctrine of Judaism about them, in which the historical idea of development in our sense has no place. This did not, of course, prevent the recognition of certain epochs in the history of the Torah, such as the work of Ezra and the Men of the Great Synagogue, or the decisions and regulations of the Soferim; but what they did was conceived to be the restoration of Torah that had fallen into desuetude and oblivion, or the bringing to light what was implicitly contained in it.

The Chain of Tradition

From this point of view the unwritten Torah handed down by tradition was revealed no less than the written Torah—it would not otherwise be Torah; and inasmuch as the universal belief at the beginning of the Christian era, and doubtless long before, was that the whole religion of Israel, in idea and act, with all its distinctive institutions and observances, was revealed to Moses at Sinai, it necessarily followed that this revelation included the unwritten as well as the written Torah, down to its last refinements, and even to the last question an acute pupil might ask his teacher.

The written Torah in Scripture had by a singular divine providence been transmitted without the minutest change, even in the spelling.

since its origin. A similar guarantee of the authenticity of the unwritten Torah was necessary, and this was found in the chain of tradition: it had been transmitted from Moses, through Joshua and the Elders and an unbroken succession of prophets, down to the days of the Great Synagogue among whose members were several prophets, and thereafter through the "Pairs" to Hillel and Shammai, from whom it passed into the carefully guarded tradition of the schools. The genuineness of tradition as a whole and in particulars could only be assured if in every generation it had been in the custody of trustworthy men, especially qualified for the task. Similarly in Christian theory, the bishops were the keepers and transmitters of the Apostolic tradition.

Authority in Jewish Tradition: Scholastic—Not Ecclesiastical

The principal task of the schools in the first and second centuries of the Christian era falls under two heads: Midrash, the study of the Scripture by which the harmony of the written and the unwritten law, and of the one with the other, was established—and Halakhah, the precise formulation of obligations and prohibitions, practical regulations for observance in all spheres of life, and many cautionary ordinances designed to keep man at a safe distance from the unwitting infraction of a law. The Midrash was not in theory and intention a derivation of the unwritten law from the written or a discovery of authority for the unwritten law in Scripture; and whatever increment the unwritten law received from this source was, in the apprehension of those who made it, only a bringing to light of the unity of revelation.

The unity of the Torah in its two branches was always assumed. The authority of all parts of it was the same; for the divine revelation was one, complete and final, from which nothing could be subtracted, and to which nothing was to be added—nothing had been kept back in heaven. In theory and intention purely conservative, the work of the schools in the interpretation of Scripture and the formulation of tradition was in fact the way of progress; through it the unchangeable Torah was adapted to changing conditions.

As in other religions which recognize tradition as a concurrent authority with Scripture—in Christianity and Mohammedanism, for example—not only is a guarantee of the authenticity of tradition necessary, but an authoritative definition, exposition, and application of tradition. But in comparison with Christianty, it is a significant difference that in Judaism and in Mohammedanism this authority is not ecclesiastical but scholastic; it was the learned who were the voice of tradition, and this, it may not be superfluous to observe, in the sphere of the Halakhah only. Dogmas, in the proper sense of the word, are only the fundamental articles of Judaism, the unity of God and the revelation of religion in the Torah, to which was now added the resurrection of the dead. The Haggadic tradition, however highly esteemed, is not binding.

The Identification of Religon With Education

Since God has made a revelation of his character, of his will for man's conduct in all the relations of life, and of his purpose for the nation and the world, the study of this revelation in its twofold form is the first of obligations, the worthiest of occupations. When pursued for its own sake, such study is a religious exercise and a means of grace. The man whose "delight is in the Torah of the Lord, and in His Torah doth he meditate day and night," is the ideal not merely of the scholar but of the religious man. Study, as well as prayer, is 'abodah, like the service of the altar. Familiar is the eulogy attributed to R. Meir in an appendix to Aboth: "He who studies the Torah for its own sake not only attains many good things, but deserves the whole world. He is called friend (of God), beloved, lover of God, lover of mankind; he delights God and men. It clothes him with humility and reverence, qualifies him to become righteous, pious, honest, and trustworthy. It keeps him far from sin and draws him near to virtue. Others have from him the benefit of good counsel, wisdom, understanding, and power, as it is said, 'Counsel is mine and sound wisdom; I am understanding, power is mine' (Prov. 8. 14). It gives him royalty and dominion and discernment in judgment; to him the mysteries of Torah are revealed; and he is made like a welling fountain and like a river that never fails. He is modest and self-controlled, and forgiving of insult. It magnifies and exalts him above all the creatures."

It would be easy to accumulate examples to show that the zeal of learning in the rabbis is a religious enthusiasm, and that the true end of learning is character. This conception of individual and collective study as a form of divine service has persisted in Judaism through all ages, and has made not only the learned by profession but men of humble callings in life assiduous students of the Talmud as the pursuit of the highest branch of religious learning and the most meritorious of good works.

The religion God had revealed was a religion for every man and for the whole of life, and the condition of the religious life, inward and outward, was knowledge of this revelation, that is of the Torah. This led to an effort, unexampled in antiquity, to educate the whole people in religion upon the basis of its sacred Scriptures. Elsewhere the religious tradition was preserved by a priesthood which made no attempt to instruct others in it and sometimes jealousy kept it from the knowledge of the laity. This was true not only of the art and mystery of the cultus, but in even higher degree of the meaning of the cultus and of the esoteric theologies and philosophies which were evolved by priestly speculation. The profounder truths of religion were—in the view of those who possessed them—not only beyond the capacity of the multitude, but were mysteries that would be profaned by vulgar access. Egypt and India in different ways may be taken as illustrations of this attitude. In Judaism, on the contrary, the ideal was a people completely instructed not only in the observances of individual and household religion, and in the form and meaning of the rites of public worship, but in the highest conceptions of the character of God, his righteous will, and his beneficent purpose, to the end that all classes of the community might do intelligently and from the right motive what God required of them, and that every individual might share in those blessings which come from the occupation of mind and heart with religion. The instrumentalities created for this end eventually constituted what we should call a complete system of education, from the elementary stage to the most advanced professional training of the doctor of theology.

A Complete System of Religious Education for All

For the Jews in the dispersion, who had lost their knowledge of the ancient tongue, the Scriptures were translated into Greek; the lessons in the synagogues were read in this translation, and the expository homily or other discourse was delivered in the same language. We are so familiar with translations of the Scriptures as well as of other books into all manner of languages that it takes some effort to realize how radical this step was. The Greek translation of the Pentateuch is the oldest piece of translation on a large scale of which we have any knowledge; and even if the age had been more given to translation of secular books than it was, the translation of sacred books has always encountered strenuous opposition not only from the jealousy of the learned but on religious grounds: the words of sacred Scripture in the original are the very words of revelation, and this quality cannot be communicated to the words of another language, no matter how faithful the version may be. That this way of thinking and feeling was shared by the Jews is evident not so much from the occasional depreciation or condemnation of the Septuagint in utterances of Palestinian rabbis, as in the Alexandrian legends which endeavor to confer upon the translation the authenticity of the original by means of a divine supervision over the translation or the miraculous unanimity of the translators. But if the religious instruction of the masses in Greek-speaking countries was not to be abandoned altogether, it must be given in a language they understood; before this imperative necessity all scruples had to give way.

In Palestine, and doubtless in Syria and Babylonia, the lessons were, in conformity with long established custom, read in Hebrew, and interpreted piecemeal in the Aramaic vernacular of the land; and in the same language the exposition followed.

The synagogue is a unique institution in ancient religion. Its services had no resemblance to the public worship in the temples; there were no offerings, no priesthood, no pompous ritual. Still less were they like the salvationist sects of the time, the mysteries, with their initiations and the impenetrable secrecy which enveloped their doctrines and their doings. To the Greeks the synagogue with its open doors, its venerable books, the discourses of its teachers on theology and ethics, seemed to be a school of some peculiar philosophy. A school it was in Jewish apprehension also—a school of revealed religion, which was itself for Hellenistic Jews like Philo the true philosophy.

Elementary schools for boys were early established, some supported by the community, some private enterprises. It was from the Hebrew Bible that the pupils learned to read. The lessons in the synagogue were read by members of the congregation, and the regulations for this part of the service which we have from the latter part of the second century assume that ordinarily there would be several present competent to participate in it—an indirect testimony to the existence and efficiency of the Bible schools. Many, doubtless, did not progress beyond this stage; but others continued their studies until they had acquired a more extensive knowledge of the Bible, for which the Bet ha-Midrash, where the better educated part of the community gathered especially on Sabbath afternoons, afforded additional opportunity. Those who aspired to what we should call the academic career frequented the rabbinical schools, in which they learned Halakhah and Midrash, and at a more advanced stage Talmud (in the older sense of that word). These studies demanded unusual accuracy of memory and an acute intelligence, and many fell out by the way; only the elect few carried their learning to the point where they were recognized as qualified masters of the law and received the *venia docendi et decernendi*. A Midrash on Eccl. 7. 28 ("I have found one man of a thousand") tells us: "Such is the usual way of the world; a thousand enter the Bible school, a hundred pass from it to the study of Mishna, ten of them go on to Talmud study, and only one of them arrives at the doctor's degree." Through the higher education was ensured a succession of qualified teachers in every stage; edifying homilists for the synagogues, and in the scholarchs and their academies a decisive authority for the definition and application of the norms of the Halakhah.

That this system of education as we know it in sources dated from the second century of the Christian era was in reality much older, whatever changes in form may have taken place in the meantime, is to be seen very clearly in Ben Sira, whose reputation as a coiner of aphorisms for the conduct of life sometimes makes us forget that he was an eminent member of the class of *soferim*, professional scholars.

The Universal Aspect of the Torah as Divine Wisdom

The Torah had, however, yet another aspect. For Judaism, while in history and in actuality a national religion, the religion of one of the smaller peoples of the earth, was in idea and in destiny universal. As there is but one true God, one revelation of His character and will, so in the future all mankind shall acknowledge the sovereignty of God, the *malkut shammaim*, embrace the true religion, and live in accordance with its precepts.

The revelation of religion, the Torah, is universal. A significant expression of this idea is the identification of Torah with Wisdom. It is the peculiar wisdom of Israel. Moses says of the statutes and ordinances which by God's command he delivered to the people: "Observe therefore and do them, for this is your wisdom and your understanding in the sight of the peoples, that when they hear all these statutes shall say, surely this great nation is a wise and understanding people" (Deut. 4. 6). But it is this because Torah is divine wisdom, or to put it in the way the rabbis conceived it, the Wisdom that speaks in the eighth chapter of Proverbs is the Torah. The identification is a commonplace in the rabbinical literature, and many passages of Scripture referring to wisdom are interpreted in this sense; it appears in Sifrè as a universally accepted truth. We can, however, trace it much farther back. In Sirach 24, 23 ff., after a eulogy of wisdom pronounced by itself as in Prov. 8, the passage concludes: "All this (that is, all the great things that he has said of wisdom) is the Book of the Covenant of the Most High God, the Law which He commanded Moses, an inheritance of the congregation of Jacob."

In Proverbs, Wisdom was present at the creation of the world, not as a passive onlooker, but as a participant in the making and in the joy of the Maker. She was at God's side as a skilled artificer, or artist. Identifying Wisdom with Torah, and taking the word *amon* in the sense of instrument, Akiba speaks of the Torah as the instrument with which the world was created. According to others it was the plan, or pattern, after which the world was made. Or again, the world was created for the sake of the Torah. It is permissible to modernize the last words: The world was created for religion; a stage on which, under the guidance of revelation, the right relation between God and men might be realized.

The identification of Torah with divine wisdom and its connection with creation made it premundane: "The Lord made me as the beginning of his way, the first of his works of old." For the Torah was *created,* however long ago; Judaism has no parallel to the eternal Koran of Moslem dogma, rival of the eternity of God. And since God foresaw that men would sin by transgression or neglect, He at once created repentance as the remedy. Without that provision He would never have created the world and frail man in it.

The Torah which was before the world is unchangeable for all time. In the World to Come, indeed, certain prescriptions for the law will have no application because the conditions they suppose cannot occur; but there is no abrogation and no supplement, only perfect fulfillment. And since perfect fulfillment supposes perfect understanding, God Himself will be the teacher there. The wisdom God has searched out and given to Israel is "the book of the commandments of God and the Law that exists to eternity" (Bar. 4. 1). "Until heaven and earth pass away not the smallest letter (a *yod*), not an apex on a letter (one ḳoṣ in the Tagin), shall pass away from the Law till it all be done" (Math. 5. 18); "It is easier for heaven and earth to pass away than for one apex of the Law to fall" (Luke 16. 47).

The Torah Intended for All Nations

The Torah was in nature and intention for all men. How then did it come that it was the exclusive possession of the Jews? The God of all mankind could not have been so partial in His revelation. The fundamentals of the Torah, it was taught, had been given to Adam; with one addition (*eber min ha-ḥai*) they had been renewed to Noah for all branches of his posterity. At Sinai, in the desert that was no man's land or every man's land, the Law had been offered to all nations in their several languages or in the four international languages, and been refused by them because it condemned their favorite sins; Israel alone accepted it. "All that the Lord hath spoken will we do and obey," was the response of the people at the foot of Sinai when Moses delivered to them the revelation of God's will he had received (Exod. 24. 7; *cf.* 3). There for the first time the sovereignty of God, which hitherto had been acknowledged only by individuals, was confessed by a whole people. The Kingdom of Heaven in its national form was founded.

Of greater religious significance than the offering of the Torah in the remote past of the forefathers of all the Gentiles is the emphatic teaching that the Torah, by virtue of its origin and nature, is for every man. R. Meir found this in Lev. 18. 5; "My statutes and my ordinances, which if *a man* do, he shall live by them." It is not said, "priests, Levites, lay Israelites," but "*a man*," therefore even a Gentile; nay, such a Gentile who labors in the Torah (or, does the Torah) is in that respect on an equality with the high priest. Other texts are quoted in the same sense; for example, 2 Sam. 7. 19, "This is the Torah of mankind, Lord God"; Isa. 26. 2, "Open the gates that a righteous Gentile (*goi ṣaddiḳ*) preserving fidelity, may enter in thereby" (*cf.* Psalm 118. 20).

The Jews were the only people in antiquity who divided religions into true and false, affirming that Judaism was the only true religion and that it was destined to prevail over all the rest and become universal. Their pretensions and the manner in which they asserted them, especially their mordant satire on polytheism and idolatry, were resented by people of other races and religions, and contributed not a little to the general prejudice against the Jews that was so widespread in the Hellenistic and Roman world. If, as Philo complains, Judaism was alone excepted from the universal religious toleration of the times, it is fair to the heathen to say that Jewish intolerance toward other religions gave great provocation. Early Christianity, it may be added, inherited the attitude, and suffered the same consequences.

Judaism as a Proselyting Religion

But if some of the methods employed to turn the heathen from the error of their ways had a prejudicial effect, on the other hand the faith of Judaism in its truth and universal destiny made of it the first proselyting religion in the Mediterranean world. The universality of the true religion, in the age when "the Lord shall be one and His name one," and "the Lord shall be king over all the earth," was not, indeed, expected to come by human instrumentality or through historical evolution, but in a great revolution wrought by God himself, a catastrophic intervention such as the prophets had so often foretold. Meanwhile, however, the Jews had a twofold task in preparation for that great event; first, to make the reign of God a reality for themselves individually and as a people; and, second, to make known to the Gentiles the true God and his righteous will and convert them to the true religion. This conception of the prophetic mission of Israel among the nations had been set forth by the prophet in Isaiah 42 and 49: Israel is to be a light to the nations, that God's salvation may reach to the end of the earth; and not only reflection but the logic of the situation led to the same result.

In the two or three centuries on either side of the Christian era Judaism made great numbers of converts throughout the wide dispersion. Various Oriental religions in that age were offering the secret and the assurance of a blessed immortality through initiation into their mysteries, and drew into their mystic societies many seekers of salvation. Judaism on the contrary, as we have seen, appeared to ancient observers to be not a mystery but a philosophy. It had a high doctrine about God which was publicly taught in its synagogue-schools, a rule of life, and venerable scriptures in which both the doctrine and the rule were contained; and it sought to make converts by rational persuasion. In this aspect Judaism is sometimes called a missionary religion; but if the phrase is used it must be understood that it was a missionary religion without an organization for propaganda and without professional missionaries. The open doors of the synagogue, a noteworthy apologetic literature, and the individual efforts of Jews in their various social spheres to win over their neighbors, were the only instrumentalities in the conversion of the Gentiles.

Polytheism and idolatry were the salient characteristics of the religions in the midst of which the Jews in the dispersion lived. More intelligent Gentiles, instructed by the prevailing philosophies, regarded both as popular errors, but made no effort to combat them, and were not hindered by their personal convictions from taking part in the rites and festivals of their cities or of the state. Judaism alone was uncompromising. The worship of gods that were no gods was not merely an intellectual error but the sin of sins against the true God, the sin from which all others sprang. Its monotheism was not a philosophical theory of the unity of deity in the abstract, but a theological doctrine of the nature and character of God drawn from His revelation of Himself. There was nothing He was so intolerant of as the acknowledgement of other gods and the worship of vain idols: "I am the Lord, that is my name; and my glory will I not give to another, neither my praise to graven images" (Isa. 42.8).

To convert men from polytheism and idolatry was therefore the prime effort of Judaism among the Gentiles, and it might well seem that the renunciation of these from religious conviction was in principle the abandonment of heathenism and acceptance of Judaism. Even from Palestinian teachers come such utterances as, "Whoever professes heathen religion is as one who rejects the whole Torah, and whoever rejects heathen religion is as one who professes the whole Torah" (Sifrè, Deut. § 54, end; *ibid.* Num. § 111, f. 31b end).

The One Treasure That Could Not Be Destroyed

Next to this the emphasis was laid upon morality, which in Judaism —one of its singularities—was an integral part of religion, and especially on the avoidance of those vices which the Scriptures persistently associate with heathenism—*'abodah zarah* and *'arayot*. If to this was added observance of the Sabbath and of certain of the rules about forbidden food, and attendance on the synagogue, a man might well be regarded as a convert to Judaism, even though he had not formally been admitted a member of the Jewish people by circumcision and baptism nor assumed as a proselyte the obligations, hereditary for born Jews, of the whole written and unwritten Torah. The number of such "religious persons" was large, and through them the leaven of Judaism was more and more penetrating the mass of Gentile society. Thus the Kingdom of Heaven was growing in the world and preparing for its consummation.

This rapid expansion was arrested by the climactic disasters that befell the Jews in the three-quarters of a century from Nero to Hadrian. But when everything else seemed to be lost, Judaism clung the more tenaciously to the one treasure that could not be taken from it, the Torah. The Temple might be destroyed and with it the whole sacrificial worship abolished, but in the study of the Torah and in good works it had the realities of which the ritual institutes of atonement were but symbols. Hadrian might suppress the schools and put the great teachers to death; the mere possession of a roll of the Law might invite the same fate; but persecution for its sake only made the Torah, sanctified by the blood of the martyrs, more inestimably precious. The disciples of the martyrs perpetuated and ordered the tradition of their teaching; and if one had to name the age in which the study of the Torah was pursued with the greatest zeal and the most epoch-making results, he would, I suppose, take the two or three generations between the catastrophe of the Bar Kokba war and the death of the Patriarch Judah. It was the supreme proof of faith in the Torah God had given to his people and in God's purpose in it. Nor has Judaism ever lost this faith in itself and in the universal nature and destiny of the true religion whose prophet and martyr Israel has been through the centuries.

The Adaptation of Judaism to Changing Conditions

Today the situation of Judaism is again somewhat similar to that which it occupied in the Hellenistic world or in the Moslem world of the Middle Ages. In the lands of the modern Diaspora, and above all in America, it has, like contemporary Christianity, Catholic and Protestant, the conflict within itself of modernism and reaction. At bottom it is the question whether the finality of a religion lies in the tenacity with which it conserves forms that it has inherited from the past, or in its capacity for indefinite progress wherein its very fidelity to its constitutive ideas enables it to adapt itself to the present and to shape the future. The great epochs in the history of Judaism have been those in which it conceived its nature and mission in the latter way. It was so, as we have seen, in the Hellenistic age, when, in the midst of polytheism and idolatry and the vices of heathen society, it presented its Torah essentially as pure monotheism and a high morality, with the authority not only of revelation but of universal human reason and conscience. Philo interpreted Judaism in the light of the religious philosophies of his time, and expounded its theology and ethics to educated men as the highest and best philosophy.

The work of the Tannaim, which appears to be the deliberate antithesis of this Hellenizing tendency, was itself a no less far-reaching adaptation of Judaism to the conditions which ensued upon the destruction of Jerusalem with the cessation of the temple worship and the calamities that befell the nation under Trajan and Hadrian. The preceding period had been characterized by an adaptation to expansion, with the ideal of universality; now, threatened with dissolution in the surrounding world, rabbinical Judaism became by force of circumstances an adaptation to self-preservation, and made of the unwritten Torah, with all its distinctive institutions and observances, not only a wall of defense without but the organic bond of unity within. The survival of Judaism through all the vicissitudes of its subsequent history is proof of the thoroughness of this adaptation.

In the Middle Ages, again, from the tenth century to the thirteenth, the Jews, especially in Moslem lands, took an eager part in the intellectual life of the times. Scholars and thinkers equipped with all the scientific and philosophical learning of the time set themselves not only to prove the truth of the religion as revealed in its Torah but its eminent rationality. This movement, of which Maimonides is the conspicuous exponent, was again an adaptation to a new intellectual environment in the progress of the times.

Finally, when, in the eighteenth and nineteenth centuries, the Jews of central and western Europe emerged from their intellectual isolation, the same capacity for adaptation manifested itself not only in the assimilation of contemporary philosophy, as in Mendelssohn, but in the field of critical and historical investigation, of which Leopold Zunz, whose name we honor tonight, was one of the shining lights. Through these studies the way was made to a new apprehension of the ancient Torah. It had been accepted as a unitary revelation, which shared in its way the timelessness of its author; it had been interpreted in the sense and spirit of Hellenistic, or Greco-Arabic, or modern philosophies; it was now to be understood as an historical growth. This way of apprehending it led to a discrimination not only in the Talmud but in the Torah itself between forms and ideas that belonged to outgrown stages of the development and what is of permanent validity and worth, and so to the conception of a progressive development of the latter elements in the future.

But, however apprehended and interpreted, Torah remains the characteristic word and idea of Judaism. The much debated question, race or religion? is a false alternative. The Jews are a race constituted by its religion—a case of which there is more than one other example. Those who fell away from the religion were in the end eliminated from the people; while multitudes of converts of the most diverse ethnic origins have been absorbed in the race and assimilated to it by the religion. External pressure would not have held the Jews together through these centuries without the internal cohesion of religion—a living and progressive religion; and apart from religion no temporary exaltation of national feeling can in the end perpetuate the unity and peculiarity of the race.

(—1922)

Jewish Thought as Reflected in the Halakhah

❦

LOUIS GINZBERG

I T WAS NOT without hesitation that I accepted the kind invitation
extended to me to deliver the Zunz Lecture* of this year. Greatly
as I appreciated the honor conferred upon me, I did not find it an easy
task to free myself from a deep-rooted conviction that, to speak in
the words of the great Frenchman, Pascal, most of the mischief of this
world would never happen if men were contented to sit still in their
parlors and refrain from talking. As a compromise with this strong
conviction, I have chosen as my subject, "Jewish Thought As Reflected
In The Halakhah." On a subject of this sort one would talk only when
one has something to say, or at least thinks so—otherwise one would
be prompted to keep silence.

To be candid, keeping silence strongly commends itself to one who
has spent the greater part of his life in the study of the Halakhah and,
believing himself to have a good deal to say about it, is at a loss how
to do so within the limited space of a single paper. It would be impossible within the compass of anything less than a substantial volume
to present an analysis of the ideas comprised or implied in the term
Halakhah, or even to set forth the various senses in which the term has
been employed. It has often been observed that the more claim an idea
has to be considered living, the more various will be its aspects; and
the more social and political is its nature, the more complicated and
subtle will be its issues, and the longer and more eventful its course.
The attempt to express the "leading idea" of the Halakhah I must perforce leave to those whose forte is omniscience and whose foible
is knowledge. What I propose to do is something less ambitious than

* Delivered under the auspices of the Intercollegiate Menorah Association at the
University of Chicago on December 29, 1920.

(32)

to sketch before you the nature and scope of the Halakhah. It is more closely connected with the problem of the nature of Jewish history.

Indispensable to an Understanding of Jewish History

The Talmud remarks: "He who daily studies the Halakhah may rest assured that he shall be a son of the world to come." The study of the Halakhah may not commend itself to everyone as a means of salvation. Some may desire an easier road thereto; but we may well say that he who studies the Halakhah may be assured that he is a son of the world—the Jewish one—that has been. Not that the Halakhah is a matter of the past; but the understanding of the Jewish past, of Jewish life and thought, is impossible without a thorough knowledge of the Halakhah. One might as well hope to comprehend the history of Rome without taking notice of its wars and conquests or that of Hellas without giving attention to its philosophy and art. To state such a truism would be superfluous, were it not for the fact that the most fundamental laws of nature are often disregarded in dealing with the Jews, and their history has undergone strange treatment at the hands of friend and foe alike.

If we further remember that Jewish historiography in modern times dates from the days when the Hegelian conception of history reigned supreme, the "peculiar" treatment of the history of the "peculiar people" is not in the least surprising. Historians who believed with Hegel that "history is the science of man in his political character," and consequently were of the opinion that there could be no history of a people without a state, could not but ignore the Halakhah, a way of life that was never sustained by the power of the state and was often even antagonized by it. What was the result of this conception of history applied to the Jews? The three main subjects dealt with in works on Jewish history in post-biblical times are religion, literature, martyrology, to which a little philosophy with a sprinkling of cultural history is added; but of actual history in the modern sense of the word we find very little indeed. History as now generally understood is the science establishing the causal nexus in the development of man as a social being. The Jew may well say: *homo sum, nihil humani a me alienum puto.* State or no state, even the Jew of the Diaspora lived for almost two thousand years a life of his own and has developed accordingly a character of his own.

A Mirror Held Up to Jewish Nature

Modern students of heredity teach us that three elements contribute to the formation of a man's character—heritage, environment, and training. What is true of individual character holds good also of national character. We hear a good deal of the importance of heritage or race, to use the favored phrase of the day, in appraising the character of the Jew and in the interpretation of his history. Dealers in generalities especially are prone to call in the racial features and characteristics to save the trouble of a more careful analysis which would show that these racial qualities themselves are largely due to historical causes, though causes often too far back in the past to admit of full investigation. The explanation of history from the narrow point of view of race is tantamount to affirming as Hegel did that the whole wealth of historic development is potential in the beginnings of mind, a view which it would be impossible to justify historically. The lessons of history indicate rather that at certain times men of genius initiate new movements which though related to the past are not explained by it, and that there are various possibilities contained in a given historic situation. Which of the possibilities is to become real would depend solely upon the training of the people confronted with the historic situation. Nothing is easier and nothing more dangerous than definitions. I shall not define what Halakhah is; yet one is safe in asserting that its chief feature is education of oneself, or training. Accordingly, the Halakhah is a true mirror reflecting the work of the Jew in shaping his character.

No man who is badly informed can avoid reasoning badly. We can hardly expect to understand the causal nexus of our history if we disregard the most valuable source of information we seek. Here is a plain example in arithmetic to prove it. The literary output of the eighteen centuries from the beginning of the common era to the year 1795, the date of the emancipation of the Jews in Holland, when the modern history of the Jew begins, contains seventy-eight percent of Halakhic material. We may easily convince ourselves of the exactness of this statement by looking at the classification of the Hebrew books in the British Museum, the largest collection of its kind in the world, prepared by such an eminent and careful bibliographer as Zedner.

Yet it is not the quantity of the Halakhic Literature that makes it so valuable a source of Jewish history; by far more important is its quality.

A Treasury of Historical Remains

Historians divide historical sources into two main groups: (a) historical remainders and (b) tradition. By the first group we understand all that remains of an historical event. For instance, we find in certain parts of Germany ruins of Roman castles, places with Roman names, burial-grounds containing the bodies of Romans, their armor, pottery and so on. Let us suppose for a moment that the writings of Caesar, Tacitus and other Roman historians treating of the relations between Rome and Germania had disappeared; these remainders of the actual life of the Romans in Germany would suffice to establish beyond any doubt the fact that at a certain time in history the Romans lived in Germany and were its masters. The second group of historical sources, tradition, is much less reliable, since it is only a subjective reflection in the human mind of historical events and can therefore be made use of only after a critical analysis has separated the subjective element of reflection from the objective facts reflected. We often hear of the lamentable dearth of sources of Jewish history. As far as historical tradition is concerned, the correctness of this statement is above dispute; but of historical remainders we have in the Halakhah a veritable treasure of material. The Halakhah, as its meaning "conduct" indicates, comprises life in all its manifestations—religion, worship, law, economics, politics, ethics and so forth. It gives us a picture of life in its totality and not of some of its fragments.

You will ask how it could happen that all the historians and scholars who devoted their lives and great abilities to the study of Jewish history ignored its most important source, the Halakhah? The answer to this question is not a difficult one. Important as the Halakhah is as an historical source, equally difficult is its utilization. Its faults lie not in its substance but in the form which the conditions of its growth have given to it. It is a system extremely hard to expound and hard to master. So vast is it and so complicated, so much are its leading principles obscured by the way in which they have been stated, scattered here and there through the vast expanse of the "sea of the Talmud," in an order peculiar to the latter, which is the perfection of disorder, that it presents itself to the learner as a most arduous study, a study indeed which only a few carry so far as to make themselves masters of the whole. Hence the favorite phrase that a general impression of the Halakhah suffices without the study of its details. Of course, this is a fig-leaf for incapacity. To understand the whole, the knowledge of its parts is as indispensable in the study of the Halakhah as in any other branch of human thought.

I do not wish to be misunderstood. Not everything that happens is history and consequently, the first requirement of the historian is to distinguish between essentials and non-essentials, between historical and non-historical happenings. The individual performs countless acts daily which the most conscientious and careful Boswell would pass over in silence as irrelevant. So also in the lives of nations and peoples, many things happen daily that are of no historical value. Not all the minutiae of the Halakhah are historical material, but to quote the saying of an old Jewish sage: "If there be no knowledge, how could there be discernment?" To distinguish the essential from the non-essential in the Halakhah, one must master it entirely, if one is not to become a prey to his subjective likings or dislikings—and we all know how Jewish history is marred by bias and prejudice.

The Haggadah: A Conflicting Mass of Subjective Views

The problem of subjectivity in the presentation of Jewish history leads me to remark on another aspect of the Halakhah—its authoritative character. Writers on the phase of Judaism that comprises Jewish theology and ethics, in post-biblical times, have based their studies exclusively on the Haggadah, which means that they erected their structures upon shifting sand. Whatever else the Haggadah may be, it certainly is either individual, consisting of opinions and views uttered by Jewish sages for the most part on the spur of the moment, or creations of popular fancy. The haggadic sayings of the rabbis belong to the first division; the apocryphal-apocalyptic writings belong to the second.

All work, it is true, is done by individuals. We have nothing beyond the dicta of definite—known or unknown—persons. Yet the great men of a people give the impulses only, and all depends upon what the mass of the people make thereof. It is doubtless as important for the history of Judaism to know what Hillel said, what R. Akiba thought and what R. Meir taught as it is important for Christianity to study the writing of Augustine, Luther and Calvin. But not all Christians are Augustines or Luthers, nor all Jews Hillels and Akibas. The great moulders of Christian thought did indeed succeed in making the masses of Christianity accept their doctrines at solemn councils and representative covenants, but that was not true of the spiritual leaders of the Jews. Even if we admit that whatever is alive in the nation finds expression in the works and words of individuals and that many individual contributions are products of the national spirit, there still remains a vast array of intellectual products that are temporary, accidental and individual, in which the national soul has but a small share. The devil, according to Shakespeare, quotes Scripture. But if he is really as clever as he is reputed to be, he ought to quote the Talmud, as there is hardly any view of life for and against which one could not quote the Talmud.

Neither History Nor Theology Can Be Formulated From Legend

No less uncritical is the attempt made by many theologians to give us a system of the religious thought of the Jew based upon the apocalyptic literature, the fantastic fabric of popular imagination. As the author of a large work on Jewish legends, I believe myself to be above suspicion of lacking sympathy for the creations of popular fancy. Theology, however, is a rational system of religious values and cannot be built up of material furnished by fancy and imagination. As often as I read books on Jewish theology, and I may say with Faust: *Ich habe leider auch Theologie studiert,* the diametrically opposing views expressed in them remind me of the following story so popular in my native counry, Lithuania. A rabbi, trying a case—for the rabbi of olden times was more of a judge than a theologian—after listening to the plaintiff, exclaimed: "You are right, my son;" and then made the same remark to the defendant, after the latter had pleaded in his own behalf. The rabbi's wife, who was present at the trial, could not refrain from remarking to her husband; "How can both litigants be right?" To which the rabbi in genuine meekness, as becoming a husband and rabbi, replied: "You, too, are right, my dear." I frequently feel like saying to the diametrically opposed theologians: What you say is so profoundly true and so utterly false! You are so profoundly right in that you tell us about the beliefs and doctrines of this rabbi or

that apocalyptic author, but you are so utterly wrong in your attempts to stamp as an expression of the Jewish soul what is only an
individual opinion or a transitory fancy.

It is only in the Halakhah that we find the mind and character of
the Jewish people exactly and adequately expressed. Laws which
govern the daily life of man must be such as suit and express his
wishes, being in harmony with his feelings and fitted to satisfy his
religious ideals and ethical aspirations. A few illustrations will often
explain better than long abstract statements, and I shall therefore
present a few concrete examples of the Halakhah applied to the study
of Jewish thought.

The Egg That Was Laid on a Holiday

At the risk of causing Homeric laughter I shall begin *ab ovo*,
not as the poet did, with the egg of Leda, but rather with that no
less famous one that, to speak with Heine, was unfortunate enough
to be laid on a holiday. He who does not appreciate Heine lacks
the ability to appreciate something genuinely Jewish, and I, for one,
greatly enjoy his merry remarks on that unfortunate egg. But grave
historians, or rather theologians, the majority of whom are not usually
distinguished by a sense of humor, do not show deep historical insight
in ridiculing the great schools headed by Shammai and Hillel for
discussing the question whether an egg laid on a holiday be permitted for use or not. We hear a great deal of Judaism's being a view
of life for which religion is law. I am at present not interested in showing the fallacy of this dictum nor in inquiring why we hear so little
about the second part of this equation, to wit: for the Jew, law is
religion. But if it be true that religion is law for the Jews, the conception underlying Jewish law must necessarily be expressive of Jewish
religious thought. The discussion of the old schools about the egg is
tantamount to the question to what extent the principle of intent is
to be applied. *Actus non est reus nisi mens sit rea,* say the Roman
jurists, and similarly the rabbis: Actions must be judged by their
intent. Since, according to biblical law, food for the holy days must
be prepared the day before, the progressive school of Hillel maintained that an egg laid on a holy day must not be used because,
though prepared by nature, it was without intent of man and hence
can not be considered prepared in the legal sense. As strong men
exult in their agility, so tendencies that are strong and full of life will

sometimes be betrayed into extravagances. It may be extravagant to prohibit an egg laid on a holy day on account of not having been prepared for food with intent. But of what paramount importance must intention have been to the religious conscience of the Jew if it could assume such an exaggerated form as in the case before us! And could there be a better criterion of the development of a religion than the importance it attaches to intent, the outcome of thought and emotion in opposition to merely physical action?

Now let us examine another Halakhah that might throw light on the question as to the relation of thought and emotion to acts and deeds in Jewish theology. Sin, we are told by leading theologians, consists according to the Jewish conception in acting wrongly, and hence forgiveness, or to use the more technical term, atonement, is of a purely mechanical nature. Originally, there were different kinds of sacrifices, the sin offerings, the guilt offerings, and so forth, by means of which the sinner could right himself with God. Later the rabbis substitute prayer, fasting and almsgiving for the sacrifices which, after the destruction of the Temple, could no longer be brought. So far our theologians. And now let us hear what the Halakhah has to say about it. In a large collection of laws treating of marriage with conditions attached, which is to be found in the Talmud, we read: For him who says to a woman, I marry thee under the condition that I am an entirely righteous man, the marriage is valid, even if it is found that he was a very wicked man, because we apprehend that at the time of the contraction of marriage he repented in his heart. For him who says to a woman, I marry thee under the condition that I am a completely wicked man—sin is homely but also attractive—the marriage is valid. For even if it is found that he was very pious we apprehend that at the time of the contracting of marriage he had thoughts of idolatry. Sin as well as forgiveness are thus understood by Jewish law to be entirely independent of acts and deeds; the evil thought in the heart turns the perfect just into the completely wicked, and vice versa, the change of heart changes the completely wicked into the perfect just.

The Halakhah A Source of Jewish Ethics

The ethical principles and ideals that shaped and formed the Halakhah have been made a subject of study by many; however, as we are still in need of a thorough investigation of Jewish ethics, a few remarks on the Halakhah as a source for Jewish ethics may prove to be profitable. I shall, however, content myself with touching upon those parts of the Halakhah that treat either of ceremonial law or of the forms of civil law; my purpose in doing so being to show to what use the knowledge of these minutiae may be put.

Whether Jewish ethics are of a positive or a negative nature is a question often propounded, and of course answered according to the nature of the quotations one is able to gather from Jewish writings. A favorite argument for the negative character of Jewish ethics is drawn from the number of the commandments, which is said to consist of two hundred and forty-eight positive and three hundred and sixty-five negative ones. I doubt whether the good rabbi who first computed these numbers was aware of the consequence of his statistics. There can, however, be no doubt in my mind that modern theologians are not aware of the fact that statistics are as fatal to theology as theology to statistics. A prompt and decisive answer to the question concerning Jewish ethics is given by the Halakhah in its ruling: that in all conflicts of laws the positive takes precedence of the negative. This legal maxim applies of course to conflicts of ceremonial laws, but it is the outcome of the legal mind, or to use the more adequate term of the Germans, *das Rechtsbewusstsein,* of a people which conceived ethics as something very positive.

The Recognition of Altruism by Jewish Law

Many of us are undoubtedly acquainted with the favorite diversion of many popular writers who deny to the Jew any claim to creative genius. His religion and his ethics are said by them to be merely different manifestations of his commercial spirit; *do ut des* being the guiding power of his life. Hence, the insistence upon the dogma of reward and punishment in his religion and the utilitarian character of his ethics. We have had enough of theology for the present and I shall not enter upon a discussion of the dogma of reward and punishment. Yet I cannot help quoting to you the very wise words of one of the finest minds among contemporary thinkers. The world, says Mr. Balfour, suffers not because it has too much of it—the belief in reward and punishment—but because it has too little; not because it displaces higher motives, but because it is habitually displaced by lower ones. To those who maintain the utilitarian character of Jewish ethics, my advice is: study the part of civil law in Jewish jurisprudence treating of gifts. While the ancient Roman law, as has been pointed out by the great jurist and philosopher of law, Ihering, knows no gratuitous transfer of ownership, but only paid, the promise of a gift attained an independence of form in the very earliest stages of the Halakhah. For the Roman law, gift is a sort of exchange; one makes a gift in order to receive a gift in return, or in the words of the Roman jurists: *ad remunerandam sibi aliquem naturaliter obligaverunt, velut genus quiddam hoc esse permutationis.* The Halakhah, on the other hand, had overcome the egoism of man, and beneficence and love dictated by altruism have come to their full right in legislation as well as in life. The importance of this phenomenon only he can fail to recognize who sees in the forms of the laws mere forms and not the expression of ideas.

The only point where liberality comes to the surface in the Roman law is in regard to wills, and it is highly interesting for appraisal of the Jewish character to notice that Jewish law is rather inclined to limit the power of the testator to the extent that it prohibits the disinheritance of an ungrateful and wicked son in favor of a good and dutiful son. It has been noticed by others that bequests have psychologically not the value of a gift—the gift of the cold hand is compatible with an icy cold heart; it is not a gift of one's own, but from the purse of the legal heir. In the long course of the development of the Jewish people the underlying bond was the family; the ties of blood were of absolute and undisputed strength. Consequently, the Halakhah is not in favor of any measure that might disrupt this bond of union. In this connection I may call attention to the fact that the Halakhah failed to develop the law of adoption, notwithstanding the fact that the Bible offers some precedents in certain forms of adoption. The idea of blood relationship forming the basis of the family was too strong with the Jew to permit the development of a law that would undermine it.

The Halakhah On the Question of Nationality

This leads us to the burning Jewish question of the day: Are the Jews a nation or merely a religious community? Of course I am not going to discuss it from the point of view of the Jew of today, but justice to my subject requires that we discuss this question from the point of view of the Halakhah. And the answer to this question is given unmistakably in the following two laws of inheritance. A Jew, converted to paganism, inherits his father's estate; a pagan, who is converted to Judaism, does not inherit his father's estate, whether the father also becomes a convert or not. The idea underlying these Halakhot is that the ties of blood binding the Jew to the Jewish people can never be loosened, and that, on the other hand, by becoming a Jew, a pagan severs his national connections with those to whom he previously belonged. There is a logical contradiction in these two laws of inheritance as formulated by the Halakhah. But what is life but a conglomerate of logical contradictions? The Halakhah was not a true mirror of Jewish life, if it were free from all logical inconsistencies. The Jew is bound forever to his people and yet anybody who enters Judaism becomes a true son of Israel.

A little reflection will, however, convince anyone who comes to the question with an open mind that both these theories concerning Judaism, that of nationalism pure and simple as well as that of a mere creed, are alike incomplete, and being incomplete, are misleading. They err, as all theories are apt to err, not by pointing to a wholly false cause but by extending the efficiency of a true cause far beyond its real scope. Considered from an historical point of view there is no such thing as nationalism in general. History knows only a particular form of nationalism. It is not the military or economic organization of a state which makes it a national body but the spiritual idea represented by its people. When we speak of the Greek nation we primarily think of the form in which the genius of this nation expressed itself. And is not Jewish nationalism an empty phrase if we do not connect with it Jewish religion and Jewish ethics, Jewish culture and the Jewish mode of life which gave it its individuality?

(—1921)

The First Encounter of Judaism with Europeanism

⧼⧽

MOSES HADAS

WHERE the Jewish community is not a self-contained political entity or endowed with an imposed stability by unfriendly pressure from without, Jews must themselves determine the extent of their participation in the general life of the non-Jewish community and the intensity of their loyalty to specifically Jewish tradition. But even where no formal restrictions are imposed it is still the climate created by the environment which controls the attitudes of Jews to their own traditions, whether religious life is shaped to minimize differences from forms generally prevalent or whether differences are emphasized more insistently than they would be if the tradition were not on the defensive; whether individuals indifferent to religion pointedly avoid Jewish organizations or whether they affiliate with a synagogue in order to conform to the mores of the larger community; whether individuals and groups retain independence of action or delegate responsibility and direction to powerful central authorities professionally administered.

The problem of achieving a *modus vivendi* has been recurrent from the time when Jews first began to participate in the civilization of Europe, which is to say from the Hellenistic age, or the third century B.C.E. And because the Hellenistic age saw the first encounter between Judaism and Europeanism, it provides the clearest paradigms for the various solutions of the problem. Later experiences are not so instructive: for when certain forms of response acquired authority they became part of the tradition rather than a tactic for confronting a new crisis. It happens too that the cultural, political, and economic climate of the Hellenistic age was strikingly like our own, and hence can afford fruitful analogies. History may not repeat itself, but (as

(43)

Machiavelli or Thucydides shows) human responses to political
exigencies are reasonably constant.

+ + +

As a premise to any consideration of the influence of Hellenism,
it must be noted that so far from resisting it, the peoples of the East
eagerly welcomed it, and the attitude of the Jews was not essentially
different from that of other peoples of the Near East. Powerful
political and economic considerations, to say nothing of the sheer at-
tractiveness of Greek ways and the factor of social prestige, made
Hellenization irresistable. Upper-class natives, who were the first to
be exposed to Greek influences, became ardent Hellenizers, to the
degree that they shared the Greek view of themselves as barbarians.
To bolster their self-esteem and win the respect of the Greeks, some
wrote books to prove that their own antiquity and culture were as
respectable as the Greek; but the language of these books was Greek,
and Greek norms were tacitly accepted as paramount. The strongest
motivation for survival was religious—religion and nationality could
not as yet be separated; but even where this motivation was most
powerful the principle seems to have been to participate as fully
in the new as loyalty to the old would permit.

Until their total loss of sovereignty in 70 C.E. and the rising danger
of the Christian heresy, the attitude of Jews to Hellenism was not
essentially different from that of other peoples of the Near East. It is
a mistake, based on the false analogy with the Jewish Reform movement of the nineteenth century, to regard the Palestinian community
as Orthodox and the Diaspora (which was much more numerous) as
Reform. For one thing, Palestine itself was deeply tinged by Hellenization; for another, Diaspora Jews never regarded themselves as in any
way abrogating or relaxing their loyalty to Jewish tradition.

Both points are demonstrable. The Hellenization of Palestine is
proved by the evidence of archaeology, which reveals Greek motifs
even in synagogue architecture and in burials; by the wide currency
of the Greek language; and, most telling, by the presence of Greek ideas
and Greek literary forms even in religious literature. These are obvious in books of the Apocrypha originally written in Hebrew, such as
Judith; in certain other early extra-canonical works such as the Testa-
ments of the Twelve Patriarchs and perhaps even the Eighteen Benedictions; and even in canonical books such as Ecclesiastes and Canticles
and perhaps Job and Jonah.

For the loyalty of the Diaspora, books written in Greek—in the Apocrypha and outside it—are significant evidence. Such devout works as IV Maccabees and Wisdom of Solomon, to say nothing of Philo, are impregnated with Greek substance and employ Greek modes of discourse; yet their authors give no slightest hint that they are in any way deviating from the mainstream of Jewish tradition. Insofar as they do deviate, it is from an orthodoxy which was formulated long after they wrote.

In one phase, Alexandrian writers of "history" took liberties with the Scriptural story (yet hardly more extensive than those in the Midrashim), but soon they resumed fidelity to the ancient texts. The authors whom Clement of Alexandria and the Church historian Eusebius excerpted from the collection of Alexander Polyhistor illustrate a shift in attitude which was probably general. Demetrius (probably early second century B.C.E.) follows the Septuagint text carefully but tries to give his work the appearance of Alexandrian scholarship. His successor Eupolemus is somewhat freer and rather shrill in his claims for Jewish priority in cultural attainments. Artapanus takes the greatest liberties of all; but his elaboration of the Moses story was intended not as history but as romance, and Greek literary theory approved the elaboration of ancient history for purposes of edification.

Presently even writers who adopted bellettristic forms used Scriptural materials more carefully. So the tragic poet Ezekielos is faithful to the story of the Exodus, though he presents it in the form of a Euripidean tragedy. Here and elsewhere we see a serene loyalty to tradition, with neither truculence nor obsequiousness, combined with full participation in the secular environment. The secure and natural *rapprochement* continued so long as the status of the Egyptian Jews was undisturbed.

Soon after the battle of Actium (31 B.C.E.) Rome began to administer Egypt as a province, and a head tax imposed on non-Greeks brought the Jews certain political and economic disabilities. The response of the Jews, as reflected in III Maccabees, was a new hostility towards their non-Jewish environment and a hardening of barriers to admit no compromise with Jewish tradition.

✦ ✦ ✦

It was in Palestine, where the Jews themselves held real or nominal sovereignty from 165 B.C.E. to 70 C.E., that something like tension between tradition and humanism ("Greek wisdom") emerged, and this too was the result of external pressures. The sequence of events shows that emphasis on tradition was a means for promoting political ends, and not politics a means for promoting religious ends. The object of the Maccabean uprising, and certainly of the Hasmonean dynasty which it inaugurated, was to establish a sovereignty that could hold its head up among other sovereignties which were rising out of the debris of the Seleucid empire. It is clear from the books of the Maccabees that Hellenization had proceeded very far among the priesthood and the upper classes of Jerusalem before the rebellion started. The banner of religion was raised to rally the populace to the national cause. It is significant that Antiochus's anti-religious decrees were issued only *after* the insurrection was under way, and significant too that when these were rescinded the religious elements in Judah's army left the movement and were indifferent to the goal of independence.

In the dim period before Alexander the Great the position of Palestine was that of a Temple State under a High Priest—a form not uncommon in the ancient world. The Maccabean rulers were high priests and so ostensibly continued ancient traditions based ultimately upon Scripture; but in the organization and administration of this State they adopted Greek usages, perhaps actually using the theory of Plato and the practice of Sparta. So the Ptolemies were ostensibly the legitimate successors of the Pharaohs but in fact adopted Greek practices.

The Maccabean rulers were no less ruthless and demanding than other Hellenistic princes, and provoked internal opposition. The dissidents, called Pharisees (literally "separatists"), based their opposition on independent and much freer interpretation of the Bible which the rulers claimed as their charter. A king like Alexander Jannaeus therefore felt justified in persecuting them as subversives. But it is to be noted that it was the "usurping" kings, not humanism, that the Pharisees opposed. There is nothing to show that they objected to humanism as such; as long as even the shadow of sovereignty survived a man could be at once a patriot and a humanist.

Regularly in politics the left moves towards the center; and when the old center was destroyed by the Romans in 70 the Pharisees became the dominant element in Judaism. The basis of their resistance under the Jewish rulers gave them a program capable of maintaining the identity of a religious communion despite the loss of sovereignty.

Their program, as exemplified in the career of Johanan ben Zakkai, was to transform loyalty to a sovereignty to loyalty to a way of life based upon a literature. It is worth noting that Johanan's contemporary, Plutarch, similarly strove to meet the challenge of Roman domination in Greece by substituting cultural for political survival.

And since the only criterion of loyalty was now adherence to a prescribed way of life, no longer to a sovereignty, prescriptions were ramified and crystallized until every act of a man's life was regulated. It was only after the loss of sovereignty that the requirements of strict observance were hardened and avenues to defection barricaded. Even so, the knowledge and use of Greek continued, so that a more literal translation of Scripture (that of Aquila) had to be procured because the Septuagint, which had enjoyed canonical authority, had proven susceptible to latitudinarian interpretation. Only after the fall of Jerusalem and the rise of Christianity was humanism branded with official disapproval. The considerable elements of Hellenism which had been received into Judaism had now become part of the Jewish legacy which must be protected from the inroads of Hellenism.

✦ ✦ ✦

To establish and enforce a regimen without secular power was a marvelous and unprecedented feat which could only be realized by a recognized authority clothed with prerogatives based upon a religious sanction. The sanction was conceived as deriving from the revelation at Sinai and as having been transmitted by Moses through an uninterrupted succession of teachers each of whom, no matter how inferior he might be to the greater lights, was clothed with the requisite authority: "Jephthah in his generation was as Samuel in his." The opening sentences of the *Chapters of the Fathers* list the succession from Moses through Joshua and the Prophets down to the newest contemporary. In the rabbinic age the heads of the schools did in fact issue binding rescripts on questions of conduct, collect fixed contributions for the maintenance of their establishments, and wield the power of excommunication to enforce their decisions.

The elaborate system constructed by the rabbis, often described as "normative Judaism," was thus conceived of as a monolithic structure, essentially unaltered from its revelation to Moses and only extended (but not added to or diminished) by generations of authorized teachers to meet new conditions. Normative Judaism was indeed such a monolith from the rabbinic age until the last century, and no significant deviation from the mainstream could be countenanced; but the antecedent portions of the chain are an artificial construction calculated to provide authority for measures thought essential to survival in a period of crisis.

Though at its inception the construction served to solidify and perpetuate a loyal core, it also cut off a much larger number whom it could not reach or who were not amenable to a new para-governmental authority; when a new orthodoxy has not yet established itself failure to acknowledge it is not heterodoxy. Our best authority on the subject has calculated that one out of ten persons in the population of the eastern Mediterranean during the late Hellenistic age was Jewish. It is likely enough that many of these would have been lost to Judaism in any case, but it is likely too that many who were lost—surely the larger portion—might have continued in the tradition if it had not become so demanding and so exclusive.

Insistence upon Hebrew not only cut off the larger segment of world Jewry whose language was Greek. It excluded from the body of acceptable reading an extensive literature in Greek at least as high in quality and as edifying as the surviving rabbinic literature, and more meaningful to our own age. The language of grave inscriptions, in Palestine and Egypt and especially in Rome, illustrates the process of concentration and reduction. Through the early centuries of the common era Jewish grave inscriptions are regularly in Greek, which was clearly the preponderant vernacular, with a few examples in Latin and only an occasional formulaic phrase in Hebrew.

Not until the sixth or seventh century do we have epitaphs in Hebrew. These are then sure evidence for the consolidation of normative Judaism, a principle of which was the use of Hebrew; but one wonders what happened to the descendants of the people buried in Greek who failed to learn Hebrew.

✦ ✦ ✦

If we attempt to summarize the experience of the first encounter between Judaism and Europeanism we must observe that Jews both in Palestine and the Diaspora welcomed participation in the cultural life of their new environment and yet maintained loyalty to the essentials of their own tradition. Their *rapprochement* with the non-Jewish environment was easy and natural, and promoted an exchange of cultural values fruitful to both parties. Tensions which disturbed this amicable relationship were initiated by outside forces, and resulted in a shortening of defense lines and strengthening of barriers.

The question is whether heroic measures undertaken to ensure survival in a time of crisis need in fact have been made part of the permanent structure of Judaism. The danger is ever present that a centralized religious organization, with large claims of authority, will blur the distinction between its own survival and prosperity and the survival and prosperity of the cause it was created to serve.

The realization of this danger is perhaps the most timely lesson that the period under consideration can afford.

(—1959)

Ghetto and Emancipation

∽⚬∾

SALO W. BARON

THE HISTORY of the Jews in the last century and a half has turned about one central fact: that of Emancipation. But what has Emancipation really meant to the Jew? The generally accepted view has it that before the French Revolution the Jews of Europe lived in a state of extreme wretchedness under medieval conditions, subject to incessant persecution and violence, but that after the Revolution a new era of enlightenment came to the nations, which forthwith struck off the bonds that fettered the Jew and opened up the gates that shut him off from civilized life. Prisoner in the Ghetto, denied access to the resources and activities of Western society, distorted intellectually, morally, spiritually by centuries of isolation and torture, the Jew was set free by the Emancipation. In the words of Graetz: "The Revolution was a judgment which in one day atoned for the sins of a thousand years, and which hurled into the dust all who, at the expense of justice and religion, had created new grades of society. A new day of the Lord had come 'to humiliate all the proud and high, and to raise up the lowly.' For the Jews, too, the most abject and despised people in European society, the day of redemption and liberty was to dawn after their long slavery among the nations of Europe. It is noteworthy that England and France, the two European countries which first expelled the Jews, were the first to reinstate them in the rights of humanity. What Mendelssohn had thought possible at some distant time, and what had been the devout wish of Dohm and Diez, those defenders of the Jews, was realized in France with almost magical rapidity."

Emancipation, in the judgment of Graetz, Philippson, Dubnow and other historians, was the dawn of a new day after a nightmare of the deepest horror, and this view has been accepted as completely true by Jews, rabbis, scholars and laymen, throughout the Western world. It

is in terms of this complete contrast between the black of the Jewish
Middle Ages and the white of the post-Emancipation period that most
generalizations about the progress of the Jews in modern times are
made. Prophecies as to the future of the Jew are also of necessity
colored by an optimisim engendered by this view. If in so short a
time the Jew has risen from such great depths, is it not logical to
hope that a few more years will bring him perfect freedom?

Unfortunately, in the light of present historical knowledge, the contrast on which these hopes are built is open to great qualification. A
more critical examination of the supposed gains after the Revolution
and fuller information concerning the Jewish Middle Ages both indicate that we may have to revaluate radically our notions of Jewish
progress under Western liberty. A wider, less prejudiced knowledge
of the actual conditions of the Jew in the period of their deepest
decline*—during the sixteenth, seventeenth and eighteenth centuries
—seems to necessitate such a revision. If the status of the Jew (his
privileges, opportunities, and actual life) in those centuries was in
fact not as low as we are in the habit of thinking, then the miracle
of Emancipation was not so great as we supposed.

In the Jewish "Middle Ages," it is said, the Jew did not have "equal
rights." But to say that pre-Emancipation Jewry did not have "equal
rights" with the rest of the population does not mean that Jewry
was the subject of special unfavorable discrimination. The simple fact
is that there was no such thing then as "equal rights." In this period
the absolute State, like the medieval State, was still largely built on
the corporations. The corporations were legally recognized groups of
people belonging to different corporate organizations, each with distinct rights and duties. The corporation of the nobility had its rights
and duties, among them that of administration and defense of the
country. The clergy was entrusted with spiritual and cultural affairs.

---

* The Jewish "Middle Ages," as Zunz soundly remarks, are not identical with
the "Middle Ages" of Europe. The "Dark Ages" of the Jew are roughly comprised by the centuries immediately preceding the French Revolution, the sixteenth,
seventeenth and eighteenth centuries; the "Dark Ages" of Europe were really
a time of relative prosperity and high civilization for the Jew. Until the Crusades
a majority of Jewry lived under Islamic rule in relatively good circumstances,
while even Western Jewry was far superior to its Christian neighbors in culture
and economic status. Only in the last centuries of the European Middle Ages did
the Jewish Middle Ages set it. The decline was accelerated and continued during
the religious wars, particularly in the countries of the counter-Reformation.

While mercenaries and standing armies had to some extent replaced feudal military, and the Church had begun to give way to secular agencies of culture, the traditional powers of both were still recognized down to the very opening of the Revolution. The urban citizenry (not the peasant or proletarian mass) formed the real third estate, and its chief function was the maintenance of economic life and the replenishment of the State treasury. Below these corporations in large was the peasant body, the vast majority of the population, in many countries held in complete serfdom, and everywhere with few rights and many duties.

It is, then, not surprising and certainly no evidence of discrimination that the Jews did not have "equal rights"—no one had them. Moreover, it may be said that if the Jews had fewer rights than nobles and clergy, their duties were hardly ever greater. Their legal status was comparable to that of the third estate, and, indeed, they were largely an urban group. In some periods they had equal, in some, fewer, in some, more rights than other town inhabitants. At the very opening of the modern period, Jewish rights after a long decline happened to be on the average lower than those of their urban Christian neighbors, yet even then they belonged to the privileged minority which included nobles, clergy and urban citizenry.

Certainly the Jews had fewer duties and more rights than the great bulk of the population—the enormous mass of peasants, the great majority of whom were little more than appurtenances of the soil on which they were born. When the land was sold they were included in the sale. None could move away without the master's consent. Like cattle they were *glebae adscripti,* but less free than cattle to mate. The larger part of their produce went to landlords or to the State. On every important occasion—at a birth, marriage or death—the landlord had rights to be considered. In every legal contest his was the only competent court. Seen by La Bruyère, the peasants in 1689 even in comparatively happy France were "savage-looking beings . . . black, livid, and sunburnt . . . they seem capable of articulation and, when they stand erect, they display human lineaments. They are in fact men. They retire at night into their dens where they live on black bread, water, and roots."

In contrast to this class, the Jews were well off. They could move freely from place to place with few exceptions, they could marry whomever they wanted, they had their own courts, and were judged according to their own laws. Even in mixed cases with non-Jews, not the local tribunal but usually a special judge appointed by the king or some high official had competence. Sometimes, as in Poland, the Jews even exercised influence in the nomination of such a *judex judaeorum* for mixed cases.

The disabilities under which medieval Jewry suffered have been made much of. Jews could not own land, or join most of the guilds, and were thereby effectively barred from certain branches of craft and commerce. But these were, in legal theory, restrictions made on the privileges granted them, and not limitations on any general rule of equal rights. Every corporation had similar restrictions, and in this respect the Jews' case was no different in principle from that of other privileged groups.

True, the Jews were *servi camerae* (servants of the Treasury), but this status can neither in theory nor in practice be compared with that of the peasants, who were serfs of their local masters. If one may introduce a modern legal distinction not thoroughly applicable to medieval conditions, this difference becomes clear. The peasants were really serfs in civil law, that is, they belonged to a private owner as a kind of private property. The Jews were, so to speak, serfs in public law, and as such belonged to the ruler as representative or embodiment of the State, and they were inherited by his successor in office through public law. The man elected to the Imperial throne was their master, and not the private heir of the former Emperor's private estates, or the heir even of those German countries which, like Austria, he could claim on dynastic grounds. Now we ought not to forget that even today we are, in effect, serfs of the State in public law, notwithstanding all theories of personal rights, natural rights of citizens, and the sovereignty of the people. In fact, even more so today than formerly. The State can levy taxes little short of confiscatory; it can send us to war; in democratic countries, and even more so in Fascist Italy or Soviet Russia, it is complete master of all lives and property. This situation, expressed in medieval terminology, is a serf relationship applying to all citizens. The Jew then, insofar as he was *servus camerae*, was in substantially the same position all modern free citizens are in. In a word, the difference in the legal status between Jew and peasant was what David Hume, writing in that period on the condition of ancient slaves, called the difference between "domestic slavery" and "civil subjection." The first, he recognized, is "more cruel and oppressive than any civil subjection whatsoever."

The Jews' status as servant of the Emperor only, which had been opposed in vain by Thomas Aquinas and Pope Innocent III (these had it that he was the property of the different kings and princes in Christendom), was based on the erroneous theory that the Holy Roman Emperors of the German nation were direct successors of the ancient Roman Emperors and thus inherited the authority exercised over Jewish prisoners by Vespasian and Titus after Jerusalem's fall. Vespasian had levied the *fiscus Judaicus,* and the medieval rulers levied a similar tax—*Schutzgeld* (protection money). In practice, the theory of Imperial overlordship of Jewry was occasionally a disadvantage, as when the argument was made in fourteenth century France that these subjects of a foreign monarch be expelled from the country. But in general it was a profitable theory, for the Emperor often did provide the protection for which Jewry paid, as when he used his considerable power on their behalf in several of the German free cities.

Indeed, the status of the Jew in the Middle Ages implied certain privileges which they no longer have under the modern State. Like the other corporations, the Jewish community enjoyed full internal autonomy. Complex, isolated, in a sense foreign, it was left more severely alone by the State than most other corporations. Thus the Jewish community of pre-Revolutionary days had more competence over its members than the modern Federal, State, and Municipal governments combined. Education, administration of justice between Jew and Jew, taxation for communal and State purposes, health, markets, public order, were all within the jurisdiction of the community-corporation, and, in addition, the Jewish community was the fountain-head of social work of a quality generally superior to that outside Jewry. The Jewish self-governing bodies issued special regulations and saw to their execution through their own officials. Statute was reinforced by religious, supernatural sanctions as well as by coercive public opinion within the group. For example, a Jew put in *Cherem* by a Jewish court was practically a lost man, and the *Cherem* was a fairly common means of imposing the will of the community on the individual. All this self-governing apparatus disappeared, of course, when the Revolution brought "equal rights" to European Jewry.

✦ ✦ ✦

A phase of this corporate existence generally regarded by emancipated Jewry as an unmitigated evil was the Ghetto. But it must not be forgotten that the Ghetto grew up voluntarily as a result of Jewish self-government, and it was only in a later development that public law interfered and made it a legal compulsion for *all* Jews to live in a secluded district in which no Christian was allowed to dwell. To a certain extent the Ghetto in this technical sense was a fruit of the counter-Reformation, having its origin in Pope Paul IV's Bull, *Cum nimis absurdum,* issued against the Jews in 1555, and in its extreme application it was, of course, obnoxious. In origin, however, the Ghetto was an institution that the Jews had found it to their interest to create themselves. Various corporations in the State had separate streets of their own; the shoemakers, for example, or the bakers, would live each in one neigborhood. In addition to their growing mutual interest as a corporation of money dealers, the Jews wished to be near the Synagogue, then a social as well as a religious center. Furthermore, they saw in the Ghetto a means of defense. Thus, it was the Jews themselves who secured from Bishop Rudiger in Spires in 1084 the right to settle in a separate district and to erect a wall around it. There were locks inside the Ghetto gates in most cases before there were locks outside. The Ghetto, in the non-technical sense, was then a district in which most Jews and few Gentiles lived long before the legal compulsion which came when Christian authority found it necessary to mark the Jews off by residence district, in order to prevent complete social intercourse between them and Christians.

In this Ghetto, before compulsion came and after, Jewry was enabled to live a full, rounded life, apart from the rest of the population, under a corporate governing organization. The Jew, indeed, had in effect a kind of territory and State of his own throughout the Middle Ages and early modern period. The advantages of this autonomy, lost through the Emancipation, were certainly considerable; they must have contributed in large part toward the preservation of Jewry as a distinct nationality.

Again, the terrors of the Inquisition play a large part in all descriptions of the state of medieval Jewry. Its horrors have been fully portrayed, and many assume that whatever normal Jewish life might have been potentially, the constant incursions of the Inquisitor made it abnormal. It should be remembered, however, that the Inquisition was legally instituted only in a few European countries, and even there had no jurisdiction over professing Jews, beyond censoring Hebrew books. Therefore, far from being a special prey of the Inquisition, Jews belonged to a small, privileged group which had virtual immunity from its operations.

In the eyes of a contemporary European, the Inquisition was no more than an ordinary court of justice, proceeding along the ordinary lines of criminal prosecution in cases of capital crime. Apostasy from Christianity, by an old law of Church and State, was punishable by death. To the religious conscience of the Western man it seemed to be a holy task to burn the body of such a criminal in order to save his soul. According to the interpretation of Canon Law prevailing throughout the Renaissance, Marranos (secret Jews) were regarded as apostates. True, the highest Church authorities taught that enforced baptism was criminal, but most of them understood by force real physical compulsion, the *vis absoluta* of the old Romans, and in this sense the baptism of few Marranos could be viewed as enforced, even though a strong *vis compulsiva* existed in the menace of deprivation of fortune and expulsion. Furthermore, many authorities contended that once baptism occurred, even by compulsion, for the neophyte to return to his former faith would be apostasy. (If the sixteenth-century Popes permitted Marranos to return to Judaism in Rome itself, theirs was certainly a laxer attitude than that of earlier and later church teachers and jurists.) At least in pure legal theory, then, the Marranos were apostates. They were, therefore, subject to the jurisdiction of the Inquisition, and the governments of Spain and Portugal were acting with strict legality in applying to them the strict interpretation of laws concerning apostasy.

As to the horrible means of procedure depicted with such vividness in the classic histories of Jewry, we must say again, with no effort to justify but in an effort to understand, that they were not extraordinary for their times. The "Inquisition" was a characteristic form of legal procedure, prevailing in civil as well as ecclesiastical courts, in which the judge was at the same time prosecutor and attorney for the defendant. The use of torture was based upon the belief that circumstantial evidence is insufficient, and that a confession must therefore be extorted. Many also believed that such bodily sufferings were salutary for the soul. Such principles are shocking to the modern mind, but in a period of such draconic secular law as the *Constitutio Criminalis*

Carolina, issued by the enlightened ruler of Germany, Spain, the Netherlands and all the New World, they are hardly extraordinary. Nor is it surprising that Jews were tortured and killed in an age when not less than 40,000 Christian "witches" were burned because they confessed to relations with demons. Regarded by itself or measured by absolute standards, the position of the Jews under the Inquisition was certainly unenviable. But by comparative standards they were, if anything, in a preferred position. For if as apostates or heretics they ran afoul of the Inquisition, they were no worse off than Gentile apostates or heretics, while as professing Jews they were beyond its jurisdiction.

Legally and in theory, we have seen, the status of the Jew was by no means an inferior one. But did actual events—persecutions, riots, pogroms, monetary extortions—reduce their theoretical legal privileges to fictions in practice? Even here the traditional answer of Jewish historians does not square with the facts.

First of all, it is certainly significant that despite minor attacks, periodic pogroms, and organized campaigns of conversion, the numbers of Jewry during the last centuries preceding Emancipation increased much more rapidly than the Gentile population.* The Jewish population in the middle of the seventeenth century probably did not exceed 650,000 out of the more than 100,000,000 inhabitants in Europe. In 1900 the Jewish population of Europe exceeded 8,500,000 while the general population was about 400,000,000. That is, the Jewish rate of increase from 1650 down to the beginning of the twentieth century (when the mass of Jewry was still unemancipated)† was three times the rate of Gentile increase. Furthermore, in the same period European Jewry built the great American center.

It may be worthwhile to analyze in some detail the population

* Pre-Revolutionary population figures given here are by no means certain. I arrived at them after a careful study of all available source material. It is impossible, of course, to give these sources here or to explain the methods of textual criticism and synthesis used in arriving at the conclusions. It has long been apparent, however, that figures given by our classic histories are far from reasonably exact, which is all that mine pretend to be.

† It must be borne in mind that Emancipation did not come to Russia, Rumania or Turkey until the present century, while in Austria (including the Jewish masses of Galicia and Hungary) it postdates 1867.

increase previous to the Emancipation. From 1650 to 1789, when no
Jews were yet emancipated, the Jewish population increased from
650,000 to 1,700,000, or more than 160 percent, while the European
general population rose from 100,000,000 to 177,000,000, an increase
of only 77 percent. During the period 1789–1848, when only the Jews
of France and Holland (less than 5 percent of all European Jewry)
were emancipated, the Jewish population increased from 1,700,000 to
3,700,000, or about 120 percent. In the same period the general population increased only 40 percent. Even more amazing are the figures
for France and Holland themselves. The chief Jewish settlement in
France (Alsace) increased from 3,300 in 1700 (pre-Emancipation) to
26,000 in 1791 (year of the Emancipation), or about 700 percent,
while in the six decades following 1791 their number rose only to
about 40,000, an increase of less than 50 percent. In Holland the
Jewish settlement started in the sixteenth century, developed rapidly
during the next 200 years, and when Emancipation came there were
about 50,000 Jews in the country. During the first decades of the
Emancipation the general population of Holland rose from 1,882,000
(1805) to 2,640,000 (1830), while the Jewish population decreased
about 20 percent. Only about 1840 did it again touch the previous
high figure of 50,000. As for Russia, Rumania, Austria and Turkey,
to which Emancipation came late, there was a great increase in the
Jewish populations century after century. Is it not clear then that,
despite the fact that pre-Revolutionary Jewry suffered massacres and
other sanguinary persecutions, the population increase went on at
least as rapidly before Emancipation as after?

As a matter of fact, a comparison between the loss of life by violence
in the two eras—pre- and post-Emancipation—would probably show
little improvement since the French Revolution. Between Chmielnicki
and Human, the two great pogrom movements of earlier East
European Jewish history, more than a century intervened, whereas
three major pogrom waves have swept Eastern Europe between 1880
and 1920, despite the coming of Emancipation. And if the Emancipation era did not relieve the Jew of pogroms, it did burden him in
addition with the obligation of military service, from which (except
in rare and temporary situations of abnormal character) he had
always been free. During the continuous wars of the sixteenth,
seventeenth, and eighteenth centuries, when even the non-combatant
Christian felt the curse of religious conflict, the Jews were neutral and

suffered few losses. If they had been combatants they might have lost more than in all the pogroms.*

✦ ✦ ✦

What of the economic situation of the Jew? Despite all the restrictions placed on his activities, it is no exaggeration to say that the average Jewish income much surpassed the average Christian income in pre-Revolutionary times. This is hard to prove, and certainly excessive wealth was rare except among high nobles and clergy. But is it not remarkable that the most typical ghetto in the world, the Frankfort Judengasse, produced in the pre-Emancipation period the greatest banking house of history? And even before Rothschild's day, such Central European *Hofjuden* as the Oppenheimers and Wertheimers, and such West European bankers as the Pintos, Modonas and others, were not far behind rich Christians in their financial power.

Paradoxical as it may seem, the very restrictive legislation proved in the long run highly beneficial to Jewish economic development. It forced them into the money trade, and throughout the Middle Ages trained them in individual enterprise without guild backing, compelled them to set up wide international contacts (the banking house of Lopez was established by five brothers in Lisbon, Toulouse, Bordeaux, Antwerp and London), and equipped them with vast sums of ready cash. With the dawn of early capitalism, and the need for ready money for the new manufactures and international trading ventures, the Jew fitted readily into the new economic structure. One need not accept Sombart's exaggerations to see that the Jew had an extraordinarily large share in the development of early capitalism, and received corresponding benefits. For several hundred years before the Emancipation many individual Jews were to profit from the old restriction which had trained them in money economy, and some of those profits were to seep down to the Jewish mass.

There were, of course, many impoverished Jews, particularly in Eastern Europe. But there were not so many of them, even relatively, as there were poor peasants. Their standard of life was everywhere

---

* It has been pointed out that the sixteenth century knew altogether twenty-five years, the seventeenth only twenty-one years, without big international conflagrations, not to speak of smaller wars. What the effects of those wars were upon the numbers of the population even in such a rich country as France, the leading empire of the world at that time, we see best in a short statement like this: "I estimate," says Hippolyte Taine, "that in 1715 more than one-third of the population, six millions, perished of hunger and of destitution."

higher than that of the majority of the populace. Particularly in Western and Central Europe the frequent complaints about the extravagance of some Jews, and the luxury laws of certain large Jewish communities, indicate a degree of well-being which is surprising. Furthermore, there existed in the Jewish corporations numerous relief agencies, a whole system of social insurance against need, in startling contrast to the often exposed and defenseless situation of the mass of the population.

Compared with these advantages, social exclusion from the Gentile world was hardly a calamity. Indeed, to most Jews it was welcome, and the ghetto found warm champions in every age. There the Jews might live in comparative peace, interrupted less by pogroms than were peasants by wars, engaged in finance and trade at least as profitable as most urban occupations, free to worship, and subject to the Inquisition only in extreme situations (as after the enforced baptisms in Spain and Portugal). They had no political rights, of course, but except for nobles and clergy no one did.

✦ ✦ ✦

When the modern State came into being and set out to destroy the medieval corporations and estates and to build a new citizenship, it could no longer suffer the existence of an autonomous Jewish corporation. Sooner or later it had to give to the Jews equal rights in civil and public law and to impose upon them equal duties in turn. After the French Revolution one state after the other abrogated their economic disabilities, and granted them full freedom of activity. Finally they opened public offices, elective and appointive, to Jews, and made them citizens with "equal rights."

Emancipation was a necessity even more for the modern State than for Jewry; the Jew's medieval status was anachronistic and had to go. Left to themselves, the Jews might for long have clung to their corporate existence. For Emancipation meant losses as well as gains for Jewry.

Equal rights meant equal duties, and the Jew now found himself subject to military service. Political equality also meant the dissolution of the autonomous communal organization: the Jews were no longer to be a nation within a nation; they were to be thought of and to think of themselves as individuals connected only by ties of creed— Frenchmen, Germans, Englishmen of the Jewish "Confession." This meant that politically, culturally and socially the Jew was to be absorbed into the dominant national group. Eventually, it was hoped, his assimilation would be complete.

In the face of Emancipation traditional Jewish ideology underwent great revision. The concept of the inseparability of nationality and religion—which had been increasingly abandoned in Europe after the bloody Wars of Religion—had persisted in Judaism down to the Revolution, and after. Now the theory was put forth that the Jewish religion—which the Jew was permitted to keep—must be stripped of all Jewish national elements. For national elements were called secular, and in secular matters the Jew was to avow allegiance to the national ambitions and culture of the land in which he lived. Jewish Reform may be seen as a gigantic effort, partly unconscious, by many of the best minds of Western Jewry to reduce differences between Jew and Gentile to a slight matter of creed, at the same time adopting the Gentile's definition of what was properly a matter of creed. The reality of the living Jewish ethnic organism was to be pared down to the fiction of the Jewish "Confession." Jewish nationality was to be declared dead and buried. Assimilation via Reform was the Jewish destiny, as the nineteenth century European, Jew and non-Jew, saw it.

There emerged at this point the new *Wissenschaft des Judentums*, intrinsically connected with Reformation and Emancipation, a movement of scholars anxious to assist the completion of the process of emancipation with their learning. Confronted by the general suspicion in which Germany and the modern world in general held the Jew, and convinced of the desirability of complete emancipation, they consciously or unconsciously sought a tool in history and evolved this argument: "The Jews may be bad, but if they are it is because of your persecution; change your attitude, welcome the Jews into the modern State on terms of perfect equality, and they will become good." Ardent advocates of liberalism and democracy, visioning a reformed society guided by beneficent rationalism, believing religiously that the world in general and the Jews particularly could be improved by an extension of rights, it is easy to see how they found it useful to take as black a view as possible of the pre-Revolutionary treatment of the Jews. The exaggerated historical picture of the horrors of the "Dark Ages" which we have been examining was the result.

This view of the Jewish past, outlined by the earliest advocates of political and social equality, was seized on and elaborated by advocates of Jewish Reform in the nineteenth century. Eager to widen the breach with the past, to demonstrate a casual relation between the treatment given the Jew and his general acceptability and usefulness to society, Reform advocates proclaimed in unmeasured terms the wretchedness of the age that preceded them. They explained Jewish "pecularities" as results of oppression. The more radical expounded the idea that to achieve a new, free Jewish religion based on the Bible, the entire literature of the Diaspora must be abandoned. The Talmud, which grew up in the Diaspora, did not reflect Judaism's innermost spirit, they maintained, but was a mirror of the "abnormal conditions" in which Jews had lived.

At the end of the nineteenth and in the twentieth century, this view, originated by the anti-nationalist leaders of Reform, was to find reinforcement, paradoxically, from Zionism. Zionism wished to reject the Diaspora in toto, on the grounds that a "normal life" could not be led by Jewry elsewhere than on its own soil. So, notwithstanding their profound differences, Zionism and Reform both found that their positions were best supported by that view of history which held that before the Revolution European Jewry had lived in extreme wretchedness. They differed only in that the Zionists denounced the post-Revolutionary period as equally bad.

✦ ✦ ✦

It should be pointed out at once that this conception of modern Jewish history is indispensable neither to Reform nor to Zionism. Indeed, each has begun to shift its ground. Particularly among the younger intellectual leaders of national Judaism one discovers a note of romantic longing towards the Jewish ghetto, its life, and its culture. In literature, the revival of Chassidism, at least as a cultural force, in the writings of Martin Buber, Peretz, Berditchevsky and others, represents the new tendency. The establishment of national Jewish minorities in Eastern Europe has done much to reverse former animosity to ghetto ideas of Jewish self-government. As for Reform, strong wings of the movement in America and Germany endeavor to reconcile it with Zionism. Even those who do not fully adopt Zionist ideology have become lar less antagonistic to Hebrew culture than were their forerunners in the *Sturm und Drang* period of Reform.

Thus medieval Jewish life takes on new values for Reform, and the old need for rejection of all that preceded the Emancipation disappears.

Such revaluations of the Middle Ages are part, perhaps, of a general modern tendency in historical studies, reflecting changes in our modern outlook. Liberal *laissez faire* is being more and more supplanted by a system of great trusts, protectionism, Fascism, Sovietism. Growing dissatisfaction with democracy and parliamentarianism has brought about a movement back to a modified medievalism. This is a medievalism on a higher plane, perhaps, but a medievalism just the same, of organization, standardization, and regulation.

That Reform and Zionism have both begun, though timidly and slowly, to reconsider the Jewish Middle Ages is encouraging. The future will certainly not see a reversal toward an obsolete and impossible corporational system. With other national minorities the Jews claimed and are claiming, not without success, the equilibrium between their full rights as citizens and the special minority rights they think necessary to protect their living national organism from destruction and absorption by the majority, a process that has often proved to be harmful both for the absorber and the absorbed.

At any rate, it is clear that Emancipation has not brought the Golden Age. While Emancipation has meant a reduction of ancient evils, and while its balance sheet for the world at large as well as for the Jews is favorable, it is not completely clear of debits. Certainly its belief in the efficacy of a process of complete assimilation has been proved untenable. Autonomy as well as equality must be given its place in the modern State, and much time must pass before these two principles will be fully harmonized and balanced. Perhaps the chief task of this and future generations is to attain that harmony and balance. Surely it is time to break with the lachrymose theory of pre-Revolutionary woe, and to adopt a view more in accord with historic truth.

(—1928)

On a Jewish Humanism

❦

MARVIN LOWENTHAL

OURS is a practical world, and of all the people in it we Americans are reputed the most practical; and if there is anything we like better than anything else, it is to prove that something or other is useful. Only second to our love of surrounding ourselves with things of use is our passion to devise ways of measuring their utility. We like to think that we are a nation of statistics, questionnaires, surveys, ballots, and competitive contests. We rejoice in dollar and cent valuations, crop computations in bushel and ton, population estimates, and percentage tables; and when we are not appraising literature through a survey of the best-sellers in the Ozarks, we are measuring religion by racing for records in Bible class attendance. There is no American so ignorant that he cannot repeat to you the Chamber of Commerce claim for the population of his home town.

This American passion for usefulness and measurement, shared, to be sure, by the general western world, is not to be frowned down or sneered away by epithets of "materialism" or "utilitarianism," for, at bottom, it is the natural efflorescence of that rediscovery of the world which historians loosely call the Renaissance and which moderns call the scientific attitude. It is the awakening to self-consciousness, faintly at first, and of course somewhat childishly, on the part of whole societies. It is a turning of the attention of men from the gods to themselves, from the Great Beyond to the Little Way Ahead, from cosmic dreams to county facts—and it is evidence, no less, of a turning from a provincial theological cocksureness to a universal skepticism. It is, in short, the essence of Humanism, so far as we mean by this word the view of life traditionally accepted as Greek. "What's it good for?" and "How much is it worth?" are largely what Socrates meant when he said, "Know thyself," and when he makes Protagoras say, "Man is the measure of all things."

It is, therefore, innocent of any pandering to a supposedly crass element in modern life that I wish to consider some elements of usefulness in Jewish culture, that I wish to set forth an attitude toward and use of this culture which I believe would serve us moderns, as Jews, Americans, and children of western civilization, in an explicitly humanistic fashion. I believe that rightly approached and employed we have in Jewish culture objects of use and measurement; stimulants to a further awakening of our self-consciousness; means to a deeper understanding of ourselves, of mankind, as the proper study of man; material, that is, for an enrichment and development of a wider humanism today.

Because I am using words devoid of any fixed meaning, culture, humanism, and the like, I will have to set forth rather precisely, without I hope becoming pedantic, what I mean by what I am writing about before I really write much about it.

I do not mean by a Jewish humanism that secular aspect of the Jewish past or present which Dr. H. M. Kallen, and perhaps others, have called Hebraism. Nor am I concerned here with that totality of ancient Jewish history, secular and religious, expressible in a body of principles, in, that is, a "philosophy of life" that with varying interpretations has elsewhere won the name of Hebraism. In other words, I do not mean by a Jewish humanism ancient Hebrew sociology or modern Hebrew poetry. So much for what I do not mean; unfortunately, what I do mean cannot be said so briefly.

Toying with the word Hebraism, I was led to re-reading Matthew Arnold's chapter on "Hellenism and Hebraism" and, on the side, the remainder of that schoolday book, *Culture and Anarchy*, in which this chapter appears. I discovered that what I had in mind as a Jewish humanism was rather similar to what Arnold meant by Hellenism. And I also discovered that the greatest obstacle to understanding—and what is equally important, to employing—what I mean by a Jewish humanism is Arnold's own conception of Hebraism accepted, as it is, by great bodies of western Jews. Because of this, and not by way of subscribing to Arnold's historically artificial categories, I shall risk repeating the distinctions he made.

Arnold conceived the use of culture as "turning a stream of fresh and free thought upon one's stock notions and habits." Upon examining these stock notions and habits, he found that the bulk of them, which differ in no great degree from our twentieth century stock, were dominated by an emphasis on conduct and a devotion to obedience, by a cult of morality in action that he called Hebraism. He called it Hebraism because he thought that this emphasis on right behavior, on what we do, harks back, through Christianity, to ancient Judaism, and that by this name it can best be distinguished from that emphasis on how we think, on clear seeing and right reason, which he conceives as deriving from ancient Greece and which he calls Hellenism.

In his pedagogical way, Arnold rings numerous changes on these two terms in order to reinforce his interpretation of them. "The uppermost idea with Hellenism," according to his notion, "is to see things as they are." It is, more ambiguously, "spontaneity of consciousness." "To get rid of one's ignorance, to see things as they are, and by seeing them as they are to see them in their beauty," is the ideal of this Hellenism, and it and human life in its hands are thereby invested "with a kind of aerial ease, clearness, and radiancy." The Renaissance, to take an example of the sort of thing Arnold means, is "the great reawakening of Hellenism," because it is an "irresistible return of humanity to nature."

Hebraism, on the other hand, sounds in Arnold's definition like an old-fashioned medicine—something bitter, unpleasant, but good for one. Its "uppermost idea" concentrates on "conduct and obedience." It is impregnated with "right acting" rather than "right thinking." Instead of spontaneity of consciousness, it is devoted to "strictness of conscience." Socrates, the Hellenist, "is terribly at ease in Zion"; the Hebraist, contrariwise, "has always been severely occupied with an awful sense of the impossibility of being at ease in Zion." If the Renaissance is Hellenism reawakened, Christianity and Puritanism are Hebraism "aiming at self-conquest and rescue from the thrall of vile affections." Hellenism lays its main stress on "comprehensively knowing the grounds of one's duty"; Hebraism on "diligently practising it." As Hellenism represents a triumph of man's mental impulses, so Hebraism represents a triumph of his moral impulses. Hellenism is "sweetness and light." Hebraism is "fire and strength."

Arnold somewhere makes a point of England's affinity with this Hebraic spirit; one can, with perhaps even closer accuracy, speak of a modern Jewish affinity with this English notion of Hebraism. Western Jews, whether they have read Arnold or not, look at Judaism

through his bi-focal glasses. Judaism is for them emphatically a profession of morals—that is, of customs and manners. Sometimes they
prefer to speak of Judaism as a matter of ethics; and here Jane Harrison's translation of the Greek root is enlightening, for ethics (*ethea*)
describes our current Judaism with uncanny exactitude when it is
understood that the word primarily means "haunts and habits."

The more orthodox insistence on the supposedly all-embracing trilogy,
Torah, Avodah, and Gemiluth Chasodim, is, except for the troublesome Torah, equally an emphasis on behavior. To go to synagogue,
at least twice a year; to give to the poor, enough to save one's self
from public shame: upon this the modern Jewish world is based. The
demands for heavy thinking inherent in the obligations to Torah,
which properly met might lead toward "comprehensively knowing the
grounds of one's duty" and land one almost plump in the Hellenist
camp, are circumvented by interpreting one's duty to Torah as teaching
numerous little children the Hebrew alphabet and an occasional
adolescent how to officiate as a rabbi. So much for the professedly
religious Jews; the more "advanced" wing have girded themselves with
the "fire and strength" of Arnold's characterization; and on the (not
altogether false) assumption that they are thereby the sons of the
prophets, they translate Hebraism into Liberalism, Progressivism,
Socialism, and general trouble-making for the public good.

In any case, the Jewish tradition is looked upon by western Jews
as a recipe for action, for something to be done, which is either to be
followed literally by doing again today whatever has been done for
some thousands of years, or to be followed figuratively by doing today
whatever you think your forefathers, especially the prophets and great
rabbis, would do were they in your shoes. And in the blare of this call
to action—to rebuild Zion, to contribute to someone's favorite orphan
asylum, to go to temple Friday nights, to join a synagogal men's club,
to teach children the *Aleph Beth* so that they won't grow up to be
gunmen, to keep the seminaries going so that there will always be
someone on hand to marry and bury us and deliver speeches against
the Klan; in short, to do the things we call a Jewish life—in this blare
it is exceedingly difficult to catch the sound of a low voice, a *Bat Kol*,
which exhorts to no enterprise, propounds no formula, offers no program, but which is instinct with a humanism generally neglected by
our practical Jewish world.

✦ ✦ ✦

This humanism, leisurely acquired and slowly matured, flowers—not, as I have said, in a program, a formula, an enterprise, but—in an attitude of mind. This attitude is at once critical, appreciative, and fructifying. It rises, to begin with, through a disinterested but enthusiastic absorption in Jewish culture, and ultimately from the confrontation of this culture with a series of alien worlds, including the world of today. This sounds complicated, no doubt, but that is because I have tried to put the matter in one mouthful; as we ruminate the ingredients in detail, they will simplify themselves.

The first ingredient is an absorption in Jewish culture. By Jewish culture I mean quite simply the totality of the Jewish experience. I mean, therefore, an absorption in not only biblical literature and the Talmud, but in the full stream of Jewish literature from "In the beginning . . ." to the latest lyric of Bialik; not only Jewish literature in Hebrew, but in every language which transmits the experience of the Jewish people, the Greek of Philo, Paul, and Josephus, the Aramaic of the Talmud, the Arabic of Maimonides, the Yiddish of Nahman of Bratzslav and Sholem Aleichem, the German of Zunz and Geiger; not only literature revealing Jewish life from within and in the mass, but likewise the experiences of provocative Jewish personalities and the manner in which they have impinged on and accepted the world, Spinoza, Maimon, Heine, Rahel Varnhagen, Beaconsfield, Lassalle, Jean de Bloch; not only Jewish history from Genesis to the Dispersion, but through the twenty centuries thereafter, in every continent of the globe, down to the last election of a Jewish bloc in Poland and the last immigration report from Palestine; not only Jewish thought glorified in the growth and crystallization of the central Jewish faith, but its exotic adventures in Hellenism, Scholasticism, Protestantism, and modern Nationalism, and its unorthodox digressions among the Rechabites, Essenes, Jewish Christians, Karaites, Kabbalists, Chassidim, and Reform Jews; not only the Jewish religious, philosophic, and literary experience, but Jewish social and economic life in its phantasmagoria of customs and taboos, imitations and survivals, cuisines and costumes (what haven't they eaten and worn, these Jews, by way of "national" cookery and dress, for variegated centuries!), trades and crafts (slave-dealers in Rome, spice merchants in Cathay, diamond cutters in Amsterdam, inn-keepers in Podolia, and tailors in New York), judicial, educational, and charitable institutions and innovations from the *Bet Din, Cheder,* and *Chevrah Kadisha* to the Federated Charities,

Rabbinical Seminary, and Fraternal Order; not only this pageant of spiritual and practical life, not only the three thousand years' experiments in truth and goodness, but the equally prolonged search and trial of beauty, with its diverse manifestations in calligraphy, illumination, decorative ritual objects, embroideries, mortuary sculpture, synagogue architecture and fresco-work, engraving, painting, music, and the dance, from the cunning workmanship of the primitive Bezalel to the eruptive fancies of Marc Chagall, from the thirteenth century Haggadah of Sarajevo to the modern woodcuts of Steinhardt, from the desert-born ullulations of *hazzanut* to the *Schelomo* of Ernest Bloch, from the triumphant dance of Miriam before the Lord to the mystic tread of the Chassidim still to be heard and seen in the villages of the Carpathians.

Manifestly no individual can acquaint himself with, much less master, all the details of this august totality. When, therefore, I urge an absorption in Jewish culture, I mean no more than a journey for a liberal distance in these many directions, a distance determined by one's capacities and interests, but—and this is the nub—always recognizing the existence of the totality, appreciating through some slight excursion, at least, its intricate diversity, and formulating some notion of the interrelationship of these infinite parts to the as yet unended whole.

It can almost be guaranteed that an immersion in this flood of three thousand years of culture will forthwith dissolve most preconceived notions of Hebraism and the like. The whole is too great for any part to claim its name, to serve as its symbol, or to convey its essence. You may make the plunge with the conviction that the Jews are essentially a religious people, but you will emerge with the knowledge that while they are emphatically a religious people they are likewise emphatically—as the Romans are reputed to be—a legislative people. And, by a pertinent selection of details, one can as readily conclude that they are—as the Greeks are famed—an intellectualizing people; and on the record of their achievements in literature and art a beauty-loving people.

The fallacy of these old and wooden distinctions lies in attributing to a people as an inherent characteristic something which is chiefly an historic and altogether an extraneous accident. Greek art has influenced the world more profoundly than Roman or Jewish, but the Greek people were innocent of a design to become the art dictators of a continent; and, if you could have strolled into the *agora* at Athens and told anyone you chose, from Pericles to the green-grocer, that of course the Greeks were not essentially a religious or a political people, you would have been lucky to escape with mere smiles of incredulity. The influence of Greek art is due as much to the receptivity of the barbarian, including the last student to graduate from the Beaux Arts, as to the creative quality of the Greek. And it is out of the receptivity of the non-Greek and the twists of history that brought about a Roman conquest of Greece and later a Roman conquest of most of Europe and the Mediterranean world, and those more recent twists, such as old Cosimo di Medici's Council of Florence and the fall of Constantinople, that we have manufactured the artistic pre-eminence and essentiality of the Greeks. If the Romans could have conquered China instead of Greece, it would have been Chinese painting instead of Greek sculpture which would have set for us the standards of artistic perfection. Nor were the Romans, popularly conceived as arch lawgivers, concerned with making laws for feudal Europe or thinking of the Napoleonic code. Nor were the sages of the Great Synagogue, painstakingly building their fence, concerned with Mohammedanism or Christianity. Neither were the Romans so engrossed in making laws that their life was devoid of religion or beauty. A pious Roman could have learned nothing of meticulous observance from a Jew, and Horace nothing of artistic devotion from Theocritus. Neither have the Jews, in their religious fervor, failed to make laws or create beauty. Despite historical generalizations, the Talmud and Judah Halevi stubbornly remain. Jewish law is still open for anyone to read and Jewish courts, too, for anyone to attend. The illuminated Haggadahs cannot be torn up, the altar embroideries unraveled, and the synagogue frescoes washed away.

This destruction of habitual notions under the shock of facts is itself a humanizing process. It is a spiritual calisthenics and limbers not only the mind, but that dim seat of our deepest instincts, the core of impulse and prejudice we call the soul. By confronting one and another of the multitudinous elements of the Jewish experience, the shocks can be kept up indefinitely. The notion, if one happens to be possessed of it, that Judaism is almost exclusively a rationalist sort of religion will go to pieces before a cursory study of the so-called new and old Chassidism. The notion that it is pre-eminently a this-worldly rather than (like Christianity) an other-worldly religion will have to be qualified as to time and place; Leviathan, Gan Eden, and the pitiful glories of the New Jerusalem were not the affair of one weak century or two. Even the notion that Jews are essentially monotheistic must submit to certain qualifications; and here enters a second, and a more profound, humanizing influence inherent in this process of absorbing one's self in Jewish culture.

Although Jews in their temples and synagogues today may repeat the same phrases with regard to the unity of God as their ancestors in the wilderness, even a superficial glance at the records will reveal a vast and ever-changing difference in what the phrases mean. The God of the desert, however one He may have been, was one among many. The gods of the Gentiles were real enough, at first; they were merely strange gods which Hebrews were forbidden to follow. One can perhaps go further back than this, and with the help of comparative studies in primitive culture, and the assistance of hints from such research as Jane Harrison's *Themis,* glimpse a time when a mere sense of holiness preceded any concept of a God at all. At the other extreme we have the God of Maimonides, a literally ineffable Being, to whom one cannot, in reality, impute any human distinctions—not even unity. God cannot, within any human meaning of the words, be omnipotent, omnipresent, all-good, or—one; He is beyond both human language and human conception. The only approach, Maimonides finds, to describing or conceiving Him is through understanding what He is not; He is not like anything man could know, feel, or tell. Between these two poles lies a series of changes, a veritable theobiography, in which one concept of divinity would hardly recognize another. The series is not even a straightaway development from a primitive god among gods to a philosophical, ineffable One. It is complicated by mystic notions of God united to Himself through a Holy Love: a kabbalistic and shadowy trinity. And the series is still uncompleted; the concept is still in the process of change. It is not beyond possibility that in the Jewish thought of the near future God will become identified with a cosmic evolutionary process, and His unity be conceived of as a continuous growth, and his Oneness a series of succeeding differences. Not a phrase in the prayer book need be altered, yet in these circumstances Maimonides would scarcely recognize the old *Shema;* it would be as strange as the *Shema* of Maimonides himself would have been to Hillel, or that of Hillel to Joshua.

Monotheism as a changing rather than a fixed thing is of course no singular phenomenon; Jewish or any other culture is a congeries of changes. Jewish culture is especially rich in these changes—which enter into every item of its law, custom, ritual, and literature—merely because of the length of its history. And the understanding of history as a process and of institutions as growths, an essentially humanizing business, is peculiarly potent in the case of an absorption in Jewish culture and comes directly home to one, because the Jewish experience is our own experience and because the institutions and ideas born of this experience are still intertwined in the fibres of our western world. Egyptian culture extended over a period as long as the Jewish, and Chinese longer; but both are comparatively remote from the western world. A mummy, the central figure of Egyptian life, has much to say to us, but not so much and nothing so pertinent as the most tattered scrap of parchment in the Cairo *Genizah*.

✦ ✦ ✦

An absorption in Jewish culture will, I have tried to indicate, suffuse one with a genial skepticism toward preconceived notions of history; that is, toward the nature and behavior of mankind, and impregnate one with an understanding of culture as a changing process with many directions in its changes. Under the guidance of this skepticism and understanding, and the consequent flexibility of mind, the Jewish experience can be relived sympathetically. No more exhilarating or richer adventure can be imagined. We pass into the minds of sages, suffer with martyrs, and agonize with heroes. We share the gusto and bloodiness of centuries of political conquest, and the chicaneries and piteousness of centuries of defeat. We sing with poets and lose ourselves in the mystic *altitudo*. The Anglo-Saxon American visits England, in fancy or reality, and captures an expansive thrill. We visit scores of lands and a century of cities, and every lane and stone is eloquent of ourselves.

A race experience, penetrated in this way, is of course an enrichment of our own experience; but its deeper value lies in the new perspectives it affords us on our own age. It becomes for us a new critical touchstone. We have a new scale. It is a tower to which we can withdraw from the overwhelming details of the immediate life in order to catch a new angle on the surrounding world. It is not a tower of ivory, but an observatory, and at times a watch-tower.

The Jewish experience is singularly fitted to give us these fresh, critical, and appreciative points of view, not merely because of its great span, but chiefly because the Jews have lived their centuries both in and with the western world and yet *apart* from it. From their first appearance in Canaan to the present day they have absorbed the culture of their neighbors and yet maintained a culture and individuality of their own. They have become the natural, if unofficial and sometimes unwelcome, critics of the western world. In the Joban sense, they are the Adversary of the nations. Because of the exceptional relations between Christians and Jews which originated in the attitude of the Church toward them and the niche they occupy in the Christian mythos, the Jew has in an intensified degree played the complementary part in Europe.

Yet, if he had been merely an outsider, a people with a different culture, this absorption in his past which I am urging would be of no greater immediate value than an absorption in Japanese culture. And if his culture had been merely one of the sources of European civilization—the religious source, let us say—an absorption in it would be, as a humanizing device, at the most on a par with an absorption in Roman and Greek culture (which usually goes by the name of humanism). But unlike the Japanese, the Jew has shared European culture throughout its vicissitudes, as fully almost as he has maintained himself against it and apart from it. And unlike the Greek and Roman, he has not only been a cultural ancestor, but he has persisted in being a contemporary. He has everywhere been a native—with a foreign past and the possibility of a foreign future. His history is a Gulf Stream through Europe, wet and salt like the surrounding waters, taking hues from the same sun, ruffled by the same storms, inhabited by the same creatures, but always with a different temperature and an individual direction. Because of this continuous presence yet separation, similarity yet difference, coincidence yet tangency, his culture becomes for Europe a basis of measurement and appreciation. It can be used as the Cartesian co-ordinates of western history.

✦ ✦ ✦

Let me suggest a few directions in which this appreciation can be utilized. A hubbub of human problems centers around the relation of the individual to a larger social unit: to what extent shall a man be loyal to his religious faith, nationality, race, class, country, and to humanity? Another vortex centers on the relation of groups to a larger unit and to each other. The whole reeks with questions of rights and duties of minorities, self-determination of peoples, nationalism and Ku Klux, racial inferiorities and superiorities, intolerance and freedom, economic democracy and imperialism, national sovereignty and a League of Nations, and internationalism and patriotism. Pick up any one of these problems, at either end, and it will lead you to the seething heart of the modern world; on these issues we make peace or war, and millions of human pawns are spared to life or hurled to death. Whether we are aware or not, they pluck at and shape our individual life at every turn.

I am not suggesting that we turn to Jewish culture for a recipe of how to mix and proportion our loyalties, nor for rules on how to make these problems behave. Not that it lacks a recipe or rules; on the contrary, the difficulty with this sort of hunt for morals up and down Jewish history (a favorite occupation of many of our spiritual leaders) is that one finds too many. It should be obvious, before one begins to look, that, in three thousand years of history, one can find precedents to justify one in being a nationalist or an internationalist, a pacifist or bellicist, a Jew first—or last, a believer in democracy, theocracy, monarchism, or communism. This sort of prescription hunting is precisely what Arnold meant by Hebraism and what I am least concerned about.

Suppose, however, that one has immersed oneself in the Jewish experience imaginatively and in its totality. This experience, it will be found, is one long posturing of these vexatious modern riddles. For the two thousand years of dispersion, the Jews have been a minority group, occupied with inventions and devices for adjusting their life to that of a majority and still preserving what they held precious. If anything, it has been their *métier*. It is not, I believe, too much to say that out of reliving this experience, there is born in one an attitude toward these questions today that, in its understanding of what any minority—individual or group—is seeking and suffering, in its sympathy for the claims of the majority, in its knowledge of the many and intricate forms the conflict has taken throughout centuries, and in its intimate recognition of all the human factors entering the problem, may best be called humanistic. And one will have seen the problem assume so many labels, appeal to so many superhuman sanctions, justify itself with such a diversity of reasons, that a genial skepticism toward the modern equivalents of these ancient dodges is certain to color this new attitude. And this is humanism.

It is true that broadly speaking, this attitude will weigh against the majority, against whatever orthodoxy—that is, belief of the majority—may be current, against principles set above men, against concentrated power and tyranny, against whatever tends to coerce the human spirit. This too is an attribute of humanism. For since the majority of men have as yet been loath to accept the necessities of human nature as their touchstone to conduct, humanism has always been a sort of heresy. But no man who has been absorbed in the Jewish experience, who has acquired a two thousand years' memory of what it means to be misunderstood, unjustly condemned, and violently coerced, can make the mistake of adopting a similar course against the current orthodoxy and majority. He will mix pity and imagination with his judgment. This is, above all, humanism.

The Jewish experience, imaginatively absorbed, will evoke a similarly humanistic attitude toward the conflict between religion and science, mysticism and intelligence, dogma and liberty of conscience. I have only space to intimate that the rabbinate was something quite different from a priesthood or a modern ministry, and that an understanding of its nature is provocative of a new valuation of the present-day conflict. And, furthermore, in certain periods, the Jewish understanding of religion was altogether different from that of the Christian poles of Catholic or Puritan, and an absorption of this point of view would yield a new criticism, a new basis for appreciation, of what we understand by religion today. Again, the problem of how to conserve our established western culture against the inroads of industrialism, or at least how happily to make an adjustment between the two, may receive fresh light from one who has acquired what I may now call a Jewish humanistic attitude. The adjustment of cultures is, I must repeat, a Jewish *forte*. But I must also repeat that I am not implying that one can find in Jewish culture an answer to this or any other of the many problems which could be enumerated. One will not find an answer; but one will acquire an attitude. And this attitude, in the liberalizing effect it will have on our sympathy, understanding, and conduct, and in the emphasis it will place on the relativity of history as a process, is the essence of humanism.

✦ ✦ ✦

Cannot all I have said with regard to the humanistic value of an absorption in the Jewish experience be said in equal truth of an absorption in any great culture—Greek, Roman, Chinese, what not?

With certain qualifications, which I have already touched on, this is
true. Chinese culture, perhaps in spite of its remoteness; Greek culture,
perhaps in spite of its destruction long before our day, can be made
to yield a humanism in an intensity equal to the Jewish; for these and
any number of great human cultures are as rich, if not richer, in every
variety of human experience and achievement.

For a Jew, however, an absorption in the Jewish experience as a
means of acquiring a humanistic attitude offers peculiar advantages.
Because it is the experience of his own people, because it has been
continuous to the present day, because therefore he has himself, no
matter how far he may think he is from being a Jew, relived fragments
of it and shared it as a living thing and not as a matter of books,
records, and monuments, because of all this he can more quickly and
sympathetically enter into the Jewish experience of the past.

This is not a matter of logic; any Jew can test the fact as a living,
glowing experience. Suppose, for example, he is studying Greek culture and stumbles on the word, vital in Greek life, *sophrosyne*. Zim-
mern translates it as Gentleness, Self-control, or the Rule of Religion.
If one understands it all, it is sheerly as an intellectual label. It does
not, it cannot, tingle with life. But suppose this Jew, in absorbing
himself in the Jewish experience, encounters the word *rishus*. Here indeed he needs no dictionary; the meaning throbs, living, in his veins.
Nor is it simply a question of words and definitions; the Jew by his
own experience is, however faultily, better equipped to understand
from within, as a living fire, the leit-motifs of Jewish history than those
of the Chinese or most other histories. The cry for justice, the search
for social adjustment, the sense and hope of an international unity to
be ultimately set over petty patriotisms and side by side with these
the burning loyalty to a group—these are, even if imperfectly, shared
in every Jew's individual life. When he encounters these humanizing
elements in Jewish culture, they are not something foreign to be
digested as best one can, but something native that will simply bring
to fuller flower what is already living within him. A Jew who chooses
to seek humanism in the Jewish experience will have a running start.

(—*1924*)

Whither Israel?

HORACE M. KALLEN

WHAT Jew, believer or not, has not once in his life heard, or himself recited, either the 126th or the 137th Psalm, or both? Let me repeat them here, in a version somewhat different from the traditional one. First, Psalm 137:

By the rivers of Babylon, there we sat down.
  Yea, we wept when we remembered Zion.
We hanged our harps on the willows in their midst.
For there our captors required of us a new song.
Our ravishers demanded of us mirth.
They said: "Sing us one of the songs of Zion."

But how shall we sing the Lord's song in an alien land?
O, if I forget thee, Jerusalem, let my right hand forget her cunning;
If I fail to remember thee, let my tongue cleave to the roof of my
    mouth.
If I prefer not Jerusalem above my chief joy.

Remember Edom, God, that said "Raze it, raze Jerusalem to its very
    foundations."
O Babylon, destined to destruction, he will be happy who serves
    thee as thou hast served us,
Taking thy little ones, dashing them against the stones!

Turn from the helpless anger and bitterness of this poem to Psalm 126:

When God brought the exiles back to Zion, we were like men dreaming.
Then laughter filled our mouths and song came from our tongues.
Then it was said among the peoples, "Greatly hath God worked with
    this folk."
Greatly indeed hath God worked with us! and we rejoiced.
O Jehovah, bring back all our exiles as streams of water to the Negeb!
Those who are sowing in tears shall reap in song,
He who weeping goes to the field, bearing the trailing seed,
Shall return thence, singing, carrying his sheaves.

Both poems are remembrances, set to music, and passed on from generation of Jews to generation, to be chanted again as tradition ordains, yet with never unvarying tone and accent. Psalm 126 is intoned at a dramatic point in the Seder ceremony. Together with Psalm 137 it fixes the poles of that axis of desire and frustration upon which revolves the enduring legend of the Jewish people. Whoever wrote Psalm 137 had obviously been an enforced exile from his homeland, victim and survivor of a war that destroyed the Jewish State and was followed by spiritual disruption in the community of exiles to whom the State was the force and form of the Jewish psyche. The author and his comrades were remembering a life that was no more. Their song was an endeavor so to reanimate a past as to nullify a present they could not accept. For the neighbor who had desired their dispersion, the foe who had worked it, they craved a fate as bitter.

Their song, together with Psalm 126, suggests something of the mood also of the Jews of our own time. There is, I think, a true analogy between the sentiment common to many twentieth-century Jewish communities and that of the exiles of close to six hundred years before the present era. In many lands of the globe, of which Israel is not the least, men and women of Jewish derivation are remembering an existence long dead, yearning to resurrect it, struggling with pitiful and ridiculous ardor to re-establish it as if it were not over and done with—as if recollection were event and event recollection.

✦ ✦ ✦

Such quixotism is inveterate in the human psyche. It imparts its own singularity to the tragi-comedy of the human enterprise, whatever direction that take. Often noble, it is always regressive, like the wish to evade the responsibilities of the mature by assuming the ways of the child. But living beings cannot go back to infancy; at most they can live out adult years childishly. Indeed, there are schools of human psychology which argue that childish ways are the prevalent ways among the majority of mankind.

We need not, however, heed the sectarian fantasies of this or that school of psychology. It is enough to regard the activities and life-patterns of any human being, of any age in any place, as they come before us. They impress us firmly enough as events of a struggle to survive and grow, with its winning daily battles, suffering perennial defeat, never doing what is done once only, but ever again and again and again. We note continual searching and seeking to still the same wants by the same satisfactions, both changing as they repeat; both altering simply because they repeat, within and without. Only with death does this self-annulling victory come to its term.

Only the dead have no need to repeat, and to alter as they repeat. Only the dead don't change and can't change; that is, don't die; and only as dead are immortal.

The living are mortal. Their mortality lives in the circumstance that their present passes into their past and stays alive as their memories, which their future transforms. They are able to grow up and grow old because their past is a living past which the future enriches and reforms by entering. Remembering and living are not separate doings but a continuing activity seen now as image, and now as action. When any part of the living past is segregated and used for a mold which the future shall fill, it is experienced as an arrested movement, an image that on-going life leaves behind; it alters from a power into a burden, from a process of passage into a retaining wall.

The natural spontaneity of vital recollection has its variations. There are those which a student evinces when he is trying to repeat for his professor what the professor has said. There are those of the witness testifying, responding to lawyers who press him to remember this and not that. There are those of the painter painting from a model or projecting a remembered pattern on his canvas for himself alone. And there are many others—echoes, conformations, transpositions, projections, recreations and creations, together with all the yet unidentified spontaneous variations of which authentic, vital recollection consists. The most familiar occur as separations and isolations, dammings and rechannelings in momentary abstractions from the vital process whose topmost turn is the stream of consciousness.

When this process is healthy and whole, the future digests and contains the past as the sound body digests and contains its food and drink, rendering them living flesh of its flesh and bone of its bone. Isolation, segregation, abstraction have the effect, among others, of stoppage. They replace the natural multi-dimensional moving image with an unnatural mono-dimensional still.

Theologians and philosophers create and adore such stills. They appraise those abstractions as mankind's ultimate safety and certainty, by definition always and everywhere the same, which is to say, eternal, universal, supreme, ideal and—absolute. So defined, these reworkings from remembrances of things past are assigned another locus than the life process whence they are drawn, thence by grace to guarantee present safety and assurance. Their faithful invest them with values and meanings incommensurable alike to their derivation and their use. The investiture renders them objects of worship—fetishes, idols, gods, emptied of life by being exalted into immortal potencies.

✦ ✦ ✦

Whatever the provocation, these are the reflections that the question, *Whither Israel?* first leads me to. Throughout the years that Israel has been the name of a historic people with a biography singular to itself, the image "Israel" that the psalmist mourned in Babylon, and the Zionist invokes in New York, has been little a living process, all too much a memory isolated and abstracted into an ideal, a vision of being, happy and high and noble, once possessed, never yet recovered, yet ever to be so recovered that the ideal might be fact again, and vision event.

Students of philosophy know, of course, even more than students of history, that ideals enacted are ideals corrupted, conceptions implemented are conceptions maculated, visions realized are visions disrupted. To keep your conceptions immaculate, don't employ them; to hold your vision intact, don't realize it; to retain your ideals, don't live up to them. Reality and its actualizations transform. They bring unforeseeable distortions and shocking shapes and colors. Their touch contaminates the eternal and universal with protean singularities of time and place. It impregnates their immaculacy with the vital corruption which alone can breed existence from conception. Whatever renders the ideal potent and fruitful deflowers it. To stay ideal is to stay sterile; and any ideal consolations and values must stay those intrinsic to sterility.

✦ ✦ ✦

The ideal which "Israel" came predominantly to signalize was distilled out of the experiences of the Exile. It was abstracted, isolated and established in Babylon, amid the lifeways and thoughtways composing the singularity of a victorious empire worshipping its victory-giving gods. The Hebraism of the prophets' urging was digested in the Judaism of Ezra's ordination, Nehemiah's enforcement, with its invidious distinctions, among others, between the people of the Ingathering and the people of the Dispersion.

Before that alteration, the lifeways and thoughtways of the Judean people had been a process shaped to a program consciously accepted and more or less successfully enacted—mostly less, otherwise there would have been no occasion for the prophets. What else was the word of any of them to the tribes of Judah and Israel, if not that they were failing to accomplish a plan of life and establish it as life's way, and that dire consequences follow failure? What else do the deliverances of the best and greatest of the prophets whom we read in the Bible communicate?

And how do we think of the record they assume and the program they prescribe, as the Bible records them? Certainly not in their totality as complete remembrance of things past directed toward the future. The totality enfolds much that, regarded in and by itself, would be unspeakable, unprintable. We think those data selectively, choosing from the compenetrated melange those which we feel most viable for our times, our places, our vital intention and personal integrity. The monotheism, the moralism, the divine election and the other stressed items of the Law and the Prophets are only portions of the record, and not the most comprehensive portions. There are also the priesthoods and their ways, the tribal customs and folkways and their prescriptions and taboos, the lusts and treacheries and cruelties of kings and nobles, the sufferings of the righteous and the prosperings of the wicked, the reciprocally contradictory claims of all to gratify the desires and obey the will of Jehovah. There is the aggregation of data which ethnologists, archaeologists and sociologists study and appraise, which together with the Judaists' own diverse selections compose into that variegated assemblage of the record, and are further continued and varied as the Judaisms of Ezra and Nehemiah, of the Apocrypha and the Talmud, of Philo and Josephus, Jehuda Halevi and Maimonides, Crescas and Baal-Shemtob, Moses Mendelssohn and Theodor Herzl and Mordecai Kaplan.

The process consists in an indefinite, diverse, and diversifying coming together and compenetration of ideals and events, of faiths and things and forces. "Jew," "Israel," receive their manifoldly conflicting meanings from the fluid constellation of lifeways and thoughtways which this ingathering presents.

Thus, although some form of the word *together* here carries, for me, the meaning nuclear to "Jew," "Israel," it does not for the leaders or spokesmen of any sect or faction within the constellation which elects to monopolize those names for its own intentions. Claiming a mission, each for itself, they use the names both invidiously and tendenciously, as designations of a chosen cluster of memories and events, which they have abstracted from the moving aggregate, arrested and isolated. In the name of that cluster they then assume to signalize themselves as the chosen ones of the Chosen People, and for the entirety of the Jewish past to substitute their selections by which to shape a Jewish future. What Christians or Moslems or Nazis or Communists choose from that entirety to denote by the words "Jew," "Israel," is notoriously something else again.

✦ ✦ ✦

Grounds of choice are as diverse, as manifold, as their times and occasions. Modernly, they are distinguishable into two not altogether exclusive groups. They may be called, without prejudice, "supernaturalist" and "humanist." There are also "supernaturalistic humanists" and "humanistic supernaturalists" in increasing numbers. But the gradient differences are signalized by the simpler divisions.

The supernaturalists form the Judaist variant of the prescientific tradition of Western culture. They sustain the organization and practice in Rabbinic Judaism which are intrinsic to a vital economy ordered to flattering, cajoling, coercing, bargaining, bribing or persuading supernatural power to preserve this economy and its members and to prosper their growth. The typical codex of this economy has long been the *Shulhan Arukh*, the compendium of prescriptions and prohibitions conforming behavior to supernatural requirements. To meet them is to merit salvation, to fail is to merit damnation, in the life to come.

As a lifeway, Judaism is in this of one fellowship with the world's other supernaturalisms. It is called "religion" because of the supernaturalism, not because of the act of faith which asserts the supernaturalism. When the act of faith is considered, it has no more claim on being appraised religious than man's attribution of saving power to any other object or idea.

Those who choose meanings for "Jew," "Israel," on humanist grounds appraise the supernaturalist orientation as one Jewish mode of man's adjustment to the changes and chances of a world no more made for him than for any other living thing. They set the supernaturalist doctrines and disciplines in the perspectives of human history and judge them by the consequences they in fact lead to. They understand the otherworldly providences which the supernaturalists postulate, the magic their ritual purports, the miracles they describe, as fear-created defenses against dangers felt to be insuperable, as lasting compensations in imagination for needs and hungers never in fact lastingly satisfied. Humanists apprehend supernaturalist realities as such stuff as dreams are made of, to be accounted for by the methods of the natural and social scientist, employing the insights of scientific psychology and the other sciences of man.

The numbers and kinds of Jews who have consciously chosen so to envisage and appraise the singularity of Israel are not very great, though perhaps proportionally greater than among others of the globe's peoples who look upon, remember and judge themselves.

✦ ✦ ✦

That "perhaps," I suspect, is a very large "perhaps." Not alone during the pre-scientific ages of Western history, but also during the scientific nineteenth century, the Jewish multitudes believed with a firm faith that Divine Providence had guaranteed the miraculous return of Israel to the Promised Land under the leadership of a Messiah, son of David, who in God's good time would, without force, without might, but by His spirit responding to magical rites, gather the exiles from all lands of their dispersion, into the land of Israel. Like these true believers, the humanistic idealists, of whom Theodor Herzl became the spokesman and the Zionist movement the instrument, also aspired to an ingathering of the exiles. But their ends and means of gathering followed from their humanism, and were as incommensurable with Messiah and miracle as humanism is with supernaturalism.

To the believing Judaists restoration could be nothing else than the repetition of a Judaistic past, hypostatized into what they variously interpreted as the eternal and universal Torah. In daily living it would consist of selections from accumulated precedents and practices, with sanctions from the Talmud and other carriers of Jewry's pre- and anti-scientific traditions, woven into a way of life. Restored Israel would thus be a theocracy, in principle committed to obeying all the commandments and performing all the *mitzvoth,* in practice doing what the folkways and mores approved. A Jew's existence would, perhaps, be regulated and policed by a Sanhedrin, and judged by a rabbinate. Whatever might be said, done, or taught would be con-

formed thus to that hypostatic Torah, its design for living infallibly
defined by the power-holders of the theocracy. Could restoration be
perfect, it might perhaps raise the Temple again and serve the Lord
with blood-offerings and burnt offerings, first fruits and gifts of money,
as well as with confession, song and praise.

But also without this consummation social control would have to
be hieratic. For if Divinity were to communicate the intent of its
Torah democratically, by direct inspiration of each believer, Torah
would be a babel of interpretations, not the one true instruction in
the best life here, and sole propaedeutic for the good life to come.

Before Herzl these idealistic Judaists traveled to their Holy Land
to die, and in large numbers lived on, making self-righteous claims
on the pious charity of the communities of the dispersion. Nor have
they quieted their godly clamor since Herzl.

+ + +

The humanists responded to it, and keep on responding. But the
ingathering their vision projects has other grounds and refers to quite
other conditions.

Westerners of diverse cultures and disciplines, those humanistic
Jews were all poignantly aware of anti-Semitism as a principle of
Christian faith and a corollary of party conflicts, economic competition
and cultural pretension in political and social practice. In their own
persons, or through their observations of such obscenities as the
Dreyfus Affair, the Damascus horror, the Beyliss persecution, the
massacres of Kishineff and Gomel, they had come to understand that
anti-Semitism suffused the entire religio-political outlook of the European peoples. Their reading of history gave added force to the evidence of their eyes. They knew from direct experience how Europe's
nationalisms, Europe's racisms, and Europe's socialisms took over and
cherished and used, for the benefit of their own power and influence,
the intrinsic anti-Semitism of Europe's religion. From Moscow to Paris
and Madrid, from Berlin to Rome and Stambul, "Jew" was a ready-
made name any spokesman for a reactionary cult or party could give
the scapegoat it needed, and win instant response. The spokesman
might be a Sebastian Brunner, a Chateaubriand, a Drumont, a
Maurras, a Jaime Balmez, a Dostoevski, a Houston Stewart Chamberlain, a G. K. Chesterton, a Franz von Papen, a Karl Marx, an Arab of
the Husseini, an Ilya Ehrenbourg, an Adolph Stöcker or an Arthur

Rosenberg. His employment of the word "Jew" would make it denotative of danger to whatever social interest he was soliciting.

The humanistic proponents of the Ingathering of the Exiles became convinced that reassembling enough Jews to form a Jewish State in Palestine would immensely weaken this groundless but potent aggression; and would in the course of time alter the anti-Semitic animus of its use of the word "Jew" to secular humanistic attitudes common between peoples not Jewish.

Such a correction of the age-old injustice might, however, be achieved anywhere; and a philosophy of territorialism, postulated on the assumption that an Ingathering in Palestine would forever be blocked by churchly and imperial interests, was proposed as an alternative to Zionism.

This philosophy—even though voiced by dedicated men of noble mind, such as Israel Zangwill, and for an interlude accepted by Herzl —found as little response among the Jews to whom it was addressed as do its expressions having currency today. It received symbolic renunciation in Herzl's dramatic recitation of the verse from Psalm 137: "If I forget thee, Jerusalem, let my right hand forget her cunning." Nor he, nor the congregation of his faith, could yet have the will to sing the Lord's song in an anti-Semitic land. But they knew also that in the land of the fathers, if ever they return to it, the Lord's song could not be the old but must needs be a new song, drawing for spirit upon the old, but prompted, not merely by a renewed, but rather by a *new* vision, wherein all the powers and virtues of the new time might enter and animate into growing new life the old Jewish vision.

These Jews' remembrance of things past elected, hence, to fasten upon the positive intent of the prophets of Israel. Their purpose became to give the admonitions of Amos and Micah and Hosea, as they abstracted, isolated and generalized them, a local habitation and a name in today's Judea.

One imaginative conception of this purpose is Herzl's *Altneuland;* a philosophical exposition and practical projection of it are A. D. Gordon's essays. Its concrete enactment was the initiation, in what was still a vassaldom of the Ottoman Empire, of a cooperative settlement which has become the model for what is now known as the *Kwuzah.* Beside the communities of the supernaturalists who had come to the land to die, because they believed that they could therefore live a better after-life, the humanistic sons of the prophets established communities of the faithful who came to the land so to live that their commune would transpose the supernatural holiness of recall and worship into the natural holiness of the works and ways of daily living. They were for the most part intellectuals and romantics, not craftsmen, artisans, or manual workers of any sort. Their strengths were verbal, their skills pilpulistic. But their Judaism had assimilated the wisdoms of humanism, and their feeling for prophetic righteousness had been diversified into socialist sentiment. They were strong in pity for the servile lot of the human multitudes; they reappraised the thankless labor which was their all of life as liberty and independence, and the leisure their lives lacked as parasitism and helplessness.

Those young Jews freely assumed a discipline that should make them over into authentic proletarians. It was their chosen way to the secular holiness which alone could establish naturalist fact in the place of supernaturalist fantasy. It was their religion, the Hebraism of the prophets in modern dress.

Their vision of it took them into the desert and swamp of Palestine to work them over into fertile acres. They began their labors as soft-bodied, tender-minded specialists of the intellect. Hungering, sweating, sickening, bleeding and dying, they builded that wasteland into their homeland as their toil transformed them into freer spirits, hard in body and tough in mind. Their communes became a fissionable nucleus of social reconstruction on a vital gradient of vision for growth. Willy-nilly, the institutions and enterprises of the Zionist movement bent to their pattern: the National Fund, the Keren Hayesod, the agencies and the colonization which the Funds financed with calculated—often not wisely calculated—risks.

Soon after Balfour published his releasing Declaration, American Zionists set the singularities of the Jewish enterprise in Palestine in the perspectives of a more general democracy by means of a group of of "Resolutions Bearing on Palestine Policy." These were resolutions adopted by the Zionist Organization of America at a Convention it held in Pittsburgh in July of 1918. This was the American organization of what are now called "General Zionists." Their leader at the time was Louis D. Brandeis.

The resolutions became known as the Pittsburgh Program. They begin with an imaginative preamble which transposes into the terms of a natural democratic humanism the supernaturalism in the Jewish tradition. Thus:

In 1897 the first Zionist Congress at Basle defined the object of Zionism to be "the establishment of a publicly recognized and legally secured homeland for the Jewish people in Palestine." The recent Declaration of Great Britain, France, Italy, and others of the allied democratic States have established this public recognition of the Jewish National Home as an international fact.

Therefore we desire to affirm anew the principles which have guided the Zionist Movement since its inception, and which were the foundations laid down by our lawgivers and prophets for the ancient Jewish State, and the inspiration of the living Jewish law embodied in the traditions of two thousand years of exile.

Then follows the realistic program:

First: Political and civil equality, irrespective of race, sex or faith, for all the inhabitants of the land.

Second: To insure in the Jewish National Home equality of opportunity, we favor a policy which, with due regard for existing rights, shall establish the ownership and control of the land and of all natural resources and of all public utilities by the whole people.

Third: All land owned and controlled by the whole people should be leased on such conditions as will insure the fullest opportunity for development and continuity of possession.

Fourth: The cooperative principle should be applied as far as feasible in the organization of all agricultural, industrial, commercial, and financial undertakings.

Fifth: The fiscal policy shall be framed so as to protect the people from the evils of land speculation and from every other form of financial oppression.

Sixth: The system of free public instruction which is to be established should embrace all grades and departments of education.

Seventh: The medium of public instruction should be Hebrew, the national language of the Jewish people.

Far as fulfillment still is from fact, neither World War I, nor the rule of the British as the agents of the League of Nations after the Balfour Declaration, nor the factional rancors of the Zionists, much deflected Jewish Palestine from forming along this humanistic ethical gradient. Here a little, there a little, the figure of vision became the flesh of fact, right alongside the communities of supernaturalist intention whose members were aspiring only to fear the Lord and

obey his commandments. Fearing the Lord consisted, indeed, in following today's version of yesterday's commandments, as tradition had
carried them from yesterday into today's meanings. Its substance was
the aggregation of *minhagim* (customs), composing the diversities of
"traditional Judaism," whose observance the elder required of the
younger generation, no matter what the cost, nor who paid it.

The British, who took the rule of Palestine from the Turks for the
greater security of their colonial empire, had long experience, alike
in Asia and in Africa, in governing submissive communities of supernaturalism. Colonial empires are possible only among such communities; the communities of humanism exact commonwealth. But the
British were without precedent for right relations with the Jewish
communes, whose humanism rendered them recalcitrant to both their
paternalism and their snobbistic bureaucratism. The men and women
of the settlements believed with a firm belief that they owed Caesar
nothing, that all the land was the Lord's land, and the fruit thereof
belonged to the workers who produced it. As their numbers increased
and they settled towns even more abundantly than *Kevuzoth* and
Moshavim, they gathered into a union whose organizational pattern
was an adjustment of a compenetration of Hebraic prophetism and
European syndicalism to Palestine's primitive, frontier-like economy.

This union is today's Histadruth Ovdim. It was the dynamic of that
government within a government which under the Charter consistently
challenged and checked the Mandatory bureaucracy, not failing to
develop, in the process, bureaucratic ways of their own, which only
the behaviors of the ill-disposed, third-rate British civil servants
stopped from growing into the full flower of the bureaucratic art.

For a long time almost three-quarters of the Histadruth's membership came from the settlements. Its enterprises added, to typical
trade unionism and agricultural cooperation, building trades, transportation and other service cooperatives, cooperatives in banking and
finance, in health and hospitalization, in consumer goods, in "culture,"
and in schooling infants and youth according to the doctrines and disciplines of their humanistically envisaged faith. Where the supernaturalists employed Yiddish or some other vernacular as the speech of
man to man and reserved Hebrew as the *loshon hakodesh* (holy tongue)
for addressing only Deity, the humanists consecrated Hebrew to the
uses of daily life, and became aggressive suppressors of other languages. They even produced for their school-children Hebrew versions

of such Yiddish writers as Peretz and Mendele. Of course, they cultivated ideological enmities and political faction: some were leftist radicals like Hashomer Hazair; others radically rightists like the Revisionists, or the later Mapam and Heruth splinter groups. But during the
always uneasy and intermittently violent and bloody operation of the
Mandate, they all learned something of the cooperative discipline of
self-government.

✦   ✦   ✦

British colonialism, skilled in the inertias which keep administration
of "lesser peoples" relatively peaceful as well as profitable, favored,
among the Arabs, the effendi over the fellah; among Jews, the supernaturalist over the humanist. The Colonial Office knew how, by keeping Arab divided from Jew, to rule with least effort, intellectual or
moral, and to make sure of serving the interest of empire elsewhere.

This was not without its benefits, however. If the Mandatory's administration did not consistently keep the peace between Arabs and
Jews, it did discourage major clashes between the Jewish supernaturalists and humanists. Over the years numbers of such clashes had
occurred, the violent initiative having always been the supernaturalists'. The Shomrei-Shabath group, for example, being sure that not
to compel an absolute observance of *Shabbath* would draw divine vengeance on Sabbath-breakers, went about, as they still do, beating
shopkeepers, destroying goods, and otherwise guaranteeing that such
as do not share their views about God's desires with respect to the
seventh day should know how painful and costly such heresy must be.

Under the British these aggressions of the "truly righteous" could
be simply a bit of disorderly conduct that an Arab policeman could
attend to. Today they signalize a confrontation of faithways and lifeways from whose antagonisms will follow whatever future meaning
Israel may have for freedom-loving mankind. The Orthodox faction of
mandatory Palestine has become the "religious bloc" of independent
Israel. Disorderly conduct of a small band of fanatics has become the
symbol of the purposes and policies of a conspirational Judaist clerical-
ism which looks for support to the great majority of the new Israel,
ingathered from the degradations and exactions of exile among anti-
Semites to the austerities and disciplines of a homeland all embattled
frontier. Frontier within, because each immigrant *landsmanschaft*
brings the language, folkways and mores of its country of origin, which

unite their members to one another and make a boundary between them and the other peoples of Israel. Frontier without, because of political delimitation and military need, also where Israel faces the sea.

If the miscellany of Israel have anything in common, other than being victims of anti-Semitism, it is the Judaist supernaturalism, although this, too, is diversified by suffusions from the cults and cultures of the lands of origin as well as by inner variations of belief and rite. But the Judaist aggregation is the central mass from which the other groups and factions—Israel has nineteen political parties alone —are deviants, as the factions of the prophets were deviants from the factions of the priests in Bible times. Each is a minority of beliefs and programs.

The position of Israel as an integral and solidary polity is inescapably a function of the relations of these groupings to one another. How each lives and works together with all presents a more fundamental problem than the foreign relations of the State. The domestic configuration cannot, in the nature of such things, fail to be an issue, as well as a determinant, of the foreign relations.

✦ ✦ ✦

For, given the clericalist conception of the Jewish role in the divinely directed course of history, it could very well have happened that, had the Judaist majority of Palestine been as purposefully organized as the Jewish minority, the State of Israel would never have been created. Indeed, when its first war for survival was imposed upon it by the aggression of Egypt and the other states of the Arab League, numbers of Judaists, certain that the creation of the State was rebellion to God, fought with the League against the Jews. And in truth, the decision to make the diverse Palestinian Jewish communities into the independent and sovereign State of Israel was a decision to bet life, liberty and sacred honor on an endeavor which neither the prudent nor the politic could see as having the slightest promise of success, and which the supernaturalist viewed as sin.

The Jews who made this bet undertook to overrule the expediencies of "statesmanship" and the timidities which are often synonyms for "practicality." They bypassed what seemed to men of experience the more hopeful way of meeting the needs of the Jewish multitudes *in extremis.* This was, for Palestine, an international trusteeship under the United Nations that would administer the trust in spirit and in truth, and would thus establish the Jewish homeland by a gradual but speedy development at a minimum cost in life, in suffering, in treasure. This was, to other lands, easement of immigration and settlement. These were held the least hazardous, the least unlikely to succeed. Statehood was regarded as too precarious a gamble.

Making that gamble postulated an idealism of a different order from both the "realism" and the idealism it bet against. It was an act of faith, far beyond any that Jews of the supernaturalist persuasion were capable of exercising. It sprang from the bettors' readiness to stake their existence on an action with no guarantees, with odds against it greater than could be measured. They launched their undertaking in full awareness of the circumstances it defied, the forces it challenged, the hazards it ran. It brought to the ultimate trial the courage which is wisdom concerning dangers.

The critical event of the trial was the war immediately launched by the Arab states. These had early formed a League, not in order to help and strengthen one another, but in order to destroy the Jews of Palestine. The word "Arab," as those fighting Jews had come to employ it, thus tended to express a feeling rather than knowledge and understanding. Usage made it a term of anxiety and aversion, deprecation and antagonism. And there are many causes—in the sinister story of the notorious double-dealer whom Britain's Sir Herbert Samuel had promoted from German-paid traitor to Britain-subsidized "Mufti of Jerusalem" (he later took service with Hitler), as well as in the course of Jewish-Arab relations—why this should be so. Whatever the causes, their effect is reflex of feeling, not wisdom of life. Even the rightly aspiring *Ihud* movement, with Judah Magnes for avatar, was impelled by sentiment rather than guided by insight.

✦ ✦ ✦

"Arab," it is helpful to remember, is a term no less ambiguous than "Jew," and, like "Jew," denotes many aggregations of conflicting needs, interests and wishes, voiced by many dialects of the Arab tongue. The peoples of the Arab League, from Syria to Egypt and from Iraq to Yemen, have lived a thousand years but as tools with life in them, of less worth to the power-holders of those lands than their camels and oxen. For the standard of living permitted them is below the level of subsistence. In skill, health, literacy and self-rule they have been among the world's most retarded, as in an older time they had been among its most forward, peoples. I say retarded, not backward. They are no less able to advance, to grow in freedom, self-help and fellowship, than their forbears of old, or the most progressive peoples of our own day. But they have been held back. Authoritarian supernaturalism and feudal rule subdue them to the credulous service of masters often absentee, who reap because *they* sow, consume because *they* produce, and live at leisure because *they* labor.

These masters, called "effendi"—the word shares a common derivation with such terms as "authentic," "authority," and suggests "power-filled"—have a vital stake in the fellah's condition. Its continuation became, as elsewhere in Britain's colonial empire, synonymous with the law-and-order which government preserves. Jewish settlement in Palestine carried, both as faith and as works, a vital threat to that order and a challenge to Christian missionary enterprise. It embraced, for the very interests that hate it, a model to emulate, a mode of life to imitate. It set a precedent for such *bona-fide* "Arab nationalism" as was permitted to develop, and it stimulated initiatives in farming and trade whose entrepreneurs were inhibited from making common cause with Jewish business by the factitious isolationism of cultist, racist or nationalist ideologies in Arab dress. In effect they served as rationalizations of the interdependence of British colonialism with vested effendi interests. They frustrated all attempts of Jewish labor organizations to unionize Arab workers more than superficially. They constricted the cooperation of citrus growers. They contributed to keeping Arabs and Jews apart on the levels of learning, art and science. They are the postulates of the aggression with which the Arab League blooded the new State of Israel. The appeal to them set off the fantastic exodus from Israel of the hundreds of thousands of Arabs, which is one of the critical chances of that War of Liberation. The ideologies crystallize the animus which the effendi élite, who control the Arab League, invoke in their unyielding aggression against the survival of Israel.

The masters of Egypt, Syria, Iraq, Lebanon, Jordan and Yemen could readily enough find a *modus vivendi* with an Israel whose ways and works were not by their instant presence a judgment in the eyes of their subjects upon the entire economy, political and spiritual, of those countries. Their own Jewries, oriented toward otherworldliness, were not such judgments; nor were the Judaist communities of Palestine; nor are Israel's *Neturei-Karta,* nor the major groups in Israel's "religious bloc." A clericalist Israel administered under the talmudic canon could without great difficulty find a *modus vivendi* with Arab feudalism, the cultural distance between the two being small indeed.

This is not the case with that remnant in Israel who are oriented towards the humanistic freedoms of modernity, who look to the Hebrew prophets for vision rather than to Judaist Torah for rules. Humanistic Israel—the Israel of the Kibbutz and the Histadruth—was seen as more than ever a judgment when Arab lands were found to be richest of all in oil; and after the exploitation of that natural resource by alien knowhow for alien interests has brought the Arabs' effendi overlords wealth and pleasures beyond their greediest dreams, whilst the generations of the fellaheen are continued as poor, as hungry, as ignorant, sickly and servile as their fathers.

Inasmuch as the Arab folk of Jewish Palestine had long been noticeably healthier, wealthier, freer and more literate than their kin in the Arab League, the judgment is of long standing. Inasmuch as the Arabs of the State of Israel are, like its Jews, automatically citizens of the State, equal in rights and freedoms, the social impact of this judgment for the millions of the Arab League is inescapable. Their unrest will keep alert the effendi consciousness that an Israel with a political economy and spiritual outlook like Egypt's or Yemen's is an ethical impossibility as well as a historical anachronism.

How aware the power-holders of those lands have become of the moral challenge of Israel is evidenced by their effort to shut Israelis out and cut them off from all communication with their subjects. They impose and enforce an economic and cultural isolationism by means of barriers against all trade, whether in thoughts or things. It is their unannounced aim not only to quarantine their positions against Israel's democratic contagion, but to destroy that nearest vital source by starving if not beating Israel to death.

Moreover, the event that Israel, poorly armed and outnumbered as it was, could yet hold its own against the Arab League's collective might and win the uneasy armistice under which it since struggles, had unexpected consequences in the Moslem world. The 661,000,000 adherents of that cult are spread from Morocco to Egypt, from Arabia to China and the islands of the Pacific. They constitute majorities or powerful minorities in upward of thirty-six states. Israel's victory over the Arab and Egyptian oligarchies aroused the fanatics among them. They initiated a "back to Mohammed" movement, a new pan-Islamism that might offset Catholic Judaism and Catholic Christianism and Catholic Communism with a Catholic Mohammedanism. They organized a World Moslem Conference, whose principles and policies are conceived in ardent remembrance of the faithfuls' "days of glory," when military victory and imperial rule went with devotion unto death to the Koran.

The potentials of this Catholic Moslemism must needs be counted in any calculation of Israel's existential hazard.

✦ ✦ ✦

The states of the Arab League comprise the closest external conditions of Israel's survival. Almost wholly inimical, they enclose it in a ring of hate, whose disposition and interests had largely determined the policies of Britain's mandatory role. In the widening circle of the powers, the states spiritually more intimate, societally similar, the states more friendly than unfriendly and the positively friendly, are the most geographically distant. Without the cooperation of the latter, the State of Israel would have been only a brief and bloody interlude between despair and impotence. Without their approval and support, Israel's existence as a nation among nations would be far, far more precarious than it is, and Israel's survival would be a risk challenging all calculation.

However, that friendly disposition of the democratic powers is in no way unconditional. Common ideals aside, it expresses the confluence of two motives. One is a consideration of advantage made by partisan politicians competing for rule within a state, and the other is a similar consideration by statesmen responsible for advancing national self-interest in the struggle for power between states. The ambiguities in American policy toward Israel follow from both these considerations. Soviet recognition of Israel followed from the latter —the Politburo's purpose to hurt Britain, not any will to save Jews.

On the other hand, the procedures of the United Nations Organization, which culminated in the recognition of Israel as a sovereign and independent state and its admission to equal membership in that Organization, were due not alone to the initiatives of the United States and Russia. The choices which those actions consummated were shaped as well by another motive. That one is intrinsic to the nature of the World Organization. It is set forth in its Charter and presumably expressed by its agencies and operations. It is especially signalized by the Universal Declaration of Human Rights which the Assembly of the United Nations Organization adopted on December 10, 1948, and which various commissions have since been endeavoring to implement via "conventions."

Charter and Declaration make statements about human relations. They lay down rules which the different peoples of the world can follow when they honestly seek to live together with each other on equal terms of peace and freedom. They embody agreements between all the states to cooperate in establishing "the four freedoms" for each, and insuring for each its inner liberties and outer safety. Although much of the history of numbers of the "high contracting parties" to these global agreements has been one of evasions and nullifications designed to save only their singular and exclusive interests, and to heighten and spread their own powers, the great majority have been as faithful as they dared to the principle of collective security, laboring as they could to apply it practically. The smaller and weaker sovereign states among them recognize that the principle is the one salvation of their freedom and independence; those which have been reduced to satellites are aware that it is their best hope of liberation from servitude. The role of all in admitting Israel to equal fellowship in the United Nations signalizes thus a common understanding of the global nature of the faith which the articles of the Charter and of the Declaration affirm, and of the obligations which the signatories to those documents contract.

✦ ✦ ✦

Perhaps we do not recognize as loyally as we might that those obligations do somewhat modify the brutalities of power politics, do clothe their corruptions with a little decency, and do promise much more. They are the hope of the world.

And they are certainly the chief hope, almost the sole hope, of Israel—that tiny state assembling a citizenry of many peoples who are far indeed from being orchestrated into a nation, upon a land barren of natural resources, with enemies for neighbors on every side, who could, if their masters win them to such aggression, overwhelm Israel by numbers alone. Although their Governments have been stopped in their war upon Israel, they have not abandoned it. Members of the

United Nations though those Governments be, and vowed to its principles, they know that to embody the principles in practice at home
would be to divest themselves of all their inequitable advantages.
They hence invoke the principles abroad in order to shut out their
application at home. They claim for their internal affairs immunity
from those principles on the ground of those very principles, that they
may preserve their privileges intact. Since they see in Israel's plans
and policies the concrete challenge to these privileges, they wage unceasing war, shifting from hot war to cold, and keeping the renewal
of the hot war imminent. Not merely have they failed to make peace;
they give every indication that they will agree only to an enforced
peace.

And it may be true that no other is possible. For the ultimate issue
between them and humanistic Israel is a way of realizing human relations. Whatever be the dogmas of a totalitarian religion—sacerdotal,
nazi, fascist, communist, or communazi—they are closer than the teachings of democracy to the beliefs and conduct of the power-holders of
the Arab League. Spiritually and practically the latter belong with
Franco and Peron and Malan and Rankin and Mao and Chiang Kai-
shek. They impose on Israel a war economy to which all its institutions must needs be conformed, and for which too many of the utterances of Israel's leaders and missioners are anxious rationalizations.

✦ ✦ ✦

One such rationalization is the oft-repeated and much-resented doctrine that for a Jew not to live in Israel is to live in exile; that the
program of the Ingathering is a program of Return from Exile, regardless of whether those whose "return" is sought agree or not; regardless of whether they are survivors of the Warsaw Ghetto, or
Auschwitz or Buchenwald, or are victims of Moslem or Marxist totalitarianism, or livers of the life of Riley in France or England or the
United States. Even if it had five million persons on whom it could
draw for armed service, Israel would still be surrounded by an enemy
that could call upon forty million, and no superiority of organization
or firepower (assuming this would be had) could in the long run offset
that discrepancy in manpower.

As a rationalization, the idea of a total Ingathering of the Exiles
is a secular projection of a religious fantasy, which the leaders of the
returning remnants from the Babylonian exile likewise had failed to

render efficacious. Psychologically, it is a cry out of the depths for help, not a utopian execution of a supernatural design. Its spring is a will to believe, similar to that which established Israel, and in no way less hazardous.

For the European majority among the actually Ingathered come from lands at best long immeasurably behind the democratic countries of the West. And those who are "returned" from the Moslem states are taken from lands of a neolithic economy anointed with petroleum, of feudal rule and a rotted culture, practicing a faith-sanctioned anti-Semitism of which Yemen probably maintains the most obscene forms. Those Ingathered bring habits of submission and evasion which have become, not a price, but a penalty of survival. Those from the concentration camps of Europe have suffered regressions of personality signalized by broken bodies not only, but by confused hearts, inert wills and lax minds. Their penalty for survival has been animalization. All groups nevertheless retain, at least vestigially, cultural singularities from their countries of origin, singularities of folkways, mores, speech, song, diet, dress, tradition and legend. These suffuse and divide whatever is common in their heritage of Judaism.

Inescapably, the State of Israel postulates its own survival as an equal member of the family of nations on converting these many, mutually foreign Judaist communions into a united Israel of soldiers and workers, all equally loyal citizens of the State, all heart and soul committed to its defenses and growth.

But the institutional form which such a conversion calls for is itself a hazard regarding which all calculations are perforce hazardous. The State of Israel had to found itself from the start on a war economy, based on gifts and loans first, and on investments only secondarily. Its rule of life has had to be a rule of austerity, even as measured by the low standard of living of the Near East; and the burdens which sovereignty and independence impose on the people of Israel outweigh the heaviest they were required to bear under the British.

Of these burdens perhaps the most ominous is the menace to the vitality and moral influence of the cooperative economy of the *Kevuzoth.* It was natural for these fellowships to avert from the dilemma of, on the one hand, choosing between protecting their corporate economy from dilution by unaffiliable newcomers and, on the other hand, the swift conversion of discoordinated, unproductive consumers into eager and disciplined producers, or at least into manpower able to learn producer arts.

Another burden is the governmental dilemma between, on the one hand, a solidarity to be created by appeasing protagonists of religious intolerance and coercion and, on the other hand, remaining loyal to the principle of equal liberty for the different to which Israel's membership in the United Nations commits the State. The exigencies of survival imposed by the Arab League may lead to shaping Israel into a twentieth-century Sparta, with war as its paramount concern, with military service as the over-all duty of every citizen, regardless of sex, faith, occupation or age, and with every other function of this common culture subordinated to its militarism. To acquiesce in militarism as the form and condition of survival might be to require developing Israel into a corporative state with freedom at best but a word for a pretension, democracy a way of talking and not of living. A continuing war economy might require coordinating Histadruth Ovdim and its institutions with the "religious bloc" and its supernaturalist prescriptions and taboos, on at least the same terms as the concordat which fascist militarism led to between the Italian State and Roman Catholic power.

One item in such a *gleichschaltung* would be the complete surrender of the critical intimacies of human existence such as birth, puberty, marriage, divorce, diet, and burial, and, above all, the education of youth, to clericalist regulation and management. Even if state and church were not completely unified, schooling would be unified, standardized and militarized. Today's control by sect or party would be replaced by an authoritarian central authority. The effort to educate as modernity understands education would be abandoned or forbidden. Instead there would be indoctrination. Guidance in the free use of reason in the arts and sciences and the faith underlying them would be rejected on behalf of inculcation of unquestioning assent to dogmatic repetition of certain principles and practices.

Still another consequence of spartanization for survival would be the projection of what is now a contingent mood among Israelis into a driving demand upon Jews and Judaists who are not Israelis. The truly representative appeal for the latter's moral and material support rests on the scientific spirit and the democratic faith. Their personal involvement is a voluntary act sanctioned by the ethics of universal human brotherhood as well as familial, cultural and cultist belongingness. The statesmen among Israelis so recognize it.

But there sounds in the anxious summons to Ingathering also another tone. This conveys compulsive demand. It asserts claims upon the Jews of the world, even where not Judaists, resembling the claims of the papacy upon Roman Catholics and its pretensions upon all Christians. Hitler's hierarchy made similar claims upon all Germans everywhere. Stalin's makes such claims and gets them served wherever there are Communists. To make good such claims upon the Jews of the world would require the organization of a "Catholic Israel," with headquarters in Israel's Jerusalem, after the manner of Catholic Christianity with its headquarters in Italy's Vatican City, or of Catholic Communism, with its headquarters in Russia's Moscow.

✦ ✦ ✦

"Catholic Israel," so intended, is a fantasy of helplessness bred in the weak by fear of their own weakness. It is a compensation in idea for strength and security lacking in fact. Though entirely unrepresentative, the idea has been seized upon by Christian alarmists and frightened Judaists, as well as by anti-Semites, to charge Israel and non-Israeli Zionists with demanding of Jews everywhere a dual political allegiance. In the United States a certain sect of Judaists employs the charge to condemn all support or giving by Americans to the Israeli enterprise, even though these be either goodwill offerings freely made, or actions to serve the national interest.

Ironically enough, this traditional argument of the anti-Semite against Jews—the charge of dual allegiance—is addressed to a world-community endeavoring to organize itself for collective security and equal liberty through the United Nations and for the system of international relations it is struggling to realize. The argument implies that recognizing and serving America's interest in the socio-political character of Israel is somehow disloyalty to the United States. That is to say, an American, be he Jew or Gentile, is held disloyal to his country if he cares whether Israel is a democracy, whether its institutions are the institutions of a free society of free men, and if he does what he can to enable Israel to grow solidly into such a society.

The argument obviously disregards precisely that which in fact makes a person an American, and that which Americanism implies for his attitude toward other states—such little weak states as Greece, for example, or Korea, or Turkey, or, for that matter, Israel. I say nothing of the parties to the North Atlantic Pact.

Now, to be an American is not an accident of birth but an act of faith. Although nationality accrues automatically to persons born in the United States, the responsibilities and privileges of citizenship do not. They are not functions of nativity. They come alive and actual when any person, wherever born or brought up, publicly commits himself to the faith and works of a certain way of life. The native is admitted to those duties and liberties at the age of twenty-one, when he becomes a voter and formally responsible for decisions, which his vote registers, regarding the officers, the policies, the entire political life and destiny of his community, of his State, of the Federal Republic—and he may have been carrying economic and cultural responsibilities long before then. An immigrant makes his commitment when he of his own free will publicly and solemnly abandons all allegiance to any other nation and takes the oath of allegiance to the United States. Thereby he becomes a "naturalized" citizen. There are not many Americans without "naturalized" forbears; there are millions who are themselves "naturalized."

Being "naturalized," rejecting allegiance to other sovereignties, becoming an American, does not mean committing oneself to any organization of party and power existing at the time. Such organizations keep forming and dissolving; they are formations in the American Way, changeable and to be changed. What the American commits himself to is the rules of human association which are to guide these changes. He vows a fighting faith in freedom whose fundamentals are written down in the Declaration of Independence and the Constitution of the United States. These first books of the Bible of America express certain principles and ideals by which the nation endeavors to shape its life. They are the articles of its faith. American history is the history of the struggle of the American people to embody its faith in works as the American way.

True, many who oppose the effort at embodiment are also called Americans. Some want to convert the country into an oligarchic republic. Others would like to reconstruct it into a fascistic corporative state; others to work it over, from Southern models, into a nazi-like racist state; others seek over-ruling power and privilege for a sacerdotal hierarchy; others conspire to turn it into a hierarchical soviet. Some make up a "Liberty League," others are "constitutionalists," others "dixiecrats," others clericalists, others communists. And unhappily, although perhaps inevitably, each such organization of passion and

interest has its echoes and its imitators, for whatever reasons, among
the nation's Jews.

Americanism, as the Bill of Rights defines it, protects all of them
alike in their rights to believe and to implement their beliefs in policies
and programs which, in the frame of reference of that very Bill of
Rights and of the Declaration of Independence, do not fit with Americanism. It is the American way for every person who is not an idiot
to be a "joiner," to enroll himself in many associations, to each and
every one of which he gives allegiance but none of which may claim
his exclusive allegiance. That they are many liberates him from servitude to any. Their numbers give efficacy to the assurance of the Bill of
Rights that he shall be free to believe, to think, to speak, and to associate with others in multiple and diverse ways: that he shall not be
deprived of that spiritual, physical and social mobility which signalizes
free society.

Americanism envisages "life, liberty and the pursuit of happiness"
as individual ends whose common means are the multiple religious,
political, economic, cultural and recreational associations which individuals enter and leave, and the multiple activities they together carry
on. Americanism envisages the Federal Union as this communion of the
different—one country, of upward of fifty diverse states and territories,
with their countless communities, each cherishing, and pooling, its own
ways, its own characteristic economy and culture, with those of the
others. The American Idea is the national faith in democracy as the
religion of religions which guarantees equal liberty to each of upward of
three hundred sects and denominations. It hence requires of them that
they should be united in common loyalty to this democratic faith. The
American Idea designs the national economy as the free coming
together of men and managements in common enterprises, moved by a
common concern so to raise the national standard of living that all may
live their lives in ever greater abundance because of the ever-widening
knowledge and truer skills wherewith they earn their livings.

Similarly, Americanism in foreign relations is postulated on the
idea of an international peace built on the equality of the different
nations who have freely come together in order that all might assure to each on equal terms its sovereignty, independence, and well-
being. This was the idea that led to American initiative in forming
the betrayed League of Nations, and that led to the renewal of the

initiative in creating the United Nations Organization, and this time sharing the international tasks and responsibilities.

In sum, Americanism envisages the entire human enterprise in America as one civilization created by the communion of its many cultures, a self-orchestration of all the diverse works and ways of the spirit of man into the singularity of the American way of life. This way of life America wants its arts and sciences to express, to symbolize and to fulfill, and its schools to teach and develop. It locates any American who has become aware of the nature, the ideals, the powers, and the relationships of his country, in a consciously realized network of connections and belongings which centers in his family and joins him to all the peoples of the globe. The network gives substance to the American credo, and direction to the believer's commitments who would live by the credo. It is intrinsically a commitment to a struggle aiming to conform fact to faith, to Americanize existence in America, and by works to communicate the faith to the world. From the battle for the Bill of Rights in Washington's time to the fight for the program of President Truman's Commission on Civil Rights, and for the propositions of the Universal Declaration of Human Rights adopted by the Assembly of the United Nations, the struggle has been unremitting. Its one aim has been, and remains, to free the different from penalties for being different; to unite them as equals in free association so that they might work out and maintain together equal liberty for each.

This religion of equal liberty has never been an easy one. Its faithful have always been confronting entrenched and greatly preponderant power, fear, inertia. They have always sweated, suffered and bled for their belief. Violence has been thrust on them, as in the American Civil War, as in the two World Wars, as in the Korean betrayal.

Recurrent violence is a fact of the history of liberty which Jews can least afford to ignore. Penalized for being Jews on the basis of a religious dogma which demoted them from God's Chosen to God's Rejected People, they were in many ways more conspicuous beneficiaries of the struggle for equal liberty than women or the darker peoples. For they had been excommunicated from the natural fellowship of mankind on the basis of supernatural revelation. The Democratic Idea is the ground of their release from this segregation, of their full restoration as Jews to human fellowship. Not unnaturally many of them took freedom to be a Jew without penalty to be the same as ceasing to be a Jew at all. They interpreted defeating anti-Semitism into liquidating Judaism.

This was both a sociological error and a subversion of the Democratic Idea. Anti-Semitic aggression changes its forms but gives no sign of dissolving its powers or abandoning its purposes. The Democratic Idea affirms the equal right of the Jew, fully as Jew, to "life, liberty and the pursuit of happiness," not as fleeing Jewishness but as achieving it more abundantly.

Morally, the Jewish Americans' commitment to the Democratic Idea is double. It is both American and Jewish, and Jewish as American. This twentieth-century world he lives in is one everywhere of a life-and-death struggle for democracy. Totalitarianisms threaten wherever a free man turns. It is not so long that one such, with horrible cruelty, exacted from Jews six million lives for being Jews. It is still the case that in much of the world where Jews survive they are at the mercy of a ruthless power which nullifies the very idea of freedom on the grounds of an economic myth exalted into an infallible religious dogma—which may similarly penalize them.

That nullification of freedom is not the first, since 1776. In 1820 there was the Holy Alliance. When its plans of aggression came to the knowledge of the Government of the United States, it declared: *You shall not pass.* It declared that since the rule and program of the powers of tyranny were antipathetic to American liberty, they should not be imposed in the Americas, and pledged itself to resist such imposition. The pledge is called the Monroe Doctrine. A century and a quarter later the Nazi totalitarian aggressor turned all his resources of force and fraud against the ongoing struggle for equal liberty. The President of the United States called upon all Americans and all free men everywhere to *quarantine* the aggressor. Little more than a decade later this call was developed, on the precedent of the Monroe Doctrine, into the Truman Doctrine, which tells Stalin's imperialist tyranny: *You shall not pass.*

This Truman Doctrine is at once a weapon in the nation's war for survival as a free society of free men, and an aspect of the nation's commitment as a member of the United Nations. It accepts the American people's partnership in the reconstruction of free Europe. It implements their commitments as one of the insurers of free society in Greece, in Turkey, in all the Near East, and particularly in Israel.

Not in their own right only did the American people acknowledge the claim of the Israelis to sovereignty and independence. They did it also as a member of the United Nations Organization of which they are both among the prime sponsors and the sincerest supporters. They voted hence for admitting the new State to that international fellowship with its rights and duties. The action was based not alone on the usual motives joined to lagging humanitarian sentiment, but in no small degree also upon the democratic pattern given the Jewish homeland in the past, upon the new State's avowed design to extend and fortify democratic ways in the future. The American action assumed Israel's integral commitment to liberty and democracy as the American Declaration of Independence affirms them, and as the Universal Declaration of Human Rights, for which Israel voted in the Assembly of the United Nations, extensively defines them.

That Americans have a vital stake in this commitment of Israel's goes without saying. National interest is joined to disinterested devotion to liberty in the requirement that Americans shall, as in China and elsewhere, challenge totalitarian tendencies in the Land of Promise and nullify or avert their causes. Americans have a moral obligation to do whatever they freely can to nourish the springs of liberty in Israel and enable its peoples' growth to self-reliant strength and cooperative union with other free societies.

For Americans who are Jews or Judaists, the stake in Israel has additionally, psychologically and socially deeper, older, motivations. And, for that matter, so it has for Judaists wherever they make their homes. They may not forget, and most certainly may not forget in Israel, that the chief, not uncommonly the sole, difference for which Jews have been penalized is religious; that to lay this sort of penalty on any one, Jew or non-Jew, in a land dominated by Jews is a blasphemy beyond pardon. Their leaders might well emulate the example of Purshottamdas Tandon, the orthodox Brahmin recently elected President of the Indian Congress Party.

Tandon was the candidate of Hindu fanatics who stood intransigant against the rule of equal liberty for all faiths which the Hindu Government was endeavoring to apply. But in his presidential address Tandon declared: "The administration of this country cannot be run from the communal standpoint or on the authority of any fixed religious book. Even thinking on these lines will increase internal dissensions and weaken our administration." The

Congress accepted this view, and by resolutions affirmed the principle and policy of toleration.

What holds for India holds far more momentously for Israel. It is inadmissible that the spirit of equal liberty and equal responsibility, which initiated Dagania and created the *Kevuzoth* and the city communities, shall not inform and shape into a free society of free Jews the diverse Jewries of Israel. It is inadmissible that the cultural economy and educational establishments of Israel shall, on the score of exigencies of national survival, be made instruments of a Sparta-like totalitarianism. To permit this to happen at all would be to forfeit all claim on the United Nations' support, without which survival would be forfeited anyhow. But more, it would be a betrayal of the integrity of the humanist freedom from which Judaist supernaturalism has everywhere drawn so many benefits. It would be a moral nihilism. For the action undertaken to realize ideal as fact would nullify the ideal in the name of the ideal.

✦ ✦ ✦

A consequence inadmissible to faith or reason may readily find admission in perception and fact. The logic of discourse is congruent with the logic of life only by a happy chance; the dialectic of belief can lay down hardly any gradient for the succession of events. Things happen. One leads to another, but not as reason ordains or the heart demands. They move on with a blind contingency which only the retrospective look of some philosophical historian composes into a logical pattern that he then attributes to God's providence or Nature's laws. Beliefs and reasonings are also happenings. Once in a while, they find other happenings from which they receive vindication of their own certainties and confirmations of their own foregone conclusions. At their functional best, they fuse into the form of calculated risks. Supernaturalism verifies the calculations by superseding the experienced with the desired, thus feeding invincible hope on ineluctable illusion. Humanism verifies the calculations by proving the desired on the hazards of experience, forging the valor of idealism on the contingencies of events in such wise as to toughen hope without invoking illusion.

The humanist and the supernaturalist modes of religion span the life of man and together give it shape. Their synergy compounds into the predicament which is human existence in every age, in every culture. It is conspicuously the predicament of free societies. For these, events every so often move to a climax of options which are both momentous and forced, between irreconcilable alternatives and self-defeating programs. The movements follow from the fact that the rule of equal liberty, by which free societies live as free, protects also enemies of liberty who employ their freedoms in order to destroy freedom. Since their ways of living together are ways of toleration, also of the intolerant who aim to put an end to tolerance, the ways could be the murder of tolerance at the hands of the intolerant; while if free societies themselves were not to tolerate the intolerant, they would bring death to toleration at their own hands. When men in the predicament of the free are confronted also by unappeasable aggression from without, what they must needs do to resist and vanquish the aggressor may often involve such a regimentation of all the people, such limitations upon thinking, communication, movement, and assembly, as first to contain, then to suppress, ultimately to destroy, the liberties in whose defense the regimentation has been devised.

The condition is endemic to free societies. Between World War I and World War II, thinking men have become radically conscious of it, again and again and again, in the United States, in Great Britain, in France, in all lands that affirm freedom as their rule of thought and life. The pressure is constant, within and upon them, toward either moral abdication or enemy victory.

These are the horns of the dilemma between which the people of Israel are placed by the being of the State of Israel. The alternatives are to accept the murder of freedom at the hands of its foe or to kill freedom in order to save it from the foe. They shape up a predicament which is no news in the Jewish tradition. Jeremiah could understand it; the second Isaiah could interpret its global import; the author of Job could characterize the strength that can overcome and dissipate it and free the state to form itself into a free society of free men.

The precise way to that fundamental liberation is neither clear nor easy. It cannot be other than one which will both defeat the enemy and preserve freedom as alike the end and the means of Israel's continuing as a different and equal member of the international community. It cannot be mapped as other than the enduring strategy of a discipline of freedom whose tactic and logistic shall be willingly fitted by all whom it engages into the configuration of the common enterprise.

This is not now the case. The record shows a polarity, as well as cross-purposes, among the Ingathered of Israel and among Zionists elsewhere. It shows too ready a disposition to lose the design of the whole in the daily round of dirt and drill and disputation, with their habits, their hazards, their aggressions, their evasions and their impatience. It shows too prompt a willingness to ignore the long run for the short run, and to import fabrications instead of cultivating a greater growth of the freedoms already sprung from the soil.

In the communities of free agreement which Dagania initiated, in the primary associative structure of Haganah and Palmach, there may be data of experience from which an economy of free men in arms, loyal to freedom and dedicated to a just peace, can be designed. Made confluent with the Pittsburgh Program of the American Zionists, they may provide a base in thought for a strategy and tactic of Israel's indispensable discipline of freedom.

Israel's logistic, however, is conditional upon investments and loans and gifts from the free world, particularly investments, since investment brings with it a lasting concern of the investor that his venture shall prosper and grow. He knows now that his best risks are those conditioned upon the human freedoms. The free world, certainly the American variety of it, no longer cares to hazard either material or spiritual capital save in the safeguarding of freedom. To win its cooperation, professions with no practice to confirm them are no longer enough, as the Kuomintang has discovered. Unkept or broken promises by Chinese rulers have lost the free world the whole of China.

Not one Israeli sect or party by itself, but all the people of Israel must set themselves the arduous task of learning how, in the day's work and the day's fight, "to perform justly, skillfully, thoughtfully and magnanimously, all the offices, both private and public, of peace and war."

The words are John Milton's. They are his definition of education. But they also signalize the discipline of freedom. If the people of Israel can freely perfect themselves in this discipline, they have more than a fighting chance to achieve the definitive victory over freedom's foes, which a just peace could crown by agreements, under the United Nations, of mutual cooperation and support with the Arab States. Or, if Israel's God wills that the foe should prove too strong, Israel will have held fast to its integrity and not paid for some form of physical survival with moral suicide.

(—1951)

FIRST AND LAST THINGS

Ibn Gabirol: Poetry and Philosophy

⤪⤳

ISRAEL ZANGWILL

I N HIS well-known *Romanzero*, the greatest modern poet of Jewish birth, Heinrich Heine, satirizing the ignorance of Hebrew literature, wrote—I cite an early translation of my own which preserves the meter of the original—

> Jewish girls of wealth and fashion,
> Future mothers of free burghers,
> Culling all the latest knowledge
> In the dearest Paris *pensions,*
>
> Know by heart the names of mummies,
> All the stuffed Egyptian Pharaohs,
> Merovingian shadow-monarchs
> Whose perruques were yet unpowdered,
>
> Also pig-tailed Kings of China,
> Porcelain-pagoda princes,
> Pat from tongue it all comes tripping.
> Clever girls! But, oh, good heavens!
>
> Should you ask about the famous
> Names that formed the golden triad
> Of our Jewish constellation,
> Our Arabic-Spanish singers,
>
> These three stars if you should ask of,
> Our Jehuda ben Halevi,
> Or our Solomon Gabirol,
> Or our Moses Ibn Ezra,
>
> Should you bring up names of that sort,
> Then with large eyes will regard you
> All the girls, the pretty darlings,
> Dumb-struck, mud-struck, disconcerted.

Later in the same poem, Ibn Gabirol is singled out as the thinker among poets, and the poet for thinkers; and finally our eleventh-century singer is compared to that troubadour, that medieval nightingale, who delicately in the dusk of the Dark Ages sang *The Romance of the Rose*. Gabirol, says Heine, is the nightingale of piety, the consecrated Minnesinger whose rose was God.

+ + +

This is the essential fact about our Hebrew minstrel. But if, not content with it, we seek for the prosaic details of his biography, we shall not, I fear, be exploring on very firm ground. True, a quite elaborate book on Gabirol has been written by Geiger, but the Germans are famous for their ability to evolve the camel by intuition, and how little is really known about our Hebrew worthies I had long ago realized when studying the life of Spinoza. Since Pharaoh set the Jews to make bricks without straw, many Jewish biographers have brilliantly illustrated the possibilities of the manufacture.

Gabirol was a contemporary and fellow-countryman of the Cid, Spain's national hero, and the age has become fabular for Jew as for Christian. Heine assumes that Gabirol lived and died in Cordova; but Gabirol's own poems show him in other parts of Spain, and Malaga is now credited with his birth and Valencia debited with his death. According to Moses Ibn Ezra, his successor in Heine's triad of stars, he died, like Keats, in the heydey of youth. Graetz gives him half a century. The latest scholarship—expressed through Dr. Halper—cuts him off in middle age. That he was born about 1020 is only a deduction from an elegy he wrote in 1039. In truth the only thing we know in full detail is his name—Abu Ayab Sulaiman Ibn Yachya Ibn Gabirol—a name which in its plenary resonance would have satisfied that hidalgo of Bevis Marks, my friend, the King of Schnorrers.

Happily as with Shakespeare we have his works, and although to deduce an author's life or opinions from his dramas may be illegitimate, we are on surer ground in dealing with his lyrics. One need not hesitate to believe, for example, even had we no other evidence, that Burns loved not wisely but too many. And on opposite grounds we may believe that Ibn Gabirol, though a son of Spain, was no Don Juan. Even his enemies—and they were not a few—accused him of nothing but a reckless disrespect for conventional values. He seems indeed like Lycidas "to scorn delights and live laborious days." Moses Ibn Ezra records his chaste devotion to philosophy and the higher mathematics and he himself protests as to remonstrant friends:

"Better that my strength shall be sapped by love of study than of
woman."
Only once he seems to yearn for the comfort of a woman's breast.
"Open the gate, my love," he cries almost in the very meter of "Come
into the garden, Maud." But it is not because "the black bat night has
flown," but because it has swooped down upon him. "My soul is dismayed" he wails, and in agonized accents he laments his lot. And his
personal grief flowing over into his people's sorrow, he asks why the
wild ass of Islam should now pursue what the wild boar of Rome had
trampled on. And the sealed fate that awaits him and Israel adds to his
unrest and his pain.

✦ ✦ ✦

The lad had drifted to Saragossa, and at sixteen already laments
that he has the heart of a man of eighty. It was the morbidity of the
early teens. For at nineteen—as we see from the preface to his versified
but invaluable Hebrew grammar, that marvelous *tour de force* all in
rhyme and in one rhyme at that—he is full of the optimism of youth.
Beholding, he tells us, the scatterings of his people and the ruin of its
language, and seeing the ship laboring in the waves, he resolved with
God's help to be the instrument of salvation; to dress up in verse the
laws of pure Hebrew speech, so that his poem might be as a well-
watered garden in a day of drought, that the language of angels,
prophets, and holy singers might again live on his people's lips, that
the handmaid Hagar should not outstrip the mistress Sarah, and that
Sarah should no longer tend the fruit of strangers and forget her own
vine and fig-tree.

But, alas, that 'heart of eighty' is a more substantial fact when the
poet, disillusioned and embittered, finally shakes off the dust of the
then commercial capital of Aragon. To find a parallel to the pessimism
and vituperation of his poem on leaving Saragossa we must go back
to the early chapters of Jeremiah. One's pain at reading it is alleviated
only by one's pleasure at the marvelous rhyming, which no doubt
softened equally for the poet the sorrow to which it gave vent.
Indeed, he himself wrote:

"Perchance to utter my grief will still the edge of the tempest."

✦ ✦ ✦

Two centuries later, Alcharizi, the author of *Tachkimoni*, looking
back wistfully—a *laudator temporis acti*—to Gabirol's period as to a
literally golden era, sings in his easy jingling fashion:

The fathers of song
Were a fortunate throng.
From Gabirol to Moses,
Their bed was of roses.
They shone in the West
In that period blest
And rich men abounded who purchased their poems with zest.

But obviously Gabirol did not take advantage of his opportunities. A
wanderer, without wife or child, without sister or brother, with no
companion—as he laments—save his thought, urging himself in his
song to dissolve his tears in his blood and both in his wine, Gabirol
has no material center of happiness. Though as a youthful prodigy
he had been patronized by the vizier Jekuthiel Ibn Hassan, one of
those wonderful figures—Hebrew scholar and Gentile statesman—
which Jewry has always thrown up, he could not pander to the great,
even when they played the Maecenas; still less could he hold truck
with those prosperous pillars of the Community, those leather-manu-
facturers and cloth-merchants—whom neither Heine nor Matthew
Arnold had yet called the Philistines. He could not suffer fools gladly,
especially when he saw them exalted, applauded and revered, as was
sometimes so strangely the case—in those days. His noble-souled
successor, Moses Ibn Ezra, whose homage to the departed Gabirol was
only equalled in magnanimity by his welcome to the coming Jehuda
Halevi, and who pronounced his predecessor unsurpassed in every
species of poetry, elegy, panegyric or philosophic contemplation, who
declared that "his songs of friendship are full of tenderness," that "his
religious poems move to tears," and that "his confessionals abase the
soul to humility," yet cannot away with the acridity of the Master's
satirical moods, complains that he repays the contempt of the powerful with too bitter a disdain. It is clear that Gabirol belonged to the
genus irritabile vatum—"dowered with the hate of hate, the scorn
of scorn, the love of love."

Particularly is his motto "no compromise" where poetry is in question. He even flutters the dovecotes of orthodoxy by doubting the wisdom of Solomon himself when the poet of "The Song of Songs" perpe-
trates that characteristically Oriental comparison of a set of white
teeth to a flock of sheep. But of his own genius he has no shadow
of a doubt, and when a scribbler steals some of his own lines he writes
with sublime assurance:

Poor thief, would you my door break through,
And shine with gems not shaped by you
    And with the rays from me you stole
    Make for your head an aureole?

Fool, would you up to heaven run
And with your hand blot out the sun?
    I watch your raids without emotion—
    A bucket cannot drain the ocean.

There was indeed something oceanic in the man, both in his depths and his tempests. At one time he resolves to leave Spain for the more glamorous Jerusalem or Babylon, but his resolve finds expression only in music. Like Heine, he makes his little *Lieder* out of his great sufferings, and as with Shelley, his sweetest songs are those that tell of saddest thought.

Those were the days before the printing press. The poet lived from hand to hand, when not merely from mouth to mouth. But the synagogue was not yet dead and the poet might find his reward in seeing and hearing himself incorporated in the ritual, which was still a living growth. It says much for the Jewish congregations—despite Gabirol's carpings at his contemporaries—that they eagerly seized upon these new lyrics of his, which still stand in the Machzor among the tortured and obscure Piyyutim of his predecessors, like palms waving over rocks. Those old Spanish Hebrews had indeed no mean flair for poetry. And the poetry of young Gabirol passed not only into the Spanish ritual, but also into the German and Rumanian, and penetrated even to the Karaite Machzor.

✦ ✦ ✦

All the arts began with religion, and in Gabirol we catch sight of Hebrew poetry at the moment of transition when, as in some Ovidian metamorphosis, it was passing from a purely devotional to a secular character. Even the devotional begins to root itself not in tradition but in the individual experience. In a remarkable poem beginning "Three witnesses have I," Gabirol speaks of the starry world without and the moral law within almost with the modern cosmic mysticism of a Kant or a Wordsworth. There is thus a double movement by which the devotional is freeing itself from the hypnotism of the biblical and liturgical *Anschauung* and taking on a personal quality, while at the same time the subject-matter is enlarging itself with elegies, epigrams, and

Horatian epistles. Gabirol's Hiawatha-like jingle on the meanness of
his host who failed to give him wine—

> May the man, his son or daughter
> Be for ever doomed to water.

—is sometimes cited as the first secular lyric in Hebrew poetry; but although this is not literally accurate, it is not easy to find anything
prior but what partakes of a gnomic if not a pious character. While the
Bible itself is full of matchless poetry, both primitive and cultured,
the purely profane element was so discountenanced in this thesaurus
of national literature that "The Song of Solomon" slipped in only as a
religious allegory; "Ecclesiastes" scraped through under the aegis of
Hezekiah; while "Job" was ascribed to Moses. And this tendency to
make Hebrew literature synonymous with sacred literature was aggravated by the limitations of Jewish life in the Diaspora, whose sole
organ of common consciousness was the Synagogue with its holy lore.

The Jew, living as a "Son of the Law," and continuing to live only
because he was a "Son of the Law," did not readily develop a lay
literature. Torah, not wine, woman, or song, was the poet's expected
theme. Luther's trio of themes came along more copiously in Moses
Ibn Ezra and Jehuda Halevi; in Alcharizi we get a semi-burlesque
Hudibras method, modelled on the Arabic *Makama;* and in our own
day this evolution from liturgical literature has reached its climax
in the nature-poetry of a Jacob Cahan, the sensuous strains of a
Shneour, or the skeptical bitterness of a Bialik.

But in the best Spanish-Hebrew period we see the poet, like some
tropical lung-fish that can breathe either in air or water, moving
equally between the sacred and the profane. Gabirol is the first
Hebrew poet to use the secular image of the Muse, which he figures
as a dove, white as the lily of Sharon, with golden wings and a bell-
like voice. He is the first to paint the sunset or the autumn, and in
a Shelley-like image to show us Night spreading her wings over the
tired Day. And he is the first Hebrew poet to handle philosophy.

✦ ✦ ✦

In Judaism proper there is no philosophy. Sufficient to obey and
adore the unknowable Creator. Philosophy is the attempt of the human
intellect to circumscribe what circumscribes it, and is thus a sort of
Irish bull chasing its own tail. As Montaigne put it, "To stride further

than our legs can reach is both impossible and monstrous. . . . Man cannot see but with his eyes nor seize but with his power." But the Greeks boldly grappled with the unseizable, and the Arabs clinging to the Greeks brought their dependents, the Jews, into the great gymnastic. Gabirol with his Arabic treatise, best known by the Latin name of *Fons Vitae,* was the first Hebrew philosopher in the West, indeed the first Andalusian philosopher. Even in the East only Saadia and a few obscurer Jews had wrestled with metaphysics. Gabirol's book was moreover the first Hebrew attempt—obviously on the lines of the *Kalam*—to work out a theological system, irrespective of Revelation. His poetry is only too full of biblical quotations. But in his *Mekor Hayim (Fons Vitae)* he ruthlessly avoids even a biblical reference. His philosophical system must stand exclusively on its own legs— theological must mean purely logical. That is enough of itself to explain the non-influence of this book upon Jewish thought, the odor of heresy that clung to it, even had it not been inspired by the Enneads of Plotinus.

"Go not near the Grecian wisdom," sang Gabirol's successor, Jehuda Halevi. It was a futile warning. A large part of Jewry was destined to receive the Grecian wisdom through Maimonides' refraction of the Arabized Aristotle. But all Jewry shrank from the neo-Platonic mysticism refracted through Ibn Gabirol.

Ibn Daud of Toledo in the next century remarked caustically that Gabirol seemed to think many bad arguments equivalent to a good one. But *habent sua fata libelli,* and the stone rejected of the ghetto became a corner-stone of Christian scholasticism, while the author long figured as "the Moor, Avicebron."

Though the *Fons Vitae* is a work of Pure Reason, it is composed in the livelier Platonic form of a dialogue between a Master and his Disciple. Its main originality consists in the thesis that Matter and Form underlie everything except God; from whom, however, Matter is an emanation. There is a Cosmic Soul, almost as with some of our latter-day philosophers, and man, as combining soul and body, is a microcosm. Birth obscures our vision of the cosmic soul, much as in Wordsworth's great Ode, "Intimations of Immortality." This philosophy is not—like a growing school of modern thought—one of the evolution of God, but one of devolution from Him, with a return through Ecstasy. It would seem that Gabirol figured God rather as Will than as anything intelligible—thus foreshadowing Schopenhauer and perhaps Bergson—but this section of the treatise, if it was ever written, is lost. It was only through such glimmerings of his system as he could work into his great religious poem, the "Royal Crown," that all this mysticism reached Jewry.

It is worth remarking, however, that Gabirol's other prose Arabic work (*Improvement of the Qualities of the Soul*) was rapidly translated into Hebrew and as the *Tikkun Middot Ha-Nefesh* became a popular classic. That was because it showed that after all philosophy and orthodoxy were not incompatible. His contemporary, Al Ghazzali, had sought to prove as much for Islam by his book, *The Overthrow of the Philosophers*. But while Ghazzali's method was to doubt the philosophers, Gabirol, like Philo before him and Maimonides after him, beclouded the Bible. It did not mean what it said. Allegory was the reconciling principle.

Gabirol's ethical system is as labored as this explanation. He seems to have confusedly supplied Aristotle's doctrine of the Mean as the test of virtue with a physical basis. Every sense is viewed as the medium through which two Virtues and two Vices find expression. But granted that Sight may evoke Pride or Meekness (according presumably to the face one sees in the mirror), or that Touch may be stretched to cover Liberality and Niggardliness because of the closed or the open hand, good sense must draw the line at connecting Love with Hearing, when the evocation comes not even from the voice of the beloved, but from the fact that the injunction to love God follows on "Hear, O Israel." This is to confound words with realities. The sole merit of this popular work is that it varies its Hebrew quotations with citations from "the divine Socrates" and his disciple Plato, so when we find Mr. Claude Montefiore pleading so earnestly for the Jewish recognition of the best in Hellenism, it seems a curiously belated plea. The catholic temper of Gabirol likewise admitted there was wisdom in Islam, for it is largely from Arab sources that is culled the popular florilegium associated with his name, entitled *Mibhar ha-Penninim*, the *Choice of Pearls*.

✦ ✦ ✦

If it is necessary to envisage the philosophy of the *Keter Malkut* ("Royal Crown") in its historic perspective, still more is this necessary with the astronomy of the poem, which German translations leave out as though in shame. But the science Gabirol absorbed at Saragossa was of the eleventh century. And Copernicus did not publish his system till the middle of the sixteenth. Dante in the thirteenth gives us in his *Convito* Ten Heavens, each symbolizing a branch of study, and the last corresponding to the Divine Science, Theology. These Ten Heavens reappear in his *Paradiso,* nine revolving round the earth, with a fixed all-encircling Empyrean. Gabirol's chart of the celestial vault is of the same order as the Tuscan poet's, and his poetry in its aesthetic aspect is as little affected by the inaccuracy of his astronomy—if indeed in these days of Einstein there is anything but a relative inaccuracy.

Maimonides, born half-way between Gabirol and Dante, in his introduction to the Mishnah Tractate Zeraim, remarks on the astonishment of the ignorant on learning that the sun, which appears to them as a small, flat sphere, is a round body one hundred and sixty-six and three-eighths times greater than the earth, and the philosopher himself is amazed at the unerring science which can calculate celestial dimensions even to a three-eighth. We now believe that "unerring science" was wrong by considerably over a million; not unlike a modern Chancellor of the Exchequer. But the religious emotion which the poet desires to evoke by his figures is as little impaired by such errors as the beauty of his poetry: on the contrary, the emotion is augmented by our enhanced sense of the vastness and mystery of the universe. If a sun one hundred and seventy times as large as the earth sufficed to arouse Gabirol's cosmic rapture, how much more overwhelming is a sun over a million and a quarter times the volume of the globe that holds our petty fortunes, a sun down one of whose rifts, as a Royal Society lecturer said the other day, the earth would be dropped and lost like a boy's marble.

Nor need we be put off by the poet's astrology, that pseudo-science which has still not been slain outright, and of which our "Mazzol tob" is a survival. In Gabirol's day, and long after, it occupied no less proud a place than astronomy, and Jews, owing to their Chaldean origin, were regarded as peculiarly awesome masters of the horoscope. And in truth they both produced famous astrologers of their own and translated the Arabic astrologers into Hebrew or Spanish. A century after Gabirol, Maimonides derided astrology, but a century after Maimonides, Dante is found still ranking it as the science of the seventh heaven, above Grammar, Music, and even Geometry. Indeed Gabirol and Dante are at one in their conception of science, which differs literally *toto caelo* from the modern. For if Gabirol admits planetary influences, these are but secondary agencies: the force that set the planets in motion has never abdicated, and he still proclaims, like the great last line of the Divine Comedy,

"The Love that moves the heaven and all the stars."

(—1922)

The Intellectual Love of God

MORRIS R. COHEN

I wish in this paper to urge the validity of the Spinozistic ideal of the intellectual love of God—the *Amor Dei Intellectualis*—as an ideal which may still serve as a beacon to illumine current tendencies in life and thought.

It would be difficult to mention any contemporary issue in metaphysics or ethical and political philosophy in which Spinoza has not said something that is still laden with pregnant significance. On the questions of humanism or anthropomorphism, naturalism and idealism, on the relation of mind and body, on the method of ethics, on the relation of democracy to government by law, and on the ever-burning question as to the proper scope of governmental activities and the freedom or toleration of political and religious differences, few philosophers contain so much that is still so apt and modern. Spinoza is a central figure in the world's great stream of religious, political, and scientific thought. More than any other philosopher, Spinoza has impressed the imagination of Europe and its literature—witness Lessing, Goethe and Heine, Shelley, Coleridge and Arnold, Taine, Renan and Leconte de Lisle. Hence the neglect of Spinoza in contemporary Anglo-American philosophic discussion is itself a significant fact for those who wish to judge the intellectual temper of our age, and it is not altogether irrelevant for our present purpose to consider the possible causes of this neglect.

In the first place we have the linguistic difficulty, the fact that since Locke and Kant we have lost the old meaning of terms like subject and object, substance and essence. This offers great difficulty at a time when there is a general disinclination to see how our problems appear when translated into another philosophical dialect. The linguistic difficulty, however, is connected with a real difference of attitude. The struggle between science and theology since Spinoza's

(121)

day has made it difficult for us to understand his naive union of radically thoroughgoing naturalism in both ethics and science with the genuine piety toward that which has been held noble and sacred in the spiritual history of man.

Back of this difficulty, which makes naturalism and spiritualism antithetic terms to us, is the development of the modern conquest of nature which makes the modern American and European look exclusively to the control of material objects for the way to happiness, where ancient wisdom sought self-control by spiritual exercise. Metaphysically this shows itself in the tremendous emphasis that modernistic thought places on the category of time. The kernel of my contention in this paper is that if we recognize Spinoza's distinction between time as a category of existence and eternity as a category of essence or meaning, we can reconcile naturalism or, if you please, materialism with the piety which has distinguished genuinely spiritualistic views of life. The doctrine of the intellectual love of God, the central doctrine of Spinoza's philosophy, offers a convenient point of orientation for this contention.

The Spinozistic Ideal

If the *Ethics* makes anything clear it is Spinoza's rejection of all anthropomorphic theism. The view that God has any personal traits like will or human intellect, that he can act with a conscious view of promoting what is good for us, is repeatedly and most emphatically rejected. By the term "God," Spinoza obviously denotes what we call today the realm of reality which is the object of all science, the system or necessary concatenation of nature. Matter and meaning (in Spinoza's terms, "extended body" and "idea") are but two aspects of the unimaginable whole called God or Nature. When Spinoza calls the logical aspect or "attribute" of the universe the intellect of God, he expressly warns us that the term intellect does not at all mean the same when applied to God as when applied to man. Nor is there any anthropomorphism in the saying that man's intellectual love of God is a part of the love with which God loves himself. The most consistent atheist—I mean one who denies a personal God, rather than one bent on rejecting any and every use of the word God—can agree with Spinoza that the universe contemplates itself to the extent that it actually contains or involves intellectual contemplation.

All this, however, seems a dreadful play on words to those who complacently assume that the term God has not been and cannot be used in any sense other than that of a magnified human person to whom we can pray for recovery of health, or victory in war, and who will be pleased or displeased by the course of our action.

So thoroughly has this language of piety become associated with supernaturalism and pre-scientific superstitions, that there have not been wanting historically unimaginative souls to accuse the fearless Spinoza of having purposely put his atheistic doctrine into pious language in order to ward off personal annoyance. This is pathetically absurd. There can be no doubt that Spinoza was profoundly sincere in rejecting and resenting the charge of atheism which is associated in his mind with the pursuit of wealth and material goods. Now it would be hard for me to overemphasize the importance of language and the consequent duty of avoiding the confusion which always results from giving new meanings to old words, a confusion which De Morgan has keenly satirized apropos of theologies that convert the stories of the the Bible into transcendental psychologies by methods which can make anything mean anything else. But this objection cannot be justly brought against Spinoza, who is the pioneer of our modern historical methods of interpretation. On the contrary, those who object to Spinoza using "love of God" to denote devotion to philosophic or cosmic truth would cut us off not only from understanding the great neo-Platonic tradition in which Spinoza was nurtured, but the great human insight of teachers since the days of the Buddha and Jesus who have insisted that the kingdom of heaven is within us.

William James, who did inestimable good by insisting on thorough-going naturalism in psychology, seems to me to have produced untold harm by the unhistorical assumption that religion must necessarily rest on the belief in the supernatural. To insist that God must necessarily be a person who, if we pray to Him, will help us against our enemies and whom we in turn might help or please by believing in Him, seems to me to rest on an appeal to the unenlightened multitude against the judgment of all reflective thought; an appeal as unjustified as the parallel appeal to the multitude in questions of natural science. The unreflective judgment of the multitude is no more decisive on the question of the ultimate values of life than it is decisive in matters such as the motion of the earth around the sun. The unutterable miseries and wretchedness of mankind should emphatically

silence the claim that natural ignorance and unreflection is the road
to blessedness. The God of Spinoza is clearly not the God of Abraham,
Isaac and Jacob, precisely because, on reflection, it is impossible for
honest thinkers to believe literally that the infinite ground or rational
cause of the universe can sit down to dinner, get angry and punish
innocent people, or be guilty of the other absurdities which the
consecrated popular conception of God contains. The eternal cannot
become identical with the temporal. It is not democracy, but rather
the height of sophistication, which can lead a philosopher to appeal
here to the judgment of the multitude, very much as the disgruntled
political aristocrat sometimes appeals to the mob.

On the other hand, those who call themselves naturalists are intensely suspicious of such language as that of Spinoza because of their
fear of other-worldliness. But, if other-worldliness means despising
the joys which a wise use of nature can afford us, on the ground that
mortification of the flesh is in itself preparation for a higher life
hereafter, no one has more vigorously opposed such other-worldliness than Spinoza. The popular conception of Spinoza as an ascetic
must be corrected by his explicit teaching (*Ethics*, Props. 41-42, 45
note) that mirth is something of which we cannot have too much.
The rejection of wealth, sensual pleasures, etc., as absolute ends,
is always accompanied with the reservation that a wise man will
rationally use them as means to happiness.

Those, however, who are exceedingly afraid of other-worldliness
frequently use that term in a wide sense to denote any way of life which
tends to minimize the importance of immediate gratification of the
impulses to which man in natural or artificial society is subject.
Other-worldliness, in that sense, is the antithesis of that worldliness
which wise men in all generations have called a state of spiritual
death. Worldliness is, indeed, the most emphatic denial of the value
of philosophy; and no greater blight can fall upon philosophy than to
become so preoccupied with human affairs as to become worldly.
When naturalism becomes positivistic and loses the speculative or
cosmic interests of philosophy, it falls into deadly traditionalism, devoid of all freedom or liberality in ethics. It may sound paradoxical,
but in a complex world it seems the sober truth that philosophy
can help the man in the market-place only by turning its face and
fixing its eyes on larger vistas. It may seem cruel to indulge in metaphysical speculations while the great masses are chained to the grind-
stones; but, as Spinoza has well pointed out, unreasoned pity is a

passion of weakness. The physician can help the patient only after hours devoted to impersonal or theoretic issues.

If by materialism we mean to denote the doctrine that every existence is (or refers to) extended body, I do not see how any student of Spinoza can deny that he, like Hobbes, was a materialist. What distinguishes Spinoza from Hobbes and later materialists is his constant distinction between time or duration as a category of existence, and eternity as a category of essence or meaning. This distinction prevents Spinoza from falling into the nominalistic logic which cuts up the universe into a number of hard mutually exclusive terms that have no genuine internal connections, and can therefore be united only by a *deus ex machina*. His insistence that ideas, as logical essences or meanings, are eternal or timeless (that is, not subject to the processes of material change of which time is the measure) enables him to save all the profound human values of neo-Platonism and spiritualism generally.

Modern nominalism arose when physical science was compelled to break violently with the scholastic doctrine of substantial forms. That revolt against scholasticism was humanly necessary and brought much good to mankind. But like other revolts it was also very destructive, and it would have been even more so if mathematics (nourished in the neo-Platonic schools) had not developed the principle of continuity which enables us to see the threads of identity running through the diverse existing things. By taking mathematical method seriously Spinoza was able to maintain—despite some flings at the frailties of scholastic realism—that universals, meanings, or essences (laws, in ultra-modern language) unite infinitely different existing terms, but do not form additional particulars, and are not, therefore, subject to the temporal changes of such terms. To see things "under the aspect of eternity"— *sub specie aeternitatis*—is to see their actual meaning. All existing terms are bodies subject to change and therefore located in the time series. But if the whole time order has any meaning at all, the order of meaning includes it and is not exhausted by it.

As subordination of time to eternity (the latter is not to be confused with the everlasting, which endures through all time though in it) distinguishes Spinoza's philosophy from most modernistic thought, some reflections on the modernistic emphasis on time, which we may call temporalism, will not be out of place.

The consciousness of the importance of time separates the modern

European from the Oriental as well as from ancient and medieval man. It is intimately related to our modern industrial life. Reflection, however, shows that overemphasis on the importance of time is the root of nearly all the distinctive fallacies of modernism. These can be summed up in the false assumption that the existence of historic antecedents or psychic states does away with the importance of logical reasons. Formally this can be stated more generally by saying that the distinctive error of modern metaphysics is the false elevation of time, which is the necessary condition or aspect of all existent things, into the sufficient condition of all meanings. But it is easy to see that what is an indispensable order for all existing things need not and cannot be exhaustive of all possible orders of meaning.

A bare reference to the typical forms of this fallacy will perhaps make my point clearer. The old fallacy of supposing that you have refuted the truth of anyone's contention by showing that he has an economic motive for saying it has become generalized into a system of politics and historic interpretation. Substitute general psychologic motives for concrete economic ones and you have Freudianism instead of Marxism. Generalize this fallacy still further by saying the existence of temporally antecedent states contains all the significance and value of anything, and you have historicism, geneticism, or universal evolutionism. All these movements are professed revolts against abstract rationalism. Yet what can be more naively and baldly rationalistic than the assumed laws of Marxian social economics or the simplicity with which the different stages of the Marxian dialectic succeed each other; and what could be more crudely rationalistic than the way the subconscious or Freudian unconscious invariably acts like a logical automaton without any emotional disturbances? Popular evolutionism also shows its crude rationalism not only in constructing history into dialectic stages, but also in assuming that all the irrational acts of man are merely survivals from acts that originally served a useful purpose or were thought to do so.

Clear Spinozistic or mathematical rationalism saves us from such vain efforts. The relation of means to end is not at all a characteristic of the order of physical existence. Good and bad are relative to man; and man's power to secure the good depends upon his knowledge. The mathematical form into which Spinoza casts his ethical doctrine is an expression of the faith in universal truth. All forms of professed irrationalism avoid this faith. They passionately embrace some brute particularism, leaving no real ground for rational discussion or toleration or for the ideal of an ever wider integration of our natural interests which is set by the *Amor Dei Intellectualis.*

It is instructive for an understanding of the true character of naturalistic religion to contrast Spinoza's love of God with the Positivist love of humanity. The latter, if humanity denotes the actual human beings we know, involves us, among other difficulties, in the impossible obligation of loving the brute imperfections of our own nature. Now although it is possible to love human beings despite their imperfections (because of the better possibilities which enlightened love can discern), it is not possible to love the unlovable imperfections themselves. Any love that is rationally feasible must involve some norm which will enable us to discriminate that which is admirable from that which is not so; and that is exactly what the *Amor Dei Intellectualis* effects. (The command to love our neighbors needs the love of God as a norm of that which is lovable in them.)

The Spinozistic love of God or nature does not involve a love or acceptance of the world as it is at any particular moment. An intellectual love or understanding of the universe is not possible if our view is limited to a single moment. Such a limitation may help us to form definite images but not adequate ideas which, Spinoza emphatically insists, must not be viewed as lifeless pictures on a panel (*Ethics* II, 43 note). So far, then, as the love of God involves acquiescence or an acceptance of the universe it is in no way inconsistent with rational effort to improve any particular state or mode of being. Spinoza is as far removed from the violent optimism of Leibnitz as he is from the light-hearted pessimism of Schopenhauer. His doctrine is rather the reccognition that all rational effort involves an acceptance of the universe; we cannot improve nature except by nature's means. Hence there can be no true happiness or freedom that is not based on a recognition of the causal relation or necessary order which binds together the various parts of nature in time and space.

Though Spinoza's ethical ideal is fundamentally naturalistic, that is, aims at a rational synthesis of natural interests, his insistence that man must visualize his task *sub specie aeternitatis* distinguishes his doctrine from the type of progressivism formulated by the American national poet, Longfellow, in the "Psalm of Life." The latter rejects enjoyment as the end of man and formulates the categorical imperative: So act that each tomorrow finds you one day further than today. This type of popular progressivism rests on the optimistic belief that the cumulative results of personal or communal achievement can endure indefinitely—a belief which appears fantastic in the light of the robust knowledge of the variations of nature. The naive faith in temporal continuance can only increase the anguish of inevitable disappointment. Of course a certain amount of progressivism is an indispensable aspect of practical life aiming at commonly attainable external results. In the field of politics, I for one can see no other feasible program. But when progressivism becomes exclusive in its claims, pretending to fill the whole life of man as a religion, it becomes a foolish effort to impoverish life by robbing men of sustaining vision and moral holidays, in the effort to make them satisfied with the petty improvements which is all we can confidently expect from the uncertainties of nature. Here we certainly need Spinoza's reminder: "Human power is extremely limited and is infinitely surpassed by the power of external causes; we have not therefore an absolute power of shaping to our use those things external to us." But we can conquer nature by the act of understanding it.

Some Difficulties

I have thus far roughly sketched the concrete Spinozistic ideal without regard to the traditional difficulties which famous expositors have found in the structure of the Spinozistic system. An important group of these difficulties center about the supposed incompatibility between the terms of God, love and intellectual.

Love having been defined as a pleasure or joy, and pleasure as a feeling of transition towards greater perfection, how can it possibly be predicated of God who is all-perfect? We may of course answer this by textual distinctions between the intellectual love of God and the love that is not so qualified. But too sharp an antithesis between the two kinds of love may not help us much to understand Spinoza's doctrine. Let us admit, in the spirit of Spinoza, that any intellectual love which can be actual must have a physical or physiological location in our bodily organism. This physiologic process, so far as it is a transition to greater perfection or a heightening of our vitality, is a bodily process or mode. Like other modes it exists in nature or God, that is, it has its locus in some point of the temporal series. But the

essence or meaning of intellectual love of God is the adequate idea
or ideal of a complete intuition or insight into the system of nature
to which a study of the implication of existing things and especially of
our own emotions may lead us. The meaning of this idea is certainly
part of the ideal essence or intelligible structure of nature which
Spinoza calls God.

But how can love which is an emotion, or passion, be intellectual?
Spinoza's explicit declaration that intellectual love is not a passion at
all, but an intellectual activity, carries no conviction to the present
generation. For since the romantic movement we no longer look upon
passion as literally suffering, but regard it rather as an intense consciousness, expressive of an enhanced vitality. The ideal of passionless
reason seems to us, therefore, that of a logical machine without any
vital power. To Spinoza, however, passion means suffering due to the
absence of the light of reason, and the adequate ideas which remove
this suffering are not outside of the active conation which is the
essence of our being, but are this very conation or will perfected. Here
again Spinoza's identification of intellect and will is misunderstood
today because we identify the expression of will entirely with external
physical motion of practical affairs and exclude thought itself as an
expression of human and indeed cosmic energy. This makes us view
intellectual insight as a passive state, whereas to Spinoza, as to Aristotle and Dante, it is the most intense activity. The issue here is the
same as that concerning the nature of classic art. It is best answered
by recognizing that the serenity or absence of distorting passion in
classic art is not due to a lack of vitality, but to the literal perfection
of it by the mastery of form. If the word passion then be used in the
modern sense as an intensification of life, intellectual love is the passionate pursuit of truth, which is also the highest expression of the
conatus to self-preservation.

This will enable us to dispose of those who complacently deny any
religious value to the *Amor Dei Intellectualis* on the ground that it is
merely the scientific interest. This facile and fatal use of the word
"merely" was easy in the days when to the transcendental snobbery of
theologians scientific knowledge was a relatively unimportant affair.
Doubtless, also, so long as the term scientific is so often applied to particular investigations which leave the investigator hardly richer in the
wisdom of life outside of his narrow specialty, it seems rather violent
to identify the scientific and the religious motive. But when we recall

that the *Amor Dei Intellectualis* is not knowledge of isolated details, but the union of our mind and nature attained by self-knowledge, we need not hesitate to recognize the profoundly religious value which Spinoza's thought has had for so many.

The Spinozistic Ideal in Contemporary Thinkers

It may, perhaps, make my conception of Spinoza's position more clear if I indicate briefly to what extent contemporary thinkers seem to me to embody this *Amor Dei Intellectualis*.

The first name that will readily occur is that of John Dewey. No one today is doing better service in calling attention to the indispensable role of the intellect in making possible a life that can fitly be called human. This is more clear in his recent work, where the emphasis is no longer on the unfortunate term "practical," but on philosophy as vision or illumination of the *significance* of events. In his opposition to authoritarianism, to the romantic return to primitive or natural unreflection and to other forms of anti-intellectualism, he certainly embodies the Spinozistic spirit. Mr. Dewey's divergence from Spinoza results mainly from a too great concentration on the problems of practical education and empirical psychology. Concentration upon practical or social applications have, for instance, led Mr. Dewey to belittle, if not to ignore, the interest in physical or cosmic issues.

For the thorough acceptance of naturalism, both in morals and in science, perhaps no one today represents Spinoza as closely as does George Santayana. Though Mr. Santayana sweepingly rejects Spinoza's claims at the beginning of his *Life of Reason,* the latter work comes as near being a translation of Spinoza as it is possible for an independent thinker trying to envisage with his own eyes the human scene and its natural background. That the chief human good is not in perpetual physical motion, but in the vision of the essence or significance which illumines the natural scene, is brought out by no one more clearly than by Mr. Santayana. The difference between the latter and Spinoza is not so much in the emphasis that Spinoza placed on the rigorous or mathematical procedure of science as in the historic circumstance of their respective times. Spinoza wrote at a time when there still flourished the great neo-Platonic tradition which, despite its crust of superstition, had kept alive, while it somewhat cramped, the wisdom of antiquity. Certainly Spinoza's Hebrew teachers, as well as Giordano

Bruno, embodied that tradition as a living doctrine. Santayana writes at a time when that tradition, after having nourished the founders of modern science, Copernicus, Kepler, Galileo and Newton, had run itself into the intellectual underworld, and when the demand all around us is for novelty or originality above all. Santayana, to be sure, has aptly characterized this demand for originality as such as most deadly, and his genius for direct vision into the common life has stood him in good stead. But in a time of general insistence on novelty for its own sake, genius alone is insufficient. One needs also historic study to make the continuity of human life and thought so vivid as to save us from vain efforts. Such study Santayana has not adequately pursued. Hence the results of his thought often appear as illustrations of that which he is most anxious to combat, to wit, impressionism and willfulness.

Mr. Bertrand Russell, in his more strictly philosophical work, has given us a vivid illustration of the Spinozistic belief in the potency of thought and a striking example of what devotion to the truth really means. In this I cannot help thinking his mathematical training has been a great aid. While Mr. Russell's position differs from that of Spinoza in fundamentals, especially in his pluralism, the great difference seems to me rather temperamental. This shows itself in his famous essay, *A Free Man's Worship.* Mr. Russell is at one with Spinoza in rejecting the temporalism back of the effort to build up an abiding place for the human spirit in external nature. Nature cares not for our human hopes, and destroys the just and the injust. Hence there can be no enlightened human happiness without an element of wisely cultivated resignation. But while Spinoza recognizes that human hopes and aspirations are themselves the outcome of nature, and that even in thought we cannot transform nature except by the means with which nature supplies us, Mr. Russell too often allows himself to speak as if nature were an anthropomorphic being, consciously bent on defeating us.

Finally, I must mention one who, perhaps better than any other man, in candor and self-restraint, in depth and profound simplicity, illustrates the Spinozistic *Amor Dei Intellectualis*—F. H. Bradley. Mr. Bradley is at one with Spinoza in the view that insight or intuition into reality is possible only through rigorous intellectual exercise. Mr. Bradley also most thoroughly represents Spinoza in holding that the knowledge of particular things or modes (parcelled out among the special sciences) is in itself inadequate for philosophic insight, and needs to be submitted to that persistent inquiry into the nature of the absolute or the whole, which we call metaphysics.

By his profound devotion to the pursuit of truth in close reasoning, Mr. Bradley has prepared the way for philosophic modernism, over-throwing the complacency of neo-Hegelians and of the followers of the self-styled critical philosophy. Yet he has not been justly dealt with by this generation. For it is easier to ignore him or revile his doctrine of the absolute than to read him, understand him, and meet him on his own ground. May the recent reprint of his *Logic,* forty years after its first publication, serve to impress contemporary thinkers with the permanent value of his philosophic work.

(—1925)

On Creeds and Wants

◒〜◐

MORDECAI M. KAPLAN

M OSES MENDELSSOHN was the first spokesman of Judaism to react affirmatively to the Enlightenment. His general culture was that of eighteenth-century rationalism, which in its entire approach to religion and morals negated traditional Judaism as much as it negated traditional Christianity. Notwithstanding this negation, Mendelssohn made a heroic effort to work out some reconciliation or synthesis between Jewish tradition and modern scientific rationalism. This was the first attempt of its kind.

All who help to bring about a harmonization between the old and the new are innovators, whether they like to admit it or not. Throughout the past, in matters of religion, the innovator stood not the least chance of getting a hearing. If he had something new to say, he had to persuade himself that he was merely bringing back to life the pristine truth which had become overlaid with error. Even those who in the past posed as political and social revolutionaries claimed that they were only urging the restoration of the normal. Nor were they always certain in their own minds whether what they regarded as normal was actually ever realized, was chronologically prior to the state of affairs which they were condemning, or was merely logically prior, existing as an ideal, be it in the mind of God or of some human being. A case in point is the "social contract" theory. The eighteenth-century philosophers, including Rousseau himself, who drew some very significant conclusions from that theory in his *Contrat Social,* considered the social contract not as a real past event but as "a concept of a continuous social transformation," as an ethical postulate. This peculiar confusion of logical with chronological precedence, of what ought to be with what was supposed to have been, was inevitable before the concept of evolution was clearly grasped and applied to the affairs of human life.

Only when we bear in mind this peculiarity of eighteenth-century rationalism can we appreciate what Mendelssohn meant by asserting, in his *Jerusalem* (published in 1783), that Judaism was without dogmas. This was but part of a new orientation that he was unconsciously formulating. The distinction he drew between belief and revealed law was the first attempt to give Judaism a place in the world outlook which was permeated by the spirit of the Enlightenment. It is not my purpose to prove that Mendelssohn's attempt was successful. On the contrary, it is all too apparent that in trying to hold to the assumption that the laws of Judaism were supernaturally revealed, he became entangled in numerous contradictions. The merest tyro can discover those contradictions. But to expose his failures is not the way to appraise Mendelssohn's interpretation of Judaism. It should be judged rather from the standpoint of a deeply felt, though unformulated, urge to reconstruct Judaism, to readjust it to the needs of a newer day, which he was the first in Jewry to experience. Judaism without dogmas was to him not an actual part of the past, but Judaism as it ought to be. He wanted to make it possible for Jews to retain their Jewish individuality without having to surrender their freedom to think and believe in accordance with the dictates of reason. He did not want any Jew to feel that his Jewish loyalty was impugned as soon as he found that he could not accept certain beliefs which the rabbis and the medieval philosophers had declared to be essential.

Mendelssohn was well aware of the part that dogma played in the Judaism which he had inherited, but it was precisely this aspect of Judaism which he wanted to change. The thought, however, of changing anything in Judaism could not but appear as presumptuous to a man like Mendelssohn, who lived at the beginning of Judaism's conflict with modernism. Under these circumstances, such a thought begins to lead a subterranean life and to operate in disguised form. The usual disguise which it assumes is that of an anciently accepted truth. Thus Mendelssohn, wishing to rid Judaism of all elements of irrationalism, found refuge in Scriptures. On the face of it, the Torah contains no dogmas which the Jew is commanded to believe. That was for him sufficient proof that dogmas were alien to the spirit of Judaism, and should never have been introduced into it. But proof or no proof, Mendelssohn could not have remained a Jew had he been obliged to accept beliefs against which his reason revolted. He therefore found it necessary to establish the principle that, whatever demands Judaism had a right to make upon the Jew, there is one demand it cannot and in fact genuinely never did make upon him, namely, that he accept beliefs which his mind cannot affirm.

As was to be expected, this innovation which Mendelssohn unwittingly introduced into Judaism could not at first have anything but a destructive effect upon the complex of Jewish beliefs. Due to the undermining of traditional beliefs, many of the age-old institutions of Jewish life were bound to be swept away. All that Mendelssohn did was to legitimize the reliance upon the dictates of reason. He did not take the next step: he did not indicate in what way the dictates of reason could be synthesized with a life of obedience to the laws of the Torah. Little, however, as he can be blamed for having failed to take the next step, even less can he be blamed for what many, calling themselves his disciples, did with the principle of "dogmalessness." Although they utilized it to exempt themselves from the need of subscribing to traditional Jewish beliefs, they did not avail themselves further of the right to follow the dictates of reason; consequently, they were unable to achieve anything constructive in Judaism.

Nothing, however, has been gained by merely attacking the untenability of Mendelssohn's position from a historical standpoint.

Granted that Judaism was historically just as dogmatic as Christianity and Mohammedanism, is that likely to augment our loyalty to Judaism? How does the insistence upon dogmas help Judaism nowadays to deal with the challenge of modernism? It is difficult to gather from Mendelssohn's critics what inference they would have us draw from the point they labor so hard to establish. Do they mean that Judaism is still committed to the traditional creeds? Did Dr. Schechter, for example,* want the modern Jew to accept as binding upon his conscience the dictum in the Mishnah that one loses his share in the world to come if he denies that the doctrine of resurrection is to be found in the Torah? What of those Jews who find themselves unable to accept the belief in resurrection altogether, or in the divine authorship of the Torah (which Mendelssohn himself accepted)? Are they to be excommunicated?

If it is not on the traditional dogmas themselves that the opponents

* Solomon Schechter, "The Dogmas of Judaism," in *Studies in Judaism*, First Series (1911). Among other leading critics of Mendelssohn are Leopold Loew, *Gesammelte Schriften* (1871) Band I, 133-176, and David Neumark, "The Principles of Judaism in Historical Outline," published posthumously in 1929.

of Mendelssohn would insist, but on the contention that Jews have some kind of dogmas or principles to differentiate them from non-Jews, what are these dogmas or principles to be? Is the authority of the past, or of reason, to be binding?

The only way we can hope to arrive at some well-grounded conclusion with regard to the whole question of the place of dogmas, principles or beliefs in Judaism is to try to understand exactly the nature of this element of assent which Mendelssohn, on the one hand, seems to regard as unnecessary to Judaism, and which his critics, on the other hand, consider so indispensable.

✦ ✦ ✦

Belief is an attitude not confined to religion; it is evoked by a variety of situations. These two simple facts about belief seem to be entirely ignored in the discussions concerning the place of belief in Judaism. In all such discussions belief is stressed as though it were peculiar to religion and constituted part of its very essence. But it is a commonplace that belief plays as important a part in science and in all social relationships as it does in religion. How would it be possible for a scientist to draw conclusions from what he sees if he did not trust both his senses and the general laws of reason? Granted that scientific belief is less implicit and much more contingent upon verification than religious belief. That is only a matter of degree. For even the most implicit faith in any religious teaching will be shaken by a series of contradictory facts. And the part that faith plays in our human relationships is too well known to require proof. How is it possible to live on terms of cooperation unless we believe in the integrity of those we deal with, or have confidence in their good will?

Since belief is not limited to religion, it cannot constitute its differentia. Then why so much ado about its presence in Jewish religion?

Indeed, from the standpoint of attitude, denial is quite as important a part of religion as belief. In Judaism it was just as imperative to deny the existence of many gods as to believe in the existence of one God. Do not the rabbis say that he who denies the godhood of strange deities is as though he had acknowledged the authority of the entire Torah? (*Kiddushin*, 40a.) To say that denial is only affirmative belief concerning the non-being of objects, powers or qualities would be mere quibbling. Why should the issue hinge only upon beliefs of an affirmative, but not upon those of a negative, character? In any case, it is just as absurd to discuss whether or no there are beliefs in Judaism as to discuss whether or no there are emotions in Judaism, or practices. The presence of ideas, attitudes of belief and denial, is an integral part of every phase of human life. Among the elementary facts the merest beginner in psychology learns is that there is no manifestation of conscious life wherein either cognition, emotion or conation is altogether wanting. So why labor the point that Judaism is inconceivable without ideas or beliefs?

Perhaps we shall get at the significance of Mendelssohn's idea about dogmas in Judaism if we differentiate the types of mental reaction that are included within the category of belief, and identify the one particular type which, according to his opponents, is indispensable.

The designation "dogma" would seem to point to the importance in religion not of belief in general, but of a particular type of belief. When David Neumark—in his essay on "The Principles of Judaism in Historical Outline" (published posthumously in 1929)—calls attention to the fact that his predecessors in the criticism of Mendelssohn fail to note the meaning of dogma, he gives promise of dealing with the differentiæ that distinguish the kind of belief which has never been wanting in Judaism and, we are led to infer, continues to be indispensable. "What is 'dogma'?" he asks. His answer is: "The most *essential* feature of dogma is the insistence of a religion on a certain belief." Disregarding the looseness of the wording, what Neumark probably means is that the question at issue is not whether Jewish religion includes beliefs. The question is whether Jewish religion insists upon particular beliefs. This element of insistence is what turns a belief into dogma; and the way to recognize this element of insistence is by the presence of fixed formulas, of the duty to recite a fixed creed, of authoritative books, of controversy, of authoritative decision and anathema.

In all of this there is not one ray of enlightenment as to what actually differentiates "dogma" from other kinds of belief. All the features Neumark considers as the earmarks of dogma are only expressions of the insistent attitude which the religion takes toward a specific belief. Now, this insistent attitude is not an intrinsic part of the belief or attitude of the believer, but something entirely external to it. According to Neumark, the social attitude of insistence, which is a concomitant of certain beliefs, converts those beliefs into dogmas. Thus all the arguments marshalled by Neumark reduce themselves to the thesis that Judaism has been no different from Christianity and

Mohammedanism in bringing pressure to bear upon the individual to give his assent to specific beliefs. The individual's part of the transaction does not seem to interest Neumark at all. If that is all Neumark tried to prove, what has he added to the understanding of that aspect of the present problem of Judaism which is due to the refusal of many Jews to accept beliefs against their reason?

If we be guided in our classification of the different types of belief by differences in the attitude of the believer himself, we find the following types and their characteristics:

(1) *Unreflective beliefs.* These are ideas to which the mind gives assent merely because the mind at the time contemplates their subject-matter exclusively. William James has pointed out that the human mind tends to accept as fact or reality whatever is presented to it in such a way as to shut out all conflicting ideas. This explains why the mind accepts as real all the ideas that occur to it while it is asleep. This quality of mental somnolence also characterizes the majority of people, especially the untutored, when they are awake. For that reason the ideas occurring to them in the course of their daily experience, especially those prompted by the emotion of fear which tends to narrow the mental perspective even of the alert mind, are accepted uncritically. To this tendency of the human mind is to be ascribed the rich variety of superstitions and beliefs concerning the mysterious powers supposed to reside in the various objects of the environment, and the practices whereby they can be induced to ward off harm and confer benefits.

(2) *Reflective beliefs* are of two kinds: (a) rational and (b) intuitional. Both kinds presuppose the element of reflection. In both of them the mind is sufficiently awake to be able to contemplate possibilities which contradict the idea presented to it. Nevertheless, the mind adopts an affirmative attitude toward that idea. When it adopts that attitude because the laws of logical reasoning make all opposing ideas untenable, then we have reflective belief of the rational kind. But most ideas seldom present so clean-cut an issue between themselves and the alternatives that come to mind. For example, the beliefs we entertain concerning people, from the most intimate to the most remote, do not usually lend themselves to rational upbuilding and analysis. When we trust a friend, and rely upon his willingness and ability to help us in trouble, we do not indeed ignore the possibility of his disappointing us. If we allow our minds to assume the affirma-

tive attitude, it is not on grounds so compelling as to destroy completely the case for his unreliability. We merely make our choice of attitudes on intuitional grounds. This kind of intuitional belief is the basis for the majority of the practical decisions we continually make, decisions which cannot wait for all the facts necessary to furnish them with a perfectly rational basis. An important consideration which should be remembered throughout is that intuitional beliefs are, no less than rational beliefs, part of the personal experience of the one who holds them.

(3) *Traditional beliefs* are ideas communicated from one generation to another. Those who communicate such beliefs may themselves hold them either unreflectively or reflectively; and if reflectively, either rationally or intuitionally. The traditional belief itself may be accepted unreflectively or reflectively; and if reflectively, it may be through reason or intuition. In either case it becomes part of one's personal experience. We begin our conscious thinking with beliefs that are transmitted to us by parents, teachers, and acquaintances. Tradition is the basis not only of religious knowledge but of all knowledge. It is conceivable that among the traditional ideas there might be those which stress the importance of thinking for oneself and testing the ideas one acquires from others. The implication that a belief transmitted from the past which is found incapable of being fitted into the framework of one's own experience should be abandoned without any compunction might itself be part of a tradition. So far, however, no system of traditions associated with the life of any group, whether nation or church, ever included an idea which tended to encourage doubt or questioning. On the contrary, every such system has carried with it the implication that it is the duty of the individual to accept implicitly what he has been taught to regard as truth.

It was only with the entrance of Greek philosophy that this demand of group traditions was challenged. Ever since then group traditions have been laboring under the necessity of coming to terms with this challenge of reason. We must remember that group traditions originally dealt with all phases of life, with facts of nature, of history, as well as with norms of behavior. They were all in some way related to the God-idea; all group ideas were identified with religion. This situation created difficulties for those who in their eagerness for the truth refused to confine themselves to what they learned on the authority of the past and went off to explore on their own account. When conflicts arose, the spokesman for the group traditions would insist upon members of the group accepting those traditions as an evidence of loyalty. The group or community in whose name these spokesmen made their demands was little concerned that the individual member could not make the traditional beliefs part of his own experience. He had to accept traditional belief more as a mark of obedience than of mental assent. *When traditional beliefs carry with them the authority of the group which insists that they be accepted as a sign of loyalty and obedience, they acquire that connotation, and nowadays also the odium, which is associated with the term "dogma."*

There can be no doubt that each and every one of the types of belief enumerated functioned in Jewish religion at some time in the past. But the question is: To what extent did each type function during the different periods of the religion?

An adequate reply to this question presupposes a more exact knowledge of the history of the Jewish religion than we at present possess. The traditional account, especially of the beginnings of the religion, is such a mixture of fact and fiction that it cannot serve as a basis for a study of this kind. Nor is there any reconstructed account which can be regarded as sufficiently plausible for this purpose. Besides, it is not the main purpose of this essay to deal with the past. Therefore only the most salient and generally accepted facts about the past of the Jewish religion will be recalled to indicate how far each type of belief prevailed in the various periods of Judaism.

It is safe to assume that the unreflective type of belief was responsible for many, if not most, of the elements that constituted the religion of the nomadic ancestors of Israel. These unreflective beliefs were acquired to some extent personally, but to a larger extent traditionally. The moment we deal with an already existing group we assume the functioning of tradition, for it is only through traditions that a group comes to know itself as one and continuous. The belief, for example, that YHWH was the deity whose presence had been made manifest in the volcanic eruption of Mount Horeb arose, no doubt, in the same naive and unreflective fashion as did the belief among the aborigines of Greece that Olympus was the seat of the gods who figured later in the mythology of the Greeks. The idea that conspicuous places and objects on the earth's topography were inhabited by deities came just as naturally and unreflectively to the Israelitish nomads as the idea comes to the child that a doll responds to being fondled and caressed. Those to whom the storm over Mount Horeb and the accompanying earthquake and eruption signified the presence of YHWH were indeed wrong in their interpretation of these phenomena, but that made their unreflective interpretation or belief no less a matter of personal experience. Their descendants accepted the belief uncritically, and in their imagination lived through again the experiences which were recounted to them. The presence of YHWH on Mount Horeb was no less real to them than to those who actually witnessed the storm or the eruption.

Thus from the very beginning traditional belief was undoubtedly an important factor in Israel's religion, although from the standpoint of credibility there was little difference between tradition and personal observation. Their lack of reflection made everything told them by others as credible as anything they personally experienced. With the same unreflective docility with which the Israelitish nomads accepted the belief in YHWH's presence on Sinai they accepted the belief that all the vicissitudes they encountered were in some way related to their obedience or disobedience of the laws which were ascribed to YHWH.

When the Israelites on entering Canaan came into contact with the natives who had other religious experiences, traditions and customs, there set in a twofold process of unreflective syncretism and reflective antagonism to the native worship. Those who were conscious of something incompatible between the worship of YHWH and that of the native deities resisted the syncretistic tendencies of the majority, doing all in their power to accentuate the difference. This led to the further development not only of the traditions which they had brought with them but also of those traditions which sprang up in answer to the need for such contrast between the religion of YHWH and the religion of the native *baalim*. Acceptance of the YHWH traditions, which vindicated the superiority of YHWH over all other gods, was necessarily a result of reflection. But the considerations which determined the YHWH zealots were far from being of the kind we usually call rational. Their preference for YHWH was probably determined either by the intuition that it identified them with the invaders instead of with the natives, or by conservative leanings toward the simple life of nomadic ancestors in contrast with the socially corrupting tendencies of the more complex civilization of the natives.

But whatever the considerations that led them consciously to choose the religion of YHWH and to denounce the *Baal* religion, those considerations belonged to the class of reflective beliefs of the kind described above as intuitional. When these beliefs were transmitted to subsequent generations, they entered the class of traditional beliefs of the reflective type. The godhood of YHWH was not imposed upon those generations, nor was their consent demanded as a matter of blind obedience. On the contrary, that godhood was always validated by an elaborate system of narratives which told of the great wonders whereby YHWH had demonstrated his power and the great kindnesses whereby he had proved his love for Israel. This is anything but dogma.

Mendelssohn does go too far when he says the Torah does not demand belief that is in conflict with reason. For the truth of the matter is that no such issue could have arisen in those days. Reasoning— namely, that process of logical or scientific deduction which leaves one no choice as to the conclusion—had not yet been cultivated anywhere in the world. The only kind of reflective belief was that wherein the choice was determined by practical considerations, which were in turn governed by intuitional ways of thinking.

Thus, throughout the stories of the Exodus, we find that the Israelites are not expected to believe Moses on his mere say-so. They were merely expected to acknowledge the miracles he performed. It is not in dispraise of Israel that the Torah says: "When Israel saw the great execution which YHWH wrought among the Egyptians . . . they believed in YHWH and in his servant Moses" (Exod. 14.31). The doctrine that there is no god but YHWH is represented as having been proved to be true beyond doubt (Deut. 4.35). The reason given in the Torah for God's coming down on Mount Sinai is that the Israelites might hear Him speak to Moses (Exod. 19.9). This was the form in which the tradition of the revelation at Sinai was transmitted from generation to generation. That tradition did not say, as did Maimonides later, "Don't expect to understand it. It is a mystery which you have to accept on faith." (Cf. *Guide for the Perplexed*, Book II, ch. 33 end.) On the contrary, the tradition tried to explain the revelation in terms of the experience or world outlook of those to whom it was communicated. The Torah does not merely encourage demanding proof from anyone who presumes to speak in the name of YHWH. It actually insists on such proof being furnished (Deut. 18.21-22).

What the great canonical Prophets regarded as YHWH's message must be treated, from the psychological standpoint, as the sum of the intense convictions which came to them with such irresistible compulsion that, in the light of the then prevailing ideas, the Prophets interpreted those convictions as emanating from YHWH. The compulsion was not merely that of cold logical necessity but of such inner urge as is associated with profound moral or spiritual intuition. No belief could more integrally be a part of one's own experience than the belief arrived at by the Prophets in their effort to articulate YHWH's message. Likewise those in Israel who had faith in the Prophets acted of their own free will. Their belief belongs to the reflective type, since the alternative of not giving heed to the words of the Prophets was not only present to their consciousness but was actually adopted by the majority of their contemporaries. When those priests who were in sympathy with the aims of the Prophets brought together the laws that had been attributed to YHWH, they made use of traditional beliefs to translate the teachings of the Prophets into a practical program of social and religious life. Those beliefs conformed with the ideas of the time, though they were by no means exempt from challenge. Their acceptance, therefore, presupposes a considerable amount of reflection.

Under the head of reflective belief, also, we may well include all those ideas which came to the Jews under the stress of conditions during the Babylonian captivity. Later the hardships suffered by those who returned to Palestine led to serious questioning. When the possibility of recovering their ancient prestige and attaining peace and security seemed remote, they grew skeptical of God's power. Was their God really the creator of the world and did He actually dispose the destinies of the nations? If the Israelites are His people, had they not suffered enough for the sins they had committed against Him? Why then were they still at the mercy of the great kingdoms of the world, and why were they compelled to live in dispersion away from their land? All these questions were dealt with and answered by the anonymous Prophets. These answers became a part of the growing ideology of Judaism. In that ideology were included such important beliefs as the ultimate return of all Israel to their land, the spiritual hegemony of Israel, the mission of Israel.

In the centuries immediately after the return, the scope of beliefs was enlarged as a result of the questioning that had set in when the contradiction between the fate of many a righteous man, and the reward which the Jews had been led to expect awaited the righteous, became too flagrant to be silenced. First came the beliefs enunciated in some of the Psalms and by the friends of Job—the attempt to explain away the contradiction as being only apparent and due to a lack of careful observation. And when this solution proved unsatisfactory, the difficulty was resolved by the doctrine of resurrection, emanating from Persian and Egyptian circles, and by the reinterpretation of the older messianic ideals in terms of the newer apocalyptic and eschatological teachings. All this is very far from what we usually understand by "dogma." It belongs as much to the class of reflective beliefs as the belief, for example, which men nowadays arrive at, that the ills of the present economic order would be healed by a juster distribution of wealth. Rightly or wrongly, beliefs of that kind are arrived at not so much by strict logical or scientific considerations as by the method of intuition. When a civilization is productive of such beliefs, it is alive and creative. That was the case with Judaism during the centuries of the Second Commonwealth.

✦ ✦ ✦

By the beginning of the common era Judaism was well launched on its new career as an otherworldly civilization, that is, as a method of life whereby any human being could attain salvation, which meant a share in the world to come. During that period the greater part of Western civilized mankind was in a state of spiritual ferment arising from the disintegration of the old nations, empires and city states, with the consequent breakdown of the pagan religions. Amidst the economic and social upheavals which followed, most people lived under conditions of severe want and danger. In despair of seeing any improvement in this world, men turned to the hope of a better and happier future world either upon this earth or in some other sphere of existence. In that new world wherein all who lived in accordance with the will of God would have a share, in that life in the hereafter, the state of bliss would compensate for all that men suffered in this, their earthly existence. Meanwhile, the grave quest upon which all men set their hearts was to discover the true and dependable revelation of the God who controlled the destinies of human life. Various mystery religions, philosophic religions, national religions, laid claim to being the

true road to bliss and immortality. Judaism, which had given battle
to polytheism and had reason to feel that it possessed in the Torah the
key to salvation, came to figure for the Jews more than anything else
as the surest means of qualifying man for the world to come. It was
this function of Judaism that enabled it to weather the crisis which
befell the Jews when they lost their Temple and their State. No people
more than the Jews so needed the compensatory solace that was offered by the new function which the Torah had taken on, for no people
was so completely on the verge of despair.

It was in the wake of this new meaning which Judaism took on
for the Jews that there came dogma, or the insistence upon certain
traditional beliefs as mandatory. Now it is evident that the power of
any agency or instrument to confer otherworldly bliss is contingent
upon its acceptance as such. Nothing could so vitiate that power as
the failure to bring to the agency or instrument the implicit belief in
its supernatural origin as a means of qualifying man for a share in the
world to come. This will enable us to understand why the denial of
the particular dogmas mentioned in the Mishnah of *Sanhedrin* dis-
qualify one from a share in the world to come. "All who are of Israel
have a share in the world to come, for it is said: 'Thy people shall
also be righteous, they shall inherit the land forever' (Isa. 60.21).
The following, however, have no share in the world to come: he who
says that the doctrine of the resurrection is not derived from the
Torah, and that the Torah is not from Heaven. R. Akiba said: also
one who reads uncanonical works, or whispers incantations over
wounds. Abba Saul said: also one who pronounces the Tetragram according to its letters" (Sanh. X.1).

In other words, to deny that the Torah taught or assumed the doctrine of resurrection negated the potency of the Torah as a means to
salvation in the hereafter, for the resurrection was conceived as the
prelude to the world to come. Further, it is obvious that denial of
the supernatural origin of the Torah would destroy one's qualification
for the hereafter, since it was its supernatural origin, according to the
rabbis, that endowed the Torah with the power of salvation. R. Akiba's
amendments, quoted in the Mishnah, can also be understood in this
light. To treat extra-canonical books as though they were sacred is
tantamount to negating the exclusive potency of the Torah. Likewise,
by utilizing the words of the Torah for healing wounds one also
negated its more important function of giving life eternal. The amend-

ment of Abba Saul also probably refers to the use of the Tetragram for incantation purposes.

This intrinsic connection between otherworldly salvation and the emergence of dogmas, or mandatory beliefs, seems to be verified by the fact that the Mishnah, which deals with the heresies that cause one to forfeit salvation, served as occasion for Maimonides, in his commentary, to set forth his well-known creed. In his lengthy introduction to the statement of what he regards as the thirteen fundamentals, he gives his conception of salvation, or the world to come. This is not the place to enter into the question whether Maimonides' conception of salvation coincides with that of the Tannaim and Amoraim. Suffice it to say that his conception approaches more nearly the philosophic ideal of immortality than the Jewish ideal of a recreated world. Yet we must not lose sight of the fact that the entire discussion of fundamental principles is motivated by their character as a prerequisite to salvation. In that regard they are more important than obedience to the precepts! Disobedience even of those precepts whose violation is punishable after death does not deprive one of salvation. (Cf. Maimonides' commentary on Mishnah Sanhedrin XI.3. Such statements as those in *Ethics of the Fathers* that he who puts one to shame in the presence of others forfeits his share in the world to come are merely hyperboles.) On the other hand, it is only logical that heresies which impugn the saving character of the Torah *should* deprive one of salvation.

Though the place assigned to dogma by the Mishnah in Sanhedrin is the same as that assigned by Maimonides in his commentary on the Mishnah, there is a considerable difference in content between the specific dogmas enumerated in Sanhedrin and those in Maimonides' commentary. That difference in content is indicative of the development which had taken place in Judaism as a result both of its contact with Greek philosophic thought and of the challenge from Christianity and Mohammedanism. To appreciate the significance of that development, it is necessary to measure it against the background of the universal quest for salvation which during the Dark and Middle Ages was centered upon the belief in the world to come which God Himself was to usher in, in some cataclysmic fashion. The usual omission of that background from the consideration of medieval Jewish philosophy places completely out of focus the Jewish contribution to medieval theology.

The only way to get a proper perspective is to study that contribution in the light of the purpose which the Jewish medieval philosophers set before themselves. Their purpose was to uphold the function of the Torah as a means to salvation in the face of a twofold challenge: one, that of philosophy, and the other, that of Muhammedanism and Christianity. Philosophy, to those who studied it, was the source of incontestable truth. Since some of its ideas and conceptions conflicted with those of the Torah, the Torah was apparently prevented from being a source of salvation, for surely only the truth could save. The Jewish philosophers were thus faced with the necessity of interpreting many parts of the Torah figuratively or metaphorically in order to bring it into line with the truth as promulgated by the outstanding philosophers.

In doing this the Jewish philosophers unconsciously transformed some of the characteristic teachings of the Torah. For example, the Torah treats miracles as acts of God analogous to the acts of man called forth by some immediate exigency. This conception of miracle implies a change in the will of God. Such a change, such vacillation, is a mark of imperfection. Consequently, the idea is evolved that the miracles in Scriptures were not elicited *ad hoc* but were anticipated and provided for in the very structure of the world when it was created. An even more remarkable transformation of traditional doctrine was the change undergone by the conception of theophany. The philosophic conception of God attained by the Jewish philosophers precluded the naive notion of theophany conveyed in the various stories of God's self-revelation or of His speaking. They overcame the difficulty by positing that God created a luminous body which served, for those who experienced theophany, as a representation of God. When God wanted to communicate anything to the Prophet or to Israel at Sinai, the Jewish philosophers maintained, He would create a Voice for that purpose. The fear that the anthropomorphic conception of God in the Torah might continue to be taken literally, and that as a consequence the Torah would cease to be regarded by the philosophically-minded as a medium for salvation, constrained the Jewish philosophers to enunciate as dogma the absolute negation of any anthropomorphic conceptions of God. Thus, a philosopher like Maimonides, who felt the full force of the philosophic conception of God and at the same time was bent upon guarding the prestige of the Torah, saw no other way of combatting anthropomorphism than by formulating the doctrine of incorporeality of God into a dogma,

implying that anyone who conceived God anthropomorphically forfeited salvation.

But that was only half of the task which the Jewish philosophers
set out to accomplish. It was not enough to prove that the Torah could
be harmonized with the accepted philosophic conceptions of God. It
was also necessary to point out the imperativeness of those beliefs
about the Torah without which it could not function as a means of
salvation in one's life. The Torah's supernatural origin had to be emphasized. Likewise the belief in resurrection and in the coming of the
Messiah. But, in addition, the counterclaims of Christianity and
Mohammedanism made it necessary also to affirm the finality and
infallibility of the Torah.

In short, what we would gather from a detailed survey of medieval
Jewish theology (which cannot be attempted here) is that its main
interest, like that of the Tannaim and Amoraim, was to present
Judaism as a system of life that qualified the human being for other-
worldly salvation. It was with that end in view that the theologians
designated the specific beliefs the Jew must accept, if the Torah was
to help him obtain a share in the world to come.

✦ ✦ ✦

When we turn to Mendelssohn, we encounter an ardent Jew who
is thoroughly imbued with the spirit of rationalism and enlightenment. The outstanding idea of the Enlightenment—which he could
no more ignore than Maimonides could ignore Aristotle's metaphysical
conception of God—was that salvation, or life immortal, was the reward the individual human soul achieved through a life of reason and
righteousness, both of which were inherent in the very soul of the
human being and were not dependent for their exercise upon any
special supernatural revelation. Mendelssohn broke with what had
been the traditional conception of the Torah as the sole means to salvation. "Judaism," he says, "boasts of no *exclusive* revelation of immutable truths indispensable to salvation, of no revealed religion in
the sense in which that term is usually taken. Revealed *religion* is one
thing, revealed *legislation* another. The voice which was heard on
Sinai, on that memorable day, did not say 'I am the Lord, thy God,
the eternal, self-existing Being, omnipotent and omniscient, who re-
wards men, in a future life, according to their works.' All this is the
universal religion of mankind and not Judaism. And it was not the

universal religion of mankind, without which they can be neither virtuous nor saved, that was to be revealed there." (*Jerusalem,* translated by M. Samuels, London, 1838, page 102.) In that sense Mendelssohn was a Deist, for the essence of Deism is the rejection of the idea that salvation is contingent upon subscribing and living up to any particular supernatural revelation.

If, then, the Torah was no longer to be viewed as the exclusive means to salvation, how was it to be regarded? His answer was: the Torah must be viewed as divine legislation and as setting forth the historical background of the Jewish people. The Jews were to him, as they had been all through history, a nation. As a nation the Jews required a legal code. They were more fortunate than other nations in possessing a system of law which emanated direct from God. That fact, of course, made those laws binding and authoritative for all time. It is obvious that this belief concerning the origin of the Torah called for the acceptance of everything in the Torah. It was forbidden to doubt the stories of the miracles, including the miracle of the theophany on Mount Sinai. Nevertheless, these beliefs, according to Mendelssohn, belong to a different category from the one to which belonged the dogmas about the Torah as essential to salvation promulgated during the Middle Ages. In Mendelssohn's view, those were simply ideas to be accepted on the strength of the honesty and reliability of those who transmitted them. The loyalty of the Jew to Judaism should express itself chiefly through the observance of the laws of the Torah. Salvation the Jew can attain through the universal religion of reason. Thus, by saying that Judaism had no dogmas, Mendelssohn meant that henceforth Judaism should not be expected to function as a means to otherworldly salvation. It should function as the Jews' way of life in this world.

Mendelssohn's critics, who marshalled all the evidence of belief and dogma in Judaism, simply failed to realize that he was trying to give a completely new orientation to Judaism. The first to articulate the new orientation, he lacked the very categories needed to convey its true significance. Living at a time when there was insufficient knowledge of the history and nature of religion to enable one to comprehend its relation to group life, he could not but leave the question of the relation of universal religious principles to the Torah in a worse tangle than before. It is this peculiar fact about Mendelssohn's philosophy of Judaism that has puzzled most of his biographers when they come to

relate him to the Reformist movement. On the one hand, his evident
desire to occidentalize the Jew, his advocacy of tolerance and of freedom to think for oneself, make him fit progenitor of the Reformist
movement. But, on the other hand, his assumption that the Jews are a
nation, that the Torah was supernaturally revealed by God, and that
it is the duty of the Jew to live up to its precepts, prevents his being
classed as pioneer of the Reformist movement.

The truth is that Mendelssohn did inaugurate a new era in Judaism,
and he laid down the general lines of the reconstruction necessitated
by a new world in which Judaism must find a habitat. But the particular movement which developed under the name of Reform Judaism
did not proceed along his lines. True, Reformism is indebted to
Mendelssohn for having taken up the question of Jewish self-readjust-
ment, but the spirit in which it carried out that readjustment was
radically different from the one he had in mind. As soon as Reformism
began to formulate its philosophy of Judaism, it repudiated his assumption that the Jews were a nation, it abrogated supernatural revelation
as the basis for the authority of the Torah, and it took issue with
his declaration that Judaism had no dogmas. Instead of treating the
Torah as divine legislation, the Reformists treated it together with
the rest of the Bible as the basis of universal religion. Judaism as a
universal religion had to have definite beliefs, principles, and dogmas.
It was perfectly logical for Einhorn, another of Mendelssohn's critics,
to consider a Judaism without general or fundamental principles as
not Judaism at all, because to Einhorn Judaism was essentially an
ethical monotheism or a religious philosophy.

We may correctly say, I think, that Mendelssohn's attempt at reorientation proved abortive because it did not harmonize with either
of the alternative conceptions of Judaism that have been current:
neither with the one, namely, that it is a supernaturally revealed
religion intended for the salvation of mankind, nor with the other, that
it is a religious philosophy of life which could help mankind attain
salvation if they would regulate their lives in accordance with its
principles. Mendelssohn himself was not in a position to supply a third
category for his orientation because, first, as stated above, the nature
of religion was then not sufficiently known and, secondly, because he
was too much in the momentum of traditional Judaism to be able to
conceive Jewish life possible without the belief in the supernatural
origin of the Torah. If he did momentarily question the historicity of

miracles and theophany, he was too devoted to the welfare of his people to cut himself off from them by openly expressing his doubts.

Since Mendelssohn's day, however, many changes have taken place which have greatly reduced the momentum of tradition and have demonstrated that Jewish life is compatible with the denial of the traditional belief in miracles and theophany. Were he living today he would, I believe, define Judaism as a civilization, the individual and unique culture evolved by the Jewish people in the course of its three thousand years of history. He would redefine the conception of salvation. Although salvation had ceased to mean for him a share in the world to come which God was to create in the same way He created this world, he still continued to regard the soul as a spiritual entity, individual and apart from the social medium, and its personal well-being as the only worthwhile objective of salvation. By this time he would have learned to think of salvation as an affair in which man as individual and man as a race are inextricably bound up together, and as something which has to be consummated on this earth.

In such a scheme of salvation, Judaism can easily find its place as a civilization. For, if a civilization is defined in terms of function, it is the process that weaves the web of social relationships whereby the individual is realized through his human environment, the environment itself being an ever progressive, organic, spiritual structure built up from what individual men and women contribute. This conception of Judaism undoubtedly calls for a reappraisal of the part it has played in human history. That reappraisal need not minimize in the least what mankind has gained from Judaism. But if Judaism is to make itself felt as a force for good in the present, a revaluation expressed in the current idiom is more likely to point the way. Moreover, Mendelssohn would have realized that while religion as the affirmative reaction of the individual soul to the cosmos is not to be conceived as limited to any civilization, any civilization which means to play its part in the furtherance of salvation in the socialized sense in which we now conceive salvation cannot help but be religious. For religion as a social phenomenon is the self-consciousness which a civilization attains when it conceives the ambition of helping its adherents to achieve salvation.

In the light of this relation of religion to a civilization, the Jewish religion is not a collection of abstract universals about God and Man,

universals which have a power to confer salvation upon those who
accept them unquestioningly. The Jewish religion is the self-conscious
aspect of Judaism, Judaism being the civilization of the Jewish people.
According to this view, the Jewish religion must be articulated not in
terms of beliefs, which represent nothing but static and passive reactions to life in general, but in terms of "wants," which represent pur-
posive decisions to bend the course of Jewish living in the direction
of salvation both individual and social.

Of course, "wants" include and assume beliefs. As active desires
to change an existing into a hoped-for situation, they presuppose judgments and beliefs concerning the existing situation and judgments and
beliefs concerning the desideratum. But it is in the wants, rather than
in the judgments and beliefs, that the entire personality, the emotions
and the volitions and the cognitions, are implicated. It is in wants,
therefore, that the individual is most self-conscious.

When we speak of a civilization being self-conscious, we are obviously using a figure of speech. Literally, the meaning of such a
phrase is that there are times when those who live by a certain
civilization become most conscious concerning it. If their attitude
toward their civilization is affirmative, it takes on the expression of
religion. The individual glories in his power to redeem not only himself but also others from the evils that beset mankind. If he contemplates with gratitude the past of this civilization, it is mainly
because he finds there the seed of great things in the future.

Hence, if we wish to render the Jewish religion articulate and
communicable today, nothing could be quite so pointless as to insist
on the beliefs we may hold concerning the Jewish civilization of the
past. Some would be commonplace, some boastful, some disputable.
This does not mean that we can forego holding general beliefs about
the history, the mistakes and the trends of the Jewish civilization; on
the contrary, knowledge of that civilization is imperative. But the
conclusions of such knowledge cannot be set up as a program on which
a whole people can unite, nor can they serve as a definition of what
the Jews really mean to do with their Judaism. That can only be set
forth in terms of wants on which all Jews can unite, though they may
variously express these wants in ways best suited to their several
temperaments, backgrounds, and abilities.

The question we should ask ourselves is: What do we as religious

Jews really expect from Judaism for the salvation of both the individual and society? What do we consider the proper functioning of its social structure, its authoritative texts, traditions, institutions, sanctions, and arts, if all these elements of the Jewish civilization are to justify themselves from the standpoint of human welfare and progress? In the very act of putting such a question, the Jewish civilization begins to attain self-consciousness in us and begins to crystallize itself into fresh Jewish religion.

The specific demands we should then make upon Judaism would constitute the analogue or equivalent of the creeds by which the Jewish religion in its otherworldly stage was wont to identify its loyal adherents. The sum of these demands would then serve as the criterion of Jewish loyalty in our day, when diversity of beliefs and world outlooks has made agreement on a creed neither likely nor desirable. The affirmations of Judaism would no longer be assent to "facts," the truth of which is often challenged by reason or transcends its powers. Rather, the affirmations of Judaism would constitute the expression of the highest demands of the individual Jew upon his civilization. They would set forth what he expects of his civilization if it is to inspire him to perpetuate it, to enrich it, and to make of it a source of blessing to mankind.

(*—1933*)

A Mystical Approach to Judaism

CRAVE

MORDECAI GROSSMAN

In the first flush of Emancipation, when the new social order—bourgeois, industrial, scientific—was in its early stages, liberal Gentiles and hopeful Jews predicted that the "Jewish problem" was on the verge of solution. A completely isolated living, they said, had stamped certain characteristics on the Jewish group. But these characteristics were not indelible. First of all, was not the Jew a man? That he was specifically a Jew (in any concrete sense) was due to an accident of history which could, by means of human intelligence, be corrected. All that is necessary, it was thought, are freer relations—economic, political and cultural—between Jews and their neighbors, and the distinctly Jewish in Jews will disappear; and out of two distinct groups, Jews and Gentiles, strangers to each other, irritating each other, will arise one community, sharing in a common civilization, a common culture and a common destiny.

To what extent has this prediction of the liberals—Jews and Gentiles both—been fulfilled? Certainly the Jews have been absorbed into the general political, economic and cultural life of the peoples among whom they reside, at any rate in the Western world. Further, the conscious content of the mind of Jews, their tastes, their habits, their creative expressions in the realms of thought and art, are for the most part indistinguishable from those of the non-Jews.

Yet, after more than a century of Emancipation, there is still a separate Jewish group with a separate life. Liberalism, in a word, has proved itself strong enough to empty Jewish group existence of its positive content; but it has not been able to bring about the annihilation of Jewry as a distinct social entity. But that is not all. Emancipation has not merely proven itself something less than a panacea for ancient Jewish ills. It has resulted in the crystallization of a new problem, distinct from the old "Jewish problem," which concerned the

(154)

social, political and economic situation of the Jews. This new problem is "the problem of Judaism."

Increasingly, of late almost obsessively, the character and fate of Judaism has haunted the minds of modern Jews. What has the impact of modern Western civilization done to Judaism? What actually is its present strength and character? Has it anything to give us as citizens of a twentieth-century world? Does it enlarge, fructify, enrich our life? Does it make it more creative? If it is not satisfying, what *might* it be, what should it become?

That the century and a half which has seen the progressively accelerated process of emptying Judaism of its life-content has also seen this ever-increasing consciousness of and preoccupation with Judaism seems paradoxical, but it is none the less natural. Before the days of the Emancipation the Jew was not intensely concerned with his Judaism, any more than he was with the house in which he lived, the bed he slept in, the food he ate. When one lives an experience, when one identifies himself with his activity, there is little conscious preoccupation. There was no Judaism distinct from Jews; Judaism was simply Jews in a state of living. There was no distinct Jewish culture; Jewish culture was the substance of living, undifferentiated from the spontaneous interests and acts of living. There was not even a Jewish religion, in the sense of some separate spirituality outside of daily Jewishness; religion was so evenly diffused in the total of integrated Jewish life that it was impossible to say which aspect of Jewish life was religious, which not.

It was with the new order of things, and out of the conflict of old habits and old attitudes of Jewish life with the new Jewish absorption in the general life, that a consciousness of those experiences once lived on the non-conscious plane was born. In the process of change, conscious Jews analyzed themselves out of Judaism. Thus the distinction between Jews and Judaism came into being and Judaism began to be thought of as something that appertained to Jews, yet was distinct from them. Its nature and contents were analyzed and formulated. There was the Reform movement, the Wissenschaft des Judentums, the Haskalah movement. There were decades of exposure to Western culture and Western life. What is the character of the "Judaism" that has emerged?

Judaism, at present, is thought of as a distinct, ready-made entity, visualized by some, the Orthodox, chiefly as ritual, by others, the

Reformed, primarily as a platform of idealistic-religious dogmas. To
most Jews, however, it is merely a name, a vague memory of a
group experience once lived, the ghost of what was once a living
organism. Impalpable, insubstantial, it still cannot be shaken off.
In times of crisis it may yet have power to create group solidarity
—troubled ghosts are very potent; but between pogroms it leads
only a spectral, remote existence. It adds nothing to the largeness and richness of our living. It is obviously a bar between us
and free activity in the Gentile world. Yet we do not give it up.
Why? Partly because of Gentile fear of and contempt for the ghost;
partly because of Jewish inherited loyalties, too deep-rooted to be
eradicated by verbal logic and the superficial contacts of Jews
and non-Jews. Primarily, we do not banish the ghost because we cannot. In its mysterious, inexplicable way, it still masters us.

✦ ✦ ✦

Perhaps the most promising feature of contemporary Jewish life is
the search for means whereby to clothe this ghost of Judaism with
muscles, bone and sinews—to recreate Judaism into something real
with which we might identify ourselves in such a way as would enlarge and enrich our life. The Menorah effort toward rediscovering
and revitalizing Jewish culture is one manifestation of this search.
Professor Kaplan's project (the Society for the Advancement of Judaism) to rehabilitate a Jewish religious civilization is another. The
Zionist program—though now under the stress of circumstances almost
completely submerged by fund-raising activities—to utilize the act
of building a Jewish community in Palestine as a means of restoring a
full, creative Jewish experience, was an earlier. For words, forms, and
a ghost, they would substitute a Judaism able to form the palpitating
rich life-content of modern Jews.

This search is promising in that it indicates a life-urge toward a real
Judaism. It is now articulate only in the leaders of the various move-
ments, but possibly it is present also latently in large masses of Jewry.
For where there is a life-urge there is always the chance of the crystal-
lization of an organic living Judaism capable of enhancing the lives of
Jews.

That such a Judaism may crystallize the writer thinks possible. But
that the Menorah, Advancement of Judaism, and Zionistic efforts are of
themselves adequate to give birth to a Judaism that will be the content

of the life of a people, he considers unlikely. Interesting as these efforts are, they lack at present that intense emotional motivation which alone can give birth to far-reaching creative achievements. Ultimately, of course, they flow from the unreasoned source of the will to a creative Judaism. But the source is not sufficiently present in the tributaries to give them a driving force. On the whole, the approach of these movements to the task on hand—the vitalization of Judaism and its reintegration with living modern Jews—like their motivation, is rationalistic. Reason, however, essential as it is as control and guide to creative energy, can never generate the *élan vital* itself. These movements, therefore, must get their drive from other, deeper well-springs in human nature. Thus vitalized, they can become potent techniques of a process to create a living Judaism. Otherwise they seem to be destined to make only superficial changes on the surface of Judaism.

Moreover, there are currents running in Jewish life and in the life of mankind today of such strength as to make it seem probable that the dreams, hopes and ideals of the would-be rebuilders of Judaism along the lines of Jewish culture, "religious civilization," and autonomy of Jewish experience in Palestine, *if unsupplemented by that creative something,* are destined to be largely frustrated. Contemporary tendencies disclose forces of a magnitude and character such as to reduce these programs, if based only on rational design and direction, to a gallant but ineffective gesture.

Each day the content of the Jewish experience becomes more and more like that of non-Jews. In their economic, political and social activities and interests, in language, customs, habits and attitudes, the majority of Jews are becoming less and less distinguishable from their Gentile neighbors. As the process continues, it is increasingly less possible to revive and to continue a unique Jewish culture. Culture, when alive, is to the gifted a process of creating values, ideas and ideals, and of giving them expression. To the less gifted it is a process of appreciation of values experienced by them and made articulate by creative spirits. Now, there is no immaculate conception of values, ideas and ideals; they are not gifts from heaven. They are born of the clash of experiences, of an effort to organize conflicting experiences into a harmonious whole. They are made of the stuff of experience. It is clear, therefore, that where there is no uniqueness of experience there cannot be uniqueness of culture. Jewish culture was the flower of Jewish life, and in turn was a stimulus for richer living. Where there is no soil of Jewish life, there can no longer be fruits of Jewish life. Old values cannot be transplanted from full Jewish living in the past to function creatively in the present in the face of non-Jewish modes of living.

Moreover, we live in a world that is hostile not merely to the uniqueness of Jewish life, but whose whole tenor is toward the dissipation of those elements that make possible any unique life and culture for any group. There has always been a tendency toward the standardization of culture; even in those days when groups were largely isolated, separated from one another by racial, industrial, political and geographical boundaries, culture values spread beyond the group in whose experience they originated and shaped a more or less uniform human culture. Today with the annihilation of time and space by new means of communication and transportation, with the ever-increasing mechanization of the economic life, with the outreaching of economic interests beyond national boundaries—all making for a uniformity of individual and group experiences—the process has been tremendously accelerated until the prospect of a uniform culture for mankind is no longer remote.

This standardized culture which social forces are now in the process of making will not be a culture in the old sense of the word. Old cultures were homocentric. Out of the events and experience of group life, inarticulate values grew. Creative individuals gave these values an articulate expression in art, poetry, religion and ethics, These inner subjective values and their artistic, philosophical, religious expression rendered the unique *quality* of the group and formed the cement of the life of the group. They made civilization organically whole by giving it, as it were, a cultural soul. Thus Hebraic culture was the qualitative aspect, the soul, of Hebraic civilization, as Catholicism was the soul of feudal-medieval civilization.

A culture in this qualitative sense is today impossible. Present-day culture tends to center about the quantitative and material. Every external event leads to new external events. Every physical conquest leads to new physical conquests. Mechanical organization is supreme; the personal is ignored. Reduction of quality to quantity—and not the personal qualitative re-living of physical events—is the central *motif*. Subjective quality values have, indeed, become almost irrelevant. Atomization and not integration is the·spirit of the age. Man is broken up into stimulus-response units, drives and mechanisms and complexes.

Religion, once an aspect of life, is now a distinct department of life. Art, once the flower of living, is now a compensation for the unsatisfactoriness of life. Life is conceived now as a process of adjustment. What works mechanically, and now what is satisfying personally, is the criterion of evaluation. There is lacking, in short, that feeling of wholeness, that quality of looking into oneself, essential to the making of the old type of culture.

It is clear that such a civilization and culture as is developing will not be an attractive edifice for an individual or a group that still cherishes the emotional coloring of life. Nevertheless, it is coming, this mechanical *Golem* which human intelligence under the stimulus of the material aspects of experience is creating before our eyes. Nor may we any longer think, as we did once, that this *Golem* will be an instrument in the hands of man. It is now apparent that it is he who will be the master of life, which he will mechanize, Golemize.

Now it is with this *Golem*, with his cosmic sweep, no less than the assimilation of the unique life of the Jews into the life of the community in the midst of which they happen to live, that such movements as the Menorah, the Society for the Advancement of Judaism, and Zionism, with their programs for the recreation of the old-new content of Jewish living, must contend. Are they potent enough to oppose it? Much as we may wish they were, much as we wish that Judaism could be made vital, as we desire cultural variations, as we yearn for quality in life and shrink from the prospect of the *Golem*-empire, we cannot help thinking that our wishes and our intelligent plans are puny compared with the stupendous tendencies they are called upon to deflect. There is no hope, we feel, for direct creation of Jewish culture, or for a Jewish religious civilization. Or for a fully unique Hebrew culture in Palestine —the *Golem* will invade Palestine. Even were there some charm to keep him out, even were the renewal of Hebrew culture in Palestine achieved, how could its effect on the Golemized Diaspora be anything but negligible?

No, we cannot cold-bloodedly and intelligently re-create, re-manufacture a Jewish culture, a Jewish civilization, an autonomous Jewish experience. For intelligence is an instrument of organization and not a creative drive. It has given birth to a mechanical civilization that in its spread is submerging unique culture. It is bound by the anonymity, the impersonality, the unspirituality of this civilization. Conceivably, human intelligence may direct a creative urge in culturally fruitful channels. Without such urge, however, intelligence by itself is culturally barren. The urge must come from man's inner resources, from the unsolidified, creative center of personality, rather than from habitual, impersonal reason. To release it, more than concepts, ideas and words are necessary; only gripping experiences, with which the rich and palpitating inner life can identify itself, are adequate.

✦ ✦ ✦

If, then, the pure intellect is our only resource, we can look for no Jewish culture, no Jewish civilization—unless a profound change takes place in the present processes of history. But the intellect is not our only resource; there is another way: the way of mystic impulse—of emotion, art, religion. If the process of grafting externally on the body of Jewry the tissues of an extinct group life seems doomed to frustration, life must be restored from within. If the vital impulse can be reawakened, the disintegrated parts will be sloughed off, and new tissues organically developed.

Less metaphorically, we wish to inquire if a renewed emphasis on certain Jewish religious elements, linked up with certain philosophic and spiritual tendencies already making themselves felt in the world at large, might not, in spite of the *Golem*, restore the human quality to our life. From this, a rebirth of Jewish culture would probably follow, and thus a heightening of the Jewish religious spirit might achieve indirectly what seems outside the capacity of the more deliberate approaches by intellectual means.

By the Jewish religion we do not mean the practice of any special ritual, no matter how time-honored; nor do we mean the vocalization of certain verbal formulas purporting to be the religious philosophy of the individual and the race. Mechanical observance, having no meaning, has no human value. As for a reasoned Jewish philosophy—that is a contradiction in terms. Reason has no patience with unique things—it removes the peculiarities of individual experiences in the interest of arriving at general concepts that are calculated to mean the same to all human beings. To the extent that Judaism is rationalism (and not rationalization) it is non-Jewish. Neither philosophic dogmas nor forms of ritual will serve our purpose.

What then? We mean the emotional element in religion, the urge to largeness of life, the urge to beauty, the quest for a universe in which men are important and of which human values—subjective and imaginative—are the core; the imaginative reconstruction of the universe into one embodying our wishes, aspirations and hopes. What we have in mind is religion as poetry and religion as mysticism.

Religions are born as cultures, as civilizations. They disintegrate in the process of cultural evolution into lifeless dogmas and forms. They may possibly be revived as mysticism and poetry. In the first stages of the development of a people, there is no distinction between its civilization and its religion. Its mores are its ritual. Its institutions are its churches. Its outlook upon life, when expressed in words, its dogma. Its poetry, its Bible and prayers. Primitive religion is neither dogma nor ritual, neither reason nor mysticism. Ritual and dogma, philosophy and mysticism are its aspects merely. With the evolution of cultures from the simple to the complex, from the homogeneous to the heterogeneous, these aspects of life become independent entities. Institutions become laicized. Reason becoming separate from value develops into philosophy and then science. Ritual and dogma become mechanical and meaningless; religion degenerates into nothingness.

The urge to full, whole, valueful living, however, still remains. The urge seeks expression. There is a residual imagination which has not become conceptualized, institutionalized, petrified. It expresses itself in poetry and art. Art and poetry do not, however, fully exhaust it; they are too limited in their medium and scope. Fragments of matter, complexes of sounds, portions of wishes, they can give an ideal form expressing human values, but there remains the universe as a whole, the total strivings of a person to power, dignity and meaningfulness of life. No art can conquer this territory.

This urge to create a dream universe in which the dream individual of his own imagination can find a place, this reaching out for beauty only hinted at in crude natural events and objects of art, this imaginative effort to constitute a universe of pure beauty is the legitimate empire of religion.

We suggest religion thus conceived as the primary content of Judaism. If we can revive the mystical elements of Judaism in this sense, we will have a modern Judaism of vitality and power. And possibly the emotional life it will bring with it will result in the re-creation of a new-old Jewish culture.

But is not Judaism essentially a religion, not of mysticism, but of practice? Did not Yahweh say, "Would they had forgotten me and fulfilled my commandments"? Is not the appeal of Judaism to reason rather than to emotion? Will not the revival of mysticism constitute an act of violence against Judaism rather than one of continuation of its spirit? We are conscious of Graetz's appraisal of mysticism and its embodiment in Chassidism as a fungus accretion on the body of Judaism. We are equally aware that Reform Judaism is primarily rational, and of the hypothesis that the relatively large number of neuroses and psychoses among Jews is an evidence of the lack of imaginativeness in Judaism. We are ready to admit that Judaism as a religion now lacks in imaginativeness, in an urge to beauty. But we are constrained to deny that historical Judaism is unmystical. In the first place, while there are no purely mystical religions, there are, on the other hand, no religions without a mystical element. In the second place, the attitude of Graetz and the majority of Reform rabbis is obviously rather a reflection of their personal needs and tastes, of the special social situation in which they shared, than of Judaism as the continuous religious experience of the Jewish people.

✦ ✦ ✦

The historical fact is that mysticism is an important, perhaps the most important, continuous and fruitful aspect of Judaism. The Bible is neither history, nor a rational editorial on history, but rather a poetic reconstruction of history. The prophetic view of the world, the destiny of the individual and mankind, was not based on fact but on wish, not on reason but on emotional, creative imagination. The known world is interpreted by the prophets in the light of an imagined and willed world. In the universe of their knowledge only physical force counted; observation discovered no place for human values. But in their prophetic ecstasy they created an imagined universe of holiness, a universe in which there was room for the realization of human ideals—beauty, reason, righteousness and peace. They humanized this universe by projecting it into the universe of every-day practical life. In the Talmud, particularly in the Aggadah, we find a continuation of this mystic strain. In medieval Hebrew poetry we discovered the same reaching out for a world not given in ordinary experience. The willed imagination strives to create a universe in which man's inner yearnings may find their haven. And in the *Zohar* and the *Sepher Yetzirah*, in the practical and theoretical Kabbalah, we see the culmination of this effort to substitute an imaginary universe of beauty and harmony and values for the universe of matter and conflict and force.

All kabbalistic systems have as their dominant note the mystic denial of the dualism of human values and dreams on the one hand, and cosmic processes on the other. The real universe, as revealed in the ecstatic imagination of the mystic, is affirmed as continuous with the innermost cherished nature of man. Universal processes are not mechanical occurrences but the expression of a creative impulse akin to, and continued in, human activity. Universal laws are human potentialities, cosmically projected, in a state of becoming actualities on a universal scale. The Infinite is a creative urge expressing itself in its emanations, which partake of its own creativeness, and are thus inseparable from it. Human beings are among the clearest emanations of the Infinite. The attributes of the Godhead are nothing more than the ideals of human values. The kabbalic man—Adam Ha-Kadmon—is an epitome of the divine nature of existence.

Thus man, being a continuation of God—or stating it the other way, God being but the idealization of man's creative imagination—is cosmically important. New heavens are created by means of his mystic contemplation; new earths by the action of his intelligence; his dreams assist in the process of the ever-renewal of the universe. By an effort of heightened imagination, he can bring back the ray of the Infinite, that is himself, to its source and thus wield even greater power over the universal flux. His loves—even his sex loves—are of cosmic character. The love urge is a real cosmic urge emanating from the Infinite; it is at the basis of the universe itself. Earlier universal systems, in which the infinite creative urge had expressed itself, all fell into chaos because it is not until this present universe that the different emanations are held together by a love akin to sex and parental love.

The dream world of the kabbalistic mystic lived in the isolated minds of religious poets until the advent of Chassidism, when it became the vital content of the lives of great masses of people. Originating in Ukrainia in the need, on the part of the masses of Jewry, for a compensatory universe for the one in which they were ground between *pans*, peasants, poverty, a rising Gentile bourgeoisie, and a religion of mechanical ritual and barren, wordy talmudical scholasticism, it was formulated by Besht, spread by his disciples into Poland and Galicia, and introduced in an intellectualized form in Lithuania by Shneur Zalman of Ladi. The Chassidic dream world, stuff of the creative urge of man, a world with which he is continuous, and with which he can unite by means of his aspirations and prayers so closely as to wield an influence in its transformation: this world, shot through with human values and the joy of living, became in a short time the common possession of half Jewry.

Chassidism degenerated into Zaddikism (the worship of the rabbi-saint, or Zaddik), but its original impulse still continues among the Galician and Polish masses. A rich folklore, numerous folk songs and folk melodies, many religious-poetical ideas were the fruit of the vitally shared emotional life of the Chassidic communities. It was a creative force which found wide expression in literature, music, dance, painting and the plastic arts. Nor has this impulse limited its creativeness to its literal votaries. Artists in many fields have found in the crude expression of the Chassidic genius the stimuli, the environment and the material of their art.

+ + +

It is curious, when one sees how important a part the intense mystic strain has played in historic Judaism, and when there is so striking a modern example as Chassidism of its power to revitalize and render meaningful Judaism for large masses of Jews, that among the various present-day efforts at revivifying Judaism the mystical Jewish world view has not been utilized. Especially when one considers that a renewed emphasis on the Jewish effort at imaginative reconstruction of the universe and on the expressions of this effort in mystical lore and art with a mystical motif would have its appeal to the intellectual as well as the non-intellectual, would be culturally fruitful, and would, moreover, fit in with certain powerful intellectual and spiritual tendencies now gaining ground that seem to possess the potentiality of redeeming mankind from the threatened dominance of the *Golem* of mechanism.

Of course, we cannot now have the same attitude toward the imaginative Jewish world structures as the Kabbalists and the Chassidic Zaddikim had. To them their dream-universe was a literally true universe, completely substituted for the impersonal universe of natural events indifferent to human values, to the world of goodness, righteousness and beauty. They literally believed in the magical potentiality of their dreams to transform even the physical world of action. This we cannot do.

Brute facts, we realize, are real as brute facts. But strivings and dreams, on the other hand, are real as strivings and dreams. We can take the Jewish dream structures as poetically true, even if we cannot take them as physically true. Physics will present to us the world as outside of us, as subject for our external observation. Jewish mysticism may give us the world that is at one with us, the world which we do not merely observe but live. For control we shall employ physics; for free living, mysticism.

Nor can we consider the dream structures already created as final. No. We would rather consider traditional Jewish mysticism as stimulus for further dreaming, its symbols of our inarticulate yearnings as prototypes for the creation of new symbols. For our mysticism, the recent scientific achievements—relativity, the electronic constitution of the universe, the larger view of cosmos given by astronomy, and the mechanical achievements of the conquest of time and space—may be material for a richer imaginative structure than the kabbalistic and Chassidic dreams attained. But the spirit can be the same. Their dreams can form the impulse and the beginning for our poetic efforts. If it is not exactly Chassidism, this revised and extended human striving and dreaming of cosmic dimensions, it will be a continuation of that last and greatest embodiment of Jewish mysticism—it will be neo-Chassidism.

✦ ✦ ✦

Aside from its elements of positive appeal, the mystical approach to Judaism will recommend itself to the present-day Jew because of the absence in it of certain aspects of other contemporary types of Judaism which clash with his modern attitude. The neo-Chassidic approach to religion lacks those insuperable stumbling-blocks common to Reform and Orthodox Judaism—the anthropomorphic ideas of God and the universe, with their anti-scientific and anti-evolutionary implications. Since it does not ask us to accept the Bible as scientifically and historically true, but rather as a poetical reconstruction of physical and historical events, there is no conflict between religion and science: religion as poetry cannot clash with science as fact.

The Infinite of the Kabbalah is not a personal God; no human qualities can be attributed to him; indeed he has no form by which we can conceive him. Thus it is that the Ain Soph (the Infinite) is said to be Aiin, non-existing. In modern terms, we might quite properly identify this Ain Soph with the infinite material basis of the universe, or still better with the impersonal energy basis of the universe of events of modern physics.

Likewise, the stress in the Kabbalah is not on creation but on the eternal evolutionary process of the creative energy which forms the basis of the universe. The Infinite did not create, did not manufacture the universe. The universe is a progressive series of emanations emerging from the Infinite. Yahweh, Elohim and Adonai Zebaoth are, in this view, not creative entities; they are among the prime emanations of the Infinite, as is the world and man.

It is clear that there is nothing in these views which conflicts with the attitudes, methods and teaching of modern organic and inorganic science. Rather they are totally in harmony with them, and as such are surely more acceptable to the modern man than are other contemporary forms of Judaism.

But neo-Chassidism has positive potencies of its own, which go beyond mere agreement with certain modern ideas. Its great strength is the universality of its appeal. It is a commonplace that our present-day Judaisms have lost their hold on the masses. Orthodox ritual is meaningless to them; Reform dogma is uninspiring and alien. Projects for the revival of Jewish culture and civilization appeal only to the intelligentsia, since they alone have the mind and the creative capacity for such endeavors. But the content of neo-Chassidism has the mystic appeal of emotion and the urge for beauty; and these are universal. In a few decades Chassidism transformed the lives of half Jewry; with a similar appeal, neo-Chassidism, if it cannot hope for such rapid success, could also achieve much. Certainly it is on the level of emotion that the disunity of Jewish life must and can be overcome. Emotion unites, where reason divides. Those who dream of a "Keneseth Israel" might realize their dream if they would identify the essence of Judaism with the emotional striving for a world of beauty.

Moreover, a mystical Judaism has power not merely to unite Jewry; it—and it alone—can vitalize it, make it fruitful, creative. The drive of individual and group life is not in reason, but in emotion. The intellect may direct the creative urge of emotion, it may compose emotional clashes into an harmonious expression, but without the propulsive drive of deep feeling it can only reflect what is going on, it can in no sense transform the stream of experience. Neo-Chassidism would provide a propelling, creative Jewish experience. Its imaginative reconstruction of the mechanical universe given in physics and in every-day experience, would express itself in language. These statements of its vision would not be dogma in the sense of articles of faith, but would be looked upon merely as efforts at expressing something whose nature cannot be exhausted by any and all expressions. As such they would be symbols of the inner experience, and true only symbolically. These symbols would be reconstructed in the light of ever-growing emotional experience and of creative power constantly searching to express itself in newer forms. Nor would the emotional experience of the dream world limit itself to words. The need for dramatization will create ritual, which instead of being empty form will be the stylized representation of the immediate group experience and of the poetical reconstruction of its historical experience. Some of the old ritual will be conserved, vitalized; new rituals will evolve.

Nor will the drive of the emotional experience necessarily end with symbolic dogmas and ritual. In the first stages the dream world will be a compensation for the world of crude actuality. The impulse will continue itself in an intense striving for the organization of the world of empirical events in the light of the ideal born of imagination and quest. The conception of man as an emanation of the infinite energy, expressing itself in cosmically creative processes, will give the individual a greater dignity. He will become, as a man, cosmically important. The experience that the reality of things lies in the continuous and unitary creative force inherent in them, may well lead to an emotional realization of the unity of the human race. This in turn may tend to eliminate conflicts between races, classes, nations and individuals. The realization of the creative nature of the Infinite and its immanence in man might lead human beings to consider themselves not as machines, but as creators, and thus shift the emphasis in industry from production and distribution to creativeness. Thus an ethic—larger, freer, more colorful than ethical-monotheism—may be a fruit of the neo-Chassidic Judaism. Scholarship will be transformed from contemplation of creative experiences that once were, from subtle distinctions between Tweedledum and Tweedledee, into a search for gripping experiences that can continue themselves in an act of creation of wisdom and beauty. Instead of contemplating Jewish life once lived, Jewish scholarship would become a phase of creative Jewish living. Finally, neo-Chassidism should find expression through sensitive and esthetically creative persons in art.

Thus, beginning as emotionally-driven, imaginative reconstruction of the universe of non-human events, the impulse of neo-Chassidism might well create a symbolic system of ideas, an ethic, a ritual, a new way of social and Jewish living, a new Jewish scholarship and a new Jewish art. Beginning as a striving for a world of beauty, it might conceivably result in the creation of a cultural environment of beauty and goodness and wisdom. For while old cultures cannot be revived by intellectual processes or new cultures manufactured direct through the heightening of the emotional mystical strain of Judaism—its most universal and most enduring element—a creation of a new Jewish culture continuous with the old may be hoped for.

✦ ✦ ✦

Granting the desirability of neo-Chassidism, is it possible, is it practical? In the first place, can the neo-Chassidic position withstand analysis? Can there be a rich emotional Judaism in a machine age? Can we experience a dream cosmos in the face of a universe of inexorable mechanical laws given by our science? Will not the *Golem* of industry and intellect frustrate the spread of a movement like neo-Chassidism?

First, then, neo-Chassidism must meet the attack of those who will contend that, purporting to reconcile the dualism of the universe, it is itself guilty of bifurcating it. It will be said that the neo-Chassidic position divides the universe into one given in fact and one created by the imagination: into one of events and one of values. Possibly. But what of that? If one way of looking at the universe gives us only brute events, and if we have a longing for a universe that will embody values and an imagination capable of envisaging a universe of beauty, why should we not supplement the universe of mechanism with one which is in harmony with our yearnings? After all, as we realize now, there is no absolute and ultimate validity in any fact or any law. Validity is never anything but relative; it is determined in terms of method, point of view and purpose. The immediate experience is valid as immediate experience; the reconstruction of experience by the scientific method is valid from the scientific point of view and purpose; the imaginative and aspirational reconstruction is equally valid as human imagination and reconstruction. Science as a body of knowledge in itself is no more than a specific type of reconstruction of immediate full experience, and as such is no more valid than poetry or religion, which are other types of reconstruction. Such aspects of varying unique experiences are chosen by the scientific method as will give continuity, uniformity and causality. Since the universe it posits differs from the universe of immediate experience, it, too, bifurcates the universe. Why, then, shall not the full vital imagination be given scope to construct an imaginary universe different from that given in science and in ordinary experience? All that can be reasonably demanded is that there be no conflicts, and the universe of neo-Chassidism does not conflict with the universe given in other aspects of human experience.

But, we assert, we are not actually guilty of the sin of bifurcating the universe. We are aiming at envisaging it fully and uniting with it harmoniously. There is one universe, and in it and as an integral part of it there are human beings, experiencing, valuating, thinking, abstracting, *imagining*. In a variety of ways these human tendencies impel us to harmonize more fully with the world of which we are a part. This effort at harmony is also an effort at living fully and universally. An approximation of harmony of the universe in which we live and of fullness of life can emerge only from the full interplay of all our tendencies. Thus the imaginary reconstruction of the world which our other tendencies have given us is essential to a creative functioning in a dynamic universe. Far from neo-Chassidism conflicting with other ways of living, it will, therefore, actually enter into the creative harmony of life.

But what chance can a rich emotional Judaism have in a twentieth-century industrial civilization? Of course, we cannot be sure; but we believe there is at least the possibility of success for a movement like neo-Chassidism. Besides the factors already discussed, its success or failure will depend on the strength developed by the anti-intellectualist, anti-mechanistic revolt lately growing in philosophy and science.

Bergson's emphasis on full experiencing, on living dynamically as opposed to observing, reflecting on experiences, his thesis that reason is an instrument of control rather than a way of life, that instead of revolving around things and events and reducing their dynamic reality into static concepts we ought to identify ourselves sympathetically with the inner fluxing reality, is one manifestation of this revolt. (It is interesting to note that Bergson is a scion of a Chassidic family.) Whitehead's realization, as expressed in his *Science and the Modern World*, that scientific laws and concepts are merely symbols of experience viewed from a certain angle, but do not describe the ultimate nature of the universe, his thesis that the validity of the symbols depends on the adequacy with which they signify the fullness of our immediate experiences, is another manifestation. The present-day tendency in physics to reduce matter, substances, atoms and electrons to events and energy behavior is still another.

Should this anti-intellectualist revolt succeed in changing current modes of thought, neo-Chassidism would find it possible to thrive as a Jewish poetical epitome of the new spirit. In the progress of this revolt neo-Chassidism would be a re-enforcement aiding materially in the direction of overcoming the threatened dominance of the mechanical *Golem.* For the *Golem* draws his strength from the fact of the mechanization of man. His power comes from man's own identification of experience with thinking, of creating with manufacturing, of shared living in society with mechanical control through force and propaganda. A renewed emphasis on the emotional, imaginative life of man may result in the isolation of the *Golem* and his death by attrition. Should the revolt fail, civilization, culture and man face universal mechanization.

The outcome of historical processses cannot be predicted. We cannot possibly know what the destiny of the anti-intellectualist revolt will be. All we know is that there is such a revolt and that it has in it the possibilities of human redemption. Those who strive at this redemption will identify themselves with it. If a modern Judaism can harmonize with it, this Judaism will be far more vital and creative than it could otherwise be.

Neo-Chassidism, in its spirit and content, is in such harmony with the declaration of independence of the human spirit from the bonds of mechanism. A movement like neo-Chassidism would be, therefore, not merely Jewishly creative; it would be at the same time a movement auxiliary to the large human movement making for a freer, more creative human life. By its own life it would help in the creation of human conditions necessary for its continued living.

(—1929)

In Defense of Skepticism

❧

FRITZ MAUTHNER

THE greatest skeptic among poets, Henrik Ibsen, portraying himself
in his drama *The Pretenders*, characterizes himself as a northern
skald, Jatgeir. So thorough is the skepticism of Ibsen—kin to Nietzsche
in his transvaluation of all values, even the values of poetry—that he
is never entirely convinced that he himself is a poet. Ibsen-Jatgeir values skepticism as one of the great gifts that lead to great achievements.
He names four such gifts: the gift of suffering, the gift of faith, the gift
of happiness and the gift of skepticism; but of course, none of these
gifts, neither suffering, happiness, faith, nor doubt can be small-spirited.
We feel here the birth of a new spirit—a poet paying homage to the
greatness of skepticism.

Public opinion is still unfriendly to skepticism. Skeptical thinkers
and even skeptical spirits are decried, almost without reservation, as
men of little ability, who tear down and destroy, who have lost the
power of positive construction. If skeptics are not exactly devils they
are probably at least Jews! Now, since I am considered a skeptic, not
only by myself but also by a number of other persons, and moreover,
since I am by birth a Jew, I have for many years pondered whether
skepticism is really so evil and dangerous a philosophy of life and
whether there is really a relationship between Judaism and skepticism.

The last incentive for me to express my views on this subject (that
is, prior to the request that has resulted in the present article) was a
posthumous book by Christian Morgenstern, a poet not yet esteemed
at his real worth. His book, entitled *Stufen* (*Steps*), was published in
1918. I had always had a deep regard for the wanton seriousness of this
mystisches Kobold without suspecting that he, on his part, had an interest in my own writings. The relationship pointed out by the phi-
lologist, Leo Spitzer, between the creative work of Morgenstern and my
own *Critique of Language,* came as a happy surprise to me. For in his

(171)

posthumous work I found two passages concerning me in particular (pages 70 and 105), which flatly contradict each other. They affected me deeply because of the spirit of wrathful love which they displayed toward my life work. For, on page 105, Morgenstern, who certainly entertained no ill will toward me, says:

Everything that is Jewish is preponderantly destructive. Jesus, the greatest Jew, is also the greatest destructive element in the world. Spinoza has a similar spirit, and for this reason is acclaimed by the most recent Jewish iconoclast, Mauthner, in his capacity as anti-theologian, the greatest of thinkers. In Mauthner, himself, we find perhaps the maddest spirit of destruction which the world of thought has encountered. In opposition to these diabolic revolutionists stands Nietzsche, the critic of morals, and we have here two completely antithetical worlds, antagonistic as fire and water. . . . The Jews are the opponents of the constructive spirit. They are its hecklers, its bad conscience.

But, on page 70, Morgenstern lauded me for the decisive step I have taken beyond even the creative Nietzsche. If both statements are true then surely I must be both fire and water.

I cannot allow myself to be dazzled by the embarrassingly flattering juxtaposition of my name with those of Jesus and Spinoza. Let us rather disregard names and consider the matter itself. I only wish to insist that so far as my writings are concerned the word *destroyer* can have only one meaning, *skeptic;* for, unfortunately, neither in act nor in theory have I played the iconoclast.

If, however, we consider the problem itself, and examine the basis for the reproach, it is necessary to answer several questions consecutively and deliberately. First, what is the aim of the higher skepticism and how is it distinguished from petty doubt? And second, what part have the Jews played in the liberation of the human spirit and in particular in the victorious struggles of skepticism? Finally, it will be difficult for me to avoid answering the question to what extent I may be conscious of any influences of my Jewish descent determining my own skepticism—even though such attempts at self-examination can only with difficulty lay claim to any scientific value.

✦ ✦ ✦

According to the literal meaning of the Greek word, skeptics are persons who keenly and attentively look about and deliberate before taking a definite stand concerning any proposition. Much time must certainly have elapsed before this clear-sighted method of skeptical inquiry was directed towards original thinking. In the modern languages we have the analogous expressions: *Mistrauen, soupçon, suspicion*—which refer for the most part to the moral trustworthiness of an individual, somewhat to his usefulness, but almost never to his intellectual powers. Petty doubt is practically parallel to suspicion; the petty doubter—who must never be confused with the skeptic—has no faith in the sincerity of his fellowmen, no trust in the honesty of business men. Anyone suspicious in this modest sense easily qualifies for a shrewd business man. The fact that the Jews are said to be suspicious in business and to make excellent tradesmen might seem to have something to do with our question, but both these assertions are maintained of all commercial peoples: proverbially they are attributed with even greater emphasis to the Greeks and Armenians than to the Jews. Both suspicion and acquisitiveness could quite generally be also attributed to the peasants of the so-called Aryan peoples, to the peasants of Eastern and of Western Europe. Furthermore, it was the course of European history which first developed the Jews into a commercial people, which also educated them in suspicion, and in the miserable, petty doubt involved in anxious discretion.

A more highly developed stage of doubt, but not the great skepticism, is the doubt concerning inherited notions, and in particular concerning universal concepts—scientific doubt. Visual experience had taught that the sun revolved around the earth, that the earth was a flat disk, that empty space forcibly drew all bodies to itself. A tremendous mental effort combined with the spirit of scientific doubt was required to arrive at some of the elementary facts of nature: for instance, that the sun was stationary in relation to the earth, that the earth was approximately a sphere, and that no force whatsoever inhered in empty space. This form of practical cleverness, for the last five hundred years, from the rediscovery of nature up to the present time, has been regarded as wisdom or science. It had led to increased comfort for the human race through the discovery of different means of controlling nature; it has loosed the spiritual hold of the Church; but as a philosophic contribution it has produced merely a materialism which only in the last few decades has begun to give way.

The Jews in proportion to their number and endowments have had their share in the achievements of this restricted scientific doubt. For the most part, however, they were followers rather than leaders along the road to materialism. When in the Middle Ages the dominant

Church fought with fire and sword precisely this scientific form of doubt, and succeeded finally in reducing it to silence in the Christian Occident, the Arabs were the world leaders in the effort to find a materialistic explanation of the universe, and the Jews, their supporters and interpreters in Europe.

Later, when the emancipation of school from Church—and, in close relation to this, the emancipation of Jews from bondage—was slowly achieved, Jewish scholars (in disproportionately great numbers) took part in the development of the mechanistic interpretation of the universe, but again as disciples rather than as revolutionary thinkers. Here, just as in the religious enlightenment, the pioneers in Holland, England, France and Germany were Christians—although they often found their best audiences among the Jews. But the champions of the Church, in their anger, did not hesitate to declare, falsely of course, that the outstanding religious freethinkers—Lessing, Strauss and Renan—were Jews.

These two forms of suspicion or petty doubt, to the short-sighted observer entirely dissimilar, nevertheless possess a close relationship in origin and effect. Both commercial and scientific shrewdness arise from an unwillingness to be deceived by appearances, whether by the lies of men or by the lies of nature. Both common and scientific doubt have a practical aim and seek their own advantage. In the egoistic struggles of commerce, in the common struggles for existence, both seek to become master of these illusions with which the world about us—the living as well as the seemingly dead—wreaks evil upon our head. Both seek to master the deceitful and importunate realities of Nature.

There is an essential distinction, however, between this petty common doubt and this inferior pseudo-scientific doubt on the one hand, and on the other, that lofty type of doubt which in learned terminology is called *skepsis,* or skepticism. Properly speaking, this too is a type of doubt, but it does not impugn the veracity of the individual, the honesty of one's contemporaries or the credibility of nature; it is rather the appalling doubt of the possibility of humanity ever attaining knowledge through the use of language.

The origin of this great and lofty kind of doubt seems to be very ancient, for as far back as the days of Socrates such speculators may be found who even then were called Skeptics. These philosophers taught, with some wit, the three-fold impossibility—the impossibility inherent in the concept of being, the impossibility of knowing, and the impossibility of communicating knowledge. These speculators were the so-called Sophists, critical thinkers, iconoclasts, who acknowledged no authority and who, in their method of demonstration, often resorted to subtle means which even then were characterized by their pedantic or alarmed opponents as "sophistic" or quibbling.

What still distinguishes the ancient Greek Skeptics from the modern doubters, whose speculations concerning the world have been growing in importance for the past four hundred years, is probably more a distinction of mood than of thought. Among the Skeptics or philosophers of classical antiquity there reigned a spirit of obstinacy in regard to the infallibility of skepticism, a slavery to words, a sheer language superstition, which since the days of the completely emancipated liberators, Montaigne and Hume, we no longer tolerate. The Greeks denied being and yet possessed no critique of knowledge; they denied the possibility of true experience, and had as yet no idea of psychology; they denied the possibility of communicating experience and had nevertheless failed to formulate a philosophy of language. Thus ancient Skepticism furnished only a few half-formulated propositions to the higher skepticism.

The solution of these problems could only be approached thirty generations later by a new race (after the tyranny of the medieval Church had been overthrown) over a road painfully built upon an unbiased theory of knowledge independent of the notion of a "soul," and leading toward a critique of language. This higher skepticism does not offer the individual the obvious commercial advantage of protection against sharp practices in business; it seeks, moreover, no gain for humanity by the conquest of nature through a knowledge of her laws; it desires nothing, it creates nothing; all that it teaches is an ultimate resignation to an inarticulate humanity, the calm and serene insight that with our poor human language we shall never understand what language can only hint at with the words "Being" or "Knowledge of Being."

Generalizations are always dangerous, but most dangerous on questions which lie on the borderline between philosophy and religion. In answer to the question whether or not the Jewish race has shown a particular tendency to skepticism, one could say quite readily: the Jewish race cannot by any means be considered skeptical, because it was the first to establish in the world the tremendous hypothesis of the one and only God as the creator of heaven and earth. But it might immediately be urged that the acceptance of a single nameless God (*Yahwe* connotes "The Eternal" and is not, accurately speaking, a proper name), that is an unknown God, in contrast to the many anthropomorphic gods of the heathen, proclaimed, or at least prepared the way for, a deism which already implied doubt of a personal God. One could say, with rather less plausibility, that the Jewish religion in its original form did not, either before or after the Babylonian captivity, preach the immortality of the soul, but fostered a morality completely divorced from the conception of reward and punishment in the life-to-come, and therefore made practical reason autonomous thousands of years before the founders of a religion of reason, before Kant. We could, indeed, rather substantially support this view by reasoning that if man has, in truth, no immortal soul (that is, no soul at all according to the Christian conception) then it follows that the gods or God can likewise be denied a spiritual nature, and it becomes possible to doubt even the immortality of God or of the gods. Thus, the disavowal of immortality has, historically, very often opened the way to atheism. If, on the other hand, an imperturbable faith in the existance of God and in his attributes (eternity, goodness, omnipotence, etc.) characterizes the sacred books of the Jews, there is among them at least one to which those who doubt the ardor of Jewish faith can appeal in support of their contention that the Jews are born skeptics. It is true, of course, that a conclusion drawn from this one instance should not be generalized. I refer, naturally, to Solomon the Preacher and the secular book Ecclesiastes, which with its godless, pessimistic and skeptical aphorisms appears strangely enough in the Holy Scriptures. One is reminded of Greeek skepticism: all is vain, worthless, and fruitless—existence, thought, and the achievements of thought. In the first century of the Christian era there arose among Jewish theologians a serious dispute as to whether Ecclesiastes should be suppressed. Rabbi Shammai cannot be criticized for his condemnation of the book; it is un-Jewish in its attack on life and knowledge. Schopenhauer, that hater of Jews, that complainant against the world, could quote no book of the Old Testament as readily as Ecclesiastes. "Better is the day of death than the day of birth" and "He that increaseth knowledge increaseth sorrow."

We must not overlook the fact that the discontent with life revealed in such sayings—and their bitterness can hardly be surpassed—is not merely an articulation of the wretchedness of the human lot, but is at the same time a violent expression of doubt of God's justice and goodness. The most devout Christians of the eighteenth century, the true pietists, became confused with regard to the Bible as soon as they reached Ecclesiastes. They were filled with despair over the destiny of the individual: "I saw all things that were done under the sun and I saw that it was vanity and vexation of spirit." They were filled with equal despair at the fruitlessness of thought and investigation, at the vanity of the history of the world:

The thing that has been is that which shall be; and that which is done is that which shall be done and there is no new thing under the sun . . . As it happeneth to the fool, so it happeneth even to me: and why was I then more wise? Then I said in my heart, that this also is vanity . . . there is no contentment in seeking . . . no man can find out the work that God maketh from the beginning to the end . . . Who can make that straight which he hath made crooked?

One might well call Ecclesiastes the Song of Songs of Skepticism. That King Solomon could not possibly have been the author of Ecclesiastes is immaterial; it would be enough if this book of accusation against God and the human spirit (disregarding the pious retractions of the closing passages, which most certainly were appended later) originated in the Jewish classic age.

Such, however, is not the case. I do not trust the philological critics of the Bible unreservedly; nevertheless they have proved with some certainty that the language of Ecclesiastes no longer possesses the compact vigor of the older poetry of the Jews, that it probably was produced roughly as late as 300 or 200 B.C., that it was influenced superficially by Greek philosophy and that it was written not in Jerusalem but in Egypt, in the dissolute Alexandria of the Ptolemies. When Renan, in his worldly fashion, once called the poet of Ecclesiastes an amiable roué, he should have added: a roué of the capital of Egypt where the Jews had rapidly become Hellenized.

I have tried to distinguish between the petty doubt of commercial cleverness and the great lofty doubt of skepticism. I have warned against pronouncing sweeping judgments on the Jews or other races. Let me return briefly to the grotesque idea of Morgenstern, that master of grotesque poetry, that Jesus and Spinoza were, as Jews, negating, skeptical spirits. At the same time, I am loath to mention again that negation is here regarded—a trick and habit of only small minds—as something especially despicable as evil. Nor do I wish to undertake any vindication of Jesus and Spinoza. They do not need it. I only wish to attempt a few corrections.

Very little is known of Jesus and his philosophy of life, however much Christian theology tells us concerning both. At no time was the Christian religion the religion of Christ. Morgenstern reinforces his theory that Jesus, the greatest of Jews, was also the greatest destructive spirit in the world, by the simple device of confining his references to the temporal world; the possibility remains then, that Jesus in the spiritual world was not a destroyer. But Morgenstern later betrays his real intent, when he speaks of the Jews as the opponents of the creative spirit, its hecklers, its bad conscience. But this, alas, could only be said of Mephistopheles, that evil spirit *der stets verneint*. Jesus, in fact, was never a destroyer; he was a master builder. Not once did he repudiate the "law" of the Jews, a fact of which old Reimarus was aware. And he laid especial emphasis upon that other law, the law of love. This surely is not negation. Our knowledge of the historical Jesus is meager; but from a few individual traits of his character there has been formed during the past two thousand years an ideal image, and this ideal has been one of affirmation, of creative leadership for generations of men.

The philosopher Spinoza, the second greatest Jew, stands fully revealed in the light of history, and only a complete frivolity could accuse this quiet, heroic sage of being a destroyer, a negator, a petty doubter, an enemy of mankind.

I do not wish to repeat what I have said concerning Spinoza elsewhere, but let me recall that this much-reviled Jew of Amsterdam, appreciated at his true value only long after he lived, advanced beyond the materialism of his Latin teacher, beyond the cowardly dualism of his master Descartes, whom he far surpassed, and finally attained his godless mysticism, his so-called pantheism, the overwhelming feeling of the All-One. To call this all-embracing spirit a negator is senseless. Besides his main work, Spinoza with a view to a study on public law devoted his attention to a criticism of the biblical law, and in particular to the Old Testament. But criticism is not skepticism: if it were we should be obliged to confer upon skepticism the right to claim for its own any one who furthered the spiritual life. And in his life work, the so-called *Ethics*, Spinoza was a creator, a master builder for hundreds, perhaps for thousands of years. Even here he was not vigorously skeptical but continued to use the old scholastic expressions without critical examination. He laid only ghosts. Among those ghostly antitheses which as critic he overthrew (such destruction is one of the first tasks of a builder) we may happily count not only Good and Bad, but Order and Disorder, Affirmation and Negation. Jesus as a preacher, Spinoza as a thinker, stand high above such miserable confusion of human words.

Moreover Spinoza himself, in his early shorter writings, had expressed himself often and decidedly against skepticism. Like Descartes, who was also no true skeptic, he maintained that truth is knowable, that every clear and distinct idea must be true, because truth reveals itself as immediately as light and error as darkness. It is the fault of his too scholastic manner of speech that here he again confuses a logical with a psychological concept, falsity with error.

✦ ✦ ✦

In order to refute the assertion that Jews brought also into the world—together with all evil—doubt and negation, it will not be necessary to write a complete history of skepticism. A few observations will suffice to show that skepticism is no more bound by national spirit than other philosophies.

As is generally known (or at least should be, since Lewes) the Greeks were quite uncritical thinkers; they were, indeed, never in a position to verify ordinary natural observations, much less to test the higher concepts of their language. This accounts for the great amount of verbal superstition in their pedantic skepticism. These ancient skeptics were so little bound by a Greek national spirit that at the time of the Renaissance when nature was rediscovered, and with it man, their work could be borrowed from and translated by the new races, as easily as the works of those altogether non-skeptical philosophers, Plato and Aristotle. There were now to be found Italian, English— and soon even German—Platonists, Aristotelians, and Skeptics.

Already in the sixteenth century, at the time of the bloody anti-Reformation, as a result of the rebirth of skepticism, two works appeared, almost at the same time, written by half-Jews—the *Quod Nihil Scitur* (1581) of the Spaniard Sanchez, and the *Essays* (1580) of the Frenchman Montaigne. This coincidence need not be considered accidental, it could in fact be made to explain skepticism as a national Jewish trait, if only . . . if only there existed any inner resemblance between the skepticism of the Spanish Jew and that of the half-Jewish Frenchman.

We read superficially. There are flashes of almost identical thought. "We know nothing," says Sanchez. "What do I know?" asks Montaigne.

But as I have pointed out elsewhere, Sanchez knows only the ancient form of doubt, verbal logic is his only weapon against the trustworthiness of the scholastic sciences; Montaigne, on the other hand, is seized and permeated by the higher doubt—he really knows nothing; he questions only; he questions with a smile of resignation; he questions only for himself: "What do I know?" Sanchez, who was perhaps a full-blooded Jew forced into baptism, a Marrano, merely repeats in a keen and witty manner the ancient paradoxes, as if with excessive gesticulation. In form only is he a man of the Renaissance; in content, a fanatical dogmatist not differing from the fanatics of Spanish-Christian theology. Montaigne, the son of a rich merchant—whose real name was Equem— and of a Jewess who apparently had turned Protestant, was inspired to the authorship of his imperishable works because he had not merely learned but had experienced the rediscovery of nature and of man, because he had accepted nothing from Christianity save one idea, unknown to the ancient world, namely, the *search* (the root of *skepticism* means literally *to search*) for the secret impulses of the individual soul. But Montaigne was no destructive, no negating spirit, though he was the greatest skeptic of the new era, in so far as it was concerned with doubt of the moral values and values in general. In wisdom, in lack of bias, and in incorruptible goodness, he was as worthy of honor as Goethe. But Goethe was a poet in addition and certainly no skeptic.

Despite the anti-Reformation, the spiritual emancipation proceeded steadily, not along the dogmatic road of Sanchez, but by the modest and reflective path of Montaigne. Doubts arose concerning the principles underlying human thought and action; in addition came a rapid increase in scientific skepticism, and criticism of the accepted laws of nature. Until finally in the middle of the eighteenth century the higher skepticism produced its masterpiece in David Hume's analysis of the ideas of necessity (or causality) and universality. If it were at all permissible in philosophic discoveries to speak of the merits of a particular people, then we should speak of the nation to which Hume belonged, because a path leads directly from the nominalism of Occam through Locke's early critique of language to the radical skepticism of

Hume. But nominalism—the doubt concerning the value of language—
originated internationally among the scholastics, and at a time when
the cultivation of science had not yet developed on national lines.

In Germany soon after, Kant (who was probably of Scottish descent)
alarmed at Hume's precipitation, made it his life work to surmount,
point by point, the dogmatism of Hume, to apply himself to a criticism
of human thought and action, a criticism unequalled in profundity, to
show the subjective origin of all conceptions of space, time and necessity (or causality) even more sharply than the Briton had been able to
do, but to rescue the old God (along with freedom and immortality)
and furthermore to proclaim the existence of the thing-in-itself, the
absolute beyond the subjective or relative world of phenomena. Men
were to think and act in spite of Hume, as if all had still remained as it
was of old.

Kant, with unusual power, had laid the foundations of a critique of
reason, but he had not erected a system. Nevertheless, the profound
impression created by his critique resulted in clever youths with
vacuous mentality presuming one after the other to surpass Kant, and
continually to erect their own systems and elaborate those philosophic
flights which ever since comprise what we ordinarily mean by "German philosophy." Englishmen and Frenchmen have never been able
to enter into the spirit of the work of Fichte, Schelling or Hegel.

Soon, however, doubt arose as to the conclusiveness of Kant's
critical philosophy. And it is a strange coincidence that besides
Schultze, of pure German stock, who is still known as Aenesidemus-
Schultze from his chief work, a Jew appears as the second most
vigorous critic of the *Critique of Reason,* as the restorer of Hume, as an
advocate of the latest skepticism. He was not an assimilated half-Jew
like Montaigne, but rather a thoroughly Eastern, Polish Jew, who in his
youth had learned to speak, besides Yiddish jargon, only Hebrew, and
who according to the local customs had been married at the age of
thirteen. Half-mad with intellectual thirst, he passionately devoted
himself to the German language, to a few sciences and to the new
Kantian philosophy. Solomon Maimon was the name of this talmudic
Jew, staggering about in the labyrinth of German philosophy. Maimon
was an original thinker; his critique of Kant appeared about two years
before that of the famous Gottlieb Ernst Schultze, and emphasized even
more strongly his main point, the incompatibility of the thing-in-itself
with the *Critique of Reason.* Aenesidemus-Schultze probably borrowed

the important part of his attack from Maimon, together with the watch-word—to be sure not directly expressed—Back to Hume! And never-theless . . . if there were any truth in the assertion that the Jews are born skeptics, then the native Eastern Jew, Maimon, when he cast the stone of skepticism at the giant Kant, should have been much more successful than any German Schultze. For Maimon was endowed with a truly miraculous ability to enter into the most abstruse problems, to sport with the most abstract propositions. Kant, himself, after he had read—superficially, it must be said—the manuscript of Maimon's first work, recognized almost enthusiastically the philosophic ability of the author, only, of course, later to reject this embarrassing op-ponent. But Maimon's work, though highly praised from time to time, has not remained a living source, whereas Schultze's *Aenesidemus* may still be recommended and is still read today as the first and foremost critique of Kant's errors. But the curse which prevented the glowing zeal of Maimon from exerting a decisive influence on the self-emancipa-tion of the human spirit lay in the tendency which has been attributed —quite falsely—alone to Jews, to what is called Talmudism. There are ancient Greek writers, and scholastics of the Middle Ages, who are as extreme in this matter as the scholastics of the Talmud. Jacob Fromer, the greatest living authority on the Talmud, has given us in his introduction to an edition of Maimon's biography an excellent joke characterizing this kind of subtilizing: God asks a Talmudist "What do you know?" And the Rabbi answers "Say something and I will refute you."

Maimon, however, had this tendency, not alone because he was an Eastern Jew but because he was at the same time Solomon Maimon. Many sophists, many Fathers of the Church, even Agrippa of Nettesheim, were equally disputatious. But Maimon's miraculous eye was focussed so sharply upon particulars, he noted so microscopically the most hidden subtleties of a single word, that he had no view of the whole; he formed for himself no picture of the problem he wished to consider. He was a virtuoso of fleeting detail, but a deficient virtuoso. He divined but did not master the great skepticism of Hume. But with all his nominalistic formlessness he was an independent thinker, who was concerned solely with truth. He stood alone, above the industrious plodders of philosophy, as he did above his Polish countrymen.

Solomon Maimon remained such a thoroughly Eastern Jew that he never learned to write nor speak German properly. When excited, he would drop back to his Yiddish jargon. This, however, did not prevent him from striking off epigrams caustic as acid, epigrams such as a non-Jew could never have coined. As an example let me quote the profound blasphemy: "God knows what God is."

✦ ✦ ✦

I have still the minor task of tracing, to the best of my knowledge and understanding, the possible relationship between my own skepticism and my Jewish blood. Since I believe that skepticism is neither an inherited trait nor a national gift, for I have never discovered it to a marked degree either among the French and English nor yet among the Greeks and Jews, I might answer very simply that there is no Jewish skepticism, either in me or any one else. My innermost conscience obliges me, however, not to rest content with this brief answer. I am neither able nor willing to deny that my *Critique of Language*, which I once called an infallible Lie Detector—or a Criminal Code on Cosmic Sins Against the Truth—developed first and foremost around religious concepts, that the deliverance from religious falsehoods has always seemed more pressing to me than other forms of emancipation. And, indeed, it may be a historic fact if not even ultimately a national privilege that today the average educated Occidental Jew stands in a position whence he can advance, whereas the average Occidental Christian, after a desperate struggle of more than a thousand years, cannot yet move without encumbrance and opposition. The Jew stands on the ground of Deism, I might say on the ground of an impersonal monotheism. From this position which, for the most part, was already the inheritance of Heinrich Heine, it is but a step to the criticism of those most holy concepts, God, freedom and immortality. It was not necessary for Maimon, the son of a Polish rabbi, to free himself from as many dogmas as the son of a German pastor would have encountered.

In my autobiography I have ventured to relate how my grandfather, who, as a Frankist, belonged to the sect of Sabbathai Zevi, already at the close of the eighteenth century stood outside Orthodox Judaism. But when the authorities offered him the alternative of orthodoxy or baptism he chose the former. In my first novel *The New Ahasuerus*, I have pictured the comparatively rapid enlightenment of a Jewish boy.

The purpose of all these allusions is to show that my *Critique of*

Language is an outcome of a critique of religion, and that the path to a critique of religion and to religious skepticism does not diverge greatly from the path leading to a deistic natural religion, which, after all, since approximately the time of Moses Mendelssohn, has been the motive underlying modern Reform Judaism. Moreover, the outer hindrances, like the inner, are fewer for the Jewish than for the Christian youth. The power of the theologians is relative to the power of their Church. The power of the Catholic theologians is still at the present day dangerously strong; the power of the Protestants is also still mighty, although based almost entirely on the consideration and courtesy of the ruling classes; Jewish theologians, however, at least in Western Europe, are quite powerless: neither by moral nor even by disciplinary measures can they exert any pressure against religious skepticism. Furthermore, they are themselves often freethinkers. In the Amsterdam of today Spinoza would no longer fall under the ban of the synagogue.

And there is a final point, not entirely unrelated to a tendency toward skepticism, which might be attributed to my Judaism. Many even of those well disposed towards me have often regretted that the three volumes of my *Critique of Language* is not organized in the approved academic manner, that my philosophy of language does not possess the systematic form so dear to the professional heart. I might appeal to the fact that a radical distrust of linguistic expression, of the word as the instrument of thought, must obviously produce a similar distrust of the verbal architecture of a system. But this involves a further consideration: the Jew has—whether to his advantage or not—a certain aversion toward systems and the solemnity of robes of state: he takes things easily. It is, perhaps, only in the field of political economy, in socialism, that the Jews have produced a system. The systematic is not exactly typical of the incomparable Spinoza. And Solomon Maimon's thinking, focussed as it is on atomistic and microscopic particulars, even if it often produces grotesque results, may nevertheless be held in certain respects typical of Jewish philosophizing. And so finally we could construct a traffic-bearing bridge between skepticism and the Jews, and the bridge could indeed be built, were it not for the fact that all that has been said could be applied equally well to Nietzsche who, we have learned in the introduction from Morgenstern, was not a destroyer but a positive and faithful German (Nietzsche himself boasted of his Polish descent); were it not for the fact that this very Nietzsche passionately loved such negating spirits as Voltaire and Heine; were it not that this very Nietzsche was more bitter than any Jewish skeptic in his warnings against systematization (the will to systematize is, for him, a lack of honesty); and once more, were it not that the Norse skald Henrik Ibsen, that first poet-skeptic, derided more harshly than any other modern writer the value of systematic truth —at least in morals—and like Nietzsche commended to the living the Lie of Life as salvation.

Translated from the German by Adolph S. Oko.

(—1924)

Race and Culture

❧❦❧

IRWIN EDMAN

T HE question of race is a depressing illustration of the difficulties in the way of an effective social science. It is not to be expected that, for the layman, race any more than politics or religion should be a matter of dispassionate and objective inquiry. A man is born willy-nilly of a given race; he acknowledges perforce a given ancestry. This promiscuous human fact holds true of anthropologists as well as of editorial writers and drug clerks. And the usual miscellaneous emotions that are corruptive to the thought of the layman seep not unnaturally into the professional work of the student of races. It is, perhaps, for this reason that, despite the careful empirical investigations of the last fifty years, race remains a matter for excited propaganda and superstition even in circles allegedly scientific.

This short paper cannot undertake a detailed or even a summary enumeration of all the latter-day theories of race. I shall attempt merely to indicate one or two of the extremes of current opinion, and to indicate the implied or conscious motivation, the intended or inevitable consequences of each, especially for Jews. In social science, still largely a matter of elaborate language and simple, often simple-minded guesses, the natural history and the social consequences of a belief are perhaps even more important than its alleged truth.

At the one extreme lies the popular conviction, articulated in impressive terms by more or less literate sociologists, that a man is eternally marked off, distinguished, made what he is by virtue of the race in which and of which he happens to be born. It is, of course, not the color of the hair or the contour of the skull that is italicized as a distinguishing mark. The Jew, the Chinaman, the Negro and the "Nordic," are considered to be eternal psychological types, revealing characteristic and invariable traits. These are ranged in a given order of superiority, the choice of God or of some current chauvinism. The order of preference is, of course, variable, and is strikingly coincident with the origin or allegiance of the scientist making the analysis or the man in the street subscribing to it at fifth hand. From this point of view the signature of race is the most striking and ineluctable fact about a man. The tempo of his life, the turns of his thought, the coursings of his emotions are determined and controlled by his racial, that is, his biological inheritance. Let him be subjected to any wind of doctrine or current of culture, let his personal contacts and affinities be what they may, he remains, like the Englishman in Gilbert's *Pinafore*, "in spite of all temptations to belong to other nations," eternally and inescapably true to his racial type.

It is important, irrespective for the moment of the merits of the contention, to consider the sources of this age-old belief and the psychological reasons for its intellectual or popular maintenance. The simplest and most coercive ground for the popular conception of races as eternal types is the brute fact of physical differences. To superficial observation, even of the supposedly trained and emancipated mind, marked physical differences are immediately, almost instinctively correlated with pronounced differences of mental and emotional disposition. The mental processes that go on inside a characteristically Slavic, Jewish or Indian face must certainly be different from those that go on behind the blond regularity and normalcy of Nordic features. The kink of the hair, the lines of the jaw, the shape of the eyes, these are for the generality of opinion clear indices, unmistakable symbols of the kind of psychic life to be expected from an exemplar of that given physical type. When members of one race observe members of another acting remarkably like themselves, as whites watch Negroes at a church service or Chinese in a theatre, these evidences of a common humanity are matters of amused and condescending surprise.

A little education or a modicum of travel sometimes helps to eradicate this naive identification of color and contour with deep-seated racial characteristics. There is a more radical popular confusion, long made by professional anthropologists and still insisted on by a few who go by that name, that is, the identification of race and culture—I am using culture in the broadest sense of the social inheritance of a given group, not in that polite sense in which Matthew Arnold wished to butter it thinly over the world. When we commonly speak of the mind and imagination of a race, we seldom make clear just what we are referring to, whether something radical, indigenous and biologically transmissible among members of a given racial group, or something that is merely a definitive and constant tradition, so pervasive in its details, so early acquired by individuals of the group that it comes to appear a native biological character. It is carelessness of this distinction that leads historians of European culture to speak glibly of the passion for clarity as a racial character of the Greeks, of monotheistic fervor as an ineradicable trait of the Jews, of the invariable lucidity of the French mind, the changeless tenacity of the English, the unhurried stolidity, the steady contemplativeness of the Chinese.

The newer school of anthropologists, given its original momentum by Boas, assure us that so far as devisable tests can show, there is, apart from different social and cultural traditions, no notable or discoverable difference among races. Sensory discriminations, emotional reactions, mental adjustments, seem strikingly the same wherever carefully controlled tests have been made. The character of a reaction seems to be altogether dependent on social rather than on biological facts, on the environment, milieu, culture, to which the given individual has been exposed.

It is impossible to consider all the testimony on this point. Some of it is doubtless debatable. The tests that have been made cover, after all, only the more obvious external reactions, and leave untouched those more pervasive and intangible qualities which are commonly selected as racial qualities. The facts of different rates of maturing among different races, of the apparent differing medians of intelligence among different races, still offer legitimate food for controversy. But the evidence of expert opinion is increasingly on the side of equality among races, so far as net biological equipment is concerned.

It is important to note, however, that there persists even among the educated the feeling that whatever, so to speak, laboratory facts may be, in the empirical light of daily experience, racial differences— waiving for the moment the question of racial superiorities—are there. "You may talk as you will," the average man says to himself, "about the essential humanity of all humanity, the superficiality and purely social character of racial differences. Those differences exist; they are as much facts controlling human behavior as if they were transmitted biologically from generation to generation. Call racial differences simply cultural differences; those variations nevertheless remain. A Jew and an Indian, a Chinaman and a Celt are obviously and fundamentally different. If these varieties of human type are not explicable in terms of racial inheritance, let some other explanation be found, but do not let the absence of an explanation blind us to the presence of so patent a fact."

The layman has the logic of unsophisticated observation on his side. He is not measuring skulls or studying statistical averages. He is thinking of the people he has met and known, of the races whose stories and traditions and character he has studied and detested or loved. The abstract racial uniformity insisted on by the scientist he simply does not see. The world seems to him, in fact, the more interesting for the variety of racial types he finds in it. He is even grateful that the common theme of humanity has so many characteristic variations played upon it.

Recent psychology has come to the aid of the layman in his pertinacious conviction that racial differences are not to be explained away by measurements and questionnaires. We are assured by the Freudians that the habits acquired by a child before his fifth year are so deeply and quickly integrated into the bedrock of his character that for all practical purposes they are fixed traits of his character. When the layman speaks of racial characteristics, apart from physical traits, he refers to these primary and apparently native reactions, these unconscious and inflexible strands of character. Much of what goes by the name of a racial flair or frailty is simply the fixed residuum of early acquired habits, the deposits of a stable and pervasive tradition.

It goes without saying that most of these early habits are traceable to a cultural tradition itself so complex and interwoven that it is hardly fair to call it racial. The marked differences present or alleged between Jews brought up in varying cultural traditions would be a case in point. Much, for example, of the passionate intellectuality that is supposed to mark the Jewish student turns out on examination to be the expression of a Russian background rather than of the Jewish race, and Jews whose families have for generations been domiciled in this country exhibit to the interested observer almost no traits that mark them off from the "Nordics" from whom or by whom they would be segregated.

The Jew offers indeed a peculiarly apposite illustration of the meaning (or is it meaninglessness?) of racial differences. Here is a racial stock that has been distributed in a variety of cultures and "races" and whose most marked "racial characteristic," if any, would appear to be its easy assimilation of any and all the characteristics of the culture to which it happens to be exposed. It will be cited in answer that the Jews have, nevertheless, appeared to maintain an integrity, a unity, a racial timbre, that sets them off. I think this will be found in most cases to be the result of a commonly maintained religious interest, or a separatism fostered by an exclusion of Jews from the cultural and social life of the people among whom they have lived. But where there has been opportunity for cultural assimilation and for diversion of the interests of Jews into habits and traditions not specifically Jewish, I think it would be difficult to find a residuum of traits that could be called essential to the Jewish character.

Less immediate, less innocent, less directly the result of observation are the reasons why these racial traits, observed or said to be observed in common day-to-day experience, are exaggerated and, depending on the point of view, vilified or glorified. The insistence and emphasis on racial traits come largely not from first hand experience, but from a preferential or inimical analysis, from a chauvinistic adherence to or a chauvinistic opposition to a given race. Perhaps biological uniqueness has never been insisted on more than in the case of Jews.

The reason for the emphasis on so-called racial traits on the part of Jews themselves has, it appears, partly a sad and partly a seductive origin. The Jews have, in the first place, for reasons thousands of times discussed, been set off as a distinctive minority. They have been told so often by members of their own race and by outsiders that they are a race apart that they have come to believe it themselves. They have been accused so often of impossible racial defects that they have, in self-defense, ascribed to themselves wholly imaginary racial virtues. The sad accidents of their history have been converted by a facile logic of defense into unvarying strands of a biological inheritance. They have added to the unfavorable myths invented by outsiders a whole folklore of favorable myths about themselves. It has often been averred—and truthfully—that the doctrine of racial differences has been fostered by the illiberality and provincialism of jealous, of conquering, of dominant races. An interesting study might be made of the contributions to fairy tale anthropology that have been made by the passionately defensive members of minority races themselves.

But there is a more generous and inspiring source for the belief on the part of Jews themselves in a specific racial quality. A Jew, from the simple circumstance that he is like other human beings, likes to have the roots of his intellectual and imaginative life somewhere, just as he likes to have a physical and social place he can call home. The physical wanderer and cosmopolite is traditionally a lonely figure, and so is the wanderer and cosmopolite in spirit. Ranging over the broad area of spiritual experience, drawing imaginative nourishment from all quarters of the European tradition, an intellectual Jew comes to feel, or, more accurately, comes to desire to feel, a moral homesickness. He puts his ear to the ground hoping for some resonance from his racial past. He feels, or hopes he may feel, that it is not simply he but his race that is speaking through him. He senses or thinks he senses it speaking to him not merely verbally and intellectually, through a recovered cultural and traditional background, but that it is sounding intimately through the tempo of his mind and the beat of his emotions. It is part of the pounding of his heart and the coursing of his blood. It is not merely, he realizes or hopes to realize, that there is a Hebraic tradition which an alien Matthew Arnold can externally contrast with Hellenism. He wishes for, and so finds, a Hebraic spirit which utters itself in his innermost moral idiom, reveals itself to him and to others in his fundamental spiritual idiosyncrasies.

The Jew is not alone in this. The last century and especially the last few decades have revealed the same phenomenon happening in many nations and among many races. The revival of Gaelic learning and the fanning into flame of a Gaelic spirit, the uprush of nationalism and of nationalistic psychologies all over Europe and the East, have been noted with varying degrees of sympathy or alarm by those interested in the common prospects of humanity. These movements have a seduction and warming intimacy to those in them or observant of them. The doctrine or fantasy of a racial psyche seems to knit a man more closely to a human group; it enables him, imaginatively at least, to discover an undying current vitalizing him with the common warmth of his racial fellows in this and past generations.

The fascination of this racial sense has a perfectly natural and plausible basis. Few men are really cosmopolitans in spirit, or citizens of the wide world of thought. There are not many so completely objective, emancipated and intellectualized, that they can stand on their own feet and draw food freely from any nourishing quarter. The human animal, even in his most abstruse and sophisticated moments, remains a creature of the herd. He cannot lead even the life of the spirit in isolation. Few are sufficiently sure of themselves or sufficient respecters of the uniqueness of personality to believe their lives or ideas can be of much substance unless they derive from some deep and ancient wellspring of race or tradition which they can call intimately their own.

This longing for the moral warmth of close esoteric association is an intelligible and controlling factor in the lives of many sensitive and imaginative Jews. It is none the less, I think, a form of sentimentalism, and of danger, especially when it invents a psychology of racial uniqueness to justify a devotion to a culture and traditions for which there are more cogent justifications. The Jew, educated in America, is brought up imaginatively on all the various strains and elements of the European tradition. The color and dimensions of his education are, by the time he reaches manhood, indistinguishable from that of other broadly educated men of his time, nor, so far as I have been able to observe, are the processes of his mind or the turns of his temperament different. He discovers, rather late, perhaps, the interest and scope of his own tradition, becomes, sometimes factitiously, sometimes out of all proportion, interested in the Hebraic elements in the stream of Western culture. I am thinking, of course, of those cases, very general now, where the religious factor is, as in the analagous cases of non-Jewish intellectuals, neutral or negligible.

Now a Jew or a non-Jew may, for all sorts of reasons, become primarily interested in Hebraic culture, history and imagination. In either case such an interest has as little moral reverberation as a passion for a study of birds or of Beowulf. It is, however, natural that for a Jew the Hebraic tradition should have the nearer interest that the history of one's family has as compared with the history of one's friends. That is a natural weakness and a clear human gain, but the Jew need not, therefore, lose a sense of proportion. He need not, because he has a more familiar and homespun curiosity about the heritage of his own race, exalt that heritage or suppose that a minor strain in the history of civilization, of which his own life happens to be a note, is by virtue of that personal accident really the major theme. He can be curious about Philo and Maimonides without ranking either of them above Plato, or finding them necessarily more congenial to his own temper.

Above all, he need not make the sentimentalist's or the chauvinist's fallacy, the identification of history with biology. He need not translate an absorption in his own traditions into a mystic psyche that vibrates somehow through the heart of his essential being, and through the heart, as he eloquently imagines, of all those of the Jewish race. That there exists a racial mind, I am quite convinced, but it is a mind in the sense of being an intellectual and imaginative history. It is the complex of ideals that have been articulated in the literature and poetry, the philosophy and the political and social experiments of the race. It is a legacy, not a neural eccentricity, nor need it become a neurosis. This is exactly what it does become when it is considered as being a mental process unique to the physical nature of the Jews. There are dozens of reasons why the contribution of the Jews to the common civilization of the world should be studied, explored, given scholarly and creative expression. There are important psychological factors which recommend that this work can be better, more sympathetically done by Jews, and why Jews would be stimulated and morally vivified by doing it. But there is no reason why this enterprise should be accompanied by fanfare of foolishness or superstition. There is no call for the Jews to play right into the hands of reaction by insisting on a psychological uniqueness, the net profit of which would be nothing but a psychical isolation from the rest of a strangely similar humanity.

(—1924)

Marxism and Religion

ᥫᩬᥬᩭᥩ

ROBERT GORDIS

WHEN Lenin died and came to Heaven, Marx met him at the gate to guide him through the celestial regions, as Virgil had escorted Dante. In their progress they met a crowd of people who made profound obeisance before Marx. "Master," said Lenin, "who are these people?" "I do not know," Marx answered with a puzzled look, "they are too many to be my readers, but too few to be my commentators."

This possibly apocryphal incident may serve as the starting point for a discussion of Marxism and religion, for it emphasizes the truth that Marx must be clearly differentiated from his interpreters. Anyone who has ever worked with a sacred text knows what a wide gap frequently exists between the meaning of the author and the exegesis of his commentators.

Even within the body of Marx's writings some ideas are central while others are peripheral. Unquestionably, the two basic conceptions are the economic interpretation of history and his program of social action. Karl Marx was the first social scientist to recognize with perfect clarity that the economic conditions of society are the fundamental factors in human affairs. This insight is independent of social philosophy or religious preconception. Perhaps the most lucid exposition of Marx's thesis was written by a leading conservative economist, Professor E. R. A. Seligman of Columbia University.

Unfortunately, this brilliant contribution to the science of history was obscured, because it was exaggerated by his followers. Marx had said that the primary motivation for human activity is the desire for food, shelter, and security; what is more, the economic facts of a given society, such as the distribution of wealth, the living standards, the workers' wages, and the stage of technological advance, *condition* the other elements of civilization: the moral code, scientific research, literature, art and religion. Marx's followers took this to mean that economic forces *determine* the culture of society.

The difference between "condition" and "determine" is elementary, but it was coolly ignored by the most militant of Marx's disciples. If the economic order *determines* the culture, and is found to be untenable, both must be destroyed root and branch, since all the cultural manifestations are merely the hypocritical masks of selfish vested interests. Morality is nothing but bourgeois hypocrisy; scientific research, the slave of the propertied classes; and religion, the instrument for keeping the masses contented in their slavery.

If, however, it be recognized that while economic forces condition, they do not determine, culture, the consequences are radically different. Then it follows, indeed, that economic interests may exploit science, religion and morality for their own use; but these and all other expressions of the human spirit have a genuine, independent *raison d'être*. Culture needs to be redeemed from its economic shackles, not destroyed, if civilization is to endure.

Naturally, religion refuses to consent to its own destruction. It has, however, no quarrel with the economic interpretation of history, even as far as religion itself is concerned, if kept within the bounds of truth. In stating that religion has often been used to bolster up economic privilege, Marx is only making explicit what religion has implicitly recognized in the most vital chapters of its history. A classic illustration for the Western mind is the incident of Jesus driving the money-changers from the Temple. Centuries before Jesus, however, this recognition existed among the Hebrew prophets. When Amos was expelled from Bethel by the priest Amaziah, the prophet knew that the priest was only protecting the political and social system he was attacking. A century later Isaiah castigated the unholy alliance of plunder and piety:

> And when ye spread forth your hands, I will hide Mine eyes
> > from you;
> Yea, when ye make many prayers, I will not hear;
> > Your hands are full of blood.

His younger contemporary Micah denounced with equal fervor the false prophets who invoked God's favor on the side of the best-paying battalions:

> . . . the prophets who lead my folk astray, who cry, "All's well" if they get food to eat, and open war on any who refuse them.

✦ ✦ ✦

The most significant aspect of Marx's thought lies in his program for social change. He was an acute critic of the present economic order; his diagnosis of the ills of capitalism must be recognized as epoch-making, despite errors in detail. The defects of capitalism, Marx held, are inherent in its nature. Economic competition, which is the starting point and theoretical creed of capitalism, inevitably goes over into combinations of ever smaller groups of industrialists and financiers. With the inexorable concentration of wealth, the great middle class would be forced into the ranks of the proletariat, where they would intensify the competition for jobs in the labor market and thus further depress the living standards of the masses. But ultimately the people would rise, take over the means of production, and usher in a non-profit economy, called socialism.

Now in the seventy years since Marx wrote, it has become clear that he exaggerated the speed of the process of monopolization, since he was unaware of countless factors operating to decentralize certain types of industry. Besides, he could not foresee the rise of the service industries, like electrical appliances, automobiles, radios, that created a new and large class of entrepreneurs. Nor was his theory of the progressive deterioration of working-class living standards borne out by the facts. Technological improvements increased productivity very considerably; while the strength of the trade union movement, sup-ported as it has been by the liberal and humanitarian attitudes among large sections of the middle classes, compelled the employers to grant labor a larger, not a smaller, share in the products of industry.

These exceptions notwithstanding, the essential truth of Marx's diag-nosis is amply attested by the phenomenal growth of trusts, combines and cartels, the development of chain and department stores, and the increase of interlocking directorates in finance and industry.

Such being the malady, Marx's remedy is the collective ownership of the means of production, to be operated not for the profit of the few but for the welfare of all. Both within religion and without, men are divided on the feasibility of Marx's program. But it seems clear that its goal agrees with the aspirations of religion. Increasing numbers of religious leaders feel that the socialization of economic resources is the practical technique for realizing social justice. If the cardinal doctrine of religion is the Fatherhood of God and the Brotherhood of Man, then all human beings have an equal right to share in the blessings of God's world.

This is no modern rationalization. It is encountered in the most primitive religion we know, that of the Australian bushmen. When the first English settlers came to Australia, they acted the part of justice as well as discretion by buying the land from the natives instead of driving them off. In a few years, however, the natives returned, demanding to be paid over again. Children had been born to them: they too had a share in the soil, no less than earlier generations. This very conception meets us in the Bible as well. Much in the spirit of the Social Contract, Palestine is described as having been divided fairly among all the tribes of Israel. To prevent the monopolization of land through sale and foreclosure, the Jubilee Law was enacted, whereby all land reverts to its original owners at the fiftieth year. In justifying this apparent confiscation of private property, the Bible enunciates a higher law: "And the land shall not be sold in perpetuity; for the land is Mine; for ye are strangers and settlers with Me."

Indeed, in all its vital periods religion has demonstrated its zeal for justice and freedom. The Pentateuchal ordinances regarding the sabbatical and jubilee years were practical expedients for dealing with the problem of the concentration of wealth and the impoverishment of the masses. The prophetic note is essentially the arraignment of political tyranny and social misery, from Elijah to Jeremiah, from Amos to Isaiah and Micah. To be sure, we do not find in these pages of Scripture a practical program for our own day. But adherents of religion derive from them the social passion to labor on behalf of a cooperative commonwealth, where exploitation and misery may be replaced by cooperation and universal plenty.

Thus it is clear that religion *per se* is not opposed to the basic aspects of Marxism, whether in its economic interpretation of history or in its program of social action. Why, then, are there such undeniably deep sources of conflict between Marxism and religion? The answer lies in the tendency of all movements to grow beyond the original core of essential ideas. They absorb peripheral conceptions and historical associations that often are merely accidental in character. Communism, the most militant form of Marxism today, has not remained an economic program pure and simple. On the contrary, it has made the destruction of religion a cardinal doctrine, contending that science is sufficient to solve all human problems.

Before analyzing the communist objections to religion, it is worth noting that Marx himself has been treated in a religious and not scientific spirit by his followers. This becomes sufficiently evident by contrasting the fates of Isaac Newton and Karl Marx, each an outstanding thinker in his field. During his long life Newton engaged in a variety of intellectual enterprises. He formulated the laws of gravitation, warmly defended the corpuscular theory of light, and also spent many years in the calculation of the Second Coming of Christ based on the predictions of Daniel. His gravitational laws have become basic in modern physics; his theory of light was rejected in favor of the wave theory; while his fantastic biblical writings are not even mentioned in modern exegesis. The method of science is to accept the true, and reject the rest, no matter how august the authority. Marx, on the other hand, has been canonized by his followers, who insist that the Master can do no wrong. Every aspect of his thought and activity—including his "excess baggage" of Hegelianism as well as his attitude toward religion —must be accepted as sacred, if one is to be admitted into the community of the faithful.

Marx, as every schoolboy knows, is the author of the aphorism, "Religion is the opiate of the people." Quite at variance with the Marxist method, few have sought to investigate the social background of this statement. Karl Marx's father belonged to that generation of German Jews who, during the brief heyday of the Emancipation, thought they would be received into Western society as equals. To prepare themselves for citizenship in the general world of liberty, fraternity and equality, they cut loose from the Jewish people and its heritage. When the first flush of idealistic enthusiasm subsided in Europe and reaction resumed the saddle, they discovered that the millennium had not quite arrived. The academic and professional world, Western society generally, still remained barred against them. Their only hope of admittance lay in adopting the dominant faith, which would not be difficult, since they believed in no religion. An epidemic of conversion swept through the intellectual classes of German Jewry, including the children of Moses Mendelssohn himself, and Heinrich Heine, Ludwig Börne, and countless others. That this step proved fruitless for most of them is beside the present point.

Karl Marx was six years old when his father and whole family became nominal Protestants. It is more than doubtful whether Karl ever visited either a synagogue or a church. In common with many of his contemporaries, he saw Judaism as a tragedy and Christianity

as a joke. Moreover, the science and history of religion had not yet
been born. He certainly made no attempt to determine whether religion was always marked by the mystical other-worldly character
and by the alliance with privilege and reaction that it bore in his day.
He never suspected its great vital sources of inspiration. In any case,
Marx's attitude toward religion was one of indifference rather than
active hostility. Religion is rarely the subject of his thought, and even
his famous aphorism was coined in passing, in a review of Hegel's
Philosophy of Law. Marx doubtless had a right to his prejudices; what
is unfortunate is that this particular prejudice became invested with
the sanctity of dogma.

That the phrase became a slogan for the destruction of religion
was largely the result of the situation in tsarist Russia. Here was
the most absolutist reign on earth, abetted by the most fanatical
and obscurantist of Churches. Obedience to the Little Father in the
Kremlin was inculcated by the priests with no less fervor than devotion to the Great Father in Heaven. The Greek Orthodox Church had
never met with the corrosive acids of modern thought. It reeked
with superstition and corruption. It exemplified Marx's epigram in a
more striking fashion than he could have imagined. Thus organized
religion everywhere was taken to be the ally of exploitation and
tyranny, whose destruction must precede the advent of a just social
order.

When this thesis is considered on its merits, however, its inadequacy becomes patent. Undeniable, of course, is the fact that religion has been used as an opiate to deaden men's sensibilities to the
physical ills of the world. But cannot that charge be leveled with
equal truth against every phase of the life of the spirit? Music has often
enough proved an isle of refuge in a bleak sea of poverty and suffering. Some of the noblest spirits have found in science an ivory tower
of isolation from the fever and fret of the world. Literature has served
as an anodyne for troubled men and women in every age. Indeed,
Freud has argued with a good deal of plausibility that artistic
creation of every type is a means of compensating for frustration and
failure in the practical world.

Every non-economic desire has at times put material interests in
the background. Did not the caresses of Delilah deaden Samson's
zeal against the Philistine oppressors? Was not Antony's vigilance
against Octavian relaxed before the voluptuous charms of Cleopatra?

From the august Justices of the United States Supreme Court, who read detective stories, to the Italian barber, who buys standing room at the opera, men are always seeking "escape" from care and responsibility. Some forms of escape are essential if life is to go on; others are dangerous. Religion has undoubtedly afforded both kinds.

But the other side of the picture cannot be overlooked. Religion is not a thing apart from life; it receives its style from the temper of the age. Religion has had its periods of revolt as well as its eras of acquiescence. Readers of the Old Testament know that it is completely this-worldly in character, and conceives of salvation as human happiness here and now. Never did the legislators and prophets of Israel urge submission to present misery for the sake of future bliss. There is no word for "resignation" in biblical Hebrew. Nowhere in Hebrew religion is there the slightest warrant for Lenin's contention that "religion teaches those who toil in poverty all their lives to be resigned and patient in this world, and consoles them with the hope of reward in Heaven." On the contrary, the whole burden of prophetic teaching is a flaming protest against social injustice and political tyranny. Even the war against idolatry was more than purely religious. Wallis, one of the acutest of modern biblical students, points out: "The struggle for justice and the struggle against other gods [in biblical times], instead of being two separate movements, are logically one and the same."

Salvation became other-worldly when the national hopes of the Jewish people collapsed beneath the Greek and Roman oppression. Only a miraculous intervention from on high seemed to hold out any hope for the future. This tendency was reinforced in both Christianity and Judaism during the medieval period. But it was not religion that made the Middle Ages other-worldly; the process was rather the reverse. Men and women of the Middle Ages, tormented by the constant succession of famines and plagues, wars and persecutions, steeped in chaos and ignorance, groaning beneath the brutality of feudalism, were driven to find in their religion an escape to a happier existence in another world.

Nevertheless, the prophetic note did not die. It lingered on in the phrases of the Lord's Prayer, "Thy will be done *on earth,* as it is in Heaven." It received expression in such Jewish prayers as the Adoration: "to order the world after the Kingdom of the Almighty"; or the New Year's aspiration for the day "when iniquity shall close her mouth, and wickedness be consumed like smoke, and the dominion of arrogance shall pass away from the earth."

Nor was it merely the soulless echo of prophetism that endured. Whenever men fought oppression and injustice, they found their inspiration in the Bible. Such movements as those of the Lollards and the Hussites, and the Lutheran Reformation in its earlier folk-character, were grounded in the Bible. The Puritan dictum "Rebellion to tyrants is obedience to God" was based on biblical precedent, and the American revolutionsts compared their struggle for freedom to the exodus of the Israelites from Egypt. The influence of the Bible on American ideals is so marked that Lecky has said, "Hebraic mortar cemented the foundations of American democracy." During the first half of the nineteenth century, attempts by Congress and the Courts to enforce the Fugitive Slave Act were balked by the creators and supporters of the Underground Railroad, who pointed to an older and higher law in Deuteronomy: "You must not hand back to his master any slave who has escaped to you from his master; he shall live with you wherever he chooses, in any of your townships as he pleases; you must not wrong him." In the latter half of the century the Christian Socialists like Kingsley in England and Bellamy in America, and the larger and more influential movements for social reform that derived support from the Church, all demonstrated that the social dynamic of religion was not dead. And today religious bodies of all denominations are deeply concerned with our economic and social problems.

Radical critics of religion are sometimes, indeed, disposed to admit that religious ideals have occasionally served the cause of human betterment. They contend, however, that religious institutions have a vested interest in the status quo, and must of necessity be defenders of inequality and privilege. The bond between religion and the dominant classes is especially marked in countries having Established Churches; but the bond also exists everywhere else, since the Church is supported by the wealthy elements.

This accusation against organized religion cannot be lightly dismissed. It has contributed largely to the falling away of radical and labor circles from religion. In his book, *Capitalism and Its Culture*, Professor Jerome Davis has painted a graphic picture of the interrelations of religion and business, and of the capitalist character of religious corporations. Nevertheless, this charge too is based on a half-truth. Bertrand Russell has said, "It is the fate of idealists to obtain what they have struggled for, in a form which destroys their ideals." To achieve a given purpose an organization must be created, which inevitably develops vested interests of its own that are often at variance with the ideal. The solution to the dilemma lies not in destroying the organization, but rather in maintaining a perpetual vigilance against its degradation. All the great heresies and reformations in religious history have attempted this very thing—to quicken the wells of spiritual power that have congealed into organized forms, and make them the source of free-flowing inspiration once more.

For that matter, religion is not the only form of culture that is largely maintained and controlled by the propertied classes. Journalism, literature, art, music, science and education are in the same position. Men being more than economic animals, there is nevertheless a great deal of untrammelled expression and free action in all these fields. There is nothing strange in the fact that religion, like other cultural manifestations, has so often been a handmaiden of economic interests. What is noteworthy is that religion has been demonstrating with increasing frequency its vital concern for social reconstruction. The Pension Fund of the Congregational Church is invested in fifty-four railroads, nine government agencies, two industries, and forty-three public utilities. That, however, did not prevent the meeting of the Congregational and Christian Churches in 1934 from asking for "the overthrow of the present economic system, including the principles of private ownership," and voting $60,000 annually for social action. The pronouncements of the Federal Council of the Churches of Christ, the Methodist Episcopal Church, the Congregational and Christian Churches, the Central Conference of American Rabbis, the Rabbinical Assembly of America, and other religious bodies, both lay and clerical, differ in their points of view, but they all show an increasing awareness of the social implications of religion. In doing so they are not breaking with tradition, but are directly in the line of vital religion that cannot die, because it ministers to life.

+ + +

Nevertheless, even after the inadequacy of the communist attack on religion is laid bare, a wide gulf remains between religion and Marxism because of the grave objections religion has to communism in several of its phases. Religion not only teaches the inalienable right of all men to share in the blessings of the world, but its stresses equally the sanctity and value of the individual human personality. In practice, communism has often suppressed the latter ideal for the sake of the former, and has used violence to achieve the social revolution.

Radicals point out that violence is constantly being used by the present system to throttle civil liberties, to smash strikes, to prevent orderly social change. Fascism is capitalism with its back to the wall, or, more specifically, the violent destruction of democracy, in order to preserve the profit system. Under such circumstances, it is not always easy to draw the line between violence and self-defense.

This argument, however, cannot be invoked to justify the violence inherent in the dictatorship of the proletariat, the theory that a majority may be coerced in order to achieve a goal desired by a minority. Religion opposes such manifestations as the forcible collectivization of peasant holdings in Russia, the brutal liquidation of the kulaks, and the callous indifference to the declassed groups, most of whom were the victims rather than the beneficiaries of tsarism. Religion sees an affront to the human spirit in the rigorous suppression of all divergent opinion, and the tyrannous control of the press, literature, and education in Soviet Russia. In spite of all its weaknesses, democracy alone offers the hope of peaceful and orderly social change, thus advancing the collective good without submerging the individual.

Not only is violence unjust; it is impractical. At short range, violence does seem more effective than persuasion in getting men "to turn over a new leaf." One erases the old and starts afresh. Unfortunately, there is no starting with a clean slate in human affairs, and the "erased" materials are human beings, who deserve life and happiness. After nineteen years of forcible methods against "counter-revolutionary" ideas, the Soviet Government has recently established a School for Propaganda. Apparently, violence is not much more rapid and efficacious than education in transforming human nature, and it suffers from the additional defect that its victims remain dead a long time.

However, the root of the conflict between communism and religion goes deeper than the problem of violence. It lies in the fact that they are both rival systems of absolute values. Observers have noted many striking parallels between communism and conventional religion. Communism has its God, the socialist state; its lawgiver, Marx; its

Bible, *Das Kapital;* its major prophets, Lenin and Stalin; its minor prophets, Engels and Bukharin. It believes in the Last Judgment (the social revolution) when the righteous (the proletariat) will at length triumph over the wicked (the bourgeoisie). In its missionary zeal, its impassioned hatred of heresy, its sectarianism, the psychological phenomenon of its conversions, and the heroic self-sacrifice of its devotees, communism is the Church Militant of our age.

In communism the economic interpretation of human history has been generalized into a materialist conception of the universe, which is based on notions current in scientific circles back seventy-five years ago. The newer trends in modern science, represented by Whitehead, Eddington and Jeans, have undermined materialism and tend to find a vital intelligence at the core of things. These tendencies are branded by communists as bourgeois attempts to bolster up religion or, more charitably, they are viewed as retrogressions to childhood fears and fancies.

Communism insists that it is an absolute system of values, extending over the entire sphere of culture, including science, art, ethics and metaphysics. The length to which this idea is carried is illustrated by the statment of Nemilov, the Soviet biologist, in *The Biological Tragedy of Woman*: "Not only should every good Marxist be a biologist, but one cannot be a good biologist unless he be a Marxist." The recent "postponement" of the International Eugenics Congress by the Soviet authorities, because of the danger that the communist dogma of the mental equality of all races might be subjected to scrutiny, is a perfect obverse of the nazi insistence that the doctrine of Aryan race superiority is an *a priori* truth that dare not be questioned.

Religionists, on the other hand, may well see in Marxism a valuable technique for achieving economic justice, and thus clearing the decks for the unhampered spiritual development of man. A century and a half ago, when the French Revolution burst upon the world, the slogan of Liberty, Fraternity, and Equality seemed the trumpet-blast of the Messiah. Today we know that it heralded only the enfranchisement of the middle classes. Nevertheless, it marked a great advance toward the day of justice and freedom for all men. The creation of a cooperative commonwealth is the next step in human progress—but it is not the last.

Let a reconstructed society solve the problem of food, shelter, and security, and it will only become evident that the long trail is not yet ended. Russians today can grow lyrical over a new power plant or factory, as Americans did not so long ago over skyscrapers and suspension bridges. But ultimately the great aspirations of the human spirit reassert themselves. Men will seek after the purpose of human life, and resume the eternal quest after the meaning of the universe. There will still be selfishness and cruelty and envy to combat, the lust for power and the power of lust to restrain. Men will continue to meet frustration and unhappiness in life, and will need resignation in the face of tragedy and death. Men will always crave the support of a moral universe in their striving after ethical perfection. As the state grows more and more powerful, it will be more and more essential to champion the right of the individual as a sacred personality, and to free men from the inevitable tyranny of the mass. Religion antedates the passing economic order; it will survive the new.

As an advanced program of economic justice, Marxism may liberate but it cannot replace the great enterprises of spiritual discovery that we call science, philosophy and religion. In sum, religion commits the heresy of viewing even Marxism in the light of eternity. If this heresy could be forgiven, the conflict might be resolved.

(—1937)

Kierkegaard and Judaism

❧

MILTON STEINBERG

As a thorough Christian—or, as he would have put it, infinitely interested in becoming one—Soren Kierkegaard (1813–1855) addressed himself neither to Jews nor to Judaism. But they have overheard him. In part because they could not help it. Is not Kierkegaard the begetter of Existentialism? Is not the school he fathered all the vogue of late? Are Jews less submissive than others to the tyrannies of fashion?

But Kierkegaard, though made into a fad, was himself a highly original and richly endowed spirit, the author of various fresh critical judgments and insights. But every new truth, every reformulation of an old one, constitutes a challenge to all inhabitants of the universe of discourse on which it bears. In effect then, even if not by intention, Kierkegaard has confronted Jews with a twofold *mai ko mashmo lon*: "What has this to teach us?"

He needs to be considered first of all for his theses of which Judaism has been inadequately aware heretofore. "From all my teachers have I derived understanding"—that is a norm for traditions as well as individuals. Kierkegaard demands appraisal also in still another frame of reference. If Fichte is to be believed, it is from the non-Ego that the Ego becomes conscious of its own nature. Now whatever else Kierkegaard may have been, he was a Christian, marginal and idiosyncratic perhaps, but a Christian none the less. For each of his positions, no matter how eccentric, some authoritative warrant can be found, whether in his immediate Lutheran-Calvinist heritage, or in such a tangential Catholic as Pascal and before him in Duns Scotus and Augustine, or, as is to be expected in a Christian theologian, in Paul, the fountainhead of all Christian doctrine. But if so, if in Kierkegaard we have an *anima totaliter Christiana,* then he constitutes a non-Ego against which the Jewish Ego may whet its self-awareness.

Nor, to this end, is his extremism an impediment. To the contrary, it is an advantage. Just because Kierkegaard represents Christianity at its most intense and distinctive, his evocative effect on the Jewish spirit is all the more pronounced. Approaching him, therefore, Jews are well advised to be on the alert for what they can learn not only about him but about themselves also.

Among the more consequential of Kierkegaard's affirmations are these:

A. That man's plight is desperate, beset as he is by sin and bewilderment, dreading his freedom, shrinking from death, confronting Eternity; forever seeking, never finding, mitigation of his dire lot in the pleasures of the body, the conceptions of the mind.

B. That among human delusions none is more common and baseless than the belief that reason is capable of grasping reality at all, let alone achieving certainty. In this connection Kierkegaard criticizes conceptual thought with such acumen and thoroughness as to win for himself a place in the high tradition of anti-intellectualism stretching from Pyrrho of Elis and Sextus Empiricus to William James and Henri Bergson.

C. That of all conceptualist errors none is more bizarre than the notion of man as a thought-machine who cannot say *sum* ("I am") until he has first asserted *cogito* ("I think"); or the notion of man as a depersonalized, devitalized "something in general" into which philosophy loves to congeal him; whereas, in fact, he is always something particular, dynamic and passionate, more *sentiens* (emotional) than *sapiens* (intellectual).

D. That the crucial determinations of the human soul are reached in privacy and in decisive instants, not in the public domain and the unfolding of events. This thesis, aimed at Hegel, constitutes the first sortie in modern thought against "historicism," the doctrine that the social and the temporal are somehow involved in salvation.

Such are Kierkegaard's premises, from which flow as consequences:

A. An importunate appeal for subjectivity, for the soul's turning away from the outer world and externalized ideas to its own immediacy.

B. The renunciation of the hope of finality, of attaining to a resting place. To the contrary, man's destiny is to be always "on the way," that dialectical ingress and progress penetrating without end to ever deeper levels of inwardness.

C. And finally—or, more accurately, first of all—a revolutionary re-envisagement, in the light of the foregoing, of the religious life.

The sole principle of religious truth, according to Kierkegaard, is subjectivity. For Christianity is "spirit, spirit is inwardness, inwardness is subjectivity, subjectivity is essentially passion, and in its maximum and infinite, personal, passionate interest in one's eternal happiness." Whence it follows that externality, intellectuality, objectivity—call them what you will—are all obstructive to the religious purpose. Scholarship, biblical and doctrinal, may be an appealing and sometimes illuminating enterprise; but so far as salvation is concerned—and that is man's only serious business—of no account. So also with formal creeds and rituals; so also with the church as an institution; so even with ethics and all its apparatus of rules and principles.

The religious quest, Kierkegaard insists, is neither so easy, so impersonal, mechanical or self-limiting. It demands within man a burning with what Pater called "a hard gem-like flame." Even that does not suffice. For God must respond, and who can commit or compel Him? That, too, if granted, is not enough. For salvation and grace are not "things" to be given once and thereafter owned by their recipients. They are not possessions to be held in fee simple: they are ever-receding goals which, once won, must be won again. Hence the most stupid of all complacencies is that of "believers" who suppose that no more is asked of them than the performance of the right commandments or the recitation of the proper confessions. And the most arrogant of offenses is to cease, out of religious pride and self-assurance, from that anguished striving which is the mark of the human soul and its hope of salvation.

Man's freedom therefore is his peril, his misery and his grandeur. His peril, since all depends on it; his misery, since it consigns him to an infinitely toilsome and ultimately endless task; his grandeur, for its goal is nothing less than eternal bliss in God.

But there is more to Kierkegaard, much of which is philosophically questionable and some, from the Jewish point of view, nothing short of perilous.

Consider, first, Kierkegaard's radical anti-rationalism. This, to be sure, is far from total. For Socrates his admiration is as warm as his antagonism to Hegel is deep; and if he has no high regard for the physical sciences, he recognizes them as legitimate fields of human interest, with the intellect as the proper tool for their exploration. But though he pays obeisance to reason and gives abundant evidence of expertness in it, on the climactic issues of living—religion and human salvation—he repudiates reason totally, radically, with zest.

Faith for Kierkegaard is not supplementary to the intellect but its antagonist. This, be it noted, is something different from the usual conflict between faith and reason, whether in religion or philosophy. Here we are not dealing with the *noesis* of Plato or the *theoria* of Aristotle, which, reaching beyond the discursive intellect or *logos*, nevertheless carry it along in their very transcendence of it. Nor are we handling here that more commonplace collision between religious dogma on one side and science on the other.

Kierkegaard makes a different and much more radical point. He argues not merely the conventional thesis that faith and reason can have no traffic with each other, operating as they do in different realms, separated as they are by a "disjuncture" which may be "leaped" but not bridged. His is the revolutionary contention—and it is the core of his doctrine—that faith *of necessity* must "affront" reason, must "spurn" and "scandalize" it. Nor could it be otherwise when faith's climax is the twin declaration (a) that God became man and (b) that His death on the cross, an event in time, is the occasion of eternal salvation.

Can any assertion, Kierkegaard queries again and again, be more paradoxical and absurd? But if the supreme affirmations of faith be absurdities and paradoxes, then manifestly reason is not only insufficient to faith, reason must be faith's natural enemy.

An anti-rationalist, Kierkegaard turns out something of a nonmoralist also. As in logic, so in ethics, he discloses great forensic virtuosity. Witness the case for marriage and traditional morality in general, which he sets forth in the latter half of *Either-Or*.

But again it is another tack he takes once the issue becomes salvation. As before he sprang from reason to faith, spurning the intellect and trampling it down in his leap, so now he springs above morality. Goodness, he asserts, whatever its other utilities, does not save; it cannot even help to salvation. What is more, when God asks it as He may, or faith requires it as it sometimes does, moral principle must be jettisoned. This is the "teleological suspension of the ethical," propounded by Kierkegaard in his *Fear and Trembling* as the final meaning of Abraham's readiness to sacrifice Isaac at God's behest. This, be it observed, is such a *midrash* on the *Akedah* as no rabbi in two thousand years ventured to put forth.

Closely related to such "secondarizing" of the ethical is that aspect of Kierkegaard's thinking which Buber has analyzed in *The Question to the Single One*—its near-solipsism. This is no morally neutral solipsism (the metaphysical view that the self is the only knowable, or the only existent, thing) such as might derive from the epistemological question of how one can know anything. It is rather a projection of self-centeredness, so total a concentration on one's private existence and salvation as to leave no room for concern over anyone else. Indeed, in Kierkegaard's writings "others" simply do not exist as objects of solicitude. There is no community, no society. There is only the soul alone with God.

But if the relation between the individual soul and God be all, then "horizontal" history—the succession of happenings in time— embraces only one true event, the self-revelation of the Eternal. Obviously, however, a history composed of a single and unique episode is not history at all. As for internal or "vertical" history— the soul's confrontation by God—not only is this not history in the usual sense, but Kierkegaard, in addition, leaves unresolved whether this is the culmination of a progress in which time is involved or of an instantaneity, a "leap," in which time is not involved. But what manner of history can it be in which the status of time is left questionable? In sum: nothing, or at most next to nothing, remains of history when Kierkegaard is through.

Consistently, therefore, he strikes the study of history from the roster of earnest concerns. Historical research is not only an irrelevance to the quest after salvation: it can be a hindrance, interposing a "century-long parenthesis" into the urgent business of faith. Indeed, it may prove an active peril, a "most dangerous enemy," eventuating as it does in objective knowledge rather than inwardness and passion.

The main point however remains, that history effects nothing toward man's salvation. As Kierkegaard puts it in his *Philosophical Fragments*: "The first and last [generations] are essentially on the same plane. . . . Immediate contemporaneity is merely an occasion. . . ."

From all the foregoing, the anti-clericalism and anti-ecclesiasticism of Kierkegaard's last phase, his attacks on institutional Christendom, follow inevitably. That is not an expression of mere unsociability or eccentricity, not even of an ambivalence to the world's esteem which he affected to despise, though all these were factors in the case. Given his points of departure and the direction of his tending, he can arrive at no other terminus. His logic gives him no choice but to reject all churches, regardless of character and denomination. Are they not institutions, externalizations of faith, and so objectivity incarnate? Are they not, further, social entities existing in time, whereas both the social and the temporal are alien to essential religion? So it came to pass that this ardent Christian ended up as Christendom's intransigent critic.

Finally, it should be recorded that when Kierkegaard speaks of the desperateness of man's plight he is indulging in no rhetorical exaggerations. To him the human condition is one of desperation in the most literal denotation of the word. It is, so far as man's own capacities are concerned, simply and starkly hopeless.

For what is it that man can achieve for himself? As all the historic religions have agreed, aesthetic gratifications, whether crude or refined, are unlikely to effect tranquility in this world, let alone eternal life in the next. And if one seek his salvation in virtue, what man is there on earth who doeth only good and sinneth not, whose righteousness is sufficient to redemption? What can remain then except to transcend pleasure and the good alike, perhaps even—and here Kierkegaard leaves the main road of religious affirmation—to spurn and repudiate them, and go seeking elsewhere?

Only now does the true desperateness of man's plight become apparent. For his very desire and ability to seek belong not to him but to God. As much as the finding is a gift of divine grace, so much is even the setting out to find. Or, to put it in the figure employed by Kierkegaard himself in his *Philosophical Fragments*: Man is not only "destitute of the Truth up to the very moment of his learning it; he cannot even have possessed it in the form of ignorance . . ."; the teacher, that is, God, "gives the learned not only the Truth but also the condition for understanding it. . . ." Which means that facing the alternatives of eternal salvation and damnation, man is all dependence, all impotence; for what he can do for himself is of no avail, and of what avails he can do nothing. Was ever a plight more "dreadful"?

The essence of Kierkegaard, then, at least in so far as he constitutes a non-Ego to Judaism's Ego, consists of the five following antinomies, in each of which the first term is affirmed as against the second:

1. Faith *versus* Reason
2. The Religious *versus* the Ethical
3. The Individual *versus* Society
4. The Moment *versus* History
5. Man's Need *versus* his Powers

It is important that these positions be seen for what they are, not the eccentricities of an individual but the expressions—extreme perhaps, and certainly not exclusive, but none the less authentic —of the Christian *Weltanschauung*. Kierkegaard is not properly understood unless he be taken for the Christian he claimed to be. Nor does our discussion center on anything so unequal as a single person *vis à vis* a historic tradition. What concerns us here is nothing less than the timeless dialectical interchange between the Jewish and Christian faiths.

That it should be necessary to argue now what was asserted earlier in this essay—namely, the Christian character of Kierkegaard—is itself astounding. Few authors have been more explicit about their purposes. He was forever declaring and underscoring his Christian intentions and temper. Of his expositors, however, many have simply refused to take him at his word, some because they have come to him with special interests of their own, others because they were not themselves Christians, or else not Christians of his stripe. Whatever the reason, the role of Protestant doctrine and spirit in Kierkegaard has been consistently underestimated.

The fact is that Kierkegaard was a Christian *ab ovo*. He was raised in a devout Lutheran society, steeped in Christian learning, schooled in Reformation theology, attracted as well as repelled by the prospect of becoming a pastor. The issues of Christian faith and practice burned in him, all the more fiercely for the fierce troubled piety of his guilt-ridden father. Under such influences, under the dynamism of his own genius, Christianity became for Kierkegaard in the end—though not without a terrible struggle—the living heart of his thought, the *pathos* and *telos* of his entire existence.

As for the antinomies above listed, there is no accounting for them in terms of the idiosyncratic or capricious, nor as reactions to Hegel nor as responses to Kant or Schelling or Schleiermacher. They can be explained adequately only as Christian affirmations, restatements in individualistic phrases and insights, of the key assertions of Protestant Christendom in its Lutheran version.

That subordination of reason to faith, that denial of one for the sake of the other, what is it except an exultant obeisance to the mysteries of the Christian faith, the Incarnation foremost among them? On this article the less steadfast believer turns apologist or rationalizer. Not Kierkegaard. Recognizing that any attempt to make sense of it is foredoomed to failure, foreseeing that the sole sure result is to strip away its supernatural power, he elects the bolder course. He sets forth faith not only as beyond, but as radically opposed to reason. His repudation of the intellect turns out, then, neither wanton nor philosophically motivated, but rather a doctrinal necessity.

It is also impelled by another, equally weighty consideration. Within Christianity, within all theisms, there have always been two states of mind as to the nature of the divine essence. One holds it to consist in reason and the rational. To this school the Christian Platonists and Thomists belong and, in a drastic metamorphosis, the Hegelian idealists also. In the alternative view, God is Will before He is Reason. What He determines, by the very fact that He determines it, becomes the reasonable and the good. In this line stands Duns Scotus, Calvin and Luther. This is the foundation-stone of all those theologies which teach that salvation is of God's election only.

The logic behind this doctrine is clear. On two grounds salvation cannot be by man's merit. First, all men are sinners and, if the dogma of "total depravity" be granted, none is consequentially better than any other. Shall they then be saved by a righteousness no one of them possesses?

Second, were salvation by merit, God would be *bound* to confer it on those who had earned it, in which case God would not be free; which is a palpable absurdity. This is the classic Augustinian-Lutheran-Calvinist argument. Its effect is to present God as arbitrary in His bestowal of grace. He saves whom He pleases, and for no other reason than that He pleases. But if so God is not only intellectually absurd but morally irrational also.

Little wonder that it comes easy to Kierkegaard, who was reared in such conceptions, that indeed he finds it necessary, to make faith the antagonist of reason; for such, in his scheme, it is.

In his non-moralism, too, Kierkegaard voices an authoritative Christian judgment, one as ancient as the Pauline Epistles.

Having asserted Christ to be the sole medium of salvation, Paul found himself confronted by a dilemma. Obviously, none but the good man should or could be saved. Yet salvation was now a matter not of morality but of faith. But suppose a man had faith but not goodness? The problem was too much for Paul, who ended up by insisting that if the believer were truly a believer he would inevitably be good also. But on the choice between faith and morality, on the issue of what it is on which salvation ultimately depends, Paul was all explicitness. "He who believeth shall be saved; he who disbelieveth shall be condemned."

The "secondarization of the moral" in Kierkegaard, therefore —his "teleological suspension of the ethical," about which such a fuss has been made—that is basically no more than a restatement of a doctrine as old as Paul. Revived by the Reformationists in their rebellion against the "works" of the Catholic Church, it was a conviction imbibed by Kierkegaard with his father's first instruction.

Nor is it otherwise with his near-solipsism. In the Pauline-Protestant tradition the crucial tension is always between the individual and God, to which relation other persons and the community are irrelevant. This conception of primitive Christendom, interrupted for centuries by the Catholic Church with its communalizing of the anchorite and its theologizing of society, was revived in an extreme form by Luther. That was indeed, so far as practical consequences went, one of the major differences between the German and Swiss Reformationists: the former yielded up politics and economics to the secular powers and so arrived, by simple subtraction, at a religious life centered on the private soul. Eventually, in the nineteenth century, Lutheranism turned from Luther's precedent toward Calvin's. Some of its communicants evolved a "social gospel." Revealingly enough, to achieve this they had to reach beyond Luther, beyond Paul, beyond even Jesus, to the Hebrew Prophets for sanction and content. But though in the end a rebellion arose against the non-sociality of the Lutheran way, it came after Kierkegaard's time and too late to affect him.

To confirm the already marked individualism of the Reformation religion went its doctrine of the Church. Under the Catholic dispensation the Church was conceived as indispensable to the soul, there being no salvation outside it and the dogmas and sacraments it administered. Religion then, even though it might seek the salvation of the individual, was necessarily social in its expression. With the Reformation, however, that theory was displaced by a congregational conception whereunder redemption became a transaction between each individual man and God. It was Christ directly, immediately, who was the mediator. As for the Church, its proper function was now to serve, before the saving moment, as a guide in its direction; and, after, as an assembly of the Elect in the eyes of men. But since even this limited role could be construed as an invasion by a human institution into the redemptive prerogatives of the Christ, among some Protestant sects the Church was whittled down further until it all but ceased to exist.

Thus, when Kierkegaard ended up an anti-ecclesiast, he was doing no more than traveling the same road to the same goal which other tangential Protestant groups had arrived at before him.

In the case of his next antinomy—the Moment *versus* History—its traditional Christian derivation, while less obvious than with the others, is nevertheless not difficult to trace. The prevailing Christian tradition has always been strongly historicist. How could it be otherwise with a faith which reaches its apogee in an event regarded as the fulfillment of the ages, and expects an even higher climax in a second event at the end of days? The Augustinian schematization of history as an interplay through the centuries between the City of God and the City of Man—Apocalypse, Millennarianism, Eschatology—these are all expressions of the deep Christian preoccupation with time. But against that there is another, a narrower yet no less authentic stream of Christian thought, which flows not downward through the succession of incidents but circularly about one, which considers as consequential not time and its episodes but a single Moment only, that of the Cross. These were the waters of Kierkegaard's baptism.

As for the texture of man's temperament, as Kierkegaard described it, dread is the warp, powerlessness the woof. A dark fabric to begin with, it is rendered darker still when interwoven with such threads of Christian dogma as Original Sin and *sola gratia*. Under these doctrines man, born in corruption and predestined to damnation, is altogether without the power to save himself. Which is the meaning of the anti-Pelagianism of the Catholic Church, and of the anti-Arminianism of the Protestant. Under the former, Christendom rejected as heresy the suggestion that man can achieve anything toward his salvation outside the Church. Under the latter, he is conceived as standing in even a more parlous pass, first because he is now adjudged a creature of total depravity, without a single merit, and second because not even the Church can aid him. Only God can save; and, since man is deserving of naught, God can save only as an act of pure grace.

This is original Protestantism. Witness the repudiation by the Protestant world of Melanchthon's proposal of Synergism: the thesis that man may cooperate with God in his own deliverance. This is the teaching of the neo-Reformation school in our own time. Witness Barth's insistence that man, the drowning swimmer, is incapable of even a single feeble stroke to keep afloat; that the rescue is to the last effort God's.

Here, then, is the root of Kierkegaard's despair as to man's capacities. It is a despair deriving in part from the precariousness of the human situation, but even more from the inability of the individual to do anything about it—a despair, in a word, which, like the rest of the antinomies, comes to him from the Lutheranism of his rearing.

Now historic Judaism and historic Christianity, being kindred religions, share all sorts of presuppositions. The fact that a thesis is Christian does not exclude it from the possibility of being Jewish. The probabilities, in fact, are quite the reverse. Yet the distinctive points of Kierkegaard's position, those caught in the antinomies, are one and all, non-Jewish; indeed, so far as they go, they are the crucial issues at stake between catholic Judaism and universal Christianity. But in varying degrees.

Least clearly definable is the position of Judaism on the first of the five antinomies, that between faith and reason. Of conflicts on the philosophy-*versus*-religion or science-*versus*-religion level Jewish thought has its quota. Such is the purport of the first chapter of Saadyah's *Emunoth v'Deoth* and of the entire Maimunist controversy. Like other men professing a revealed religion, Jews have debated whether speculative inquiry is necessary or permissible and, if so, what may be the status of its conclusions *vis à vis* religious verities. But the possibility that faith and reason should be ideally exclusive of each other has little troubled traditionally minded Jewish thinkers.

They neglected to consider that possibility for one simple reason: they had no reason to. Paradox may inhere in all religious affirmation; but where Christianity must glory in it, Judaism need not. Its central position is neither "absurd" nor an "affront" to reason. It is involved in no mysteries like that of the Trinity-Unity, of which one has no choice but to say *credo quia absurdum est* ("I believe because it is absurd"). It sets forth no Gods who are yet mortals. It does not rest on the premise that the death of one man can atone for the sins of other men. All these are notions truly impenetrable to reason. Against them Jewish theology is purely of God, an object of faith to be sure, but by no means of faith against reason; of revelation, miraculous of course, but scarcely a scandal to rationality; of the election of Israel and human redeemability by moral effort, positions complex and difficult enough, and undemonstrable to boot; but, in every case, compared to Christian dogma, comprehensibility itself. As is attested by the fact that "natural religion" approaches many of these basic Jewish positions.

Historic Judaism does include some elements totally impenetrable to the intellect; such a tenet, for example, as Resurrection; such a ritual as the *Parah Adumah* (the red heifer, Numbers 19). But even with these, neither virtue nor principle is made of obscurity or mystery. To the contrary, the prevailing effort has always been to rationalize.

Not that such efforts were regarded with universal favor. Some of the ancient rabbis objected to inquiring into the *taame hamitzvoth*, the purpose of the commandments. The anti-Maimunists sought to ban all philosophical inquiry. But these rabbis, whether ancient or the medieval, were motivated by a kind of anti-rationalism worlds apart from Kierkegaard's. Their objection to speculation was pragmatic: that with revelation available it is superfluous; or, by its stubborn questioning, disturbing to faith; or, given human limitations, foredoomed to failure. No Jewish thinker is on record as advancing Kierkegaard's contention of the radical incompatibility of religious truth and reason. To the contrary, the common Jewish assumption has always been that the two for God are one, as they would be one for man were his powers of comprehension equal to the theme.

Nor is the Jewish conception of God at all conducive to anti-intellectualism along the lines of the Lutheran-Calvinist.

Kierkegaard, we have already seen, was predisposed to such a conclusion by, among other things, the notion of a God who is Will rather Reason. Admittedly, the Jewish tradition shows traces of a similar position on the part of some Jewish thinkers: such a characterization of God as in Exodus 33.19: "I will be gracious to whom I will be gracious, and will show mercy on whom I will show mercy"; such ideas as the *En-Sof* of Kabbalism, whereunder God is pure Being before He unfolds moral or intellectual qualities. Notions of this sort, however, are the exception.

The prime distinction among God's attributes drawn in rabbinic literature is between His justice and His mercy. Medieval Jewish philosophers as a rule demonstrate first the existence of God and then His other attributes, intellectual and moral. That is a matter of forensics almost altogether. The fact is that those thinkers agree one and all, whatever their argumentative procedures, that God is simultaneously and co-essentially existent, moral and free; that, in sum, whatever He is or does or ordains, all makes equal intellectual and moral sense.

From the Jewish viewpoint, God remains beyond man's reason, perhaps beyond all reason. He cannot be counter to it, rationality pertaining to His nature.

Kierkegaard's anti-rationalism is thus altogether a Christian, more exactly a Lutheran-Calvinist, but not in the slightest degree a Jewish, necessity. Nor does anything in Judaism correspond to Kierkegaard's teleological suspension of the ethical.

From the Jewish viewpoint—and this is one of its highest dignities —the ethical is never suspended, not under any circumstance and not for anyone, not even for God. *Especially not for God!* Are not supreme Reality and supreme Goodness one and co-essential to the Divine nature? If so, every act wherein the Good is put aside is more than a breach of His will; it is in effect a denial of His existence. Wherefore the rabbis define sin as constituting not merely rebellion but atheism as well.

What Kierkegaard asserts to be the glory of God is Jewishly regarded as unmitigated sacrilege. Which indeed is the true point of the *Akedah,* missed so perversely by Kierkegaard. While it was a merit in Abraham to be willing to sacrifice his only son to his God, it was God's nature and merit that He would not accept an immoral tribute. And it was His purpose, among other things, to establish that truth.

In sum, the secondary antinomy of Kierkegaard turns out, like the first, alien to Judaism.

So equally with the third, disjoining the individual from others and society.

In the Jewish view, as Buber has demonstrated, it is a false exclusion of which Kierkegaard has here been guilty. The fulfilled human life requires, in both theory and fact, the simultaneous affirmation and sanctification of both the self and the community. "If I be not for my-self," asked Hillel, "who will be for me? But if I be for myself alone, what am I?" Each man, the tradition insists, must seek the redemption of his own soul; but at the same time the "perfecting" of the world under the Kingdom of the Almighty."

In his fourth antinomy, the negation of history, Kierkegaard, as we have observed, is out of harmony with the dominant Christian tradition itself. As to Judaism, the discrepancy is total. Contemplating a Creation and Revelation in the past and a Resurrection and Kingdom of God in the future, the Jewish tradition is historical throughout. This is not to say that it is "historicist." Judaism does not hold that mere time re-generates men, or history by itself redeems society. Only the decisions of the human spirit are determinative—of the individual to his own salvation, of all men to the achievement of the Kingdom; and neither, of course, ever without God. Yet time and history, like the air men breathe and the space in which they move, are the necessary preconditions for the working out of their destiny.

They are not merely inert, environmental media. They are living, even if not crucial factors, both in the career of the soul (here Kierkegaard might assent) and in that of society (here he would dis-agree altogether). Indeed, no sharper contrast than on this score can be found between Judaism and Christianity in its Kierkegaardian version. On the latter side is the insistence that "the history of the race" is a merely "quantitative accumulation," that is, a meaningless piling up of more and more of the same thing. On the other hand we have such teachings as Isaiah's "end of days," the rabbinic "future to come" and the "merits of the fathers," and the kabbalist schema where-under each soul that lives hastens or retards, by the tempo of its return to its Primal Source, the descent and ascent of the last soul, the Messiah's.

Poles apart on whether the Moment is all, Judaism and Kierkegaard are if possible even further apart on the fifth antinomy—the issue of man's own ability to do anything of consequence towards the allevia-tion of his plight. The plight is one of anguished intensity, Judaism agrees. But that the human condition is beyond hope Judaism denies, with fourfold warrant.

In the first place Judaism does not, like Kierkegaard, set up a dis-juncture between the aesthetic and ethical, and again between the two of them together and the religious. Nor is this a matter of theoretical import only. Kierkegaard is thereby impelled to regard all pleasures, whether sensual or aesthetic, as at best spiritually indifferent, more likely deleterious; all principled morality as at the most a preparation for something else, rather than as anything in itself; all scientific and speculative thought as a diversion from the religious encounter. Once so much that contributes to the joy and meaning of life has been depreciated or rejected—in any case, ruled out as a field of God's service—little wonder that the human prospect comes to appear inordinately limited and bleak.

Judaism takes a stand of clear opposition to all that. It maintains that God can be encountered, and accordingly salvation can be furthered, in anything man feels and does, so long as it is felt and done "in holiness," that is, in obedience to God's will.

With its pleasures and activities legitimized, its opportunities for service of the divine multiplied times beyond number, life very naturally takes on another, a brighter guise. If the evil in it is still as grave as in the Kierkegaardian view, its good is larger, more variegated, more readily accessible.

Secondly, where Kierkegaard can discern but one hope for man, the deliverance of his soul, Judaism espies another also, the regeneration of society. This is no little thing, this goal of the Kingdom. It throws a second light and warmth on all human existence.

Third and fourth, Judaism has greater confidence than has Kierkegaard in God and in man.

This is the Deity which Kierkegaard, after the pattern of Paul and the Reformationists, depicts: a God who first made men imperfect and then demands sinlessness from them—wherefore he took on flesh and died as an atonement for them—who offers them deliverance but on the condition that they believe, a capacity however which lies not in their power but in His to give or withhold. The greatest thing of all, Salvation, is altogether by Grace, since no man has the least shred of righteousness to plead for him. Does not this account of God's administration of His world make Him out as questionably just, incontrovertibly unmerciful?

Judaism's appraisal of man's powers is far more generous. They are not unlimited, to be sure; they are often severely circumscribed, as we too well know. But always, the Jewish tradition insists, there is some margin of self-determination. Always a man can do something, no matter how little, with his own soul. And that something may suffice to transform him into a *b'riah hadashah,* a new regenerated crea-ture. If nothing else, a man can do *teshuvah,* he can repent—repent of the evil which heretofore he has loved and affirm the good which up to now he has scorned. By that the whole import of his life may be remade. He may even thereby, and thereby alone, come to merit salva-tion, according to the rabbinic teaching concerning those who "acquire Eternity in one moment."

How can this be? First because man is a free agent. Everything may be pre-ordained for him, said the sages of old, but not whether he will be righteous. That crucial issue is left to his own decision. It is a determination which not God Himself will coerce. A man's failure to attain perfection is no insuperable obstacle to his vindication. For, being just, God asks but does not exact perfection from one whom He made frail and fallible. "He remembers that we are dust." Not im-peccability is required of man, but earnestness of striving toward it. "Not thine to finish the work, but neither art thou free to quit it."

Then is man not in need of God's grace? Of course; all the time and in everything. But that grace is not to be supposed as only exceptional and crucial, as it were, a lightning flash of redemptive mercy breaking unpredictably into and through normality. There is that grace described in the *Siddur* as the "miracles which are daily with us, the wonders and goodnesses which are at all times, evening, morn and noon." This is the grace manifest in the Torah's guidance and in "the merits of the fathers," the examples and admonitions of the righteous, in the *yezer tov* (good instinct), conscience and aspiration toward the good, and, above all, in the uninterrupted magnetic pull of God. It is a grace always at work, ever available, never failing. All a man need do to have it is to call for it in truth. Even as it is said: "he who setteth out to be purified, from heaven do they help him."

This is the supreme and ultimate reason why Judaism, conscious with Kierkegaard of the human ordeal and peril, does not yield to his despair. It knows that man is stronger, and God is greater in justice and mercy, than he allowed.

Analogies in history are never exact. Yet in many respects Existential-ism of the Kierkegaardian stripe is to Judaism in our day what Gnosticism was at the beginning of the Common Era—an alluring but dangerous heresy. There were virtues in that doctrine as in this: inwardness, mystical sensibility, a passion and groping for truths but coldly or imperfectly comprehended by conventional religion, a returning to the primary experiences from which all formal faith stems, and a penetrating feeling for the dilemmas and torments of human existence.

But there were grave failings also. Gnosticism, like Existentialism, abandoned natural reason, the one for esotericism, the other for faith. Like the latter the former also suspended and secondarized and so, in the end, perverted moral values; abandoned the group in its concern for the self; considered only the saving moment but not history, personal salvation but not the Kingdom of God; and, out of despair, surrendered the world to the demiurge, looking for salvation in flight.

To one doctrine as to the other the proper Jewish response is that of Rabbi Meir when he said, concerning the teachings of his heretic master Elisha ben Abuyah, "As with a pomegranate, one eats the seed and throws the rind away."

(—1949)

Looking to the Future

❧❧❧

VISCOUNT SAMUEL

Having now reached an advanced old age I find that, when I am invited nowadays to give a broadcast* or an address of some kind, I am usually expected to be retrospective: to talk about events in which I have taken part, in more than sixty years of public life, or to recall anecdotes about eminent people. But I am not really interested in the past, except as a guide to the present in its most important task, that of making the future. So I am by no means willing to play the part of a link with the quaint and remote days of long ago. I feel myself a contemporary of today. I would rather say with Walt Whitman, "I stand in my place, with my own day, here." That is why I have taken as the theme and the title of these talks "Looking to the Future."

I will start with one observation that is obvious and will be generally agreed: that our age is a time of upheaval, political and social, religious and moral. In countries that include one half of the human race the upheaval has been marked by armed violence, by rebellions, civil war, international conflict. Everywhere, in the present century, it has brought great disasters: two World Wars, the most widespread and destructive in the history of men; and even now the risk of a third, which the nuclear bomb might make still more terrible.

To try to deal with these problems, and to forestall and prevent these catastrophes that menace us—that this is our most urgent duty no one will dispute. My first proposition is that we must take that as the standpoint from which we shall view the future.

My second proposition—and this is the foundation for all I have to say in these talks—is that the causes of the present troubles and future dangers that afflict this age can all be traced back to the lack

* This essay consists of four talks delivered in 1958 over the British Broadcasting Service.

of any root principles, generally agreed, in philosophy, in religion, and in politics, both national and international. The whole structure of our civilization is unstable because its foundations are crumbling. Everywhere the old class structure of society has been undermined by the advent of democracy. At the same time the European empires in Asia and Africa are yielding place to independence or to partnership. Most important of all, in religion, the simple faith in the ancient theologies and their sacred writings as the explanation of the universe and the foundation and sanction of morals has been shaken and often destroyed by the impact of modern science.

Civilization has to adjust itself, if it can, to the new conditions. Meanwhile confusion prevails. The ordinary man is often not interested in these high topics. He does not expect to be able to understand them: he expects leadership from the intellectuals—the statesmen, the philosophers, the men of religion. But these, too, are confused, contradicting one another; engaged more in criticisms, negations, refutations, than in the positive work of constructive thought. If there is one point on which mass opinion appears to be definite and agreed, it is that the present age is mostly concerned not with this World of Ideas but with the World of Things—the material things that we make and use, sell and buy.

But the view that I would offer for your consideration is that this attitude is altogether wrong. While recognizing the immense value to mankind of physical science, technology, economics in general, I would submit that it is not anywhere in that world that we may hope to find solutions of our problems, but in the World of Ideas.

Our first principle must be to realize that men's actions are determined by their ideas. This is so now, always has been so, and always must be. Right ideas are those that lead to good actions. Good actions are those that experience shows will lead to welfare. Wrong ideas lead to bad actions, and bad actions are those that lead to suffering and disaster.

I use the word "welfare" in its widest meaning, to include everything that is worth while: material welfare certainly, but also intellectual, moral, and spiritual welfare. To discover in what true welfare consists, and to find the ways to attain it—through good conduct in individuals and wise policy in the state—is matter for continuous study, discussion, and argument.

This, we shall find at once, must require the reopening of some of the ancient problems that have for hundreds, or even thousands, of years vexed the minds of men, and which still remain unanswered. But the attempt may be worth making, because the advent of science can open a new line of approach for present-day philosophers. Theology also has become less rigid in its doctrines in an age of wider toleration of religious differences.

I will conclude this first talk with a review of one of those fundamental problems which has again been brought into the forefront. The two World Wars, taken together, have undoubtedly been the dominant event of our times. That such a monstrous event should be possible could not fail to be a challenge to all the monotheistic religions. They hold as their basic doctrine the existence of a Divine Providence, transcending the world, yet working within it: a Providence, just and merciful, caring for mankind as a father cares for his children. If that is true, and if God is both omnipotent and benevolent, the question presents itself insistently: if God is Love, why are there wars? This is the gist today of what has always been termed "the problem of Evil."

The Problem of Evil

Theologians often give the answer of the Book of Job—so magnificent as a poem, so sterile as a philosophy: the ways of Providence are inscrutable; it is not only impious, it is also absurd, for man, with his intellect knowing so minute a part of all that there is to be known, to dare to sit in judgment upon the Creator of the universe.

But to say that a question ought not to be put is not to answer but only to evade it. The philosopher must attempt a different approach.

If he is a realist, he may say, in the first place, that we mislead ourselves when we speak of "the problem of Evil." That is to assume the actual existence of a mere abstraction. The imagination then personifies it. We are asked to believe that there has been let loose in the world—for the Hindus a goddess Kali; for the Zoroastrians a deity Ahriman; or the Adversary of the Book of Job, the Devil of medieval Christianity, the Satan of Milton, or the Mephistopheles of Goethe. But all this is myth, is nothingness; and it is difficult to understand how it can be thought that the cause of religion can be advanced by first offering for the worship of mankind an All-Creator who is just and loving, gracious and merciful; and then laying upon Him the responsibility for having created also this maleficent Power, to prey upon mankind. For if not by His creation, how did it come to exist?

Putting aside, then, the conception of *"the* problem of Evil" as an unreality, we are confronted by "problems of evil" in the plural—all too many and only too real. Viewing them more closely, we shall do well to recognize in the first place that they must be divided into two kinds, which can only be considered fruitfully if they are separately discussed. One category consists of evils that come upon us from natural causes, the other of those that we bring upon ourselves.

All we are and do, all we enjoy and suffer, depends at bottom on astronomical and terrestrial conditions. The earth that we inhabit is a planet as well as a home. The stage of evolution it has reached as a planet makes it sometimes unsafe as a home. The cooling surface of the globe has not quite settled down. Now and then, here and there, an underlying rock stratum slips a little, and up above there is for us a disastrous earthquake. Or a volcano erupts and a city is destroyed. The atmosphere also is in a constant state of flux: climate and weather cause all kinds of misfortunes—hurricanes and cyclones, raging floods, droughts bringing famine; occasionally, for individuals, strokes of lightning. At a different size-level the lowest forms of life, often our servants, are sometimes our enemies. Microscopic bacteria and viruses are more formidable than the earthquake and the volcano.

But against some of these natural evils the energy and ability of man enabled him to make headway. Gigantic engineering works, harnessing the flood and fructifying the desert, save vast populations from misery. Against storms at sea we build ships large enough and powerful enough to outride them. We can even grasp the lightning and make it harmless. Greatest of all man's triumphs are those won in the incessant battle against the micro-organisms. Plague and pestilence, and many diseases that had always been the scourge of mankind, have been almost eliminated: there are high hopes that many among the rest may be conquered soon.

Other calamities arising from the character of the planet will indeed still remain, beyond possibility of control. As to those we can only say, in the concluding words of one of the great Greek tragedies: "Lament no more: these things are so."

By far the larger part, however, of the ills that beset us belong to the second category—those that we bring upon ourselves: those that result from our own ignorance or misbehavior or inactivity, our own follies and errors, vices and crimes. And so we find that the scene has shifted. The so-called "problem of Evil" is no longer to be seen simply as a problem for theology. It has shifted to ethics and the moral law; and so to the field of practical affairs—to politics, economics, and technology, to social and personal conduct; finally, it involves the responsibility of the individual and his power of choice.

But is that power of choice anything more than an illusion? In actual fact, does the individual carry any real responsibility? Or does modern science require us to substitute a philosophy of Determinism for a philosophy of Free Will? To that fundamental and formidable problem I will turn in my next broadcast.

The Problem of Choice

In the first talk of this series I started from the fact—obvious enough —that our present age has been afflicted by constant troubles and sometimes by catastrophic disaster, and that it is now beset by grave anxieties. Men's actions are determined by their ideas, and these troubles and disasters must be the outcome of ideas that have been proved by their results to have been wrong.

Seeking the root cause we may assign it to the fault of the intellectuals—the philosophers, the scientists, the men of religion, the statesmen—who should have taken the lead in forming and establishing right ideas, but who have failed in that duty. It cannot be denied that they have been—and still are—continuously at cross purposes; busy with contradictions and controversies; concerned with criticism and negations rather than with any persistent effort to arrive at some positive body of constructive thought which might be generally acceptable.

The hope of anything better must lie in an endeavor, at the very beginning, to clear up certain philosophic problems which are fundamental, which have for centuries troubled men's minds, but which still remain unsolved. As an example, I ventured to attempt an inquiry into what is termed "the problem of Evil," which led to a conclusion that responsibility for the choice of sound ideas that shall lead to right actions must lie upon individual persons, on leaders and followers, intellectuals and ordinary people acting singly or in groups through social institutions.

Arising out of that, we cannot escape re-examining another of the ancient unsolved problems, one which challenges the whole of this conception of individual responsibility. This is the problem of determinism: or of free will, as it is usually called.

It is contended by some philosophers that the individual person is not in fact the self-contained, self-controlled unit that he thinks he is. Theologians also, in some periods, have given support to this position in the doctrine of predestination. At the present time modern science itself is often invoked in much the same sense.

Science, we are told, has now established, beyond all doubt, that the individual person is the product of his heredity and his environment. Biology has discovered the inner mechanism of heredity in the fertilized germ-cell and its genes; and all the organic cells that make up the body, including the brain and the nervous system, are of a pattern inherited from parents and ancestors. Psychology also has revealed the existence of a subconscious mind, below the level of the conscious. This is the seat of instincts, intuitions, and emotions, accumulated during a race evolution of millions of years, which are a determining factor throughout man's life. Furthermore, from outside the individual, the social environment into which he happens to have been born is continuously active, influencing and moulding his mind and his character, and therefore his choice and his conduct.

But I would venture to suggest that a realist philosopher, who accepts the scientific outlook, may have something to say about determinism different from the views that are today widely current.

In my previous talk I began by questioning at the outset the term "Problem of Evil," contending that there is no such thing; but that there are only "problems," in the plural, of "evils," and that our business is to get to close quarters with them. In the same way we should recognize that we have misled ourselves by talking of the freedom of the will. That seems to imply—and does indeed imply—that the human will is uncaused and unconditioned. That plainly is not so. Heredity and environment are facts. The genes and the individual characteristics they control; the subconscious mind and its influence on the conscious; the society and its institutions—schools, churches, laws—are facts. In any description of the actual situation, the existence, and the importance, of all these must be agreed.

But when that has been said, not all has been said. The psychological argument, as stated above, is fallacious. Because the subconscious is accepted as important it does not follow that the conscious mind is now to be discarded as unimportant. Each of the two mind levels is incessantly interacting with the other. Because the external factors of ancestry and environment are essential elements, it does not follow that the internal factors—reason, conscience, will—are unessential. As Radhakrishnan, the philosopher of Hinduism, has said: "All life is a commerce between Self and Not-self."

Consider for a moment a new-born infant. Its development as an embryo is finished, but it remains small, helpless, and passive. Through its own inherent vitality the development continues. In the next few weeks or months the infant will have doubled its weight, and many of its future capabilities will have begun to appear. The psychologist tells us that there are two critical points in this development—at about the age of eighteen months and between the ages of seven and eleven —which mark the beginning of new phases. Meanwhile, and afterwards, there grows up the capacity for judgment and the power of will.

Every father and mother can see this happening with their own children; each, in due course, will develop, as they will say, "a mind of its own." This independent power to choose and will to act does not come miraculously, at a particular moment: it comes gradually and relatively late, but it comes as easily and normally as the growth of flower or fruit in a plant. And this spontaneity is just as much as anything else the outcome of heredity and environment, of the genes and of the society.

Similarly with regard to the subconscious. We have only to look round us and within us to see abundant proof of its reality. Often one's mind may be the theater of a definite conflict. Whenever we feel an inclination towards an action which we may perhaps think it would be better not to take, we may confirm our first view, or we may finally decide for the other. We have a choice between the first prompting, that may have come from the subconscious, and the later influences of the conscious. Sometimes we may watch in other people such a conflict between conscious and subconscious: for example, some acquaintance, who has been an addict to alcohol or to nicotine, may tell us of a prolonged struggle within his own mind, which may have been successful or unsuccessful, to give up his habit.

If the subconscious is real, so is the conscious, and there is no reason *a priori* why the first should be allowed the final word and not the second.

Viewing the process as a whole we see that every human thought and action may be attributed ultimately to a combination of four factors. They are, first, the working of the physical universe, as basis; second, the activities of the surrounding society; third, the characteristics inherited by the individual; and, fourth, his own autonomous will. An essential point is that the event that is happening is indeed a combination, not an aggregation: not merely the result of a number of prior causes, added together like a sum in arithmetic. The effects of all four are interfused. As the consequence, something new and different has appeared. Through the act of volition a new event has been born —real and unique. It will help, in conjunction with others, to give rise to other new events in the future.

We find, then, that we need not regard ourselves as in the grip of pre-ordained necessity. Included in our heritage is the capacity to go beyond the heritage. We are not living in a closed system: within limits that are given, we ourselves are shaping the environment. And this is what matters most.

Discarding the term "free will" as ambiguous, we may prefer to speak of the independent power of choice—which is what we really have in mind. And if we are able to re-establish individual responsibility on an intellectual foundation that will hold firm, we may be helping to clear up one at least of the many confusions that bewilder our troubled age.

Our conclusion will be that the modern mind ought not to accept defeat on this matter. We ought not to ignore or evade the issue by saying that the arguments for free will and for determinism are both unanswerable. We ought not to say that the ordinary man would be wise not to reopen this particular argument, because he could end only by accepting simultaneously two opposite conclusions, and so his confusion at the beginning would only be worsened at the end. He would do well to discard the term "free will" altogether, and to speak rather of the power of choice. But if the old expression is too firmly rooted, then he should make it clear that by freedom is not meant that the individual's will is uncaused or unconditioned.

Then the philosopher may firmly decide in favor of free will— as so interpreted—and would be able to go on to a continuous study of the causes and conditions and their several effects. And from this view neither the scientist nor the man of religion need have reason to dissent.

Reason and Imagination

These discussions started with a frank realization of the grave faults in our present civilization, and they must have been grave indeed since they have given rise to the appalling calamities of the first half of the present century and the terror still facing us in the second half. I have said that, in my view, all this has been caused by the acceptance of wrong ideas and mistaken principles, resulting in the bad conduct of individuals and the disastrous policies of nations, and that what is now needed is active guidance into better courses by the leading minds among the peoples.

But this teaching must be accepted and acted upon by the ordinary average men and women, here and everywhere. Also, it must be acceptable to science, which is the dominating factor of the present age; and to religion, which appeals to the fundamental instincts of hundreds of millions; to philosophy as well, bringing in the element of pure reason. On that basis, I suggested that we must consider afresh some of the oldest of the intellectual puzzles which have ever vexed mankind and which many look upon as still unsolved.

Already we have tried to arrive at clear-cut conclusions on two of these: the first, often rather confusingly called "the problem of Evil"; and the other—also misleading by its title—"the problem of Free Will."

Now I ask you to consider a factor which is not usually taken into account in a discussion of this kind. Our troubles, I believe, have been due in large measure to the errors into which man has so often been misled by his own imagination.

No doubt I shall at once be told that imagination is one of the most precious qualities of man, distinguishing him from all the rest of nature; and the origin of all the arts. It is indispensable, too, to both science and philosophy: for it enables us to speculate, and speculation is the pioneer of discovery. Also, imagination was the origin of religion among the primitive peoples, and it is still rooted deep in the subconscious of the civilized.

Nevertheless, experience shows clearly that imagination, if it is allowed to run loose from reason, has again and again led the human race into disaster. In religion there were the idolatries which dominated the ancient world. In the mighty empires of the valleys of the Euphrates, the Tigris, and the Nile, as well as in India and China, or again among the Aztecs and Mayas, there were those powerful priesthoods, dominating men's minds, often for thousands of years. They rested upon the worship of invented deities that had no real objective existence at all. Some mythologies—those of Greece and Rome in particular—may have had features of beauty and charm; but all of them, in greater or less degree, were the sources of abominable cruelties and of what are now regarded as odious vices.

If we pass from religion to politics, from those long dead paganisms to recent history and the public affairs of today, we may quote any number of examples of imagination—irrationalism—causing great calamities. As an example I would take the theory of the Divine Right of Kings. For centuries Europe was plagued by that myth. It was the prolific source of tyrannies, followed by rebellions and revolutions, and of many wars between rival dynasties. This went on all through the Middle Ages, right into the modern world. The tragic experience of England during the century when the Stuarts were on the throne will at once come to mind. Many other examples could be given all over Europe, and in other parts of the world as well.

Moreover, we see how imagination separated from reason has been the cause of disaster in our own time. Undoubtedly, the greatest evil that has beset the modern world has been war. And in our two World Wars it has been carried to a record of destructiveness unmatched in all previous history.

The responsibility is generally assumed to lie with a sinful and foolish mankind. But that, too, is a figment. "Mankind?" said Goethe. "It is an abstraction. There are, always have been, and always will be, men and only men."

We come back again to our basic principle, the responsibility of individuals, and their actions, or their inactions, based upon their ideas.

The two great wars were the outcome not of the folly of mankind as a whole but of German militarism; and German militarism was based upon a philosophy of life. This was developed and impressed upon the nation by the state-appointed professors of the German universities,

led by the University of Berlin. This was not the humane philosophy
of Goethe, which was brushed aside and forgotten, but the barbaric
philosophy of Fichte, Treitzchke, Oswald Spengler, and their followers.
The whole of it, at bottom, rests upon myths. It was inspired by
Hegel's theory of the state—his doctrine that the state is a living entity,
real in its own right and supreme. "The state," he said, "is the divine
idea as it exists on earth . . . It is the ultimate end which has the
highest right against the individual."

This is nothing better than the Divine Right of Kings over again,
with a philosophic camouflage; and with no more substance; for any
state is nothing more than an organization of individual human beings,
who have come together to establish institutions for the better conduct
of their common affairs, and to maintain them generation after generation. A parliament, a government, law courts, military forces, local
councils, police, civil servants, schoolmasters—all these, and the like,
make up the state. About them there is nothing abstract. Without
their individual personal activities the supposed "living entity, real in
its own right" would vanish. It would no more exist than the dead
empires of Pharaoh, or the King of Kings of Assyria or of Persia, exist
today.

The great subversive movements of the present century—Fascism,
Nazism, and Marxism—all share a belief in this myth: indeed, it is of
the essence of their creeds.

In addition, it is allied with another figment—an imagined force or
principle that is supposed to govern human affairs, with such names
as "destiny" or "fate" or, more recently, "history" or "economic laws."
This renders all that happens "inevitable"—another keyword of the
communists. It is a revival of one of the basic ideas of Greek philosophy—"Necessity," *Ananké*—to which even the gods were supposed to
be subject.

As the outcome of all this, we have Mussolini, in June 1940, harangu-
ing a vast crowd in Rome and proclaiming "the hour marked out by
destiny is sounding in the sky of our country . . . The declaration
of war has been handed to the Ambassadors of Britain and France."
A month later, in Berlin, the Nazi Foreign Office issues a statement
saying: "Nobody now contests that Germany and Italy are predestined
to reorganize Europe on a new basis."

This faith in destiny by Fascist Italy and the Germany of Spengler
and Hitler resulted indeed only in defeat and utter ruin for its devotees;

but after how much physical suffering and mental anguish for tens of millions of people in Europe and over a large part of the globe.

Nevertheless the myth continues, under the name "history," which is imagined to be not only what it truly is, the record of past events and human and natural experience, indispensable to the present as a guide for the shaping of the future, but something more. History is regarded as a force, formless, undefined, but irresistible, which intervenes in human affairs and can *do* things. What is so formidable is that this idea has become the essential basis of a dynamic political creed, which is held by the effective leaders of nations comprising more than a third of the population of the globe.

I may quote chapter and verse, not from textbooks or newspaper articles, nor from anything said long ago, but from recent speeches by the two men who, at the present time, have together more power than any other two in the world—Mr. Khrushchev and Mr. Mao Tse-tung. The following passage is from a letter by the Russian leader which appeared in a London weekly journal in March 1958, in reply to letters from Lord Russell (Bertrand Russell) and Mr. Dulles. Mr. Khrushchev begins by saying:

Emotions are always emotions. The logic of facts is an entirely different matter. . . . If we base ourselves on facts, we have to admit that in our world today there are two world systems—the new Socialist system and the old capitalist system. Each is developing in accordance with its own inherent laws. And these systems were not born today or yesterday. . . . If you take a look at history you will soon become convinced that the new system was disliked by many at the time. History, however, did its job.

As to the Russian Revolution, he writes:

The people themselves acted on the arena of history, proclaiming their legitimate rights. And, in the long run, this is what will happen in other countries. This is what will happen both in the United States and in Britain, though there are no Soviet Communists there, nor will there be. Such is the relentless course of historical development, and no one can halt it.

The declaration of the Chinese leader was made on November 6, 1957, as the culminating passage in a speech in Moscow, where he had gone for the celebration of the fortieth anniversary of the Russian Revolution. I quote from a full report issued by the Chinese official news agency. After asserting China's hatred of war and firm opposition to a new world war, he said:

We firmly stand for peaceful competition between the Socialist and the capitalist countries, and for the settlement of the internal affairs of each country by its own people in accordance with their own desires.

But when he came to state the foundation on which their whole movement is based, he did so in these words:

In the end, the Socialist system will replace the capitalist system. This is an objective law independent of human will. No matter how hard the reactionaries try to prevent the advance of the wheel of history, revolution will take place sooner or later and will surely triumph.

I would draw your special attention to these final sentences, closely parallel to those of Mr. Khrushchev: "an objective law independent of human will," and "the advance of the wheel of history," bringing revolution which "will surely triumph."

All this is pure myth. There is no such "objective law"; there is no such thing as "history" imagined as an entity, a force, an agency, capable of bringing about political results on this planet, at this time, irrespective of what may be the opinions, ideas, and actions of any, or even of all, individual persons.

Here we have an example—and the clearest and most dangerous of any—of imagination running loose from reason. Accepted as a faith, by leaders wielding such power as these, it may do immeasurable mischief. Marxism, which claims to be based on reason, logic, and above all on modern science, is really based on a philosophic figment. The West, and almost all other countries which have not been prevented by military force from forming free opinions, have always seen clearly that communism is a tyranny. We should realize also that it is a tyranny based on a myth.

Man in the Cosmos

The prevailing frame of mind of the present generation—at all events in the Western World—is clouded by pessimism. I should like to argue, in this last talk, that there may be less justification for it than we sometimes think.

That there are some good reasons for pessimism cannot be denied. The two World Wars, and the Cold War still, with its terrible risks, the ever-growing armaments of the Great Powers, especially the nuclear bomb, threatening to poison the whole atmosphere of our planet; to this, many would add a weakening of religious faith, and a lowering of moral standards; with the daily catalogue in the newspapers—reported on the instant from every quarter of the globe—of riots, revolts, outrages, hideous murders and other crimes of brutal violence, famines, floods, air disasters—all this casts over our civilization a dark shadow of pessimism. One of our leading historians, G. M. Trevelyan, speaks of this era as "the fall of European civilization."

All this is not new. There have been such phases of opinion before and they have passed away. The stoic philosophy of the Roman Empire, for instance, holding that life is something to be endured, not enjoyed; or the asceticism and detachment of medieval Christianity. But there is one new and important difference between the pessimism of the ancient world, or of what has rightly been called the Dark Ages, and the pessimism of today.

In the present age science is predominant. And in the eighteenth and nineteenth centuries science was accepted by the intellectual world as assuring material progress and greater happiness through wider knowledge. But now it is different. Among the consequences of the scientific discoveries, some are seen to have brought new evils and the threat of unlimited disaster. There are even some who say that the world would be better and happier if modern science had never arisen. We find a mood of apprehension, of alarm, even of despair. But as an over-all view of the present situation and the prospects of the future, I think this is as wrong as wrong can be.

Let us consider some of the reasons that may account for this attitude.

In the first place, the aspect of the universe now given by astronomy is frightening. We know that the universe includes millions of galaxies, like the Milky Way of which the solar system is part, each with millions of stars, and possibly planets. Sir James Jeans—whose books popularizing science had great influence—drew the conclusion that "Man must reconcile himself to the position of the inhabitant of a speck of dust, and adjust his views on the meaning of life accordingly."

This seems to me an entirely false conception. From the philosopher's point of view, size is not what matters. Our measurements of size are arbitrary, and relative to ourselves. Nature knows nothing of our standards of distance large and small, or of time long or short. That we should feel "humble" because we are so much smaller than a galaxy would be as absurd as if we were to be puffed up with pride because each of us is so much bigger than an electron, in about the same proportion. It is not material bigness or smallness that is significant, but the range of mind—and, for us, of the human mind. Not humility because our planet is but as a speck of dust and our bodies infinitesimal in relation to the cosmic vastness, but rather a pride and an exaltation that our minds can transcend it—that is our right demeanor.

But astronomy has brought us another nightmare besides that. To quote Jeans again, he gave to the first chapter of another of his books the title *The Dying Sun*. In it he states, as the definite teaching of science, that our sun, like all the incandescent stars, is a wasting asset. It is continuously diffusing into space, at a prodigious rate, immense quantities of its initial stock of energy; the process has an enormous time still to run, but the end is inevitable. Bertrand Russell quotes from Jeans: "With universes as with mortals, the only possible life is progress to the grave"; and he adds that "from such depressing conclusions" he himself "sees no escape."

Nevertheless, further investigations have shown that what was regarded not long ago as an established fact is now found perhaps to be a false conclusion. The new nuclear physics has discovered that a countervailing process may be going on all the time. As fast as the sun's heat is being dissipated in space, it may be that the fusion, at enormously high temperatures, of pairs of hydrogen atoms—the same process that makes the hydrogen bomb possible—may be replenishing it.

So the nightmare that man and all his works, and all forms of life on this planet, and ultimately everywhere else as well, are doomed to an inevitable end, passing through universal cold and darkness to eternal death—that is now found, possibly or even probably, to have been too hasty an assumption. So that the spirit of man need no longer feel itself oppressed by this one, at all events, of the sources that have been at the root of the philosophy of pessimism.

The next point arises from the acceptance of the theory of evolution. No scientists, and few well-informed laymen, would wish now to challenge the main principle of Darwinism, that of natural selection, with its "struggle for existence" and "survival of the fittest." But one conclusion that has often been drawn from it, and still is, may rightly be challenged. At first, indeed, evolution was regarded as a powerful reinforcement for the optimists. Admittedly cruel in its method, it was welcomed as beneficent in its results. The individual might suffer, but in the long run this was of benefit to the species: it was a guarantee of the automatic progress of all forms of life to ever higher levels. But it is now realized that that is not so. For in the millions of years of evolution, as many kinds of plants and animals have declined and suffered extinction as are still surviving today.

Further, in the sphere of world history it was too hastily assumed that wars between nations also played a part in the evolutionary process; that they led in the end to the predominance of the more efficient and courageous peoples and therefore to the progress of mankind. But there is, in fact, no resemblance at all between the wars among nations and the biological struggle for existence; and when it comes, as now, to indiscriminate slaughter of tens of thousands, perhaps even millions, of people by nuclear bombs, the idea that war can be justified by such an argument is seen to be sheer nonsense.

So it is currently believed by some people today that we are left with a "nature red in tooth and claw," essentially cruel and callous. So far, at all events, the pessimists are on firm ground.

But that is not the end of the argument. To stop there would be to accept a complete misinterpretation of the facts of the case. To argue that conflict, struggle, death and elimination is the only, or even the main, mechanism of the evolutionary process at any biological level is to ignore opposite factors that are obvious all round us, and in the life of every one of us. Cooperation is not less essential to animal existence than conflict, and it is prior.

When the pessimist calls upon us to denounce Nature as callous and cruel, without mind, morality, or purpose, let us pause for a moment and ask what meaning we are giving to "Nature." In ordinary talk we are accustomed to speak of Man confronted by Nature; of Man sitting in judgment on something outside himself; and it is useful to have some word which can be used to express that idea. But such a differentiation is arbitrary and unphilosophical. When we take the universe as a whole it knows nothing of any such division. Man is himself a part of nature.

A. E. Housman, the author of "The Shropshire Lad"—a fine poet but the arch-pessimist of English literature—wrote of the hard fate of Man,

> For nature, heartless witless nature,
> Will neither care nor know.

But this is not really so. Man is himself the organ of nature which does bring heart and wit, which knows, at least partly, and does deeply care.

A present-day philosopher is nearer to the truth when he tells us that we are not reduced to a choice between two opposing views —either that the world is ruled by superior powers, by "essential destiny," or else that it is irrational, a gamble, governed by a mere wheel of chance. There is a third possibility: that *we* may introduce reason into it.

Throughout animal nature the care for mate and offspring, the family with its mutual aid; within human civilization, the whole vast structure of institutions for promoting the general welfare, the instinct of sympathy, the emotion of love—all these are as much a part of the evolutionary process as self-assertion, competition, and the failure of some as the price of success for others. Let me add a reference to the tremendous efforts now being made to meet the rapid increase in world population by a vast increase in food production, through irrigation and better husbandry, and the improving health of the cultivators in what have been the backward regions. Biologists will agree with this: they will tell us that cooperation no less than conflict has helped man to survive. But, more than this, they will tell us that man's conscious choice has become a factor in evolution.

In other words, we must realize as an essential factor that men, by their own decisions, affect the course of their own evolution.

It is true that, when we come to the conclusion of the whole matter, we cannot fail to see, as the main feature in the existing world situation, the possibility of war. If men have not learnt their twice-taught lesson, if indeed the world is to be devastated by another general war, or perhaps by a whole series of them, then, indeed, we must look to a future when all our hopes and plans must fail. Therefore our efforts in all countries, through all creeds and philosophies and political schools, must be to secure the elimination of war—not this war or that war, but war itself, from among the accepted institutions of the civilized world.

But if we can suppose that the time may come when we may be able to survey the human situation relieved from that obsession, then no ground would be left for pessimism. For when we try to view the cosmic process as a whole; when we envisage the birth of the worlds, the history of our planet, the coming of man, the growth of civilization; when we take account of the value of human free-dom, individual self-reliance, the moral law; and when we look round and see the achievements of science and art, and the profusion of simple things that make people happy—then, indeed, it seems a perverse folly to contend that the evil in the world outweighs the good.

(—1960)

THE SPELL OF MEMORY

The Portrait

❧⚬❧

FRANCIS HACKETT

H<small>E WAS</small> a big man, powerfully built, with a gaze peculiarly direct. In the tedium of our railway journey, as we sat together, he asked questions. I have met many people who ask questions, but this man was the most relentless, at any rate for a casual acquaintance. And what could be so casual as this acquaintanceship, not yet ten minutes old and carrying itself to me on the frail plank of his English?

But he had personality, this handsome Jew, he had force. The very fact that he slung his questions into me like a boathook, and dragged me to account for myself, had a certain boldness in it. And the queer thing was, he did not seem particularly interested in my answers. He listened, but without savoring what I was telling him. Something was on his mind.

All right, I said to myself, something is on your mind. I'd like to know what it is. Why shouldn't I ask a few questions myself?

He had pinned me down as to who I was, what I did for a living, how much rent I paid in New York, what I paid for my hotel last night, how much I expected to pay for my hotel in Rome, who I knew in New York, this judge, that financier, that Supreme Court Justice, this newspaper owner, that politician. . . . Well, why not turn the tables, why not delve into his soul?

So I began. In a few aggressive moves of my own, sweeping away the pawns, I had him back in Russia, back in his young manhood, back in his childhood. He was that most sympathetic and romantic of all Jews, the Russian Jew. But he had not been a radical. He was telling me about Odessa, and about his early struggles. It was a career of the old régime. Against what odds he combatted, and how he mounted, with what a power to grasp, yes, to grasp, ideas, money, opportunity, everything. It was formidable—and terrifying. He did not raise his voice. His shapely hands, well-cared-for, merely sketched an occasional gesture. But he talked freely. It relieved him to talk.

He needed this relief. Still vibrating with unspent force, restless with projects, he had been flung out of the world of success. The whole system he had won in was overthrown—he had been carried overboard, like a sailor in the typhoon. Yesterday he had been in control, a ruler. Today he was floundering outside. His very hand-bag was a bit of salvage from the old régime.

I became interested in him. He concealed nothing. He was definite. He was completely himself. I felt I was worthy of him, as he developed his story, since I was admiring him. And perhaps my admiration helped him, because pretty soon he was actually revealing himself, revealing the inmost passion of his nature, confessing the great love of his life.

"One thing I understand," he said, with his eyes alight. "One thing I love. Banking. I am a banker by instinct. I live, I feel myself live, when I walk into a bank.

"And I can tell men. In ten minutes' talk I can tell whether a man will ever make a banker. All over Russia there are men I singled out, men I discovered. That was my big work. I found the right men, I brought them out, I gave them their start, I knew them . . ."

He boasted. But there was passion in his boasting. It was as if he told of the great buildings that his people had once built, under the whip of the conqueror. It was like the Pyramids, like the Coliseum. He saw his banking grandiosely, and he enlarged on himself until he fitted his conception of his work. What was there for me to say in the presence of so luxurious a will? At first I had felt contemptuous of him, he was so coarse, so banal, so ostentatious, so impressed by the world of onyx pillars, velour hangings and shining chandeliers. And yet, as his judgment of New York began to appear in what he said, as he revealed the place of newspaper editors and idealists and politicians and national leaders and bankers, exposing the vast manipulation to which he had come as a stranger and yet which he had taken a hand in within a few weeks, I began to diminish in my own estimate, to see myself as a small ingredient in the frightful mélange of New York, to feel feeble, amateurish, under-energized. Unwillingly, and knowing my own reluctance, I thought: After all, this man knows. He has dealt with his Roosevelts. He has had his big industrials in his mesh. He just missed a gigantic dominion. Why didn't I understand the forces at work, why didn't I cut through the pious formulas as well as this stranger? I think I know life, and what is essentially important. But I see that I am simply a fly that crossed the window of New York, on the outside.

But now he was telling me something. It was about Art. Of course, art. Good God, so he knew Art too! Yes, grand opera, pictures, portraits. He was telling me about his own portrait, and in a queer, rather querulous voice.

"You must know the painter," he was saying. "I brought him over. He's my fellow-countryman, one of my people. He painted me. I have the painting at home. I'd like you to see it some time. It's a real portrait, but I don't know why, he's painted me with my hands dripping with blood!

"Dripping with blood. I—I don't really understand it. But it's as if I were a beast of prey!"

The man's whole face was changed. He was no longer certain. He was hunted. He turned his eyes on me, and in their depths I could see agony and bewilderment.

I pitied him.

"You know," he said, so low the noise of the train almost drowned it, "I asked him why he did it."

"Why did he do it?"

"I don't know. First he said it was the light of the sunset reflected on my hands. But I pressed him. Then he said, 'Well, that's the way I see you, Vladimir!' That's all he'd say."

There was silence. He watched me closely, but I could not speak. I looked at him, with his sombre face, his faintly curved body, his slightly red lips. His compatriot had seen him.

We passed through a tunnel.

Now his voice was clear again, as we came out. He was back on banking. His face became animated.

"Do you know how much I was earning by the time I was thirty?" he asked in the simplest of mild voices, with a light smile, "one million francs a year!"

(—1924)

Seder

BERNARD GORIN

PALTIEL, as his wife would often remark, let nothing eat his heart. "Passover? Why are you worrying now about Passover? Here winter has only just begun, and you are already breaking your head with worry." And shifting his heavy cap to one side, he scratched his head meditatively.

But that was in early winter. Before its end, even Paltiel was disturbed. Even he began to wonder where the few extra *groschen* for the holidays were coming from.

Paltiel was a carrier. Each week he made the trip from Rapshansk to Vilna and back again, leaving early Sunday morning, and, if the roads were good, returning Thursday before dark. But if the way was bad and the roads muddy with rain, as they often were, he was lucky to get home in time for the Sabbath singing of *Lecho Dodi* in the synagogue. But after the raw, cold road there was home, with the rooms hot as a bath, as Paltiel liked them. Off would come his greatcoat and Paltiel would expand in the heat.

But with Passover so near at hand and with wood so dear, he was forced to be content with a house almost as damp and chilly as the road itself. But Paltiel did not complain. He would climb to the top of the oven and play there with the children their favorite game of "Fools," while Sosye sat and stripped goose feathers.

For Sosye had done more than worry—she began to deal in geese, and if what she made was little enough, at least there would be *gribenes* for the children to eat with their bread and goose-fat on the coming Passover.

Paltiel, too, was willing to do what he could to add to the weekly income, but what more could he do? He had never been one to refuse an extra passenger or an extra bundle of goods, even when it meant giving up his own seat; and often it happened that he went all

the way from Rapshansk to Vilna on foot, walking alongside the
wagon. And if the way was bad, as when was it not, he would help
the horse by giving the wagon an occasional shove, from which he
gained that odd habit of his of suddenly lifting his right shoulder every
once in a while. . . .

Paltiel began to look around for odd jobs which ordinarily he
wouldn't have bothered with. No parcel was too small, no errand too
trivial, if it promised an extra *groschen* or two—a pot of goose-fat for
a married daughter in Vilna, a loaf of black bread and a few cheeses
for a son studying in the *Yeshivah*—a little package here, a little
package there. Passover was coming and Paltiel could not be particular.

Yet with all his efforts, and pinch and scrape as Sosye might, they
could manage to save nothing. During the long winter months, Mirel
took sick and the doctor had to be sent for, at ten *groschen* a visit;
and there was medicine, which was not cheap either. Purim came and
passed, and Sosye, more worried than ever, declared with a sigh that
only through a miracle could they hope to bring in the Passover.

By now Paltiel was not so optimistic. He pulled at his pipe, filling
the air with thick clouds of bitter smoke from his cheap tobacco and
said nothing. Sosye coughed.

"What about the *podrad?*" asked Paltiel at last. "They should be
starting to bake *matzo* any day now."

"I have already spoken to Ephraim. I shall work as a roller. Moshe
can pour water, and Mirel sift flour."

"P-f-f-f!" He blew another cloud of smoke, turning his head to one
side for his wife's sake. "Then why, stupid, are you so worried?"

"The children's earnings can't be depended on. Besides, Moshe needs
a new pair of boots, and Mirel a new dress. They are children and
their holiday must not be spoiled."

"Sh-h-h. Don't worry. With God's help we will manage everything,
and we will have a Pesach such as all Jews have. Goose-fat you have,
and *matzo* you will get for nothing at the *podrad*. So now the only
thing you need is flour. I say, don't worry. We will yet have such
kneidlach as. . . ."

He shoved his pipe in his mouth, and it remained a matter of con-
jecture what sort of *kneidlach* they would have.

That night Sosye could not sleep for a long while, marveling at
how wisely God had ordained the world. If there was a Passover, there

was a *podrad* where poor people could earn a few *groschen* to prepare for the Passover. True, it was miserable work at the *podrad*. One stood on one's feet fourteen hours of the twenty-four, and kneaded dough until one's hands were swollen and one's whole body ached. But what did it matter, so long as one could make Seder. She fell asleep with the calm thought that He who dwelt in Heaven was watching her from above.

It was quiet in the *podrad*. The workers stood around a long table, swaying their bodies back and forth like so many shadows. Their feet were heavy; their arms were like stones; their palms were puffed up like pillows; their limbs ached; their heads were as if filled with lead; their faces were sleepy, white and tired.

No one jested; no one tried to be witty; it was quiet except for the slight noise of the rolling pins, and of the perforating wheel over the metal sheet of the table. Sometimes there was a sigh or a yawn— a long drawn-out, weary yawn.

The heat was suffocating. The sweat dripped from them, but no one fanned himself; it was too much effort even to wipe the sweat from one's brow.

They were finishing the last of the customers' *matzoth;* the chief kneader had flung himself at last upon a stool; the roller girls, too, were finishing up; only Sosye, too tired to finish the last piece, was still kneading dough—dough which seemed iron in her hands, so tired she was. The roller girls sat down, one after another; the work had stopped at their tables; the man at the perforating wheel was finishing off a few remaining *matzoth*. These done, he quit the wheel at last, giving a joyous bang on the metal sheet with his rolling pin, and stretched himself full length upon a bench. Only the baker remained standing at the oven.

The few remaining *matzoth* were taken from the oven and gathered together for the packages. The baker straightened himself out, placed his hands upon his hips and delivered himself of a long, drawn-out *"oy!"* which began at the top register and descended to his lowest.

The fire was stirred afresh. The baker seated himself on a corner of the bench, and folding his arms, puffed at his pipe and stared thoughtfully into the fire. Moshe, who had been pouring water for the dough, crawled under the wheeler's table, and straightway fell asleep. Mirel, too, was fast asleep, with her head on a heap of empty flour bags.

For an hour all was quiet. It grew dark and the proprietor lighted the lamps. Sosye and her children were up again, and busy near the huge batter dish. The roller girls began to waken, and as they awoke, to grumble.

"Where is it written that at *bedikas chometz* one must be kept standing at the *podrad?*"

"Such an injustice has not occurred since the world began," murmured another, "to be tortured in the *podrad* at *bedikas chometz.*"

But the work went ahead with a vim. The *matzoth* they were now baking were for the employees of the *podrad*. Things were livelier now. The wheeler began to sing a shady song. The roller girls tittered; the young married women smiled; and the older ones hurled maledictions upon his indifferent head.

"May he strangle! . . . He sings. . . . May he sing for the last time!"

Toward daybreak, the work waxed even more furiously. The wheeler sang and jested with more spirit; the roller pins beat a merry tattoo upon the hard metal sheet: the wheel squeaked as it turned—and no one, watching the workers, could have told that all of them were more dead than alive.

Suddenly they were through. Sosye and her two children with the rest immediately received their wages and their *matzoth* and ran home as quickly as their legs could carry them to prepare for the Passover.

Arriving home, Sosye hardly knew where first to turn. She worked in a frenzy, complaining as she worked. Housewives worked for weeks, cleaning and making ready, and she had the one day. Forgetting her aching body, her tired feet, she dashed about like mad. Lucky she had somehow cleaned the bed and table and scrubbed the floor the Saturday night before. Otherwise God alone knows how she would have managed.

She drove the children from one place to another, giving them not a minute's rest. Run here and borrow a mortar, borrow a strainer, borrow this and that. Moshe wanted to sneak away to the cobbler's to see how his new boots were getting along, for which he was paying with his own money. Mirel was dying to look at her new dress. But there was no time. They must help mother.

And Sosye did the work of ten. By two in the afternoon, all *chometz* was out of the house; sand had been scattered over the clean, scrubbed floor and a piece of matting thrown over it. The freshly scoured pots hung shining in their proper places; the beets were scraped of their greyish film; the oven was cleaned; the fish and meat prepared for cooking. And still Sosye could not rest.

All day they had run to the window and looked out. But finally the sound of approaching wagon wheels caught them unawares. Moshe and Mirel ran hastily to the window, and before Sosye had time to turn her head away from the oven, they had cried out together.

"Look! Father! Father has come!"

Sosye's face glowed with happiness. She ran to the window. Moshe and Mirel were already out in the yard, opening the gates for the wagon.

Paltiel rubbed his horse dry, and led him to the stable.

"How are you? *Ai!* I am late; so late today." This was his first greeting as he entered the house.

His hands, his boots, his coat bound around his waist with a leather strap, were all covered with mud. What a luxury it would have been now to be able to wash, to change his clothes, but there was no time. There were still several bundles to be delivered to the shopkeepers, and money to be collected. And it was late, late. He hurried out with his bundles.

Returning, dead tired, there were other tasks for him to do: fresh hay to be prepared for the horse; wood to be chopped for the holidays; the Passover dishes to be carried down from the loft; his boots to clean and grease. These done, it was almost dusk.

"Snatch a *kartoffel*," begged Sosye. "Take a potato; you must be famished."

He complied, and burned his mouth in his haste.

"*Nu*, Moshe," he said, with his mouth full of hot potato. "Take the bottles, and come with me after wine."

Moshe seized the two bottles, one for mead and the other for wine, and departed gleefully, knowing well that the wine dealer would give him a glassful for himself. Paltiel took a small flask in his pocket for Passover brandy. "Let us have a Passover as becomes *people*." Paltiel and Moshe hastened away.

On the way back there was the bath to be visited. From it they both returned, red and glowing. It was now quite dark.

No sooner had they entered than "Run! to the synagogue," cried

Sosye, driving the men folks from the house, "You may yet snatch a *brocha!* And don't forget to bring *choresis* from the *Rov.*"

Paltiel donned his gaberdine, once of black satin, but now green with age, Moshe his new boots; and together they hurried away to the *Beth Hamedresh.* When they returned, the table was already spread, with a clean tablecloth over the matting. Four *Ma Nishtanah* candles burned brightly in the center; the *matzoth* were prepared and covered with a white towel; in a plate was placed a boiled egg, and the half roasted neck of a goose. The bottle, and the cups filled with wine were at hand. All was in readiness, except the horse radish, which Paltiel grated in the opening of the chimney, that the odor might not enter the room.

Paltiel covered his shoulders with his white prayer shawl and seated himself at the table, leaning on two cushions. Mirel ran to put on her new dress. Sosye went into the kitchen.

"Eh-eh, you are sleeping already," said Sosye, approaching the table.

"Who—I? No," said Paltiel, awakening with a start from his half doze.

He filled the cups with wine; one for himself, one for Sosye, and one for Elijah the prophet. The cups for Mirel and Moshe he filled with mead.

"Moshe! you sleep."

"No, no . . ."

Paltiel opened a dusty Haggadah.

"*Kiddush!* When a Jew returns from *shul* he says *Kiddush!*" And he began the benediction.

"Blessed art Thou, Lord our God, King of the Universe, Who hath chosen us for His people . . ."

"I can't find the Haggadah," said Sosye, and Paltiel turned the pages of her *Korban Mincho* to the proper place. Meanwhile Sosye fell asleep.

"So, now you are asleep," said Paltiel triumphantly, turning to show her the Haggadah.

"My eyes are like glue."

At the end of the *Kiddush,* Paltiel drank his cup of wine with relish. "Marvelous wine!" And he smacked his lips.

The preliminary prayers come to an end at last, "*Maggid!*" exclaimed Paltiel suddenly, and they began the Haggadah.

Keholachmo was finished. Moshe asked the four questions in a sleepy voice, and Paltiel answered sleepily.

"Slaves we were unto Pharaoh in Egypt . . ." The last word trailed. Paltiel caught himself with a jerk.

"Slaves we were unto Pharaoh in Egypt, and—the Lord—released—us—with a mighty———ha-a-and. Ch-r-r-r."

"Paltiel, you—are sleeping—already?"

"Ha! Slaves we were unto Pharaoh in . . ."

"Paltiel! Moshe! Wake up!"

"Slaves we were unto Pharaoh in Egypt . . ."

For a while all was quiet.

"Are—you—sleeping?"

"Ch-r-r-r."

It is daybreak. The horse in the stable neighs. Paltiel and Sosye and the two children sit drugged with sleep around the festive table.

Paltiel is dreaming he is still on the road. It is thawing; everywhere are great pools of water; by the side of the road the snow is still hard, and covered with a dark film. The pale rays of the sun are glowing, melting the snow, and the dirty water trickles to the center of the road.

Paltiel walks by the side of the wagon. The poor horse can hardly drag his feet along, and steps heavily and slowly. The wagon is loaded to the very brim. Paltiel is worried. How late it is and he still so far from home! He has not had a wink of sleep for many hours, and his heart bleeds for the poor horse; he has not been able to spare the time to give him his fodder.

Far off a verst-post is visible. Still twenty versts to be crawled over before the end of the journey—twenty versts over such a road, with such a load, and a worn-out starved horse! But the fear that the holidays might find him still on the road makes Paltiel forget his weariness; summoning up all his remaining strength he pushes the wagon along with his broad shoulder. The horse, as if thankful for the help, steps faster; the wagon moves more speedily. Paltiel becomes hopeful; the horse has yet strength to go on.

Another verst-post is seen in the distance. That was good time, says Paltiel happily, but all at once—Stop! Heavenly Father! A wheel of the wagon has stuck in a hole filled with mud and water. The horse strains to pull it free, twists about and stamps, but all in vain.

"Up! Up!" cries Paltiel in a hoarse voice. He bends low, gathers up his strength for one great effort, pushes his shoulder under the side of the wagon, and lifts it with all his strength into the air.

✦ ✦ ✦

Paltiel, Sosye, Moshe, Mirel awake with a start. The table is over-turned; the bottles and plates are broken; the wine is spilled. An egg has rolled away, over to the threshold.

Translated from the Yiddish by Elizabeth Gorin

(—1927)

Mrs. Sigmund Freud

꧁꧂

ESTI D. FREUD

"**F**RAU PROFESSOR! Frau Professor!"
"Yes?"

The frail distinguished old lady at the Chippendale desk raised her eyes from a letter in surprise as the door of her living-room was opened suddenly, without even a knock.

"Why are you so excited, Paula?"

"Thirty Nazis armed with guns are storming our entrance door!"

The frail lady's eyes returned to her letter. "Surely, Paula, you did not expect the Nazis to come with flowers."

The Nazi gangsters ransacked her home so thoroughly that there was not enough money left to buy food for the next day. This outrage was neither the first nor the last of her trials; but to keep perfect calm amidst the most turbulent situations was one of the remarkable qualities of Mrs. Sigmund Freud.

As her daughter-in-law, I had the pleasure of living in close proximity to her for twenty years; and during those years, through war and revolution, through sickness and death, again and again I was able to observe her self-control and equanimity.

I was told that her greatest attraction for the young Sigmund Freud had been not her slender grace or charming features but her inner peace and serenity. She radiated calmness; and he sensed instinctively how wonderful it would be to have her near him after a day of hard work.

When they became engaged Freud was not yet established as a psychiatrist. He did scientific research at the Physiological Institute in Vienna, a poorly paid job in the old Austrian Empire. Consequently, Mrs. Freud's family tried to discourage her from marrying a man whose prospects seemed so poor.

She is now eighty-six and lives in London. In her most recent letter

to me commenting on the pending marriage of my son—her grandson
—she wrote: "Do you remember the prediction the family made for
my future? It turned out differently than they expected! We were
obliged to wait four years to be wed. It was such a torture! Today
youth is more courageous; they marry and go to college, and somehow it works out. How shocked everybody was when the first rent
of Dr. Freud's office and apartment was paid with the little sum I
brought with me as my dowry."

"How was *Pappá* when he was young?" I once asked.

Her face lit up with a smile; she was eighteen again. "Oh, he was
the most charming and fascinating man I ever met. Everybody who
came to know him wanted to do something nice for him."

For me, the newest member of the family, the most striking impression of the Freud household in 1919 was its unchangeable, rhythmic regularity—so compulsory that everyone who lived there was
caught up in it. At five minutes before the hour my mother-in-law,
Mammá, would look at the clock and say: "In five minutes *Pappá* will
be through with his patient; I hope he is not tired."

If a visitor was with her whom she knew Dr. Freud liked, she
would say: "You stay! The Professor will be glad to meet you." But
if it happened to be somebody who might be bothersome, she said:
"You had better go now. I am sorry, the Professor will be in a hurry
and can't see you."

At the stroke of the hour the door of Dr. Freud's office, which was
connected with his private apartment, opened and Dr. Freud came out.
My recollection of his walking through all the rooms is still vivid,
just as if it happened yesterday. He was a tall, slim, slightly bent man;
his blue searching eyes and a tremendous forehead dominated his
face. A small well-trimmed beard was the only concession he made
to the typical "Viennese professor."

Dr. Freud would greet the children and their friends with a cheerful
grunt, smile at his wife and, leaving in his wake the smoke of his
inevitable cigar, return to his office. When the door closed behind
him, my mother-in-law sometimes said with a sigh: "It is too bad
Pappá has a headache; maybe his office is overheated. I had better
check on it." Mrs. Freud needed neither words nor complaints to
know how her husband felt.

The performance of this hourly cycle was something like a holy ritual. It seemed to me that Dr. Freud walked through the apartment on a visit to his family once every hour to gather new energy for his difficult task, just as the giant Atreus must needs go down and touch Mother Earth to regain strength before he could go on fighting.

Dr. Freud had to lead a most carefully planned life to be able to accomplish his tremendous amount of work. From nine to one he saw his patients. At one o'clock sharp he was served lunch. From two until seven he again had office hours. At seven he dined, and then until midnight he wrote the books in which he proved to be the Columbus of the human mind. Observing him I learned that to be a genius it is not enough to have the creative spark; one must also have the courage and physical energy to persevere.

In the choice of his wife Freud was guided by his lucky star. She knew how to remove from his path all the common annoyances of everyday life. He was not permitted even to take a tie or a handkerchief from a drawer: everything was prepared for him. Mrs. Freud understood how to imbue the household—children, family, guests, servants—with such love, admiration and respect for the great man who was her husband that all of them submitted with pleasure all the circumstances of their lives to Freud's work and well-being. (My mother-in-law's attitude contrasted sharply with what I had been accustomed to see at my own home where my father, in worshipful adoration of my mother, adjusted his life to all her wishes.)

Mrs. Freud's task was not an easy one. She had six children to rear, three boys and three girls. In addition, the family nephews and nieces were left in her care. "I had enough trouble with all those children," she admitted. "They had the measles and scarlet fever at the same time, and I had to watch out that those with the measles did not catch the scarlet fever. We were twelve at the dinner table during these years."

But, whatever happened, nothing was permitted to disturb Dr. Freud's work and schedule. During all the fifty years the Freuds lived in Vienna there was never a day when the soup was not on the table exactly on the minute. At each meal Mrs. Freud had a pitcher of hot water and a special napkin at her place, so that if anybody made a spot on the table cloth she could hurry to remove it. Only her husband was permitted to make as many spots as he wished.

Although Mrs. Freud did not directly cooperate in Freud's work, she was to a great extent his Egeria. Readers of the *Interpretation of*

Dreams, which appeared in 1900, may remember that some of Freud's fundamental discoveries were made by observing his own children. Mrs. Freud was his assistant in helping to transform the nursery into a psychological laboratory. But the children were not to know they were being used as guinea pigs. "Above all, the family must be normal," she said.

For many years the world would not admit the validity of Freud's discoveries. He thus shared the hard unjust fate of many scientific explorers. He stood alone amidst a sea of hostility. It was Mrs. Freud's unshakable admiration and unfaltering belief in her husband which made that isolation easier to bear.

If God has favorite children, Mrs. Freud is one of them. Nevertheless she was not spared the cruel strokes of a merciless destiny. Her beloved young married daughter Sophie died suddenly in February 1920 from an attack of Spanish influenza. Four years later Dr. Freud underwent his first palate operation, from the effects of which he never completely recovered; it was followed by a series of painful surgery throughout the rest of his life.

About that time, however, Dr. Freud suddenly became world-famous. Patients, pupils and celebrities from all over the world flocked to see him. These guests brought many new responsibilities for his wife, since Viennese hospitality required that they be entertained. Moreover, she had to help many of them find their way around Vienna since they could not speak German. She helped them find apartments and buy tickets for the opera. She went with the ladies to the dressmaker and to the beauty parlor; she gave advice to funny "Hokinson women" on how to transform themselves into seductive and chic *femmes fatales*—sometimes a rather strenuous job.

At Christmas and other holidays, as a sign of grateful appreciation, Dr. Freud's admirers deluged the house with flowers, mostly orchids, as they were known to be Freud's favorite. The apartment looked like an exotic tropical garden. "If they would only send their flowers on the installment plan," Mrs. Freud remarked wistfully, "we could enjoy them all the year round."

People with vivid imaginations, averse to bringing "commonplace" flowers, thought of more personal gifts. Princess Marie Bonaparte, for instance, surprised the Freuds with two precious chow puppies. My father-in-law loved to play with them and enjoyed them very much;

hence, to keep them in good health became a constant concern of Mrs. Freud. Nevertheless she held the opinion that somehow *Pappá* spoiled them too much.

Every day she went to the most exclusive delicatessen shop in the city to get fresh tender ham for Dr. Freud. But when, during the meal, he fed the chow dogs with Vienna's best ham instead of eating it himself, she was justified in remarking that the ham from the neighborhood store would have been good enough for the dogs, and anyway their favorite dessert was the edge of the antique Persian rug in the dining-room.

So when an eccentric patient brought an exotic viper from a South American snake farm, she categorically refused the gift with the excuse: "I don't know a thing about the diet for reptiles."

Freud's last birthday in Vienna was overshadowed by the threat of Nazi persecution and by impending emigration. Books were packed, furniture moved; the beautiful home built up with so much work, love and artistic understanding was in a state of disarray. Everyone was depressed.

My birthday present was intended to cheer them up a bit. I brought a huge cake on which was cleverly painted in icing a map of the "Western world." This world was populated with readers of Freud's books. A tiny sugar Eskimo sat on the North Pole reading *Totem and Tabu.* On the South Pole a penguin lingered over *The Interpretation of Dreams.* In South America an Indian labored over *Civilization and Its Discontents;* while Uncle Sam studied a volume of *Psycho-pathology of Everyday Life.* When after much hesitation Mrs. Freud cut the cake, she reasoned: "This is a nice present, Esti; at least it is something I don't need to pack."

In June 1938 they departed for England, where Freud became the recipient of various international honors. Mrs. Freud never accompanied her husband to receptions at which these honors were bestowed upon him; she always sent her daughter Anna in her place. Once, when pressed to appear, she argued: "I shun any kind of publicity. I believe in the proverb that the best wife is the one about whom the least is said."

She certainly was the "best wife." In one of her latest letters to her granddaughter she wrote: "I wish for you to be as fortunate in your marriage as I have been in mine. For during the fifty-three years I was married to your grandfather, there was never an unfriendly look or a harsh word between us."

This letter is truly a document of a successful life. To be loved and cherished a lifetime by one's husband is indeed an accomplishment of which any woman may be proud. If the husband happened to be Sigmund Freud, this accomplishment made Mrs. Freud *par excellence* "a grand woman."

(—1948)

Fish Suppers

✦

EDWIN SAMUEL

A<small>N</small> earnest young man was John G. Branson, Junior, with red hair and a crew cut. He called at my office in Ramallah with a letter of introduction from an American I had known at Oxford. The note said that Branson was coming out to Palestine to get material for a thesis on American influence in the Middle East, and would I help him.

I was delighted, of course, as the Ramallah Sub-district thirty years ago never got any publicity. There were no Jewish settlements in it—it was far too mountainous and arid. Under the Turks there had been a steady drain on the manpower of this impoverished area. Some young men had been drafted for life into the Ottoman Army; others had got away to the United States to make some money.

But the Ramallah emigrants had not done too well on the whole. Only a few had made any money and had returned to their villages to build a house, buy a horse and an extra wife. Most had come back with little more than a broad American accent and flashy ill-fitting clothes. A few were too poor even to be able to get back to their wives and families.

There was, however, a steady trickle of remittances from the United States into my sixty hill villages. According to the banks in Jerusalem, it amounted to at least a third of the income of the sub-district. America, even in those days, helped to feed Palestine's hungry mouths. And their minds as well. For, back in Turkish days, the American Quakers had founded a large boys' school and a large girls' school in the little town of Ramallah itself. It was in the boys' school, with the amiable Mr. Clarke, that John G. Branson, Jr., stayed for a week during his investigations.

Of course I had to invite him round to the house several times for talks. He lunched with my wife and me the day he arrived; he came round a couple of times more for a drink. I took him in the car to the more accessible villages; and we called, of course, on the new Mayor of Ramallah, Elias Eff. Shehadah.

The Mayor received us effusively in his office in the Municipal Building. That was a grand name for a two-roomed stone house at the end of a narrow cobbled alley. The Mayor—when he was not out in his vineyards, supervising his laborers—sat in one room. The chief clerk, accountant and typist sat in the other. This was not as crowded as it sounds, as they were all one person.

Elias Shehadah had, of course, been in the United States—in the city of Shicawgo—as he called it; but many years before. He had forgotten much of his English and relapsed into Arabic from time to time. I had to translate, which wasn't too easy, as the Mayor poured out an endless list of improvements he was about to effect in the town. As I knew he had nothing in the till, I wondered how he was going to finance all this. But I didn't want to belittle my sub-district in Branson's eyes; so I kept quiet, which was unfortunate.

For Branson was immensely taken with the Mayor: an excellent example of how modern American ideas of city development were finding their way into the remote recesses of Asia. Branson wrote everything down, and I was terribly afraid he would put it all uncritically into his thesis and make us all look ridiculous. The last straw came when Shehadah declared, just as we were leaving, that he had been elected Mayor by the largest majority ever known in Ramallah.

So on our walk back to my office, I took the opportunity of telling Branson the facts. "It wasn't at all like that," I said, "really. It's true that Shehadah was elected last January; but so were half a dozen other Councillors. He wasn't elected Mayor at all: I appointed him. Between ourselves, he's rather an old humbug, especially with visitors, if you'll excuse my mentioning it. I only hope that a tenth of those plans of his will be carried out. It'll take years, anyhow."

"But isn't it true what he said—that he's the most popular man in Ramallah?" Branson asked, looking up at me with troubled gray eyes.

"There isn't such a thing as general support for anyone in any Arab town. In spite of their European clothes, they're still in the Scottish Highlands of the sixteenth or seventeenth century. Everyone belongs to a clan; the different clans are all struggling for ascendancy. There's hardly a village around here where I can appoint a single headman. Usually I have to have two Mukhtars, one for each clan. In one village

I have six! Ramallah's not a village any more: it's got 3,000 inhabitants —quite a town by Palestinian standards. But it's still got its clans— seven of them. That's why there are seven members on the Municipal Council, one for each clan or *Hamuleh,* as we call them round here— although three of the clans are very small, and hardly count.

"So, you see, none of the Municipal Councilors could possibly have any support outside the members of his clan. And the worst thing about it is that each owes loyalty primarily to the clan, not to the town, much less to Palestine as a whole. And all those public works the Mayor talked so glibly about, they'll be jobs for the boys, if I'm not careful; you know—most of the laborers on the new drains he wants to put in will be the poorer members of his own *Hamuleh.* Not that he'll really go ahead with drainage: he's out for something flashier, that everyone will see, like street lamps. He knows nothing about drainage and cares less. He even asked me if he couldn't econo- mize by using the same pipes for water by day and drainage by night!"

"Say, that's good!" said Branson. "Do you mind if I make a note of that?"

"Well, I'd be happier if you didn't. It'd be bound to get back to him. Let's call it off the record."

"O.K., if that's how it is. But why did you decide to appoint Mr. Shehadah as the Mayor and not someone from another clan? Do they take it in turns or something?"

"Well, look here, Branson: if you'll promise not to put this in your thesis, I'll come clean and tell you the whole story. It's rather amusing, really. It all came about accidentally, I'm afraid—through the Fish Suppers."

"What on earth are they? Arab feasts?"

"Not a bit of it, I'm afraid. On the contrary, you might say—the thin end of the wedge of Westernization. There isn't any fish up here in the hills. It has to be brought up specially from Jaffa at vast ex- pense, all covered with ice. There isn't even a fish shop in Jerusalem. So it's the greatest mark of hospitality—if you want to be really ostentatious in Ramallah—to give a fish supper.

"Well, I only came here six months ago myself. And as ill luck would have it, the old Mayor, George Odeh—a grand man he was, it seems—died the week after I took over. Threw a spanner in the works. Everything upside down for weeks. We had to have new elec- tions and then *I* had to choose the Mayor. You can imagine the intriguing that went on! The three smaller *Hamulehs* didn't count. But the other four! The wire-pulling that went on, even in Jerusalem. One of them was clearly out, as he came from the previous Mayor's family and I couldn't possibly allow a family claim to the job. Another was an old scallywag—a building contractor who narrowly escaped being jailed last year for bribing Public Works. That left two contenders— Elias Shehadah and John Marroum. Both big landlords: both been in America: both terribly anxious to be Mayor. Hardly anything to choose between them."

"How did you choose?"

"It was an accident: but for God's sake don't tell anyone that. This is *really* off the record. The four leading *Hamulehs* all knew I was trying to be impartial. I told them so in a speech I made at old man Odeh's funeral. I took the best advice I could, here and in Jerusalem. I asked everyone what they knew about Shehadah and Marroum— even our friends at the school, the Clarkes. Some plumped for one, some for the other. I was being very careful and was terribly afraid of making a mistake so soon after my arrival.

"Then one of the families took a bold step in inviting me to dinner, so that I should get to know their Councilor. I couldn't, of course, go to one house and not to the others. Within a few hours the other three families all invited me too. (Everyone knows everything in this town.)

"Perhaps it would have been better if I hadn't gone to any of them. But I really did hope to be able to make up my mind this way; and I must confess that I'm very partial to Arab food.

"The trouble was that there wasn't any. All four families wanted to appear terribly sophisticated. Shehadah and Marroum had both been in the States; and there were several leading members of the other two clans who'd also been there. They all knew how one entertained in America. Western food; knives and forks; everyone sitting round a table. And, of course, a fish supper. No chicken, or anything local like that, not even a lamb stuffed with rice. That might do for the villages. Ramallah was a town: *they* were civilized. It must be a whole fish brought up from Jaffa. And if one family had it, all the other three had to, of course.

"And that's where the absurd business all started. The little hotel in Ramallah—the Bellevue they call it, but they spell it *Bellview* now that we British have arrived—couldn't cope with real dinners. Or, at any rate, was not considered *chic* enough. So they sent in to Jerusalem for a cook.

"But there's really only one good Arab hotel in Jerusalem—the New Grand Central, by the Jaffa Gate. So out they bring the Grand Central's cook, a funny little man who had a waiter's black jacket. After he'd cooked the dinner in the kitchen of the host's home, he came into the dining room and served it. All very civilized.

"Well, *the pièce de résistance.*"

"The what?" asked Branson.

"I'm sorry: I meant the main dish. It was, of course, this whopping great fish—about two foot long, and flat, on a great silver-plated salver the cook-waiter had brought out from Jerusalem for this purpose. He'd made gallons of mayonnaise and had poured it all over the fish and the dish. After it had set, he had decorated the fish in wonderful geometric patterns with bits of black olive, green pepper and red tomato. Looked magnificent. At least, the first time I saw it I was so surprised at this *chef d'oeuvre*—I mean masterpiece—that, in my formal speech of thanks, I complimented the host lavishly on the superb fish, and the wonderful mayonnaise and the beautiful way it was decorated. The cook-waiter stood there against the wall, his face covered with perspiration, beaming with pride.

"A few days later, I went to the second dinner and there was the same waiter and the same fish on the same silver dish.

"I pretended, of course, that I'd never seen any of them before. I gasped with well-mannered surprise when I was asked to help myself to the fish. They all knew that I'd had the same thing only a few days before; but that didn't matter. So I got through that evening somehow, without making a blob.

"The third was already a bit of a trial. I caught the waiter's eye as he struggled round the table—they always invite many more people than they have room for. He gave a slight grin and I'm afraid I did, too.

"The fourth evening—at Shehadah's—was really the limit. I'd got tired by then of that fulsome speech. So I cut it down a bit. I said it was a superb fish: that I'd never seen a finer [*loud clapping by the assembled company*] and left it at that. I then went on to talk about my host's career. I'd learnt quite a lot about the four families and their Councilors at these dinners; but I still couldn't make up my mind between Shehadah and Marroum. Anyhow, I was as complimentary as usual; but I noticed the rather perfunctory applause when I sat down. Or was it that I was getting a bit tired myself of all this hospitality and particularly that self-same fish?

"Anyhow, when the dinner was over I walked home alone in the brilliant moonlight—you know how fantastic these moonlit nights out here in the hills are: you can read a paper without any other light. As my wife was waiting up for me, I was hurrying up the road. She, of course, hadn't been invited: it was men only, in the usual Arab way.

"Just as I turned the corner into the main road—over there, where we've now come from—I heard someone running after me. 'Ya Hakim! Ya Hakim! Oh Governor! Oh Governor!' I stopped and turned. It was the cook-waiter. 'What's the matter?' I asked. 'Has anything gone wrong?' 'Yes, indeed,' he gasped. 'You have blackened my face to-night: Elias Eff. is furious with me.' 'I have blackened your face?'

" 'Yes, Your Excellency. Tonight, for the first time, you didn't say anything about my mayonnaise and the patterns I made on the fish with black olive, green pepper and red tomato. Weren't they good too tonight? What have I done wrong? You have cost me my tip, Your Excellency, and much future customers. Oh, Your Excellency!'

"I couldn't explain to him the real reason—that I was so heartily sick of him and his fish, too. But I had to be impartial: I'd promised to. So instead I made Elias Shehadah the Mayor."

(—*1956*)

That Evening in Taurus

M. Y. BEN GAVRIEL

WHENEVER I escape from that prison in the city called my home and find myself walking at sundown through a valley overcast with the violet glow of twilight and with a sky streaked in shreds of drifting copper clouds—then that evening in Taurus comes back to me, poignant, vivid.

A jagged, narrow, saddle-back ridge falling between steep mountain cliffs and immeasurable canyons. On the saddle a barracks, over whose roof flaps a red flag bearing the crescent. Gurgling camels laden with mighty packs. Turkish Askeri hurling themselves in prayer upon the bare ground. A masked Kurd with his gun swung crossways over his saddle. Hindu prisoners with thousand-year-old visages and incredibly noble bearing. Over it all the sun, pouring gleaming metal on the cliffs, sinks behind the pine stockade. It is evening in Taurus.

Below, close to the steel rails they were laying, the Hindus sat shivering around a small fire, holding their palms over the glowing faggots. The reflection of the flames crept straight up against the surrounding pines and intermittently lit up their faces.

One of them spoke in low tones (he had been a student in Oxford). "That is our enemy who thinks himself above us, who does not understand us, and who clutches at our throat; this is the spirit for whom we are preparing the way." He pointed to the steel rail on which he sat. "Here Europe rolls over us, to coin greedy riches from our soul, sets brother against brother, wholesale murder, callous efficiency, eternal misery. In its mad pursuit of activity, the destructive urge of this inhuman civilization reaches out for the soul of Asia."

He looked up and stopped short when he realized that I was listening. He did not know that I was a Jew, an Oriental like himself, in whose veins flowed the spirit of the East, despite centuries of European life.

I walked over toward the camels and sat down on one of the packs.

Fifteen Hindus squatted around the fire and looked mysteriously into the flames. Out of fifteen Hindus, one is sure to be a Sikh—a fanatic whose cry of despair is a bloody knife. His pulse is too swift, he cannot wait until our Oriental spirit, victorious, will imbue the world with the idea of an asiatic Asia.

As though seized by a cramp the Sikh threw himself suddenly into the air. He hurled a cry into the night which lingered curdling and bloody, a mad desperation and an uncontrolled will.

The cry startled the Askeri out of their huts. Terrified and not knowing what was happening, they stood above in the dark, staring at the Hindus below. Then a drunken German under-officer drove the Hindus to their sleeping quarters.

A Sikh was surely among them, they obeyed so unresistingly.

The last of them to pass me was the student. I took courage to greet him: "I am Jew."

He understood me. He reached out his hand and answered, "Brother?"

Half of Europe lies between you and me, Mother Asia, and more than that the bitter failure of my blood-brothers to understand; they hear not the call of Asia and do not recognize the heart-rending cry of a mother for her children.

I will be gone from this earth a long time and all traces of me wiped out in the Great Nameless, but the Idea will live on from the east sea to the west sea, from Pekin to Jerusalem. Bridges will be flung from one to the other over which will pass the new man of Asia, free from Europe, chaste and noble. And where once Europe's profit-sucking "progress" raged, the soul of the Orient will dwell, that soul for whom the moral life, love and spirit are more than business, efficiency, and the bestial gluttony of utilitarianism.

Hearken, my brother, hearken then to the call of our Mother: *Choose!*

(—1925)

Seder at Grandpa's

❧⧫❧

MARGHANITA LASKI

W E ALWAYS came up from Manchester for Passover, myself and
my brother and sister, Mummy and Daddy and Nanny. And
coming from Manchester to London was to us, as to those original
Israelites, the release from bondage, the arrival in the Promised Land.

In Grandpa's house the old night-nursery was made over to us. His
house was tall and square and had six bedrooms. One belonged to my
great-grandmother, one to the maids, and one of course to my grandparents. My grandparents had thirteen children, and in the early years
seldom more than one was away. I can't remember or begin to think
where the others slept.

The preparations for Passover had begun long before we arrived.
Every piece of table-china normally used by the household had to be
put away and others brought out. The table-silver—at Grandpa's a
confusion of heavily wrought Georgian and Penny Bazaar—had to
boiled and purified. Every scrap of pre-Passover food was given or
thrown away. For the eight days of Passover only food that had been
passed as entirely clean and pure by the Beth Din could be eaten
either in the house or out of it.

For at least a week the Passover brown eggs had been simmering in
huge saucepans at the back of the kitchen range. These were eggs
stewed in a broth of cinders, coffee-grounds and onion skins until they
were dark brown from shell to the center. We ate them as an *hors
d'oeuvre,* sometimes with salted water, sometimes mashed up with
potato and goose-fat. They were entirely delicious, and we never had
them except at Passover.

The food began to arrive. Cheese and white unsalted butter from
Holland; pale translucent goose-fat from Rumania; unbelievably nasty
wines from Palestine; and *matzoth* from the same East End shop that

had been supplying them to English Jews almost since Cromwell allowed us to come back here again.

These *matzoth,* which had to suffice entirely for bread during the whole Passover week, were of infinite variety. Some people had heavy squares, hardly to be distinguished from those biscuits served with cheese in railway trains. But we had round ones, some huge, about two feet across, lying like cartwheels in piles down the dinner-table; and little thin six-inch *matzoth* for tea.

Plates, with *matzoth,* were a mockery. The *matzoth* were as fragile as eggshells, and only the very light-handed could spread a whole circle with butter or chicken or goose-fat without them crumbling to pieces under the knife. They seemed to get everywhere—all over the tablecloth, all over your plate, even into your wine glass. You ate much too much of them because there was nothing else to take the place of bread. True, there were little round sweet cakes called prelatoes that arrived fairly fresh and soft; but by the end of the week they were as hard as the stalest sponge cake, and as they were believed by Nanny in the nursery to be more digestible than *matzoth,* we had them with milk instead of porridge in the mornings and for every other meal when she could conveniently substitute them. By the end of the week we could hardly swallow the sandy lumps. But as an additional precaution Nanny always took care that Passover began and ended for us with a whopping great dose of Syrup of Figs.

It began with going to bed after lunch in our combinations.

Each year came the same argument. "Nanny, please mayn't we read? Nanny, must we go to sleep?"

Normally Nanny insisted on sleep. The curtains were drawn and through them the afternoon light filtered into the room. One lay in bed and stared at the picture of the stork with a beswaddled baby in its beak striding gravely through a reeded lake—why, one wondered, had it come down from its flight, or hadn't it started yet?—and at the bulbous crimson-and-white and emerald-and-white urns of Nuremberg glass that stood on the grey marble mantlepiece. Occasionally a drip would fall noisily from the tap in the corner; from the mews outside floated in the strange raucous cries that to me, at least, meant London once more.

Downstairs a furtive "Here we go round the mulberry-bush" was being played.

We never sat down to dinner much less than forty. Tables were placed end to end in the drawing-room to make one continuous if frequently uneven festal board. Whether the chairs were hired or pulled out from here and there I don't know.

But there remained the placing of the name-cards.

In a good year when the youngest aunts were feeling cooperative we had some beauties. One year Lulu drew an appropriate emblem on each, another year Bertha identified us with Shakespearian quotations—I had "She was a vixen when she went to school"—and as Bertha's knowledge of Shakespeare was infinite and her sense of fitness frequently in abeyance, a great many cards had to be altered before they could appear on their plates.

So Granny, accompanied by a responsible daughter, would revolve slowly round the table with the name-cards. I don't know the principle on which she worked, but it was probably that trouble must be avoided and personal feelings mustn't be hurt.

There were certain well-established precedents as fundamentals: an unmarried daughter must dish up at the lower end; a married daughter could help Granny up at the top; Great-Aunt Alice must be next to Grandpa in the middle, and on his other side must be the son who would read the prayers for him that night, for Grandpa was blind; space must be left for temporary migrations from the children's table in the corner when the sense of loss on the part of parent or child became intolerable; and the year's batch of cousins from Germany and Rumania must be fitted in somehow.

After Granny's perambulation was over a married daughter would slink in. Contemptuously, authoritatively, yet with an uneasy furtiveness, she would shift a card here, a card there. Mother had put her little daughter next to a profligate uncle: must the past year's careful teaching be undermined all over again? Mother hadn't tried to split up the younger ones at all: it would be intolerable if their so-called witty conversation should again dominate the table. Did Mother really think that one's husband would be happy next to old Miss X who was an intolerable bore but had been young when Mother was young? The cards were slipped from plate to plate and the married daughter left the room, sternly assuring the maids that *no one* else was to be allowed in.

But somehow the maids had gone down to the basement when the youngest uncles and aunts came to impose the final order. That impossible Rumanian cousin with the perfumed hair-oil could be stuck next to a great-aunt. Young Rudi from Hamburg could be slid into the bottom and best end of the table. And sometimes, if uncles and aunts were particularly kind and Mummy particularly busy, I could be slid in there too.

With such a large family there was nearly always the bridesmaid's frock from the latest wedding to be worn for Seder night. Combination sleeves were rolled up, only to slide down again during prayers; the top combination button was left undone and the flap safety-pinned back; there were silk knickers and bronze dancing-sandals. My long and mousy hair was released from its curling-rags to fall in uncertain ringlets topped by a new bow. We were already feeling over-full from our first tea of prelatoes, for no *matzoth* could be eaten till after the evening service. Uncles and aunts were dressing all over the house, the older ones into proper evening dress, the younger into afternoon frocks and neat suits. Each man provided himself with a hat to wear during the prayers when no male head must be uncovered. Grandpa would wear his crimson fez with the black tassel, and some of the men would wear black silk or paper skull-caps. Even the little boys must bring down their school caps or, at the least, a mother's hand must lie over their heads while prayers were being read.

Grandpa and the men came back from synagogue and slowly, with constant readjustment and comment, we were all in our places around the long table.

To a child the Passover service, which so unfortunately preceded the meal, seemed interminable. One recognized its high spots—the glasses of wine drunk with this or that blessing; the *charoseth*, a thick spiced jam handed round in little parcels of lettuce-leaf to remind us of the mortar our ancestors laid between the bricks in Egypt; the herbs dipped in salt water to remind us of the bitterness of their affliction; the lamb-bone lifted from the dish in memory of the slaughtered Pascal lamb. There was the moment when I carried round the water ewer and slashed a few drops over the hands of each guest; the moment when the youngest child able to do so stood on its chair and, prompted by a proud and anxious parent, asked in Hebrew, "Wherefore is this night different from all other nights . . . ?" and was given an incomprehensible answer. There were the questions asked by the sons, the wise son, the foolish son, the wicked son who said, "Wherefore do *ye* do these things?", thereby dissociating himself from the company. And there was that grand moment when the door of the room was flung open and we knew that one year—and it might be this year—the prophet Elijah would walk in and foretell the coming of the Messiah.

It was, I believe, at this moment when no stranger who comes may be refused that during the Middle Ages and very very much later a stranger would come with the body of a dead child hidden under his cloak. Later the law or the soldiery or the mob would arrive and discover once again that the Jews slaughtered Christian children for their Passover feast. A great many of us would be killed and next year the rest of us would sit round the table again.

Each guest was provided with a book of the service—a Haggadah. At Grandpa's some of these were very old indeed. There is a counting rhyme in the service—"Who knows one? I know one. One is the unity of God. Who knows two? . . ."—and in the older books *nine* were the nine months preceding childbirth and if you were lucky you got a book with a woodcut of a massive woman in a farthingale swooning into labor. But the modern editions that came from America said that nine were the nine holy festivals of the year.

At last—and how long it seemed every Jewish child will remember—the hats and prayer-books were cleared away. Up the red stone stairs from the basement clumped the maids with the brown eggs and mashed potato, with the traditional soup with its *matzoth kleish,* bullet-heavy little savory balls—but that was the stage when the children were cleared off to bed.

As the oldest grandchild, I was usually allowed to stay. I would sit, admiring and envying, among the younger uncles and aunts while they argued, shouted, disputed, quarrelled, always with the utmost wit. I heard better talk at Grandpa's on Seder night than ever since, and I can remember the passing of the years as I remember the things they talked about.

In the earliest years they talked about Barrie's *Peter Pan.* Then it was Bernard Shaw, and then the I. L. P. to which they all then belonged. With this last, of course, went Maxton and a weekly paper called *The New Leader.* One year it was Katherine Mansfield, then *Lady Chatterley's Lover,* then *Ulysses.* Lately it was the Labor Party; but soon those who were members would not publicly discuss such esotericism and fell back on the old sport of laying bets on the probable protagonists of the first family row to break out that evening.

But dinner was finally over and soon prayers would start again. While the débris was being cleared away the younger ones would sneak up to the old nursery at the top of the house for a surreptitious cigarette and I, if I could evade my mother's watchful eye, would go with them. There would be endless shoutings and fetchings before we were all assembled round the table again, the men's heads covered once more, for Grace.

Grace was almost as long as the service before dinner. But it was infinitely gayer. Once the really serious Hebrew prayers were over we settled down to singing Hebrew and Yiddish nursery-rhymes with wild enthusiasm. The tunes were good, the words were fun, the years had hallowed both with the status of prayers and such prayers we could wholly enjoy. Till we came to the last song of all, a sort of "House That Jack Built" with far less climax, that was invariably sung by one of the lady guests in an over-trained and over-fruity soprano, assisted on the last note of all with a cacophonous chord from the entire family.

Then quickly my mother succeeded in packing me off to bed. And I would usually go without too much reluctance, knowing that a whole week of *matzoth* and brown eggs and goose-fat lay ahead.

But it was always annoying that we couldn't buy buns to eat when we were taken for our annual visit to the Zoo.

(—1947)

Zudechkis Makes Himself Useful

❧

ISAAK BABEL

THE house of Liubka Schneeweiss, nicknamed Liubka Cossack, is located in the Moldavanka part of Odessa, at the corner of Dalnitsky and Balkovsky Streets. The place contains a wine shop, an inn, a feed shop, a number of other shops, and a dovecot for one hundred couples of Kriukov and Nikolaiev pigeons. The shops, as well as Section 46 of the Odessa quarries, belong to Liubka Cossack, but the dovecot is the property of the watchman Yevzel, an ex-soldier with a medal on his breast. Besides this watchman there live in Liubka's place also Pesia-Mindl, cook and procuress, and Zudechkis, the manager, a tiny Jew, whose size and beard make him look like our celebrated Moldavanka rabbi, Ben-Zechariah. . . .

I know a number of engaging tales concerning this Zudechkis, but none better than the story of how Zudechkis became the manager of Liubka Cossack's inn.

Some ten years ago Zudechkis acted as broker in the sale of a threshing machine to a landowner. In the evening he took the landowner to Liubka, to celebrate the purchase of the thresher. His client had tufts of whiskers prolonging the line of his moustachios, and he wore patent leather boots. For supper Pesia-Mindl served him Jewish gefilte-fish, and later she brought him a very nice young lady, named Nastya. The landowner stayed for the night. Toward morning Yevzel, the watchman, woke Zudechkis, who had snuggled up in the form of a pretzel by the threshold of Liubka's room.

"Look here," said Yevzel, "yesterday you bragged of the landowner buying a threshing machine through you. Well, know you then that he ran away at sunrise like the last scoundrel. It's clear that you're a fraud. Shell out now the two rubles for refreshments and four rubles for the young lady. It's clear that you're a tricky old rogue."

But Zudechkis refused to pay. Yevzel pushed him into Liubka's room and locked the door.

"So," said the watchman. "Stay there. By and by Liubka will come from the quarry, and she will, with God's help, pull your soul out of you. Amen."

"Convict," answered Zudechkis, and began to examine his new abode. "You don't know anything, you convict, outside of your pigeons, whereas I also trust in God who will bring me out of here, as he brought out all the Jews, first from Egypt, then from the wilderness. . . ."

The little broker had a lot more to say to Yevzel, but the soldier took the key out of the keyhole and departed, clattering with his boots. Zudechkis turned around and observed Pesia-Mindl, the procuress, reading by the window a book entitled *The Miracles and the Heart of Baal Shem.* She was reading this Chassidic book with gilded edges, rocking with her foot an oaken cradle. In the cradle lay Davidka, Liubka's son, and he was crying.

"A fine order of things I see on this convicts' island of Sakhalin," said Zudechkis to Pesia-Mindl. "Here lies a baby and tears itself to pieces, so that it's a pity to look, while you, fat woman, sit there like a rock in the woods, and you can't give him the nipple."

"Give him the nipple yourself," answered Pesia-Mindl, without turning away from the book, "if he'll only take the nipple from you, old fraud that you are. See how big he is already, a regular rowdy, but he wants only mama's milk, while his mama is galloping through her quarries, drinking tea with Jews in the Bear Tavern, buying contraband at the wharf, and thinking of her son as much as of last year's snow."

"Yes," the little broker then said to himself. "You're in Pharoah's hands, Zudechkis."

He went over to the eastern wall, mumbled through the whole morning prayer with the supplements, and then he picked up the crying child. Davidka looked at him in bewilderment, and waved his raspberry feet wet with baby sweat. The old man began to pace the room, and swaying from side to side, like a rabbi in prayer, he struck up an endless song.

"Ah-ah-ah," he sang. "Here's figs for all the babies, and here's cracknels for our little Davidka, that he may sleep day and night . . . Ah-ah-ah . . . Here's fists for all the babies . . ."

And Zudechkis showed to Liubka's son his tiny fist covered with gray hairs, and proceeded to repeat about figs and cracknels, until the boy fell asleep and the sun had reached the middle of the shimmering skies.

The sun reached the middle and trembled like a fly overcome by heat. The savage moujiks from Nerubaysk and Tatarka, who were stopping at Liubka's inn, crept under their carts and sunk into a savage sonorous sleep. A drunken artisan staggered to the gate, hurled apart his jack-plane and saw, flopped to the ground, and launched into a snoring challenge to the whole world, his face and body all in golden flies and blue July lightnings. Nearby in the shade sat a group of wrinkled German colonists, who had brought wine for Liubka from the Bessarabian frontier. They lit their pipes, and the smoke out of their twisted tubes began to stray in the silvery bristles of their unshaven aged cheeks. The sun hung down from the skies like the pink tongue of a thirsty dog; far off an immense sea was rolling up on the strand, and the masts of the distant ships swayed in the emerald water of the Odessa bay.

The day was seated in a many-colored skiff, the day was rowing up to meet the evening, and only toward evening, about five o'clock, Liubka returned from the city. She rode up on a roan nag with a big belly and a shaggy mane. A young chap with thick legs, clad in a calico shirt, opened the gate for her, Yevzel held the horse by the bridle, and at that moment Zudechkis shouted to Liubka from his jail: "My respects to you, Madam Schneeweiss, and good day to you. Behold, you've gone off on business for three years, throwing a hungry baby into my arms . . ."

"Shut up, you mug," answered Liubka and came off the saddle. "Who is that there gaping out of my window?"

"That's Zudechkis, a tricky old rogue," spoke the soldier with the medal on his breast to the mistress. He began to tell her the whole story about the landowner, but he did not bring the story to its end, because Zudechkis broke in, screeching at the top of his voice: "What impoodence," he screamed and threw his skull-cap to the floor, "what impoodence to throw your baby into my arms and for you to go off to perdition for three years. Come up and give him teatie."

"Here I am coming to you, old fraud," muttered Liubka and ran up the stairs. She entered the room and scooped the breast out of the dust-covered waist.

The boy drew up to her, bit sore her monstrous teat, but got no milk.

On the mother's forehead a vein bulged out. Meanwhile Zudechkis was saying, shaking his skull-cap: "You want to grab everything, greedy Liubka. The whole world you drag to yourself as children pull a table-cloth with crumbs on it. You desire the first wheat and the first grapes. White loaves you want to bake in the heat of the sun, while your little child, such a baby, like a little star, has to languish without milk . . ."

"Milk nothing!" bellowed the woman, turning aside and pressing her breast. "What milk can there be when today the *Plutarch* came in port, and I made fifteen miles in the heat! And you, it's a long song you're singing, old Jew—better come out with six rubles."

But again Zudechkis refused to pay. He rolled up his sleeve, bared his arm, and thrust into Liubka's mouth a lean and dirty elbow.

"Choke on that, you female convict," he said and spat into the corner.

Liubka held that elbow in her mouth for a moment, then took it out, locked the door, and went down into the courtyard. There she had been already expected by Mr. Trottiburn, who resembled a pillar of ruddy meat. Mr. Trottiburn was the *Plutarch*'s first engineer. He had brought along two sailors, one an Englishman, the other a Malay. Together the three of them dragged into the courtyard the contraband which they brought from Port Said. The box was heavy, they dropped it to the ground, and out fell a shower of cigars entangled in Japanese silk. A throng of women rushed toward the box, and two stray gypsies began to flank it, swaying their hips and rattling their beads.

"Away with you, trash!" Liubka shouted at them, and she led the seamen off into the shade, under the acacia. There they seated themselves at a table. Yevzel served them wine, and Mr. Trottiburn unwrapped his wares. Out of the pack he produced cigars and fine silks, cocain and files, unlabeled tobacco from the state of Virginia, and black wine bought on the island of Chios. Each and every ware had its price, and after each and every figure they drank Bessarabian wine that smelled of sun and bedbugs. Already twilight tripped across the courtyard, twilight ran across like the evening wave on a broad river. Full of astonishment, the drunken Malay touched with his fingers Liubka's breast. He touched it with one finger, then with all the other fingers, one at a time. His yellow gentle eyes hung over the table like paper lanterns in a Chinese street. He began a song under his breath, and dropped to the ground. Liubka nudged him with her fist.

"Look at him, how well he knows his ABC," said Liubka about him to Mr. Trottiburn. "I am losing the last drop of my milk because of this Malay, and that Jew over there has already gobbled me up for that very milk."

She pointed at Zudechkis who was standing by the window and washing his socks. A little oil lamp was smoking in the room, and a small tub was frothing and hissing in front of Zudechkis. Sensing that they were talking about him, he leaned out of the window, and screamed with desperation.

"Help! Save me, people!" he screamed and waved his arms.

"Shut up, mug!" Liubka guffawed. "Shut up." She threw a stone at the old man, but missed him. She grabbed then an empty wine bottle, but Mr. Trottiburn, the first engineer, took the bottle from her, aimed carefully, and threw it into the open window.

"Miss Liubka," said the first engineer, rising and gathering up his drunken legs, "many worthy people, Miss Liubka, call on me for goods, but I sell to no one, neither to Mr. Kuninson, nor to Mr. Baty, nor to Mr. Kupchik, to no one but you, because your conversation pleases me, Miss Liubka."

Firmly establishing himself on his tremulous legs, he gripped the shoulders of the two sailors, the Englishman and the Malay, and started dancing with them across the cooled-off courtyard. The men from the *Plutarch* danced in profoundly pensive silence, while an orange star that had rolled down to the very edge of the horizon gazed at them with wide-open eyes. Then they received their money, and holding one another by the hands they went out into the street, swinging like suspended ship lamps. From the street they could see the black water of the Odessa bay, toyish flags on the vanished masts, and piercing lights kindled in the spacious bowels of the sea. Liubka had seen her dancing guests to the crossing, was left alone in the deserted street. Laughing at her own thoughts, she went back home. The sleepy young chap in the calico shirt closed the gate behind her, and she went upstairs to sleep.

In her room she found Pesia-Mindl, the procuress, dozing, and Zudechkis rocking the oaken cradle with his little bare feet.

"Akh, you've tortured us to death, heartless Liubka," he said and picked the baby up from its cradle. "But learn from me, nasty mother."

He placed a fine comb to Liubka's breast, and laid the baby by her side in the bed. The son drew to his mother, the comb pricked his mouth, and he began to cry. Then the old man offered him the nipple of the milk bottle, but Davidka turned away from the bottle.

"What sorcery are you playing over me, old fraud?" mumbled Liubka, falling asleep.

"Keep still, nasty mother," he answered. "Be still and learn from me, may perdition come upon you."

Again the baby got hurt by the comb, hesitatingly it took the nipple of the bottle and began to suck greedily.

"Behold," said Zudechkis, and laughed loudly. "I've weaned your baby. Learn from me, may perdition come upon you."

Davidka lay in the cradle, sucked the bottle, and exuded blissful saliva. Liubka awoke, opened her eyes and shut them again. She had seen her son and the moon that was breaking in through the window. The moon was skipping amid the clouds like a lost calf.

"Well, all right," Liubka said then. "Pesia-Mindl, open the door for Zudechkis, and tomorrow he may come for one pound of American tobacco."

On the next day Zudechkis came for one pound of unlabeled tobacco from the state of Virginia. He got that and in addition a quarter of a pound of tea, extra.

And one week later, when I came to buy pigeons from Yevzel, I noticed a new manager in Liubka's courtyard. He was as tiny as our rabbi, Ben Zecharia. The new manager was Zudechkis. He kept his position for ten years, and during that time I learned many stories about him. And if I can, I shall tell them all, because they are very engaging stories.

Translated from the Russian by Alexander Kaun

(—*1929*)

An American Boy in Keidan

❧❧❧

BERNARD G. RICHARDS

M Y FIRST childhood recollections go back to early mornings in my grandfather's house at the end of Smilga Gass in the Lithuanian town of Keidan. I remember fearfully cold mornings when the windows were covered with ornate designs wrought by the frost, allowing but little daylight to enter the dim large *stoob,* or living room. It was lit up only by a smoky kerosene lamp, sometimes augmented by candles and burning *balonas,* or faggots, stuck into crevices of the huge brick oven. I recall the crunching of the snow and ice under the creaking wheels of the peasant wagons passing our front door on their way to the market to dispose of their products. After a while the blazing fire in the stove would add illumination and warmth and cheer to the room.

My maternal grandfather, Yakov Herz Sirk—everybody called him Herze Yankel—usually rose with the first signs of dawn. Often he got ahead of the dawn. "I work fast, I eat fast, I sleep fast," he would say. He loved company and conversation so much that whichever grandson was staying with him at the time was roused from his sleep soon after the fire was lighted and the morning activities begun. His method of waking the children was to walk through all the rooms and call out, "Get up, children— it's six, seven, eight, nine o'clock! Get up, children." Or he would announce to my grandmother that it was high time to get up and start household affairs going because *"Der bettler is schein in ziebetin dorf"* (The itinerant beggar has already since morning reached his seventh village!).

For the visiting little grandson to climb down from the high warm sleeping perch built into the oven, to dress and wash and hurry through the morning prayers, the incentive was to participate in all the early household operations. There was wood chopping, there were odd repair jobs around the house, butter churning, preparations for cheese making, to say nothing of feeding the cows and the chickens and perhaps a goose or a couple of ducks. If the domestic animals—including the all-wise Spitzka, the dog—had been increased in numbers by the arrival of a new-born calf, then the barn back of the house was the special center of attraction.

My grandfather was not satisfied with the regular arrangement for the pasture of his cow in summertime. A Polish shepherd boy would come every morning, assemble all the "Jewish cows" from the street in a vacant lot, and then drive them all to a field "up the hill," a distant and nebulous spot. At the close of the day the shepherd would bring them back to the border of the town; then, ready to be milked and fed, the animals would come plodding through the streets and find their respective homes and barns. My grandfather, however, must needs get in an hour of pre-official pasture. When it was still dark he would take the cow out and give her a special treat of some high, sweet, luscious grass, in a spot near the town that only he knew how to find.

In all the household chores, multiplied by the restless energy of my grandfather, the six-or-seven-year-old grandson somehow was credited with making practical suggestions and thus was prematurely promoted to chief assistant and adviser. In this elevation he undoubtedly found compensation for the minor status bestowed upon him by two elder brothers, who always played more vigorously, fought harder, and ran faster and swam better than he did.

My grandfather's intrusions and improvisations in the housekeeping tasks of the family were largely actuated, aside from the need of letting out his surplus energy, by the special interests of the domestic animals. Whether in handling cereals, cutting bread, preparing vegetables or fruits for cooking, he would so manage as to leave behind sufficient surplus or waste to benefit beast and fowl. My grandmother Reva, rising much later than her husband, would be horrified to find several pots filled with peeled potatoes, turnips, carrots or beets, with the peeling so thick and lavish as to redound only to the advantage of the livestock. Then too, as the amount of vegetables prepared was far above the immediate needs of the family, the animals would benefit some more. Grandmother would scold in her mild, restrained manner. Grandfather would explain and apologize. But he remained incorrigible to the end, just as he never ceased being proud and boastful among his neighbors of the fine sleek appearance of his animals. As for the exploits of Spitzka, faithful guardian of the home, protector of the chickens and the ducks, the children and the grandchildren—Spitzka, who one dark night returned from a distance of over fifty miles, after having been sold for a sum much needed by the family to a dog-fancy-ing *poritz,* or landowner—how could one stop talking about Spitzka?

My grandfather's home, where I spent so much of my childhood, is more familiar to me than the successive domiciles of my parents. Grandfather's house, built of logs partially covered with boards in the primitive manner of the time, was the last but one on the street named after the river Smilga and paralleling its winding course. In the rear of the houses were truck gardens extending to the river's bank. This was the lower end of the town. The last house on the street, also built of logs with straw-thatched roof, belonged to my grandmother's brother, Baruch Kamber, whose family hailed from a *dorf,* or farm settlement, not far from Keidan, called Kanebersz. The road at the end of the street, passing the soldiers' barracks and stables on the right and the drill grounds on the left, led to the open country with fields and woods on all sides.

A quarter of a mile below the town was the bridge which crossed the deepest and widest section of the Smilga. Farther away, about four miles from the town, was the railroad station, a place of special wonder to the children, who would occasionally be taken there. The arrival of the train pulled by a bellowing and clanging engine, the ceremonial waving by the flagman to hold all bystanders back, the formal salute of the station master to the conductors in their military-style uniforms as they alighted from the cars and in most resounding Russian announced the name of the station and length of the stop, the emotional meetings between arriving passengers and their friends, the frantic farewells as the loud bell over the engine signaled imminent departure —this was enough thrill and excitement to last a young lifetime.

The railroad was of course our chief means of communication and contact with the great world outside, or at least with the large cities of Russia, which then held Lithuania as well as Poland under its domination. Beyond were far-off marvelous cities and lands about which we children spun our fancies, drawing upon tales we heard from our elders about Germany, France, England and, above all, miraculous America to which a good number of natives had betaken themselves and from which they sent letters describing incredible happenings.

Up this open road, which connected with all the outlying farm settlements of Lithuanian and Polish peasants, came all the traffic from those sections. The farmers, with their crude wooden wagons heavily loaded and drawn by stalwart country horses, wended their way up Smilga Gass to the center of the town and the main market place.

It was the practice of the small traders and brokers, the *hendlers* and *meklers,* of Keidan to converge on this street and walk down the road as far as the bridge in the early morning of the market days, usually Mondays and Thursdays. There, accosting the incoming farmers, they would start negotiations with them while in transit. *"Zo mas pseditz?" "Ko turo pardot?"* (What have you to sell?) was the usual question, spoken in Polish or the more difficult Lithuanian.

If the two parties struck it up right, or if they knew each other from previous dealings, the peasant would invite the prospective purchaser or agent to jump on the wagon and take a seat beside him. They continued their discussion as they rode on together toward the center of the town. The subject of the bargaining might be several bushels of wheat or corn, or a few bags of potatoes, or some pairs of ducks or chickens contained in a covered basket in the back of the wagon. If a price was agreed upon, the trader would ride with his host into the town, looking proud of his capture of business. In less favorable circumstances the trader would walk along beside the farmer's wagon until his last offer was either accepted or rejected.

Some of these *hendlers* and *meklers* were old colleagues and cronies of my *zaide,* and his warm and always hospitable house at the foot of the street, in the path of their pursuit of trade, offered a welcome retreat on stormy and severely cold winter days. These early morning visitors would be asked to join us at the meager breakfast table and offered some hot tea or coffee with perhaps a *beigel* or a slice of *chala.* After hours of exposure to the raw and biting Russian frost this was a most grateful opportunity to warm up and relax for a few minutes.

Above this drab existence of uncertainty and privation as I now recall it, over this sordid haggling and bargaining, rose a gleam of hope for those harried people, beckoning like a rainbow of promise—from far-off America. To that land of mystery and wonder some of our younger neighbors and friends had emigrated, traveling singly in advance of their families; while the less adventurous denizens of our town had sent their sons to explore the new country. These husbands and sons soon sent rosy reports and remittances that served not only to raise the spirits of their families but to keep the Russian wolf from the door.

During their fleeting moments of rest the motley and weary chasers after the perambulating market would stop to dilate on their news from the distant and incredible land. Not the least quaint in these conversations was the naming of the various centers of population in the New World, from which letters and messages and moneys were received. Outside of New York and Brooklyn, cities less known, like Philadelphia, Boston, Baltimore, were bewildering appellations. Philadelphia was called "the Second America," Boston "the Third," Baltimore "the Fourth"; and any new city discovered was given an additional number, until perhaps Chicago became "the Sixteenth America."

Reflecting upon other episodes of those distant days I recall, more distinctly than other incidents in my boyhood, not the turmoil attending my arrival in America—with the excitement of entering Castle Garden and being taken on another long journey to a place called Brooklyn—but the return from the United States to my native town of Keidan in old Lithuania. Then I had the thrill of being hailed as "an American boy," a strange phenomenon who was followed and admired for months, and whose unheard-of English speech was listened to with awe and wide-eyed wonder.

Like most immigrants of that time before the turn of the century, my father had sailed for America ahead of the family with the expectation, which all those doughty explorers shared, of sending for their wives and children a year or two later, after securing some economic foothold. But my father did rather better, or worse. He had proceeded to the New World with the eldest of three boys, and sent for the rest of the family after a little less than one year, long before he was well enough established in his small dry-goods business.

My mother's shrinking nature, with an almost morbid dread of noise and excitement, her rustic small-town habits of life, her utter inability to adjust herself to the bustle and rush of New York existence —even in those calmer days—served to aggravate a situation which was much more difficult and complicated than the average problem of adaption to a new bewildering environment. After prolonged discussion in the family circle and consultations with *landsleut*, it was decided that my mother and the two younger children—myself, aged eight, and a younger sister of seven—return to the home country to live with our grandparents in Keidan. Since the old folks had their own home, with some small means of subsistence, it seemed best that we stay with them for a year or two, or until such time as my father would be more firmly settled in the new land.

Traveling back to Europe we experienced anew all the hardships, perplexities, and mishaps of steerage passengers. Then the long train journey through Germany, from Hamburg to Kovno, with many changes, stopovers, and losses of baggage, gave our mother such anxiety and anguish that she was driven to distraction. Whatever luggage was left, after most of it had been lost or stolen on the way, was taken in charge by traveling agents or guides who pretended to befriend us in the name of some society. They offered to take us across the frontier all right; but they never came back with the bags and satchels of clothes they had promised to deliver. We were pushed and hustled into another train before we could ask any questions.

At the station four miles out of Keidan we arrived with only one traveling basket of belongings. But we wore American clothes, and that was enough to attract attention.

No sooner had the crude wooden wagon which served as a *droshke* driven up to our grandfather's house than we became the cynosure of all eyes. All the neighbors of Smilga Gass flocked to the end of the street and surrounded the house to catch a glimpse of the new arrivals from the far-off land of wonder. Those who were not invited, or could not be accommodated indoors, shamelessly stared in through the low windows of the small log house to see the guests from abroad. All day long people went back and forth peeping, tiptoeing, expostulating and chattering about the Americans who had come to Keidan, and especially about the "American children."

After a day or two the hubbub subsided. No longer afraid of the advances of the curiosity-seekers, my sister and I at length ventured out of doors to renew our acquaintance with the street, the things around the house, the vegetable patches in back of the row of houses. These sloping grounds, now cleared of their harvests, were trampled on by the youngsters of the neighborhood for a direct route to the pebbly and purling River Smilga running below. But instead of their usual frolic and play at the river-side, the children persisted in following around the two young *Amerikaner,* plying them with questions, and above all straining their ears to hear the strange outlandish American language they spoke.

Whether, pathetically enough, we strove to retain our knowledge of the few precious English words we brought from the marvelous land whence we had been ruthlessly torn away, or whether we sought, child-like, to show off our accomplishments, we did lapse into English, such as it was, every now and then, and our former playmates listened in awe and wonder. How pitifully limited that vocabulary was, how halting the speech, how hopelessly intermixed it was with Yiddish expressions (it may have been only Americanized Yiddish), there was no one present to determine. Nor did anyone within our hearing know that, while I attended public school in Brooklyn for several weeks, my sister Rosa had no such advantage and picked up the few words she knew from hearing them pronounced, or rather mispronounced, at home or on the street. Yet our conversations in the unknown tongue were listened to by young and old with intense interest and admiration.

Then came that red-letter day which may have been entered in the *Pinkus,* the official chronicle of the community, among the records of expanding relations, transactions and communications between obscure Keidan and the grand New World beyond the seas. That day a full-grown American, an adult native who had returned, walked up the road with our little man. Both displayed their American attire, and both conversed in the outlandish but fascinating language. Getzel Glusonock, back from the United States after a sojourn of four years, may have wished only to question the boy about where he had lived there, and at the same time perhaps indulge in a little practice in the baffling and fast-slipping language. Whatever his motive, he surely was not conscious of the sensation he was to create.

It was on a Saturday afternoon when many of the burghers with their families were out for their Sabbath walk, wending their way up the road at the end of the town that led to the highway, the railroad station, and the great world beyond. Some boisterous and romping youngsters had passed the word, *"They are talking English!"* There was a rush of old and young to follow them closely, to overhear their talk, so that the conversationalists were plainly disconcerted by the eager intruders. Nevertheless, Mr. Glusonock was too proud of his knowledge to quail before the distraction of many eyes and ears. So the dialogue, meager and monosyllabic though it was, went on until the two enthusiastic pursuers grew weary of hearing sounds whose meaning they did not understand, and the cluster of people gradually fell away. Walking back, my fellow American and I reached the city-line and parted.

As far as hazy memory can reproduce, our talk proceeded something like this:

"How long you in America?"

"One year nearly."

"Where you live?"

"Brooklyn!"

"You go to school?"

"Yes, four weeks."

"What grade?"

"I no remember."

"You like America?"

"Very much!"

"Why you come back?"

"My mother don't like."

"Oh. Here you like to stay?"

"Am glad to see my grandma and grandpa."

"You going back to America, by and bye?"

"Sure when I grow big."

This and more, calculated to satisfy all curiosity and to supply the town with any missing information.

Mr. Glusonock often noticed and spoke to me on the street. It was always: "Well, how you getting along here? When you go back to America?"

I would answer in a vague and general manner, not being able to announce any family plans. But it was enough of an incomprehensible conversation to make bystanders prick up their ears and listen. After a while, however, these salutations became less frequent, and the English words and sounds and names gradually faded and became obliterated from memory, just as my American *kapelush* (blocked hat), my jumpers, jacket, knickers and shoes grew discolored and dilapidated.

My heart sank as these outward insignia of the new life abroad were gradually discarded. I donned long pants with the bottoms shoved into high boots, put on a Russian shirt and longish coat and a cap with a shining black visor, after the fashion of Keidan. I was no longer an American.

With forty-odd other little boys of similar appearance I was soon seated at the long tables of the *cheder* (Hebrew School), reciting our Bible lessons in singsong and plaintive melody, and there was hardly any trace left of my former distinction among these pupils and playmates.

It was five years before I was shipped back, as a lone boy-passenger, to the United States; and it took much longer for the other members of the family to return to the New World.

(*—1950*)

A Hoosier Twig

RUTH SAPIN HURWITZ

A T SCHOOL in Indiana half a century ago, when children were asked to bound the State, we might be vague about lines to the north, and east and west, but the southernmost boundary was pie even for the class dunce. For we lived on the Ohio River which separated Indiana from Kentucky; and we were as familiar with near-by Louisville, and the meandering molasses-colored river which was so much a part of its life, as with our little city of New Albany, just a few miles to the northwest.

Sometimes, indeed, during the early spring thaws the southern boundary of our State got over-familiar, coming right into our front parlors. But far more than flood and disaster the river was associated with moonlight excursions and happy daytime picnics in the paddle-wheeled steamboats that plied back and forth past wooded shores and flourishing fields.

This proximity to Kentucky served to give our entire section of Indiana a decidedly Southern flavor. The Negro population was large, many of the men and women working in the tobacco plants and distilleries across the river. There were separate schools for whites and blacks; no State law this—just local custom. Negro camp meetings were held regularly on the Knobs near New Albany, and in Negro churches the religious fervor and "coon shoutin'" were taken as a matter of course. Our language was a mixture of mid-West drawl and the "you-alls" and lopped-off participle-endings of the South. Our summers were long and hot. All in all, life was gracious and its tempo far more leisurely than in the bustling Indiana cities up north, near Chicago.

This somewhat atypical Hoosier background is only half the story of my varied origins. The family tree was no native sycamore but had grown far across the Atlantic, in Lithuania, where my parents and their parents before them were born and bred. And Lithuania—for those whose memory of the history of eastern Europe in the nine-teenth century is not too exact—was then part of Poland, which in turn was part of Russia.

About to be conscripted into the Tsar's army, seventeen-year-old Jacob Sapinsky decided to leave for America. Sailing vessels were on their way out as passenger transport, but their fare was the cheapest obtainable; so it was on a ship with billowing sails that he arrived in New York in 1867. Though a sturdy youth, he was decidedly sea-weary after his two-month voyage, with the monotonous kosher diet of herring, sausage, and black bread.

"Jake" did not linger long in New York. He had an older brother in the South, near Louisville, Kentucky, and thither he proposed to go.

"But you haven't enough cash for train fare," objected a New York relative.

"I can talk English, can't I?" replied the self-confident lad. "Wherever I can talk I can get along."

Accordingly he set out over the Baltimore and Ohio Railroad with a ticket to a point determined solely by the number of his silver dollars. The rest of the way he hoofed it or got hitches on passing wagons.

The brothers Jacob and Aaron became purveyors of the small com-modities needed by rural Kentuckians. Their peddling and farm lodgings brought them in close touch with young men who had recently fought in "The War between the States," most of them serving on the Confederate side under General Thomas Jonathan Jackson, the famed "Stonewall Jackson." The youth from Lithuania listened avidly to their battle experiences, and some years later was to tell his chil-dren thrilling stories of Stonewall Jackson—his mettle, ingenuity, tenacity, and finally his tragic death on the battlefield, shot down by his own men through a mistake at the very hour of victory. I was captivated by the very name "Stonewall Jackson," and boldly adopted him as my hero during the Spanish-American War in 1898, when my Indiana schoolmates worshiped Dewey, Sampson and Hobson, while their parents stubbornly remained loyal to Ulysses S. Grant and General Sherman. (Indiana being on the Northern side, many of the children had fathers or grandfathers who had "marched with Sherman to the sea.")

In four years Jacob Sapinsky had prospered sufficiently to think of importing a bride. An older sister, just married, was planning to come to America with her husband. So Jacob wrote to her, naming the girl of his heart and at the same time enclosing the thriftily saved sum for the maiden's passage.

But in the little Lithuanian village of Lidvinova there were complications. The girl vacillated, not at all sure she wanted to journey to faraway America and marry Yankele. This was Aunt Rivie's cue. She hadn't been too enthusiastic about her young brother's choice anyway. In the near-by village of Marienpole there was a pretty seventeen-year-old girl who seemed far more suitable. She was slender, with soft black hair falling in natural waves, and with a clear, fair complexion and gentle green-brown eyes. And she was bright and industrious: she not only helped her mild-mannered father in his onerous task of running a *cheder* (Hebrew school) but she had learned and practiced the trade of making *sheitels,* those wigs pious Jewesses donned as soon as they were wed.

Wise Aunt Rivie "proposed" to Dinnie Charlap on her brother's behalf; the maid and her parents accepted. The little matter of consulting the bridegroom about the switch of brides was cannily overlooked. Besides, the time really was quite short. So when Jacob came back to New York to meet his sister, brother-in-law and fiancée, he looked into the tender and anxious eyes of a complete stranger.

In a few weeks his chagrin wore off; he married the girl; and they lived in unusual harmony for over half a century until Mother's death. "Minnie" (thus her Hebrew name Dinah had been mistranslated) bore her husband eleven children. Three of them I was never to know, for they died in infancy or early childhood some years before my advent.

As Thanksgiving Day of 1888 approached, the coming of another baby was not enthusiastically anticipated by six brothers and sisters. The youngest, nearly four, had been considered the last. Therefore my arrival in the early hours of December 1 made no particular impression on anybody except that I had spoiled Thanksgiving. (The holiday that year fell on the last day of November.) In a year and a half still another baby arrived, the really final one.

Outwardly it was a quite Americanized home I came into. Father and his brother-in-law Julius Steinberg (husband of the match-making sister) had settled in the little town of Scottsburg, Indiana, where they ran a stave mill, a small plant that turned the local saplings into staves and hoops for flour barrels. Save for adherence to the dietary laws, the only Jews in the town—my parents, aunt and uncle—had seemingly adopted all the ways of the Hoosier community about them. In fact, my name, originally of course from the Bible, had a different immediate origin. When I was born, Grover Cleveland was President; long a bachelor, in 1886 he had married the beautiful Frances Folsom in the White House. Their little daughter, born not long before me, had been christened Ruth. It was after this darling of the country that I was named. Subsequently, during my brief Sunday School days, hearing about Ruth the Moabitess, I transferred my allegiance to that more ancient and exotic namesake.

When I was three my parents, urged on by the older children, made a momentous decision. Scottsburg really was too countrified a place. My brothers wanted more education; my sisters wanted husbands. Several of Father's brothers had settled in near-by Louisville and were beginning to prosper there.

We didn't quite make the leap to Louisville, but settled instead in New Albany, Indiana, a small city then numbering about 20,000. This cleaving to Indiana, it must be admitted, came from no special Hoosier loyalty. Father and my brother Julius had a good opportunity to acquire a men's clothing business in New Albany.

So the Sapinskys and the Steinbergs separated, each taking a half portion of the earnings of the stave mill and sundry other village enterprises, one family settling on this side of the Kentucky line and the other going a few miles further on to Louisville. The relationship between the two families in Scottsburg had been unusually close: everything was share and share alike. When one family built a house, the other built one precisely like it; the horsehair parlor sets, huge "mahogany" bookcases, golden oak sets and soft coal stoves for the dining-room (general gathering-place) were the same; and the girls of both families were garbed in silk and wool and calico dresses cut from literally the same cloth.

Now we were separated by the Ohio. But never mind. The trip "over the river" took less than thirty minutes. Two carriers—one a short spur of the Pennsylvania Railroad known locally as "the dinky," the other an electric line called "the daisy"—provided transportation every half-hour.

✦　✦　✦

Since my older brothers and sisters were now all at school, my favorite make-believe was that I too was learning the "three R's." I would sit out front on the stone steps pretending to do sums on my slate or read from my books—a discarded almanac, *Ivanhoe* with pages missing, and *The Last Days of Pompeii* minus binding. As soon as I was five Mother yielded to my pestering, took me to the near-by school, and bade the teacher examine me. The older children at home had taught me the alphabet, to spell a few simple words, and count by fives and tens. So to my delight the teacher put me, not in the first term "first," but in the second term "high first." This premature start meant that I was to be in high school by the time I was twelve.

During the seven years of my elementary schooling we lived on Pearl Street, in a neighborhood that provided unusual means for a child's amusement. Across the street a livery stable was an endless source of fun. In the summer broken-down surreys and traps and racing sulkies were left outside for repairs or for sale, and in and out of these vehicles we children scrambled in various games of "pretend." Incidentally, this livery stable was among the first establishments in town to acquire a newfangled contraption called a telephone, and I was allowed by the pimply stable boy to stand on a wooden box, ring up "Central," and talk into the awesome thing nailed to the wall.

In one corner of our street a tombstone maker and his couple of helpers worked away at their melancholy craft. But the cemetery monuments suggested nothing macabre to my playmates and myself. On the contrary, big stones were just right for hide-and-seek; square stones made a fine base for a see-saw; and tall columns were perfect pillars for our royal palaces.

At another corner of our street was the Opera House. Here I wept over little Eva in *Uncle Tom's Cabin* regularly every year for at least five years; here I saw my first *Shore Acres* and my first minstrel shows. These "Negro Minstrels" (sometimes with colored actors, at other times with white men in blackface) brought the latest songs and dance steps. Long after the shows left town we continued to sing the minstrel songs and do the new figures from the "cake walk." An older girl next door, hoydenish pretty Virgie Rice, seeing I could carry a tune and quickly pick up dance steps, became my enthusiastic teacher. Besides my "coon songs" and "coon dances," I learned the "Skirt Dance" (a Parisian number) and a Spanish dance done with castanets that Virgie let me borrow on special occasions. In my vocal repertoire there were such tear-jerkers as "Just Break the News to Mother," "A Bird in a Gilded Cage" and "Hello, Central, Give Me Heaven." Whenever my sisters had parties I was allowed to stay up and entertain the guests.

Unfortunately my sidewalk lessons played hob with formal training in music and dancing. When Mother sent me to a dancing-school at Maennerchor Hall, I soon quit because the class was "too prissy." Nor were my first piano pieces nearly snappy enough to suit me; it was only by giving me a solo called "Sleigh Bells," played to the accompaniment of ten little bells sewed five to a band around each hand, that I was induced to take lessons for a year and triumphantly perform this *tour-de-force* at a closing recital. (Though later in high school days I was to resume piano lessons, start vocal training and attend classes in social dancing, I fear I have never quite made up for my early rebellion against drill in the arts and graces.)

Southern Indiana has long beautiful autumns. But the winters, though short, are rather drab, with no possibility for sleighing or skating in the mushy snow or fast-melting ice. Radio and movies were of course not even imagined; but we did have fascinating pictures—magic-lantern slides, with comic series about brownies and animals, and views of foreign lands. Our lantern, proudly played by my brothers on a large white sheet in the back parlor, was a boon to the children of the neighborhood.

In our kitchen—a huge room not planned to save anybody's steps—there was a slate wall that made a perfect blackboard. On this I would write out arithmetic, spelling and grammar diagrams and importantly teach them to anybody who happened to be around—Cloe Eurton, my golden-haired, blue-eyed "best friend" who lived just across the street, our hired girl (usually a maiden fresh from the farm), or Aunt Mary, the Negro washwoman, a former slave. Nobody used the term "laundress" in those days. The laundry was just two movable tubs in the lightest corner of the stable, a dank place odorous of poultry droppings. For her two nine-hour days of washing and ironing the ruffled panties, corset covers, petticoats and dresses of a madam and her four daughters, Aunt Mary received the sum of two dollars, the standard wage of those times. Her labors completed, she would repair to the kitchen, light her corn-cob pipe and patiently wait for Mother to return from Louisville to pay her.

As Tuesday was Mother's euchre club day, it was not unusual for Aunt Mary to sit around an hour or so. The kitchen would be hazy

with the smoke of frying potatoes (the hired girl was never trusted
with more important cooking), the smoke of Aunt Mary's pipe, and the
powder from my chalk and eraser. It was all so delightfully cosy and
chummy that I preferred the kitchen to other parts of the house where
my brothers and sisters and their friends were doing their lessons or
playing checkers, dominoes, crocinole or parchesi; or the dining-room
where, around the table, under the light of a chandelier containing two
"modern" Welsbach burners, my parents and their relatives and friends
would carry on their after-supper pinochle.

+ + +

As I have said, outwardly our home, situated as it was in southern
Indiana where both the Hoosier and Kentucky influences were strong,
was completely American. Any differences between my playmates and
myself were certainly not of the sort that made for what the Freudians
today are wont to call "psychic trauma." No derisory names were ever
hurled at my parents or brothers and sisters or me. No economic restrictions were ever imposed on the clothing firm of "J. Sapinsky and
Son—Where Your Dollar Does Its Duty." In fact, we were soon to
put up an imposing three-storied corner building of yellow pressed-
brick, its large show-windows made of up-to-date plate glass the same
as in the finest Louisville stores, its main floor shining with the very
latest in haberdashery fixtures. It was an "emporium" to which our
little city pointed with pride.

While there wasn't any close social relationship between my parents
and our Christian neighbors, there was always neighborliness and
good will, which often manifested itself by an exchange of little gifts
between the various households. From our store on the occasion of
big sales or "the grand opening" there would be special souvenirs for
our neighbors; from parties at their homes there would come ice-cream
forms or a Charlotte Russe. Though Mother forewent the latter since
its chief ingredient was tabu gelatin, she had no objection to her
daughters eating it and subsequently concocting it for their own parties.

By nine or ten I became somewhat more conscious of differences
between my playmates and myself. None of them were Jewish. There
were at the time only four or five Jewish families in the town. Only one
had children about my age—the meek little rag and iron man and his
booming-voiced wife, a ménage decidedly out of social bounds. My
cronies were flaxen-haired and blue-eyed, with names like Goodbub,

Zimmerman and Beck. Their parents or grandparents had settled in New Albany several decades before to work at the skilled trades of boat building and glass making. The children attended mostly the German Lutheran and German Catholic churches. Their talk contained quite a few German expressions, since both at home and in their Sunday Schools German was spoken. I didn't understand German; my olive complexion and brown eyes and thick dark hair, I decided, bespoke a "Russian" origin; my "church" was in Louisville, and I explained to my best friends that it wasn't really called a church but a synagogue.

Anyway, it was due to my "church," I made clear to the inquisitive, that our meat was never bought at the local butcher's, that Father killed our chickens with strict regard to certain religious regulations, and our meat, "cow not pig," was delivered to us twice a week from Louisville. We never had butter and milk when meat was served at our meals, and for one whole week in the spring, I explained, to commemorate the delivery of our people from bondage in Egypt, all bread even to the tiniest crumb must disappear from our homes and we must eat of the crackly unleavened squares my schoolmates called "matches."

However, there was no explaining why we didn't celebrate Christmas, since our store in December was gay with tinsel and red bells and the show-windows crammed with Christmas gifts of all descriptions. I early learned to use considerable guile in order to show off Christmas gifts to my playmates. Luckily my December birthday (which always brought gifts from my brothers and sisters), and Hanukkah (when Mother gave each child a present), and a gaily boxed scarf or belt I regularly purloined from the store, built up for me a fairly satisfactory stockpile of "Christmas gifts."

My eagerness to celebrate Christmas came simply from a longing to be like everybody else, certainly not from any dearth of holidays in the Jewish calendar. It is tempting to dwell on them all—Purim, Pesach, Shabuoth, Sukkoth, Hanukkah—every one with its rich emotional associations, its special food delicacies, the parties and best dresses of china silk and flounced challis. . . .

✦ ✦ ✦

Through the years Mother's weekly euchre club in Louisville was her chief social outlet. The club consisted of her relatives and friends who had also come to America as young girls and had shared the early poverty and struggles of their hard-working men. Now, their husbands well established in trade and most of their children grown up, they could begin to take life easy. The card games being not all such dressy affairs as balls and weddings, the women wore their second-bests of wool or silk, beaded or lace-trimmed. Their coats in winter were of black seal (real or imitation); their earrings were diamond drops, some quite huge; and they wore breast-pins of gold, set with large or chip diamonds, each according to her husband's economic status.

On one occasion, an early May afternoon when "The Races" at Churchill Downs in Louisville were as pervasive and inescapable as the weather, the euchre club adjourned to the tracks. It was before the day of the pari-mutuels. A tout prevailed on the ladies to make up a pool of ten dollars for a bet on a horse. The horse won and Mother received two dollars as her share of the windfall. "Think of it—to make two dollars so easy!" she exclaimed to the family that evening. "If I had known that horse would surely win I would have put up another dollar."

My eldest brother Simon—then a member of the Louisville law firm of Duffin, Sapinsky and Duffin—was more sporty than Mother. One fine Derby Day he placed a moderately large sum on a long shot in the chief race. His winning of over $7,000 became part of the Derby's illustrious history, along with the doings of Vanderbilts, Whitneys and other Eastern moguls. But this gave Father no satisfaction whatever. "Only millionaires and crooks bet like that," Father admonished. "Stick to your law, son." Son stuck to his law; and coming later to New York, he joined my brother Joseph's law firm, which at the time included a comparatively obscure young man named Fiorello H. La Guardia.

Father, with a firm belief that a shoemaker should stick to his last, never went to The Downs, even as a spectator. His one diversion, outside his keen interests in his home, his business and his synagogue, was membership in the Knights of Pythias and the Odd Fellows. It must be admitted, however, that he joined because it was good business. He also served for several terms as president of the New Albany Commercial Club—the Rotary Club of that day.

A very industrious man, it was Father's habit to rise at six in the morning and be at the store by seven. With his eldest clerk Mr. Streepey, he served the railroad men, the rolling mill workers, and the farmers whose shopping hours were decidedly matutinal. By mid-morning there would be a lull. Then Father, an ardent admirer of Henry Watterson and his Louisville *Courier-Journal,* would repair to a quiet corner of the store and read the newspaper methodically from first page to last. Home for dinner (our heartiest meal served at mid-day was a leisurely affair), Father would discuss the news and "Marse Henry's" editorial with my brothers. Being precociously eager to keep up with these serious discussions, I began to read for myself not only Watterson's editorials but the *Literary Digest* which came regularly to the house—when most of my schoolmates were just about able to stumble through McGuffey's *Fifth Reader.*

During those tender years my political education was also promoted by the old Chautauqua, since New Albany was one of the favored cities on its circuit. Frequently when United States Senators, Congressmen, or presidential candidates came to town "to talk to the peepul," Father would take me to hear those celebrated men. One sweltering summer day, a paper plate of brick ice-cream (then a prodigious novelty) on my lap, I sat on a circus bench under the big Chautauqua tent and heard "the great Commoner," William Jennings Bryan, expounding his doctrine of "16 to 1." I confess his economic reasoning was beyond me, though Father tried hard to explain. I only knew that the Indiana farmers and workers and small businessmen were "for free silver" and that Henry Watterson was "agin it." Always a staunch Democrat, Father was torn between the reasoning of his two idols. But though I couldn't follow Bryan's passionate views on the currency, I remember his presence distinctly—his long black hair, flashing eyes, ringing voice and easy fluent gestures, so different from the stiff thrust of hands and arms used by the high school "professors" and commencement orators at the graduations of my brothers and sisters.

Mother didn't read the *Courier-Journal* nor trouble her head with politics. Her favorite paper (and what a favorite!) was the *Yiddishe Gazetten,* a news and literary weekly from New York. It arrived, as a rule, on Friday morning, and I would stop any game to run indoors with the precious *Gazetten,* so eager, I knew, was Mom to see her paper, her link with the great outside world. On Fridays she was always up at six and busy with the *Shabbas* cooking and baking: three fat loaves of bread with a glazing of egg-yolk atop them, huge cinnamon coffee cakes, the Friday night *gefilte* fish, the Saturday chickens. By eleven o'clock (when the mail arrived) she could leave the steamy kitchen to the hired girl, repair to the screened side-porch and lose herself in her paper.

With a sad shaking of head and a sympathetic clicking of tongue she would explain all the New York news—news of tenement house fires, dire conditions in the sweatshops, stories of little children run over and killed by horse-drawn street cars and fire engines, and, most tragic of all, tales of innocent virgins waylaid in the wicked Bowery by the dreadful characters who made it a street of sin. All these melodramatic events happened to the Jews in New York; if they touched the lives of the Irish, Italians, Hungarians, Poles and other nationalities living in the East Side, Mother failed to mention it.

The favorite "continued story" which Mother read avidly from week to week appeared on an inside page. The episodes of this never-ending serial novel were not meant for childish ears. They concerned beautiful Jewish maidens kidnapped and carried off to resplendent brothels by glittering officers of the Tsar's army. I never knew until I read *War and Peace* that the Russian Army had any other purpose. Many years later my younger son, serving as a United States liason officer with the Russian Army, was to give me yet another understanding of Russian military higher-ups, not the Tsar's officers this time but Stalin's. Most often—to return to Mother's novels—if the characters were all Jewish, the customary triangle would involve a beautiful but penniless heroine, a wealthy manufacturer from Lodz (the villain), and a poverty-stricken *yeshivah bocher* (the talmudic student-hero). *Dybbuks* (souls of the dead who crept into bodies of the living and made the victims a trifle wacky, to say the least) were frequently also in the cast of characters.

I must confess I heard these stories by eavesdropping when Mother recounted them to her sister. Aunt Dvorie, a widow with five small children, was "poor relations." Her chief respite from her cares was to come from Louisville once a fortnight to spend the afternoon, have tea with home-made hartshorn cookies in winter and lemonade and vanilla wafers in summer, and remain for supper. Between her and Mother there would be transactions involving gifts of money (about which Father was not supposed to know too much), gifts of clothes (both used garments and "seconds" from the store), and saved-up copies of the *Yiddishe Gazetten*. It was when (as often) the ignorant hired girl had used one of the serial's precious chapters to start the fire that Mother, speaking in English but with many vivid Yiddish expressions for immorality and sin, would supply the missing episode.

Playing not far away from the two utterly absorbed women, I would drink in great gulps of sexy romance.

✦ ✦ ✦

Of a sudden the *Gazetten's* continued story took on a very different character. Across the pages of French and Jewish history there flashed a true story of innocence wronged, of real villains unmasked by sleuthing worthy of a tale by Edgar Allan Poe, of virtue at long last restored to its rightful place. This was the Dreyfus affair; and for many months Mother's conversation with her sister—a continued conversation in which Father joined, for this story was not just a silly romance but live, gripping Jewish history—rang with the names of Alfred Dreyfus, his loyal and persistent brother Mathieu, the great Emile Zola, and the accursed traitor Esterhazy.

From one of his trips to New York Father brought home a thick, profusely illustrated volume on "The Dreyfus Case." I hung over Mother's rocker and looked at the little French Captain, shorn of his rank and shipped to Devil's Island—not properly clad for a lonely island like Robinson Crusoe, but in the long black coat and high collar usually associated with undertakers; I saw his pretty wife and bereft children; and my tears, with Mother's, splashed down on the pages of the book.

The Dreyfus Affair led indirectly to their first visit back to Europe for Father and his brother Simon. In 1896 the Viennese journalist and playwright Dr. Theodor Herzl, galvanized into action for his people by the Dreyfus case, published his epoch-making pamphlet *Der Judenstaat*. In the following year, with the help of the famous Hungarian physician and *litterateur* Max Nordau, long resident in France, and other men whose names are now part of Zionist history, Herzl had summoned to Basle, Switzerland, the first "Zionist Congress," a meeting that marked the beginning of modern political Zionism.

Uncle Simon prevailed on his brother to go with him to the Zionist Congress in Basle in 1903. There was much correspondence with the Department of State, for the big trip was to include a visit to their native Lithuania, and the two former subjects of the Tsar, though long since American citizens, wanted no argument with the Russian Government over the little matter of their departure before serving their time in the Tsar's army. At last a friendly letter from Secretary John Hay himself, with the necessary documents, arrived. Secretary Hay, it

may be noted, was a Hoosier himself; his birthplace—Salem, Indiana—
was quite near New Albany. About this time that high-minded statesman had won the special gratitude of American Jews for his formal
protest to the Russian Government over the pogroms and for taking
steps which led to the abrogation some years later of our Treaty of
Commerce with tsarist Russia.

Father and Uncle Simon returned from Europe with two young
nieces brought out of the poverty of Lithuania, with extraordinary gifts
from Switzerland and Germany and, most exciting of all, with enthusiastic accounts of the celebrated Jews and the eloquent speeches at
the Zionist Congress. Proudly they displayed an official photograph with
Herzl and Nordau in the foreground and themselves not too far behind.
In later years I was to see many pictures of the noble white-bearded
Nordau and the handsome black-bearded Assyrian-looking Herzl.
Through my husband I was to come into possession of a fine Struck
etching of Herzl, autographed by the Zionist founder himself. But
never was I to be so impressed with the greatness of the two Zionist
leaders as when Father showed them off to us in the Congress photograph.

It is a deep regret to me that in the period from my ninth year to my
early teens, when my interest in the Jewish people was so stirred by
world events, I had no opportunity for a systematic education in
Jewish history, or even for good elementary instruction in Hebrew.
The little *shul*, Adath Jeshurun in Louisville, to which my parents
belonged, though considered "Orthodox" was then tending to a less
rigidly Conservative type. The men still wore their hats and *talethim*
at services, and the ritual was read or sung in Hebrew; but men and
women sat together, arrived at the synagogue on the trolleys instead of
on foot, and the sermon was in English. At that time the synagogue had
no Sunday School, only a *cheder* where the boys were taught Hebrew
against the day of their Bar Mitzvah. When my youngest brother Lee
was ten, a teacher was engaged to come over from Louisville twice a
week to give both of us instruction in Hebrew. Compared with present-
day methods of teaching Hebrew as a living language—a progressive
course with attractive books and art materials carefully designed for
various age levels—our instruction was indeed medieval. We began
with the *aleph-beth*, learned to recite by rote a few prayers and blessings, and then were plunged cold into portions of the Pentateuch and
Prophets!

Always able to take considerable educational punishment, I might have stuck to my Hebrew for several years had our teacher been in the least tolerable. But he was a huge, shapeless, smelly man who knew not a single word of English and was equally innocent of child psychology. Very near-sighted, he had a comical habit of first pushing his spectacles atop his head and then, when he wished to use them, dropping them down to his nose by a mighty wrinkling of his brows. There was a cup of hot tea always before him which he sipped with a noisy gurgling. Behind his back I would mimic his gestures and mannerisms for the amusement of my brother. Under these circumstances our lessons lasted only a few months. My own Hebrew education was dropped entirely (to be resumed in a fashion, under romantic circumstances, some sixteen years later). My brother was sent to the rabbi in Louisville to prepare for his Bar Mitzvah.

Since ours was a newspaper-reading family I early discovered the weekly children's pages in the Louisville *Courier-Journal* and Louisville *Evening Post*. At about the time of my abortive Hebrew education the Sunday *Courier* offered prizes for the best stories in a contest called "Stories Heard at Mother's Knee." I had a favorite story, of a pet goat my mother had when a little girl. One day when she learned that the soldiers were coming through her village (it was one of the innumerable trampings across Lithuania of Polish or Russian troops), she got a heavy chain to fasten the animal so it would be safe against looters. To her horror, upon going to the little shed next morning she found her pet's head dangling by its chain. Its body had been carried off for the warm goat's skin. This gory tale I wrote with all the unction of a later Hemingway at a bull fight and won a second prize, three dollars. When my *opus* appeared in print, its horror enhanced by some drawings made by another child, I resolved at once upon a literary career.

✦ ✦ ✦

Father was most ambitious for his children to be well-educated. Self-taught, he honored American educational institutions often beyond their worth. When I entered high school at twelve, it was taken for granted I would go on to college, just as two brothers had already done and a brother and sister were preparing to do. But high school, oddly enough, meant a sudden drop in my zeal for learning. There were various reasons. The building was superannuated, and most of the teachers were equally so. Some subjects, like "literature" and "history,"

I found too easy. New Albany had a good public library, and even before high school days, guided by my brother Joe who was eight years
older and an omnivorous reader, I had been devouring Scott, Dickens,
Dumas and Kipling, Mark Twain, Jack London, and O'Henry. Other
high school subjects were bores. I detested mathematics and physics,
both required subjects. (Later, my elder son, in revenge, was to become
a mathematical physicist.) I disliked Latin but scorned to use a pony
like many of my classmates.

A final reason for my abrupt loss of interest in school, which had
once been a passion, was that my cronies—three lush girls several years
older than I—were not only boy-crazy, they were seriously talking
of marriage. Though precocious in some respects and aware of the facts
of life (I had learned what I thought were all of them around the livery
stable several years before, and not many years later D. H. Lawrence
and Marcel Proust were to supplement aplenty), matrimony seemed a
remote, far-off state. Moreover, my parents, while voicing no objections
to their daughter mingling with *shkotzim* (Gentile youths) in casual
groups, frowned upon anything that smacked of a serious interest.
Thus cut off from the usual boy-and-girl relationships, I went in strongly
pour le sport.

That was the time when Bernard McFadden and his magazine
Physical Culture were at their height. Along with several Louisville
cousins I became a fanatic follower of the muscular McFadden. We
eschewed meat, ate barrels of apples, carloads of bananas and tons
of shredded wheat, exercised with dumb-bells and rubbery contraptions
fastened to bedroom doors, and took ice-cold baths all winter long.
We girls not only scorned wearing corsets but, most unorthodox of all,
discarded our high shoes for oxfords. Wearing oxfords in winter was
then considered far more of a health risk than toeless, backless pumps
nowadays. I was an emaciated girl at age thirteen; my zealous worship
of the god McFadden reduced me to a wraith.

Mother finally succeeded in luring me away from the cult with her
potato pancakes, home-made jellies, roast chickens and raisin-filled
coffee cake; but all through my teens my enthusiasm for sports never
wavered. My favorite high school teacher (later the Superintendent of
Schools) was red-headed, youngish Professor Harry Burke. An ardent
oarsman, he had managed to find four flat-bottomed boats, locally
known as "skiffs," in which some fourteen youths and six intrepid girls
regularly rowed on the river under his supervision. Those rowing parties

gave me a new intimacy with the Ohio—its strange whirlpools, unexpected currents, picturesque green islands which not long before had been barren sandbars. Sometimes we would row as far as "The Falls" —rapids which had given Louisville, and New Albany and Jeffersonville on the Indiana shore, the nickname of "The Falls Cities."

Shortly after I entered high school the family acquired a substantial, many-roomed brick house on East Main Street, then *the* residential street of New Albany. It had five large porches, the two front ones decorated with wrought iron, reminiscent of Spanish-type homes in New Orleans. Two of our side-porches (Indiana scorned the word "veranda") we screened, the upper one becoming, despite Ohio Valley electric storms, a good sleeping-porch; the lower one, decorated with new green mission-type furniture, flower-filled hanging baskets, rubber plants, two canary cages and a bowl of goldfish, we converted into a pleasant summer living-dining room. In the kitchen we had a specially built ice-box, big enough in its lower depths to hold, in addition to the regular food for our large family, two huge watermelons, one for our mid-day dinner and the midnight "snack," the other always cooling for next day.

Our front lawn did not boast that typically Victorian zoological specimen, a cast-iron deer; but our next-door neighbors, the Baldwins, had two; and just up the street, at the "Depauw mansion," two Trafalgar-like lions awed the passerby. (The head of the family was the local Croesus who had founded New Albany's chief industry before the 1890's—the Depauw American Glass Works.) It was our backyard that drew everybody's envy. Here my brother Julius had a good clay tennis court laid out. Since he bountifully provided all guests with the latest in racquets from New York, the best of tennis balls, and large Turkish towels with a shower in the barn, the court was a popular place, particularly on Sundays and holidays when a contingent of Louisville youths regularly appeared for speedy sets of tennis with my brothers until dusk.

One of our neighbors on East Main Street was a prosperous and much-travelled lawyer, Colonel Charles Jewett. He had fought in the Philippines during the Spanish-American war, was something of a force in both the State and national Republican party and, not least, a *bon vivant*, spending much time in Louisville at the Galt House and its successor the Seelbach, or the Pendennis Club. Having grown up in Scottsburg, he knew Father well. Late one evening when we were returning from Louisville, "Uncle Charlie" got on the trolley and, looking at me as though seeing me for the first time, said: "Jake, your little girl is growing up. Getting personality. Getting to look like something." No great compliment, surely, but coming from the cosmopolitan, tweedy bachelor, it gave me a decided lift.

Occasion to assert my personality came the very next day when the senior class held its all-important meeting to make Commencement plans. A few of us, chiefly the rugged rowers, had decided to graduate in cap and gown. That was a bold new idea, as no class in high school annals had ever "embarked on the sea of life" in academic robes. We brought it off, but not without a compromise. The girls were to be allowed to carry large arm bouquets, just as at other commencements.

Being one of the six honor students, I had to be on the Commencement program. If my number—a Maytime song filled with birds, bees, butterflies and trills—won only polite applause, and deserved even less, everybody said my brilliant red rambler roses "went" much better with the black cap and gown than the large pink roses most of the other girls carried.

✦ ✦ ✦

As my four years at high school were drawing to a close I debated "What College?" Credits from our school would admit me to the State University or other mid-Western universities. But I was bent on going East to college, though women's colleges of standing had more language and science requirements than I could offer. Just then *The Ladies Home Journal* began to run a series on Eastern women's colleges. For no reason except that I liked the pictures of Wellesley better than those of other colleges, and preferred to be near Boston rather than New York or Philadelphia (having seen none of these cities), I decided on Wellesley.

My sister Bertha, who had graduated from high school several years before, now decided she too was going to college. We sought out Professor Abraham Flexner, of Louisville, owner and principal of one of the first progressive schools in the country. Here my sister prepared for Wellesley during part of a year, and I followed her in 1905.

About this time, however, Dr. Flexner accepted an invitation from the Carnegie Foundation for the Advancement of Teaching to make a two-year investigation of the medical schools of the United States and

Canada.* Thus it happened, to my regret, that when I entered "Mr. Flexner's School," it had been merged with a private school for boys, the Thorpe School. It now bore the name "University-Flexner School"; and though it retained some of the former Flexner School teachers and many of the former students, Abraham Flexner himself was no longer actively associated with it.

Attendance at this school brought me into daily association with the upper-class youths of Louisville, whose grandparents and great grand-parents had given to city and state the names of streets, counties and institutions, whose fathers owned its great tobacco plants, distilleries, and the wholesale businesses that lined the Ohio River. But, needless to add, I had little enough social relationship with these gilded young Kentuckians. Indeed, their presence outside school and sport hours was almost wholly demanded at balls and hops and the late afternoon *thés dansants* for debutantes then coming into vogue. Nevertheless, as my stories and articles which appeared in the school monthly, *The Varsity,* often had to do with bicycling, rowing, swimming and tennis, it was inevitable we should meet sometimes in the field of sports.

This led to a lesson in the futilities of social climbing that was to stand me in good stead the rest of my life. One spring day I invited three of the school's lions and a girl classmate nearer to my own social level for an afternoon of tennis at New Albany. Before their arrival I was as much in a dither as though my guests were to be the Prince of Wales and his entourage. What if it suddenly began to teem? The weather was perfect. What if Rick, our young blood of a Negro house-boy who rolled and lined the court, should be in jail (from which brother Julius had periodically to rescue him)? Rick showed up cheer-ful, free of any snarled *affaires d'amour*. But perhaps the pineapple frappé and the angel food cake that I made myself would suddenly turn out a fizzle. The cake was of a heavenly lightness and whiteness, and the ice-cream, turned by Rick to just the right solidity, was golden and velvety. But in the tub those last minutes, before putting on my starched ankle-length tennis clothes, I suddenly remembered to my hor-ror that this was the afternoon for Aunt Dvorie's fortnightly visit, and Mother had gone to her dressmaker's. Whenever Mother wasn't home,

* This brilliant study led to Dr. Flexner's permanent residence in the East, his long association with the General Education Board subsidized by the Rockefeller family, and finally his establishment of the Institute for Advanced Study in Princeton to give a home to Professor Albert Einstein and other distinguished Nazi-driven scholars.

Aunt Dvorie, fortified with jelly bread and tea, would invariably seek me out to ply me with questions about my parents, my seven brothers and sisters, and our *Shapinsky* aunts, uncles and cousins in Louisville (there were over fifty of them, all told.)

Heaven be praised, Aunt Dvorie was not on the trolley with the tennis party, so I had a half hour's respite. But two of my young gentlemen were openly critical of the court. It was too short by at least a foot; moreover, a rise of ground just beyond one end should have been graded to give a better runback. "But that would mean cutting down the silver maples," I protested. Two fine tall trees stood on the hillock and the Kentucky cardinals, handsome crested birds of olive green and red, made the spot their home all summer long. "The maples make no difference," snapped the youth. "Either you have a good tennis court or you don't." Another complained, "Your crazy calliope gets me off my game." (This calliope, on an old river boat, "The Queen City," which had been recently acquired from Cincinnati, was one of our town's prides; the calliope operator, a friend of brother Julius, gave us a tune every twenty minutes or so when he passed our neighborhood plying to and from a Louisville amusement park.) Only one of my guests politely refrained from criticism, but she so far outclassed me that mixed doubles were out of the question.

My spirits were at their lowest ebb when I suddenly heard Aunt Dvorie's voice. No Southern lady's gentle drawl was hers. My aunt lived in a crowded, ghetto-like neighborhood in Louisville, and her English was not only broken, it was shattered.

But just as I was about to pass out, I heard Mother's voice. The seamstress had disappointed her, so she returned home early. Meanwhile my Southern gentlemen were so busy wolfing ice-cream and cake they paid not the slightest attention to my little aunt hovering at the edge of the court.

When at supper that evening Julius asked me how the big party went I answered ruefully, "Catch me ever again inviting those snobs to play here!" But in my heart I knew it wasn't only the criticisms of the court that had riled me. I realized that the lives of the young Kentuckians were utterly different from mine. Aunt Dvorie, a part of big-hearted Mother, belonged, whether I liked it or not, to the pattern of my life.

There is a humorous and touching Jewish folksong about an *arme Tante* who comes unbidden to the wedding feast. Why shouldn't she be there, she asks. Didn't she give the bride some feathers for the bridal feather-bed? Isn't she part of the family? Why shouldn't she be present at the wedding? Well, I owed my aunt no feather-bed. But I admitted her right to visit her sister on a lovely spring afternoon. I suddenly respected the bright-eyed, courageous little widow. She was giving her five children a decent bringing-up, despite all obstacles. To be ashamed of my relative before my supercilious guests was to lose my own self-esteem.

The following month, clad in a simple white dress (no flounces and furbelows for me at that serious period of my life) I sat on the stage of a pretty club auditorium in Louisville ready to graduate from the University-Flexner School. The audience was wealthy and fashionable. With an air of affected boredom and indifference I rose to read my essay on "The Child Characters in Dickens."

In September, when the hot mid-western summer was nearly spent, I donned a wine-colored tweed suit and a stiff black sailor hat, and carrying several popular novels, a new suitcase and a long-handled silk umbrella (patterned after the parasols in the famous musical comedy of the day, *Floradora*), I took the Louisville and Nashville for Cincinnati. There I boarded the Pullman that would take me East for the first time in my life—East to college.

(—*1947*)

Memories of Boston

⟿

CHARLES ANGOFF

HISTORY is democratic. It parcels out its gifts impartially to small and large sovereignties alike. Indeed, something of a case might be made out for the contention that history is partial to smaller communities. After all, the fountainhead of Western culture was Palestine, a small, struggling country buffeted by its bigger neighbors and finally conquered by Rome, but not finally extinguished. Athens in its most glorious days probably had a population less than that of Utica, New York, today. The Republic of Venice put its enduring stamp upon human history—and its total population was never more than 650,000. It was swallowed by the Italian Empire, but that empire is known to history largely by the great contributions of the city states that were swept into it by the strange logic of history. Italian culture is a conglomerate of the cultures of the previously sovereign states of Naples and Florence and Piedmont, to mention only three principalities that come to mind. Germany? Goethe and Beethoven and Schiller were the products not of the empire Bismark built, but of the little kingdoms that comprised it. Denmark, Holland? Where did Spinoza and Rembrandt and Kierkegaard come from?

Of course, this thesis must not be pushed too far. There are exceptions. The great Elizabethan Age in England coincides with the England that leaped to the forefront of great world powers. Similarly, Molière, Racine and Descartes flourished in the period when France was a mighty power. Still, on balance, it would seem that the world owes somewhat more to small nations than to large ones.

Something of the same sort is discernible in Jewish-American history, even down to the present time. In a very real sense, the center of Jewish Orthodoxy is where Rabbi Joseph B. Soloveitchik lives, that is, Boston. And our greatest scholar, by common consent, has for decades lived in nearby Cambridge, Massachusetts. It is difficult to imagine Professor Harry A. Wolfson living elsewhere. On the other hand, Reform Judaism in America continues to have its headquarters in Cincinnati, and Dropsie College is in Philadelphia. The finest Hebrew poet, Ephraim Lisitzky, who recently died, made his home in New Orleans. But to talk about Louis D. Brandeis one must come back to Boston, and to talk about Boston one has to talk about the center of American Jewry at a crucial time in our history here.

Between 1910 and 1920, the total population of Boston was less than 500,000, about a tenth of whom were Jews. Compared to the Jewish population of New York City, this was a very small community indeed. But what a center of activity it was! For almost twenty years it was the cultural capital of American Jewry. There were superb Hebrew schools everywhere, and one of them, Ivrioh, was probably the center of the whole *Ivris b'Ivris* (Hebrew-speaking) movement in the country. Its teachers included some of the finest pedagogues in Jewish-American history. One need only mention Hirsch and Tumaroff and Pollack. How did they differ from the Hebrew school teachers of today? In many ways. They were enormously learned in their subjects. If some of them lacked technique they more than made up for it by their complete and contagious dedication to their calling. Teaching in Hebrew school was to them not merely a vocation or a profession; it was a mission.

Perhaps I am influenced by the fact that I attended Ivrioh Hebrew School in its golden days. Nevertheless, I think that there is objective truth in what I say. The school was a great spiritual force in the lives of all who worked for the welfare of Jewish culture. When Dr. Shmarya Levin came to this country, he of course stopped off in New York for a while, but my uncle, I. C. Pollack, who taught at the Hebrew School, told us young ones that Dr. Levin was most anxious to come to Boston—and to Ivrioh, for at this school he felt he could get in closest touch with the meaningful commotion in the American Jewish community. And the same was true of Nahum Sokoloff and Eliezer Ben Yehuda.

To all of us at the school, these men represented Jewish history, Jewish hope, Jewish endurance, Jewish drama. To me they also had a special personal meaning. For I came from a totally Jewish home, a home, besides, that was, in a sense, magnificently maladjusted. Some modern psychologists would perhaps say that my type of home is hardly conducive to mental health. But conducive it was, at least in my case. I found what went on in my house enormously stimulating. My father was of the old school: he was dubious of Zionism, he was willing to wait for Palestine to be ours once more by the way of the method sanctioned by Orthodox tradition. He did not literally believe that the Messiah would come on a white donkey and lead all the Jews in Exile back to Palestine, but he did believe that it would happen in some supernatural way.

My mother, on the other hand, was more "worldly" in her views about Palestine. She was an ardent Zionist and a Hebraist. But she was also a good wife, and she did not openly argue with her husband. She "stooped to conquer." Precisely how she did it I still don't know, but she managed to have her way and to maintain the love and respect of her dissident husband. We children went to Ivrioh Hebrew School, we learned Hebrew grammar and language, we knew all about the various Zionist congresses and the conflicting Zionist personalities, we bought trees in Palestine, we contributed to the Keren Hayesod and various other funds. And when we said *Leshono Haboh B'Yerusholayim* (Next Year in Jerusalem) on Yom Kippur we meant it with all our hearts.

Hebrew, Jewishness, Zionism—these were all parts of our daily living. A picture of Dr. Theodor Herzl hung above our kitchen table, and since the kitchen in our home, as in so many other homes, was the family center, we children were always under the influence of Dr. Herzl. Mother's own upbringing had been unusual. Her father was both a pious and a worldly Jew. He knew several literatures, not only Yiddish and Hebrew but Russian, German and English. He read foreign magazines and newspapers, and he was active in virtually every Jewish nationalistic movement. He was in correspondence with Dr. Herzl. Dr. Weizmann was a visitor to his home. My mother was a favorite of her father's, not only because she was the oldest in the family, but because she was a girl of extraordinary interests. She was married when she was only seventeen but she already had a vast fund of information about world as well as Jewish affairs, picked up from reading her father's books and periodicals, and she was an ardent Zionist. I still remember the November morning in 1917 when she brought home the Boston *Post* on whose front page was the announcement of the Balfour Declaration. She sat down by the kitchen table, put the paper on it, pointed to the headline, and softly said, *"Derlebt . . . derlebt,"* ("We've lived to see it,") as tears of joy ran down her face.

She made our home what it was. But apparently thousands of other Jewish homes in Boston were under a similar influence. Boston was a sort of Jewish Athens, a civilization within a civilization. To us boys the singing of "Hatikvah" was not a humdrum song forced upon us; it was a declaration of purpose for our whole lives. When we participated in Hebrew plays—there were many such in those days—we felt as if we were in training to play real parts as Jews in real life later on. I was a soldier in the play *Bar Kokhba.* I carried a spear and the only words I said were *"Kain, Kain,"* ("Yes, Yes,") but I said them with conviction. They were my answer to the call to duty to all Jews made by the Zionist leaders.

To change the metaphor, Boston was the most influential platform in American Jewry. The great *maggid* (itinerant preacher) Zvi Hirsch Masliansky, who had been a childhood playmate of my Alte Bobbe (Granny), once said to her, "Aye, New York is New York, but Boston is Boston, and Boston is all by itself. When I talk in Boston, when anybody talks in Boston, one talks to Jews all over America, to Jews all over the world." Masliansky often spoke in Boston, and he always visited Alte Bobbe. I adored him. To my nine-ten-year-old mind, he was Moses and Aaron and Samson and Joshua and all the Maccabees. He had so splendid a face, so overwhelming a beard, such deep-seeing eyes—and a voice that was now thunder, now a violin. "He thinks like a great rabbi, and he speaks like a *chazan* [cantor]," my Alte Bobbe said of him.

The time came when Masliansky was announced as the chief speaker at a drive for the Keren Hayesod, to be held in Faneuil Hall. Of course our whole family went. The hall was filled to overflowing more than an hour before the meeting began, while several hundred people stood outside waiting to hear the speeches over the loud speaker. Across these many decades I still recall the profound impression Masliansky's words made on me. In substance what he said was this. "I am not pleading with you, my friends, the great Jews of the great city of Boston, to contribute to the Keren Hayesod. I never plead with Jews to help other Jews, to help Palestine, to help Zionism. I tell them that here is another opportunity for them to be the good Jews they want to be. I tell them here is another opportunity for them to justify the high honor that comes with being called a Jew. Here is another opportunity for them to join the company of Moses and Aaron and Bar Kokhba and Maimonides and Dr. Herzl. The city of Louis D. Brandeis doesn't need me to tell them. They already know. I come here to honor myself by being among you as you decide to give still more to your Mother—for the Jewish tradition, the Jewish people, Jewish history, our Torah is the Great Mother of us all."

He related in great detail the many wonderful things that the Keren Hayesod was doing. Then he came to his peroration: "You are here doing what the Fathers of America, of the United States did, three hundred years ago. You are building the future of the Jewish State, which will surely arise in Palestine. *Leshono Haboh B'Yerusholayim.* Maybe not next year, maybe not the year after next year, or even the year after that. But the year will come. It will surely come . . . We are finished, the world says. We belong to the distant past. Well, we do belong to the distant past. But we also belong to the present. And to the future. Once more will light come from Zion, and not the Zion now ruled over by wandering, shiftless Arabs who allow the land to decay and to go to waste. No, light will come from a Palestine that is rich with resources, rich with people, rich with hope, rich with imagination, rich with learning, rich with Torah, rich with that most glorious of all things in this world, Jewishness, the Jewish Soul."

There was a moment of silence. Then, as if someone had pushed a button, the entire audience burst into applause.

Boston was a beehive, not only of Zionists of the Dr. Herzl variety, of what might be called Orthodox Zionists, but also of other Zionists of various degrees of dissidence: there were Poale Zionists, Mizrachi Zionists, Yiddishist Zionists, and still others, as I had heard. They all had their special headquarters and their own publications, some put out in mimeographed form—and there was considerable strife among them. But an important part of the strife was heated discussion. I listened in on a great deal of it, at meetings of these dissident organizations and also at home.

At Ivrioh we were encouraged to go to the meetings of these heretics, to see how mistaken they were and to be prepared to answer their arguments, for, as one of our teachers said, "How can you answer an argument if you don't know the argument?" I had a special interest in listening to arguments because at the time, in English school, I was a member of the debating team, and I was eager to get pointers in the art.

Nowhere did I get more pointers than at home and at the homes of my aunts and cousins. If my own immediate family was maladjusted, the family at large was a senate of conflicting opinions, all of them usually expressed in grandiloquent oratory. Thus I knew the Jewish world was divided into many parts long before I knew precisely what the parts were and exactly in what respects they differed. An aunt of mine had been active in the Russian revolutionary movement and for a time, I think, was a Bundist. Then she become a Poale Zionist, after that what we would now call a General Zionist, and then switched back to Poale Zionism, for the rest of her life, I think. My father was especially opposed to her brand of Zionism. To him she was wrong on two major counts: Zionism and Socialism. He was especially vehement in his opposition to the Socialistic part of Poale Zionism, for to him Socialism meant atheism, and that was the worst of all diseases. My aunt insisted that she was a Jew even though she didn't believe in "the superstitions of the Bible and the Rabbis." My father said that no one could be a Jew who didn't believe in the Bible. Whereupon she brought up Dr. Herzl, who, according to her, was even more of an *apikores* (heretic) than she was. To which my father said, "What you say about Dr. Herzl only makes me feel surer that Zionism is not good for Jews, but he's really not in this argument. I don't really know about him"—he said this, not out of conviction but out of respect for my mother—"but I know about you, I know about all Poale Zionists. From them no good can come."

This particular aunt was a Hebraist, but another aunt was a Yiddishist. My father hardly knew what to make of her. He objected to her Zionism and her Socialism, but he was ambivalent about her Yiddishist philosophy. My father was in a precarious position in this respect. My mother was a Hebraist, her father was a Hebraist, and my father saw a great deal in the Hebraist movement. After all, Hebrew was *Loshen Kodosh*, the holy language. The painful fact, however, was that so many *apikorsim* were using Hebrew as part of their Zionist propaganda. Further, there was my father's early upbringing, according to which he more or less believed that Hebrew would be spoken only when the Messiah came to earth in the tradi-

tional way, and that meanwhile Yiddish was the proper language of
the folk. Hebrew speaking was but another step to atheism. My
father, who knew Hebrew well, occasionally read Hebrew books
and periodicals, but I always felt that when he did so he gave in to
his *yetzer hara* (evil inclination). He read the *Tageblatt,* which, of
course, was in Yiddish, with a much clearer conscience. Very often he
would read the *Forward,* and that presented various special difficulties to his conscience. He liked the *Forward* very much as a newspaper, much more than the *Tageblatt.* He thought its foreign news was
superior, and he liked the stories and poems. But he did not like
many of the editorials and articles. They preached a brand of Socialism
tha was anathema to him. Occasionally they also offended his religious sensibilities, for the *Forward* was quite nonreligious. At the
same time he sympathized with the *Forward's* non-Zionist stand,
though he did not agree with the paper's reasons. Father, I imagine,
envied mother's freedom from such problems. She was a General
Zionist and she was a Hebraist, but she also read Yiddish and English
and Russian, and she had no sense of sin. She did think that Hebrew
was the real language of the Jews, that in the future it would become
the Jews' chief language, but she did not disdain Yiddish. In fact,
she was a great admirer of the writings of Sholem Aleichem and
Mendele and Peretz and Reisin and Opatashu. In other words, she
was not a fanatical Hebraist. She also enjoyed the Yiddish drama,
and Boston at the time was a center of Yiddish drama.

For a period of about ten years, 1905–1915, there was a Yiddish
play to be seen in Boston almost every weekday. Artists like Maurice
Schwartz and the Kalisches and the Tomashefskys and the Adlers
had a special fondness for the Boston Jewish community. I heard my
mother report that Maurice Schwartz once said, "In New York people
come to the theater to amuse themselves. In Boston Jews come to learn
something, to get ideas. That's the difference!"

Boston was rich in Jewish journalism. There was *Der Amerikaner,*
there was the *Leader,* there was (and still is) the *Boston Jewish Advocate.* They were all in one way or another admirable, reflecting the
vibrancy of Jewish life in Boston. Perhaps the best of them all was
the *Advocate,* which was edited by Jacob de Haas. De Haas has been
insufficiently appreciated in Jewish-American history. Besides being
the man who, probably more than anybody else, "converted" Louis D.
Brandeis to Judaism and Zionism, he was an editor of rare talents.

The *Advocate* was a delight to read. It was truly Jewish, truly intellectual, broadly and profoundly Zionistic, and excellent journalistically. It made far less money then, I imagine, than it does now, when it devotes so much space to purely social matters and to columns of finance and sports and "personal interest" items. But it made history. Reading it was a weekly education in Jewish affairs on the local scene and also on the national and international scenes.

A word about the Boston synagogues. I knew them all, I loved them all, for from my earliest days I was a *shul* shopper. I loved the variations in the cantorial chants and cantillation, the divergencies in the little and big things that go on in a synagogue. The Boston synagogues were not merely houses of worship, they were also houses of study. The Beth Hamidrash in every synagogue was its main concern, in accordance with the ancient Jewish tradition that if there is a choice between building a chapel and a Talmud Torah, the chapel can wait. I went to many of the study conventicles when I was a boy in Boston. Those that remain in my mind down the years are the North End Shul, the North Russell Street Shul, and the Phillips Street or Vilner Shul. The North Russell Street Shul is still in existence, but its neighborhood is now far different from what it used to be. The Jewish population is tiny, and the great name of the synagogue is now somewhat diminished.

In its days of glory it was one of the great synagogues of America. To me it has special significance on various counts. First of all, its vice-president was a great-uncle of mine, the son of my grandmother. He was the nabob in our family. He ran a soda and candy store on Leverett Street and did handsomely. It was he who first introduced my father and mother to the Yiddish stage in Boston, and it was he who first took them to the band concert in the Boston Common, something that stamped America as truly a "golden land" in my parents' eyes. "Music, and such wonderful music, for nothing, for everybody to hear! What more could a government do? And Jews are allowed just like any other people in America! A blessing on this land!" This great-uncle of mine offered to get my parents into his synagogue on the High Holy Days at a reduced rate, but my father refused. He preferred to go to his little Vilner Shul.

But my father did accept my great-uncle's invitation to come to the North Russell Street Shul to hear great cantors. When the word went around that one was coming, the synagogue naturally filled up quickly, and that's when my great-uncle came in handy. He took my father and me into the synagogue with him, and father and I had, so to speak, orchestra seats. It was there that I got the full meaning of what it meant to get *dem emessen nigun* ("the true melody") into a prayer. Never will I forget Sirota singing "Lecho Dodi" (Come, My Beloved) on Friday night, and Quartin singing "Ovinu Malchaynu" (Our Father, Our King), and Rosenblatt singing "Adon Olam" (Lord of the Universe). I once heard Sirota chant the *Kiddush* on Friday night with such profound sincerity that I felt shivers of delight pass up and down my spine. I was only a boy, under thirteen, but intuitively I grasped what was being done by these great cantors. I grasped, for all time what Jewish prayer meant, and in a vague way I understood why the Jews have lasted all these years and will last to the end of time.

There was something else I learned in the North Russell Street Shul. On Saturdays, before I was Bar Mitzvah, I was, so to speak, my Alte Bobbe's *Shabbes goy* (Sabbath gentile). I would go with her to the North Russell Street Shul, carrying her prayer-book, and she would wind her handkerchief around her hand or her wrist. That relieved her from any possible charge of carrying something on the Sabbath, and hence performing manual labor. Now and then I would look upstairs at her, where she sat with the other women, and I saw on her face a joy and a delight such as I have never seen since. She looked at her son, the vice-president of the synagogue, and she was happy, as only a woman of ninety can be happy. Her son was a *gabbai* (important functionary) in a synagogue. What greater joy was there for a mother?

But it was in the Vilner Shul, I think, that I was most deeply imbued with the heart and soul of Jewishness. It was a *kabtzonishe shul* (poor man's synagogue), where people of my father's modest circumstances belonged. Since there was no reason here why one Jew should look down upon another, the morale of the synagogue was good. And this equality did something for the young boys as well. The parents couldn't afford a Sabbath Bar Mitzvah and our own Bar Mitzvahs were on Mondays or Thursdays, when the Torah is read at morning services.

I was Bar Mitzvah on Thursday. My father woke me up at 6:30 in the morning, and took me to *shul*. There were about thirty people at the service. I was called to the Torah for the first time—and that was

Bar Mitzvah. Some of the other congregants came over to me and wished me *mazol tov*. My father bashfully put his arm around me and also congratulated me. Then he and I walked a bit and he went off to work. I turned toward home feeling terribly lonely. I had become a full, mature Jew—and most of Boston was asleep, and didn't care. The few people who passed me on the street didn't care either. When I reached our house, as soon as I put my hand on the door knob my mother opened the door and threw her arms around me and kissed me and hugged me and kissed me again. Her arm around me, she took me to the kitchen, which was also our dining room, of course, and there on the table was the *Shabbes* tablecloth. To my mother it was *Yom Tov* (holiday). She had the usual *boolkes* (hot rolls) on a platter, of course, but there was also a platter of the kind of cinnamon cakes I liked, and there was a smaller platter of ginger jam, another favorite of mine. There was also a cup of cocoa. "Eat, Shayel, eat," said my mother. I suggested she have some cocoa too. "No, I'm not hungry." I ate. I was conscious that she was looking at me with great appreciation of what had happened to me. Her oldest son was now a full man in Israel. I was embarrassed, but I was also delighted. I finished my cocoa, and mother said, "Have another cup." The last time she had suggested I have another cup of cocoa was when I was convalescing from a cold that had almost turned into pneumonia. I had another cup. When I was finished with my special breakfast mother said, "Father had to go to work. He had to. You understand."

"Sure," I said.

"But we'll have a small reception on Saturday night, after *mincha* [afternoon prayer]. We've invited the relatives and some friends. So we'll have a little reception."

"Oh," I said, too moved to say anything else.

She got up, came to me, patted my head, and then kissed me slowly. "Maybe you're a little sleepy, Shayel. Maybe you want to sleep a little more. I'll wake you up in time for your school."

"Yes, I think I'll have a little more sleep," I said.

I didn't want any more sleep. I lay down on the bed. I was profoundly happy. Everything was good. Everything was very good.

The rabbi at the North Russell Street Shul seemed aloof to me. I'm sure he wasn't that way actually. My great-uncle said some very nice things about him to my father. Yet I would not have dared to smile at this rabbi. I wouldn't have dared to come up to him and say how nice a day it was, or ask him a question about some puzzling matter in the Bible, or about a matter of ritual or custom. The same was true of the rabbis in the other bigger synagogues that I used to visit. But Rabbi Sharfman in the Vilner Shul was different. The synagogue was small, the people were unpretentious, and they prayed as if they were at home. They held back nothing. If they felt like it, they swayed to and fro to their heart's content, while saying the Eighteen Benedictions or any of the other prayers. If they felt like looking at the ceiling when saying some other prayers, they did so. Of course, they followed the congregational prayer, but they were also themselves. They remained at home, so to speak, while at the same time they were members of All-Israel.

Rabbi Sharfman was the same. He was homey, he was quiet and intimate. He was approachable. Indeed, he was often the first to approach others, young and old. He used to sit to the left of the *Oren Kodesh*, the Ark holding the Torah scrolls, which faced the audience. The president and vice-president of the synagogue sat on top, a few steps above the floor, and to the right and left of the *Aron Kodesh* respectively. But I seldom looked at them. I always looked at the rabbi. I liked his face better. I liked him better. He was a man of mysterious feelings and powers and insights. He was capable of sorrow, and he was capable of joy. The president and the vice-president had ordinary faces. I saw such faces every day in the street and in the grocery store. The rabbi had a synagogue face. He had a synagogue gait—slow, quiet, deliberate. He had a synagogue voice.

His *droshes* (sermons) were brief, gentle, to the point. He pointed out to his small congregation that the Bible was very much up to date; that the principles of Deuteronomy and Leviticus were the abiding principles of mankind—and of the United States in particular; that the labor laws in the Bible were the freest in all human history —truly human, truly democratic, truly kind. He pointed out that it simply wasn't true that the New Testament was a document of love and the Old Testament a document of strict duty and strict justice, that in fact the doctrine of lovingkindness appears in Micah and in Isaiah and in Samuel and in all the other books of the Jewish tradition. He pointed out time and again that it was no accident that the words inscribed around the Liberty Bell came not from the New Testament but from the Old Testament, Leviticus (25.10): "Proclaim liberty throughout the land and to all the people thereof." He

quoted parables and other sayings of the Sages. I was astonished, in
my early youth, at how well read he was, how well he had digested
what he read, how unfanatical he was despite his orthdoxy. I remember well what he used to say when people brought up the fact that
this or that Jew didn't always go to *shul* when he should, or observe
too many of the 613 *mitzvahs* (good deeds). He said, "Eh, I don't
know. A man should observe. Of course a Jew should observe. But
we must remember that it is an *avayreh* [transgression] to cast asper-
sions upon any man who performs deeds of charity. Such a man is good
in the eyes of God. A charitable man in the eyes of God, is like all the
613 *mitzvahs* put together."

Rabbi Sharfman was more than a spiritual leader. He was a job
hunter and an apartment hunter, he was a lay analyst, a home saver,
a social worker, and a doctor. In our poor neighborhood, people generally made use of the "lodge doctor" for ordinary ailments, but when
a family was large the permitted number of doctor calls was pretty
much used up by the early winter. Then the lodge doctor would be
called anyway. He would be paid first with Passover wine, then with
Passover wine and *lekach* (honey cake), then with boiled eggs and
home-baked bread. Then the doctor would not be called any more.
The poor were just ashamed. So they went to the rabbi, and the rabbi
went to the Talmud, which is full of medical lore. I remember my
father asking the rabbi for a remedy for a sour stomach. The rabbi
thought and then said, "It says in the Talmud that a man's stomach
is made up of three parts: one for liquid, one for solid foods, and
one has to be empty. Maybe, Reb Yid, you have put something in the
part that has to be empty? So eat a little less bread, a little less herring,
and if you skip a meal, it won't hurt so much. Try it for a couple
days, maybe three days, don't starve yourself, just eat a little less,
and then let me know." My father did as he was told, and it helped.
Of course, when there was a serious illness the rabbi told the man to
see a doctor, and when the man said he had no money for a doctor
or he had used up the lodge doctor calls, the rabbi would get in
touch with a neighborhood doctor, who would visit the man and
charge him nothing: "Eh, pay me when you can." Or the rabbi
arranged for the sick person to go to the clinic in the neighborhood.

But it was in the spiritual realm that the Vilner Shul rabbi was at
his best. There was a Jewish *meshuggener* in our neighborhood who

converted to Catholicism. Eventually his life was made so miserable that he moved out of the West End. But once in a while he would return and, from the back of an ice wagon, hold forth in behalf of conversion to Catholicism. We boys and girls always gathered around him, not to hear what he had to say—we barely listened—but because he was a good show. Not one of us had enough money to go to a movie more than once a month, so this convert was our entertainment. He would hand out leaflets arguing for the superiority of Catholicism over Judaism, and we would roll the leaflets into balls, soak them in our spit, and throw them at him.

Our parents, however, were afraid we would fall for his arguments and, God forbid, leave the Jewish faith. They went to our rabbi and asked for his advice. The rabbi listened, and then said, "Eh, I wouldn't worry. The children don't care about his arguments. Besides, I know them all and they are all very intelligent. And you should know that this convert is really miserable. We don't like him, and his new Catholic friends don't trust him either. Why? Well, I'll tell you. There was once a convert, a very intelligent man—I mean otherwise intelligent—his name was Heinrich Heine, a fine German-Jewish poet. He was baptized, but as he himself said, he was never really converted. Anyway, he once said that there are two classic ways of wasting water. One is trying to roll it uphill, and the other is baptizing a Jew. So don't worry. After a while, this convert won't come around any more." Of course, that is exactly what happened.

Boston Jewry showed many such rabbis. Boston was a wonderful, tightly knit little Jerusalem. The magazines of the whole Jewish world, and the books and newspapers too, could be bought in the numerous book stores on Leverett and Chambers and Green Streets. The New York Yiddish newspapers even had special Boston editions. Every Jewish home in Boston boasted many *pushkes*—coin boxes—for the Keren Hayesod, the Hebrew University, for a yeshiva here and there, for the orphans of this or that former center of pogrom outbreaks, for a new Talmud Torah in Atlanta, for a new synagogue in a distant town in Texas, and of course there were special *pushkes* for Hadassah . . . and more and more *pushkes*. The cupboard in my parents' kitchen had about a dozen, and although pennies in our household were rare and precious, mother and father managed to put some into every one. It was a *mitzvah* to do that. And the *pushkes* kept the spirit of Bar

Kochba and the Baal Shem Tov and Maimonides and Dr. Herzl ever present in our hearts.

There are not so many *pushkes* now. The Hebrew schools are not what they used to be—perhaps, pedagogically speaking, they are better. The *Jewish Advocate* is not the *Advocate* it used to be. Leverett Street and Green Street have hardly any bookstores now. The Yiddish theater is a memory. Fanueil Hall seldom echoes to the oratory of a Zvi Hirsch Masliansky. Nobody has filled the shoes of Louis D. Brandeis. The present-day rabbis are fine, but how many of them have the nobility, the sense of dedication and sacrifice that, say, the rabbi of the old and now vanished Vilner Shul had?

And yet, some of the old spirit of Boston Jewry persists. Community glories diminish in richness, but they do not completely vanish, certainly not in a few decades. The Golden Age of general American culture is no more in Boston, but who is there, sensitive to echoes and bouquets and aromas, who does not see in his mind's eye, as he walks through the Boston Common or the Public Gardens or along the Charles River or up and down Beacon Hill, the grand and towering figures of Emerson and Thoreau and Lowell and Theodore Parker and Margaret Fuller? And what Jew who is sensitive to Jewish values and to the *Zeitgeist* does not see in his mind's eye, even now, the figures of Brandeis and Jacob de Haas and Hirsch and Tumaroff and Pollack and dozens of others who, for almost two decades, made Boston the Jewish capital of the United States?

(—1962)

My World, and How It Crashed

ᐸᗒᗝᐳ

BERTHA BADT-STRAUSS

A SCHOOLMASTER married his erstwhile pupil, who had in turn become her teacher's teacher. Such was the simple but solid basis on which my parents built their house.

There was quite a lively discussion concerning the wedding date.

"A teacher should marry only in his vacation," insisted the prospective bridegroom. "How can you expect him to concentrate on Gaius Julius Caesar while his heart is 'singing hymns at Heaven's gate' "?

But Grandma, pale and refined in her neat black dress, was adamant. "How can you expect me to get a decent linen trousseau for my daughter in a few short weeks?"

And her daughter was torn between conflicting emotions. "Sometimes she was her mother's dutiful daughter, sometimes the dearest girl on earth," my father wrote in a letter I read many years later.

Well, Grandma won; and the wedding took place on February 3rd, 1885.

How did it all come about?

My mother was a little girl in her teens, and her abundant light-brown hair fell in two smooth schoolgirlish pigtails all the way down to her knees, when she first met the man whom fate had destined to become my father. Little Martha seems to have been a sort of "star" pupil, ambitious and industrious and, I am sorry to add, rather spoilt by her teachers. Like all her girl friends, she was in love with all her Sabbath-school teachers; they amounted to the sizable number of thirteen, as Father often smilingly reminded her. But most of all she adored one teacher who died in his early years. To replace him a young man came who had been highly recommended as a sound scholar as well as a friend of youth.

At first the young Dr. Badt found no favor in Martha's eyes. Like all her school friends, she used to keep a diary. I can see it now, the faded little book, with pages closely covered in her neat, orderly handwriting. On the day of her first lesson with the newcomer, the loyal little soul started a new page in her diary and wrote on the first line: "Today Dr. Badt, the unloved successor of my beloved Professor L—, taught the class . . ."

No, it was not a case of love at first sight; very decidedly not.

Was she perhaps sorry for her rash verdict when she saw all her friends "in love" with the new teacher? He did seem a peculiar sort of man. Dr. Benno Badt was one of eight children of a teacher in a tiny town in Posen, the eastern border province of Germany which is all Polish today. His father had not always been a schoolteacher. He had started his career as a businessman, and only after his commerical enterprises failed did he decide to turn to teaching. But with a clean slate: he paid off all his creditors first. It seems he did a very good job in his new vocation. Anyway, when his granddaughter came to America many years after his death, she met several successful businessmen in Texas and Louisiana who were proud to have been pupils of her grandfather.

His wife Bertha, tall and brown-eyed, was as quick with her needle as with her mind. Family rumor has it that she used to borrow the clothes of her wealthy friends' children and copy them overnight. For it was her ambition to see her eight children looking just as well clad and well fed as the rich neighbors' children. Her sons adored her; and when my father came to America in later years he was deeply moved to see his mother's brown eyes come to life again in the eyes of his little nieces, who had never seen their grandmother. For she had died in early years, killed by that dread disease of the 1850's, the cholera; and as her husband had died before her, the orphans would have been lonely indeed but for some kindhearted relatives in America, the wonderful land of refuge for the Jews of the nineteenth century— and of the twentieth century too.

So my father, who was a student at the Breslau Jewish Theological Seminary, did what he could to get the little sisters well equipped for the new world. He borrowed some cash to buy them decent clothes; and then he used up his own last pennies to buy them complete editions of Goethe and Schiller. For he wanted them to carry the best treasures of the old world to the new.

After some years the young student of theology and classical philology won his Doctor's degree with a learned treatise on the Sybilline Oracles, a mysterious book which united Jewish and Greek ideas. At the same time Dr. Badt was, as all the mothers in Breslau knew, an eligible bachelor, a witty conversationalist who had inherited his mother's sense of humor; she had been so fond of laughter. His favorite book was one of the quaint works written by J. P. Richter, better known to the literary world as Jean Paul—a book entitled *The Merry Life of the Schoolmaster Wuz from Auenthal*. It might have seemed as if Dr. Badt's own life was fashioned in a way on Old Wuz's. Old Wuz loved to buy books, as did my father; but as Old Wuz's pockets were empty, when he badly needed a book he just went ahead and wrote it himself. Thus I remember there was one particular year when Master Wuz had to be very busy indeed: he had to write the romantic tragedy *The Robbers* by Schiller and, not much later, the epoch-making new philosophical book, *Critique of Pure Reason* by Immanuel Kant.

Now I don't mean to say that my father went as far as his favorite hero in getting the books he wanted. Still, often I heard him complain, with a smile, about the efficiency of the old master Wuz from Auenthal.

Although the then unknown American slogan "Keep Smiling" might have been the young scholar's own, at heart he was a lonely man. He felt like an exile in his native land, as he wrote in his Latin *Vita*, which in those days had to be added to each thesis for the Doctorate. He determined to visit his three sisters and two brothers in America.

It was then he recalled a little girl whom he had taught in Sabbath School some years before. Might she not be able to teach him that strange language which his sisters and brothers had learned to speak in the land of their refuge? He himself spoke Latin, Greek and Hebrew; but there had been no English classes in the *Gymnasium* of his youth.

Little Miss Martha Guttmann seemed well fitted for the undertaking. Hers was an old and respected Breslau family. About 150 years before, her grandparents had come from Muensterberg in Silesia. They were successful business people who at one time owned a stately house in the Karl Street in Breslau. But times had changed; the family came to know the ups and downs of commercial life. When Hermann Guttmann died early, his widow, a well-educated, refined woman—

"always the lady!" as her old cook said—was forced to earn her own living. She set up a boarding-school for girls, which soon became one of the most popular schools in Breslau.

She was helped by her two daughters Martha and Gertrud. It was the younger daughter Trudel who led the girls in their social activities; Martha, erstwhile pupil of Dr. Badt, had acquired a brand new degree from Queen's College in London, which entitled her to teach Art and Literature. That was a great thing in those days, when young girls (with few exceptions) were supposed to stay at home and "mind their own business." But after Martha graduated with high honors from the Teachers Seminary (*Lehrerinnen-Seminar*) in her native city, she had not hesitated to go to England, all by herself, and attend Queen's College. Her friends were not a little proud of her; and well may her prospective pupil Dr. Badt have felt, on that Spring day in 1884, that she was just the teacher he needed for his conversational approach to the English language.

In the course of their meetings the student-teacher, as he later on confessed, found out some things about the energetic little girl. Once he even surprised her painting the walls of her bedroom. Anyway, on June 29th, he put the all-important question to his erstwhile pupil. Her answer was a clear-cut No. (She mistakenly thought he was under obligation to marry another girl.)

The next day Dr. Badt sailed for America.

It so happened that many years after my father's trip to America in 1884 I had the good fortune to find a printed report of this visit of a young German professor to the United States. It was written by one who was to become a very famous American woman—Miss Henrietta Szold, lovingly known as "The Mother of Ten Thousand Children." For, in later years, after Hitler came to power in Germany in 1933, she and her helpers organized the emigration of more than 10,000 Jewish children to Palestine and provided for their education in agricultural settlements. Thus Henrietta Szold saved those thousands of young lives from the horrors of concentration camps and gas chambers.

However, in the sunny summer of 1884, in Baltimore, Hitler had not been heard of, was not yet born. Clever and charming Henrietta, the eldest daughter of the learned Baltimore Rabbi Benjamin Szold, was thrilled at meeting the first German professor she ever saw. All the more as this young scholar came from the famous center of Jewish learning in Germany, old Breslau. Her own father had attended the same Theological Seminary in Breslau a generation earlier. Here was a young man who had lived in the same scholarly atmosphere that Henrietta knew so well from her father's memories.

The young Dr. Badt captivated them all by adding to the old remembrances the breath of a new generation, Miss Szold's own young generation, alive to all the problems of her own day. And the "messenger from old Breslau" revealed the same love for both classical antiquity and traditional Judaism, for both German and Jewish culture, which the Szold sisters had known and loved in their father's stories. The visitor and his charming hostesses felt an almost perfect harmony of ideas and ideals. None of them ever forgot those halcyon days of Baltimore in 1884.

My mother never revealed to anyone how the traveler from overseas succeeded in changing her decided No into an equally decided Yes. Anyway, it happened; and on February 3, 1885, the young couple moved into a little house situated near the green trees of the Breslau "Riverside" (*Stadtgraben*). Their furniture was plain and rickety, as they often remarked; but all the more solid was the moral and cultural basis on which this schoolmaster built his house, which seemed to augur an eternity of pleasant days of learning and laughing. Soon a group of interesting friends found themselves assembling in those unassuming rooms.

In spite of household duties and the care of three lively children, my mother continued to teach. Twice a week a group of young girls met in her living-room to study English literature and history of art, as was required of every educated girl in those days. I remember how "Mother's girls" often left the living-room all flushed and excited about a new book or a new idea. Oh, they were well educated, my parents and their friends and pupils. "They had read an awful lot," as Goethe's Faust put it.

We children naturally imbibed this atmosphere. At a very early age we were introduced to the whole Olympus: Greek gods and goddesses decorated our "best parlor." And so "Uncle Apollo" and "Aunt Athena" were no strangers to me, who at that time of life imagined all the world, and heaven too, to consist of one great family. I had to unlearn some of those dreams when I went to school a few years later.

Anyway, in the early years of her marriage, my mother had proudly decorated a wall of her living-room with a reproduction of the Acropolis in Athens. But the opposite wall was adorned with an embroidered picture which she prized just as highly. It was "Jerusalem at Dawn," made by the skillful hands of my great-grandmother. Here were the two centers of her life, Mother used to say. This was the bi-cultural world in which she had grown up and in which she raised her children. It was a friendly world.

In those years a new trend toward liberalism breathed through old Germany. Even an ordinary German citizen often knew Goethe's *Faust* by heart, as well as the Bible. Jews were no exception. Many among our Jewish friends saw in their *Faust* a sort of secularized Bible. Never shall I forget the unassuming Jewish businessman whom we used to meet each year at our summer home on the tiny island in the North Sea. A stately man withal, bearded like a patriarch, he used to walk alone on the beach every afternoon, near sundown, and his lips could be seen to move silently, constantly, slowly. You never knew. Was he saying his afternoon prayers, which he never missed? Or was he reciting all by himself the famous sunset scene from Goethe's *Faust*? Both were possible. Often I heard him recite the famous passages from *Faust* in his native Frankfort dialect which, as he proudly maintained, must be the one and only way to recite them. For was not the poet himself a Frankfort boy too? And then, of course, our friend would switch from Goethe to the Frankfort poet Stoltze, who had wondered all his life at nothing so much as the fact that anybody could have been born outside of Frankfort.

All of us shared the belief of our Frankfort friend that it was not only possible but highly desirable to unite German and Jewish culture —"Shem in the Tents of Japhet," as our Sages expressed it. This general atmosphere of cultural comradeship pervaded my childhood home. Looking back now it seems to me that we took part in the holiday pleasures of our Christian friends without ever forgetting our own Jewish holidays. Our friends lighted their Christmas tree; and at the same time we lighted our Hanukkah candles. There was a friendly competition between the two customs, often discussed among us.

Yes, the Christmas trees in our Christian friends' homes were lots more gorgeous and resplendent than our tiny Hanukkah candles in the *menorah*. But our candles lasted longer, they were lighted seven days in a row, and each day brought a new present to the children and an hour of merry games before the flaming *menorah*.

On a day every spring our faithful maid of all work (generally called Marie or Ida) would step around with a certain purpose to our next-door neighbor, who was the principal of the Johannes *Gymnasium*, where my father taught Latin, Greek and Hebrew. Marie had a covered dish in her hand, wrapped in a clean white towel. It contained a sample of our "unleavened bread," our *matzoth*, which we were accustomed to eat instead of bread for the seven days of Passover. Our neighbors loved to eat *matzoth*, regarded them a delicacy.

On the other hand, we children had a standing invitation to come to Herr Direktor's on New Year's eve. This night the Christmas tree was lighted for the last time; and all the neighborhood children were allowed to despoil it of its various sweets—"to plunder," as we put it. Never shall I forget the scene of the big directorial drawing-room, brimful of noisy children; nor the taste of the special delicacy, the marzipan, a heavenly mixture of almonds and eggs and sugar. The dignified Herr Direktor himself used to cook it, according to an old family recipe. For he came from Koenigsberg, town not only of Kant the philosopher but also of marzipan, the Christmas delicacy. To our youthful palates marzipan was the only dish which could be compared with our own Passover delicacy, the *matzohkrimsel*.

There was not only a sort of "kitchen harmony" between the homes of Jews and Gentiles in those friendly years. Underlying it all was the genuine will to unity based on liberal scholarship on both sides. It was Father's university friend, Professor Hermann Cohen, one of Germany's greatest philosophers, who replied to his friend the Protestant Professor of theology: "What you call 'New Testament ethics'—well, I read all that in my Isaiah long ago."

So we all felt free to share our household holidays with our Christian friends. Always there were some of our little friends around to add to the audience at Purim, the festival of Queen Esther and Mordecai. How they opened their eyes wide when Mother's bridal veil, carefully stored in tissue paper, came out of the attic to serve a new Queen Esther. Our big swing in the vestibule represented the gallows; and well I remember how the villain of the Purim story was supposed to meet his condign punishment there. However, we were not cruel-minded; Father's old overcoat, swinging from the pseudo-gallows,

was quite sufficient for our patriotic enthusiasm. My little sister, with
all her might and main, danced around it chanting the triumphal ode
which was made to order by the reluctant family poet:

> See, oh see, the villain's fate!
> God's hand punished him—not too late!

But all those early spring festivals led up to the big event of our
year, the solemn Passover Seder night. Our house never looked so
beautiful; no wonder, we had been scrubbing and cleaning it for weeks,
because not the least crumb of bread—or of dirt either—was allowed
to remain in our precincts. On the great night, at Seder, our father was
a king and our mother a queen, according to the old saying. We
children did feel in all sincerity as if we had just been liberated from
Pharaoh's slavery: was not the winter over and gone, and was not
spring come with its flowers and birds? All the age-old customs were
alive not only for ourselves but also for the guests who came. Especially
memorable to me will remain that Seder night when my Christian
friend Maria "the God-seeker" happened to drop in; how she enjoyed
the hymns! For were they not addressed to the One God whom the
Christians revered as well as the Jews? Even the language was the
same: some of our Passover songs were sung in a friendly pidgin
mixture of the two languages, old German and older Hebrew:

> *Ail bené, Ail bené,*
> *Bené beth'ha bekarov*
> (Build, O God, build, O God!
> Build Your temple soon again!)
> *Bau O bau . . . bau O bau,*
> *Deinen Tempel schiere!*

This was the world in which I grew up. And looking back it seems
to me that the same friendly interfaith understanding and fellowship
prevailed during my college years. "Don't you know that I am a
philosemite?" said the most famous of my Professors, Erich Schmidt,
the Lessing-biographer. His utterance, often quoted, remained alive
among his disciples and friends as a sort of motto of long forgotten
years of liberalism and good fellowship in old Germany.

Many years after my childhood and youth the crash happened, in
June 1938. At that time our little family of three, my husband and
my little boy and myself, lived in a quiet street in western Berlin.

It was a lovely summer day. The chestnut trees were in full bloom all along our street. Already the first linden trees were beginning to shed their sweet romantic perfume all over the town.

But there was no romance, alas, when I happened to look out on the street from my bedroom window early in the morning. Now I am not at all a habitual window-lookerout. But that particular morning something had awakened me and driven me to the window. What could it mean? Three men were walking briskly side by side along our quiet street. To this day I can hear the sharp clicking of their boots, nailed boots, on the pavement. Two of the men were unknown to me. Their faces seemed almost expressionless, the image of officialdom. But who was the man whom they held all too closely encircled, as if they would like to handcuff him? Goodness gracious: he was none other than our fat, friendly neighbor Mr. B., a well-to-do Jewish businessman. Well did I know how Mr. B. prided himself on being the soul of honesty, not owing a cent to anybody, and paying his taxes to the last penny. Still, there he was, arrested like a common criminal. What in the world could be the matter with him?

It all dawned upon me, and it was a terrible awakening when Mrs. B. rushed into my living-room some minutes later. Mrs. B. was always gracefully poised. Now she was dishevelled, tear-stained, as I had never seen her before.

"They arrested my husband! The Gestapo! They came for him and took him away. What in heaven shall I do? Help me, oh do help me. Dear God in Heaven: if I should never see him again. . . ."

Everybody now knows, or ought to know, what the dreaded Gestapo, the Secret Police, meant. They called it Gestapo in Hitler's Germany, they call it OGPU in Stalin's Russia of today. It can maim your life, it can kill the innocent man just as if some heathen deity, a new kind of Moloch, were claiming his victims. Murder without trial, without the slightest chance of justice for the innocent man who dies not knowing why he dies.

At that instant, for the first time, with a cruel flash I felt the world of my childhood days was about to crash, and all of us were in mortal danger of being buried underneath its ruins. Up to that day in 1938, ever since Hitler had come to power in 1933, so many of our kind had been living in a sort of daze and nightmare: we waited with anxiously beating hearts for all the evil ghosts to disappear, and then how we should awake and rejoice! Oh, it was a dream only . . .

Now for the first time in our lives we saw that *our* world was no more. Now the evil ghosts reached right to our doorstep. And there was nobody who cared enough for our welfare, nay for our bare existence, to drive them away.

That was the beginning of the darkest days of my life. But no more than a beginning. Mr. B. did have the rare good fortune to come back after some time, from a mysterious jail. He was strangely changed, and never told anybody what had happened to him. Then after some months they returned to arrest him for the second time. And he never came back again: we never heard any more about him.

Yes, that was the beginning of the earthquake in my life, but it was by no means the end. The Moloch claimed his sacrifices among our friends and neighbors. Soon his gruesome arms reached out for our very selves.

Soon we all were to realize starkly what I but dimly sensed on that morning in June: that our world, the world of justice and goodwill, was gone from Germany: and nobody seemed to care . . .

A tearful dishevelled little schoolgirl came to our house some months later. We knew her well: her father was a well-known physician, who had helped most of the babies in the neighborhood to enter this sorry world. Chubby little Elsie herself was a pupil of my husband's and a friend of all the family. But today she was almost unrecognizable. Deathly pale, she grasped both of my hands and hoarsely whispered: "Send him away! . . . oh, do send the Doctor away! . . . Don't let him sleep in his own bed to-night! They will kill him . . . they will kill all the Jews in Germany!" And she choked with tears.

At first we did not understand what she wanted. In vain we tried to calm her. Then, slowly and stammeringly, she told us her story. Some Gentile friends of her father's, grateful patients of his, had divulged the secret plans of the Nazis: every male Jew in Berlin was to be arrested and sent to a concentration camp. By this time we all knew that meant a fate worse than death.

"Now, now, take it easy, little Elsie!" said my husband, even-tempered as always. "Let me first have my cup of coffee, and then we shall see about it."

Nevertheless, even my husband lost his usual good cheer when he tried to call the members of his faculty on the phone and found that the very first man he called had just been arrested by the Secret Police. The man's sister answered the phone, and her voice broke with sobs.

From that day onwards we lived the life of hunted animals, all the Jews of Germany. Never before had I understood the passion of the hunter, nor the fear of the hunted. We began to feel what hunted animals must feel. We knew not why we had to suffer, nor how to end our sufferings. Was this country, with its green valleys and lush woods, the same country which we loved, which our parents and grandparents had loved? Where they and their fathers before them had lived in peace and good fellowship with their Gentile neighbors? Where our sons and brothers had fought side by side with their fellow-citizens . . . yes, and died with them? Here was my own brother, who was wounded in the First World War at its very beginning in August 1914. Now he was hunted like a criminal along with all his fellow-Jews.

No, we could never understand it. Had the Middle Ages really come back in the year 1938 to our enlightened times? Oh yes, we had learned all about the medieval persecutions of the Jews in school. But we had forgotten it all, and had been glad to forget.

However, whether we understood it or not, we had to get accustomed to a totally new and peculiar manner of living. None of our husbands, brothers or sons dared sleep in his own bed at night. Sometimes, of an afternoon, a slightly disguised voice (alas, we were no experts at Robin Hood stories!) asked the housewife over the telephone: "Did you have any visitors?"

Sure enough, on the very afternoon little Elsie brought us her warning I did have a visitor, two of them. Two husky men in civilian clothes came and asked for the master of the house. They searched all our closets, as though they suspected I had hidden my husband underneath a bundle of old clothes.

Luckily, our buxom cook sent them off in her brusque way. "Herr Doktor is not here—do you think he tells me where he goes?" Reluctantly, they went away.

After a while one of them came back. All of us shook with fear. But it turned out he only wanted to date our cook. A little comedy amidst all this horror!

Those were the days when in Paris an unhappy, half-demented Jewish boy from Poland, whose parents had been murdered by the Nazis, tried to take his revenge by killing a clerk in the German embassy. None of us knew the boy or his parents. But here in Berlin the diabolical Doctor Goebbels welcomed this unique chance to unleash "the people's fury," as he called it. And—one, two, three—on November 10, when the German people were wont to celebrate the birthday of their great Protestant reformer Martin Luther, and of their great poet Friedrich Schiller, the singer of human dignity and liberty—on that very day the windows crashed and the candelabras broke into a hundred pieces in most of the Jewish synagogues and temples all over Germany. Oh yes, it was great fun for all the schoolboys in our neighborhood. Shall I ever forget the venerable schoolmaster whom I saw in the block of the Levetzowstreet-Synagogue? There he was, marching at the head of all his pupils and commanding in his shrill officer's voice: "One, two, three!" And each boy threw the rock from his grimy palm into the windows of the famous synagogue.

Those were the days when good friends and neighbors of yesterday blushed on seeing us in the streets and looked the other way. Their youngsters had long ago joined the Storm Troopers (SS) and were happy to howl their favorite song on Friday nights right in front of half-demolished synagogues: *When Jewish blood dyes red our knife, All will feel twice as good. . . .*

Those were the days when my childhood world crashed, never to rise again. And God looked on. . . .

It was then that a hand reached out from across the ocean to save our lives. After a long delay—caused by all sorts of red tape—we were at last allowed to enter this blessed country across the seas, which had saved our father's brothers and sisters before. Nor shall I ever, ever forget the day when we first looked upon the Lady who "lifts her lamp beside the Golden Door."

We were among the pitifully few, the fortunate ones, who were given the chance to build up a new life in a new world, after our own world had been destroyed. It was Thanksgiving Day in America when we landed: for us Thanksgiving Day in the most literal sense of the word.

But very soon after the first wave of relief and happiness had laved our hearts, we felt ourselves tormented with the haunting question: Why? Why were we saved while most of our friends had to perish?

We had left our native land on a sultry day in August 1939. A faithful little group of friends and relatives had assembled at Charlottenburg Station to see us off. They were hoping we would all meet in the new world to build up a new life. There was the Old Professor, our next-door neighbor, his frail body sustained by an indomitable will, and there was his brave wife, kindest of hospitable souls. There was the upright lawyer to whom we entrusted the care of our few worldly goods. (He tried in vain to save them from Nazi robbery.)

And there was my close dear friend, the tall lovely woman who had been a famous society belle in her youth, who had now become a selfless social worker and proud Jewish enthusiast; lover of German poetry, who knew Goethe's *Faust* by heart.

Why did all these pure souls have to perish? They still haunt my dreams at night. They will haunt me as long as I live.

Could it be that this is the meaning of ourselves having been miraculously saved from death: that there should remain some people, scattered all over the world, who do not sleep at night, and are haunted by the souls of the innocent millions who had to die? Some people who did not just read in the newspapers, "*Six millions have been murdered*" . . . and forget all about it in a happier world? Some who knew deep in their hearts: this man and that woman, whom I loved and admired, they were murdered in cold blood. Some people who must continue to tell the world about the unbelievable crime, and ceaselessly implore: Watch out! Never let it happen again!

This is why I had to tell you about my world, and how it crashed.

(—1951)

Riots or Lamps

ᏸᎧᏁᎧ

JOSEPH WECHSBERG

Always when the going gets a bit too tough and I feel run down by the wheels of a hostile world, I try to think of what Uncle Absolon would have done under the circumstances. This method generally restores my belief in mankind.

Uncle Absolon always looked on the brighter side of things. He wasn't the one in the family who said all the wise things; this was Grandfather, as in most families. But we of the younger generation were fascinated by Uncle Absolon's faith in humanity and the bizarre ways it was manifested. He made the best even of the most dreadful time of his life, the seventeen months he spent as an Austrian prisoner of the First World War in a Siberian camp: he went to Vladivostok and thence to San Francisco, where he wisely interrupted his eastbound trek and settled down for good.

Uncle Absolon's pre-American life was closely connected with the small Austrian-Moravian town of Weisskirchen, where he had founded and owned the thriving firm of Krauss Bros., Textile and Cotton Goods. The "Bros." was a typographical error. When he founded the firm, Uncle Absolon intended to take one of his brothers in as a silent partner, but they quarreled and separated. Unfortunately, the business stationery had already been printed at considerable cost; and rather than reprint the letterheads and envelopes, Uncle Absolon decided to keep the "Bros." in the firm.

The textile and cotton trade provided my uncle with an ever-ready pretext to evade, temporarily at least, the harsh regime of Aunt Melanie, his wife, and to undertake "business trips" to such places as Paris, Venice and Monte Carlo, although the commercial connection wasn't quite clear. From these journeys Uncle Absolon always came home full of zeal and startling innovations. Back from a philatelic exhibition in Stockholm he persuaded several owners of old houses in

Weisskirchen to break up their roofs because there might be some
letters hidden up there. They didn't find any Cape of Good Hope or
Wuerttemberg, and Uncle Absolon had to indemnify the enraged
house-owners for new roofs. A visit to London and Hyde Park resulted in an effort to establish complete freedom of speech in
Weisskirchen's Town Park—a venture promptly suppressed by the
Austrian Police.

From Paris Uncle Absolon, greatly impressed by the charm of the
boulevards, returned eager to embellish Weisskirchen's main street in
a boulevard-like fashion. The city fathers readily agreed. Uncle Absolon, who was Assistant Mayor, promised to cover all expenses. The
first step of the embellishment program was to put meter-high, circular
iron plates around every third oak tree, providing the street with a
great many gents' rooms, and thus creating a definite Parisian atmosphere. But when the shocked womenfolk of Weisskirchen threatened
to picket the "scandalous, immoral establishments," Uncle Absolon had
to tear down the iron enclosures.

This was the end of his career as city builder. Proclaiming that
from now on Weisskirchen would have to provide for its own embellishment, he retired to the meetings of the City Council. This
august body consisted of Mayor Havelka; Uncle Absolon as Assistant
Mayor; Dr. Kugelmann, physician and city treasurer; and Father
Jaromir, the town's cleric. The Council met every night at Anton's
Beer House, where momentous local matters were discussed during
a game of whist.

About this time the town of Weisskirchen was perturbed by strange
rumors from Vienna. Herr Lueger, the *Buergermeister* of the capital,
was eager to rouse the masses for a crusade of liberation from "the
brutal yoke of Liberals, Jews and Freemasons." Another Aryan named
Bielohlavek proclaimed, amid cheers from guttural throats and beer-
glasses, that literature was "what one radical copies from the other."
Thus they ushered in a "new phase of life."

Soon the new phase was illustrated with minor riotings and broken
windows in some Austrian and Moravian towns.

Weisskirchen faced a dilemma. The only impressive two-story building in town, with a large plate-glass window and a definite liberal-
Jewish-freemasonish aspect, was Uncle Absolon's house and place of
business. His living quarters were on the second floor; the ground
floor and mezzanine were occupied by the Krauss Bros. salesrooms

and stockrooms. Now, should this house be the target of the attack? No one dreamed of doing any harm to Uncle Absolon, the town's benefactor and best-liked citizen. However, as pressure from Vienna continued, things began to demand a peremptory solution. One night, after the whist game, Mayor Havelka put the matter before the City Council.

"There has been rioting in all the neighboring towns. Leipnik, Prerau and Sternberg have had their demonstrations. In Neutitschein they almost wrecked a coffee-house." He sighed. "Weisskirchen cannot stand behind. They'd say we are sissies. We'll have to do something."

"There will be no violence against Uncle Absolon. We are all children of the same Father," said Father Jaromir with emphasis. An energetic as well as religious man, he wasn't afraid to mention the personal issue. "Do you know that Uncle Absolon has agreed to buy five hundred egg yolks which will provide a new coat of paint for the church?"

"Make it six hundred, Father," said Uncle Absolon, grateful.

"Gentlemen, gentlemen!" said the Mayor. "I am the last man to encourage violence against Uncle Absolon. To me one religion is as good as the other—"

"Or as bad!" said Dr. Kugelmann, the town's leading atheist.

"—but something has to be done," said the Mayor, with finality. "More beer, Anton!"

Gloom settled down on the assembly. They all liked Uncle Absolon, but the fact remained that he was the prominent non-Christian citizen, and the crusaders in Vienna wanted to see action.

Finally Uncle Absolon had an idea. "You know, I've always believed in people. They are not as bad as Schopenhauer made them out. Why don't you organize a nice little riot? Nothing serious, of course. The angry crowd could be formed on the Market Place and would then march down Main Street toward my house. There they could demonstrate an outburst of spontaneous rage and throw a few stones at my windows. Afterwards the crowd will dissolve. Thus serious harm to my other, non-Christian, friends will be avoided."

The City Council thought the idea was acceptable.

"We'll of course reimburse you for the broken window from city funds," said the Mayor.

"How?" asked Dr. Kugelmann in alarm. Like every treasurer he hated the word "reimburse." "We don't have available money. There's just a little in the lamp account."

"We'll pay it from the lamp account," said the Mayor.

"But people in the park district demand two new gas lamps."

"Riots or lamps," decided the Mayor. "They can't have both. They'll have to wait another month for the lamps, until additional money comes in."

"Don't break the large window," said Uncle Absolon. "It would be too expensive. Concentrate on the smaller one. It's cracked in the upper corner anyway."

There was a lengthy discussion about the time of the riot. Mayor Havelka suggested Sunday morning at ten would be best, when nobody had anything else to do. Uncle Absolon pleaded for eleven o'clock. On Sundays Aunt Melanie always needed an hour for her hair-do, he explained, and no one would like to expose his wife to public violence in an improper state. The gentlemen present agreed fully with that. The Mayor and Dr. Kugelmann had wives too.

At this point my uncle always stopped to emphasize that Mayor Havelka was a great organizer. Calling in the members of the *Turn-und-Gesangverein*, the three firemen, the football club and the youthful poolroom crowd, the Mayor informed them that next Sunday at eleven there would be public rioting instead of bowling. Dr. Kugelmann supervised the selection of stones to be used in the assault. He eliminated all big ones which might result in injuries and keep him from his Sunday afternoon nap. Father Jaromir was to appear toward the end of the demonstration in front of Uncle Absolon's house and send the mob home with harsh spiritual condemnation and a few Bible quotations.

Meanwhile Uncle Absolon faced the truly difficult task to inform Aunt Melanie. As he expected she was aghast.

"Rioting, Absolon? A pogrom perhaps! Do you know what this means? They will kill us, burn down the house, destroy my garden . . ."

"Now, now, now, now," said Uncle Absolon. "I've always told you that you don't have faith in your fellow-creatures . . ."

"I don't care for the creatures. I'm not going to let them kill me! I'm going to leave town. I'll spend the week in Prague, with cousin Jarmila."

"You'll do nothing of the sort!" My uncle straightened himself to rare greatness. "Can't you learn that people are *good*? You'll stay right here and bake three loaves of strudel. After the thing's over they will all be hungry. I told them to come up for a bite. We'll give them goulash and beer and your strudel. Don't you know they are all crazy about your strudel, Melanie?"

Aunt Melanie smiled, reconciled.

Everything went almost according to schedule. The mob assembled, got into affected rage and demonstrated. But a man named Schultes became really excited and threw two very large stones against the plate-glass window of Krauss Bros. The glass broke. At that, the mob made for Schultes, who wasn't a native and had come to the town only eight years before from Bavaria. But Mayor Havelka appeared on the scene in time and made a speech. Father Jaromir supplied impressive Bible quotations. A few members of the poolroom crowd knocked down Schultes. At that, Mayor Havelka adjourned the meeting; and the ring-leaders of some social standing went up to Uncle Absolon's for a *Gabel-fruehstueck,* while the mob went home to their Sunday dinners. Weiss-kirchen could proudly boast of its share of wild rioting.

"You see, Melanie," said Uncle Absolon that night, after the guests had left and the maids were busily washing dishes, "there *is* some good in mankind. If you'd only learn to believe in people!"

"What about the large broken window?"

"The Mayor said they'll pay for a new one. I guess the folks in the park district will have to stumble around in darkness for another couple of months."

(—1942)

Reb Leib Sarah's Explains

༄

I. M. LASK

Some time ago I reread one of Martin Buber's versions of Jewish folk stories. And very good, impressive reading they all make, I must add. That glowing, luminous style which he spent over forty years in adapting to his manifold and multifarious needs had not yet mastered him. (This, I should add, is based on the admission of the sage Professor himself.) Here he was retelling tales of angels, spirits and demons in a German guaranteed to make the hyperintellectual Jews of the Stefan George climate feel that maybe their ghetto ancestors had had something on the ball in spite of everything. The sense of a vast brooding universe in which Man may nevertheless achieve meaning and purpose was brought home in every line. Here was a slow, solemn dance, now of death, now of life, now of those potencies and contingencies which lie beyond either; and more than all else, one's sense of awe was guaranteed to commence operations. It was writing that was thoroughly *zielbewusst*, streamlined after its fashion for its own particular purpose.

And there I came across the story of Reb Leib Sarah's and the corpse. A remarkable person was Reb Leib Sarah's. He was the intermediary, the messenger of the great Chassidic saints and wonder rabbis in the middle third or so of the eighteenth century. The *Meshullah* or Emissary of Ansky's *Dybbuk* is a pale shadow of him. He knew the secret of shortening the roads; and so he could drive a horse and cart all the way from Brody to Vienna and back on a brief winter's Friday afternoon. He could manage to be seeing but unseen, and when necessary would descend on the Austrian Kaiser Joseph and give him a sound drubbing in the presence of the full but uncomprehending court. Then he would return to Brody or Cracow or Lemberg or wherever it might be and cheerfully hallow the Sabbath and sit down to the Friday-evening repast feeling that a good job had been well done.

He could do wonders, but if anybody came along while he was doing them he would incontinently vanish. At markets and fairs he would open a shop which he kept empty. If anybody came to ask what he was selling, he would reply, "Faith." All in all, a by no means unimpressive gentleman.

And now I read once again, in Buber's version, how Reb Leib Sarah's came to one such fair and went up to a zombie-like man standing mutely behind one of the merchants. He raised the man's long *kapote* and displayed to all and sundry the cerements which the fellow was wearing. Thereby he broke the spell by which the poor corpse had been brought from the grave; and the corpse was able to return to its rest.

An awesome, creepy tale. Warlocks and enchanters stand round about even in the Jewish business world and twice-weekly market. Beware, beware, "or the gobberlins'll getcher if you don't watch out."

Reading it, I thought of the tale in the fashion I had first heard it. The busy market, full of carts and wains and wagons and booths and stalls and peasants and dealers. The mud and straw underfoot. The communal inspectors of weights and measures striding officiously from one Jewish booth to the next. The *Yor-eidus* or market witness seated gravely in front of the communal offices or being summoned to an inn to attach his name to some agreement between two merchants. The bargaining, the cheapening, the tricking and cozening, the shrewd eyes of bearded peasants measuring the Jews they knew and the Jews who were trying to muscle in, and reckoning which would pay a better price. And in the middle of them all an excited cadaverous Jew edging into one deal without knowing what it was about, offering eight instead of the other fellow's seven; dashing on and poking his nose into another transaction in which he offers to supply the goods for fifteen while the other chap is standing on his twenty; darting across the market between the carts and booths and horses and men and beasts to dig his finger in the ribs of some oxen and pile some barley on his open hand or pick up a fistful of meal like the priest in the Pentateuch; saying, "What muck you've brought here!" and dashing off again.

All of a sudden someone taps him on the shoulder. He turns round. It's Reb Leib Sarah's.

"Excuse me, Reb Jew," says Reb Leib Sarah's. "You're dead but you don't know it."

The Jew's jaw drops.

"*Tackeh, tackeh,*" says he. "Quite right, quite right." "I've been so busy I've clean forgotten."

And he toddles to his tomb, nice and quiet and peaceful-like.

And so Reb Leib Sarah's brought rest to a soul that had lost its way.

Two versions of the same tale. Which was more likely to mirror something of the actual happening? Naturally I preferred the story which had come my way, with all its symbolic significance. Apart from anything else, the story of sorcery and gramarye belongs to the sixteenth and seventeenth centuries of Jewish folklore, not to the eighteenth. The vital thing about the Chassidim was that they found wonder immanent in the everyday, while their forebears, more like our own selves, tended to be overwhelmed and dismayed at the sheer precipitous perils of very existence.

But did it simply mean that a man can lose his soul without even gaining the world if he strains after the world too much? My feeling was that something or other had once occurred; and like most real occurrences, it was susceptible of as many interpretations as there are interpreters.

Who could know what really happened? Clearly, the dead Jew and Reb Leib Sarah's. But the Jew was nameless and in any case dead; while nothing is recorded in legend and fable of the death of Reb Leib Sarah's; a significant fact which puts him in the category of Enoch, Elijah the Tishbite whom it is good to refer to, and Rabbi Joshua ben Levi who pinched the sword of the Angel of Death and entered Eden alive.*

In that case Reb Leib Sarah's could not be beyond reach. All that was needed was to know how to establish contact.

There are various methods, including those of imagination and extrapolation. But they are not all. The important thing is that if a Jew wants to contact another Jew of any age or clime, he can do so. I may go further—sometimes the contact is virtually instantaneous. In the case of Reb Leib Sarah's it took a little time, I must admit. But in due course we found ourselves in touch, *yoshvim shevet tahkemoni;* which may mean slightly more to those who know Hebrew than to those who don't.

---

* I afterwards found, in the course of desultory reading, that two communities claimed the honor of housing Reb Leib Sarah's bones in their graveyards. Which makes matters even queerer.

Reb Leib Sarah's was pretty much what I expected, but not quite. To my surprise he wanted to know all about my stock; and only after I mentioned the family grandsire Reb Zalman Taub did I pass muster.

"You'll do," said he. "Zalman was a good boy and did his time in the Lamed Vav, the Thirty-six. He pulled off some good pieces of work, what's more."

"Do you mean that the old yarn's true and he really was one of the Thirty-six Saints?" I asked in surprise.

"Saints? Who's talking about saints? That's not for you and me," said Reb Leib Sarah's. "Maybe they could have handled the saints' end of it too, but it wasn't their job. No, they were the *Nistarim,* the hidden ones; and with good reason, considering what they had to do from time to time. When you had to release a captive or get a Jewish child out of Gentile hands you couldn't always just walk up and offer a price, the way we did with the Tartars in Crimea or at the Stamboul slave market. No, you had to find other ways and means now and again, and so it was better to have it aitch you ess aitch, meaning keep your trap shut."

"Then he did—"

"Yes, and plenty more"—Reb Leib Sarah's nodded—"or I wouldn't be talking to you now. And whatever's going on in your time, I'm sure the old rule applies—aitch you ess aitch, keep your trap shut."

"But I'm living in the state of Israel," I protested.

"Maybe so," he replied, unimpressed, "but when?" And he went into a brief definition of Messianic doctrine in Kabbalistic terms that upset quite a number of my notions about the meaning of revolution.

"In fact," he finished, "not only maybe so but all the more so if you've merited to live in a state of Israel.—But to come back where we started. What did you want to talk to me about? Just plain everyday chatter of the disciples of the wise, or something specific?"

"Well," said I rather hesitantly, "I wanted to ask what you really used to do that all those stories got out about you."

"Lord of the Universe!" exclaimed Reb Leib Sarah's. "Don't you know the meaning of *Behadrag* any longer?"

"*Behadrag?*" said I thoughtfully. "Why, that's the initials of *Beherem Derabennu Gershom,* under penalty of Rabbenu Gershom's ban. Of course I know. But what's that to do with it?"

"Don't you still use the formula with letters?"

"No. Why should we? We have the public postal service."

"And do you mean to tell me that you are prepared to trust anything of that kind? Something must have changed. We certainly didn't in my day. Oh, no! *We* weren't prepared to let any of our correspondence pass through the hands of any Gentile government—not if we could help it! No! Every Jew knew that if he had to send a letter he just had to fold it. If he wrote *Behadrag* on it he didn't even need to seal it. Then he'd hand it over to the nearest Jewish wagoner for delivery. And from then on it was my affair—in my time at least."

"Meaning that you were a kind of postmaster in the Jewish postal system?"

"Not a kind of Jewish postmaster," said he proudly. "I was the last person appointed by the Council of the Four Lands to supervise the postal system we maintained, and the other things that had to be run along with it. That way I had to move about a lot and had to be in touch with people who were on the move. After the Council was abolished I made it my business to keep the post going. The job was easiest in Austria because as soon as the Austrians took over Galicia they began building roads; but I kept it going elsewhere too."

"Didn't that involve you in smuggling?"

"Not me. My share of the job was kept clear of that. It wasn't advisable for me to be involved personally, not if I wanted to keep things going. That some of my carters did a little shifting and fetching and carrying on the side I'd be the last to deny. No, it wasn't with the customs departments I personally had anything to do. My contacts were elsewhere. From time to time I had to be prepared to do some personal favors to make sure our boys had free right of passage. A colonel here and a high judge there might need to send a letter that didn't pass through official channels but reached the right quarters just the same. I found it always paid to do a favor in that respect."

Now I remembered a mid-nineteenth-century hypothesis about Reb Leib Sarah's; namely that he had been a secret agent of the Austrian government, which would account for his visits to the Royal Palace in Vienna. I taxed him with it.

"A secret agent? I? Oh, no! Not even a courier! They traveled fast, they did, but somehow the letters that passed through hands arrived just as fast; and the Chancellery could always be sure that they had not been opened and read on the way."

"I suppose the connections must have been useful."

"Yes," he agreed. "With the right bit of paper showing at the right place I could pass through some very tight spots. It didn't always have to be a bit of paper either. After all, I suppose a bit of gold or silver is just as lucky a charm as it used to be. Everything taken together helped to make me invisible when necessary."

"And how about the shortening of the roads?" I wanted to know.

"Isn't it obvious? I was the best informed person in the country on the state of the roads and the weather. And besides, I was lucky. I had a kind of sense of direction, not only by day but at night as well. And there were many occasions when carts and wagons traveled by night, for all kinds of reasons. Most carters knew their own districts, but beyond them they were stuck. I was lucky. I knew the short cuts."

I remembered the old phrase about Polish roads; and I remembered how my own father had once set out with a cartload of goods, at least a century after Reb Leib Sarah's time, which he had to deliver in a neighboring town. He started out on Sunday night and should have been back Tuesday morning, but he didn't get home until Friday just before the Sabbath, because the carter consistently lost his way.

"Exactly." Reb Leib Sarah's nodded again when I told him the tale. "It was the kind of thing that was happening all the time in my day. Everybody who started out on a journey had good reason for saying the Prayer for the Way. But I knew more than most and was lucky into the bargain. After all, merchants went to the fair once a year, but I was likely to be at ten markets and five fairs in that time."

"And what was this business about an empty shop and you saying you sold Faith?"

"Well, what else would you say I sold? There was bound to be an official post office there, and was I going to stick my finger into their mouths by proclaiming out loud what my business was? Of course those whose job it was to know, they knew all about me and would be waiting for me. And besides, it was very useful to have a place where Jews could drop in and say their prayers and do a little studying on the side, particularly when it came to passing on information connected with *Pidyon Shevuyim,* the ransoming and saving of captives.

"I'll show you how it worked," he went on. "Someone had to cross the frontier with news and information. It was a rather risky business just then and I had no idea who the messenger was to be. (If you want to know, it was just after the Gonta massacres, and the ordinary carters weren't allowed to cross.) I had no idea who the fellow would be this time, but we had the password, *Ani hashuv kemet,* A poor man's as good as dead." (He didn't pronounce it that way, but why be a purist?)

"I waited the first day, and nobody came. I waited the second day and no one turned up. It occurred to me that the Russians might have somebody on the watch, so my man would prefer not to come in. Out I went into the fair to see what was happening, and if I could strike it lucky.

"Now a fair's a fair. I walked round inspecting this and pricing that and keeping an eye open. Before long I noticed a Jew who was much too busy at his affairs, and everybody else's. He was poking his nose into each bit of business, trying to edge a piece of commission for himself. But halfway through he seemed to lose interest and shifted over to something else somewhere else; trying to lose himself, as it were. It struck me he was acting just like one of those lost empty souls of the world of void and chaos. Could this be my man on the lookout for me, I wondered? And over I went to him, and tapped him on the shoulder.

" 'Poor Reb Jew,' I said to him. 'You're in such a rush, I think you must be dead, only you're too busy to remember.'

"The fellow turned black in the face. 'Me dead?' he shouted. 'Me dead? Why, where's my shrouds and deadclothes? Would I be chasing round in the market polluting every Cohen in the place if I were dead? Me, a decent godfearing Jew like me!'

"Suddenly he stopped a moment. Then he flared up once again with burning eyes. 'A poor fellow like me trying to make an honest living he has to insult! Why, you—you're a putrid carcass yourself!'

"In that case, said I, 'let's both go for purification.' For I knew I'd found my man."

"But explain one thing to me," said I. "You say the Lamed Vav weren't saints and didn't do wonders. Now take my ancestor, Reb Zalman the tailor. When he saved children he gave each of them an amulet to be opened only on the child's wedding day. And in due course the amulets were opened and thanks to them a sister was saved from marrying her brother. How did he know in advance?"

Reb Leib Sarah's stared at me in astonishment.

"This *is* a queer dream I'm having," said he at last. "Talking to someone out of the future who claims to be a descendant of our Zalman, and who knows enough to get on to me, but doesn't understand the elementary facts of Jewish life! Well, I've told you so much, I'll explain that as well. Can't you understand that the danger of incestuous marriages due to lack of information and common sense was *the* thing we had to guard against in the circumstances? Could we take more than one child to the same safe place? Could we let the child keep his real name?"

He outlined the whole situation and technique to me. Then he added:

"When you get down to brass tacks, only one thing really counts—that Jews and Jewesses know exactly who and what they're marrying. How can you be sure of the holy sparks otherwise? What kind of state of Israel is it going to be where a fellow like you doesn't realize that?"

Truth to tell, it is only during the last few months, years and years after our conversation, that I have come to understand how correct he was.

(*—1962*)

FICTION AND TRUTH

The Prayer-Book

⚜

MARTIN BUBER

IT WAS the custom of the rabbi of Dynow when he stood up to pray before the Ark of the Covenant on the two high holidays known as the Awful Days, that is, the Feast of New Year and the Day of Atonement, to open the large prayer-book of Master Luria and to put it on his lectern. It lay open before him all the while he prayed, though he neither looked into it nor touched its pages, but let it lie before the Ark and the eyes of the people, large and open, so that its strong unblurred black letter glared forth from its wide yellowish background while he stood over it in his sacred office like the High Priest celebrating before the altar. Such was his habit and the eyes of the people saw this time after time but no one of the Chassidim ever dared to speak thereof. Once, however, a few took heart and asked the rabbi: "Master and Teacher, if you pray from the book of Master Luria why do you not look into its pages and follow the order of its prayers? But if you do not, why does it lie open before you all the time?" And the rabbi said to them: "I will tell you something that happened in the days of the holy Baal Shem, blessèd his memory.

"In a certain village there lived a Jewish landholder with his wife and little son. The lord of the manor was fond of him, for he was a quiet man, and granted him many favors. Evil days, however, came on him. Summer after summer bad crops followed, and want grew and swelled in his house till the grey waves of misery dashed over his head. He had held his own against hard work and poverty, but beggary he could not face. He felt that his life was ebbing away, and when his heart stopped at last it was like the dying of a pendulum-swing whose steady slowing passes unnoticed until its final lull seems to take one by surprise. His wife who had passed with him through the good and evil days of his fortune soon followed him. When he was buried she could no longer restrain herself; she looked at her young son and not even then could she smother her longing for her dead husband. So she lay down, saying to herself all the time that she was not going to die—till she was dead.

"Little Nachum was three years old when his parents died. They had come from a faraway country and no one knew their kinsmen. So the lord of the manor took him into his house, for the boy with his small face shimmering blossom-white out of his golden locks found grace in his eyes. He soon came to love more and more this delicate, dreamy child, and brought him up as his own. And thus the boy grew in light and joy, and was taught in all the arts and sciences. Of the faith and nation of his parents he knew nothing. Not that his foster-father kept from him the knowledge that his father and mother had been Jews, but when speaking of this he would always add: 'But I have taken you and you are now my son and all that is mine shall be yours.' This Nachum could well understand, but what was said of his parents seemed to him to be one of those fairy tales told by the servants, stories of wood-spirits, mermaids, and gay elfin folk. That he himself should be involved in such a story was dark and wonderful to his mind, and he felt wrapt in a strange twilight, and fear and longing arose in him, a yearning which seemed at times to bathe his soul in light dreamy waves, which was always weird and marvelous to him.

"One day he suddenly came upon a deserted room of the house, where there lay a heap of things which his parents had left behind. Strange and unknown these were to him. He saw a curious loose white tunic with long black stripes; a woven kerchief of fine yet simple workmanship; a large many-branched candelabrum of faded splendor; a richly chased, crown-shaped spice-box about which there still seemed to linger a faint aroma. And there was finally a large thick book bound in dark-brown faded velvet with silver-trimmed edges and silver clasps. These were things which his parents could not part from even in the extreme of poverty. And little Nachum stood and looked at them, and the messengers of dusk seemed nearer than ever around him. Then he took the book, shyly and carefully, and clasping it with both arms he carried it to his room. There he unfastened the clasps and opened it wide. The large black letters stared at him, strange and yet familiar, winked at him like a group of young friends, beckoned to him like a cluster of dancing playmates, whirled around him, twined through the pages, flew up and down, swam before his eyes—and lo! the letters vanished, the book was like to a dark sea, and two eyes gazed at him from its depth, tearless yet full of eternal sadness. And Nachum knew that this was the book from which his mother had prayed. From that day on he kept it hidden in the daytime but every night would take it out from its hiding-place and, by the light of the lamp or, better, by the living light of the moon, he would look at the strange letters which danced before him and flowed into a sea whence the eyes of his mother gazed at him.

"And thus came the days of judgment, the days of grace, the Awful Days. From many villages Jews traveled to the city to stand before God with the clamor of the multitude, to bring Him their sins together with the sins of thousands and burn them on the fire of his mercy. Nachum was standing by the door of his house and saw numberless wagons hurry by, saw men and women in festive garments and a spirit of expectancy over all. And he thought that these were messengers to him, no longer envoys of darkness but of light now and peace of soul, and that they passed him by because he failed to hail them. And he stopped one of them and asked him: 'Where are you going, and what day is this for you?' And the man answered and said: 'We are going to the Day of Rebirth, the Day of Beginning when our deeds and their forgiveness are recorded in the Book of Heaven. And now we journey to plead to God in great multitude and to join our voices into one prayer.' The boy heard these words but, stronger than these, another Word flew to him, a greater Call that came to him out of Eternity. From this hour forth the Call was always with him, roaring in the silence like a mighty stormwind, silent amidst the noise like the winging of a silent bird. And the Call lit up the darkness which had surrounded his world for so long a time, and his fear lost itself in his longing, and his yearning was like to a young green blade in the sun. So passed by the Ten Days of Repentance, and the Day of Atonement was on hand. And the boy saw again the Jews of the villages going on the road to the city. Still and hushed they sat on their carts, and their faces were paler than before. And again Nachum asked one of them: 'Where and why are you going?' And the man said to him: 'This is the day we hoped and waited for, the Day of Atonement, when our sins melt away in the light of the Lord and He welcomes His children in the House of Grace.'

"Then the boy rushed into his room and took the silver-trimmed book in his arms and ran out from the house and ran and ran till he came to the city. There he directed his steps to the house of worship which he entered. When he came in it was the hour of Kol Nidre, the prayer of absolution and holy freedom. And he saw the people standing in their long white shrouds, kneeling and rising before the Lord. And he heard them crying to God, crying from the depth of their hearts to the Light, crying from the hidden places of their souls to the Truth. And the Spirit of God touched the boy, and he bowed and rose before Him and cried unto Him. Then he heard around him the sound of words in a foreign tongue, and he felt that he could not pray like the others. And he took his mother's book and laying it on the lectern before him he cried out: 'Lord of the Universe! I do not know what to pray, I do not know what to say. Here lies before you the whole prayerbook, Lord of the Universe!' And he put his head on the open book and wept and spoke with God.

"It happened on that night that the prayers of the people fluttered on the ground like birds maimed of wing, and could not soar heavenwards. And the house was full of them, the air was close; dark and gloomy the thoughts of the Jews. And then came the Word of the boy and taking all the prayers on its pinions rose with them to the bosom of God.

"The Baal Shem saw and understood all that happened, and he prayed with great rapture. And when the Atonement Day was over he took the boy along with him and taught him the meaning of life and all open and secret wisdom."

Such was the tale the rabbi of Dynow told his pious followers. And then he added: "I too do not know what to do, and how much to do, and how to achieve the purpose of the holy men who first uttered these prayers. That is why I take the book of our blessèd Master Luria and keep it open before me while I pray, that I may offer it to God with all its fervor, ecstasy, and secret meaning."

Translated from the German by Simon Chasen

(—1936)

Making the Crooked Straight

CHAIM NACHMAN BIALIK

IT WAS evening, and three of us were standing on the front platform of the street-car; on one end an elderly Jew, tall and gaunt; I, on the other end, facing him, and between us a fledgling lieutenant—about whose person everything cried, "new!"

At first I paid no attention to the old man. He was leaning, cane in hand, against the wire-meshed grill, keeping himself far in the shadow, where the faint light of the outer lamp hardly reached him. The young officer, who stood between us, shut him off from my view, so that I could see little of him beyond his gray hair fluttering with every jolt of the tram. But when, quite casually, I happened to look in his direction, he turned his head slightly to a side and nodded—and instantly I recognized him. He was the old gentleman that I was always running into on the street, and who always nodded to me so politely.

Somewhere I must once have been introduced to him, but when and where I could not remember; nor could I recall ever having exchanged words with him; I knew neither his name nor his occupation. Occasionally I would come upon him standing, he and his cane, on some street corner, or sauntering along, pausing to look at posters or the show-windows—and seeing me, he would nod.

His clothes would be threadbare, but fairly clean; his shoes patched in places, but polished. Every morning, it was obvious, the brush had worked assiduously over his clothes, seeking to remedy today what yesterday had spoiled. But never, apparently, with complete success; for whenever he became sensitive to some detecting gaze, the palm of his hand would move quickly to cover a patch or a stain. Sometimes I met him carrying a book or bundle, but his walk would be no more hurried than usual. Passing me, he would nod his head in silence, fix me for a moment with his soft, melancholy eyes, and plod quietly on his way. . . .

Yes, I said to myself, this man is one of those unfortunates who, having no permanent employment, wander all day long, from the time they arise in the morning to the time they retire at night, in a dead emptiness—lose themselves in it and wander about lost, like a tiny cloud in infinite sky. Or, more unhappily, they manage to attach themselves somewhere: through someone's pity, say, or through some casual introduction, they succeed—after numerous rebuffs and refusals—in gaining access to the homes of well-to-do people. From whom, after being sent away repeatedly with a "come back tomorrow," they eventually obtain some sort of work for some sort of pay. They cannot help but see, poor souls! that the work given them—whether it be cataloging the house library or arranging the family records (already done for the tenth time), or copying manuscripts (copied already eleven times) or tutoring a youthful *gymnazist* through his Bar Mitzvah exercises—is neither essential nor suited to their abilities: is given to them in fact out of charity. They can make no terms, they must accept what is offered. Entering the rich man's house, they steal in through the back door like trespassers. And when they receive their pay, they lower their eyes, their faces flush, and all self-possession leaves them. They mutter an abrupt goodby, and suddenly find themselves out in the street, without knowing how they got there or through which door they came.

Some, as this man here appears to be, are men of breeding, with refined and gentle souls. Some are hypersensitive and sick with hopeless pride. But all of them suffer from the same sense of inferiority, the same self-consciousness, which conquers their spirit during the day, and gnaws at their bowels in the night. It is not so much poverty that humiliates them, but its outward signs: every patch in their clothing conceals a smarting wound, every stain scorches the flesh underneath it. . . .

So, I thought, one who pities men such as these, who does not wish to aggravate their torture, does well not to look at them any longer than formality requires. And that is how I was careful to act towards my elderly gentleman. I returned his nod with a slight nod and fixed my eyes on the front of the car.

The car stopped. Two more passengers, an older army officer and his wife, mounted the platform. The young officer drew to attention smartly and saluted. They diverted my attention, and I forgot all about the old man.

A few minutes later, however, I saw the young officer suddenly turn to the old man with a polite bow and a genteel wave of his gloved hand, at the same time saying softly:

"Sir, I beg your pardon."

This excessive politeness, like the new uniform he wore, betrayed the tyro. Here was a product of the military academy so recently graduated as to be still punctilious about the rules for a gentleman and an officer that he had learned in school, just as a Bar Mitzvah boy is careful with his *tefillin* the first few days he puts them on. How glad he must have been for the opportunity to display his academy manners in the presence of a senior officer!

What had made him beg the old man's pardon? Probably he had unwittingly jostled against him, or elbowed him by accident, or stepped on his toe. Whatever it was, the old man had not been aware of it. Taken aback, therefore, by the junker's unexpectedly courteous attention, he inclined his ear forward, and asked timidly and respectfully:

"What did you say, sir?"

"I humbly beg your pardon, sir," the junker repeated with even more exaggerated politeness than before.

"What? What?" the old man asked in amazement, refusing to believe his ears, and he bent forward even further, until his head was quite close to the young officer's.

Even then the junker did not quite lose his patience, and only his raised voice betrayed his irritation. He repeated his request for pardon a third time, stressing each word by itself:

"I do ask your pardon, sir, very . . . very . . . much."

Now the old man grasped the matter. This handsome, elegant, young officer was begging pardon; not only that, but had been forced twice to repeat himself. And all on account of him. The old man was terribly embarrassed. Meeting, at this moment, the puzzled stare of the young officer, he was like one who is caught in some shameful act of weakness. With his lips he made a strange sound—pfffff—accompanying it with a threefold gesture: shrugging his shoulders, spreading out his arms, and twisting his mouth in an odd fashion, all at the same time. It was hard to tell what he meant to convey, whether amazement, or apology, or humiliation, or disdain. Maybe the gesture included them all, and each of the four witnesses—the officer, his wife, the junker and myself—was privileged to choose for himself the interpretation he liked best.

The old man stood there pitiably restless and ill at ease. That he had brought so much attention upon himself, that so many eyes were looking at him, seemed to hurt him beyond measure. He seemed to feel that all eyes were examining him from head to foot, that he was revealed before everyone in all of his shabbiness and inferiority. It was as if all the humiliating poverty of his life, all the wounds on his soul, and all the wounds on his honor, had suddenly opened mouths and cried out in one bitter voice: Why not? Is it so unusual that a young officer should ask pardon of a man like me? Do I not deserve, for once in my life, some measure of courteous attention? Can I never hope, not even for once in my life, to experience the feelings of a complete man, without patch or stain?

The old man's eyes moved about incessantly, in tortured embarrassment. The palm of his hand moved nervously over his thread-worn clothes. It was obvious that he suffered excruciating pain. Yes, every patch had under it a deep sore, and each stain burned the brand of shame into his raw flesh.

He made hasty and furtive efforts to tidy himself. He resorted, all at one time, to all the devices he had ever employed. He hurriedly drew himself straight, smoothed his beard with a hasty gesture, straightened his hat on his head. Then he managed with the same quick motions to button his coat, covering thereby a yellow stain on his trousers. He moved his feet close together, concealing, in the one act, two large patches on his shoes. All these actions he performed hastily, almost all at one time, and, as it seemed to him, secretly, so as to attract no attention from his observers.

And at last he suddenly drew out a handkerchief, not over-clean, from his pocket, and blew his nose upon it so violently that all the by-standers were shocked, particularly the polite and elegant young officer.

Poor man! In one moment he wanted to straighten out what so many years had made crooked!

Translated from the Hebrew by Aaron Frankel

(—*1930*)

A Tale of Heaven and Hell

⁓

ISAAC LOEB PERETZ

ONE evening before nightfall a servant of Gan Eden, an angel veiled in light, withdrew from his seat and soared, as angels do, to one of the windows of heaven; he opened it, in anxiety poked his head out to the setting sun, and asked: Sun, do you know what's happened to our Lebel?

The sun goes down in silence. He doesn't know.

The angel drew his head in slowly, closed the gate, and returned to his place, sadder in spirit than he was before.

Not without reason was the angel's heart saddened.

Three times a day Lebel's voice was heard in the firmament, three times a day he would shake the world with his prayers, and his *echod* when he cries out "Hear O Israel" quivers and exults through all the seven heavens.

Only this morning Lebel's voice had been heard praying *Shachris,* but at the hour of *Mincha* it was missing. And the angel greatly wondered but in his heart he said: It must be that Lebel is busied in some good deed and has forgotten to pray *Mincha.* He'll pray the *Shemoneh Esreh* twice at evening.

But lo, the day departs and prayers arise from all of Israel's dispersion, but his voice, the voice of Lebel, is wanting. And the prayers of the world are weakened, its song is lessened. And sorrow shadows the angel's heart.

The sun sets in stillness, and the shadows imprisoned in coverts are free now to come out of their hiding-places. They creep out of clefts in the rock by the seashore, out of pits, out of shrubs, out of desert caves, out of the forest thicket of branches and leaves, and rise spreading themselves over the eye of the earth.

Sleep your sleep, O earth. Night is sovereign now.

The gates of heaven are softly opened and the souls of men take wing. Countless multitudes soar to fulfill the task that is imposed upon them, to write in the book of heaven all that they have done from morning to evening. . . .

The plumes scratch on the backs of parchment.

Through the spaces of the seven heavens spreads the low clamor of prayer, repentance, yearning, love, hope, fear, and black terror.

Then suddenly all is still.

From the breach under the Celestial Throne waves of darkness roll and lift upward, enwrap the Chair, enfold it and hide it from sight; from the darkness which covers the Throne is heard a low gentle voice, a voice like the cooing of a dove:

> *Woe unto me*
> *For I have destroyed my dwelling*
> *I have burned my palace*
> *I have banished my son*
> *My only son.*

A quiver of compassion passes from firmament to firmament, fills the sky and all the heavens. The voice is stilled and a deep silence awakens as if the world were holding its breath. Everything attends, waits hope, strives for a new creation, a reversal of the old order, a new tiding—but nothing happens; from below rises the crowing of a cock.

Slowly the darkness slips from the Chair and rolls downward; gone is the hour of grace, and the gates of heaven are opened again. The souls have completed their task and they fly down unwillingly, sorrowing and weeping. Light-winged angels prod the laggards with rods inlaid with precious stones. Hence to the gateways. . . .

And down below is heard a knocking at gates and tapping at windows: Get up, pious Jews, get up to serve the Maker. In the east a fine thread glows, a path to the rising morning star.

As though out of a deep dream, the sun awakes and races forth.

Once more the angel darts his head out the window and contemplates the faintly twinkling stars.

Before you go out, O stars, is there no one among you who can tell me what is the matter with our Lebel?

One star flamed with delight and shyness.

I passed over the city, he answered, and by chance peered into the window. He is sick, our Lebel, lying abed, his snow-white beard trembles on the quilt, his face turned saffron and then green. I even saw them put a feather to his nostrils, but I passed before I saw whether it moved. It seems to me it did not move.

And the star went out.

The angel trembled. On his own instance, without waiting to receive permission from the One above him, he flew to receive the soul of Lebel—to bring a joy to the saints of Gan Eden.

Pure angels are swift in their flight; but neither do the evil ones tarry.

And when the guardian angel of Gan Eden alighted on the threshold, the evil angel was already sitting at the bedside of the dying man— an angel black as the blackness of night.

What are you doing here? the pure angel said in wonder. Why, this is Lebel.

Well, and if so? said the evil one, grinding a white tooth in laughter.

I am the servant of Gan Eden.

Very pleased—and I'm one of the lesser demons of hell.

This soul is mine.

That isn't certain yet, answered the hairy demon. And, as he spoke, his nimble foot kicked under the bed of the sick man—and a tied sack rolled out.

Pray guess, you good kind angel, what is in this sack?

Praying-shawl and *tefillin,* of course.

Such things aren't put under the bed! One doesn't hide the law and one's good deeds.

The demon kicked the sack again. It burst open—and from it shone forth a flash of ducats! They jingled as they rolled out. . . .

Stolen money—deceit, robbery, defrauding the widow and orphan! And look at the sick man—how he shifts and stretches—his gold has been touched, his idol.

The sick man turns on his bed.

In shame the angel tries to hide his face between his wings.

At that moment a ray of light pierced through a crack in the shutter and touched the eyelids of the dying man; he half awoke, and through his scorched lips an ebbing voice questioned, Who is there?

I, answered the evil one. I have come to take your soul.

Where to?

To Gehinnom.

Out of fear the dying man's eyes closed again.

Confess, repent! cried the good angel, give up your gold . . . .

And the dying man begins, *Shema* . . . .

He'll pray—but he won't give it up, laughed the fiend, and he covered the face of the dying man with his heavy black pinions and choked him . . . .

The bright one recoiled, ashamed . . . .

Midnight. Dense darkness on earth.

In hell tumult. Hissing of fiery tongues, seething waves of burning pitch, savage laughter of tormentors, the groans and shrieks of the tortured cleave the air.

Nachmenke is dying. The end of Nachmenke on earth is near—a creature who cut his nails only at odd times, who was careless about ritual ablution of the hands, who even forgot sometimes to pray.

Whom shall we send? Who will go to get his soul?

I, answered a demon, and at once they set up a cauldron, poured pitch into it, stirred the fire, and the demon ran off.

Swift in their flight are the evil ones; but neither do the good angels tarry. They are farther away from us, but the spur of compassion quickens them.

And when the demon came under the shadow of Nachmenke's roof, the good angel was already at the bedside. He was whispering consolation into the ears of the dying man.

Be not afraid of death, miserable man, for death is very good. It is a bridge from darkness to light. It leads from sorrows and pain to eternal rest.

But the sick man does not hear. His face is aflame and his burning eyes wander about the walls.

The demon stands in the doorway and listens in wonder.

Haven't you erred, my friend?

No, answered the bright one. The God of mercy sent me hither, for this man was merciful and charitable always.

He did not pare his nails according to ritual.

But his nails were those of a man and not of a beast of prey.

He was careless about ablutions of the hands.

But his palm was clean and nothing stuck to it.

How many times did he forget to pray the evening prayers!

He was busy comforting the bereaved. The merciful Father will forgive him. He forgot himself too, and took no heed for his own flesh. See there! He had not time even to mend the roof over his head. He did not know the love of woman. He has not even left a name after him. His only desire, his only wish was to help the poor, to dry the widow's tear, to sustain the forsaken orphan.

Outside the storm raged. The lightning flashed and tore through a thick cloud. Its light pierced the room of the dying man, touched his eyelids and awakened him.

Who's here?

I, answered the good angel, in a tremulous voice. The Lord, praised be He, has sent me for you. Come with me.

Where?

To Gan Eden—to heaven.

Why?

To receive your reward.

Reward—heaven—Gan Eden? And what will I do there?

You'll live a good life, a life of peace and goodwill. The saints are enthroned there. They sit and enjoy the splendor of the *Shechinah*.

And what will I do among them?

You won't do anything. There is no need of doing anything. No need at all.

The dying man, with the remnant of his strength, turned in his bed and faced the angel.

No, angel, that kind of life is not for me. Is there anyone there crying for help to whom I may hasten? Are there fallen ones to raise—wounded to bandage—thirsty to give drink—starved ones to revive?

There are none.

Then what will I do there?

The evil one listens, hangs his long tongue from his mouth like a dog on a hot day, and grins from ear to ear.

In consternation the good angel is silent, and the sick man repeats again and again: And what will I do there? What will I do there?

The good angel turns to the window and looks up to the heavens seeking an answer. There is no voice, no sound. . . .

The evil demon takes advantage of his embarrassment.

Perhaps you will come with me, Nachmeke?

Where to?

To the place your soul seeks—to the unhappy—to the tortured —to the hunted—to those who cry out and receive no answer—to the lost—to the stray—to the drowned—to the burned—to Gehinnom. You won't be able to help them—but you can suffer with them. You can share their sorrow.

Here I am, I'm coming! cried the dying man.

The pure angel withdrew, disappointed. . . .

Translated from the Hebrew by Edward Robbin

(*—1937*)

Two Mothers

JAKOB PICARD

ONE of them was Mrs. Fradel, Tante Fradel, as everyone called her, whether they were related to her or not. There was really no reason for expecting her to be what she was—the greatest benefactress of the Jewish community in that little town of Werblingen in southern Germany. But the word "benefactress" is probably too general in its meaning to characterize her properly. You see, she was always there when she was wanted; and she "certainly had no need to do it," as people always said, because she and her husband were counted among the wealthiest in the community. It was not that she gave money, or other things that had to be procured with money —food for the poor, or clothing, new or worn—wherever she found they were needed. Others did that too, for the sake of the holy commandments, if for no other reason, even if not as extensively as she. No, you see, it was just that she was there whenever there was need of assistance, with deed or good counsel; one thought of her first when one did not know which way to turn.

What was it, then, that she really did? Well, there are many things besides those which can be had for money alone, or which have only monetary value.

Who, on Sabbath eve, in summer as well as in winter, brought red *kiddush*-wine and home-baked twistbread covered with poppy seeds, just before *shul* time, to Salme who could hardly walk any longer and had to live alone, getting a little daily attention from Balbine, the mute? It was Fradel.

And who, skillfully and with a special knife, and never asking any reward, removed the pip from the tongues of chickens, so that they could swallow their grains again like the healthy ones? Fradel, of course, when trusting women came to see her, their agitated birds under their arms.

Who was visited every week, at *Speisig*-night, after the end of Sabbath, by Black Ella, who long since had grown white under her wig—because her children, two daughters and their husbands, in their greed for money had always disdained her—who brought a few pennies, twenty, maybe, or even ten, she had saved during the week? To whom did she say almost every time: "There's no one I have more confidence in than you, Fradel; save this money for me until they bring me to the good place, and use it for a headstone for me, because my daughters would never do it. God will surely bless you for it."

And whom did the doctor send to help those people who were a little awkward when an epidemic struck the place, like diphtheria among the children, for instance; for there were no dependable injections, as today, and powdered phosphorous had to be blown into the little throats, not too much and not too little. It was Tante Fradel.

Yes, she knew about that and many other things, and she fulfilled her self-conceived obligation, which is a duty by eternal law.

Can you see her hurrying along the path in the meadows, because she has heard that Menke Gump's Jewish hired man, while mowing, had cut his leg with the scythe? "You have to be pretty smart," they had said, "to do a thing like that." So she had to be there, if only because he was strange and knew no one in the village. Or, on a bitter winter day, when the clouds in threatening gray masses are pressing down upon the small town, can you see her, bare-headed and only a black woollen shawl over her shoulders, going quickly around the corner toward the little back alley, carrying a bit of kindling wood in her apron? She has suddenly remembered that perhaps there is not enough heat in old man Salme's rooms, in this weather, in this miserable cold.

But, withal, her own house was always in order and as clean as any —you only had to see the pewter jugs that stood on the shelf in the entrance hall, scrubbed and shining during the whole year as on the day before *Pesach*, or the brass lamp with the four arms that hung from the center of the ceiling. Contentedly married they were, she and her husband, whose name was Simon; and that, after all, was as it should be. And they had a son who, for many years now, was assisting his father in the cattle business, an only son whom his mother, in her secret heart, looked upon as a special reward for her own life, as she conducted it.

Of greatest importance to herself, however, was the burden she had agreed to carry ever since she began to take care of Hannchen Lipschitz, the old woman who lived with the Weils in two attic rooms, behind the synagogue. Lipschitz? It was a name, to be sure, one never meets up with where we live, not even now. No one any longer knows where this little woman came from. But there she was, and she was alone, a sort of companion-piece to little old Salme. She spoke a language that sounded somewhat like the language of our brethren who came from the East and who were very pious, more pious than our own people believed themselves to be, so that they respected old Hannchen. But not only for that.

There was quite another, a special reason why she was respected: she, too, had a son, you see; to be sure, no one had ever met him, but there was proof that he was really living; and in America, too. And everyone knew the name of the place where he lived, and the foreign sounds had a strange effect upon all, mysterious even. Keokuk was the name of the town, located in a state named Iowa; Keokuk and Iowa—yes, there were words like that. And someone, sometime, had said that they were spoken in a manner quite different from the way they were written; but he, too, did not know how. And—this is very important—for all this there was proof in the fact that every month there came a letter with foreign postage; and it was not an ordinary letter, but it came registered, and contained not only messages, written pages, but every time there was a five-dollar bill in it—five dollars, they told each other, again and again. Yes, now you will understand what an effect that must have had in that little town. From far away, from America itself, someone received money, and so much that one could live on it a whole month, as Hannchen could. This, then, was the principal reason for the respect they had for her. To herself, however, what was of far greater importance was what she could read in the letter, what it told her about her son, who lived, these many years already, so far away across the sea.

In all probability, all went well with him. No, it was even certain: how else could he have sent the money, regularly, every month; and over and above that he must have enough for himself. It was said that he was away for over twenty years already. But, the mother sometimes pondered, he was still unmarried, though he had been around twenty when he left. Everyone knew all about that, and they knew his name, too; it was Heinrich; only how he made his living, that remained a secret. The mother alone knew, but she never spoke of it to any one; because, for some reason or other, her son had been obliged to leave the country, and over there he had finally found work with a shoemaker, as a sort of apprentice or helper; anyway, he was not in business for himself. Hannchen was ashamed of that; but she loved her son dearly, as one can love only the last remaining child of one's blood.

But the old woman, who always wore a black lace headdress with a lilac-colored velvet bow, had never read one of the letters herself. What sense was there, then, in writing her? To make it quite clear: you see, she could not read, had never known how, quite aside from the fact that for a long time already her eyesight had not been any too good. And who had been the one to help? Tante Fradel, of course. Ever since the letters began to arrive she had taken it upon herself to read them to the lonely mother. That was a task after her own heart. Every time a letter came the mother would send a message to Fradel, usually by one of the children playing before her house; and Fradel always made haste to go and read the news and have the money changed by her husband who sometimes visited the city across the frontier, in Switzerland.

To tell the truth, there was not very much to read in the four small pages of the not exactly distinguished looking paper: that he was doing well, and that he was working, the son informed her regularly at first; and during the first years he had not sent any money, either. And then, one day, he wrote that he was in good health, and that he was on his own now, and that he had opened a shoe business of his own, and that soon he would be able to send more money. But it never became more, and Tante Fradel drew her own conclusions; though— this must be mentioned particularly—never did she tell anybody else any details about the letters, so that it was really as if they were read only by the mother who was now very proud of her son, a son who even was a businessman in America. Fradel finally proposed that she should advise him—he called himself Harry now—to address his letters directly to her: it would be more simple, she said, for thus she would be most quickly informed of their arrival. Because, we forgot to mention, she had also taken it upon herself to write him, of course. Now, this was by no means done as if she herself were addressing him, no, it was his mother who talked to him, encouraged him, gave him good advice, advice from the little home town Werblingen, that did not even have a railroad, to him, way over there in far America; Tante Fradel only supplied the writing.

Thus, the years went by, and Fradel was happy in the role she was allowed to play. But, at the same time, she always thought of her own son who was at home with her, and who had turned out so well, and deep in her heart she was grateful.

But once, the letters did not come, one month, two months. Tante Fradel tried to pacify Mother Lipschitz: America was far away, and a whole ocean lay between them and the son, and a ship, or even two, could have been wrecked, and whatever other consolation she could think of. And finally there did come another letter; but it was addressed in a strange hand; and inside it said—written in German by a fellow-countryman—that the son had died of tuberculosis, which had plagued him so long already; and that he had left nothing except working clothes of little value, because, like the writer, he had worked in a shoe factory. There was nothing in the letter about a shop, or other such great matters, to say nothing of questions concerning inheritance. Well, it can be easily understood, and even condoned, that the son had merely given substance to his mother's dream of his having gone into business again—let's just mention that in passing.

But now, Tante Fradel, as we would expect of her, found herself in a bad dilemma. For several days she walked about, thinking, taking counsel with herself, with a heavy heart. How could she be expected to harm the poor mother, tell her the bad news, especially since the old woman's health had lately been failing more and more? And finally she decided all by herself that she would have to lie, hard as that would be, but she was confident that God would forgive her because of the good she would accomplish in that manner. She went to Hannchen Lipschitz and from the letter she had brought, without the envelope, she read what would be agreeable to the mother, invented a reason for the tardiness, and told of things which the son used to write about before. The old lady, relieved and contented, listened . . . .

But then a month passed, and the time came for the arrival of another letter; Mother Lipschitz had already asked about it. So Tante Fradel sat down and wrote a letter from America, and later read it to the worried lady. And the next month she repeated it. To make it easier for herself, she began one day to write to the son who did not live any more. And answered herself as the dead son. So she continued to do for a long time . . . .

But now you will ask, what was done about the money that should have arrived? But there, too, Tante Fradel knew what to do. Was not her husband in the Chevra Kadisha? She laid everything before him, and he, in turn, informed that benevolent society of the situation, with the result that every month a certain amount of money was allowed which sufficed for the few simple needs of Hannchen Lipschitz; and Tante Fradel told her once and for all that now the dollars were being changed as soon as they arrived.

Thus, more time passed, and one day there was a war, the first war against the French. And Tante Fradel's son—who had served with the mounted soldiers with the red collars—had to go, too. Well, now there was another kind of writing going back and forth, back and forth; we know how that is from our own war. Tante Fradel, now just another mother, had her own great worries; we need not say another word to make that clear. But through them she did not forget her other great duty, her correspondence with America, and every month she went with the forged letter, up the worn, creaking, wooden steps to Hannchen Lipschitz, in the house behind the synagogue. And, though she was getting on in years herself, she now took to visiting the old lady even more often, because, as everyone was aware, the end was drawing near. She really kept on living only through the expectation of her son's letters, yes, by even hoping to see him just once more. Because Tante Fradel, having heard, when reading the preceding letter, of her innermost wish to see him again, had read her an answering letter in which he promised to come soon, "if my business gives me the slightest opportunity."

But it so happened in that bitter winter that on the same day on which Hannchen Lipschitz started her final struggle with death, Tante Fradel and her husband Simon received a message from the front, saying that their son had been killed in a battle that had lasted several days; and it had been fought, the letter continued, near a river, Lisaine by name, which flowed past a certain fort, named Belfort. And that happened on just the day when within only a few hours the old woman would be dead, she whom the other mother had nursed through all these years, as we have told. The dying woman was very weak but still conscious of the thing that had been most important in her life: the son who, for her, was still living. And she spoke about him, demanded his letter, as if that could save her.

And her condition was described to Mother Fradel, herself so greatly borne down by the anguish of her own loss. But she arose, arose from the low bench on which, in accordance with the holy law,

she had sat beside her husband. Feeling the great sorrow over their
own son, and with eyes almost blinded with tears, she stepped down
and, in her black dress, went over to the dying woman, sat down beside
her bed and read her a cheerful letter from a son who did not live
any longer: everything went well, and soon he would return to visit
her. And so, until old Hannchen quietly slumbered away, she now,
for the last time, brought her the consolation she had always supplied
her during all these years.

But she, Mother Fradel . . . .

Translated from the German Ms by Eric Seligo.

(—1942)

Old Man's Choice

❧

WILLIAM SCHACK

A CREASED bundle under his arm, a little old man hurried along the street looking straight before him. Mrs. Stern, 1346 East 19th Street, Apartment 16. He saw neither houses nor hedges, neither people nor dogs. The landscape blurred by him as if he were in a train, not looking out of the window but straight before him; his mind's eye fixed on an overcoat at Mrs Stern's, 1346 East 19th Street. He had the name and address in his pocket, but he wasn't taking any chances on forgetting and he couldn't think of anything else anyhow. Walking along at top speed, he kept mumbling them like a prayer.

For it wàs growing dark and he had no time to lose. Cautious though he usually was, at the corner he challenged an auto zooming along in high and trotted across before it. Mrs. Stern, he had been told, has a very good overcoat to sell and wouldn't haggle with him over a dollar more or less. With only the one shabby suit under his arm to show for a whole day's tramping, and if he made fifty cents on it he would consider himself lucky, this was a customer worth getting to. Though his breath grew shorter, he didn't slacken his pace. His face flushed, and his hatband was lined with sweat, but he kept on. . . . Suddenly his chest choked with pain. He couldn't breathe; he couldn't move. Not another step. Not if his life depended on it. He stood still, listening to the pounding of his heart, not frightened, not pitying himself—only wondering and anxious, like an animal which doesn't yet know it is trapped.

Glancing around for a place to sit down, he saw a stoop but hesitated: they would regard him as an intruder, perhaps a beggar. What of the curb? It wouldn't be nice, respectable, though for his part it was good enough: he wasn't proud. Children sat on the curbstone: why not he? Still, no one was on the stoop; no one was in sight. Apologetically, as if someone were there, he made his way to it slowly and sat down, the bundle in his lap. Now he felt the sweat pouring down his face and took out a sweaty handkerchief to wipe it. He lifted his hat and wiped his balding head too—all the way down to the nape of his neck, between which and his collar there was room for a bath towel.

Queer! Such a thing had never happened to him before. Tired? Naturally he was tired at the end of every single day. After walking up and down streets and stairs, what would you expect? There were times when he could hardly get up from the chair to go to bed. But he slept it off and was fresh again in the morning. This, however, was a different kind of tiredness—peculiar, ugly. . . .

Herschel began to breathe easier.

What was he trying to talk himself into? A man who hadn't been sick a day in his life, he ought to be ashamed of himself for making a fuss about a trifle. He couldn't catch his breath for a minute—what was so terrible about that? He wasn't so young; he had been on the go all day long; and he had gotten winded. That was all there was to it. So why was he beginning to imagine that it was a peculiar, an ugly thing?

That was all there was to it, but when he got up to move on to Mrs. Stern's his legs were as if paralyzed. He wanted to walk and yet his legs wouldn't go: peculiar, wasn't it? He absolutely intended to move on and yet. . . . He put his hand in his pocket for a consoling cigarette, but his groping fingers could find only a few crumbs of tobacco. He recalled then that he had already smoked both of the cigarettes which were his daily allowance, but his fingers continued to reach blindly, as if he couldn't quite believe that there shouldn't always be one there, as if he couldn't believe that he could actually only afford two a day. There was a time when he smoked cigars, fine brands too—ten cents apiece—and he didn't have to count them. But what was he making such a fuss about? What was the sense of smoking anyway? Making a fire in your mouth! Smelling up the house! It was absolutely foolish. He could do very well without it—he could do without more important things. A cup of hot coffee in the morning, a plate of soup at night, a quiet corner to read the newspaper in, a place to lay his head: that was all he wanted of life. Five years ago —was it really only five years? it seemed in another life—they had lived in a fine apartment, full of furniture with carving and gold and fringes, of marble lamps and rugs, with a radio like a castle, and men in uniform at the door like officers in the Tsar's army. And they had an automobile which took you from Brownsville to the Bronx and you didn't have to transfer at 149th Street. Not that he cared for all that, though it was pleasant to sit back on soft cushions and be driven around like a king. But the children wanted it, and he didn't have the heart to deny them. Not that they would have listened to him . . . To hear them talk now, you'd think that he was responsible for the market crash. They blamed him for mismanagement of their investments—that's what they called the crazy business of getting good money for nothing; and they blamed him for lack of foresight—did he ever pretend to be anything more than an old clothes dealer? But that's the way children were. You prayed for their birth; you stayed awake nights over their sickbeds; you snatched newspapers out of wastepaper cans instead of buying them, to save pennies—all for them. And then . . . But still he didn't hold it against them: they weren't such bad children, really not. Joe's wife was a bit uppish and he didn't reproach her for it; Sam didn't come around as often as he should to see his ailing mother; Nathan was a kind of loudmouth; and Pauline was twisted in her mind, always asking for things she knew they couldn't afford any more. But still, they weren't bad at heart; they didn't disgrace the family as certain others he could mention. And the boys, married now and with children of their own —darlings they were, too—had each his own little bundle of troubles. To hear them talk, you'd think they'd been rich all their lives instead of for two swift years. But he himself had been poor a long time before—he'd never forgotten that; and he didn't regret the loss of luxury. Honestly he didn't. If he could have his coffee and rolls for breakfast, his plate of boiled beef for supper, his Sabbath fish and chicken. . . .

Herschel heard a squeal above him: the door had opened. An imposing young man in tortoise-shell glasses stood looking down at him —with disfavor, he thought. He stood up to go, but pain shooting through the chest fixed him to the spot.

A raucous authoritative voice said, "Were you coming to see me?" and as Herschel blinked at him, "I'm Doctor Miller."

"Excuse me, doctor," said Herschel, "I didn't mean to—I was only . . ."

"That's all right," said the harsh voice, and as an afterthought, less brusquely, as if in anticipation of trade, "Don't you feel well?"

Herschel hunched his shoulders in denial. "It's nothing. I'm a little tired, that's all."

Losing interest in him, Dr. Miller loped down the steps and on to the sidewalk, looking first in one direction, then in the other, as if out of sheer curiosity and not as if he were trying to conjure up patients.

Should he go in to see the doctor after all? For two dollars . . . But suppose he asked three or even more? And why should he throw away even two dollars, which he came by with such sweat and travail? He was getting foolish and self-indulgent. There was nothing the matter with him. He had been walking too fast and gotten out of breath. Was that something to run to a doctor with, like a child with a bellyache? If Pauline found out about it she would make life miserable for him.

At the thought of his termagant daughter Herschel again stood up to go, as if he were afraid she might think he was soldiering on the job. At that moment Dr. Miller turned back and confronted him. "You'd better let me examine you," he said.

"It isn't necessary, doctor. Believe me, I feel . . ."

"I won't charge you for it, old man," said the doctor laughing. It was better to have a patient, even if he didn't pay, than to read the sporting page over again.

"I thank you very much, but honestly, doctor . . ." With benign gestures of protest, he kept walking up the steps.

Listening to his sluggish pulse, Dr. Miller asked him about his family, his business, his age. He couldn't believe that the old man was seventy-two, but Herschel assured him that it was so, positively: he was born the same day as David the miller's second son Pincus, a month before the fire that. . . .

The stethoscope skipped from nipple to nipple, down to the ribs, around to his back, down below. Pleased to be the object of so much attention—and it tickled!—Herschel stood quietly imperturbable, like a cat being caressed. Mrs. Stern, would she still have the coat tomorrow?

"That's all," said Dr. Miller, removing the instrument from his ears. "And enough, if you ask me."

Herschel, as he dressed himself, listened for the physician's verdict. It wasn't for him to question a doctor: he must wait till he was spoken to. But he had put on his undergarments and his top shirt, straightened out the tails, buttoned his pants and swung the suspenders into place, and still no word. The physician was at his desk and seemed to have forgotten all about him.

"Well, doctor? . . ."

Dr. Miller stopped writing for a moment and looked in his direction. "It's nothing, nothing special."

Herschel smiled; he didn't catch the equivocal tone. "Didn't I tell you so, doctor? I'm taking up your time for nothing." He kept on smiling, but Dr. Miller's face didn't crack.

"Just the same," he said, "you'll have to remember that you won't be forty again."

"Of course, doctor, of course. A man in my years has to have the sense to know that he's no young buck."

"I'm writing you out this prescription, but you don't have to take it if you don't want to. There's no medicine for old age. But if I gave you some advice, would you follow it?"

Herschel smiled humbly. "Who am I not to listen to a sage?" he said, worried.

"Well then, you musn't walk too much——"

What did he mean, too much? A man walks as much as he has to, to make a living.

"—or too fast."

But suppose you hear of a good buy—don't you feel like running there all the way? 1346 East 19th Street.

"You musn't climb stairs."

Herschel nodded slowly with a fine pretense of candor. If everybody lived on the ground floor . . . Apartment 16 must be on the third.

"And you mustn't drink——"

A nip of brandy, a sip of wine for the Sabbath: you couldn't call that drinking.

"—or smoke."

Herschel stood very still. Don't do this and don't do that; don't walk and don't climb stairs; don't . . . "But there's nothing the matter with me, doctor?"

"No, nothing special. Only, as I said . . ."

Herschel kept his eyes on him searchingly, hopefully, but the more the doctor talked the more uneasy he became. He stood very still; the light went out of his face. So he was really a very sick man and hadn't long to live? He had seen many dead men. As a member of the synagogue's burial committee, he had washed their bodies and wrapped them in shrouds. He had helped lower them into the ground and cast the ritual handful of soil over them to symbolize their reunion with the earth from which they had come. But Herschel was so much absorbed in his duties, he was so anxious to wash the corpse perfectly, to wrap it neatly, to direct the mourners into the proper coaches, that he had no time to reflect on death. On the way home, at the same time that he grieved for the departed and his wife and children, he might try to snatch a moment's thought on the great mystery. Afterwards it was too late: he was too tired and sleepy to think about anything at all. And the next day, and the day after? The next day and the day after he had to make a living.

The thought of his own dying came with a shock, but he quickly absorbed it. It was natural to die, and he was willing, because when a man's time comes he should be willing, because it is God's will. And with his children all grown up and in a manner of speaking provided for, really what was there for him to live for? He shouldn't have said that—he should not deny that life is good. A hot cup of coffee for breakfast puts fresh blood in your veins. The voices of his grandchildren, of all little children, were like the chanting of Psalms. The light of the morning sun, spreading on the pavement, was like the Song of Songs. And a good smoke was like—what should he say? No, one should never let it pass one's lips that life is not good. But still, what had it brought him, that in his old age he must. . . . What was he standing there for, wasting the doctor's time? He ought to be on his way. Somehow his feet wouldn't move. He noted the physician's impatient glance, but he stood there stricken, like an animal that knows it is trapped.

Dr. Miller dug into his pocket for his cigarettes. Herschel gazed, fascinated, at the flame flaring and dwindling in the doctor's cupped hands as he puffed, and after the doctor had shaken the life out of the light he gazed at the glowing cigarette end. Shyly he put out his hand. "Please, doctor, if can you spare one."

Dr. Miller stared—incredulous, angry. After all his warnings, the old boy deliberately. . . . But his anger subsided into awe as he observed the profound resignation in the old man's face. Without a word, he proffered the cigarettes and struck a match for him.

As Herschel puffed slowly, his face grew serene. "Thank you kindly, doctor. I mustn't disturb you any longer." He picked up his bundle and shook hands. "Good-bye, doctor, and let me thank you again."

"Don't mention it. Remember what I said about not walking too fast and . . ."

"Certainly, doctor, certainly not."

Dr. Miller watched him go down the steps and called out, as the old man turned to wave to him again, "Good luck!"

(—1937)

A "Goy"

LUIGI PIRANDELLO

DANIELE CASTELLANI, Signor Daniele Catellani, a friend of mine (splendid head he has, curly hair and plenty of nose—the hair and nose of his race, you understand), has one disagreeable habit: he has the habit of laughing, away down in his throat somewhere, and there is something so irritating about this laugh of his that people often feel like cuffing him.

All the more because, after he has laughed that way, he agrees with what you have been telling him—agrees with a nod of his head and with a string of hurried, half eaten, "Jusso's":

"Jusso! Jusso! Jusso! Jusso!"

As though what you had to say had not been the cause of the bitter laugh with which he greeted it!

And, of course, you're nettled! Of course, you're taken aback! Though that is not because Daniele Catellani, Signor Daniele Catellani, will not do exactly as you say. He has never been known to object to an opinion, judgment, remark, or observation, of anyone.

But, first—he laughs!

Probably because, when you catch him off his guard like that, there in a dream world all his own, a word so different from the one to which you suddenly recall him, he feels as horses must when they curl their upper lips sometimes, and whinny.

That Daniele Catellani, Signor Daniele Catellani, is a man of the best intentions, anxious to get through this world of other people without unnecessary friction, there are no end of proofs—proofs, moreover, so convincing that to doubt them would, I think, be an indication of too cynical a nature on your part.

In the first place, to avoid giving any possible offense by wearing an evidently Jewish name about—his name was Levi—well, he changed it, for a more Gentile sounding name—Catellani.

And, in the second place, he went farther still. He threw in his lot with a Catholic family, clerical among clericals, by contracting a so-called "mixed marriage," on condition, that is, that the children (he has five of them, so far) would be baptized in the faith of their mother and thus irreparably lost to his own religion. They say that that curiously irritating laugh of my friend Catellani, he laughed precisely on the occasion of this "mixed marriage."

Oh no! Not on account of his wife! Oh no! A thoroughly good woman is Signora Catellani; and she thinks the world of him!

But on account of her father, his father-in-law, Signor Pietro Ambrini, nephew of the late Cardinal Ambrini no less, and a man of most uncompromising clerical principles.

How in the world, you will say, how in the world did Signor Daniele Catellani ever think of getting into a family fortified with a future father-in-law of that caliber?

I give up! But he did!

You see—well, it was this way, probably. With the idea in his head that a "mixed marriage" was advisable, he thought he might as well make a real one while he was about it. And then, who knows? Perhaps he thought that by choosing a girl from a family so notoriously devoted to the Holy Catholic Church, he could show, even to the most particular, that he considered it just an accident—an accident quite beyond his control and responsibility—that he was born a Jew.

And what a time of it he had in arranging this marriage! But isn't that the way it is with life? The greatest trials and tribulations we have to put up with are those we make for ourselves—in an effort to build a gibbet to hang ourselves on.

Even at that, my friend Catellani—at least so people say—would never have succeeded in hanging himself, had it not been for the interest (not wholly disinterested) that the young fellow, Millino Ambrini, took in the matter (Millino Ambrini is the brother of Signora Catellani. He emigrated to America a couple of years ago—we'd better not ask why).

The point I'm driving at is that the old man, Signora Catellani's father, in finally consenting, *obtorto collo*, to the match, laid down the indispensable condition that his daughter should vary in no single jot from the precepts and practices of her faith, and that she should respect with greater meticulousness than ever all her religious observances. Not only this! He demanded, and obtained, formal recognition of his own personal right to supervise religious matters in the Catellani household, to be sure that the contract would be scrupulously fulfilled, not only as regards Signora Catellani, but as regards any children that should eventually be born.

Now, this was all some nine years ago. In all these nine years that have passed, and despite, as I said, the most convincing proofs of good will on the part of Signor Catellani, Signor Pietro Ambrini has not agreed to an armistice. A cold, cadaverous, bloodless fellow, his sallow face painted up to look more human, and always the same suit of clothes that he has been wearing longer than anyone can remember, and a certain perfume of musk and talc about him, like a woman fixing up for a walk in the square—he has the effrontery to turn up his nose whenever my friend Catellani goes by, as though for that pair of ultra-Catholic nostrils the unfortunate son-in-law had not yet purged himself of his pestilential *foetor judaicus.*

Now I know, because I have often talked the situation over with my friend Catellani. . . .

He laughs the way he does, not so much because the obstinacy of the old man in regarding him, Catellani, as an enemy of the faith, seems funny to him, but because of what he has been noticing in himself for some time past.

Is it possible—I leave it to you!—is it possible that in this day and age, and in a country as enlightened as ours, a man like Catellani should be made the victim of a religious persecution—all the more, since from the time he was knee high to a grasshopper, he has shown every willingness, on his own part, to respect all religions—be they Chinese, Indian, Lutheran or Eskimo?

And yet, that's just the case. There's no use talking; his father-in-law has been and still is persecuting him. Call it ridiculous, as ridiculous as you please, but poor Catellani is confronted with a bona fide religious persecution in his own house. Persecution from one man, granted, and against one man, a man who came forward unarmed to submit, but none the less a persecution—a regular religious war waged by that old man in his house, every day in the year and on every possible pretext, and with a hostility and relentlessness maintained to the bitter end.

Well, now, let alone the fact that if you keep at a fellow all the time that way, he's bound to feel it in the end; and in Catellani's case, the *homo judaicus* has been gradually coming to life again in him,

despite his refusal to admit it. But the worst of it is, you see, that
Catellani is becoming the joke of the town, in a certain way, on account of the exaggerated religious ostentation of his family—a piety
that is in no sense sincere but is forced upon him as a gratuitous insult
by his father-in-law; and Catellani cannot help noticing that people
are laughing at him. The worst of it? Not quite the worst! The worst of
it is that his children, tormented with all the religion that is being
crammed down their throats by their grandfather, are beginning to
suspect, in their childish way, that the cause of all this church-going,
praying, and catechism, is in him—in their papa. Just what the cause
is they haven't the slightest idea. But something is wrong—wrong
with him! Today it's the Good God, and tomorrow it's the Dear Jesus
—the Dear Jesus especially. But it's also the Saints, now this Saint and
now that one; and they have to go to church with their grandfather
to pray to one or the other of them every day of their lives. And why
all this praying? Because he, Papa, must have done something very,
very bad indeed to them. So now, when they are taken in hand in the
morning to be marched off to church, they turn, poor little devils, and
look at their father with eyes of perplexed and anguished reproach;
so that he would lose his head and let out who knows what blasphe-
mies, were it not that he prefers to throw back his head with its curly
hair and its plenty of nose and give that little laugh of his somewhere
down in his throat.

Well, yes, there's something to that, I grant you; he should see he
did a cowardly and a useless thing in turning his back on the faith of
his fathers, denying the Chosen People in his children—*am olam*, as the
Rabbi says. And he ought to realize that he is a *goy*, an outsider, in
his own family; and he ought to take that Most Christian jackass of a
father-in-law he has and point out to him that it's not fair to see a
Christ-killer in him, Catellani, when in the name of this God, who was
crucified two thousand years ago by the Hebrews, the Christians, who
ought all to feel themselves brothers in Christ, have been slaughtering
each other for five long years in a war, which, with no disrespect to
the wars we are going to have, has hitherto had no equal in history!

But—not at all, says he. He just laughs, and laughs. "Besides,"
says he, "you wouldn't say such things yourself, would you, if you were
in my place?"

My friend, Signor Daniele Catellani, knows how things go in this
world. Jesus? Well and good! Brothers? All of us! But then, we turn

around and cut each other's throats! Why not? Natural enough, isn't it? Logic, perfect logic, on both sides! So that if you go over from one camp to the other you can't help approving over here what you disputed over there. So it's always: "Jusso! Jusso! Jusso!" Of course, when you're caught that way, all of a sudden, you laugh! But afterwards—"Jusso! Jusso!" You approve, you approve always, everything! Even a great war, you approve! Jusso!

However (and oh, it was a good long laugh this time!), however, Signor Daniele Catellani decided all of a sudden (it was the last year of the war), decided that he would play a joke on his father-in-law, Signor Pietro Ambrini, nephew of the late Cardinal; one of those jokes that you don't forget so easily.

You must know that, in spite of the great throat-cutting that was still in progress, Signor Pietro Ambrini, with the most brazen face in the world, had planned to celebrate the anniversary of the Holy Nativity with greater pomp than ever for the edification of his dear little grandchildren. So he had a lot of china dolls made to represent the shepherds bringing their humble gifts to the manger of Bethlehem in honor of the new-born Christ Child: baskets of fresh white cheeses, baskets of painted eggs and candy, and, in addition to the shepherds, flocks of little china sheep and donkeys (laden with more offerings and tended by old stable keepers and boys). The Three Wise Men sat there, solemn and gorgeous, on their camels, coming from afar in the wake of a comet that had stopped over a barn (made of cork), and inside the barn was another wax doll with pink cheeks—the Infant Jesus, lying between Mary and Saint Joseph, with an ox and a donkey looking on from their stalls.

To make the Holy Manger as large and as true to life as possible, Grandpa devoted a whole room to the purpose this year, with everything in proportion—hills and precipices, and fields with roads, sycamore and palm trees, with the shepherds and their flocks and donkeys and the Three Wise Men all of proper size. And he had worked in secret with a mason and a carpenter, who had taken out the wooden ceiling in the room and covered it with plaster. And he had strung blue lights around in great festoons and hired two pipers to come all the way down from the Sabine country, to play a flute and a bag-pipe.

The little ones were to know nothing of all this. On Christmas Eve they would go to church for midnight mass; then, coming home, cold and chilly, they would step into this warm, cosy room, where the pipers would be playing and the incense burning, with the Manger on one side all bright from the blue lights. And the neighbors would come in, with all the relatives of the Ambrini clan, and there would be a great banquet—a celebration, in short, that would cost Grandpa Pete a pretty penny.

Signor Daniele, however, had seen the old man all preoccupied with these mysterious doings about the house, and he had laughed. He had heard the mason and the carpenter at work on the ceiling of the room, and he had laughed. The Devil he kept somewhere down in his throat would give him no rest at all during all that Christmas season. He laughed and laughed and laughed! Signor Daniele did his best to quiet him, warning him in vain not to go too far.

"No, we won't go too far!" the little Devil whispered to him. "Don't worry! We won't go too far! All those shepherds, eh? And the baskets of cheese and eggs, and candy, eh? And they are all on their way to the Manger of Bethlehem, eh? How cute, and how cunning, eh? But we will have our little joke, too. However, we won't go too far! We won't go too far!"

So was Signor Daniele tempted of his Devil.

On Christmas Eve, the moment Signor Pietro Ambrini, with Signora Catellani, the children, and all the servants, had started off to Church for the midnight mass, Signor Daniele rushed into the room where the Manger was. He took away the shepherds and the sheep and the camels and the Wise Men and the cheeses and the candy and the painted eggs —all people and things which the Devil in his throat deemed quite inappropriate to a Christmastide to be celebrated during a great war like this one. And, in place of what he took away, he put, with greater propriety—oh, nothing much—just a few other toys—tin soldiers, but dozens, hundreds of them, soldiers of all nations, German soldiers, French soldiers, Italian, Austrian, Russian soldiers, English, Serbian and Rumanian soldiers—Belgians, Turks, Bulgarians, Americans, Hungarians, Montenegrins—all with their rifles leveled at the Manger of Bethlehem, and then toy cannons, of all sizes and shapes, all trained likewise on the Manger of Bethlehem. And there was no denying it: the spectacle they made was quite as gorgeous as the other!

Then Signor Pietro Catellani crawled in, out of sight, behind the Manger.

And how he laughed and laughed and laughed, when Grandpa Pete and Signora Catellani and the children came back from midnight mass, with all the neighbors and relatives of the family, and walked into that room, where the incense was burning and the pipers were playing their flute and bagpipe under the festoons of blue lights! How he laughed and laughed and laughed!

Translated from the Italian by Arthur Livingston

(*—1924*)

How Many Angels . . .

IRVING FINEMAN

IT WAS always in the kitchen that my father took his ease. The kitchen was as large a room as the parlor (for those were the days when there were parlors), and warmer. And it was less encumbered than the parlor, where, suited to the needs of neither mind nor body, were many pieces of carved mahogany—a sofa with uncomfortably curving back and legs, and chairs stiffly upholstered in tufted apple-green velours, a music stand, and a lamp with a stained-glass dome by the draped, gleaming length of the piano, a what-not in the corner surmounted by the bronze figure of a handsome harvester nude to the waist and sharpening his scythe. Thus it was that my father took his ease in the kitchen and that it was always in the kitchen that we had those memorable nocturnal meetings, my father and I.

Memorable, I say, for when we sat, my father and I, on opposite sides of the square kitchen table (and kitchen tables in those days were generously large) whose white oilcloth cover, stamped in blue with a florid design of an intricacy endlessly tempting to explore, shone under the soft brilliance of a Welsbach mantle glowing in the gaslight, those meetings appear to have been informed with a high significance that, it seems now, could then have been only deliberately ignored; as one comes to the theater prepared to see a play but willing to forget it is a play. To me now it seems as if we came, my father and I, deliberately, to sit in the bare brilliance of that austere room, with its bright central light and diffused reflections—from white crockery ranged behind glass doors, from the scrubbed linoleum on the floor checkered in endless diagonals of blue and white, from the nickel trim on the black polished stove, from the pale buff-tinted walls and the spread of oilcloth on the table between us—as surgeons come to a chamber, brightly lit and isolated (for the rest of the household would be fast asleep in the darkness of the bedrooms), to conduct a clinic, to dissect, to examine something laid before them. It seems so to me now, I say; at the time there seemed never anything deliberate, anything anticipated about our meetings. Never on departing from some rowdy, boyish party, walking home along the dark canyons of city streets, or, as I was fond of doing, crossing the Brooklyn Bridge, slung like a huge web of vines between the tops of monstrous trees high over a black jungle river, or returning in the noisy, swaying progress of a belated street car from a long evening's work at some distant library, never would it occur to me to look forward to one of those meetings.

I would enter and, from the dark hall while I put up my hat and coat and glanced as of habit toward the bright rectangle of the kitchen door, I would hear perhaps the clink of glass against saucer as my father reached for them in the cupboard and closed the door with a familiar click of the latch. Setting these and the sugar bowl by an open book he had been reading on the shining expanse of the table, he would peer at me, stooping a little from under the bright light that shone on the fringe of his hair around the black skull-cap he wore on the back of his head; and, after exchanging a few words of greeting or inquiry with me, he would continue his customary pacing back and forth, back and forth, around two sides of the table, stopping now and then as he passed the stove in his progress to lift the lid of the white enameled tea kettle and peer down into the cloud of steam that rose from it. By limiting somewhat the extent of his pacing, he would leave me free to repair to the ice box by the sink. While I stood leisurely examining its chill, fragrant contents, I could hear behind me the measured tread of his walk, the comfortable creaking of the floor under his feet, and the first murmurings of the kettle that would soon, with a rushing plume of steam from its spout, bring him to a halt. And as I made my choice from the left-overs—a remnant of fish, or a wing of chicken with, per-haps, a saucer of stewed prunes—I must have heard without listening (for why should one listen for such things, and yet I can hear them now) the opening and closing of a drawer, the clink of a spoon in the glass (which, he believed, prevented the glass from cracking), the trickle of the essence, and, at last, the hot gasp with which the water rushed from the steaming spout.

Then he would sit and wait for me, his hands folded to catch the warm cloud that rose from the ruddy glass in which the silver spoon appeared curiously orange-tinted and bent. He sat there thinking; in-

deed he had been thinking all the time, I always knew, of something
he wanted to discuss, and very soon we should begin to talk. But as I
brought myself bread and a knife and, cutting a crisp slice, enjoyed in
advance the seasoned tang of the frozen amber sauce clotted about the
edges of the fish, or the delicate flavor of the tender white meat on the
wing bones under their yellow skin, or stood gazing as if fascinated at
the light reflected from the black pool of prune juice from which the
prunes rose wrinkled and glistening like islands of worn and polished
basalt, never once (and I should remember, if I had, as I remember
the rest) did I wonder what he and I were about to say, or why it was
that we should meet to talk as we were bound to. I should remember,
if I had, as I remember the sensual delight it was to sit down then in
the bright silence of that room after the evening's fatigue, to feel the
radiant warmth of the stove at my back, and smell the delicate odors
rising into the air as if reflected from the shining table—the cool fragrance of the food before me, the warm fragrance of my father's tea,
and the musty fragrance of the old Hebrew book before him (that
smell of an old Hebrew book which is like that of no other old book)
that rose in an unforgettable cloud as he turned its yellow leaves and
examined the lines of heavy black characters that, I could see clearly
across the table, lay swimming like islands in the middle of a sea of
commentaries in fine print. . . .

It was the Talmud. My father sipped his tea as he turned the pages,
and nibbled at a lump of sugar between sips. "Tomorrow night," he
may have begun, "is the first night of Hanukkah." My mind and
senses, curiously intermingled and playing like a vague phosphores-
cence successively over the chicken wing I was gnawing and the problem in dynamics I had been studying all evening, floated off and, as if
alighting at his words, came to rest on the Maccabees—on a picture of
lusty men, fighting, not like shrewd Jewish lawyers with their wits,
but like gladiators with broken swords in their fists. I liked the Maccabees. . . . "Now the Gemora says," he continued, looking over my
head at the stove, " 'What is Hanukkah!' "
The Gemora, I understood, was not asking a question. "What is
Hanukkah" was a ball tossed into the air, as in a game, between eager
waiting minds. "When the Syrians—that is to say, the Greeks" (my
father had picked up the ball and was carrying it to me; and, finding it
at the moment difficult to recall the history of that period, I wondered

as I picked at the delicious chicken bones if he was justified in that archaeological assumption) "took Jerusalem, they sacked the Temple and desecrated all the holy utensils including the holy oil for the lighting of the *Menorah*. Afterwards, when the Maccabees retook the city and put them to flight, but one container of the holy oil was to be found, a single small cruse with the seal of the high priest upon it intact, a quantity ordinarily sufficient for but one day's lighting of the *Menorah*. Then, it is said, occurred the miracle that, during the eight days required for the manufacture of a new supply of the holy oil, the one small undesecrated cruse provided sufficient to keep the holy flame alight. It is for this reason that the victory is celebrated for eight days and candles are lit." I pushed away the plate with its remnant bones, listening as it were with one ear. For this seemed a childish game, this speculation concerning a miracle and a monopoly of holy oil manufactured by canting, white-robed high priests. Doughty old Mattathias battling on the Sabbath, and Judas Maccabeus, "the Hammer," with his followers, fighting like gladiators with their hard fists, desperately, against superior numbers, would, I was sure, have had none of that nonsense.

I considered simultaneously going ahead with the dish of prunes and sending the ball back to my father. But he was turning the pages searching some particular reference, wetting a finger-tip now and then to grasp one of the thick yellow leaves, and I, for the moment, lost myself in consideration of a pretty question in hydro-statics, namely, to what extent the viscosity of prune juice affected its buoyant action on the prune which it surrounded: was it then transmitting an upward pressure through a thin film seeping in under the prune as water would? . . .

"Ah!" said my father; he had found the place. "Now with reference to the lights, one Tanna says here that each family should have at least one light each night; but among those more advanced in spirit, there will be one light for each member of the family. And those still more informed should, says Shammai, have eight lights the first night, seven the second, and so on down to one light on the eighth night. But the great Hillel says precisely the contrary: one light the first night, two the second, and so on to eight on the eighth night. Now come the Tannaim attempting in their commentaries to interpret these two contrary opinions, in this manner: Shammai, one says, tells us to light each evening as many candles as there are days of Hanukkah still

coming, while Hillel instructs us to number them as the passing of the
days. Again another Tanna points out that Shammai's plan parallels
and probably takes as a precedent the ancient system of burnt offerings
sacrificed on the altar at Succoth: fourteen oxen the first day, thirteen
the second, and so on down to seven on the seventh day; but Hillel,
he says, was always of the opinion that holy things should be increased
rather than decreased." My father bit a hard corner from a lump of
sugar and took a sip from his steaming glass as he turned the page.
"Then follows," he continued, his eyes running down the page, "a
dispute as to whether it is permissible to perform any work by the light
of these Hanukkah candles." (I considered that there were, of course,
no candles in those days; but I forbore to interrupt.) "One says yes,
and another no. Then in the name of the Tanna Rab it is laid down
that above all it is not permissible to count money by the light of the
Hanukkah candles. . . ." My father's voice descended into a studious
sing-song murmur and his lips moved as he searched again the finely
printed commentaries on the page. "And that argument just about fills
this page of Gemora," he said at last, taking another sip of tea and looking up at me.

I swallowed the last of the prune juice and, still savoring its heavy
sweetness, looked at my father and said: "How many angels can dance
on the head of a pin? . . ."

He smiled indulgently; for my father knew what I meant by that
signal of scoffing criticism. I had used it before. He smiled indulgently
and shook his head. "Surely," he answered, "you do not believe that
such minds, such authorities as Hillel and Shammai, would stoop to
controversies over literally worthless matters. Hillel, who said: 'The
uncultivated man is not innocent; the ignorant man is not devout . . .'
was himself neither uncultivated nor ignorant; would he, you think,
concern himself unworthily with discussions which are indeed (and my
father's eyes twinkled) only as meaningless superficially as the pages of
mathematical symbols in your book on mechanics are to the uninitiate
like myself?"

"The symbolism in my book on mechanics is a necessary mathematical convention for convenience in elaborate but logical discussions.
But why should presumably intelligent men have resorted to far-
fetched, apparently meaningless metaphors when they were speaking
of things of the spirit?" I was warming up; feeling no longer tired, and

a little belligerent after the food. "It looks to me as if they had so far removed themselves from life that . . ." My father's nod of comprehension saved me the end of that sentence.

"There is no accounting reasonably for the particular forms in which men choose to express themselves. I have seen," said my father mildly, and thoughtfully wiping his brow as he pushed the black skull-cap still further back on his head (for the tea had warmed him too), "I have seen Chinese pictures in which ladies are shown stepping into boats which, in proportion to their bodies, are about the size of teacups. These pictures are, I suppose, not ridiculous to the Chinese. They must be seen with the eyes of one trained or accustomed to that peculiar convention to be understood and appreciated. Now, I have, I think, been in my early days in a *yeshivah* very close to the spirit of these controversies of the Tannaim. Let me try to give you," he said, and as if to reinforce his wish and to hold my attention with a gesture, he handed me as I rose his empty glass, tinkling precariously on the saucer whose round it did not quite fit, so that in pouring myself a cup of tea I might give him another, "let me try to give you what I think is the real significance of all this discussion. To begin with the miracle itself: the *Menorah,* and its modern representative the Hanukkah light, is the symbol for Torah, for learning and culture, for civilization. The Temple was the one lighthouse in a world of spiritual darkness, and it drew toward it the animosity of the rulers of the Greeks, who hated it for its moral significance and desired to destroy it, and to reduce the Jewish folk to living in the state of darkness in which they themselves then existed."

To have destroyed my father's metaphorical lighthouse (it was one of long standing) would, it occurred to me, have been for him a personal disaster as dire as the one he was describing. I was myself tempted to shake it by calling his attention to the arts, the philosophy, the science of the ancient Greeks (thinking vaguely of the pure marmoreal beauties of Praxiteles and Phidias, of the clarities of Plato and the geometricians—darkness indeed!), but having always had a weak head for historical dates, and being uncertain of the chronological relation between the time of the Maccabees and the heights of Greek culture, I held my peace. In all likelihood, my father would, I knew, have countered with an irrefutable reference to their moral decadence, to nameless and indescribable practices . . . irrefutable because those were matters not to be carefully examined between father and son.

And I should then have been prompted to retort with a demand for the riches of art, of philosophy, of science, bequeathed to mankind by that ancient, austere, Jewish morality, which had shone uniquely, like a lighthouse. A lighthouse, I might have said, is usually founded upon a barren rock . . . But I held my peace.

"And so successful were they in their determination to destroy the detested Jewish morality, to undermine the fundamentals of the irritating Jewish religion that it appeared that neither would last more than a brief day, a single generation." My father looked at me then and smiled, assuring himself that I was grasping the parable. "But then, when the Maccabees succeeded in overpowering and dispersing the barbarians, occurred the miracle that the light of Judaism, very nearly extinguished as the barbarians had thought, continued to burn, has continued even to this day to illumine the world despite all the adverse winds and storms which, from time to time, have blown so frightfully upon it. That," and my father's face glowed as if in the light of his own poetic concept, "that, then, is the significance of our Hanukkah lights. And if every Jew obeyed this injunction and, following this ancient and significant custom, placed a little light in his window, it would make the loveliest illumination in all the world as well as the most powerful demonstration against those barbarians in spirit who, to this day, hate Jewish morality and law—it would be the beautiful sign of the persistent miracle of their survival . . ."

I sipped my tea in silence, fixing my eyes as he paused on the colorful package of Quaker Oats on the lowermost shelf of the cupboard behind my father's head. For had I looked at my father then, I should have been impelled to ask him: "What is this miraculous light of Judaism of which you speak; where is it now, in these times, to be seen other than in the poetic imagery you have evoked? Let us," I should have had to say, "have done with metaphors and talk fact. And as for illuminations—in another month or so you will be seeing again as pretty and as insignificant a lighting of windows as ever warms lyric souls to singing 'peace on earth, good will to men' and betrays the optimistic into rhapsodies over the progress of human kind." But not wanting to say such things to my father's face, glowing triumphantly over the steaming glass in his hand, I waited for him to continue, diverting myself the while with an ancient boyish speculation as to how far, working with the aid of a powerful magnifying glass, the

engraver of the design on the box of oatmeal might have carried his
ingenious conceit—a scroll inscribed with the words Quaker Oats and
the trademark, a reproduction of the figure of William Penn holding
in his extended hand a scroll, similarly inscribed and carrying in minia-
ture another William Penn extending his smaller scroll with its
minuscular inscription whereon the eye, infinitely intrigued, searched
a minute spot for yet further glimpses of progressively infinitesimal
reproductions of William Penn extending his cosmic scroll. . . .

"When the Tanna says that each family should burn at least the
one light, he means it for those who have conserved the spirit of the
old days when the father's Torah was also the children's Torah, when
the one light of learning sufficed for all the family. Now, however, in
more advanced times, says the Tanna, each member of the family
should burn his own light; for the concepts of ancient days must not
be forced upon the newer generation; the Torah, he means to say,
must be adapted to the new spirit of the times." My father looked
across at me now with an earnest benevolence shining from his eyes,
and the bright light overhead reflected from his forehead. He wanted
me to understand him. I listened now, attentive only to his words.
"Now," he continued, "come Shammai and Hillel, teaching the new
generation, each according to his lights. And Shammai, it appears, was
a very strict teacher, a hard master. He says: Young man—your future
lies before you; but make haste. Burn all your lights now: learn all
you can now, for as time passes the lights become fewer and one cannot recapture them. But Hillel, gentler, more liberal, says: Be thorough;
learn one thing today and tomorrow add another to what you have
learned, and thus steadily increase the light of your wisdom. Thus
only, in time, shall you learn all. Another Tanna"—my father set down
his glass to consult again the finely printed commentaries—"suggests
that Hillel and Shammai had still other meanings hidden among their
various ideas. Shammai interprets the reduction in the number of oxen
sacrificed at Succoth as the symbol of the failing powers of man as he
grows older, and as his strength grows less in his later days so too does
his ability to study, hence his injunction to study to the fullest extent
in youth. But Hillel replies that though it is true of physical power that
it decreases with age, with Torah, that is, learning, it is quite the contrary. A learned man becomes wiser with age. . . ."

I perceived suddenly that the Maccabees had, alas, disappeared
from view; and even the Hanukkah lights were no longer substantial

tapers but ideas that danced in the heads of men—firm Shammai and gentle Hillel, those vague anonymous Tannaim, and my father—lighting their faces. . . .

"Then comes the question whether study is permissible for the purpose of making a living from it. One Tanna says no; one must study solely for the purpose of knowing. Another says it does not matter why, so long as one studies; one may even draw sustenance from it. But the last word comes from the great teacher: that one may not count money by the light of the Hanukkah candles, which means simply, that one should not draw back from a course of study which does not pay as well as another."

Ah! There were still the candles after all; though the hard-fisted Maccabees, I perceived, were indeed hopelessly lost.

"You see?" said my father, and he swallowed the last of his tea. "These men were in their field as scrupulous, as unselfish, as your scientist who today spends his time in the laboratory speculating on— say, how many atoms can dance on the head of a pin"; and, holding up the book so that I could see its mottled brown leather binding, worn and broken, looked keenly over its edge at me, and, curiously, in that glance he seemed to be setting me inexorably between himself and the leaf of Gemora as between two mirrors where each was reflected in the other—my father in the printed page and it in him—and where I beheld myself reflected endlessly in both. . . .

"And now," he said, "let us see if we shall have enough lights for this Hanukkah." So I went to one of the deep drawers under the cupboard and after tugging at it (it always stuck because of the hammer, the ice pick or a screw driver lodged in it) and displacing tins of tacks, odd nails and screws, bits of discarded hardware and twine found at last the box of Christmas candles (there was a green tree and a red-clad Santa Claus on the box) left from the year before. This I brought to the table and, disclosing the colored layers of spiraled as if twisted candles, bright red and pure white, translucent cream, pale green, dark blue and yellow, removed the broken ones. "We shall need," I said, "one and two and three and . . ." adding it quickly in my head, for I was proud of my arithmetical prowess, "thirty-six."

"And eight more for the Shammes," added my father, "makes forty-four; and, after all, the amount of light is the same whether you follow Hillel or Shammai."

But these were not metaphorical lights I was counting. The brittle, greasy feel of them and their bright colors recalled the childish delight it used to be to be permitted to hold the Shammes, to communicate that soft yellow flame, to make, as if magically, two flames out of one. There were just about enough. I poured them back into the box.

"Next year," said my father, "we shall need new lights." He rose and, as I passed into the hall, reached up and slowly turned down the gas light that first glowed red in the mantle and then vanished.

(—*1929*)

The Year of Abundance

MOSES STAVSKY

GOD RELENTED. And the whispered prayers of the toiler returned not empty, and the tears of the sower reached to heaven.

With great, with manifold mercy the windows of heaven were flung open, flung wide by a generous hand to abundance and rich blessing.

At the beginning of Cheshvan the rains began to fall, beautiful in their order and pleasant in their seasons. Week in and week out, Sabbath to Sabbath, Sabbath to Wednesday, and Wednesday to Sabbath alternately, with slight pauses until the plowing and sowing were done, and again from week to week, Sabbath to Sabbath, Sabbath to Wednesday, and Wednesday to Sabbath, as in the generations of complete purity and God-fearing men.

And when Tebet came, the fields were all plowed, plowed and sown, pregnant with fruit, rich in blessing, and drunken with rain.

To the farthest horizon, as far as the eye encompassed, it fed on verdure, bright green and yellow green. Soft and gentle and pale were the first sprigs of wheat which cracked the crust of the earth and shot forth their heads into air, delicate, languid and tender.

Light green and dark green, sun bright—beans and barley, vetch and barley, vetch and oats—light green and dark green. Sun and rain —deep-rooting, high-stretching, black-spreading—sated and over-sated, filled to overflowing. Like a well-favored child who rests on the knees of a mother blessed with abundant milk and sucks his fill, and being replete pushes away the breast without sucking to the end— not half—not a third—and falls with his head thrown back, weary of fullness, and foam dribbles from his mouth and about his neck, foam and saliva, sweet foam, sweet and white.

Joy, satiate joy rises from the earth, fills the spaces of the air, rises and pours itself over the face of the earth like the savor of good ointments—joy and blessing.

To the village abundance reached and to the colony, to the large colony and to the small colony, to the *moshav* and to the *kvutzah;* it knocked at the doors of the Arab *husha,* at the doors of mansions and huts, at the tent flap and the wooden barracks. It knocked exultingly, with exceeding joy. It shouted, "Here am I. I have come to you with blessing. Once in seventy years. Few are the graybeards that remember me.

"Behold your prayers are answered, the tears of your babes have reached me. I have come to you—and with me grass for the cow and the goat, milk for the suckling and the calf, seeds for the hen and pigeon, grain for the millstone, grain for sowing, grain for the granary."

At once worry fell away, strife ended, and hate was torn up by its roots—complete strangers with careworn faces looked at one another joyfully—delight and gladness were companions—exultation met with rejoicing.

People heavy with age and full of trouble sought out the tenderest words and the pleasantest names to call their happiness. In ringing voices like the clinking of gold against silver—

> The most blessed year, the greenest year—
> Year of milk, year of corn!
> The whitest year, the greenest year,
> Year of the lamb, year of the calf—
> The rainiest year, the most blessed year!

In the oldest of the settlements, the mother of the settlements, abundance overflowed its banks. Mud to the neck. And it was easy and pleasant to wallow in abundance, to leap from stone to bank, and hop from bank to stone, amused and smiling lightly: Did you ever see a wanton like this, such a bully—ever in all your days?

Easy it was and pleasant, for the fields were already sown, sown correctly and in their appointed time, the harvest was growing prettily, and many were eager for it.

Pleasant it was and easy. For the ditches in the vineyard were open already . . . wide open . . . they stretched from tree to tree, ditch touched ditch . . . the price of almonds was higher than last year . . . new vines will be planted this year . . . grapes are paid for in advance . . . there are great preparations in the winepress . . . every one has his hands full of work.

Pleasant it was and easy. For there was so much water that it was impossible to get to the orange grove. One could only go out and stand far off by the acacia hedge, and from there gaze at the long, entangled, heavy-laden rows of greenage. Laden with abundant blessing, a green, ripening and yellowing. And while you are standing, as a thief might stand outside the fence, your own fence, you take account, you reckon and set prices, you grow fantastic, exaggerate, and know that you exaggerate, and understand your folly. And you are satisfied and brimming with pleasure at this folly of yours.

Pleasant it was and easy. For this week a donkey sank in the swamp of the *hamrah*. Bells clanged and people gathered. Noise and tumult. The village folk rushed to the *hamrah*, some on foot, some horseback, some with rope, some with sticks. But they could not pull the donkey out. At last they harnessed a pair of mules and tied them to the donkey, jerked him out, dragged him through the whole village, pulled him from street to street singing and clamoring. People came out of their houses to whistle and hiss after them. Loafers beat on tins, trilled with their fingers on the lips, shrill feverish shrieks like the wailing lament of Arab women mourners.

Idle days they rode to the city to amuse themselves, one to the tailor or dressmaker, another to the theater or movie. Anyone who owned a horse wore riding trousers. His legs encased in boots, a kafia on his head, and an abya on his shoulders. He and comrades his own age go down to the threshing floor, the one dry spot in the village, to sport with the horses. One remembers his friend in a neighboring village, puts double sacks on his saddle and gifts in the sacks, a branch loaded with oranges, some green and some ripe, branch and leaves and fruit together. In the evening he comes home with a gift to the house, honey, eggs and chickens that peep out of the sacks.

In the evening neighbor visits neighbor, housewife visits housewife, to sip tea, eat sweets and gossip.

The old men pass their time in the synagogue; one pondering over a holy book, another in secular talk.

And the village band, from its room in the council house, from early evening until late at night, booms through all the village with its great brass instruments. Out of satiety and pleasure, with childlike folly and innocent joy—boom boom—till midnight and later—boom boom—we are blessed this year, a wonder like this comes but once in seventy years.

Boom—boom—boom—

Slow moving as the waters of Siloam, abundance poured itself out over the face of the earth. Lovely in its order and pleasant in its season.

Week after week, Sabbath after Sabbath, every Sabbath and every Wednesday. When Shevat comes the wells of Jerusalem are brimful of water, and every throat hoarse with praise and song. Every shoe and every sandal torn with dancing.

And the pasture floods over the face of the earth like a green river. Like the waters of early spring in western lands. Like the Nile at the end of summer. Wherever grass could strike its roots it climbed, sand, stone, mountain, valley, tree and roof.

The dew is still on the ground and the herd returns to the village to be shut up in the stalls a day and a night, until the morning of the morrow. Filled, glutted, every belly a barrel's width. All day and all night, they chew and ruminate. Until their jaws are tired and white foam, greenish foam dribbles from their mouths, weary of chewing, and paints all the ground about them green and white.

The calves suckle and do not empty the tits, not half, not a quarter, and they weary of sucking—they grow weary from too much sucking.

The flock are weary of carrying their fatted skins, and because of the heaviness of their fleshy rumps the lambkins move lumberingly and lazily.

In the middle of Tebet a letter was sent from brother to brother— from Ain Hai, which is in Kfar Saba near Petach Tikwah, to Tel Adashim, which is in Emek Israel, saying:

"Cauliflower is plentiful here. We have so many that we could pave the streets with them. I talked it over with my wife Zipporah and she says perhaps it would be well to send you some, for who knows whether cauliflower has grown well with you this year."

And the man in Tel Adashim, which is in the Emek, answered his brother who is in Ain Hai, which is in Sharon:

"We have packed cauliflower in cans. We collected all the cans of Nazareth and Haifa, and it is impossible to get any more. And as for carrots, we have more than we can pull up, more than we can gather. I beg you to come to us. You were fond of *tzimmus,* and my wife Tobah will cook *tzimmus* for you as you liked it in the old days, as mother cooked it, may she rest in peace, for the Sabbath meal when we were still in our father's house."

And in the beginning of the month of Shevat a message was sent by word of mouth from Kfar Saba, which is near Petach Tikwah, through a worker going to Tel Aviv. By word of mouth, because the sender was not in the habit of writing. Nor had he the time, for he was alone at his work. And there was his vegetable garden and tree nursery of orange trees on which he must keep an eye, and the cowshed where the cows must be fastened, watered and milked.

The message was addressed to the house of the produce agent in Mercaz Mischari, Tel Aviv, who was to give it to a comrade who kept cows in Tel Nordia; and it was phrased in these words:

"The calves which were nearly dead at the end of last summer from lack of pasture in the fields will not die. Their skin is almost bursting with fat. And so I beg you to send your cattle to my pastures. For there is too much grass and the blessing of God is going to waste."

And a comrade of Magdel brought his old mother and young sister up to Eretz Israel from Motomashav, which is in the kingdom of Poland. He harnessed his horse and cart and drove to Tel Aviv himself to fetch them from the ship. Himself: first, because pennies are scarce among workers on the land and he hadn't the price of an auto; and, second, because he longed to show off, to boast, to strut before them like a child.

"Just look, what a driver! How handsomely he manages a horse!"

And they the whole way could not fill their eyes with looking, nor their hearts with marveling.

"See, see, what a driver. Look at the farmer, no evil eye upon him. . . . Look, look how sunburnt and how dirty he is! Look, how cracked his hands are, his dear hands."

And the sister who had been a comrade of the *chalutz* in Poland laughed through her tears and wept in her laughter. She took the reins in her hands and learned how to drive the horse, and then in the softest, gentlest voice she called to the horse, the big horse who was pulling the cart—my dove, my bird, my cat, my darling, my love. They got home late, tired from the journey, and overwrought with joy. And long they spoke and much they recounted, questioned and answered, until drowsiness fell upon them, and they slept.

And an old peasant, a man of Bertuvia in Shephelah, which is in Judah, returned at sunset from the fields, unyoked his oxen, watered them, put fodder before them, washed himself, prayed *mincha* and *maariv* peacefully and earnestly. And when he had refreshed himself with food, he sent to a neighbor for pen and ink. He tore an empty page from a notebook that belonged to his grandchild, mounted his glasses on his nose and sat down to write a letter to his son who lived in Nahalal, which is in the Emek, in a fine Yiddish seasoned here and there with bits of Russian. And this is the translation:

"First, I wish you and your wife and children peace and good health.

"Secondly, Mother, long life to her, asks how you are and how your wife and children are, may they be found worthy of long life and good health. Also I must tell you, my son, that the barley has come up beautifully this year, higher than a man's head. Perhaps you would lose nothing if you were to come to me, you and your horse and your wagon together to help us to reap our fields."

And the son who dwelt in Nahalal, which is in the Emek, returned from the fields to his house, set the yard and cowshed in order, and after he had washed and dressed, eaten and drunk, he turned his step to the council house. (Once there had been pen and ink in his house, but the pen rusted and the ink dried from the heat—and the boy was still in kindergarten, so there was no notebook to tear a piece of paper from.) And from the council house he wrote a letter to his father, who was in Bertuvia, in pure Hebrew—and this was its content:

"To my honored father and teacher and my mother who bore me— may you have long life. The barley and vetch have grown this year beyond all other years. We are tired of too much labor. Perhaps my father would consent to come to his son to help him gather the fruit of his fields."

The letters met at the station Lydda and separated, one in one direction and the other in another direction, this one to Bertuvia, which is in the Shephelah, and that one to Nahalal, which is in the Emek.

And a Jew who dwelt in the settlement Hederah, a firmly planted Jew, broad-boned, a solid rich peasant, wrote to his daughter who was a shopkeeper in Jaffa, in Beneve Shalom:

"Lock the store and come, you, your husband and your children. There is plenty of work and plenty of food . . . milk and eggs and vegetables . . . more than we can eat . . . no one buys and no one sells!" . . .

And a farmer, a man of Ekron, met a former worker of his in a street of Tel Aviv. And they recognized one another—by the smell of the field and cowshed they knew one another. The smell clung to them and they carried it with them amid the sand and stone of the city. Both strong men, bent in stature, sunburnt faces. One in boots and the other in jacket, vest and *tsitsiyot*. They knew each other and rejoiced—they rejoiced whole-heartedly.

The plow had bent both their backs and made them equals.

"Do you know that in Mansorah each dunam gave two full sacks of wheat?"

"Do you know that with us in Ain Tivon the oats have grown higher than a man's head, so that when the watchman gets off his horse among the grain both horse and rider vanish?" . . .

And the comrades of Tel Hai wrote to their comrades in Tel Josef.

"Perhaps you can send us a few scythes. Our scythes broke this year. Each stalk of hay is thicker than a finger, and is almost impossible to cut."

And the comrades of Tel Josef, which is in the Emek, answered their comrades in Tel Hai, who dwell in the mountains of Upper Galilee.

"We have set up a carpenter to make handles for the scythes. Perhaps you are able to send us oak wood. For it is impossible to get any wood here except eucalyptus wood." . . .

And the writer of the story, who was shut up between the sand and stone of Tel Aviv, met a comrade of his, one day in Allenby Street, a comrade of many days gone by, a companion of the plow and scythe, broad-shouldered, sturdy and sunburnt. And he remembered his first month of work, that sweet, as it were, honeymoon of his workdays, that bright singing month rose in his heart—horse, cow and cowshed, plow, scythe and field, grass, sun and rain—earth—and sky—and God—

And the comrades rejoiced—rejoiced exceedingly—tears came to their eyes out of excessive joy. They questioned each other, told one another stories. Until the writer grew silent and his friend, the man of the colony, continued to recount, to relate joyously, out of his great joy.

"Beyond belief.

"Beyond conception.

"One year in seventy, one year in eighty, weary is the earth of great blessing, tired are the sowers of overwork, and every hand is heavy with overabundance."

The writer listens and is silent, tears choke in his throat, and his heart murmurs a prayer and a silent blessing.

"Blessed be the hands that have chosen hard labor for their lot.

"Blessed be ye in your houses, blessed in your gardens, blessed your garners and baking troughs, blessed your flocks and your herds, blessed your plows and your scythes—

"Even to the smallest weed of your field that grows by the wayside."

Translated from the Hebrew by Edward Robbin

(—1930)

Young Writer, Remembering Chicago

❧

ALBERT HALPER

Fall

STARK days these. Stark nights too. In the parks the trees stand firm, the bare boughs creaking in the wind. The gravel paths, clean from many rains, are neat against the dead brown of faded grass. The wind blows, the leaves fall, and smoke rolls up from factories.

Through the South Side the trains come in at night, long gray metal monsters, racing from off the plains, thundering over viaducts, small squares of light glittering from their windowed steel bodies.

And mist hangs over the lake, drifting to the shore. Tugs creep up the river like water beetles, blunt-nosed, going under bridges, chugging. Fog hangs over the Loop all night. The empty iron streets are gray and dead.

Big buildings go up, rearing themselves in the morning, the steel framework clear against a dirty sky. The chatter of pneumatic hammers, the coarse casual language of men who earn two dollars an hour and like hot beans, drop from the height, but never reach the street.

The nights are blue and chill, with foggy air to breathe. The Elevated goes west, south and north, spanning the miles, returning to the Loop, the crowded Loop, where big buildings stand lank, showing their thin sides, their flat buttocks. Cool shadows fall against the walls and the bricks are pressed down hard for strength.

Well, what about Chicago, what about the tough town by the lake, the Windy City, the burg with the bad reputation? What about Chicago in the fall? Who knows Chicago? There's no wind. No answer.

A sprawl of shacks nibbling at the prairie, then came the smokestacks and the noise. A blare and a crash, and the hum of engines speeding toward the river.

(403)

Fall comes, the hurly-burly season, the wind-howling season. The freights come in from Texas, loaded to the doors with fat steers that stamp upon the flooring, rubbing sides, grunting in the swaying, roaring trains. Everything comes into Chicago. The long-legged cowboys in charge of the cattle, lads who like plug tobacco, walk through the Loop on high-heeled boots, see the classy legs on Michigan Avenue, feel their bluish chins and swallow. Oh you Panhandle boys, how do you like the Windy City? What do you think of the big noisy town?

And after harvest the farm boys come in, big lanky fellers in overalls, with wide mouths and great brown hands, all eager to bite into Chicago, all hoping to get a job. They walk south along State Street, reach Harrison, stare at the photos in front of the cheap burlesque shows, see the penny arcades, the pimps standing in the doorways. They walk slowly under the street lamps at night. Chicago has enough women to go around, women whose job it is to make big awkward farm boys happy, women with hard eyes and tight mouths, sloppy dames with loose breasts. The cops say nothing, look the other way, twirl their clubs, and think about getting on the day shift.

Oh you farm boys, what do you think of the tough town by the lake? Corn sways when the wind blows over the prairie, but the wind in Chicago howls down the street; it howls over the rooftops of factories and office buildings; and during lunch hour the young fellers stand on the corners with toothpicks in their mouths and watch the girls waiting for the traffic signal, watch the wind act naughty-naughty. Why go to a burlesque show, folks, when you live in the Windy City? You see, my friends, I am a booster for Chicago.

And now folks, my own people, let me tell you my story. I was born on the West Side near the Northwestern tracks; there were factories and big livery stables in the neighborhood. My old man ran a grocery and once a week I sprinkled sawdust on the floor, throwing out the grains like golden seeds. That was before the chain-stores were popular, that was a long time ago. My old man carried a lot of book-trade, customers who paid every Saturday; and when the wage-earner of the family came home drunk, why of course my old man had to wait until the next Saturday. He marked down the items in his big book, then marked them in duplicate in the customer's. Everybody was satisfied, fair enough, fair enough.

There was the Polish janitress who lived on Lake Street near St.

John's Place. She bought half-a-dozen rolls every morning. She used to pinch my cheeks and feel my buttocks and say it was too bad I was only nine years old. She had a rosy face and dark eyes and was always walking fast, always out of breath. Her husband was a plumber's helper; he was tall and skinny. One day she ran away with a husky shipping clerk.

We kids used to make fun of Lumpy Louie, the old cracked gent who had three bumps on his head that looked like three small eggs. He used to stand in front of the wooden Indian in front of Sutton's candy store, arguing and lifting his cane at it; sometimes he scolded the Indian for not keeping his appointment the evening before. He would rap the fire-plugs sharply and grow very angry, and once in a while we threw stones at him and he cried.

I used to go swimming in Union Park, in the old lagoon with the cement bottom, that bottom that got slippery because the water wasn't changed often enough. There was a stone bridge over the neck of the pond and people used to toss pennies down into the water on Saturday afternoons and we dived for them. There was quite a scramble. When we got a few we stuck them in our mouths and dived for some more. One day a husky girl, a good diver, pushed us little fellers aside and got almost all the pennies. I remember she didn't wear a bathing suit, but an old dirty suit of clinging underwear; she was about twelve years old. We ducked her and kicked her, but she wouldn't go away, and the men on the bridge tossed pennies near her all the time.

George Hurrell, the kid who turned out to be an artist, the short, strong kid who was always drawing pictures on the sidewalk, was my buddy. Every night we went up the alley, crept near the rear window of Healy's and looked into the back room. The window had a coat of black paint, but there were a few scratches that let us see fairly well. We saw two women showing a few men a good time, and though the men changed from night to night, the women were always the same ones, the tall stout one and the one with black hair; they sat on the laps of the men, squeezed the boys hard and made them dance to the tune of the old mechanical piano. We watched them drinking, saw old hunch-backed Paddy Curly bring in the bottles, and when the women started smoking our eyes popped. That was the first time I had ever seen ladies smoke, that was when I was a kid. Sometimes the dancing looked like wrestling; and when I told my mother about it, she slapped my face, telling me not to go back in the alley.

Yes, folks, I know many stories—stories that run down the streets of my brain, baying. Every day, every night there's the soft quick pad of feet; the echoes die over the buildings and lose themselves around the corners. Sometimes I have the notion that my mind is a long, long corridor with small, neat doors on either side. Stories come and rap against the panels, but some do not knock hard enough and after waiting a while they go away. They walk softly all the way down the narrow hall, reach the end and pause a bit, then disappear quietly. Maybe my ears aren't sensitive enough, maybe so; but a man can't hurry, he's got to take his time. Speed is in the wind, but the world rolls dead and heavy.

The days come, the days go, and big ships sail into the harbor. . . .

And here I sit, in New York, typing these lines, my money almost gone, the room chilly, two limp towels hanging from a rod. My arms are heavy, I'm a thousand miles from home, I've got the blues; there's a locomotive in my chest, and that's a fact.

New York can go to hell for mine. I belong to Chicago, that's where I belong. Folks, if you ever have kids, don't let them try to become writers. Slam them over the heads with a big hammer, if they say they want to write. Send them to sea, ship them by parcel post to New Zealand, but don't let them look at a portable typewriter. You'll be doing them a big favor.

For every shout upon the mountain top there's a million miles of wailing wind. Panes of glass rattle in their sockets, a roomer from the third floor goes tramping down the stairs, turns the knob and slams the door, while outside the street-lamps throw their cold white glare.

Winter

In the winter all things do not die. The waves leap up along a cold shore and the wind blows hard. The gulls band in flocks, swerving, wheeling to the right, and the bright sunlight glances from their bellies.

Oh the iron streets are cold, cold. The raw wind whistles over buildings, rattles the laundry signs, swirls the snow into high drifts in the alleys and long, blue sparks fly from the third rail as the Elevated goes over the frosty tracks.

Jake Bowers, coming from down-state, walks along Madison Street, stands on the corner of Clinton, takes his hands from his pockets and begins blowing on his fists. Jake is broke. His overalls are getting frayed, his hair is long, and he is getting thin. He shuffles in the cold, bucks the wind, thinks about the big wheat-cakes he has eaten all summer, thinks about the farmer's big stout wife, and when he reaches the Salvation Army headquarters his mind is warm all right, but his legs are like wood. He sees the long line of broken men, all anxious to get a bed, and when he blows on his fists again, his chapped lips split open in several places and he begins sucking the blood coming from the cracks.

When the wind blows over the prairie the cornstalks make a dry rustling sound, but in Chicago the wind whistles through your pants and you shiver plenty. Ask Jake Bowers the tall, lanky boy from downstate. Hey, Jake, how do you like Chicago? Tell the folks about it. Jake doesn't answer; he wets his dry, cracked lips, stands in line with the others and thinks about a bed for the night.

At dawn the day breaks, the cold, dark sky cracks slowly. Now the iron streets are noisy, the trucks pound hard, teamsters swing their heavy whips through the frosty air and long columns of vapor come from the nostrils of the horses.

Hey, hey, Chicago. Go on, you devils. Drag your loads, pull them through the streets, pull them along the shiny car tracks. At night I'll turn you toward the barn, I'll give you hay and water, I'll whack your steamy rumps. Hey, hey, Chicago. Go on, you big fat devils.

And the big whips swing through the frosty air while the Elevated booms by overhead. The rear legs of the horses bulge with strength.

When I was a small kid only a few autos were on the streets. I saw the big horses leaning forward, pulling; I heard the swearing teamsters swaying on their seats. Race-horses are nice to look at, nice to write about, but what of the brutes that pull heavy loads, what of the animals that fall and break their legs on slippery streets, kicking weakly until a cop comes running with a gun in his hand? Hey, hey, Chicago. What about those poor devils, pulling?

At noon the cracked sky is wide open. Small-faced flappers hurry in the cold, their long thin legs moving very fast. They head for the drug stores, the long narrow stores lined with high stools. They crowd at the counters where prim sandwiches are sold, nicely decorated, good stuff to nibble at with small teeth. Some gals smoke now, swing their legs and eye the soda-jerker, a tall slick lad with a turned-up shiny nose. The gals look down from the office windows, hoping for a rich feller, hoping the boss won't have too many letters to dictate.

I once worked in a factory. There were punch-presses near the wall. One noon I sat talking to a man who spoke broken English, but had good jaws. It was snowing outside and we watched the big flakes floating down. Next to me a big Swede yawned, closed his mouth slowly, sighted at the factory cat like at a target, then spat a good stream of rich brown tobacco juice. The cat was white. But it was half-brown as it sprang away. The Swede did not laugh; he yawned, hoping the snow would stop at half-past five.

And I once had a job as order-picker for a mail-order house, my first job after graduating high school, when I was eager to conquer the world, to advance with the times, as it were. I went along aisles of merchandise and picked the orders, reading the sheets sent in by customers from Arkansas and Minnesota. There were many items to pick, cheap work shirts, rubber collars, corduroy pants, fedora hats that the firm picked up at auction. I used to stand in the aisles when the supervisor wasn't looking and read the letters accompanying the orders. Some of the customers could not spell; they had scrawly handwriting and wrote in the personal vein; they told the firm that the last pair of pants was a bit too small for Tom—Tom liked more room around the seat. Yes, folks, those were the days. Another fellow worked with me, he was a big Hollander, his name was Big Bill Mesland; he had to leave Holland because of a certain girl there. Big Bill was fiery when the boss was not around, but as soon as Kerton walked by Bill became meek in manner. He used to coax the packing girls into the darker aisles, and none of them hollered very much. And at Christmas, when the orders grew heavy, when we had to work overtime until our eyes were red, Big Bill cursed the firm, standing in the aisle. And one night, a clear starry night as the poets say, after we had checked out, he and I walked toward the car-line, and at the corner he wheeled around, raised his big fist in the air and cursed the building behind us, cursed it in his broken English. I laughed at him. But one year later, when I had another job, I heard that the firm of Phillipsborn had gone bankrupt. Well, maybe Bill was a medicine man after all. Who knows? He went away to California and wrote me a letter, but I didn't answer it and I don't know why.

I once had a good friend, but he left town, left his job at the Post Office and is now working as a seaman; he once wrote me from Brussels. Before he left he told me this: he said big hills are not small mountains.

We had a long argument, but I don't recall who won. I told him he was a fathead, called him a mystic, but now I'm beginning to understand what he meant.

The point is, never go to New York, my friends. Stick in Chicago where you belong. New York can go to hell for mine. They say it's a great town, that it's the greatest thing in America, but that's all a lie, and a bloody lie at that.

Let the subways roar on, let them rumble underground, let the big boats sail into the harbor bringing freight and people. But the wide mouth of hell can swallow it whole for all I care. I've got your number, New York. You're just a big small town, a burg full of suckers, swollen with yokels. Dear old Manhattan, sweet papa Knickerbocker. Eighty black years on you and yours.

But now it's winter, good old winter in Chicago. The wind howls and snow is whirled into drifts back in the alleys. A strong boat goes up the Chicago River, breaking the ice, keeping the way clear. And every Saturday afternoon races are held in the parks, the bands play on platforms, a few cops on skates keep the crowds back, and sometimes the favorite falls at the last lap and people feel sorry for him. The wide oval pond glitters dully under the sun and the wind blows fine snow over the ice. People stamp to keep warm, some slap their sides. . . .

But here I sit in New York, typing these lines. The windows rattle in their sockets. The sun comes up in the morning and rolls over the western rim by night. Words are nice to look at and you can't beat neat black type against a sheet of clean white paper. And folks, now that I have written a few lines here, I've got something off my chest. I feel better. Maybe I still feel blue, but not as blue as before.

But what about this stuff I'm writing? Won't the critics say this stuff of mine is raw and awkward and unfinished and slangy? But, by cripes, why shouldn't it be? Since when is life in America lived in Greek temples?

I was born in a raw slangy city, in a raw slangy neighborhood. I lived near railroads, and on warm nights I could smell the strong odor from the stockyards rolling in heavy waves all the way from the South Side. Try to write polite literature with that stink in your nostrils; sit down and spin smooth poetic sentences with the roar of railroads in your ears.

When I was a kid I saw sluggers pull down teamsters from the seats of wagons during the big strikes. I watched the bloody brawls at the polls at election time, and some of my old buddies are now successful gangsters. I was an errand-boy working after school when the race riots broke out on the South Side, and, coming from a home where I had just delivered a package, I saw five whites chasing a Negro up the street. The Negro was howling, waving his arms. He ran so hard his shirt worked loose from his pants and flapped in the summer wind. They chased him up an alley off Indiana Avenue, cornered him near a shed, and one white kicked the coon in the mouth as the dark boy got on his knees to beg for mercy. The nigger begged hard. He said he had never done harm to any white man; he howled and then stopped, and for a while it looked as if he were trying to swallow his own lips. That was when one of the whites pulled out a gun, a shiny revolver that caught the sun. It took two shots to finish the business. The whites stood grim. The coon, his arms spread out as if nailed to a cross, lay quiet near a pile of horse manure. The whites chased me out the alley, told me to beat it, to keep my mouth shut. Then the cops came, didn't ask me a question, and forced me to ride in the patrol wagon until we passed the danger zone. Soldiers of the National Guard stood on the corners. Many papers were sold.

I'm not a snooper, I don't go round looking for stories, but I know what I know, know what I have seen. If I was born in a raw and slangy town, if I happened to see raw and slangy things, why shouldn't my stuff be raw and slangy? Why the hell not?

And meanwhile it's winter in Chicago. The wind blows over the frozen lagoons, whirls thin fine snow toward the pavilion, and out on the ice a small man wearing a round fur cap tries to perform fancy turns with dull skates. And the days go by, the gray days, the cold days, the windy days too. They all go by.

And here I am in a New York room, tapping on a portable. Two limp towels hang from a rod. I've got a locomotive in my chest, and that's a fact. It's pretty chilly now and I pull an old sweater on, that old sweater I wore when I quit a job over four years ago and went bumming all summer with Davis, asking folks for rides along the highways. But it's winter now, my friends. It's a gray day and the traffic pounds down Eighth Avenue. Across the way, level with my window, a woman sticks a mop out and shakes it hard; she isn't much to look at, kind of middle-aged and her hair is hidden in an old house-cap.

Now a few peeps of steam come up, thin and faint, a drawn-out

whistling sound. The landlady's heart has melted, she's a good sport
after all. When I become famous, when I learn to write that slick
tricky stuff, I'll type her a nice letter, a letter that will make her proud.
"Dear Madam," I will say, and I'll say plenty nice things. She's a tall
thin old lady, and once upon a time a young writer from Kentucky
beat her out of two weeks rent. A few more peeps come up, drearily
like lost pieces of fog drifting down a river on a sunny day.

Spring

The wind blows, but it is not so cold now; its howling mood is gone,
gone down that twining river which disappears into the trees. On the
left bank lies a rowboat, bottom up, like a fat man's belly. The paint
is peeling, small worms crawl along the seams.

The wind is warm now, a little wet too, and small buds, hanging
from the branches, tremble there like heavy drops of water.

When the damp wind blows over the prairie the tall new grass nods
in the breeze, but in Chicago people sniff the air, begin walking
through the parks again, and a few married young fellers hit the boss
for a raise.

And it's nice to walk up a street at night when the warm wind blows.
There goes the Windy City Kid, coming home from work on the night
shift down at the Post Office. It's four o'clock in the morning, the street
is quiet. He takes his time, walks with his hands in his pockets, and
when he sees the police squad he hurries a bit, smiling to himself as
he lures them on. Ah Windy City Kid, you're no greenhorn, you know
your onions. The police car bears down, swings over toward the curb,
the cops leaning out, and then they call halt! The Windy City Kid
halts. He feels frisky, stands firm, and has a mocking look about his
eyes. The cops get out, slap his body to feel if there are weapons,
question him, tell him to talk up, threaten to run him in. But the
Windy City Kid holds a trump card, he works nights, sleeps days, and
he's got to have his little joke now and then. When the cops grow ugly
he pulls out his Post Office badge, flashes it under their noses, tells
them he works on the night shift, dares them to call up the supervisor
if they doubt it. The cops swear. They get in their auto and drive
away. And the Windy City Kid stands at the curb laughing. He calls
himself a crazy nut, but he feels pretty good. Then he begins walking

up the dark silent street toward home. He has turned this trick a few times; he works nights, he's got to have his little joke once in a while.

And so spring comes to Chicago. The lake boats sail away like ocean liners, cruise a few hundred miles along Lake Michigan and bring back a load. Smoke trails them, hangs in the air, follows them over the water, and on clear days the horizon seems as boundless as the open sea.

And the warm wind blows, whirling dust along the street, into the public's eyes, into the eyes of those young fellers who stand on the corners during lunch hour, chewing on their toothpicks.

Yes, folks, it's spring. The curbs along Madison Street are lined with men, husky fellers and broken geezers. It's spring and they also taste the warm wind. They stand east of Halsted Street, where the cheap employment agencies, with their flaring signs posted outside, are doing a big business. Men are wanted, big raw fellers for the railroad gangs, men for road building, men to go north to the lumber mills. Forty dollars a month, board free. Well, bohunks, what do you say? Come on, what do you say? Take it or leave it. Hey, you, the big guy with the high shoulders, do you want a job? Your fists are big, you've got small angry eyes, maybe you've had a tough time this winter, eh? Want a job, want work? Here we are, men, forty bucks a month up north in the camps, or forty-five with the road gang. Hey, bohunks, what d'ya say? Hurry, hurry, hurry, men. Hey, hey.

But Jake Bowers from down-state says nothing. There he stands, his eyes half-sunken, pretty thin now, his country color gone, his big brown hands are white now. Hey, Jake, what do you think of Chicago? Tell the folks about it. Send your story singing against the wind. The breeze blows gently over the prairie, but in Chicago a man's got to think about a job. Hey, Jake, how about a job up north? Forty bucks and cheap booze every other Saturday. How about it? Jake says nothing. He stands lank, shoves his hands in his pockets, then shuffles away. Jake wants to go back home on the farm, Jake wants his wheat-cakes every morning and the sight of the farmer's tall stout wife. Jake wants to go home. He has had a tough winter, the raw lake wind has whistled through his pants for a long time. Now he wants to go back to the soil. He has been going to a quack doctor, trying to get cured of a dose, and he wants to go back awfully bad.

Spring comes. The brisk wind flaps the colored signs of the employment agencies, and the men walk by. Merchants wash their windows, advertise bargains, hire extra clerks, and stand behind the counters waiting for business.

Blow, wind, go on blowing. Whistle through their Danish whiskers, blow the black smoke away from factories, sweep it out upon the lake.

Who knows Chicago? There's no wind, no answer, but this is what I say:

If you have seen pigeons wheeling in the sky, if you have looked at heavy sunlight warming the naked branches of trees, if all the sounds of a city merge, swelling into one great tone, if after you come back to your room, that room with the two towels hanging from a rod, if after all this has come about and you sit on your chair, your arms heavy, the keys of the typewriter staring at you—if you've gone through all this, I want to tell you that in the winter all things do not die, but death takes many things in the spring. I want to tell you that if warm wind is sticky with new life, it also suffocates the old. It drives the young writers home, the brave boys who came to New York. The young writers pack their grips, pay the landladies, take the subway to the station, and stand waiting for their trains. Youth does not always win, it rides home and tells the folks nothing, gets a job and lets the days go by.

Spring comes. The wharves along the coast lose their hard lines and whores walk through the woods on heavy stumpy legs, squinting at the blossoms, smelling the fresh damp earth. The odor of clean rain is in the air. Then comes the smell of cheap scent; for whores are walking through the trees. Don't be afraid of the word, folks; words are only words after all, even if there is a town called Boston.

Once upon a time I thought that sincerity and simplicity were all that mattered, that if a young writer was honest and had a little talent, that was enough. In my high school days I used to dream in class, thinking how to make myself a great writer. There was an English teacher, a tall strong woman of Scotch descent, who always talked to us of honesty. That's how I got a bum steer, that's how I learned out-dated stuff. What does honesty mean to the three-score wise men in the East —the publishers, the critics, the editors. . . .

Days go by. The warm prairie wind blows toward Chicago, blows up the river, blows over the West Side and keeps on blowing. Women in back yards hang clothes out to dry and old man Sutton thinks about painting his wooden Indian.

And here I sit, a fathead, typing these lines, wishing I had a job where I would never have a chance to write another line or read another book. I need a hair-cut, I hear the traffic pounding down Eighth Avenue, I've got the blues; there's a locomotive in my chest, and that's a fact. I do not believe in heroes, I do not believe in valorous deeds. I've been hurt many times, and a few more jabs won't make much difference. But why must death take so many things in the spring, why must the young grow weak fighting the old? The walls of New York are high and thick, many young people have fired their loads of buckshot at them. Out of the west they come, up from the south, but they all go back, they all go back to where they belong.

And behind the polished desks the wise men of the East sit cackling, the editors, the publishers, the critics. They scratch their thighs, screw up their little eyes and cackle silently.

Roar, New York, keep on roaring. Some day I'll write a book about Chicago, a big raw, slangy, crude book, a book that'll knock your wise men off their chairs. I'll make Chicago America. Walt Whitman was all right, but he never knew the Windy City, he never saw the stockyards, the railroads, the big dance halls, the streets and streets of factories, the lines of broken men in winter. So roar, New York, roar on. Your rumbling dies over the harbor, fades away in Brooklyn, disappears in Astoria.

And all the while the wind blows over Chicago. People come home from work and eat big meals, roast beef and fried potatoes are washed down with strong coffee. Eat, Chicago, sock it in your belly. You'll need plenty of meat, lots of coffee in the spring.

For in the winter all things do not die, but death takes many things in the spring.

Summer

Now the days are hot, the sunlight is intense. Heat quivers upward from the asphalt in crinkly lines. The tin roofs of garages glitter in the light. When the sun goes down women take their clothes from the lines and the windows in the east are blood-red. The street cars during late rush hours are jammed to the doors, box-cars for human freight, swaying packing-cases made of steel and glass.

The days are hot in Chicago, even though a breeze blows off the lake. The green grass in the parks is short and thick, and oars dip slowly as the rowboats go along.

Pop-corn venders take their stands near the parks, draw their small white wagons toward the curb, and send their little whistling sounds into the hot dark night. Pop, kernels, keep on popping. The Greek puts another scoop of kernels over the gas-flame, gazes at it vaguely, shakes the pan a bit, then begins twisting his big mustaches very slowly.

Folks, did you ever go strolling with a gal through the park? Did you ever stop with her at the curb, hand the Greek a nickel, sit on the bench under those thickly set bushes where it was dark, and have your girl shake small handfuls of pop-corn and give it to you? When the bag was empty you blew it up, then smashed it with your fist; there was a great noise. Your girl laughed. She gave you a shove and when you kissed her, you tasted the butter from the pop-corn on her lips. The night was dark, brethren, and warm.

Pop, kernels, keep on popping. Pop in the summer for dear old Chicago.

And there's outdoor public dancing in the West Side parks. Workmen have laid a cement floor and built a little platform, and a small peppy orchestra spurts hot music. Hey, hey, sister, let's go.

And around the wire enclosure stand the middle-aged men, eyeing the young gals dancing, those fifteen- and sixteen-year-old gals. The middle-aged men with their cars parked a short distance away, those men who take the kids for long rides past the city limits, those men who know their onions. Yes, folks, such is life in a big city. Lift your glass and drain it down, the sour with the sweet, the good with the not-so-good.

And a few yards away from the dance floor boys and girls get together, hold hands as they sit on benches, make a little progress in the humanities. Then they walk home along empty streets, thinking things over. Insects swarm about the arc lamps. And they reach her home.

"Farewell, farewell," he tells her mournfully.

"Good night, good night," she answers softly, then climbs the stairs, going round the back way, tells the little doggie not to bark, not even to make a squeal, then up to her room to undress, takes off her clothes, gazes at herself in the cracked mirror, feeling her breasts meanwhile, and so to bed, alone.

Yes, folks, that's the way things go in the summer, in the good old summertime.

When I was a kid band concerts were held in Union Park. That was when Flo Jacobson had a reputation as a sweet singer, that was when music publishers hired her to plug their numbers at the concerts. She wore a big white floppy hat, stood on the platform and sang the new songs. I copped a handful of navy beans from the big metal bin when my old man wasn't looking, and at the concert George Hurrell and I tossed the beans at the brass instruments. When the music was soft, you could hear those hard navy beans hit the cornets and trombones. One night a cop caught us, but that's another story, and a long sad one at that.

Oh grow, navy beans, keep on growing. Grow firm and hard for dear old Chicago.

One summer I worked nights in the Post Office, that great gray building wherein are many stories. I sweated with the others, tossed mail hour on hour, my body swaying, my arms moving, my mind going dead, my eyes reading the addresses. We were supposed to throw fifty letters a minute. Figure that out, folks. I must have tossed a few billion while I was there, and where those letters went I did not care, and if the letters had black borders, if they carried sad news, I didn't care either. I kept on tossing them into the small squares. It was some job, and it taught me plenty. It taught me how to stand on one spot until the bell rang. There were long lines of mail-cases and a thousand men on the floor, and the hard chatter of over a hundred cancelling machines went on all night. Who knows Chicago? Who knows all the big mail-order houses, those firms that dump loads and loads of mail into the Post Office? The belts rumbled on, carrying the mail away, and merchandise rattled down the chutes. Some music, folks, a symphony in the blues; the Negroes humming as they tossed the mail, the sweat rolling down their faces, the dust whirling under the lights. Can a man dance standing still? He can. He can if he's a Negro, if he's throwing mail down at the Post Office. He stands at the case, hums and sways, and pretty soon it's dancing.

Oh dance, dark boys, go on dancing. Dance on the night shift for dear old Chicago.

The windows were opened, but no wind came inside. At eleven o'clock we ate, went across the street for a big hamburger on rye, told the Greek to hurry up, folded the bread over a big slice of onion, then sank our fangs into onion, hamburger and bread. The cashier, an old guy with three teeth in his mouth, grinned at us, showing his caved-in gums. "Is the meat juicy, is the onion strong enough?"

Ha-ha, folks, I have to laugh when I remember that old boy, the ancient guy who sat behind the register grinning at us, no hair on his head. That was a long time ago, that was a thousand years ago. We left the lunch room, crossed the street again, sat on the wide stone-stairs at the Jackson Boulevard entrance, and felt the hot wind blowing up the street. We wore short aprons to protect our clothes, and Christ knows why; they flapped in the hot wind. We waved at autos going by, whistled to a few whores coming from the cheap hotel on Clark Street, and smoked a cigarette or two. There we sat on the cool stone-stairs, whites, Negroes and Filipinos, all in the same boat, our hands moist, our shirts sticking to our backs, all waiting for the bell to ring. And it rang. It rang on time too. We dribbled through the small door-way, showed our badges to the watchman, checked in again at the desk, got another tray of mail, and our arms began tossing the letters again. We worked up a swaying movement, we felt our legs go steady, and our arms seemed to flow on forever. And under the lights, those strong glaring bulbs, the dust from the mail-sacks whirled in the air.

Yes, folks, I've held down some mighty fine jobs; you've got to hand it to me.

I once worked for an electrotype foundry, stood in the office, check-ing cuts, making out statements. When work was slack I went into the shop, near the big twin dynamos where I could hear the whir of power, the deep hum of current. Back in the rear the hydraulic presses were making wax moulds for printing plates and up in front the air hammers were smoothing out the casts. The gang of workmen were good guys. I worked in the office, wore a white collar, but they treated me as an equal. Sometimes we talked about baseball. But back in the rear was a man who didn't give a hang about the game. He stood over the pots of boiling lead, pouring the hot liquid upon the copper shells. He was Pete the caster, and he had hair on his chest. All the men liked him; they called him the bloody bastard. Pete had only one eye, but that eye was so sharp that few men would sit down with him at a game of cards during lunch hour. And you couldn't blame them. He was lucky in cards and love, a tall lean man with wide shoulders, and there was hair on his chest. Every Saturday he got shaved at the lady barbers' around the corner, the shop near Polk Street.

And he always sat in Kitty's chair. She was the first barber, the big stout one, the one whose hair was dyed so red it knocked your eye out. She shaved Pete. She swung the chair back, and as the razor went over his face her big breasts nuzzled his shoulder. Every Monday morning Pete told me about it. He was a married man, had grown children, but he worked mighty hard and had to have a change once in a while. He stood half-naked over the pots and the muscles stood out on his lean powerful arms.

And in the office were three bosses, men who fought among themselves. One was a woman-hound, another was impotent, and the third was absent-minded and had five grown daughters. This third one looked over my shoulder as I stood checking the cuts, to make sure I wasn't making mistakes.

Yes, I've had a lot of jobs; you've got to hand it to me.

I was a salesman representing a southern tobacco house, doing pioneer work, as it were. I sold a brand of chewing tobacco that the public didn't buy, a brand I pushed onto the dealers. When I came around again to take fresh orders I was thrown out of the stores. The plug tobacco tasted like sour apples mixed with dried oatmeal. I tried it once just for fun; that was the time I went into a candy store run by a young widow. She dared me to chew it, and I told her the Irish never say die. We had a good laugh together.

I was once a salesman for a house selling beauty parlor supplies. Cripes, what a racket. Plenty of life, plenty hot stuff in that game, folks. I sold supplies to the little manicure girls, to the hair-dressers, the big stout women who had tasted everything there was to taste in life, who had been married three or four times and were still game, who were good sports for all that. In those days I knew all about mud-packs, astringent lotions, permanent waves and skin rejuvenator. In those days I met a hair-dresser, a handsome German girl whose father ran a farm in Iowa. She lived in a strict rooming house and had to meet me on the corner. Sometimes I think she was the finest kid I ever knew. Her name was Thelma.

That was a long time ago. . . .

Folks, I'm going strong. I'd like to tell you more, like to go on forever. But here we are in Chicago and it's summer. The heat is terrific. When a gal dances with you, her dress sticks to her back. And the small excursion boats ply between Navy Pier and Lincoln Park, twenty-five cents one way, a half a dollar up and back. Hurry, hurry, hurry, folks, the big steamer leaves in three minutes, takes you out upon the ample bosom of the lake. Kids free, madam, take 'em along. The sea air is good for their tummies, it's good for their constitutions, too.

If you stand on the Pier you hear the dinky orchestra playing as the whistle blows, you hear the banjos strummin', the darkies hummin', and once I saw a nigger gal shake her Swedish movement to get the customers aboard. Then another boat docks, more playin' and the whistle blows, the boat plows away, short and heavy toward the breakwater, and a few more Chicago souls are made happy.

Oh sail, boats, sail away. Sail out upon the lake and buck the wind. Let the dinky music hit the water sharply with a sweet smack, sail away for dear old Chicago. . . .

And what about Jake Bowers, you say, the farm boy from downstate? Well, Jake went home, got his old job back, now eats big wheatcakes and gazes at the farmer's fat wife, but his stare is rather empty. Hey, Jake, how did you like Chicago? Tell the folks about it, tell them how you stood in line, waiting for a bed while the wind whistled through your whiskers. Go on, Jake, tell the folks. Jake doesn't answer. He shoves his plate away, gets up, walks behind the barn and gulps down a pink pill. He has to take two pills a day, that's what the quack doctor back in Chicago said, the doctor who has his office in back of the dental parlors.

And the summer wind tosses the new corn playfully about, bends it slightly so that it curves golden in the sun, but in Chicago the wind is damn hot and folks walk up the streets wiping their faces.

Well, folks, I won't keep you any longer. I am sorry, very sorry that my time is up. I have much more to say, many stories to tell. Yes, folks, I am sorry. Believe me, I am sorry.

Yes, I am sorry for many things in life. I am sorry for the small folk who live thin twisted lives, who hold on to one job, who are afraid to knock about from town to town, smelling the strong sweaty odor of America. I am sorry for the broken men who stand against buildings when the wind howls down the street and the snow whirls past the arc lamps. I am sorry for clerks working in big offices, for all my buddies down at the Post Office—the whites, the Negroes and the Filipinos, who stand hour on hour tossing mail, their armpits stinking, going to the whore-houses every pay day, walking down the stairs after being with the girls, going slowly, thinking things over.

I tell you I am sorry for many things. I am sorry for all the dead jobs I have held, for lonely days in a big strange town, for long walks at night past the blazing signs of Broadway, for the dark side streets near the river. I am sorry too for the men who jam the burlesque houses in afternoons, who lean forward as the girls kick their powdered legs, those girls who are always worrying about future bookings. Yes, I am sorry. I have slept alone in a narrow bed in a small New York room many nights and have tried to think a few things out.

And now it is summer and I am sorry in the summer for many things, for those hot nights of open air dancing that had to fade, for the fall that is coming. And for all the gray dead things in life, the things that drag themselves slowly along, I am sorry.

Folks, you know what I mean. I would like to close this little piece with a grand flourish, with a blare of bugles, but I've got a locomotive in my chest, and that's a fact. . . .

When I was a kid I went camping alone through the pine woods of Michigan. There was a long trail somewhere near the lake, and now all my years seem to be going down that trail. There were short bushes on either side, like the stunted lives of small folk, and now the trail goes through my own wilderness, through strange silent trees.

I walk along. A few big needles fall at my feet, the trail turns, goes sharply to the right, climbs a hill and begins to go down again. Now the sun sets, throwing a glow over the trees, those trees that stand firm and silent, and I feel part of that glow upon my face.

A few heavy boughs creak as a wind springs up, the trail turns sharply once again, cutting deeper into the woods, beyond the glow of the setting sun, away from the western hills; and through the trees the light comes thinly while the air changes, the wind swells higher and a few birds overhead go streaking by. . . .

(—1930)

Of What We Were

❦

CHARLES E. ISRAEL

O F WHAT we are, thought Peter, of what we are and not of what
we were. Each time he looked about the grounds, saw the
neatly planted tomato patches clinging to the side of the slope, remembered the tenderness of their planting, it came back to him. Of
what we are. Of what we were in opulence and what we were in
agony blended into what we are with the opulence faded and
the agony dulled. Then, through it all, like the tiny green shoots in the
Spring forcing themselves out through the rich brown loam, the
beginning of pride and the hope born in the desperation men reach
when they feel they can go no further.

He looked at his companion. The midday sun was warm, almost
too warm. There was shade over by the grey stone Schloss. Without consciousness of their moving, they drifted toward the building, mopping
their foreheads and talking as they walked. From a wing of the
Schloss, evidently used as a dining-hall, came the sound of clattering
dishes, the low hum of many people talking, now and then a burst of
laughter. Once there was a snatch of song which died in a ragged
cheer.

The two men stopped talking when they heard the singing and lifted
their heads in the direction of the dining-hall. Then they resumed
their conversation. They spoke in melodic, guttural Hebrew.

"Listen. They're singing. Singing . . ."

He was a heavily muscled, sunburned man in his late thirties.
His face looked as though it had been hewn from rock, many-faceted,
with sculptural planes, somehow wonderfully expressive. When he
smiled or frowned, it was either muffled thunder or liquid sunshine.
Peter was ten years younger, dark, with eager brown eyes which were
never still as they darted here and there. His face was long and narrow,
having some of the quality one sees in the faces of aristocratic English-

(421)

men who have been too long inbred. In it were mingled great capacities for tenderness and cruelty, sparked together with a brief touch
of the satanic. Only in repose was his face tender or cruel. Mostly,
there was the flickering transitional satanic look, pointed up by a
widow's peak reaching far down his forehead.

"They're singing," said the older man again.

"Why shouldn't they sing? I like to hear them sing." Sometimes
Peter's voice held a spoiled-boy insolence.

The other's voice turned bitter. "Sing, sing. Sure, let them sing the
whole bloody day. Let them sing while the tomatoes rot on the vine.
Let them sing while the castle falls apart, brick by brick, and every
Jew in Germany marches off to *Eretz,* and they stay here and rot, rot,
rot. There was a *goy* named Nero . . ."

"You're poetic today, Vissotsky," Peter interrupted him, smiling.

"Peter, sometimes I could choke you with these two hands." He
displayed huge hams, making an appropriate circle of them. But there
was no rancor in his voice.

The younger man still smiled, but his face was softer. He placed
his hand gently on Vissotsky's shoulder.

"Would you really choke me, Vissotsky?"

Vissotsky took a step backward. For no apparent reason tears sprang
into his eyes.

"I would rather," he said thickly, "cut off my right arm, and you
know it. Peter, Peter, this power you have to make people love you, it
is not good for a young man to hold."

Peter clapped him lightly on the shoulder. "I won't abuse it. Don't
worry. And now, would you like to hear what happened in Munich?"

"Yes, yes." The big man was suddenly eager, and as quickly somber
again. "But what is there to hear? They turned you down, didn't
they?"

"Sure they turned me down." The lightness of his tone belied the
quick flash of anger which compressed his lips, narrowed his eyes.
"Yes, they turned me down. The bastards. And do you know what they
said?"

Vissotsky's face mirrored every nuance of Peter's. When Peter
swore, he clenched his fists. "What?" he asked.

"They said this *kibbutz* wasn't ready yet. All in good time, they
said. There are too many preferential cases and well prepared *kib-
butzim.*" He shrugged, the flickering irony returning to his lips.

"Preferential! Well-prepared!" Vissotsky exploded. His face darkened. "Five hundred Jews a month leaving this dirty land and most of them making it through, even with the blockade." He began to shout. "This is the best *kibbutz* in the whole filthy country—"

"What good does that do, Vissotsky?"

"What?" Vissotsky's mouth hung open. He stopped shouting.

"What good does that yelling do?"

"It helps me," he said, defiantly.

"It helps them to sing." Peter motioned toward the dining-room.

"Oh, they don't know about it yet. And besides, they sing like a boy whistling in the dark. What I shout about is the truth." He opened his mouth to begin shouting again and stopped when Peter lifted his hand. He went on in a lower tone. "It's true what I say, *chaver*. They'd rather take two hundred no-goods, scum, and send them off to Palestine to become public charges. Just because, out of the two hundred, fifty are leftwingers, fifty are right and one hundred are milksop herring. Just because of that they'll take them and leave this group you've built up. Just because they're good members of one party or another." He sighed and clenched his fists once more. When he went on, his voice was low. "Sometimes I wish the gas chambers—"

"Vissotsky! Stop that!" Suddenly Peter was furious, his face gone white and his eyes burning. He faced Vissotsky, breathing heavily. The other turned to meet him, rock-face impassive.

Peter relaxed, seemed to slump within himself. The color returned to his face.

"I'm sorry," he breathed. "You know what that does to me."

Vissotsky's stern expression softened. He laid a heavy hand on the other's shoulder. When he spoke again, there was no irascibility in his voice.

"I know, Peter. I know. Many of us lost our families."

The anger was back again, pulling in his mouth, deepening the lines about his eyes. "But Peter, it's not right. The Powers should know better. This *kibbutz* was nothing. It was not even a *kibbutz*. You gathered the people, out of half a dozen camps. You got this Schloss . . ."

"And you got the farm tools. And the two cows we have now."

"All right, all right." Peter was amused by the sight of a giant suddenly turned modest. "All right. If you knew the Nazis—sorry, ex-Nazis—as well as I . . ." He smiled, and his face changed magically. Then he mimicked, his cheeks puffing out as he said in German,

"'*Ja, ja, ich war bei der Partei, aber ich bin kein Nazi, nein, kein Nazi . . .*' But seriously, Peter, here you've done all this, and just because you won't make a political camp out of this farm, we stay and rot in Germany."

Peter mused. "Maybe it was wrong to make a fetish of this non-political idea. Maybe it was enough to form a *kibbutz*."

"If you're wrong, then the whole rotten system is worse than wrong. Look here, most of the group here is left of center. Not too far, but still enough to be called left. We could have easily come under the blanket of one of the labor parties. They wouldn't have cared what we did, black-marketing, murder or what have you. Just as long as we formed a balance to one of the religious groups going, the Powers would have placed us on the list, and off we'd go to Italy and *Eretz*."

He thought for a moment. "Peter, sometimes I think we're criminals. And then, sometimes I think we're saviors. When I think that because we insist on not being tied up in their lousy politics two hundred people may never see *The Land*, then I think we're criminals. And yet, when I think that the kids we're raising here will be able to make a free choice of a political belief if they do reach *Eretz*, then I'm proud. I'm proud of you for thinking of it, and proud of me for having the sense to follow it." Once again his face darkened, and he spoke angrily. "But the damned Powers should know better. Which one did you speak to this time?"

"Oh, it's not altogether their fault. They're bound by the rules of the silly little game we play. And we're breaking the rules. God, you'd think, though, that all of us would have learned something in KZ, behind the barbed wire." His forehead wrinkled up into the widow's peak of dark hair, and he laughed shortly. "I saw Rachman," he went on in answer to Vissotsky's question. "You know, the quiet soft-spoken fellow with the horn-rimmed glasses. I told him there might be trouble, that my people were getting restless."

"Which isn't true, of course."

"No, which isn't true, of course," Peter repeated.

Another song began in the dining-room and continued this time. They waited until it was over. "You know, Vissotsky, what pleases me most about this place? It's not the ten acres of crops, not the chickens, not even the nursery we've built for the kids. It's seeing these people every day, your people and my people, hounded people, Jews, beginning to stand up like human beings. Six months ago they were as cringing a bunch as you could hope to find. They had only two things in common—they wanted to work and they didn't mind taking a chance. Now, the only way you'd know them is by their eyes. They haven't lost the Look yet."

"Neither have you and I," Vissotsky commented.

"Do you think we ever will?"

"Perhaps—if we get a chance to see different things."

Vissotsky gave Peter a long glance. "You know, sometimes I wonder about you, Peter. You're the strangest combination. So young and idealistic and at the same time as heartless and insolent and tough as any Capo."

"You ought to know, Vissotsky," laughed Peter. "You and I went to the same school."

The two men turned to each other. They felt the strength of the bond between them.

People were coming out of the dining-hall. Like Peter and Vissotsky, some were dressed in cotton trousers and undershirts, but some wore shorts. All of them, men and women alike, were deeply tanned. The men were small, dwarfed by the enormous Vissotsky and even by Peter. But there was a wiry quickness about the way they walked, a restless energy in each movement. The women were different. Most of them resembled squat solid Russian peasant women, with large shoulders and bosoms, bulging calves and broad open faces that expressed sorrow in each line even when they laughed. Most of them looked healthy, well-fed. As they stepped from the building, they were talking and joking, squinting their eyes against the glare of the sun. Since they had another half-hour before going back to work, they sat on the lawn before the Schloss in little groups, gradually becoming accustomed to the bright sunlight. Peter called to one of them.

"Chayim, how long before we have a calf?"

"Two weeks," answered Chayim, a little man with a white golf cap perched jauntily on one side of his head.

"You know," shouted another, "Chayim is so worried about that cow and calf that we're beginning to wonder who the father was."

"Yes, and you know, he's been after all of us to vote in the next general meeting for his idea to build an extension to the nursery for the calf."

"Maybe we will," answered Peter.

And once more it was with him, the refrain of what we were and what we are. Never really in his own breast the bright quick melody of what we are to be nor the deep slow pleasurable nostalgia of what was once upon a time. Life was bound by the limited jerky fluctuation of a see-saw. When down again?

A DP camp is no concentration camp. A DP camp is a haven of refuge, set up and administered by representatives of the liberators, the friendly nations, who sickened when they thought of the atrocities of the Germans. A DP camp is row on row of barracks, with fifty beds in each one. And if you were lucky, you could live with your family. And you could make love to your wife, comforted by the security of numbers, because you could hear ten other men making love to their wives. When you whispered to your wife, it might be someone else's woman in the next bed who would answer you in a drowsy voice, she, too, numbed by the great wonderful security the liberators had given you.

You lined up each day for your food, also a gift of the liberators. Cereal, dried, four ounces; potatoes, dehydrated, six ounces; meat, nature undetermined, one ounce. And occasionally a gift from one of the great Jewish welfare agencies. A gift, a gift. You people should be glad you didn't die under the Nazis. Yes we should, yes we should, we are so glad, so happy, so grateful. And now, we have thanked you. Won't you please let us go? Go? Go where? What is it you want from us? You're free. We've taken you out of the shadows, brought you back to life, and now you want to go? So sorry, but we know what is best. We can't have you wandering the face of the earth, becoming a blight to every country. You must stay here. We're taking care of you. What more do you want?

What we were, what we were. Oh the wine and the music and the little cakes and the fresh voices of children playing and give us the land, give us only the land. And can't you hear the voices of our children crying for milk, can't you see the sores on their backs? Milk, milk, you want. Look, we are not a charity organization. We killed the Germans who were killing you. What is it you want? Trouble with you people, you're never satisfied. Look at that nice clean camp of Esthonians. They're *good* DPs. Why aren't you good like the Esthonians? Look at the leather bags they make, the tablecloths they embroider. Why don't you make leather bags and embroider table-cloths? Why aren't you clean? Why do you blackmarket and steal?

What? Different? Don't be ridiculous. They're DPs, aren't they? You should listen to the stories *they* have to tell. Trouble with you people is. . . .

Or the lines going in and out of the great house which sheltered the welfare organization. Here at last was succor, here at last the understanding among one's own fellows. Pity, great gushing swooping pity that rushed from one heart to another. And please wait your turn. No, there's nothing we can do for you today. Come back tomorrow. And when the great inchoate cry of hopelessness rose up in one's throat and he fell screaming to the floor of the welfare organization's hall, the pity reached its height. Quick, get him outside or Jesus I can't stand this much longer this crying it tears my heart to pieces but get him out of here before he has the whole place weeping. Next. No I'm sorry, you know we're bound by regulations. The Army watches everything we do. I've told you now, this is headquarters, we don't deal in those problems. There's a welfare officer at your camp. Go see her. Yes, I know this a welfare organization. I know we receive one hundred million a year, and we're doing the best we can to help you. What? What's that? I don't like that kind of talk, young man. I've been in welfare work for twenty-three years, and I've never had anyone talk to me like that before. What? Such impertinence. Really, you know you're not doing anybody any good with that kind of talk. I'm sorry with the raised shoulders truly sorry. You'll simply have to go. We work through your committee which you have elected, and if you can't get satisfaction from them, then I can't help you. And the next time you come in here, young man, try to keep a civil tongue in your head. The idea—how much money do I make a year. As if that mattered, when I'm over here bleeding my heart out to help you. What? Look here, young man, if you don't go this minute I'll have you thrown out of here. You know very well that if giving you my dinner would help, you could have every bit of it every day. Now please go, there are reports to write. Please go. Please please go. Klara, I can't stand it any longer. Klara, if this man doesn't go, I'm going to cry. I'm going to cry right here. Klara, please call Mr. Rubenstein and have him take this fellow down and show him where the front door is. No, no, Klara, have Mr. Rubenstein take him to the mess and give him some food. I know it's against the rules, but I can't stand it any longer. Go, go, please go. Oh dear God, I'll never get to this work on my desk. So much, so much, so much misery, so much hurt and dear God, why did you do this to me?

A DP camp is no concentration camp, and Germany is no prison. You can go anywhere you want, so long as you don't run into a border patrol of Germans who will send you back, and as long as you don't get too far away from your barracks so that you can't get back in time for your evening meal. And maybe you will join the little group of hurrying men at the Bahnhof, sly, cunning men, alert for the first sign of the uniform, brief-cases opening and closing quickly. Where, if you were lucky, you could buy from that narrow-eyed Bavarian leaning against the post a pair of shoes for one pack of American cigarettes, or a bottle of fresh milk for a pair of silver cuff-links. Or even make negotiations for a whole cow, to be paid for and received later. To keep alive, that was it. You'd done it for so many years, for so many eons, that you could go on doing it. To keep alive, to keep the sluggish heart beating inside you while the love of a note of music or a child's laugh or a woman's soft voice unhampered by a nagging worry went winging the distant unattainable way of the past, of what we were once upon a time over the gentle misty hills of the east. . . .

Vissotsky nudged Peter. His eyes followed Vissotsky's pointing finger. Coming up the steep dirt road which led from the Mitten-wald highway to Schloss Regau was an olive-drab sedan with military markings. It wound out of sight among the trees, then reappeared, leaving a cloud of dust in its progress toward the Schloss.

Peter had a deep and terrible premonition. For six months now, he had had no visits from the Occupation authorities. He prayed the car would go on up the mountain past the Schloss, but instead it turned off at the foot of the hill into the gravel driveway and came to a stop at the edge of the lawn. Peter went to meet it, accompanied by Vissotsky and about twenty of the people.

A young American major stepped out of the car. He was alone. The major was slender, about thirty years old, with dark eyes and hair, and a full lower lip which gave his face a voluptuous, almost effeminate appearance,. He walked up to the group, which immediately formed a silent, anxious ring about Peter and Vissotsky, who moved forward.

"Anybody speak English here?" he demanded.

"I do," said Peter.

"Who are you?"

"I'm Peter Dardava, the leader of this farm. And who are you?"

The major gave Peter a hard look.

"Major Stephen Adams, Executive Officer of the Altdorf Recreation Center."

"Very glad to know you, Major." He put out his hand which the major took reluctantly. "This is Mr. Vissotsky, my assistant. Unfortunately, he doesn't speak much English."

"What nationality are you, anyhow?"

"Rumanian, originally."

"I mean—you're Jewish, aren't you?"

"Certainly, Major, this is a Jewish farm." The ironic grin, approaching impudence, flickered around Peter's eyes and mouth. The major seemed uncertain how to proceed. "You don't look much like it," he ventured. Then he continued, "I want to make an inspection of this place."

"May I ask, Major, by whose authority you make this inspection?"

"By order of the Commanding General, Army Headquarters," snapped the major, becoming a little nettled.

"Will you follow me, Major?" Peter became elaborately polite. He wondered why he was going out of his way to antagonize this officer, but he sensed the contempt in the other's manner.

"Before we go through the buildings, Major, let me tell you something about the grounds. We have about ten acres here." He indicated the plateau land east of the Schloss. "We raise tomatoes, potatoes, onions, cabbage and some wheat."

"I'm not particularly interested in what you raise, Mr. —uh—"

"Dardava, Major. Very well, I'll show you the sleeping quarters."

When they came to the dining-hall in the south wing, the major could not resist running his hand along the ledge of a window-sill. It came away clean. Peter smiled and caught the major looking at him. They hurried on, Vissotsky striding along behind them like a large monkey, his bare arms dangling at his sides. Peter wondered if Vissotsky felt the same sinking feeling in the pit of his stomach that he had.

In the Lecture and Meeting Hall in the north wing, the major stopped before a large poster flanked by pictures of Herzl and Weizmann. The poster showed a picture of *chalutzim* marching with farm tools in their hands. There was Hebrew printing underneath.

"What's that say?" asked the major.

"That? Oh, that says 'A new spirit for a new land,'" answered

Peter blandly. Vissotsky hid a grin and started to sputter. What the sign really said was, "Palestine, with or without British consent." Peter flashed an angry warning to Vissotsky and they went on.

The major seemed impressed by the number of rooms, each one containing from three to five comfortable beds. Peter's spirits sank lower.

Nevertheless, he showed the officer the chickens, the nursery with its eight children and finally, the barn and the two cows.

"Where did you get the bull for that one?" asked the major, curiously, indicating the cow that was ready to calf.

"Don't worry, Major." The irony flickered and grew, broke out in a chuckle. "The father was from good Aryan stock."

"Now look here, young man—" began the major. Then he caught Peter's eye, blushed and laughed shortly. He started laughing harder. Vissotsky, tagging along, began laughing too, without knowing why. Presently the major remembered and stopped laughing.

"I must go," he said.

The people were gathered in a knot about the major's car. When they saw him coming, they dispersed hastily and formed a semicircle about twenty feet from the car, waiting.

Major Adams turned to Peter.

"You rent this place, don't you?"

Peter nodded, sick with apprehension.

"I'm sorry, but I have bad news for you. The Army is requisitioning this Schloss and grounds—for a Winter Warfare School."

There was a long pause. The people stirred restlessly, not understanding. Finally Peter said, "I rather expected that." He sighed. "How long can you give us?"

"Three weeks at the very outside."

"We'll try to be out by then."

"It's not a question of trying, my friend. You *will* be out." He held out his hand and said again, "I'm sorry. Goodbye."

Peter watched until the car was out of sight before he dared turn around to the people. When he did, he saw that almost two hundred of them, smelling trouble as they were able to after the past nine years, had gathered on the lawn. They stood watching him. The semicircle had grown and they were standing three and four deep, watching.

He stood before them, the awful sickness clutching, clawing at his innards. He looked at them and knew his strength depended on keeping that semicircle intact. If it once broke. . . .

He raised his voice and told them in Hebrew that they were going to lose the farm and the Schloss.

They said nothing, but he could see the Look deepening in their eyes. He could sense them shrinking, the edges of fear beginning to fold in on them once more.

"*Sheket!* Quiet!" he cried, though no one had spoken: "*Sheket!*" he cried once more, sensing the beginning of the break in the semicircle, trying desperately to maintain the vital power he had given them.

"What shall we do?" asked a woman quietly.

"We must get help," answered a man. His reply unleashed the tongues of the crowd. Cries of "Help, help, yes, we must get help" mingled with the despairing minor note, "But where? Who will help us now?"

"*Sheket!*" called a voice. It was Chayim, the keeper of the cows, his little white golf cap perched on one side of his head. "We must go to the Central Committee of Liberated Jews in Munich. I have heard that they have been recognized by the American Army. We must send a delegation and they will help us."

Another voice spoke out in the deep sorrowful tones of the professional orator.

"For shame!" the voice cried. "For shame! You would have us go to the Central Committee for help? For shame, indeed. After what we know about the Committee and its activities. After the long months we have fought to stay clear of them? You know that it is neither 'central' nor a truly representative committee. Have you forgotten how one of the members of the Presidium came here and offered us extra clothing if we would send him and his family fresh vegetables this summer? Committee! Help! Cheap politicians! For shame!"

"How about the ——?" asked a woman, timidly, mentioning the name of a large welfare agency.

"Do-gooders. What can they do for us?"

"They are American."

"Yes, so they will talk and threaten and say how awful it is, and we shall still lose our farm."

Peter felt again that the ring was wavering, close to breaking. The feeling was so intense that he could see in the walls of the Schloss a gray wailing wall. He shivered.

"Listen," he said quietly. They stopped talking and were quiet, so still that it seemed they had ceased breathing. "Let me tell you a story. This is a story of our Jewish people.

"There were once three Jews walking in the streets of Warsaw. One of them saw a flame from an open baker's oven. 'Look,' he said, 'there's a flame there.' The second did not even bother to look. 'The whole city's afire!' he cried. The third covered his face and shrieked, 'Oy, I'm burned to death!'"

He felt the tension relax slightly, knew that he had them with him. Strength was returning to the ring. There were even one or two furtive smiles.

"Nobody is burned to death. The city is not even afire. What you have seen this afternoon is only the flame from the baker's oven. Remember—" His glance went from one end of the semicircle to the other. "Remember. I did not bring you here to the Schloss Regau before I had the Schloss. I have not betrayed you before. I will not betray you now. . . . So let's not sit *shiva* and begin to mourn today. The potatoes need weeding and the tomatoes need spraying. Sophie, you've left the children alone. Shame on you. Chayim, the cows are forming a Central Committee of Liberated Cows of Schloss Regau. Hurry, hurry, before they steal your barn."

Scolding them, cajoling them like children, he sent them about their tasks until only he and Vissotsky were left.

"You were wonderful," said Vissotsky when they had all gone. There were tears in his big eyes, running down his broad honest face. Then he asked, "Have you any ideas?"

Peter shook his head sadly.

"I thought not."

They turned from each other. Each one took a long look about the farm, as one looks at the dead face of a loved one for the last time.

This is the first time I haven't skated beside her in this show for two months, thought Major Stephen Adams, and it hurts more than I guessed it would. He felt a bit sullen about the Colonel's having given him the Winter Warfare job and asking him to drop the Ice Show altogether for the time being. But then it also got him out of some administrative chores, which was something.

He watched Maria go through her number with the trembling inside he always got when he looked at her. Her new partner wasn't bad. A little stiff on the corners, he observed critically, but not bad. The Hungarian orchestra changed tempo, and they went into the waltz that led to the climax of the number. Stephen's feet would not be still. He felt the ice beneath his gliding skates, his arm about Maria, felt the throb of the increasing beat of the orchestra and the breathless whirl of the finish, was with her as she bowed low to the applause, smiling.

That was not *his* smile; that was what he called her "professional" smile, where her lips moved, but her lovely green eyes were still sad, unsmiling. *His* smile came in rare, blinding moments, when she turned her face up to his, swept the hair from her forehead with a quick gesture, and he could watch the radiance emerge from the slow curve of parted lips, the flash of green eyes in mounting joy. He would feel the little tongues of flame envelop him, caress him, as his own lips moved in answer to hers. He sighed. So it had been for the past two months, the minutes and hours of the measured timeglass, with the sands moving quickly, too quickly, ruthlessly down. . . .

The Arena was only half-filled with GIs and officers tonight, since it was the middle of the week. The Arena, with its glass roof that slid back to let in the stars, its three tiers around the ice rink with little tables on each tier, its long bar and the incongruous Spanish balcony where the Hungarian orchestra played. Ricky Perkins had told him proudly that it cost the U. S. Army three-quarters of a million dollars to build the Arena, and Ricky Perkins was never wrong about things like that.

He had told her this morning, before he went out to the Schloss Regau, that he wouldn't be managing the show any more. He had watched her rehearse for about ten minutes without her knowing he was watching, had marked for the thousandth time her litheness, the grace of her slender long arms and legs, the way even while she was skating she brushed the auburn hair from her forehead with that abrupt gesture. Then he skated onto the ice, took her arm and led her through the movements of their dance that had become like breathing to them. She had looked over at him, accepting the light pressure of his hand, suspecting nothing.

"Darling, I won't be in the Ice Show any more."

He felt her catch her breath. She stopped short, her skates sending up a shower of ice.

"Stephen! They're not—not transferring you, are they?"

"No, darling," he laughed. "I'll be right here in Altdorf. Just a change of assignment, that's all. I'll tell you all about it tonight. Come on, let's skate."

He should not have told her about not being in the Ice Show in just the way that he did. But he felt that he had to, that he needed her sudden shock, the drain of color from her face. He had to know that there was some vulnerability about her, that she, too, felt unsure of him, of their future together. . . .

Ricky Perkins sat down at his table, short, pudgy, dynamic as becomes a public relations man, his baby-blue eyes bulging.

"Steve, you're not skating tonight. Nothing wrong?" Ricky was always solicitous about everybody, down to the last German waitress at the Arena. Everybody liked Ricky.

"No, nothing wrong. I won't be skating for a while. Got a new job."

"Yeah, I heard about the Winter Warfare School." He became enthusiastic. "Lord, that'll be wonderful for Altdorf. Just think of it— American ski-troops in white, braving the steep Bavarian Alps in the shadow of the Zugspitz, sponsored by the trained personnel of the Altdorf Recreation Center. Think of it!"

Stephen observed drily, "Ricky, you sound like one of your own pamphlets."

"What? Oh yeah, I guess I do," he apologized, then blossomed immediately into rhapsodies again. "Hand-picked soldiers, clambering from rock to rock—hear you're going to have it out at that Schloss between here and Mittenwald. That right, Steve?"

"Um," said Stephen. "Of course, I still can't see how the Old Man in Heidelberg thinks anybody can learn winter warfare in two-week shifts. But—*c'est la guèrre*—or *c'est la* peace, I don't know which."

He turned to Ricky. "Hey Rick, I heard your new song down at the Alpenhof. Boy, it's great. What's the name of it—'Never Had It So Good,' isn't it? Got a catchy tune."

"Yeah, that's it. Thanks, Steve. Thanks. Glad you like it." Ricky was visibly moved by the praise. His baby-blue eyes bulged and he swallowed hard. "Well, I gotta be running. Got a two-star general coming in town tomorrow and a photographer from *Stars and Stripes*. Gotta make sure everything's all set. G'bye Steve."

Ricky Perkins. Stephen gazed after him. Lt. R. Richard Perkins, who had come into Altdorf with combat troops and had stayed on to become a War Department civilian employee. Ricky Perkins, whose family were mayors and governors and God knows what. Ricky Perkins, the portrait of a Rutgers man, now himself the virtual mayor of Altdorf. When would he go home? When will any of us go home?

Col. Watson's voice telling him of his new assignment. The Old Man had a real whiskey voice, like the bottom of a still. And why not? Col. Watson saying, well, boy, got a new job for you. And the thump of his heart skipping a beat when he thought he might have to leave Altdorf and Maria. Then settling down again when he learned he would stay on. The Old Man's voice telling him about winter warfare and the importance of tightening up the Occupation, just as if he were quoting from a directive. Then the order to begin work immediately and the place where he was to begin work. You'll have to kick some Jews out of the place, the Old Man said, his blue eyes boring straight into Stephen. I don't care how or when you do it, but you'll have to kick those Jews out of there. In fact, boy, I don't care how and when you do the whole shootin' match. It's in your hands.

The mention of the word Jews being the first time he had consciously thought about them since that April morning over a year ago when his unit had plunged into Dachau, the pest-hole of a place where the cremation furnace was still smoking. And he had knelt beside an old Jew with a beaked nose and had given him water from his canteen, pressed a bar of chocolate into his hand. Here, Pop, take this, it'll do you good. The old Jew muttering and jibbering, his eyes burning right past Stephen into space as he clutched mechanically at the chocolate. And then, the funny experience about six months ago outside the Excelsior Hotel in Munich, when he was just being transferred from Bayreuth to Altdorf. When he was *sure* he saw the same old Jew to whom he had given chocolate in Dachau, not so old now, and better dressed in a well-fitting grey suit, but with the same beaked nose, the same look in his eyes, tipping his hat to Stephen with an elaborate gesture.

It was amazing. That's what they probably meant when they said, give 'em a hand and they'll take the whole arm. Give 'em a drink of water, a bar of chocolate, a little firmer hold on the thread of life, and in six months they'd own Munich. At home, give one of 'em a membership in the Bangor Country Club, and in two weeks he'd have all his friends with him, loud, ostentatious. Abie, bring mine diamond-plated golf clubs ven you come, mine boy. But there were nice ones, too, ones you couldn't help liking, like that kid at the Schloss this afternoon, with all his insolence. Funny, all those sunburned people he saw standing around at Schloss Regau were Jews, and last April they must have been lying on the ground in Dachau or some other pest-hole. . . .

(—1949)

Terrorist

❧⚬✿⚬☙

ABRAHAM ROTHBERG

O RDERS *were to shoot to kill if any British soldier crossed the brook*
which cut through the green land separating the outskirts of the
city from the palm grove where Sholom Charney lay hidden with his
rifle. The sun was blistering even the blanched sands; but Sholom,
hidden in the shaded darkness of the palms, felt strangely cool.

The British soldier looked hot. As he walked he kept putting the
butt of his rifle down on the ground, holding it between his knees while
he took out a handkerchief to mop the sweat from under his beret.
Sholom adjusted the telescopic sight so that he could see the soldier's
face clearly. It loomed up, suddenly, in the cross-hairs, almost frighten-
ing Sholom. The Britisher had a young face, prematurely aged. The
lines around his mouth and eyes were stark, as though drawn in by
some actor for make-up or by some artist in an etching.

Why he had to die if he crossed the brook, Sholom Charney didn't
know; to tell the truth he didn't care. The man shouldered his rifle and
brought it up to right shoulder arms. Sholom kept him in the sights,
leading him. He began to walk alongside the brook, on the bank op-
posite, up and down, down and up. . . .

Up and down, down and up. The heavy clank of the Nazi boots was
something he could hear in his sleep. Their sound was like no other
boots Sholom had ever heard and he knew that they were looking for
him. Nazis were always looking for him. Living in Poland had been bad
enough; Poles were anti-Semites who could match the Nazis in all the
arts of cruelty except efficiency. Poles were never as clever or systematic; the pogrom was a more random weapon than the crematorium.

The guard's heels crunched on the gravel and ground it underfoot,
and each crunching and grinding was a crunching and grinding of
Sholom's heart. Carefully he counted the steps . . . six to the right,

about face, six to the left. Sholom knew that the Russian lines were nearby—seventeen miles, some of the others had said. If he could get away tonight, before they were moved, he might make it to their lines. There at least he could get a gun and die like a man, not like an animal led to the slaughter, to be exterminated in a gas chamber.

Sholom Charney watched the others in the long clap-board shack. None of them thought of any escaping. Reconciled to death, they lived in the old tradition of the head bent beneath all the clubbings of a Gentile fate. Sholom watched them gather the quorum of ten men, then more, to begin the evening prayer. They gathered in the opposite end of the barrack, the end facing the East and Jerusalem, the Land of Israel, where evening could already be seen dark-visaged against the oilskin windows. Sholom heard them begin *maariv*, the evening prayer. One of them chosen as cantor stood before them and began to chant, low and hoarse, *"Borchu es Adonoi hamvorach"* . . . "Bless ye the Lord who is to be blessed. . . ." And the forty-odd men clustered around the cantor answered, "Blessed art Thou, O Lord our God, King of the Universe, who at Thy word bringest on the evening twilight. . . ."

Sholom stopped listening to their cantillation, listened instead for the crushing, imperious footfalls passing the door. Now the guards were at supper except for a few, such as this one, who formed a skeleton watch. They didn't leave many guards for mere Jews; Jews would not even fight, much less try to escape.

Raising himself from his haunches to peer out of the oilskin window, Sholom could see the soldier: a small muscular man in the German field-green uniform with a submachine gun over his shoulder. Sholom could see the sling bite into his shoulder, the narrow leather band gathering up the material around his shoulder. It would have to be quick. Sholom knew if he missed the first thrust he was a dead one. He watched the German make two more turns, carefully noting where the man turned and in which direction he looked when he made his about-face. Invariably he looked away from the barrack over toward the mess hall of the camp, probably wishing he was at supper with the rest.

Behind him Sholom heard the congregation intone, "With everlasting love Thou has loved the House of Israel, Thy people; a law and commandments, statutes and judgments hast Thou taught us. . . ."

Yes, Sholom thought, they'd all been taught statutes and judgments, laws and commandments. That was what made them this way, readier than sheep for the slaughter. "Thou shalt not kill," it was written, and they did not kill. Even he had not killed. But now he had to kill, and in his heart he knew that the killing was right. Sholom knew he had to kill to live, to resist them by killing. And still he knew that the killing was wrong even if he did kill this one, and yet another, and still another: *the killing was wrong.*

The guard turned and Sholom was out of the spring-latched doorway with the knife out of his shirt. Back to Sholom, the guard seemed to tense, as though he heard a sound behind him, and quickly his arms went up to rip the machine gun from his shoulder. But Sholom was upon him and with a single stroke cut his throat; and the man's cry died a-gurgling in his throat.

Sholom Charney dragged the German guard back into the long barrack just as the congregation was saying, "*Shema Yisroel Adonoi Elohenu, Adonoi Echod*" . . . "Hear O Israel: the Lord our God, the Lord is One. . . ."

Sholom's call cut through the ceremony. "Jews," he cried intensely, "the German is dead. If you would go, go now."

He ripped the machine gun from the Nazi's shoulder. The sling of it stuck to his hand, sticky with the guard's blood. Sholom wiped the blood from his hand onto his trousers. He looked up and saw them all staring at him, watching fascinated as he wiped the blood on his trousers, watching horrified as he wiped the blood-smeared blade he was still holding in his hand. They stood stock still, paralyzed. It was then he got angry. "Sheep!" Sholom's Yiddish was a cry in the empty barrack. "Geese! Stupids! The Russians are nearby and the guard is dead. Why do you stand here like horrified children looking at the slaughterer killing chickens? Go! Go now!"

He turned away from them and swung the leather sling over his shoulder, feeling the heavy bit of the gun's weight on his clavicle. Crouching, Sholom slunk out of the doorway and looked quickly around him. There was no one stirring. "One at a time," he called over his shoulder to a head that came out of the doorway behind him. "Tell the others one at a time," he repeated, "but quickly."

It took Sholom Charney eight days to reach the Russian lines; eight days to make seventeen miles; but seventeen miles in eight days was good in that winter. He didn't eat very much in those days, and the hunger and freezing cold of eastern Poland almost killed him, but somehow he made the Russian lines.

Creeping craftily through the forests, on tense watch for German patrols, the machine gun hung heavy on him, dragging from his shoulder but glued to it by a mortar of ice and blood and sweat. Tremors shivered through him and his stomach rolled within him. He felt the cold ice beneath his ungloved fingers as he put them stiffly against the ice-crusted earth for steadiness and balance. Again his stomach reared in him, like an unbroken stallion's rearing. Sholom broke a small bit of icicle from a shrub twig and put it in his mouth. Perhaps the water would settle him. The icicle melted quickly in his mouth, freezingly, and all his sinew seemed turned to ice strands. Collapsing on his stomach, he lay face down on the ice, his beard making small noises against the smooth sheet-like surface as he tried to get up. He tried but could not. He retched painfully, but there was nothing in him to retch, and only a small dribble of saliva trickled down his beard, turning to ice as it flowed jaggedly away from the corner of his mouth.

Again he heard the crunch of boots, but these were no Nazi boots. By then he could tell that; he could tell a Nazi boots' sound miles off, or so it seemed to him. But he didn't know whose boots these were. Slowly, laboriously, he lifted the machine gun from his shoulder and adjusted it for firing. He couldn't sight: the peepsight was frozen and all he could see was a vague, swirling, blue-white blur. Staring over the blue frosted barrel, he lay inert; and when the Russian loomed out of the blue-white swirl Sholom Charney fainted.

The Russians picked him up, fed him and brought back his strength. The first thing Sholom could remember asking for was a rifle, but the bulky bespectacled Russian field surgeon only laughed. "Wait," he said, "now you can't hold even yourself up, let alone a rifle. You'll get your chance. There's much war left to be fought and many more Nazis to be killed."

The second thing Sholom asked for was information about the Jews who had escaped with him. What happened to them only God knew. The Russians knew nothing of them. Only much later Sholom found out from some Russian guerillas that of the forty-odd prisoners with him twelve had been killed. *Only* twelve had been killed, they said, *only* twelve. And when he fought with those guerillas, each time it was a torment in his being and a paralysis in his trigger-finger when came the time to kill. Not so with the Russian guerillas he was with; they killed with a gusto and concentration born of hatred and conviction. And Sholom fought inside himself the battle of whether killing could ever bring about the end of killing.

Only twelve, the guerillas said, *only* twelve were killed. For them it *was only* twelve. . . .

The British soldier had moved, and Sholom changed the sights so that again the man's face mushroomed into his vision, rocky and lined and weary. Sholom wondered why the man was there, if he could help his being there. The thought of pulling the trigger and killing him quickly came to Sholom, but he put it aside. He didn't have to kill the Englishman until he crossed to the other bank; but if he did cross, Sholom would have to kill him because there was ammunition buried beneath the palms where Sholom lay hidden. Through the telescopic sight he could see the British soldier prod the earth with his bayonet. A section of bank fell off into the running brook and sped away in the waters, leaving behind it a raw earth scar in the green, with severed roots of grass showing. Now Sholom knew for certain that the man was searching for something—perhaps for the ammunition.

Adjusting the range finder to twelve, Sholom noticed the number gleaming in the metal of the gun, etched in as though with acid, stark as the lines in the British soldier's face. Twelve. Twelve hundred yards: *an easy mark with this rifle.* Twelve hundred yards: *only twelve. . . .* Only *twelve, they said,* only *twelve had been killed. . . .*

"Only twelve were killed, Tzipka," Beryl Charney said to his wife.

"What do you mean *only*, Beryl?" his wife said.

"It could be more, Tzipka, no?"

"Only twelve *what* was killed, papa Beryl?" little Sholom asked, tearful already.

"Ssha, it's nothing, little son. No one was killed—and no one will bother my little Sholom," his father said soothingly. "After all, does not Sholom mean peace?"

"From where are they coming?" Tzipka Charney asked.

"I think they are coming from Danilov. Probably they are going up to Ryzpeckcha."

"Only to the all-Iddish villages they go. Why must they bother only Jews? What do they want from us—our blood?"

"Aii, Tzipkele, don't be a child. They are foolish men who do not even know what they are doing."

"Even when they kill?"

"Yes—even when they kill," he said and his voice was very tired. "They are poor and ignorant; they think we Jews are wealthy so they come to rob us so they may live a little better. They are poor—and they are very foolish."

"Perhaps—" Tzipka said hesitatingly, and then hurtling on, "but we too are foolish, more foolish even than they are. We *do* not fight back. Always we submit to them; each time they take away the few pennies we have scraped together with our ten fingers."

"What good would the fighting with them be, little wife? They are more than we are—and stronger. They have weapons and we do not. They would only kill us out if we fought with them. It would do no one good, neither them nor us. Is it not better to let them have what they want? More money we can always make but life—ah, life is another thing. Life cannot be bought back when it is departed."

"That is no life," Tzipka said and, irritated with her husband, she burst out of the large one-room wooden shack into the late afternoon sunshine. Beryl Charney went out after her, and following them both came their three children. Yussel, the oldest boy, stood next to his father. He was only a little way from young manhood. Thin and gawky, he stood looking apprehensively in the same direction that his people were squinting. Abstractedly he tweaked the first fine brown hairs of manhood sprouting from his chin. Susha, his sister, stood holding on to one side of her mother's skirt. Little Sholom hung tightly to the other side.

Their house was situated on a hill and in the distance they could see the large Gentile town of Prbovna, and close by it, almost nestling under its wing, the smaller settlement of Danilov, where the Jewish families lived. A dense column of smoke rose up from Danilov, black and thickly threatening. It had hung there since noon, clenched like a blackened fist above the town.

"Seven versts," muttered Beryl Charney. "Seven versts. By now they should be here already—if they are coming this way and going to Ryzpeckcha."

"And you stand here like an ox!" his wife exclaimed. "They will

come and take everything we have—and you stand there and say—
seven versts—uh—into your beard," Tzipka said ferociously. "Even the
Sabbath candlesticks. . . ." She looked dejected and rebellious by
turns.

"Ssha! You will frighten the children. What else can they take?
Money we don't have."

"Yussel," the mother directed sharply, suddenly thrown into efficient
action. "Come with me in the house. I will give you the silver to bury
down by Papa's brick kiln. Stay there and hide in the woods and
watch the silver!"

She went into the house with Yussel. In a moment they came out
again, Yussel loaded down with a tablecloth filled with the family
valuables. Yussel set off down the hill towards his father's brick kiln,
the white tablecloth flopping grotesquely as it hung over his slender
shoulders.

The brick kiln was in a small clearing in the woods that skirted the
base of the hill on which the house was set. Probably the Poles would
miss it. The forest around it was dense and only a footpath led to it.

Tzipka shouted to her son just before he was lost to sight in the
woods. "Don't forget, Yussel, don't come back."

"Tzipka, you shouldn't have—"

"Shouldn't have!" his wife snorted. "Why should you work for those
hoodlums? Why should you burn your hands in baking the bricks,
tear your flesh in mixing the sand and lime, for those—those—." She
could find no word of scorn sufficient for them and she spat noisily on
the ground. "Pfooo."

"You shouldn't have," her husband said gently, "because they will
be angry if they do not find any money—or any silver."

"Angry? So they'll be angry. A hundred bricks is seven zlotas. You
know how long it takes for you to make seven zlotas, Beryl. *You* should
work for *them*. Why?"

Sholom began to cry then. "Mamma. Mamma. They're coming—
over there, Mamma." With a small bunched fist, small index finger
projecting, Sholom pointed.

A crowd of men had come out of the forest, silently and menacingly.
They surrounded the house quickly, big morose-faced men armed
with knives, clubs and a sprinkling of hunting rifles. Their leader came
up to the little group of four Charneys standing before their shack.

He was a huge man, towering over the slender shortish Beryl, and wider even than the stout Tzipka. Sholom turned his face into his mother's skirt and began to cry loudly. Tzipka patted his head gently and held Susha in the small protecting semicircle of her other arm.

"Can we help you, brothers?" Beryl asked in trembling Polish.

"Zlotas. Silver. Gold, if you have," the huge man said, pushing a filthy shako back off his even filthier forehead. His eyes were red with drink, a spiderweb of blood-ridden capillaries showing in them.

Sholom looked up at him, and seeing his eyes like blood-filled sockets, hid himself again in his mother's skirt, wailing.

"We have nothing, brothers. We are very poor, just as you are. We have but two chickens—they are behind the house—but no cow. And," Beryl managed a wan smile, "we do not have any pigs because we Jews are not allowed to eat their flesh."

"Zlotas," the man insisted in his scraping bass voice.

"But I told you, brother, we have no money."

Seizing Beryl by the long traditional earlocks he wore, the leader pulled sharply. Beryl shrieked.

"Zlotas," he insisted and tore at the sideburns again.

Susha began to cry and, reinforced, Sholom even louder.

"Shut those dirty little *rsjd svena* up," the leader cried, turning on Tzipka, "before I cut them into littlest pieces." He brandished a rusted knife and pushed his glowering face almost into hers. Tzipka shrank away, holding both children tightly to her.

The leader turned and spoke to two of the men behind him, and they came up and took Beryl by the arms. Beryl made no resistance. First the men held him at the elbows and hurried him down the gentle slope toward the beginning of the woods. Then they threw him down on the ground and kicked him until he rolled like a barrel. They lifted him under the armpits and dragged him to his feet. Then they began it over again. When they got to the first fringe of trees, the two Poles tied Beryl to a slender-trunked tree. Beryl's thin body was not much wider than the trunk.

The leader called to a few of his men with rifles and four of them came towards him, working the bolts of their rifles noisily, sliding the bolts home and then withdrawing them.

"Zlotas?" the leader looked at Tzipka, recognizing mutely that the challenge was in the woman.

He spoke again to the four men when she shook her head. Only when Tzipka saw them put cartridges into their rifles did she finally scream.

"Don't shoot him," she cried. "Have mercy; we are only poor people. Who will look after my children?" Slowed by the two children who clung leech-like to her skirt, she ran down the hill and threw herself, arms outstretched, before her husband. "If you shoot him, shoot me—and the children too," she gasped.

The leader spoke a few quiet words to the four men and they raised the rifles to their shoulders and slid the cartridges into the chambers. Tzipka lowered her head. Susha was crying and Sholom could hear his father begin to pray, intensely and yet resignedly. Then the rifles cracked and Sholom began to cry again. It was not that they had been hit, for the Poles had fired over their heads, but the noise of the rifle fire had frightened him.

Just then one of the Poles came to the leader with the two Charney chickens. He had tied their legs together with a piece of string and they both hung over his arm, one on either side. Speaking with a lisp, he told the leader that the *rsjd svena* were telling the truth and there *was* nothing in or around the house beside the two chickens. The leader listened, nodding his head weightily. Then, deliberately, he took a small snuff box from his coat and put a pinch in each of his huge hair-filled nostrils. He threw back his head and rolled tentatively on his heels, and when he sneezed it was a roar of sound and a deluge of moisture. Holding one nostril with a black-nailed forefinger, he blew first that nostril, and then the other. Then again throwing his head back and cocking it into the silence that rushed around them after his uproar of sneezing and blowing, he stood listening.

Suddenly he pointed to the woods, a little way to the left. "There. There. Shoot fools, shoot!"

The men fired a straggling volley. The leader sent two of them to see what they had fired at, what it was he had heard, all the time grumbling it was probably a rabbit and four bullets wasted.

When they brought Yussel back, bleeding from the mouth and chest, Tzipka fainted and Sholom could hear his father sob, "*Ovenu Malkenu*—Our Father, our King! We have sinned before thee . . . Our Father, our King! Nullify the designs of those who hate us. . . ."

Sholom let go of his mother's skirt when she fell fainting. Now, between sobs and tears, he went to his brother and cried out, "Yussele, Yussele. Little brother." While the Poles stood around him and watched, Sholom wiped the blood from Yussel's mouth with his sleeve, and when the leader tried to touch the dying boy Sholom bit his hand. The leader picked him up, and Sholom kicked and scratched and finally spat in the leader's face. The huge Pole threw Sholom sprawling on the ground next to his brother. Then turning to his cohorts, he said, "Bah! That little *rsjd svena* fights like a Gentile. Come, these are the only poor Jews we'll find. There will be richer ones in Ryzpeckcha."

They were almost all gone in a few moments, and as the last two entered the woods on the other side of the house Sholom heard one say to the other, "Say, Jan, how far *is* it to Ryzpeckcha?"

"Only about twelve versts," the other answered, "twelve or maybe thirteen. . ."

"Twelve or thirteen," Sholom thought, feeling almost as hot as if he, and not the English soldier, were out in the sun. He flicked the range finder up from twelve hundred yards to thirteen hundred, following the man carefully in his sights. Perhaps he wouldn't cross the brook after all and there would be no need to kill him. Even now, after all that had gone before, Sholom didn't like the killing. But now, hating it still, if he had to he knew he had to, and that was all there was to it. The Tommy could still go back!

The British soldier doubled back abruptly, still poking the earth with his prying bayonet. Then he looked up, and shading his eyes with his stiffened palm, peered at the mass of trees where Sholom lay hidden. Unmoving and staring the soldier stood looking at the palms for what seemed to Sholom a very long time. And then, with a shrug of his shoulders, the British soldier put one foot into the brook. Sholom could see him clearly in the sights, the cross-hairs meeting just below the white button on his left breast pocket. Best to wait until he got to the middle of the stream. The soldier waded downstream first, along the far shore; then he came back and he was at the middle of the brook; and Sholom waited for him to reach the shore, hoping he would turn back before he climbed the bank.

But the Tommy did not turn back; instead, he pulled his legs heavily out of the water and stepped up onto the bank. This was the time and Sholom knew he ought to press the trigger, fire and finish it quickly. Still, there was time, not much time, but yet a little. He might turn back, re-cross to the other bank; he might decide there was nothing for him on this side of the stream.

The soldier was prodding the earth again with his bayonet, sharp, inquisitive stabbings. If he found nothing, saw nothing, he had to turn back. There was little time left. The soldier put his rifle down on the ground, took a small white handkerchief out of his pocket and wiped his face. He turned his back and dipped the handkerchief into the stream, rubbing it across his face, the back of his sunbrowned neck, and Sholom could see the fragile connections of his vertebrae outlined in splotches of sweat on his khaki shirt. Carefully the soldier wrung the handkerchief out, wiped his palms against the sides of his trousers as he stood erect, and then stooped again for his rifle.

Instead of the rifle, he came up with something small in his hands, holding it up to the sun to examine it. Sholom squinted through the telescopic sights to see what it was. The sun glinted sharply, brassily, on the metal thing in the soldier's hand and Sholom knew. It was a cartridge. Someone had dropped it, or perhaps it had fallen out of one of the boxes that had been carried to the oasis to be buried under the palms.

If only he would turn now—go back!

No. It was too late for turning back. The Tommy had already picked up his rifle, holding it cocked and ready, at port arms, and slowly he began to walk up to where Sholom lay hidden beneath the palms. His finger cold on the trigger, Sholom felt a sudden trickle of sweat roll down into the tense hollow of the small of his back. He watched the soldier, leading him in the sights, correcting range, adjusting. Then he knew he could wait no longer. As the soldier took another step forward, reaching the rise that led to the palm grove, Sholom Charney pulled the trigger.

(—1948)

The Son

∾

ISAAC BASHEVIS SINGER

THE SHIP from Israel was due to arrive at twelve o'clock, but it was late. It was evening before it docked in New York, and then I had to wait quite a while before any passengers were let off. Outside it was hot and rainy. A mob of people had come to wait for the ship's arrival. It seemed to me that all the Jews were there: assimilated ones, and rabbis with long beards and sidelocks; girls with numbers on their arms from Hitler's camps; officers of Zionistic organizations with bulging portfolios, *yeshivah* boys in velvet hats, with wildly growing beards; and worldly ladies with rouged faces and red toenails. I realized I was present at a new epoch in Jewish history. When did the Jews have ships?—and if so, their ships went to Tyre and Sidon, and not to New York. Even if Nietzsche's crazy theory about the eternal return were true, quadrillions and quintillions of epochs would have to pass before the smallest part of anything happening in the present would have happened before. But this waiting was boring and tedious. I measured everybody with my eyes, and each time I asked myself the same question: What makes him my brother? What makes her my sister? The New York women fanned themselves, spoke all at once with hoarse voices, refreshed themselves with chocolate and Coca-Cola. A non-Jewish toughness stared out of their eyes. It was hard to believe that only a few years ago their brothers and sisters in Europe went like sheep to the slaughter. Modern Orthodox young men with tiny skull-caps hidden like plasters in their dense hair spoke loudly in English and cracked jokes with the girls, whose behavior and clothes showed no sign of religion. Even the rabbis here were different, not like my father and grandfather. To me, all these people appeared worldly and clever. Almost all, except myself, had secured permits to board the boat. And they got acquainted unusually fast, shared information, shook their heads knowingly. The ship's officers began to descend, but they seemed stiff in their uniforms, which had epaulettes and gilded buttons. They spoke Hebrew, but they had accents like Gentiles.

I stood and waited for a son whom I hadn't seen in twenty years. He was five years old when I parted with his mother. I went to America, she to Soviet Russia. But apparently one revolution was not enough for her. She wanted "the permanent revolution." And they would have liquidated her in Moscow if she hadn't had someone who could reach the ear of a high official. Her old Bolshevik aunts who had sat in Polish prisons for Communist activity had interceded for her, and she was deported together with the child to Turkey. From there, she had managed to reach Palestine, where she had brought up our son in a *kibbutz*. Now he had come to visit me.

He had sent me one photograph taken when he had served in the army and fought the Arabs. But the picture was blurred, and in addition he was wearing a uniform. Only now, as the first passengers began to come down, did it occur to me that I did not have a clear image of what my son looked like. Was he tall? Was he short? Had his blond hair turned dark with the years? This son's arrival in America pushed me back to an epoch which I had thought of as already belonging to eternity. He was emerging out of the past like a dream or a phantom. He did not belong in my present home, nor would he fit into any of my relationships outside. I had no room for him, no bed, no money, no time. Like that ship flying the white and blue flag with the Star of David, he constituted a strange combination of the past and the present. He had written me that of all the languages he had spoken in his childhood, Yiddish, Polish, Russian, Turkish, he now spoke only Hebrew. So I knew in advance that with what little Hebrew I possessed from the Pentateuch and the Talmud, I would not be able to converse with him. Instead of talking to my son, I would stammer and have to look up words in dictionaries.

The pushing and noise increased. The dock was in tumult. Everyone screamed and shoved themselves forward with the exaggerated joy of people who have lost the standard to measure achievement in this world. Women cried hysterically; men wept hoarsely. Photographers took pictures, and reporters rushed from person to person, conducting hurried interviews. Then occurred the same thing that always occurs when I am part of a crowd. Everyone became one family, while I remained an outsider. Nobody spoke to me, and I didn't speak to any-

body. The secret power which had joined them kept me apart. Eyes
measured me absentmindedly, as if to ask: What is *he* doing here?
After some hesitation, I tried to ask someone a question, but the other
didn't hear me, or at least he moved away in the middle of my sentence.
I might just as well have been a ghost. After a while I decided what
I always do decide in such cases, to make peace with fate. I stood out
of the way in a corner and watched everyone as they came off the
boat, sorting them out in my mind. My son could not be among the old
and middle-aged. He could not have pitch-black hair, broad shoulders,
and fiery eyes—one like that could not have stemmed from my loins.
But suddenly a young man emerged strangely similar to that soldier
in the snapshot, tall, lean, a little bent, with a longish nose and a
narrow chin. This is he, something screamed in me. I tore myself
from my corner to run to him. He was searching for someone. A
fatherly love awoke in me. His cheeks were sunken and a sickly
pallor lay on his face. He is sick, he has consumption, I thought
anxiously. I had already opened my mouth to call out, "Gigi" (what
his mother and I had called him as a small boy), when suddenly a
thick woman waddled over to him and locked him in her arms. Her
cry turned into a kind of barking; soon a whole bunch of other relatives came up. They had snatched a son from me, who was not mine!
There was a kind of spiritual kidnaping in the whole thing. My
fatherly feelings became ashamed and stepped back in a hurry into
that hiding place where emotions can stay for years without a sound.
I felt that I had turned red with humiliation, as if I had been struck
in the face. I decided to wait patiently from now on and not to allow
my feelings to come out prematurely. Then for a while, no more
passengers emerged. I thought: What is a son after all? What makes
my semen more to me than somebody else's? What value is there in
a flesh and blood connection? We are all foam from the same cauldron.
Go back a number of generations and all this crowd of strangers
probably had a common grandfather. And two or three generations
hence, the descendants of those who are relatives now will be strangers.
It's all temporary and passing—we're bubbles on the same ocean,
moss from the same swamp. If one cannot love everybody, one should
not love anybody.

The passengers again began to come out. Three young men appeared
together, and I examined them. None was Gigi and even if one were,
no one would snatch him from me anyhow. It was a relief when each

of the three went away with someone else. None of them had pleased me. They belonged to the rabble. The last one had even turned round and thrown a bellicose look at me, as if he had in some mysterious way caught my deprecating thoughts about him and those like him.

If he is my son he will come out last, it suddenly occurred to me, and even though this was an assumption, somehow I knew that it would happen that way. I had armed myself with patience and with that resignation which is always there in me ready to immunize my failures and curb any desire I might have to free myself from my limitations. I observed each passenger carefully, guessing from the way he looked and was dressed his character and personality. Perhaps I only imagined it, but each face gave me its secrets and I seemed to know exactly how each of their brains was working. The passengers all had something in common: the fatigue of a long ocean trip, the fretfulness and unsureness of people arriving in a new country. Each one's eyes asked with disappointment: Is this America? The girl with the number on her arm angrily shook her head. The whole world was one Auschwitz. A Lithuanian rabbi with a round gray beard and bulging eyes carried a heavy tome. A bunch of *yeshivah* boys were waiting for him, and the moment he met them he began to preach with the angry zeal of one who has learned the truth and is trying to spread it quickly. I heard him say, Torah . . . Torah . . . I wanted to ask him why the Torah hadn't defended those millions of Jews and kept them from Hitler's crematoria. But why ask him when I knew the answer already?—"My thoughts are not your thoughts." To be martyred in God's name is the highest privilege. One passenger spoke a kind of German dialect, which was neither German nor Yiddish but a gibberish out of old-fashioned novels. And how strange that those who waited for him should chatter in the same tongue.

I reasoned that in the whole chaos there are precise laws. The dead stay dead. Those who live have their memories, calculations and plans. Somewhere in the ditches of Poland are the ashes of those who were burned. In Germany, the former Nazis lie in their beds, each one with his list of murders, tortures, violent or half-violent rapes. Somewhere there must be a Knower who knows every thought of each human being, who knows the aches of each fly, who knows each comet and meteor, each molecule in the most distant galaxy. I spoke to him. Well, Almighty Knower, for you everything is just. You know the whole and have all the information . . . and that's why you're so clever. But what shall I do with my crumbs of facts? . . . Yes, I have to wait for my son. The passengers had again stopped coming out and it seemed to me that they had all disembarked. I grew tense. Hadn't my son come on that ship? Had I overlooked him? Had he jumped into the ocean? Almost everybody had left the pier, and I felt the attendants were ready to put out the lights. What should I do now? I had had a premonition that something would go wrong with that son who for twenty years had been for me a word, a name, a guilt in my conscience.

Suddenly I saw him. He came out slowly, hesitantly, and with an expression that said he didn't expect anybody would have waited for him. He looked like the snapshot, but older. There were youthful wrinkles in his face and his clothes were mussy. He showed the shabbiness and neglect of a homeless young man who had been years in strange places, who had gone through a lot and become old before his time. His hair was tangled and matted, and it seemed to me there were wisps of straw and hay in it—like the hair of those who sleep in haylofts. His light eyes, squinting behind whitish eyebrows, had the half-blind smile of an albino. He carried a wooden satchel like an army recruit, and a package wrapped in brown paper. Instead of running to him immediately, I stood and gaped. His back was already bent a little, but not like a *yeshivah* boy's, rather like that of someone who is used to carrying heavy burdens. He took after me, but I recognized traits of his mother—the other half that could never blend with mine. Even in him, the product, our contrary traits had no harmony. The mother's lips did not pair with the father's chin. The protruding cheekbones did not suit the high forehead. He looked carefully on both sides, and his face said good-naturedly: Of course, he didn't come to meet me. I approached him and asked unsurely,

"*Atah*, Gigi?"

He laughed. "Yes, I'm Gigi."

We kissed and his stubble rubbed my cheeks like a potato grater. He was strange to me yet I knew at the same time I was as devoted to him as any other father to his son. We stood still with that feeling of belonging together that needs no words. In one second I knew how to treat him. He had spent three years in the army, had gone through a bitter war. He must have had God knew how many girls, but he had remained as bashful as only a man can be. I spoke to him in Hebrew, rather amazed at my own knowledge. I immediately acquired the authority of a father and all my inhibitions evaporated. I tried to take his wooden box but he wouldn't let me. We stood outside looking for a taxi but all the taxis had already gone. The rain had stopped. The avenue along the docks stretched out—wet, dark, badly paved, the asphalt full of ditches and with puddles of water reflecting pieces of the glowing sky, which was low and red like a metal cover. The air was choking. There was lightning but no thunder. Single drops of water fell from above but it was hard to know whether these were spray from the former rain or a new gust beginning. It hurt my dignity that New York should show itself to my son so gloomy and dingy. I had a vain ambition to have him see immediately the nicer quarters of the city. But we waited for fifteen minutes without a taxi appearing. Already I had heard the first sounds of thunder. There was nothing else to do but walk. We both spoke in the same style—short and sharp. Like old friends who know one another's thoughts, we did not need long explanations. He said to me almost without words: I understand that you could not stay with my mother. I have no complaints. I myself am made of the same stuff. . . . I asked him,

"What kind of a girl is she—the one you wrote me about?"

"A fine girl. I was her counselor in the *kibbutz*. Later we went into the army together."

"What does she do in the *kibbutz?*"

"She works in the barns."

"Has she at least studied?"

"We went to high school together."

"When are you going to marry?"

"When I go back. Her parents demand an official wedding."

He said this in a way that meant—naturally, we two don't need such ceremonies, but parents of daughters have a different logic.

I signaled a taxi and he half protested. "Why a taxi? We could have walked. I can walk for miles." I told the man to drive us across Forty-second Street, up the lighted part of Broadway, and later to turn into Fifth Avenue. Gigi sat and looked out through the window. I was never so proud of the skyscrapers and of the lights on Broadway as that evening. He looked and was silent. I somehow grasped that he was thinking now about the war with the Arabs, and all the dangers which he had survived on the battlefield. But the powers which determine the world had destined that he should come to New York and see his father. It was as if I heard his thoughts behind his skull. I was sure he too, like myself, was pondering the eternal questions. As if to try out my telepathic powers, I said to him,

"There are no accidents. If you are meant to live, you have to remain alive. It is destined so."

Surprised, he turned his head to me.

"Hey, you are a mind reader!"

And he smiled, amazed, curious, and skeptical, as if I had played a fatherly trick on him.

Translated by the author and Elizabeth Pollet

(*—1942*)

CHRONICLES

In the Days of the Sun-King

◆◆◆

ANDRÉ SPIRE

A guilty man punished is an example
. . . an innocent man condemned is the
affair of all honorable people.
LABRUYÈRE: *De Quelques Usages*

IN EARLY April 1951 I received a telephone call which intrigued
me: "This is Morphée, speaking for André Gillois."

What could he want of me, André Gillois, whose voice was heard
virtually every day over the French radio holding forth on the most
varied social, literary, artistic and political activities in France?

"Have you any family archives?" asked Morphée.

Yes, but what use . . .

"Can I see you?"

When?

"Immediately."

Half an hour later this veteran of interviewing and of broadcasting
was in my home.

"Haven't you heard the series of broadcasts, *'The Great French
Families,'* on the air every Wednesday at 10 P.M.?"

Several, not all. But in what connection . . . ?

"A forthcoming broadcast: *'The Spire Family.'*"

What! Among the great names—the Rohan-Chabots, the Gram-
monts, the Ducs de la Force, companions of kings, soldiers, ministers,
academicians; the Broglies, formerly princes of provinces, today princes
of science—to include an obscure bourgeois family from Lorraine!
People would burst out laughing at their radios all over Europe!

"You are not an attentive listener. André Gillois has explained it in
almost all his broadcasts. If up to now he has presented families of the
aristocracy, that's simply because, he says, their descendants and their

archives are easily accessible, their names in fact are on every page of our history. However, that hasn't prevented André Gillois from seeking out families with no title at all. He would have presented more of them if there weren't so much difficulty finding out such families with archives or oral traditions going back more than two or three generations."

I understand. Just to have archives entitles one to appear among the *Grandes Familles Françaises!*

"Entitles no! But without archives how can you know a family's origins, tell its story? Its thanks only to their archives that André Gillois has been able to trace their life through the centuries of a number of families belonging to the bourgeois and the peasant and working classes. In some of those families he was able to bring out the passionate struggles between Catholics and Protestants. But those struggles threw into the shade another aspect of the religious passion: the conflict between the whole of Christendom—Protestants, Catholics, Greek and Eastern Churches—and those people who to this very day have remained faithful to the ancient religion from which the others have sprung—Judaism."

In short, to your gallery of aristocratic families, and of bourgeois, workers and peasant families, you want to add a Jewish family?

"An old family of French Jews."

There are some older than mine. There are descendants of Jewish families whose settlement in Provence goes back to the days of the Roman Empire—the Milhauds, the Astrucs.

"Darius Milhaud is in America. And one of the last representatives of the Astruc family has just telephoned me that she has no document by her that could serve as a basis for an interview. Have you any?"

Yes. Not a formal genealogical tree—I've never had the time to draw one up. But I have any number of scraps of paper where I've jotted down the conversations of my parents, grand-parents, great-uncles. I have copied the records of important family events from the blank pages of prayer books, business ledgers, housekeeping account books. I have fragments of correspondence going quite far back. I even possess a portfolio containing some fifty letters and a curl of golden-brown hair, admirably preserved, of my paternal great-grandmother, an exquisite young woman who died in 1830 at Lunéville; she was a truly gifted letter-writer.

"Fine!" said Morphée. "You have everything André Gillois needs to prepare his broadcast. When will you meet him?"

Whenever it's convenient for him.

So, several days later, I met André Gillois in a studio of the French Radiodiffusion on the Avenue des Champs Élysées. He installed me in front of a microphone.

"Now," he said, "tell us about the professions of your parents and ancestors."

✦ ✦ ✦

As in many Jewish families, my earlier forebears were tradesmen, small business people. At the beginning of the nineteenth century they were wholesale merchants and manufacturers.

On my mother's side, in Nancy, there were drapers, hosiers, weavers—in the eighteenth century, glove manufacturers already living in Lunéville.

My paternal grandfather Charles Nathan, after serving his apprenticeship as glove-maker in his father's factory at Lunéville, married in Nancy, towards 1842, the daughter of a hosier born in Alsace, Isaac-Gaudchaux Picard, who had established in Nancy, at the beginning of the nineteenth century, a hosiery business, then a cloth factory.

My grandfather converted the hosiery business into a slipper factory, then into a shoe factory . . . then, around 1871, he took into the business my father, Edouard Spire, who, after serving as an advocate before the Court of Appeals in Nancy, had become a notary in the Département des Vosges. It was under the bold and skillful direction of this jurist turned industrialist that my grandfather's modest business became one of the largest shoe factories in eastern France.

"In short," said André Gillois, "there was in both your families a vocation to protect and adorn the extremities of their fellow-citizens."

That is why, I resumed, when I began to know a little Latin, I amused myself by scribbling on my father's business stationery the device "*Manu ac Pede*" ("For hand and foot") which he struck out, muttering "*Arriviste*." I replaced it with "*Dum spiro spero*" ("While I breathe I hope") which I have since adopted. Later, I had the words engraved around the turn of a spiral (in French, "spire"), lifting itself towards the sky. And indeed that could well be the motto of the intrepid Jewish people.

Gradually, as the religious and social prejudices that kept Jews out

of the liberal professions and the civil and military service of the State
grew milder or disappeared, the number of business men in my family
diminished. The family came to include engineers, university teachers,
even a member of the Institute, high-ranking magistrates, and many
Army officers, among them three or four colonels, several generals, and
even a General of the Army.

"You, yourself, before you became a writer, essayist, poet, didn't you
hold public office?"

Yes, although my father discouraged me from it, at first. A man of
very independent character, it was his opinion that a civil servant was
a "diminished citizen." Besides, I had made a mediocre record in
classical studies: at the Lycée in Nancy and at the Collège of Toul I
won hardly any prizes except in gymnastics and fencing. When I was
fifteen one teacher told my mother that I would make an excellent
student if I were permitted to pursue my studies while swinging on
the trapeze. The only things I liked were excursions into the forest,
ice-skating, swimming, boating, fishing, hunting, horses . . . But after
two years at the *École des Sciences politiques* in Paris, to the
astonishment of my parents I was successful in the competition for the
Conseil d'État, where I entered at the end of 1893 with the title of
auditeur.

I had chosen this career, which was rather difficult to enter, not for
any love of public law, but because Stendhal, whom I admired, had
been an *auditeur* in the *Conseil d'État* and a cavalryman, just as I had
done my military service in the cavalry; and I hoped to find enough
leisure to indulge the passion for writing which had been growing in
me since my fifteenth year. It was indeed by virtue of my "second
métier"—for during and after my eight years in the *Conseil d'État* I
was in several top services of the Ministries, until the day I retired as
Inspector General—that I have been able, during my long life, to write
a certain number of poems, essays, and narratives.

"How far back," André Gillois asked me, "do your personal records
furnish information on the origins of your family?"

On my mother's side, to the beginning of the eighteenth century in
Alsace, and to Lunéville in Lorraine, where my mother's great-grand-
parents were among the founders, in 1785, of the beautiful synagogue
which was destroyed by the Germans during the last War.

On my father's side my records go back to about the same time, in

Metz, which my direct progenitors seem to have left during the middle of the eighteenth century to settle in Blâmont, between Lunéville and Sarrebourg. There my great-grandfather Oury Spire, born in 1776, bought a property, after the Revolution, which he developed with the help of his twelve children—until a few years before his death, which occurred in Blâmont in 1860.

But on the paternal side I can go still further back, to the middle of the seventeenth century, to Rabbi Abraham Spire, *Ab-Beth-Din* (Chief of the Rabbinic Tribunal) of the community of Metz, where he was one of the notables. I don't know much about him except that he was the victim, along with a Jewish cattle-trader from Boulay (a Lorraine town in the neighborhood of Metz) and a number of other Jews from Metz, of an accusation of ritual crime. Joseph Reinach has written the staggering story under the title of *Raphael Lévy: Une erreur judiciaire sous Louis XIV*, published in 1898, at one of the decisive moments in the Dreyfus Affair.[1]

✦ ✦ ✦

The trial of Raphaël Lévy, is it one of those historical events in which the members of your family were involved? In the course of it did they come in contact with celebrated personalities?"

One of the historical events, yes; but not of general history. Just in the local history of the Jews of Metz. All the same, it does touch on general history—*la grande histoire*. For this trial was an episode in the struggle begun by Louis XIV, from the moment of his accession to the throne, against the encroachments of the *Parlements* and all "sovereign companies" on the prerogatives and jurisdiction of the King and his *Conseil*.

As for the persons involved, there certainly were famous names among those who appeared during this trial and its appeals: the great Hebraist Richard Simon, priest of the *Oratoire*, whose independence of character and whose free exegesis of biblical texts provoked persecutions by Bossuet; the Marquis of Berny, secretary of the King's *Commandements;* his father, Hugues de Lionne, the premier diplomat of Europe; the old Chancellor Séguier; Louvois, Minister of War; and Louis XIV, the King himself, and his *Conseil*.

[1] Paris, Librairie Charles Delagrave, 1898. A capital work, which has served as the basis for the preparation of this broadcast. To that work must be referred all who wish to get a detailed knowledge of this episode in the martyrology of the Jews of France under the *Ancien Régime*.

"Indeed, those were not unimportant people, *des gens de neant* (nobodies), as the phrase was then. You see I wasn't wrong to ask you to answer my questions. Do continue; tell me of the forms, phases and incidents of their activity in behalf of Abraham Spire."

Oh, then I shall have to tell you the entire story of the trial, beginning with the accusation and imprisonment of Raphaël Lévy. It's quite complicated, rather long, and I'm afraid of tiring your listeners.

"Let *me* worry about that! You just tell the story while I take notes; and on Saturday, April 26th, turn on the radio. You'll see how my associates and I can keep them stirred and breathless with a story from history, straight history, without fripperies or sophistications."

Very well. When Louis XIV came to Metz on September 18, 1657— he was twenty-one—with Mazarin and his mother, Anne of Austria, he visited the synagogue, "with pomp and *éclat*," accompanied by his brother, the Duke of Orléans, and a great number of dukes and nobles. On the following October fourth, renewing the letters patent which had been granted to the Jews of Metz by Henri IV and by Louis XIII, he gave them the right which had hitherto been refused them—the right to sell all kinds of merchandise, which meant new merchandise as well as old.

The Guild of Merchants, threatened in its privileges, tried to oppose the registration of the royal decisions, but the *Parlement* of Metz did not grant its request. There remained the oblique course of action, by methods mealy-mouthed or brutal, which the Guilds used so efficiently throughout Europe to crush the competition of Jews: the re-awakening of dormant religious passions, slander, falsehoods, fear. A local tragedy served their designs.

On Wednesday, September 25, 1669, on the eve of Rosh Hashanah, Mageotte Villemin, the wife of the wheelwright Gilles Le Moine, went to do her washing in the fountain; her son Didier, aged three, toddled behind her. Thinking he'd catch up with her at the fountain, she walked on and washed her linen. Then, noticing the child hadn't arrived, she ran back to the spot where she had left him. The child had disappeared. She rushed home; neither her husband nor her parents-in-law had seen him. They searched the bushes and followed the child's footprints as far as the road to Metz where his prints were lost among the marks of the carts and horses' feet. A passing mounted soldier was asked whether he had seen a child. "I saw," said he, "a Jew with a long black beard, riding a white horse and going towards

Metz, and he was carrying in front of him a child that might have been three or four years old. On my coming across him," added the soldier, "the Jew moved off the main road by a gunshot's length."

"He, he stole my son!" shouted the father.

Another passer-by, who lived in the village of Hayez, said he had met on the same road a Jew from Boulay, Raphaël Lévy, "carrying in front of him something he was covering with his cloak." Perhaps that something was food or merchandise. No! Raphaël Lévy was a Jew; and that something he hid under his cloak could only be the child he was carrying off to the house of another Jew, where he would be found "hidden in a barrel closed up with nails to extract his blood" for the preparation of the ritual bread.

Thus once again was unleashed the old accusation of ritual crime which, from the thirteenth century on, had run through all Christendom wherever there were Jews.

A complaint was lodged on October 3, 1669, with the *lieutenant criminel* of the bailiwick, who immediately permitted "information" to be given against Raphaël Lévy. No one could prove the truth of the accusations of the man from Hayez, nor of the mounted soldier (who, in fact, retracted), nor the allegations of a butcher's wife whose own husband recognized their impossibility. After a long process before the court of first instance, Raphaël Lévy was about to be allowed to produce witnesses for his defense when a technicality of procedure permitted the *Parlement* of Metz to get hold of the case.

Before the *Parlement* Raphaël Lévy, strong in his innocence, defended himself "with much boldness." Hard pressed with questions by a very skillful commissioner, he answered with "marvelous presence of mind and without contradicting himself." Then, on November 26, 1669, four swineherds who tended their animals in the woods of Glatigny found there the head, neck and a part of the ribs of a child, and nearby two little dresses, one inside the other, a woolen stocking, a red cap and a little shirt spread out on the bushes, all of these things untorn and unspotted with blood. Little Didier's father identified these as belonging to his son.

Raphaël Lévy believed himself saved. To him this discovery proved that the child, playing on the road, had entered the woods where it was devoured by wolves.

But to the *Parlement* of Metz— prejudiced in favor of the Guild of Merchants and resolved, in the interests of the Guild, to demonstrate to the King that their Jewish competitors should be banished from the country—this evidence proved, quite to the contrary, that the stolen child had been delivered by Raphaël Lévy to Jewish accomplices who probably had not put him to death until some days after the kidnapper's imprisonment, then had put the body in the woods of Glatigny in an impressive stage setting designed to make people believe in their innocence and in the innocence of their friend.

Clearly apparent though it was that this setting could only have been staged by people in the service of the Guild of Merchants, the real moving spirit of this affair, or even by the father of the missing child; though in the course of an examination which exhausted all possible methods of inquiry, including the horrible tortures of "the question ordinary and extraordinary," there emerged no smallest testimony in proof—in spite of all that the *Parlement,* on January 16, 1670, pronounced judgment declaring Raphaël Lévy "sufficiently attainted and convicted of having abducted on the twenty-fifth day of September, one thousand six hundred and sixty-nine, on the highway to Glatigny" a three-year-old child. It therefore condemned him "to make *amende honorable* in front of the grand portal of the Cathedral Church of Metz and, on his knees, naked except for a shirt, with a halter round his neck, holding between his hands a burning torch weighing three pounds, to say and to declare that he did unfortunately and wickedly abduct said child, and did take it to this city; that he repents of it, and asks pardon of God, the King, and the Judges. This done, the said Lévy is to be led to the *place du champ* of Seille, there to be burned alive, and his ashes scattered to the winds, first having been put to the 'question ordinary and extraordinary' in order to extract a revelation of those into whose hands he delivered the said child and who murdered it."

To obtain the names of these "accomplices" the *Parlement* further ordered the putting of "the question ordinary and extraordinary" to Gédéon Lévy, a Jew from the neighborhood of Glatigny who had been imprisoned since December 9, 1669, because, during the investigation, he had often received in his home Jews who had come from Metz, and because he had been seen entering and leaving the woods of Glatigny with a basket on his back. The decree also ordered the arrest, or the appearance before the court, of various other members of the community to whom Raphaël Lévy was accused of having passed notes from his prison, pleading with them to come to his aid, and informing them that the child had been "bound" (*gebunden*)—when actually he had written that the child had been "found" (*gefunden*). Among these Jews was Mayeur Schoüabbe, one of the heads and the richest man of the community.

Without even awaiting the end of the "investigations" against these alleged accomplices, Raphaël Lévy was led, on the day following the decree of January 16th, into the torture chamber. He declared and had it put into writing "that any confession which grief or torture might wrest from him was nothing but a lie; for he was innocent, and all Israel was innocent; and he accused not his judges but the false witnesses." About to faint at one moment, he was offered a drink of wine, which he refused because it was not *kasher*. During the worst agonies of his torture, while hanging with weights on his big toes, not a single confession, not a word, could be wrung from him.

The parish priest, a Capuchin friar, the public prosecutor of the bailiwick, all exhorted him to become converted. He turned his head away so as not to hear them. While being led to the torture he walked, says Dom Calmet, a Benedictine monk (in his famous history of Lorraine), "with marvellous intrepidity," refusing the wagon which was to take him there. As the priest and the Capuchin followed him step by step, "continuing to press him for his conversion and salvation, he repulsed them with blows of his elbows, saying 'I am a Jew and I want to return a Jew to the bosom of Abraham.'" At the stake he helped to put on himself the sulphur-treated garment and refused to have his face covered. And when the Capuchin and the clerk of the court still continued to press him to recognize his errors and confess his crime, he answered: "Do you not see Heaven opened and two angels ready to receive my soul?" Then he turned his head toward the executioner who, out of pity, strangled him before setting fire to the stake.

Nothing had been omitted—either in the indictment or in the text of the decree: accusations of usury, illicit traffic, corruption of morals, illegal increase of families—to arouse the fury of the populace and to transform the responsibility of a few for the alleged crime into a collective guilt of a community. To conclude, the *Parlement* ordered that a record of the proceedings conducted against Raphaël Lévy and his co-defendants be sent to the King and that "very humble representations be made to His Majesty to obtain from his Justice that the said Jews be driven from and banished in perpetuity from the city of Metz and the country around it and from other places in the Kingdom."

✦ ✦ ✦

Threatened with general expulsion, the Community of the Jews of Metz sent delegates post-haste to Paris to file an appeal, through a lawyer, from the decree of January 16th and all its legal and political consequences; and also to make inquiries about influential people who might be disposed to protect the Community against the dangers set in train by the hatred of the Guild of Merchants and by the outrageous partiality of the *Parlement* of Metz.

It is known that, from the time of their general expulsion from the lands of the Crown (in 1290), Jews did not have the right to live in Paris. Nevertheless, despite the legal prohibitions, there had always been, since the Renaissance, a certain number of Jews from foreign countries or from the Midi or the East of France sojourning in Paris or passing through by virtue of temporary authorizations. Among them, in 1670, was Jona Salvador, a Jew from Pignerol, in Piedmont. He was a shrewd businessman, "having the King's permission to stay for six months in Paris," where he was working to obtain "new-Monopols (*sic*), as he had succeeded for tobacco, which he established in Pignerol with the aid of the Governor."[2]

Salvador enjoyed "*grandes liaisons* with some courtiers" whom he had interested in his affairs. He was a frequent visitor at the home of "Monsieur le Prince," who was the Grand Condé.[3] He was also in relations with Richard Simon, priest of the *Oratoire,* savant and Orientalist who from his youth had undertaken to learn Hebrew—and the other Oriental languages which are, as it were, so many branches of Hebrew" —because he "felt very keenly its natural connection with the study of the Sacred Text, and consequently its possible usefulness for a theologian not wishing to limit himself to the thorns of Scholasticism."[4] Richard Simon considered Jona Salvador "a scholar of his Law . . . and very practiced in the reading of the Talmud which constitutes the body

[2] Pignerol belonged at that time to France. It was in its chateau that Foucquet, Lauzun, and the "Man in the Iron Mask" were shut up as prisoners of State.

[3] Richard Simon, *Lettres choisies*. Pierre Mortier (Amsterdam, 1730), Letter 2, pp. 14–15–18.

[4] *Ibid.*, vol. I, *Éloge historique de Monsieur Simon*, by Bruzen La Martinière, p. 5.

of the Law of the Jews . . ." although sinking "too much into the visions of the Kabbala and the allegories."[5]

Born in 1638, Richard Simon was then only thirty-two years old. His indomitable independence had not yet brought on his rupture with the *Oratoire,* nor yet involved him in his celebrated controversies with Bossuet. Bossuet, fearing that the liberty with which Richard Simon applied his principles of criticism and linguistics would end by ruining the doctrines of the inspiration and historical truth of the Scriptures, used the snide weapons of censorship and prohibition against his loyal adversary, and even the suppression of his writings by the civil authorities.

Although Richard Simon was himself not exempt from all the religious and social prejudices of the Christians of his milieu and his Order against the Jews, he had no hesitation in going to see Salvador "at Fort-Meulan in the rue Quincampois where he was lodging."[6] Salvador sometimes visited him in the Church of the *Oratoire,* never entering without a black satin skull-cap on his head, because he believed "that he was not permitted, without being idolatrous, to remain bareheaded in the churches of the Christians."[7]

Salvador would meet him also in the "mother-house" of the *Oratoire* on the rue Saint-Honoré, which was "at that time in a sense enclosed within the Louvre."[8] Richard Simon would take him to the Library of the *Oratoire,* rich in a great number of "Rabbins both printed and in manuscript, among them a manuscript which bore the title of 'Zohar' which, however, had almost nothing in common with the true *Zohar* printed in Cremona and in Mantua, its very style being quite different."[9]

It was "ordinarily on Saturdays after dinner" that Salvador came to visit, "for, the better to honor the Sabbath which is a day of rest, he stays abed until noon." They would spend "the entire afternoon in reading books"; and, although Jews are not permitted to carry anything on the day of Sabbath, "nevertheless, however large and heavy the book, he had no scruple about carrying it from one end of our Library to the other, holding it in his arms."[10]

On other days Salvador went straight to Richard Simon's room

[5] *Ibid.,* vol. III, pp. 11 & 12.
[6] *Ibid.,* vol. II, p. 18.
[7] *Ibid.,* pp. 17–18.
[8] *Ibid.,* p. 67.
[9] *Ibid.,* vol. III, p. 8.
[10] *Ibid.,* vol. III, p. 12.

where he would find him working, "lying on a very thick carpet, with several cushions," having "near him on the floor an inkstand, paper and books that he wished to consult."[11] There the priest of the *Oratoire* and the Jew from Pignerol talked, discussed biblical questions through the long hours—the interpretation of Scriptures, Tradition, everything concerning the Jewish Religion or Jewish Nation, in the distant past as well as in the nearest present. They discussed the Recall of the Jews, in which the French Protestants were passionately interested since the propaganda of Manasseh ben Israel for the recall of the Jews to England. Then they talked of the forced baptisms of Jewish children who had been kidnapped and sent to convents: on this matter Richard Simon's opinion was that those responsible, absolved by the theologians of the Sorbonne, would be condemned by the Court of Rome, "because more importance is attached there to civil laws than to theology."[12] Sometimes it was on the actual reading of the Bible itself that Richard Simon asked Salvador for enlightenment, on the pronunciation and intonations of this Hebrew language which Salvador had learned "by usage rather than according to the rules of grammar. It is a fine thing," said he, "to see him reading the Bible in the Jewish fashion, shaking his head and shoulders and practically his entire body, in order to animate his reading: for he sings rather than reads."[13]

As soon as they arrived in Paris the delegates of the Jews of Metz went to see Salvador at his residence in the rue Quincampois. They informed him of the martyrdom of Raphaël Lévy, of the illegal prosecutions initiated and continued against imaginary accomplices, and of the anti-Jewish agitation unleashed by the trial.

Salvador's passion for business had not made him hard-hearted, and his love for the Hebrew language and the Bible extended to all the people of Israel. Forthwith he set to work to put at their service those *"grandes liaisons"* he enjoyed with people at court and in the city. Richard Simon—"whose ardent and indefatigable genius offered itself unceasingly to great causes as well as to great studies"—was immediately won over. And the son of Hugues de Lionne, Minister of Foreign Affairs—the Marquis de Berny, Secretary of the King's *Commandements*—to whose house Salvador took the delegates.

[11] *Ibid.*, vol. I, p. 100.
[12] *Ibid.*, vol. II, p. 58.
[13] *Ibid.*, vol. III, p. 12.

They presented their request,[14] stressing the jealousy of the Guild of Merchants which had launched its accusation against Raphaël Lévy and his co-defendants only in order to rouse a popular agitation designed to bring about the banishment of the Jews. They threw themselves, they said, at the feet of His Majesty to implore his aid, and to seek from him the protection which neither the King's predecessors nor he himself had ever refused. Hence they asked the King to oppose the execution of the judgment of January 16th which laid heavy threats upon the entire Community and upon Raphaël Lévy's alleged accomplices, though their sentence had not yet been pronounced.

M. de Berny heard the delegates out with much kindness. He told them: "Your Jew is dead; why did you not appeal to me sooner?" Then, having submitted the matter to the King, he received an order from him to write to the Sieur de Choisy, *Intendant de la Généralité* and representative of Royal Authority in the province, that it was His Majesty's wish he look into this matter, and that the record of the trial of Raphaël Lévy, that of Mayeur Schoüabbe, and the public allegations against the Community of the Jews of Metz be sent to him."

But the *Parlement,* resisting the orders of the *Intendant,* not only refused to send him the information. Piling on accusations of impiety, blasphemy, and sacrilege against the religion of Christ, on March 29, 1670 it condemned Mayeur Schoüabbe, already imprisoned for over three months, to pay a very heavy fine. It decided to continue the trial for complicity in the exposure of the remains and clothing of "the stolen child" begun on March 21, 1670, against Abraham Spire, *Ab-Beth-Din,* that is, Chief of the Rabbinic Tribunal. Having been warned in time, he succeeded in quitting the city.

The *Parlement,* furthermore, decreed against several other Jews who were imprisoned "without being told the cause of their detention . . . so that, in a way, it is sufficient today in Metz to be a Jew to be accused, and being accused to be condemned."[15]

Finally, reiterating its accusations of impiety, of depreciation of the currency and usury against the Jews, the *Parlement* ordered that Raphaël Lévy's death sentence be "posted, engraved on a plate of

[14] We here sum up this request according to the text of the judgment of the *Conseil d'État du Roi* as reproduced by Joseph Reinach, in the work cited, pp. 197–203.

[15] Reinach, *op. cit.,* pp. 201 & 112.

copper fastened to a pillar of freestone to be raised in the *place* of the street of the Jews."[16]

Nevertheless, the *Intendant* succeeded in carrying out his investigation, in the course of which he interrogated a number of Jews. Having obtained proof of the good grounds of their appeal, he wrote to Hugues de Lionne—who, forewarned by his son de Berny, was strongly disposed in their favor—informing him of the dangers threatening the Jews in "the climate of riot" let loose in the countryside by publication of the proceedings, from which he had successfully protected them thus far. He begged the Minister to explain to the King the interests and the passions set in motion by the accusers of Raphaël Lévy, and the lies, calumnies, false testimony and violence which had prevailed at the conduct of the trial.

The answer of Louis XIV was not long in coming. By a decree of the *Roi étant en son Conseil,* dated at the Chateau of St. Germain en Laye April 18, 1670—completed by an *"arrêt interprétatif"* of the *Conseil d'État* dated at St. Germain en Laye August 29—Louis XIV annulled the decree of the *Parlement* of Metz rendered on January 16th against Raphaël Lévy, together with all the proceedings, charges and "informations" against the Jews of Metz. In addition, he expressly forbade the *Parlement* to carry out sentence pronounced on March 29, 1670, against Mayeur Schoüabbe and others, or to enforce the decree of arrest issued on March 21st against Abraham Spire— "under pain of three thousand livres fine and all expenses, damages, and *"intérêts."*

A decision of exceptional severity! Intentionally humiliating for a *Cour Judiciaire.* The King threatening the Court with a pecuniary reparation to those wretched Jews it had expected to have at its mercy!

One can see in the *Archives de France* the texts of these two decrees delivered by the *Roi étant en son Conseil.* The first is on fine parchment, sealed with the great Royal Seal on yellow wax and bearing the signatures of the King and of Hugues de Lionne, with flourishes. On the second, at the top left there appears the name of the Marquis de Berny, who was probably the *rapporteur.* It bears the signature of the old Chancellor Séguier, collaborating once again in Louis XIV's struggle against the encroachments of the *Parlements* upon royal authority.

[16] Reinach, *op. cit.,* pp. 201 & 112.

Other personages whose names cut some figure worked on the King's mind to become once again the protector of the Jews of Metz.

There was Louvois, Minister of War, who was in the habit of utilizing the services of the Jews of Metz for the remount of his cavalry and the supplying of his equipment. Having found these services "good, and cheaper than any other," he gave "numerous tokens of his protection."[17] It is possible, too, that the Grand Condé intervened in favor of the *protégés* of Salvador who, as we have seen, was a frequent visitor to his home. But, in the end, it was Richard Simon whose intervention proved decisive.

✦ ✦ ✦

The *Parlement* of Metz, continuing secretly to harbor hopes of reversing the King's opinion and obtaining from him an edict of expulsion against the Jews, had an anonymous lampoon circulated, which was inspired by the *Corps des Arts et Métiers* of Metz.[18] It was published in Paris on May 20, 1670, with the title *Abrégé du procès des Juifs de Metz* ("Summary of the Trial of the Jews of Metz"). A scandalous apologetic for the *Parlement's* attitude: nothing more than a piling up of profaned hosts, burlesqued scenes of the Passion, scourged crucifixes, kidnapped, tortured and murdered children, all the accusations of imaginary crimes launched from the time of the Crusades to obtain from the Kings of France, from Philippe-Auguste to Louis XIII, the expulsion of the Jews.

Richard Simon, warned by Salvador that the *Abrégé* might make an impression on the King, undertook to write the answer which the delegates of the Jews of Metz were to present to the King. "A relentless refutation," the Abbé Grégoire called it; indeed, a veritable *J'accuse* against all the fanatics who in troubled periods of history have stirred up the spectre of ritual crime.[19]

[17] Reinach, *op. cit.*, pp. 25, 63, 64.
[18] *Ibid.*, pp. 49–50.
[19] This answer appears under the title of *Factum servant de réponse au livre intitulé* Abrégé du procès fait aux Juifs de Metz in volume I, chapter VIII, of the *Bibliothèque Critique,* a collection of various critical writings, no longer in print or rare, which Richard Simon published in 1708 at Amsterdam, under the pseudonym of Sainjore.

In a note to this *Factum* he wrote: "This *Factum* was published in Paris in 1670, in the name of the Jews of Metz, who were then pressing their matter to the *Conseil.* Since only a few copies were printed for the Judges, and for several persons of quality, there are practically none extant. That is why it was deemed proper to issue a new edition."

Richard Simon showed that whenever honest investigators had the courage to seek beyond appearances, they found only false testimony. As was the case in 1338, in the Pontificate of Benedict XII. On that occasion, when a profaned host was found at the door of a Jew accused of having pierced it with a knife, it was discovered that the accuser had spattered this host with blood "in order to make people believe that the Jews had committed this atrocity." Yet it was on just such spurious testimony—in a trial where not only was there no proof at all of the kidnapping or murder of the child by the accused, but where all the presumptions were to the contrary—"that R. Lévy and his so-called accomplices, together with the entire Community, were condemned by magistrates determined neither by reason nor by the passion for justice but only by avarice, by what the zeal, or rather the fury, of Religion can produce in the minds of the people and even of their leaders."

In a letter to the Abbé de Lameth, member of the Society of Doctors of the Sorbonne—that Abbé who, in his interpretation of a case where a Jewish child was kidnapped, forcibly converted, and sent to a convent by super-zealous Christians, had taken a position completely opposed to that of his confrère at the *Oratoire*—Richard Simon, not without bantering high spirits, proudly claims the part he took in the fight for the liberation of the Jews of Metz. "A short time ago," he wrote, "the Jews of Metz boldly won a case in the *Conseil du Roi* against the *Parlement* of Metz, which had condemned a miserable Jew to the stake, and was ready to pronounce a similar sentence against two other Jews, had not the *Conseil* called for a report on this affair. Salvador, who was then in Paris, sent me the documents of the case. After reading them I had no scruple in working out a *Factum* in favor of those Jews of Metz, which contributed a good deal in winning their cause in the *Conseil du Roi*. I know that this wretched Nation hates us mortally; but it is our duty to show them that we practice towards them the maxim of the Gospel which commands us to love our enemies."[20]

✦ ✦ ✦

Such was the story I told to André Gillois, which in the form of a poignant radio drama he broadcast on April 26, 1951. It was a moment when French fascism was rearing its head, waging an

[20] *Lettres Choisies de Richard Simon*, vol. II, p. 58.

impudent campaign to restore liberty to those who had delivered the Jews of France to Nazi torture and extermination—the Xavier Vallats, the Maurras, and Pétain himself.

I am not sure it was in an access of tolerance that Louis XIV, who was to revoke the Edict of Nantes fifteen years later, intervened in favor of the Jews of Metz. No doubt he only acted from considerations of pragmatic politics, to defend the royal prerogatives and the "liberties" of his subjects against abuses of power by the *Parlements* and the various "sovereign companies," that "during the confusion of the last years of his minority and even afterwards had introduced into the kingdom a disorder in the meting out of justice."

This King, who regarded himself absolute, thus paved the way for the establishment of a jurisprudence regulating the rights of the citizen against the excesses of power of provincial authorities, of corporations public or private, and of the central power itself—a process which developed during the nineteenth century down to our own day. The modern *Conseil d'État* is the successor of the *Roi en son Conseil*, to which Rabbi Abraham Spire owed his liberty and possibly his life.

This *Conseil d'État* I, his descendant, was to enter 224 years later. It left me free—me a State official, me a Jew—to carry on, by tongue and by pen and by the sword itself, a struggle which continues still, against that degraded form of the old religious anti-Judaism—anti-Semitism sometimes dormant but always renascent.

Translated from the French manuscript
written for The Menorah Journal
(—1956)

A Clue to Chaibar

⊂⌇⋏⋏⌇⊃

YITZHAK BEN-ZWI

I HAD heard that among the Arab villagers around Hebron were some who said they were descended from Jews and who preserved memories of their origins and remnants of Jewish customs—and my curiosity was aroused. I had been told, for instance, that when the fellaheen of a certain Arab village came to make purchases in Hebron, they dealt with Jewish rather than Arab shops, and in addressing the Jews called them *Wlad'Amna,* that is to say, cousins or relatives. The fellaheen of a second village, I heard, come before Hanukkah to order a *menorah* and light candles on each of the eight nights of the Hasmonean feast. Further, that the inhabitants of a third village near Hebron have always and still do abstain from eating camel flesh, which their neighbors accept as proof of their Jewish origin. In Hebron, David Castel, a tinsmith of the Castel family of Gaza, told me that he had heard his grandfather, Joseph Castel, say that about a hundred years ago there was a family of the name of M'hamara in the villages near Hebron who professed to have been Jews until about 1700, and that the children of M'hamara celebrate Hanukkah by lighting the candles on the eight nights. But whether this fellah family lived in Bnei-Na'im (now called Dûrah), or in Juttah, he did not know.

To verify these legends I went to visit the elders of the Spanish community in the old Jewish ghetto.[*] The Hebron ghetto is no longer densely populated, teeming with life, as it was before the War. Of the hundreds of families who lived there fifty years ago, a few have removed to the new quarter of Hebron but most have left the town altogether. Not more than ten families, too poor to find an abode elsewhere, are left. The empty houses, the broken windows, give the appearance of an ancient city but lately unearthed. But the historic syn-

[*] This was written before the Arab attacks and before the establishment of the *Yeshivah* at Hebron—EDS.

agogues of Hebron still attract worshipers daily, and only their presence prevents the Arabs from seizing the property in the ghetto.

My meeting with the elders of the community took place in one of the old synagogues. My questions were answered very willingly, and Haham Jacob Mani proved especially helpful in collecting information from the inhabitants of Hebron, Jews and Arabs alike. This old scholar, a native of Hebron, knows the town and district thoroughly. From him I learned that theirs is no foundation for the Jewish legends of the villages of Beit Kahl and Tapuah. Rather, the legends about those places refer to Christians who renounced their faith and became Moslems some 150 years ago. Christian families converted to Islam are also to be found in Adoraim.

The elders of Hebron told me that there had been a Jewish settlement northwest of Hebron in the quarter of El-Haraiq, known today as Abdu-Shah-dam, which has been noted for glass making. Now, Rabbi Benjamin in the time of the Crusades had reported that he had found in new Tyre Jews skilled in the art of glass-making (the "Glass of Tyre" was much valued in all countries), and tradition has it that, as a result of the conquest of Hebron by the Crusaders, the Jews fled the city and dispersed and settled in the surrounding villages.

So Haham Mani suggested that the inhabitants of Juttah, who claim to be Jews, might be descendants of the first Hebron Jews who lived in the quarter of El-Haraiq. Even if this suggestion has not been confirmed in regard to Juttah (as will be seen further), the old legend that those who fled from the sword of the Crusaders found refuge in the surrounding villages seems to be a sound one. At any rate, it is clear that the pre-Crusade Jews of Hebron did not return to the city after their flight.

Another old man of Hebron, Haim Castel, related that during his father's lifetime a *goy*, while digging the ground in that quarter, remarked to his father: "See, there are Jewish graves here." (The difference between Jewish and Moslem graves is easily discernible as Jewish bodies lie toward Jerusalem and those of Moslems toward Mecca.)

Haham Mani introduced me to the scribe of the village of Juttah who happened to be in Hebron on that day. This Arab confirmed the story of the Jewish origin of at least some of the inhabitants of Juttah, including the families of M'hamara, who number about 1,200 souls, according to the keeper of the village records. This Arab gave me a letter of introduction to the Mukhtar of M'hamara, Sheikh Abu Ahram, and I set out in an automobile for Juttah.

Juttah, I had learned, is the second largest of the thirty-five villages in the neighborhood of Hebron, having a population of 3,179 according to the Government census of 1923. While never more than an ordinary village near Hebron, it has been known since the earliest days of Jewish history. The Book of Joshua mentions Juttah twice, once as a city of the priests given to the children of Aaron by the tribe of Judah. A considerable time after the fall of the Temple, Eusebius of Caesarea, the Greek-Christian historian of Palestine—who wrote about 330 C.E. before the final redaction of the Palestinian Talmud—described Juttah as a small village among other Jewish villages in the vicinity. Hieronimus, his disciple, quoting him a century later, also mentioned Juttah: " 'Ietan of the Tribe of Judah, a city of the priests, now a very big Jewish village, is situated at Landmark 18, south of Beit Jebrin, which is in the south." In the absence of even indirect evidence to the contrary, we may assume that Juttah existed until its conquest by the Moslems at the beginning of the seventh century. After that, there is no historic mention of Jewish habitation.

Juttah is situated nine kilometers to the south of Hebron and a sixteen-kilometer road connects the village with the town. The road, built only a year ago, is good for motor traffic, but we did not pass a single vehicle. There were pedestrians and horsemen, shying donkeys and camels unused to "this devil's means of transport" in this deserted corner of the earth. It is obvious at once that the road was built for strategic purposes: "they built them roads for the transportation of battalions." Juttah, like its neighboring villages, played a great role in the war which raged between two opposing groups of villages around Hebron, one led by Adoraim (Dûrah), the other by Dahariah.

Within forty minutes the roofs of the Juttah dwellings were outlined in the distance.

Most of the inhabitants were on the fields about the village cutting the golden corn. At harvest time even the nights are passed away from home in barns and on threshing floors, and when we reached the village we found all the houses abandoned and the streets deserted. Our chauffeur, a Hebron Arab, remained with the car, and with three Jewish companions I roamed through the streets of Juttah. Here and there a woman's voice was heard. But it is not customary in Juttah to address a woman, nor to enter a house or private courtyard when the menfolk are not present. So we went on alone.

Finally, we found a young man who said that he was one of the children of M'hamara. On our informing him that we were Jews he exclaimed, following the formula we had heard in Hebron: *"Wlad-'Amna!"*

He then led us to the quarter of the village where lived the watchman, J'abrin, the son of Abdul Rahman of the people of Sheikh Abu Ahram.

We found J'abrin at the mosque in the lower section of the village, the Abu Harim quarter. He was a tall, well-built man, forty years old, keen-eyed. His costume was that of the fellaheen of the Hebron mountains; wound around his head was a yellow turban and on his feet were scarlet leather shoes.

We presented our letter and entered into conversation with him.

J'abrin told us that he was one of the watchmen of the village and that Sheikh Abu Ahram, to whom our letter was addressed, was harvesting at a distance of two and a half hours from Juttah. I asked J'abrin whether he was one of the children of M'hamara and whether they were descendants of Jews. He replied unhesitatingly: "Yes, indeed. We belong to M'hamara and are descendants of the Jews of Chaibar. Our forefather was a Jew who came here from the land of Chaibar."

"Jews of Chaibar!" These words, so emphatically uttered by J'abrin the watchman, the son of Abdul Rahman, rang in my ears with startling effect. Descendants of the "Jews of Chaibar," therefore not of the ancient Jews, the peasants mentioned by Eusebius and Hieronimus as living in this very Juttah, nor even of the Hebron Jews who lived there before the Crusaders; but of those legendary Jews of the desert of Chaibar (who, it is recorded, resisted so stoutly conquest by Mohammed as to earn his tolerance and a covenant—broken, however, by a later Caliph), of the fabled remnants of the old Jewish community in Arabia!

J'abrin continued: "This village consists of six 'families,' among whom the land has been distributed. Three parts belong to us—the M'hamaras —and the other three to the rest. The M'hamaras are divided in two. Foremost are those who live in the upper part of the village. There is a smaller group in the quarter of Sheikh Abu Ahram. In the lower section are the children of Hushiyah. The three other families are Harizath, Sha'habin and Dajanah."

J'abrin inquired about the contents of the letter we had brought, and went with us to the village shopkeeper, who read the letter out to him. He then assumed a most respectful attitude and unlocked his heart and lips to us. We walked in the streets of Juttah inspecting its ruins and ancient sites, climbing over fences and stone heaps, descending into caves and pits, examining the acanthus ornamentation and engraved circles on the stones lying derelict about the streets or jutting out from the walls of the houses and public buildings. All of these were stone-built, some of hewed stones undoubtedly taken from ancient ruins, some of stones similar in size and workmanship to those of the Wailing Wall and the Cave of Machpelah and believed by the villagers of Juttah to have come from Carmel and Ziph. And as we walked among the houses of Juttah I questioned J'abrin and he answered me as follows:

"All of us are descendants of one man. Our forefather, Jadna El-Kadim, came here by himself from a far-distant land, from Chaibar, and by his own might and valor conquered and ruled this village. And we, the M'hamaras, are his heirs. Our forefather had two sons, Salem and Owad. Formerly they lived together but, as time went on, they separated: the children of Owad settled in the upper part and those of Salem in the lower part of the village.

"Our ancestor was a great *Jabar* (hero). When he came from Chaibar he fought against forty brigands and overcame them by killing all of them in the cave to which we will presently come. At that time there were two 'familes' in the village who fought one against the other: the Hushiyahs and the Sha'habins. The latter dominated and oppressed the Hushiyahs, who then appealed to our Jewish forefather for help. Our forebear came to their aid and helped them to throw off the yoke of the Sha'habins. The war was waged for many years, perhaps fifty. Our ancestor took away a large part of the enemy's land and all the inhabitants of Juttah were subjected to his rule, for they made him their *malik* (king)."

The last words were uttered with emphasis and great pride.

"And what was the name of your forefather who came from Chaibar?"

J'abrin was absorbed in thought. Apparently the answer required some effort of concentration. Then, suddenly, he exclaimed:

"M'heimar! And after him we are all called today 'M'hamara.'"

"Our forefather M'heimar," continued J'abrin, "married a woman of the Hushiyahs, who bore him two sons, Salem and Owad, whom I have already mentioned. And afterwards all the children of Hushiyah joined the tribe."

As he spoke, we approached the cave which now serves as an oil-press. The cave is large enough to contain a score of persons or more. Two other fellaheen entered the cave with us. J'abrin once again recounted, in the presence of these fellaheen, the heroic achievements of his forebear in this very cave.

"When our ancestor, M'heimar, came from Chaibar, he found thirty-nine persons here, all of them robbers, and at the entrance of the cave a dog stood guard. M'heimar the Jabar slaughtered all the thirty-nine and the dog—forty in all."

Then, turning to us and pointing to the fellaheen, he said: "They are not of our family. One of them belongs to the Sha'habin and the other to the Harizath. I have told nothing but the truth." And to the fellaheen: "Can you gainsay what I have told?"

The fellaheen silently approved. Then one of them said: "*Sahih!*" (It is true.)

J'abrin added with a smile: "Sometimes, when we quarrel, our neighbors tease us by saying, 'You are descendants of Jews.'"

"Do you thereby feel insulted?"

"Feel insulted!" exclaimed J'abrin in astonishment and, with a glance towards his friends of the Sha'habins, and Harizaths: "Why should we be ashamed? Had we not been Jews, we could not have conquered this village."

Our companion from Hebron asked: "What right had you to seize this land from others?"

J'abrin replied: "Since the coming of the English, curious customs have been introduced. Everything is being registered in books—nothing like it was ever known before. Surely the root of everything is action—possession follows action, and that was the way of our ancestor."

He said this quite simply and firmly, in the hearing of the fellaheen, from whose forefathers M'heimar the Jew had conquered the land and by whom he had subsequently been made ruler. These sons of the vanquished listened in silence, as if these statements were well known and beyond dispute.

"And how many years ago did M'heimar live?"

This could not be answered by J'abrin. He stood absorbed in silence for a few moments; then, in order to fix a time, he chose a method, natural and not less exact than another.

"M'heimar begot Salem and Salem begot Omar, Omar begot Amar who begot Adbul Rahman—my father; thus we are the sixth generation from M'heimar."

Then he added: "Salem had another son called Mohammed. Mohammed had a son Isa, who had a son called Salameh, who is still living. Omar the son of Salem, brother of Mohammed, made war against Ibrahim Pasha of Egypt. He fortified himself in a mosque and withstood the enemy a long time, even after Hebron had fallen. My forefather Omar possessed rifles with which he shot down the armies of Ibrahim Pasha. The Pasha then brought cannons and began demolishing the fortress until he forced Omar to surrender."

We had by now left the cave and came to the Mosque-Fortress. Here we saw the apertures through which Omar aimed at the Egyptian forces and the lintel which had been split by the cannons of Ibrahim Pasha.

From these stories, and especially by calculating from the period of Omar, the grandchild of M'heimar who fought against Ibrahim Pasha about 1834, we determined the time of M'heimar, the Jew, who came from Chaibar and conquered the village of Juttah—according to the traditions of the village—as that of the second half of the eighteenth century: the period which just preceded the coming of the first Chassidim to Safed and Tiberias.

And so it was at the time when the ancient Jewish Yishub in Palestine had dwindled noticeably that this wanderer from a distant land of wonders had arrived, had conquered the village and imposed his rule on it, had won himself adherents who called themselves after his name. For not only his descendants to the sixth generation, but also those who joined with them, are proud to bear his Jewish name.

On our way to the mosque, J'abrin showed us the house in the lower section of the village where M'heimar lived after assuming the reins of government. This house is Roumi (Roman or Byzantine). The upper part was rebuilt, probably at the time of the Crusades.

On the way J'abrin told me: "My father, Abdul Rahman, died at the age of 100 and, just before his death, he said to me, 'The most important members of our family are not here, but in Chaibar. We have had a bad harvest this last year. Perhaps we ought to return to the country of our origin, to Chaibar. But where Chaibar is situated, that, for the life of me, I cannot tell.' "

We sat down in the square facing the Mosque of Omar ben Salem. One of the children brought us a pitcher of water and greedily we drank until our thirst was slaked. From where we were sitting we could see the distant villages of Carmel, Ziph and Maôn, ruins of ancient buildings.

Days of long ago seemed to merge with each other, Bible tales with the chronicles of Eusebius, the wars of Joshua and the wars of Ibrahim Pasha, M'heimar, the mysterious Jew of Chaibar, and the shadows of his ancestors who withstood the world conquerors from Arabia. . . .

J'abrin accompanied us back to our car at the other end of the village. We parted after warm handshakings and he followed us for a long time with contemplative eyes.

All the way back to Jerusalem I could not distract my mind from the images of the strange wanderer from Chaibar: M'heimar the Jew, the King of Juttah. Might not this be a clue to the old, unsolved riddle of Chaibar? For a moment I seemed at the threshold of the solution of that ancient mystery.

(—1930)

The Slave Community of Malta

⚜

CECIL ROTH

For more than two hundred years, and as late as the eighteenth century, there existed on the island of Malta a community of Jewish slaves, protected by the Inquisition and presided over by a Gentile: this is the essence of a fascinating story which has been hitherto virtually unknown and which is now fully disclosed for the first time from documents in the hands of the present writer.

Malta had harbored a Jewish community for almost fifteen centuries after the visit of St. Paul to the island. Catacombs commemorate its existence in Roman times, and government records mark its medieval history. But the island fell, together with Sicily, under the rule of the royal house of Aragon, and the community of Malta shared, in 1492, the fate of the Jews of Spain. There was a brief interval during which there were no Jews on the island. Then followed the amazing interlude of the slaves.

In 1530, Charles V made over Malta to the Knights Hospitaler of the Order of St. John, who had been driven from Rhodes nine years earlier by the Moslems. The whole *raison d'être* of the body and of its tenure of Malta lay in the supposition of a continual state of hostility between the Moslem world and Christendom, of which its members of the Order were, in a sense, the knights-errant. Accordingly, they waged continual maritime warfare, hardly distinguishable from piracy, against the Moslem powers. Seaports were raided and their inhabitants carried off. Shipping was preyed on indiscriminately, captured vessels being brought to Malta, and crews and passengers sold into captivity. Throughout the rule of the Knights, which lasted until they capitulated to the French in 1798, the island was thus a last European refuge of slave traffic and slave labor.

The victims were any persons, of whatever standing, race, age or sex, who happened to be sailing in the captured ships. Jews made a large proportion of the Levantine merchant class and were hence peculiarly subject to capture. Because of their nomadic way of life, disproportionately large numbers were to be found in any vessel sailing between Eastern ports. Also, they formed a considerable element in the population of the Moslem ports subject to raids. So, soon after the establishment of the Knights there, the name of Malta begins to be found with increasing frequency in Jewish literature, and always with an evil association.

The island became in Jewish eyes a symbol for all that was cruel and hateful in the Christian world. Whatever the truth of the contemporary rumor that the Jews financed the great Turkish siege of Malta in 1665, certainly they watched it with anxious eyes and their disappointment at its failure must have been extreme. "The monks of Malta are still today a snare and trap for the Jews," sadly records a Jewish chronicler at the end of his account of the siege. A Messianic prophecy current early in the seventeenth century further expressed the bitterness of Jewish feeling, recounting how the Redemption would begin with the fall of the four kingdoms of ungodliness, first among which was Malta.

A typical capture, and one of the earliest mentioned in Jewish literature, is related in the *Vale of Tears* by Joseph haCohen:

In the year 5312 [1552], the vessels of the monks of Rhodes, of the order of Malta, cruising to find booty, encountered a ship coming from Salonica, whereon were seventy Jews. They captured it and returned to their island. These unhappy persons had to send to all quarters to collect money for the ransom exacted by these miserable monks. Only after payment were they able to continue their voyage.

In 1567, large numbers of Jews, escaping to the Levant from the persecutions of Pius V, fell victims to the Knights. "Many of the victims sank like lead to the depths of the sea before the fury of the attack. Many others were imprisoned in the Maltese dungeons at this time of desolation," writes the chronicler. It was not only those who went down to the sea in ships over whom the shadow hung. Of the Marranos of Ancona who fell victims to the fanaticism and treachery of Paul IV, thirty-eight who eluded the stake were sent in chains to the galleys of Malta, though they managed to escape on the way.

Arrived in Malta, the captives were only at the beginning of their troubles. A very graphic account of conditions is given by an English traveler Philip Skippon, who visited the spot in about 1663:

The slaves' prison is a fair square building, cloister'd round, where most of the slaves in Malta are oblig'd to lodge every night, and to be there about Ave Mary time. They have here several sorts of trades, as barbers, taylors, &c. There are about 2,000 that belong to the order, most of which were now abroad in the galleys; and there are about 300 who are servants to private persons. This place being an island, and difficult to escape out of, they wear only an iron ring or foot-lock. Those that are servants, lodge in their masters' houses, when the galleys are at home; but now, lie a-nights in this prison. Jews, Moors and Turks are made slaves here, and are publickly sold in the market. A stout fellow may be bought (if he is an inferior person) for 120 or 160 scudi of Malta. The Jews are distinguish'd from the rest by a little piece of yellow cloth on their hats or caps, &c. We saw a rich Jew who was taken about a year before, who was sold in the market that morning we visited the prison for 400 scudi; and supposing himself free, by reason of a passport he had from Venice, he struck the merchant that bought him; whereupon he was presently sent hither, his beard and hair shaven off, a great chain clapp'd on his legs, and bastinado'd with 50 blows.

The Holy One, Blessed be He, says a well-known rabbinic proverb, always prepares a remedy before the affliction. So it was in the present case. Among Jews, the idea that a coreligionist should be enslaved by a Gentile and forced to disregard the practices of his religion, with life and honor in constant danger, was altogether abhorrent. Thus from earliest days the Redemption of Captives had ranked high among the acts of charity which a Jew was called on to execute, and it was considered proper that, should a dying man leave money "for the performance of a good deed," without further directions, it should be devoted to this *Pidion Shevuim,* as best deserving the title.

Throughout the Middle Ages this activity continued, leaving ample traces in Halakhic and historical literature. Generally the organization of relief had been purely sporadic. Whenever need arose, an emergency collection would be made and assistance proferred to the needy. With the establishment of the Knights of Malta, the depredations on Mediterranean shipping were systematized and came to have one main center. It therefore became useful and necessary to set up a permanent organization to cope with the new permanent situation.

Now, the great entrepôt of Mediterranean commerce was still Venice, whose trade with the Levant was carried on largely by Jews. It happened, too, that there was at Venice an important settlement of Jews hailing direct from the Iberian Peninsula, whose genius for organization was famed. Thus it came about that there was set up in Venice in the course of the seventeenth century the first of Confraternities for the Redemption of Captives—*Hebrath Pidion Shevuim*—which, in the course of the next hundred years were to spread throughout the great Sephardic communities of the West.

Apparently the terrible Chmielnicki persecutions in Poland and the Ukraine in 1648 served as the immediate occasion. Thousands of Jews were sold into slavery at this time, and at Venice the charitable brothers Aboab started a fund which became permanent. By 1683 it was so successful as to be described as the most wealthy and most highly regarded among Jewish associations in Venice. The organization was under the auspices only of the Levantine and Portuguese congregations; the German and the Italian congregations, though they contributed liberally to the fund, took no official share in the labors of the Confraternity. This was not due to any lack of solidarity: it was that the two Sephardic communities had commercial and social intercourse with the Levant, and were most immediately concerned.

For its funds the association depended only partially on benevolence. Voluntary donations came in, of course, from Venice and from foreign cities as the fame of the association spread. The charitable Zaccharias Porto of Florence, among his immense charitable bequests, left it 1500 piastres. Abraham Texeira, Swedish resident at Hamburg, made an annual subscription during his lifetime, which was continued by his son after his death. Moses Pinto, another wealthy Hamburg Jew, gave a yearly subvention of twenty patacas. The Hamburg community even established an auxiliary society under the name of the *Camara de Cautivos de Veneza*, with its special treasurer or *Gabbai*. On occasions of great urgency, the Confraternity would appeal for help to communities as far afield as London and Amsterdam, which were generally glad to assist. On one occasion, in 1705, every community in Italy, except that of Rome, which was racked with oppressive taxation, contributed to the fund. Sometimes, the native city of a captive would be asked to help raise his ransom.

But all this was regarded as extraordinary income. The ordinary came as a matter of business rather than of charity. In the first place, the members of the Confraternity paid into its funds a certain proportion of their annual profits. But, above all, a special tax of .25 per cent was levied on all goods dispatched from Venice (presumably by sea) to Jewish correspondents, and .125 per cent on all goods taken away in person. This high tax is not so surprising as might appear at first sight. For those who paid it were precisely the Levantine merchants who might have occasion for the services of the Confraternity. It was, as a matter of fact, a form of insurance. That this was the case is shown by the fact that, whenever the fund was curtailed, trade with the Levant was seriously hampered.

The funds were kept in two separate chests or *caixete*, for the "Levantines" and the "Ponentines" (Portuguese) respectively. The amounts varied from time to time. About 1742, the total was 3,500 ducats, of which nearly two-thirds was in the possession of the Portuguese. The combined funds were administered by five officials, the *Deputados dos Cautivos*, of whom three were "Ponentine." These were empowered to dispose of sums up to fifty ducats on their own authority. For the disbursement of larger amounts general approbation was required. The separation of the funds having led to constant dispute, in 1742 recourse was had to the Venetian magistracy of the Cattaveri to make a settlement. It was decided that the two *caixete* should be combined; that the joint organization should continue to be governed by three "Ponentines" and two "Levantines"; and that any sum could be disposed of by four voices out of five.

This parade of internal differences had revealed the wealth of the Confraternity and aroused Gentile cupidity. The consequences were not long in showing themselves. In the same year, the *Inquisitori sopra gli Ebrei,* seeking to bolster the failing loan-banks which the Jews were forced to maintain as a condition of their toleration in Venice, confiscated the whole of the fund. A touching appeal was lodged against the raid. The sums, it was urged, were too small to benefit the banks substantially, while the Levantine merchants, deprived of their insurance, would refuse to trade with Venice. Perhaps, also, reprisals would be made in Turkey. The representations were not without effect. Henceforth, however, the organization came under the control of the *Inquisitori,* whose permission became necessary before any disbursement could be made.

The range of the society's activities was immense. In addition to captives in the Mediterranean trade, prisoners in the constant wars on the mainland of Italy or as far afield as Hungary and Poland, slaves rowing in the galleys in the Adriatic and Tyrrhenian seas from Marseilles and Elba to Corfu and Zante, victims of the Cossacks to the north and of the Tartars to the east, unfortunate Jews groaning in servitude in distant Persia or on the Barbary Coast, all turned for succor to the *Parnassim dos Cautivos* in Venice, certain to receive sympathy, and, if humanly possible, deliverance. But though many galleys slaves were redeemed at other ports, three-quarters of the Confraternity's work was done at Malta. The story of this work, as disclosed by the original documents, is not only a monument of Jewish charity at its finest but also a pathetic record of the persistence of Jewish life under conditions which could not have been more adverse.

Communication was precarious; sometimes a letter took two or three months in transmission from Venice to Malta. It was therefore necessary to have on the spot someone to represent the Confraternity. Under the Knights the exclusion of Jewish residents from Malta was not absolute (the plot of Marlowe's *Jew of Malta* was not so entirely impossible as has generally been assumed). They were, however, admitted only temporarily and under great restrictions. But the Venetian merchants had at Malta correspondents willing enough to do them a service, and a succession of these acted on their behalf as "consuls." They received no salary but must necessarily have benefited as a result of their good offices, acquiring through them business correspondents of absolute reliability whose support was valuable in dealing with Jews in other parts of the world. They had, moreover, the right to charge a commission of five piastres for every slave liberated through their offices.

The first of these agents of whom there is any record is a certain Baccio Bandinelli, namesake of the puny rival of Michelangelo, who acted perhaps from the establishment of the Confraternity down to about 1670, when he was forced to give up by reason of his years. He was succeeded by a French merchant, François Garsin, a Judge of the Tribunal of the *Consolato del Mare*. That the agency was considered desirable is shown by the fact that Thomas Luis da Souza, who had assisted Bandinelli, preferred his services in addition. He was accordingly associated with Garsin for a while (1673-74), until the latter indicated that he would prefer to dispense with assistance. Garsin's zeal was not a selfish one. He refused the commission which he had the right to charge for slaves released through his efforts. "All the greater will be your merit before God," wrote the grateful Deputados, "and by Him will you be rewarded all the more, these being of a nation diverse from your own." Nevertheless, Garsin profited from his connection. The Deputados acted as his agents for the dispatch of merchandise from Venice, and in 1671 did their utmost to procure the intervention of the rabbinate of Alexandria with some of Garsin's recalcitrant debtors in that city. Moreover, he received occasional gifts in token of their gratitude.

Garsin died in the autumn of 1706 after more than thirty-five years of devoted service. His son, Jean-Baptiste, writing to tell the Deputados of his loss, offered to carry on the work. This he did until his death thirteen years later. His successor was a certain Filippo Antonio Crespi, who served for a decade. For some years during this period, a Jewish merchant from Leghorn, Samuel Farfara, resided at Malta and aided the "consul."

When the Maltese galleys returned from a marauding expedition, the "consul" would visit the prison to see whether Jews were among the captives. Frequently there were—usually merchants or travelers sailing peacefully between Levantine ports. Sometimes when Jewish booty was in prospect, not even the flags of Christian powers were respected. The case is on record, for example, of the seizure in 1672 by a Tuscan privateer of ten Jews—seven men and three women— from a Venetian vessel sailing from Alexandria, under the pretext that they were Ottoman subjects. They were brought to Malta and shamelessly offered for sale. A petition presented by the Deputados to the Doge brought about diplomatic representations at the Court of the Grand Duke of Tuscany which were sufficient to procure their release.

This, however, was an exceptional case. Generally there was no shortcut out of the difficulty. Thus, on July 23, 1725, there arrived at the island eighteen prisoners captured while sailing from Salonica to Smyrna. All were poor excepting one—Jacob Fonseca, brother of Daniel Fonseca, Voltaire's friend, who had first been a Marrano priest and later, as a practicing Jew, physician to the Grand Vizier at Constantinople. Fonseca refused to pay ransom, and was subsequently released at the instance of the French court with which his brother had great influence. The rest were left to the charity of their fellow-Jews. Some time previously, in the autumn of 1675, ten poor Jews on their way to Palestine were captured by the treasurer of Malta and brought into the island. Five died of the plague in captivity, and the rest were ultimately liberated for 480 pieces-of-eight. Another great influx came in 1685, when the city of Coron on the Dalmatian coast was sacked;

twenty-one Jewish prisoners were brought in. But these are only a few of the most striking instances. Throughout the period, and especially in time of war (as, for example, during the heroic struggle between Venice and Turkey at the close of the seventeenth century), there was an almost constant influx of prisoners, mostly poor, to keep alive the Jewish connection with Malta and to give the Venetian community an opportunity of exercising its benevolence.

Whenever Jewish captives were found among a batch of new arrivals, the agent would give them a small sum on account of the Confraternity to satisfy immediate needs. Besides, each received an allowance of one ducat weekly until the limitation of funds forced a reduction. Even then, every Jewish slave received the equivalent of four pieces-of-eight in cash annually, distributed on the great festivals, particularly the Passover. In case of illness, they were given an additional allowance. They were housed in a special room taken for them by the agent in the *bagnio* or prison, in which they were confined.

Meanwhile, word would have been sent to Venice at the earliest opportunity to inform the Deputados of the number and quality of the new arrivals and of the sums demanded for their release. When a single individual was in question, there might be enough in hand to ransom him straightway. When a whole shipload came in, it was necessary to have recourse to all sides to collect the amount required. It occasionally happened, too, that one slave would be set free to collect money for the release of the others, or that a wealthy merchant might be able to give satisfactory security for his ransom. But more frequently the victims were indigent, and it was left to the Venetian society to look after their welfare and deliverance.

The mechanism of release was not always simple. The Jew was rarely as rich as he was reputed to be, but his reputation for wealth was greatest precisely where he was least known. The usual price standard of a slave tended, therefore, to disappear whenever a Jew was concerned. He was worth, not his value, but whatever could be extorted from his brethren. Ransom degenerated into blackmail. Fifteen centuries earlier, the Rabbis of the Talmud had realized that this was a case in which it was necessary to turn for once a deaf ear to suffering, lest a premium be put on the enslavement of Jews. They ordained, accordingly, that no captive be ransomed for more than his economic value. This was a rule to obey which was hard for Jews, "Compassionate sons of compassionate sires," and generally the price paid for a Jew was higher by far than that of a Moslem.

On occasion, the Jews were mercilessly exploited. The owner of one Judah Surnago, a man of seventy-five whose value in the open market would have been negligible, was unable to obtain the sum which he demanded in ransom. Thereupon, he shut him up naked in a cellar for two months, giving him nothing to eat but black bread and water. The old man came out blind and unable to stand. His master then threatened to load him with chains and to pluck out his beard and eyelashes if the sum asked were not forthcoming. Ultimately, the Deputados redeemed him for 200 ducats. For a certain Aaron Afia of Rhodes, bought in 1793 by a speculating owner, 600 ducats were demanded. To stimulate the zeal of his coreligionists, Afia's owner kept him in chains and threatened him with the galleys. The owners would not believe, wrote Garsin in despair, that they were poverty-stricken. The Deputados were horrified. "We are not in a condition," they wrote, "to make such exorbitant expenditure. If they do not moderate their price there will be disaster for the poor wretches, who will die in slavery, and the owners will lose their capital." For a certain Rabbi Isaac Moreno of Belgrade with his wife and three children, the Deputados were willing in 1673 to pass their usual limit and pay 300 piastres for which (so low were funds) they would have to dip into their own pockets. The owners demanded 575 piastres. "If the said masters expect to obtain more for a useless old man and a sick woman and three children, one of whom is blind, who have had nothing out of him (saving your reverence!) but lice, they are much mistaken," they wrote the "consul." The owners retaliated by attempting to convert one of the children, but the Deputados, on principle, refused to raise their offer. In another case, when one Abraham Perez and five companions were taken, one, Joseph Levy, was killed under the lash to stimulate the others to greater liberality. The rest were ultimately released, partly through their own efforts.

In 1702, a speculator had purchased three men and a woman of sixty for 350, 304, 299 and 72 ducats respectively. "It astounds us that they could be sold at such extravagant prices," wrote the Deputados. "They can be sure that they will remain on their hands as long as they live, for our resources do not allow us to order their redemption even for as little as sixty. . . . It would be as well to publish abroad what we have told you in this matter, so that no one will desire in the future to purchase at such rates."

Encouraged by a governmental order that Jewish slaves should not be sent to the galleys, an attempt was even made (with the help of a few judicious gifts) to obtain an edict fixing a fair price for Jewish slaves and forbidding their being put up at public auction. Apparently nothing came of it, for complaints continued without intermission. "Though it displeases us to see the miseries which those unhappy wretches suffer," wrote the Deputados in 1703, "we do not see how to contribute to their release with more than we have offered in the past, by reason of the calamitous times which are on us and the restriction of business. Their masters should moderate the rigorous pretensions which they have for their ransom: for if they do not they will assuredly lose all, by reason of their inevitable death in consequence of their miseries."

Such was liable to be the fate of any wretched Jew who fell into the hands of an extortionate master. Every effort was made, therefore, to purchase prisoners before they had been put up at public auctions. In the auctions, the "consul" was empowered (when there was money in hand) to pay up to sixty or seventy ducats without preliminary authorization, or, at moments of especial affluence, even more. Some of the original deeds of sale are extant, or were until recently, for example, that of Abraham de Mordecai Alvo, "white," of Smyrna, aged twenty-two, disposed of by his captors for a sack of bones "according to the use of the corsairs" and bought by the "consul" for the sum of 110 ducats. In 1677, six slaves belonging to the Treasurer were released together for 480 pieces-of-eight. For every sale a notarial agreement and the license of the Grand Master was essential. Sometimes, the unhappy prisoners were sent to the galleys, in spite of the governmental order to the contrary, and so it occasionally happened that the Deputados had the opportunity of ransoming slaves from Malta in Venice itself. Thus, in 1704, they appealed to the community of Leghorn for assistance in raising 2,000 reals for the release of three victims on a vessel then in port from pains "worse than those of death."

Despite all efforts, a long period frequently elapsed before slaves could be liberated. Thus a certan Isaac Esicrit who was released for one hundred ducats in 1716 had been captive for five years and worse cases are recorded.

Consequently, there was frequently in Malta a veritable community of slaves, as distinct from an agglomeration of isolated individuals. In 1672, for example, there were no fewer than sixteen left unredeemed at one time, while the total number of persons bought in that year was twenty-nine. Perhaps the most remarkable feature in the whole pathetic story is the way in which these miserable captives found it possible to carry on their religious life under such atrocious circumstances.

The authorities on the island were tolerant, as the ecclesiastical arm generally was, regarding Jews. There was an old authorization permitting the Jewish slaves to have their cemetery and synagogue, with scrolls of the Law. Slave-owners, however, were often less sympathetic, compelling their chattels to work on Sabbaths and holidays. The Deputados professed themselves unable to comprehend how they could do this, since they had acquired only corporeal dominion over their slaves. On March 3, 1673, they wrote to the community of Rome suggesting that some action be taken there, at the center of the Catholic faith and of ultimate authority over the Knights, to remedy this state of affairs. It would seem that something was effected, though none too speedily. In 1675 the Inquisitor of Malta issued an order prohibiting that Jewish slaves be compelled to work on their religious holidays. Thus facilities for a minimum of observance were ensured.

In consequence of this tolerant attitude on the one side and of remarkable tenacity on the other, there came into existence what is surely the most remarkable Jewish community that has ever existed —one composed exclusively of slaves, with its numbers continually recruited by prisoners brought in by sheer force, or depleted by releases effected through death or ransom. The Deputados address them in Hebrew in full form: *"To all the congregation of the groaning and captive which are in the city of Malta—may the Lord bring them out from anguish to enlargement; Amen, this be His will!"*

The community, however small, required services which could be rendered only by one who was free. Who else was available but the agent of the Venetian society? It is strange to see how this Catholic man of affairs looked after the religious welfare of these unfortunate creatures of a different faith. He worked with a conscientiousness and a fervor which would have been praiseworthy even in a Jew. On the occasion of the Holy Days, he distributed among the slaves some small gratifications, sometimes without the express consent of his principals, who, he knew, would honor whatever he did. It was the agent, too, who made provision for a modest place of worship. He took a room in the *bagnio* which was fitted up as a synagogue. At first it was used as such only on festivals, later, on the Sabbath as well. Originally, the Jewish slaves slept here, but subsequently a couple of additional rooms were taken for their accommodation. The goaler acted as caretaker, receiving regular payment. In the autumn of 1673, the Deputados authorized Garsin to have necessary repairs done to the doors of the synagogue, and, two years later, to the reading desk. In the *bagnio*, too, the slaves had their oven—which in 1685 Garsin had been ordered to provide—for baking unleavened bread for the Passover. In 1707, when the number of slaves was small and regular religious worship momentarily ceased, one of the two rooms was given up.

There was a copy of the Scroll of the Law for the use of the slaves, doubtless originally sent from Venice, though it was not unknown for one to find its way to the island with other booty. If the number of slaves fell below the quorum of ten necessary for the full formalities of public worship, the Scroll was looked after by the agent. Thus, in 1696, when the last Jewish slave then in Malta died, the agent was instructed as to the preservation of the Scroll of the Law and other appurtenances of public ritual. When the younger Garsin entered upon his voluntary duties in 1707, he was recommended to take care of the Scroll and other Hebrew books until they were needed.

But, whatever might have been hoped, the days of the Congregation of Slaves were not yet over, for there was a recrudescence of piracy. "Yesterday," wrote the Consul, on May 6, 1713, "they came to take the Law, wishing from now onwards, being eleven in number, to say their Mass. I gave them also stuff to make the mantle: and they stand in need of a table, with the pulpit." Besides these bare necessities, they went to the extravagance of having a Perpetual lamp to burn in their synagogue and bells wherewith to adorn the Scroll. They had a curtain, too, to hang for the Ark.

Another necessary adjunct of settled religious life was the cemetery, for the conditions of life under which the slaves lived in so insalubrious a climate (Malta is notorious for its fever) made this requisite out of all proportion to their numbers. In 1674, without applying to head-quarters for authorization, Garsin paid for the burial of two poor Jews who had died in an English ship going to Constantinople. This was done, however, in unconsecrated ground. For a short time afterwards the slaves complained to the Deputados that they had no place in which to bury any of their number who might die. On October 26, 1675, Garsin was authorized to purchase a plot of ground for this purpose at a price not exceeding fifty ducats. A couple of years later plague broke out in the island, and, since it was impossible to bury the dead in the ordinary cemetery, a special piece of ground had to be acquired as a plague pit. It was on March 17, 1677, that Garsin, for seventy-five ducats, purchased a plot outside Vittoriosa in the name of the Spanish community at Venice. Five slaves had been buried there previously. Arrangements were made for surrounding the cemetery with a wall. Despite this, in 1727 it was found that it was being treated as a private garden, and Filipo Antonio Crespi, the new Consul, urged the Deputados to find the title-deeds. A permanent cemetery was established in 1784 at the expense of the community of Leghorn for the benefit of the freedmen, as an inscription over the bricked-up gateway still testifies.

Even in the depths of their misery, the slaves found an opportunity to indulge in the Jewish luxury of charity. A touching appeal was made by two of the slaves, both fathers of families, on behalf of one of their companions, Solomon ben Isaac Azich (Aziz?), of Leghorn, a youth of seventeen who had been captured while on the way home from Smyrna. He was in the service of the Grand Master, being forced to carry intolerably heavy burdens and to work beyond the limits of his strength. The two elder men urged that intervention should be made on his behalf, not mentioning their own plight. Despite their miserable material condition, the slaves somehow found the opportunity to translate their charitable sentiments into works, though they were not always well-directed. The case is on record of one unmitigated scoundrel, Isaiah Orefice, probably a galley-slave, who was in the island in 1716 pretending to be a captive like the rest, and without doubt obtaining relief from the agent on that score. The tale he told was so piteous that the compassion of the other slaves was aroused. They assisted him to get away, not only by entreaties to the agent, but also with gifts from their own slender store of money. He rewarded their benevolence by taking with him the quilt and cloak of another slave, Abraham Ajet, and the prayerbooks of the Synagogue.

Even more touching was the pawning by the slaves in 1672 of the lamps and petty articles of silver which their synagogue boasted in order to assist in the ransoming of Moses Messini and Mordecai Maio, two of their brethren in distress. The Deputados rated them roundly for this action, which might have deplorable consequences in the future and ordered the Christian agent to redeem the articles from pawn. Nevertheless, there seemed to be an undercurrent of admiration in their rebuke.

The religious life of the captured was enriched frequently by the presence on the island of scholarly prisoners. The most eminent scholar of whom we have any record, as well as one of the earliest, was Jacob leBeth Levi (Jacob ben Israel the Levite), a native of the Morea and translator of the Koran into Hebrew. He was later Rabbi of Zante, where he died in 1634, leaving a considerable body of Responsa. Earlier in his career he was carried off with his household and all his property to the "den of lions and house of imprisonment" at Malta. His deliverance he regarded as a special manifestation of Providence. More than one victim redeemed by the Confraternity is referred to as Rabbi or Haham; for example, that Joseph Cohen Ashkenazi of Constantinople, who was redeemed at the close of the seventeenth century for 150 ducats. Another was one Samuel aben Mayor, purchased in Malta by a speculating Armenian and ransomed later through the congregation of Ferrara. "Emissaries of Mercy," on their way to collect alms in the Diaspora for the four Holy Cities of Palestine, were especially liable to interception at sea. Thus, an Emissary of Safed was captured irregularly with nine other persons in a Venetian vessel in 1672. In 1666, a party of rabbis from Jerusalem was captured while on their way to convey the glad tidings of the Messianic pretensions of Sabbatai Zevi.

An interesting and tragic figure appears among the slaves in the last decades of the seventeenth century. Moses Azulai was doubtless of the famous Moroccan family of scholars and mystics, some of whom had emigrated to Palestine. How he was brought to Malta it has been impossible to trace, but his presence there is attested at least as early as 1671. He must have fallen into the hands of a mild master, for there is some indication that he engaged in trade on his behalf, nor did he make appeal for ransom. His preoccupations were not for himself but for others, and for a long time he was coadjutor to the worthy Garsin. He would report what captives had been brought in, what steps were being taken to release them and who had been ransomed. The Deputados had perfect trust in him, advising their agent to rely on him implicitly for the regulation of the internal affairs of the slaves. He seems to have been a man of some learning, who corresponded occasionally in Hebrew and could not support captivity without the solace of Jewish literature. He is, indeed, first mentioned in connection with the dispatch to Malta of a copy of the *Midrash Tanhuma*. He was probably ringleader of the slaves who requested a perpetual calendar (*Sefer Iburim*), and some time after we find him obtaining another calendrical work, the *Tikkun Issachar*. A work of practical utility in another direction which was sent him was the *Pitron Halomot*, or Interpretation of Dreams, as well as the liturgical subsidiary, *Maamadot*, with a commentary. His rabbinical knowledge was at times of practical use. In 1673 and again in 1685 he was called on by fellow-slaves to draw up bills of divorcement. It was owing to his insistence that the oven for unleavened bread was provided. When any of the slaves were refractory (as, considering their misery, quite apart from their race, was no matter for surprise), it was he who was enjoined to restore discipline. From all this it would appear that he acted as religious leader of the community during the period he was on the island.

Azulai seems for all these years to have made no effort to obtain his freedom. Apparently he was content to remain in his position as guide to the captive Jews who came and departed, to maintain his post—the one constant in the shifting population.

At the beginning of the last decade of the seventeenth century, however, there came about a change in the condition of the Jewish slaves in Malta that altered also his apparent determination to make the island his home. The maritime war in the Levant was not being carried on with much vigor. Victims were fewer. The slaves remaining on the island were released one by one. The calls on the Deputados at Venice became more and more rare, the total of their outgoing letters being reduced from a maximum of forty in 1673 to as few as two twenty years later. By the end of 1691, Azulai had only one companion left—a certain Moses Joseph of Safed. He began to feel lonely. And after twenty years of captivity, during which he had been in constant communication with Venice, he asked for the first time for his own release. He was advanced in years and had for a long time served unstintingly without recompense. He had seen scores of fellow-slaves liberated while he remained in uncomplaining captivity. His demand now could not be refused. The Deputados of Leghorn added forty reals to the fifty contributed by those of Venice, and Garsin was instructed to go as high as 120 if necessary. So that Azulai's companion should not be left in utter solitude, Garsin was to negotiate his release as well. In the latter case there was rapid success and the Palestinian prisoner sailed for freedom on a French ship for Tripoli after 180 ducats had ransomed him. But over the unhappy Azulai, thus left in complete loneliness, there was some difficulty, for the anxiety of the Deputados increased the expectations of his owner. An additional contribution was elicited without much difficulty from Leghorn, and Garsin was authorized to go up to 150 reals. Success seemed at last assured. Instructions were given for the care of the communal property. Garsin was to retain the keys of the Synagogue and the custodianship of the oven and burial grounds. The Scroll of the Law and books and other ritual objects were to be placed by Azulai in a sealed chest and entrusted to the agent's keeping until opportunity should offer itself for dispatching it to Venice. For the expenses of his voyage, Azulai was to be given five reals. At last, in July, 1694, it seemed that his long sufferings were at an end. But when the Deputados at Venice were expecting to hear of his final release, they received instead the information of his death (April, 1696).

Out of the horrors of slavery there was always one easy escape—baptism. But this simple expedient was an alternative rarely chosen by the slaves. An exception was one Jacob Cardiel of Tunis. When the ship on which he was sailing was captured he fought to defend it. Fearing ill-treatment in consequence, if his religion should be discovered, he passed as a Moslem for the first year or more of his captivity. Realizing, perhaps, that he had better chance of release as a Jew, he declared himself as one, after fourteen months. The Deputados, informed of this, instructed their agent to make inquiries. Ultimately his claims were accepted; but when matters moved more slowly than he had hoped, Cardiel decided to take the shortest road out of his trouble. After three years' captivity, he was baptized—more, wrote the "consul," from desperation than from zeal. Another convert, Guiseppe Antonio Cohen (though there is no definite proof he was a slave) attained some fame, as well as a commemorative tablet and a small annuity, by betraying the Turkish Plot of 1749—a curiously contradictory historical parallel to *The Jew of Malta.*

Once a person had apostasized, the Deputados naturally lost interest in his fate. "As for the young woman from Coron, whom you were to ransom," they wrote the "consul" in 1688, "since she has passed to another religion, you are to remove her utterly from your mind."

It was not only human captives that the association felt moved to redeem. At the raid in Coron in 1685, during the Turko-Venetian War, besides the twenty-one individuals captured (mostly women and children), large numbers of books, with Scrolls of the Law and their trappings, were carried away among the spoil. The Deputados were careful to instruct their representative on the island to attempt to redeem these. In 1699, Garsin gave a woman ten ducats for five Hebrew books of the nature of which he had no idea, sure of the approval of his principals. Rabbi Jacob leBeth Levi, a century before, was able to bring away from the island an ancient Scroll of the Law, no doubt a redeemed captive like himself.

Precisely how long the Community of Slaves continued its intermittent existence it is impossible to say. In 1749 the slaves in the island were still so numerous as to make possible the Turkish plot which nearly brought Malta under the Crescent at last. With the growth of international peace and humanitarian ideas, the traffic necessarily diminished, but conditions were not fundamentally changed. Slavery ceased in Malta only at the dawn of the nineteenth century, the slaves being freed on the overthrow of the Knights, and their release being confirmed officially on May 15, 1800. The Jew, as merchant and nomad, must have remained peculiarly subject to capture until the last. The case is recorded of the release by the Deputados of Venice of Daniel de Benjamin Silva and his wife Judith as late as 1752 for the sum of 200 ducats, probably from Malta. For Jewish victims at this place were still common. As late indeed as 1768, the community of London forwarded to Leghorn the sum of £80 to assist in ransoming a batch of no fewer than fourteen prisoners, then in captivity at Malta. Similar conditions must have prevailed in some degree as late as the period of the French Revolutionary wars. By this time, however, travel at sea was becoming more secure, and the need for ransom less frequent. The duration of the Venetian hegemony covers, therefore, the most interesting portion of this community's history.

In their last days, the Knights began to show greater tolerance, and a few Jewish merchants settled in this commercially attractive center. Even some redeemed slaves remained and settled as freemen. So, when the British came into possession in 1802, there was the nucleus of a Jewish community already on hand. Under British rule it prospered and increased. Though today on the downward grade, it appears still firmly established, with a rabbi and a synagogue. Among its members, perhaps, are still to be found descendants of the slaves, who introduced a new and heartrending element into the tragic story of Israel, and founded a community the like of which no other place or age has known.

(—1929)

Herzl in Paris

༄ＡＡＯ

JOSEF FRAENKEL

I N 1891 Theodor Herzl went through a crisis. He was in his thirty-second year. He had given up his law practice and for some time had been devoting himself entirely to writing. His contributions had appeared in various newspapers and journals, but this did not satisfy his ambition. Nor was he content with his work as a playwright. His comedies "Poachers" (*Wilddiebe*) and "The Lady in Black" (*Die Dame in Schwarz*), which he wrote in collaboration with Hugo Wittman, as well as his other plays, had been produced in the Vienna Burgtheater. But this, too, was not enough for his dreams.

His Jewish experiences troubled him. His pride suffered when he heard insulting remarks about the Jews, and he heard them frequently. The "Jewish problem" gave him no rest, especially after his best friend, Heinrich Kana, too weak to fight for his existence as a Jew and a journalist, committed suicide in February 1891. He wanted to immortalize his friend in a novel, but in Vienna he could not write. Terribly depressed, he fled to a Spanish village where at last he found peace to work and dream.

While Herzl was in Spain, the *Neue Freie Presse* of Vienna decided to send a correspondent to Paris. This paper, founded by Michael Etienne and edited by Moritz Benedikt and Eduard Bacher, was the most important and influential journal in the Austro-Hungarian monarchy. Several years earlier, when Herzl was twenty-seven, he had applied there in vain for a position. Now when the editors consulted Hugo Wittman, Herzl's collaborator, on whether they should offer the post to Herzl, Wittman strongly urged them to do so. Thus, in October 1891, Herzl received an invitation by telegraph to go to Paris for the newspaper, and he went there the same month.

Herzl soon became known as the best correspondent of the *Neue Freie Presse*. His reports read like scenes from a drama, and his political surveys like essays. In 1895 a selection of his reports on the proceedings of the French Parliament was published under the title, *The Palais Bourbon*.

In later years Herzl regretted that he had not started a diary immediately upon his arrival in Paris. He knew everybody. Jean Jaurès; Barthou; Poincaré who, as Herzl thought, "would become President of the Cabinet"; Léon Bourgeois, the man "who committed no follies"; and Georges Clemenceau, who "cannot praise." He admired Clemenceau tremendously, considered him the greatest man in the French Parliament. The "Tiger" returned the compliment many years later, calling Herzl a genius such as appears only once in several generations, like Socrates, Washington or Zola.

Herzl's interest in France was by no means confined to politics. He was a frequent visitor at the Louvre, at the Mazarin Library, at the Opera; and he had friends in all the social and literary circles of Paris. He was also often found at workers' meetings or with the peasants in the villages.

The French capital was the seat of progress as well as of reaction. The Panama scandal and the Dreyfus affair aroused deep agitation. The "League for Anti-Semitism" added fuel to the fire. France stood on the threshold of revolution. Herzl's reports filled pages of the *Neue Freie Presse*. Nothing was glossed over or distorted. Paul Painlévé called Herzl "a great friend of France," and he was. But that did not prevent him from criticizing, particularly the army officers who were affected by anti-Semitism.

Herzl felt the revolutionary storm as he sat in the press gallery of the Parliament of France. The Palais Bourbon was his university. It was there he learned how the state was run, he learned about social problems, constitutions, *negotiorum gesto*—all of which he afterwards incorporated in his *The Jewish State*.

And he studied anti-Semitism. Previously in Vienna he had read the anti-Semitic works of Eugen von Duehring; in Paris he delved into the anti-Semitic works of Edouard Drumont. His attitude towards the problem changed—he felt stronger. Racial hatred was growing; he knew anti-Semitism could not be defeated by speeches and committees. What could be done? He compared the societies formed to fight anti-Semitism with the futile leagues for peace, and concluded that the discovery of a terrible explosive was a far greater incentive to work for peace than a thousand mild apostles and societies. . . .

French authorities became aware of Herzl for the first time in 1889 when he reviewed and praised, in Viennese papers, *Les Sous-Offs* ("Sub-Lieutenants"), an anti-military novel by Lucien Descaves. The author had been tried and exonerated by a French court, but the authorities apparently never forgot Herzl. When, some years later, his journalistic activities in Paris increased, the French authorities became suspicious. A police officer was assigned to keep check on his movements. After that Herzl could never go anywhere without his "shadow."

I have found in the archives of the French Police-Prefecture (Dossier No. 92,509) about twenty documents concerning the *Neue Freie Presse* correspondent Herzl before he had published *The Jewish State* and before he had founded the World Zionist Organization.

These documents have not been previously published.

On February 1, 1893, the Commissioner of Police received the following letter signed by the Premier and the Minister of the Interior:

We would ask you to give us details regarding a certain Herzl, residing in Paris, rue de Monceau 8. He sends disquieting telegrams to Vienna to the address "Etienne Vienna."

They received the following report prepared by the police officer assigned to the Herzl case:

The Republic of France
Paris, 23rd February 1893
Commissioner of Police
Office of the Commissioner
1. Enquiry Section
1. Office
No. P.P.H.

Information regarding Mr. Theodor Herzl, Austrian citizen, Reporter of the *Neue Freie Presse,* Vienna.

REPORT

The said Theodor Herzl, Reporter of the *Neue Freie Presse* in Vienna, to whom the four enclosures relate, is about 36 and is thought to have been born in Vienna. He is married and the father of two children.

He arrived in Paris in October 1891, presumably entered via Bordeaux, and seems to have considerable means at his disposal.

Before he came to Paris, Herzl had published several articles in Viennese newspapers about Lucien Descaves' book *Sous-Offs*. In these articles he declared that the author of this book had not exaggerated in his description of the French Army, and that the Tripartite Powers would, therefore, have no cause for anxiety about the result of a war with our country.

We found further that Herzl declared one evening on returning home that he had paid more than 100 francs for the dispatch of telegrams to his newspaper. These telegrams concerned a split which had just taken place in the Chamber of Deputies over the Egyptian affair.

He also apparently publishes literary chronicles in the Viennese newspaper. We have every reason to believe that the cables which he sends to the address of "Etienne Vienna" are meant for the *Neue Freie Presse*, as this newspaper had as its founder and chief editor a certain Mr. Etienne, who died in the year 1879, and who may have left a son who takes part in some way or another in the publication of the newspaper.

Herzl is little known in the quarter in which he lives. He is seldom visited. But, on the other hand, his incoming correspondence is very great. This foreigner belongs to the Jewish faith. He sometimes has slight quarrels with his parents, who are very thrifty and who are said to reproach him for living too lavishly.

The fact that he speaks fluent French leads one to believe that he has not lived in his homeland for a long time now. It is not known whether he bears any enmity towards France. He has not complied with the decree of 2nd October 1888 regarding foreigners living in France. His name does not figure in criminal records.

(*Signed*) ANGERS
Police Officer

There are several biographical inaccuracies in this report. Herzl was thirty-three, not thirty-six, at that time. He was not born in Vienna but in Budapest. These errors were corrected in later documents.

Several other inquiries about Herzl having been addressed to the Paris Commissioner of Police, a later statement was prepared about him, as follows:

Surname: Herzl
Christian Name: Theodor
Son of: Jacob and Jeanette Diament
Born: 2nd May 1860, in Budapest
Citizenship: Austrian
Married to: Julie Naschauer, born in Budapest on the 1/2/1868
Children: Three. Pauline, born 4/3/1890 in Vienna; Jean (Hans), on the 10th June 1891, in Vienna; and Margarete (Trude), born on the 20/5/1893 in Paris.

Profession: Journalist
Present address: For the last two years at rue de Monceau 8, at the
  yearly rental of 6,000 francs.
Social connections and political opinion: None.
Reference to his integrity and character: None.
Documents: Austrian Passport issued in Vienna on the 15th June
  1889, No. 26
Personal description:
  Height: 5 ft. 9 in.
  Color of hair: Brown
  Visible distinguishing marks: None
Any convictions: No
Military position in his country: Unknown
Does he receive letters from abroad: Yes, from his family and from
  the newspaper on which he works.
Can he be regarded as a suspicious character: No
Associations or Parties of which he is a member: None

In February 1895 a letter addressed to Herzl was intercepted by
the police. It was written by a Mr. H. Ilman of Graz, and praised an
article by Herzl on Herman Sudermann's *Fatherland* (*"Heimat"*).

Sudermann and Herzl were friends. They had met in Capri in the
year 1887 and had often discussed literary matters. Though Sudermann's plays were received very well by the public, many critics re-
proached him for bringing "poison and frivolity into the pure spirit of
the German people." Herzl was of a different opinion.

The police ordered an immediate translation of Ilman's letter. The
following is an extract from it:

> I have for a long time read your Paris articles with very great in-
> terest. I could say, ever since they began to appear in the *Neue Freie
> Presse*. They are written in a wonderful and most unusual language,
> curt, concise and rich in content, and show not only a most significant
> talent but also a manly independence of character. You do not court
> success but go straight to the point and see things as they are. . . .
> Let us rejoice that there still is as brave and wise a man as you in our
> degenerated business-minded journalistic world. In this spirit, I pay
> tribute to you and prophesy for you a great future. . . .

There are two more notes in the "Herzl File" of the Paris Police
Archives:

24th November 1895

Herzl has finally left Paris. His place as correspondent on the *Neue
Freie Presse* has been taken by Dr. Frischauer.

Extract from *Figaro:*

Paris, 4th July 1904

Theodor Herzl, the well-known writer, novelist and romantic, for seven years reporter for the Vienna *Neue Freie Presse* in Paris, leader of the Zionist Movement, died in Edlach, near Vienna, at the age of 44.

(*—1948*)

Memories of the Jewish Legion

MOISHE RIVLIN

H<small>E WAS</small> typical Lancashire, the British officer who reviewed us on our last parade, but he heaved a distinctly Jewish sigh. He had aged perceptibly since first he took command, on that gallant day when we had set out to recapture Jerusalem from the Turk. Something of Jewish resignation had entered into his soul.

"Another bloody war may break out, but I am certain of one thing," he said ruefully. "King George will never again indulge in the luxury of a Jewish Legion."

These were his parting words, poor man, spoken more in sorrow than in anger. He took one look at our ragged lines—at the sharp command of attention, one man had slumped this way, and another that way, one held his gun up, another down—and sadly he dismissed us. He was obviously glad to be rid of us. But we forgave him and took his prophecy quite cheerfully. Certainly there were in our eyes no tears of shame, in our bosoms no pangs of remorse. We were a Jewish army, and entirely without conscience. . . .

A number of years have passed since that memorable occasion: the tenth anniversary of the forming of the Jewish Legion has just been celebrated. Much has and will be spoken, and deservedly so, of the heroism of the first Jewish army in Palestine since the Dispersion, but one phase of the matter will, I am afraid, be somewhat neglected. Not much is likely to be said of what took place when hoarse and despairing British officers undertook to fix on stubborn Jewish necks the yoke of military discipline and the sacred British army codes. "Theirs not to reason why, theirs but to do and die"—and all that sort of thing. Expect free spirits of the Café Royal to swallow that?

What a business it all was! The sergeants swore, the captains and colonels grew puffy with rage. As for the Jewish soldiers, they were

calm: their reasons were good, their logic irreproachable. Let a British
general give them an argument—they were ready for him.

This obtuse rationality, I must say immediately, came not from the
sober and patriotic Palestinians, nor from the thoroughly obedient
English division of the Legion. All the recalcitrants, all the trouble-
makers, all the "lawyers" of the Legion were from America.

The vast majority of the English group were men who had been
long drafted into the ranks, and had received permission to be transferred to the Legion. Some few had entered directly from civilian
life, but these, too, would have been drafted in time. The British
members were, as a result, a subdued group in the main, wholly
amenable to British discipline. They might curse the war and the
army, they might curse especially Jabotinsky and the Jewish Legion,
forgetting for the moment that in the regular British army their lot
might have been somewhat worse, but they harbored no illusions whatsoever that the army was any sort of trade union. They did their duty
as they were told.

The Palestinian members of the Legion were to a man volunteers
who had joined the Legion as soon as the flight of the Turks before
the British armies left them free to do so. They were men of high
ideals. Among them were such leaders in thought and action as Moishe
Smilansky, Berel Katzenelson, Yavneeli, Dov Hoz and others. They
maintained strict discipline, not so much because they loved the King
and feared the British army officers, as from supersensitiveness to the
prestige of Jewish soldiers. They were desperately anxious to prove
their worth to England, and were willing therefore to endure soup
without salt, and make bricks without straw.

The American contingent was not so idealistic. And most of them
were from the ranks of the Poalei-Zion, and brought with them trade-
union traditions. With such a background, it is not surprizing that to
this day their proudest boast is that they organized successfully the
first strike ever to take place in the British Army. . . .

The American group supplied a connecting link between the other
two groups which greatly helped to make the Legion a military entity.
The fact that it spoke English constituted a bond with the British
group; its Zionism gave them common ground with the Palestinians.
But it was itself by no means homogeneous. Only a small minority
were American born—the majority came originally from Russia,

Poland, Galicia or Rumania. In no other group were there so many
varied elements, such a Babel of tongues, such extreme differences of
opinion. Passing their line of tents, one could hear Hebrew, Yiddish in
all dialects, English in all its accents, Russian, French, Spanish, and
one or two other languages. And one could find men like Ben-Zwi and
Ben-Gurion, perfect zealots, in a tent next to someone like "Chicky,"
who did most of his fighting for the Holy Land behind iron bars in the
guardhouse. There were Jews who entered the Legion "to show these
Irish bozos we, too, have a country to fight for." There was such a
"volunteer for Zion" as "Kid" Lobster who, being out of work, entered
one of the recruiting offices of the Jewish Legion on the East Side
to find out what it was all about. When he was told that the Jews
once had a country which had been taken away from them, and that
now they were to fight the Turks to get it back, he went into a perfect
frenzy of rage, and shouted: "These damn Turks took away our country, did they? Look here, put my name down, and let me get over
there. We'll knock hell out of 'em. We'll show 'em we're no suckers."

I have said the majority were Poalei-Zion—the *enfants terribles* of
the Zionist movement. They greatly outnumbered the Allegemeine
Zionists and came soon to dominate the entire American group, bar-
ring only those cruder elements who joined the Legion only because
the draft was threatening, and were without sympathy for Zion or
Zionism. Some of the Poalei-Zionists were confirmed pacifists, rabidly
conscientious objectors. One had come to the Legion after having spent
several months in an American prison for refusing to don the uniform
of the American Army. Another had been imprisoned even longer for
participation in anti-war propaganda, and had been deprived of his
American citizenship. Camp humor had it that before they would consent to go over the top they might call a meeting to make sure they
were properly represented. Anyone who knows their tactics at Zionist
meetings will appreciate the point.

But that was at home. In the Jewish Legion, explain it as you will,
they were veritable fire-eaters. They did themselves proud when it
came to hard and risky work, but—aye, there was the rub—they were
still terribly keen on their rights. In one respect they continued to
rebel: They had no use for the sacred tenets of British military discipline.

The Jewish Legionnaire might accept bayonet drill, and learn how to
form fours, but beyond that his reason and his conscience revolted.

When the first batch arrived in Palestine, ninety percent of the men, tired and hungry as they were, threw down their packs, and dashed off immediately in all directions, each according to his temperament: to visit the Palestinian girls, to study the agricultural experiments in the colonies, or to see the country. Scarcely enough of them could be mustered to form the camp guard.

"What the hell is this, an army or a bunch of tourists?" demanded the Commanding Officer, and threatened to court-martial the "whole damn army." There was much jeering when his threat was made known to the men. "It's our country, not his," they argued. Moreover, they reasoned, with the Turk hundreds of miles away, who'd run off with the camp if it did remain unguarded?

The outcome of the war, so far as they were concerned, was never for a moment in doubt. So they spent the first few weeks in camp arguing the Yiddish-Hebrew question. At times the argument would become so heated that armed officers and non-coms would come rushing into the barracks, prepared to quell a riot. And when they found out that all this terrible excitement was over the question of whether Hebrew or Yiddish was to be spoken in Palestine when it became the Jewish homeland, they were considerably angry, but a good deal more bewildered. What sort of an army was this?

These heated debates would be carried on late into the night, despite the most stringent British barrack regulations to the contrary. The sergeant would enter in the midst of the hubbub and threaten to lock up the debaters. There would be a moment of silence.

"What does he want?" one would ask mildly.

"*Beh, man hot ihm in drerd,*" would be the reply, and the discussion would go on as if nothing had happened.

It can be readily seen that British officers would view this new kind of fighting material with some misgivings. "A fine army I have to fight with," complained one officer. "I'll bet my next month's pay that when we get to the battle-front the whole lot will be absent without leave." Lucky for him no one took him up. For once on the battlefield, and in real action, few trained regiments could have acquitted themselves with greater regard for duty and honor than this paradoxical army. But how was any British officer—however trained on the cricket-fields of Eton—to know that?

There was one recruit, for example, who when he finally arrived in Palestine had been the first to throw away his pack, and to set out on a visit to the colonies. Yet during the now famous march from

Nimrin to El Salt, when the Legion was going into action, he steadily refused to obey the doctor who ordered him out of line. He had a skinful of malaria and his temperature was alarming. The doctor's instructions were positive. He was to fall out and wait for the first lorry to take him back to the hospital.

"A clever fellow, this doctor," blandly remarked the recruit. "I have traveled some ten thousand miles to fight for Palestine, and now that I have my first chance I am to be put to bed. Not on his life," and he continued the march.

When the commanding officer was told of this incident, he shrugged his shoulders. "A strange lot, indeed, these Americans," he said.

Not that the Legion covered itself with glory during the march. As a matter of fact, so unusual was its conduct, that it awoke grave misgivings in the heart of the British Commanding Officer. The distance from Nimrin to El Salt, where it was to see action, was approximately twenty-one miles, and an uphill climb all the way. The march was made overnight and on precious short notice.

Now, few members of the Legion had ever hiked further than to the top of Bear Mountain on the Hudson in their lives. Little wonder that of the entire battalion only fourteen ended the journey on time. The rest straggled in at all hours of the morning, and the Colonel swore he would court-martial them all.

As a matter of fact, the first of the survivors to arrive bore the reputation of being the laziest man in the battalion. So impressed was the Colonel with his performance, that he was all for giving him the Victoria Cross. He might have been less enthusiastic had he known how this hero managed the trip. He had wearied before he was half a mile on the road, but seeing ahead of him a plodding transport donkey, had hitched himself to this animal by the belt-strap, and suffered himself to be practically dragged to his destination. He swears to this day that he slept half the journey.

As for the rest of the battalion, it was treated by the Colonel to as nasty a tongue lashing as it had ever been its privilege to hear.

"It is all very well for you," the Legionnaires grumbled, but not so loud that the Colonel could hear. "You made it on horseback."

To save them, they could not understand why he was so choleric over the matter. His bitter words penetrated slightly, and they spent all day arguing over them. The popular phrase was one familiar to every *yeshivah* student. "Nu, I'll be a rabbi a day later." "Why all the excitement?" they reasoned. "The Turks will not run away."

On the other hand, once done with the troublesome business of marching and stationed in the Jordan Valley, then the third line of trenches, no Boy Scout, I submit, could have stayed more conscientiously on guard. Until it occurred to them, after three days had passed and not a shot had been fired, that perhaps the outposts were not worth guarding after all. And no sooner had they begun to doubt the superior wisdom of their officers than they began to neglect guard duty, and to steal off to explore the desert. Their first experience in the line of battle might have ended with three-fourths of them in the guard-house, had not the Turks providentially gotten wind of the location and begun to shell the encampment.

One of the men, an eighteen year-old, was on guard on the top of a hill when the enemy howitzers were first trained on the battalion. Shells began bursting all about him, and he was given up for lost, but pretty soon his voice came bawling down hill. "Captain Ried, they are shelling us!"

"What the bloody hell do you want us to do?" called back the perplexed captain. "Send them a telegram to stop firing?"

At any rate, things became less unbearably dull. The Legion could sit at the bottom of the hill, and make bets on how far the next shell would reach. Or hunt souvenirs. I wonder what the enemy would have made of them, had he been able to see that lot of wild men madly chasing after exploding shrapnel. Not even the horrible tales brought back to them by their Jewish comrades of the 38th Battalion, Royal Fusiliers, the English division of the Legion which had been in actual combat, could frighten them.

Sometimes I think they were not such a bad army after all. . . .

Complete demoralization did not set in until after the armistice. Its "contract" with King George, the Legion reminded itself, was due to expire six months after "cessation of hostilities." And when the six months had passed, and there was no move to release it from His Majesty's service, a delegation called upon the Commanding Officer to inform him that he was party to a flagrant violation of that sanctity of contract which is the Anglo-Saxon's pride. He countered with the statement that "armistice" did not mean cessation of hostilities. Whereupon someone ran off to fetch a dictionary in proof that it meant indeed just that.

Having settled this point to their own satisfaction. the Legion took life somewhat more easily. They could not win their release from military service, but at least they ran the army somewhat more after their own hearts. Even those of them who had been capitalists before the war were now strong adherents of the strike and collective bargaining.

When they were behind the lines, and the Legion was given tea without milk or sugar, they might grumble, but they could accept the explanation that the transport was days behind them. But when they were dished up soup without salt three months after the armistice, they refused to touch it. A delegation called upon the Commanding Officer with their complaints, and when he told them "to take it or leave it" a general strike was ordered.

Certainly the Commanding Officer could have broken the strike almost immediately, if he had cared to, by placing them all under arrest. But he was Colonel Margolin, a good Jew, and jealous of the reputation of the Jewish Legion. Suppose the news spread outside? What would the *goyim* say? He tactfully yielded, whereupon the boys announced with great glee that they had won their first strike.

There were other strikes of a more serious nature. Some were won; the larger number were lost, with the result that many of the strikers received long prison terms.

Ill feeling mounted as they continued to hold the Legion in service. Several men tried to desert. One unfortunate, disguised as a sailor, tried to escape by stealing aboard a ship that was docked at Haifa. He was detected and brought back ignominiously to camp. Thereafter he was given the title of "Admiral in the Jewish Navy."

This same "Admiral," otherwise the same "Chicky" heretofore mentioned, was a source of great grief to officers and non-coms alike. He spent most of his service days in the guard-house, and it was told of him that he refused to remove his effects when released, being quite certain that a few more hours would see him in again. Fortunately, since he was under age, he could never be given more than 21 days in the guardhouse for any of his offenses.

"Chicky" was a student at City College before the war, and quite the young intellectual. On one occasion the Captain threatened to write, reporting him to General Headquarters. "Chicky" brightened up at once. If it ever resolved itself to a question of writing, he was certain he could write a much better letter than the Captain. Which was no more than the truth.

A few more like "Chicky," and the officers would have deserted.

Even as it was, their lot was bitter enough, especially since, for the most part, they refused to see any humor in the situation, much to the Legion's disgust.

Less stupid was Captain ———, deservedly popular with all of the men, who used to beg them not to talk back to him while other officers were around. "You can say what you please to me in private," he pleaded, but you've got to help me keep up appearances in public." As far as I know, his request was observed. He had come to the Legion with a reasonable argument.

At Allenby's Headquarters, however, there was no disposition to argue reasonably. The Legionnaires were hated there, perhaps because they were Jews, but mainly on account of their independence and lack of discipline. Probably only fear of open scandal prevented the persecution from becoming a bloody one. The Legion, on its part, held firm. The war was over, and the Empire was detaining them at its own peril.

There are hundreds of such anecdotes to be told—to what point? To prove perhaps that Jews were good soldiers provided you left them alone. Or that they could never be good soldiers, because a good soldier does not think.

The Jewish Legion, if the truth were to be told, played little enough part in the conquest of Palestine during the World War, and King George might be puzzled to this day to decide whether or not he made a good bargain when he enlisted the Jewish Legion.

But it fought better than it soldiered, and, considered from all angles, maybe the Legion was an asset to the British army. Perhaps Vladimir Jabotinsky, its founder, was correct when he said: "The day will come when every Legionnaire will be able to stand proudly before the mirror and salute himself."

Which, some unkind person has said, many of them can be found doing this very day.

(—1928)

Lotus and Manna

❧

LOUIS GOLDING

I DO NOT POSSESS the ingenuity and arcane scholarship of those German savants who demonstrate that Jesus Christ and William Shakespeare were pure Germans; and I will therefore not try, as I am tempted, to prove that Odysseus was a pure Jew. It may seem unnecessarily modest on my part, for there is a not innumerous school of Jewish writers whom no ethnic or chronological or psychological difficulty prevents from proving that any Gentile possessed of any virtue is a Jew and any Jew possessed of any vice is a Gentile. For my own part, I am content to hail Odysseus as the most Jewish of the Greek heroes. And I should like to claim the Odyssey as a poetic pattern of the Diaspora.

It is possible that such a thought would not have imposed itself upon me, if I had been content to be a quiet clerk in London or a fervent seller of sewing-machines in Cincinnati. But waking lately in my vaulted bedroom in the island of Djerba off the coast of Tunisia, it occurred to me suddenly that I, a humble Jewish wanderer, had at length fulfilled the circuit of Odysseus' wanderings; for Djerba, the island of the Lotophagi, had been the only island of Odysseus' tribulations whither my vagrant sail had not yet impelled me. I had bathed from that desperate strand in Isebia where Circe converted his sailors into swine. I had plucked rosemary on the island where the sirens sang. I had climbed the fumy volcanoes of Lipari, where Æolus delivered the bag of winds. I had plucked the scarlet anemones of Ithaca, the beginning and end of his journeys.

It was only to the island of the Lotophagi, the Lotus-Eaters, I had not penetrated, the outer limit of his perils, and the most sinister of them all. For here the Lotophagi dwelt, that quiet people, who offered not death to the sailors of Odysseus, but oblivion. "Now whosoever of them did eat the honey-sweet fruit of the lotus, had no more wish to bring tidings nor to come back, but there he chose to abide with the lotus-eating men, ever feeding on the lotus, and forgetful of his homeward way."

It was those words that most of all jangled in my head when I awoke that morning of Rámadán, to the near cry of the muezzin on his minaret and the loud boom of the gun on the yellow shore. I had come to Djerba that I too might eat the lotus. And I met a forgotten community of Jews that had been eating lotus for two thousand years.

True that nowhere upon the diverse tempest-twisted tracks of the Odyssey had I not met Jews—whether they drank *Asti Spumante* in Capri or *rezzinato* in Ithaca, that careful distillation from glue and turpentine. But here in Djerba I had met the Jewish Lotus-Eaters; I saw them immured in ghettos more impregnable than the sunken fortresses of Verdun—more impregnable because the bastions consisted of no more than a string slung between two twigs which they themselves had suspended. I beheld the only voluntary Jewish ghetto in existence and the air was heavy with the insidious enchantment of lotus.

So it was that the thought came to me, not that Odysseus was a Jew, but that he was the most Jewish of the Greeks; not that the Odyssey was to be confused with the forty-year wanderings of the pastoral Jews in the stark desert, but that it was a pattern of the adventures of the later Jews, seeking Ithaca, seeking Zion, across a hundred seas, perilous with ogres and seductive with sirens.

A man would need little ingenuity to parallel the incidents of Odysseus' seafaring with the uncompleted tale of the Jewish exile. Who is Circe but the goddess of stocks and bonds who has converted so many of our most promising sailors into swine? How many different shapes in our history has Polyphemus taken, from Spanish Inquisitor to Tartar Cossack? How often have we too been detained in the island of Calypso, not for years but centuries, offering our bewitched hearts to Parisian intellect, London manners? Nor is our Odyssey completed. With Ithaca almost in sight, on what island of Phæacia shall we be wrecked again? And of what nature will the marvelous Phæacian ships be that will carry us home at length? The golden keel of a Rothschild bequest? The iron keel of some Napoleonic araboktonic soldier? But we are not arrived in Phæacia yet. Our sailors are dispersed. Some are reconnoitering dizzily between Scylla and Charybdis. Some of us stuff our ears with wax or bind our bodies to the mast because of the

Gentile Siren that bids us lose ourselves upon her mouth. And some are drowsed with the lotus century beyond century, and are forgetful of the homeward way.

It is of the Jewish Lotophagi in the primordial island of the lotus that I purpose to write here, of the Jewishness which they still possess and of their relations with their kinsmen in Abraham, the Muslims who encompass them. These things I intend to write, and such thoughts as may proceed from them—but they all pertain to each other as the kernel and the flesh and the skin of the lotus pertain together, steeped in a fabulous enchantment.

Once or twice a month the Compagnie de Navigation Oliver may provide a craft for you, almost as primitive as the galley of Odysseus itself, whereon you may proceed to Djerba. But I counsel you first to take the long journey by train round the flat sandy coast by way of Sousse and Sfax to the oasis of Gabes. You must not miss those strange cities nor the strange Jews who dwell in them, if you desire to build for your soul a picture of your race and for your mind a philosophy. At Gabes you will leave the train and ascend that ramshackle groaning public automobile for the south wild lands, that automobile which does not burst into flames more than two or three times a week. Squeezed in all around you on the hard wooden seats, as tight as cattle in a truck, your kinsmen in turban and burnous sit upright, the sons of Ishmael. Hour beyond burning hour they do not move, they do not speak. Strange how much more dignity is theirs in that stinking box than any lordly cropskulled Teuton lolling in his Mercedes all the way to Potsdam.

You enter now the country of the troglodytes, the dwellers in holes in the ground, whom Herodotus on his journeying found here nearly two thousand years ago. Did he find amongst them certain families of Jews, as I did, in the most lightless ghettos of all the five continents? Perhaps not. He records that they fed on "serpents, lizards and other similar reptiles," which, while they are scaled as *kosher* prescribes, have splayed, but not cloven, feet. So at length to Medenine, the metropolis of the troglodytes, where (it being the Sabbath morning) a praying-shawl may be lent you so that you may recite your prayers duly in a synagogue more like a mosque than even a conventicle of the Reform Jews is like a Baptist chapel. Now from Medenine, the Sabbath being over and the automobile not yet being reduced to three buckled wheels and a gear-box, through jackal-haunted dunes, past the forlorn half-buried forum of some unknown Roman city, you snort and thunder to the sea's-edge, even to the white miracle of Djerba across the pellucid strait.

I salute you, lovely island, of minarets white as a girl's thought, of domes curved and toppling like a wave arrested that moment before the crest splinters into the green trough, of colonnades shady as Eden, of olives transfixed in a silver silence, of bloomy peaches and burning lemons: island of the lotus, I salute you, which seduced the sailors of Odysseus from Ithaca and the progeny of Abraham from Zion.

That once there grew a fruit here, overpoweringly enticing, Homer, and to a lesser degree, Herodotus, make abundantly clear. What else attracted hither to this remote beach the first adventurous Jews? What else attracted me? It is true that whereas you gather from Homer that it was a fruit so potent and so subtle you took it for dessert only, Herodotus infers it was a sort of tabloid food which did away with the necessity of breakfast, luncheon and dinner. "The Lotophagi," says he, "live entirely on the fruit of the lotus-tree." Entirely, you observe. "*Mán hu?*" indeed, as the Hebrews asked when they first saw manna upon the ground. "*Mán hu?*" What is this?" I wonder that some scholar has not attempted to prove that manna and lotus were the same vegetable.

What then was the lotus? Had I not come to Djerba to feed on it? No man today shall decide what it veritably was, saving he enter, as I did, into the dwelling-places of the Jews. Certain learned half-wits declare the lotus was no other fruit than the date (though Herodotus explicitly declares that in sweetness it *resembled* the date, ergo it was not the date). More dangerous patients prove laboriously it was the olive. Some incline to the berry of the *rhus oxyacanthoides*—a theory which bears its condemnation in the very sound of it; few to the inspired conviction that it was a clover whereof the sailors grazed like the beasts of the field. And there are some finally, speaking more wisdom than they know, who declare it to be the fruit of the wild jujube— *zizyphus lotus.*

I say they speak more wisdom than they know, for if they were to pluck the fruit of that tree and devour it straightway, they would abandon their theory. The raw lotus, as Rawlinson correctly says, looks and tastes like a bad crab-apple. I refuse to believe that the sailors of Odysseus forgot the name of their native land in the stupefaction caused by an overdose of crab-apples; or that acute stomachic pains were the cause of their languor. The fact is that, precisely as Herodotus remarks with a somewhat audible sniff, "the Lotophagi even succeed in obtaining from it a sort of wine." Exactly. It was the wine distilled from the lotus which was the secret of it all, the most potent wine I have ever tasted. And it is not the few French colonials of Djerba who distill it, or drink it. They drink the imported poisons from the Tunisian vineyards, and should a real French wine wander into their exile, their bosoms shake with sobs. It is not the Muslims of Djerba who are responsible for it, the Supreme Teetotaler having turned their talents in other directions.

It is the Jews of Djerba who distill the lotus. They are the Lotophagi, by which you must translate lotus-drinkers. Whether it was the Jews in the Jewish villages of Hara-Kebîra and Hara-Serîra who seduced the sailors of Odysseus from Ithaca as they themselves are seduced from Zion, I will not decide. So early as that I do not believe that the peoples of Israel in the north and Judah in the south had sunk their differences. It may be that the people of Hara-Kebîra were a colony of Israelites and the people of Hara-Serîra a colony of Judeans and that they first joined forces to entertain the Greek strangers from the Ionian islands. All that seems to be rather hazardous theorizing. I merely wish to make it quite clear that if you would now desire to partake of the lotus even where those old sailors partook of it, it is from the hands of a Jew you must receive it in the far island of Djerba, hemmed in by yellow sands.

Not even a Jewish stranger will find room in either of the Haras, or ghettos, of Djerba. He must pitch his tent in the Gentile village of Houmt-Souk, where there are one or two primitive hotels. This is the metropolis of the island, though only in so much as the population, which is pretty evenly distributed among the orchards and the olive-groves, coagulates here rather more thickly than elsewhere. The villages are, in fact, hardly more than local markets of which Houmt-Souk is the chief. Here gather the bronzed Maltese with the sponges wrested from the fretted bases of the island, and the poorer Muslims lay out their vegetables and fruit. The richer Muslims and the Jews sit cross-legged in the bazaars among the rugs and carpets woven in those curious gabled workshops that are a unique feature in the architecture of the island, breaking so unexpectedly into the familiar lines of soaring minaret and curving dome. The Jewish goldsmiths also foregather here with the gilt trinkets they have hammered and fretted and bejeweled, squatting in their vaulted rooms in the Haras several miles away; or they fasten on some dusky Libyan leg, precisely as Herodotus records, "a ring made of bronze." How many shadowy centuries back extends the Jewish tradition of jewelry in Djerba? Whence derived? From those primal goldsmiths who bedecked the heart of a priest with twelve jewels in rows? For though most of the conventions they work in are Arabic or Byzantine in nature, others are earlier than the Hellenic from which the Byzantine are derived; sacerdotal they seem, as if the artificers had an uneasy memory or that thaumaturgic jewelry which winked with its own fires in the precincts of the Lord, the Urim and Thummmim. . . .

But let it not be understood that though they have distilled the lotus and are masters of its secrets, the Jews of Djerba have had their business instinct spirited away from them by that enchantment. I heard a story from a young Muslim of a felucca beating its way up the fringes of Africa with a cargo of pots and oranges. The boat carried three passengers, a Negro, a Muslim, and a Jew from Djerba. They had not proceeded far on the journey when a sea-serpent was described opening and shutting its jaws ravenously. Regretfully but swiftly the captain threw his cargo of pots and oranges overboard, hoping to appease the monster's hunger. The monster duly devoured the pots and oranges, but made it abundantly clear that he was still hungry, whereon the captain threw the benches overboard. Having swallowed these, the serpent made signs that he was rather hungrier than when he started. The captain had no alternative but to throw over successively the Negro, the Muslim, and the Jew from Djerba. The serpent was now convinced that he had never met a more engaging captain in his life. He looked like he would swallow the whole ship when fortunately a man-of-war appeared and blew the monster's head off. There was a general rush to see what the interior of the creature looked like. It did not disappoint them. The pots and oranges were all neatly arranged on the benches and the Jew from Djerba was busy selling them to the Negro and the Muslim.

It was in a beautifully disposed company we set forth southward from Houmt-Souk to explore the ghettos of Hara-Kebîra and Hara-

Serîra. We were a Protestant, a Muslim, a Greek Churchman, a French Catholic and a Jew. I could not help pointing out to my friends that I felt like a hen shepherding the chickens she has hatched into the hen-coop they have deserted. They could not repudiate the analogy. "But you seem to forget," said the French Catholic, a somewhat cynical young gentleman, "the part the Divine Chanticleer played in the fecundation of your eggs." When we approached the entrance into the first ghetto, the Muslim, being a native of the island, said a little uncomfortably he would wait for us outside the village. I am certain his motive was not a sense of social superiority. The official shiekhs of the island are Muslims, it is true. But the élite are a small handful of Jews. Indeed a tiny house was pointed out to me in the Hara owned by a certain Jew who was a preponderating influence not only in the politics of Djerba but in the whole colony. His property in the Faubourg St. Honoré was considerably more extensive, but he preferred squatting on a Djerba rug with a decoction of lotus beside him to sitting stiffly in his gilt Louis Quinze salon amid the plop of Veuve Cliquot corks.

My friend's motive was not a sense of social superiority, I repeat, even though every Jew he would meet in the village wore a garment of shame to distinguish him from all Muslims. But it was a garment of shame from which the shamefulness had departed, a distinction retained as deliberately as the string suspended between two twigs marked off the deliberate ghetto. The days were gone when the wearing of that white smock was attended by the easy danger of cuffings and spittings in the face. But even when the danger was at its greatest, in the dark days before the Powers extracted their Pacte Fondamental from Mohamed Bey, I doubt if the most ferocious Muslim did not pause and draw back at the threshold of the ghetto, with whatever jeers and flinging about him of his camel-hair rope he had reached thither. It will not be imagined, of course, that the Muslim, as such, was forbidden entrance into the ghetto. But however he may dawdle with his camels and asses on the high road on either side, he does not linger in the ghetto itself. A certain awe is upon him, he walks swiftly through, urging his beasts and looking neither to the right hand nor to the left.

No, not for any social reason did my friend, the Muslim, forebear from entering the ghetto. And I can assure you it was not for any dread of physical violence. I say this not only because the Jews and Muslims of Djerba have of late lived on terms of scandalous amity, but because this particular Muslim was an *Aïssaouïa* and therefore very readily subjected himself to more deadly violence than any Jew, or indeed any Christian, could possibly have conceived. In certain conditions of religious ecstasy he would transfix his whole body with swords till he looked like a bull in the arena after the banderilleros have finished with him. Moreover, and I have seen him do it, he could devour live scorpions with the utmost relish in attestation of the glory of Allah and the superiority of Mahomet over his predecessors, Moses and Jesus.

It was not fear, therefore, that kept my accomplished friend beyond the circuit of the ghetto. It was taboo. It was the piece of string suspended between the two twigs stuck into the opposite corners of the ghetto street. His friends, the Jews, respected his own taboo. He respected theirs. But as foreigners to the island, the Catholic, the Greek Churchman and the Protestant permitted themselves to proceed with me into the places of my kinsmen.

The houses of the Jews in Djerba are indistinguishable from the houses of the Muslim. A blind wall faces upon an unpaved narrow lane, and the dark door is opened not a second longer than will allow you to enter. You find yourself in a sunny court crowded with multitudes of children. There are few trees and no flowers in the court, for there is no living water in Djerba. The water supply of the island consists exclusively of wells and rain-cisterns, which helps to explain why the Djerba Jewesses are much slimmer than their sisters in Tunis. The Djerbans, like Rebecca, must make their way to the well, balancing the clay jar on their erect heads. The Tunisians have water laid on, which absolves them from their sole opportunity of exercise. Not that their menfolk mind. The Jewess of Tunis is valued by weight. In Djerba she is more frequently valued by her headdress of gold coins, and still more frequently by charms more impalpable. But I must quell my impatience to arrive at that theme. I must endeavor first to compose her setting.

A number of small archways on three sides give upon this central court, and each is the entrance to the single vaulted chamber which is the whole territory of a single family. The walls above the archways of this central court are sometimes inlaid with rows of colored tiles, but only among the more elaborate jewelers and the master carpet weavers. The building consists of one story only. Usually the patriarch of the family with his spouse occupies the chamber nearest to the door, so that the constitution of a house is only a single stage removed from a tribal encampment, the tents merely being stiffened into dried brick and whitewashed. The cooking has no ampler machinery than a few three-pronged clay shards not many inches high, heaped up with charcoal. There are no chimneys in the rooms, of course, and the open court is the sole kitchen. Water is stored in the shadow in great clay amphorae, of precisely the shapes that the Romans introduced into the island, and they themselves introduced from Greece.

As you enter, the first thing you set eyes on is the patriarch of the household seated upon the capital of some pillar which once held up a Roman temple; he turns over upon his knee the pages of a holy book expounding an earlier creed, a creed worshiped in a temple earlier than the Roman temple, in a temple overthrown by the Roman worshipers. Little does that old man know what a symbol he is of one of the great revenges of history. He is more potent than Samson with the ruins of Dagon about him. For Samson was slain with Dagon, but this old Jew of Djerba has his foot on the neck of Jupiter and his quiet murmur is in truth a hosanna of victory.

A brightly-striped hanging suspends in each archway. You push this aside to enter a small shadowy vestibule, and turning right or left you enter the chamber proper, one half of which is occupied by a low and deep recess. In this recess the whole family sleeps upon piled rugs, and in a higher and smaller recess in one of the side walls the rest of the family's rugs are stored against the keen winter nights. Other belongings than these they do not possess. It is as if they had inherited from some remote exodus the knowledge that he travels swiftest who carries least; as if their lotus-heavy somnolence were sometimes for a sharp moment disturbed by the fancy that the whitewashed brick of their vaults had sagged of a sudden into the brown camel-skin of a nomad tent; as if the wandering from Palestine into Arabia, from Arabia across the torpid sea to Abyssinia, from Abyssinia to this quiet fringe of Libya, must on the morrow be resumed; and the way to the Pillars of Hercules is perilous and the breath of the enemy is hot upon the neck.

We had not left taboo behind us at the insubstantial portals of the ghetto. It was true that my Catholic friend, on account of his grace and good spirits, was persona grata among these Jews of Djerba; moreover, they spoke little French or none, and he a certain amount of their Judeo-Arabic (so that I, incidentally, had an easy channel of communication with them). And yet the moment we swung aside the curtain that shielded from the sun the household of his friend, Sidi Pinhas Sabban, a sense of taboo once more asserted itself. It was an arcane sensation, difficult to describe, and I can vouch that my own little conscious mind had no part in it. I can only speak with certainty of its effect, and its effect was to exclude my three Christian friends from that dark vaulted room as certainly in the spirit as the Muslim was excluded some hundreds of yards away in the flesh. It was not that my friends, and least of all the Frenchman, became in the slightest degree embarrassed or ill at ease. It was merely that they knew that they were outside, excluded, and we, Sidi Pinhas Sabban and I, were within, held together in a mystery till the end of time.

When I come to reflect upon that uncanny moment, it strikes me as a more beautiful corroboration of his most desperate allegations than any professional anti-Semite ever dared to hope for. That little goldsmith who twists gold thread in the Island of the Lotus-Eaters off the coast of Libya, and I, the chance wanderer from misty England—we *were*, indeed, the Elders of Zion. We *were* the agents of a wide-world conspiracy. And what made us more dangerous was that our complicity was a thing so subtle; secret, spiritual, spontaneous. We had not sent letters to each other in invisible ink detailing the latest stages in our plans for the assassination of all the Gentile financiers in Lombard Street and Wall Street. We had made no swarthy arrangements for the exchange of Muslim and Christian children between our countries to be ritually murdered on the coming Passover. And yet, not having conveyed a single syllable to each other by any medium, or having been in the faintest degree aware of each other's existence until the swinging aside of that curtain, having as common superficial currency not more than five words of French on his side and five of Arabic on mine, we could have organized in the knowledge of our oneness vaster projects than those. Drugged as he was by his African lotus, drugged as I was by my Hellenic asphodel, we had a potency which had already performed great things and will perform them again. It had made their creeds for our Catholic and Greek Orthodox and Protestant friends in the room with us and for the Muslim beyond the gate. It had made their creeds. It will unmake them. Who knows to what ultimate creed it will then address itself, even until the fires of the sun wane and the glaciers thrust their snouts from the saddles of all the hills into the grey nipped lands?

And, I repeat, all this was uncanny. For how little had I in common with this shy brown-eyed besmocked little Jew from Djerba, and how much with my three Christian friends! For the Protestant was an Englishman and we had all English literature in common from Beowulf to James Joyce; and the Greek and I had in common the memory of the cloven cliffs above Delphi and the blue rapier of the Gulf of Corinth beyond the olive-groves. And if the Frenchman and I had no more in common than the memory of a bottle of Château Lafitte, what a bond was there!

Yet soon, soon, verily, in the bond of the wine distilled from lotus were the two Jews to pledge their race and in the sweetened lotus preserved whole in spirit to record the mystic benefaction of manna. Yet I confess myself baffled by the nature of the taboo which imposed itself in Pinhas's small room. First he brought forth two three-legged stools and sat himself down on one. He expected, I gathered shortly, that I should assume the other. But I did not do so until I had pressed the three Gentiles to occupy it singly or divide it between them. "No, no," whispered the Catholic. "It is not right. We Christians must sit on the floor. It is expected here. Do you sit upon the stool." I did so, my head somewhat in a whirl. I had never known in general history or personal experience the Gentile so assume or so submit to disabilities with regard to the Jew. I had a feeling that we had attained antipodes, or the secret side of the moon. Yet I could not suppress a certain sense of self-satisfaction that I and my brother should be enthroned on stools and the Christians lie at our feet upon the floor. It was as if we were the twin Kings of Israel and Judah and the outer tribes had come in to pay us dues. The badge of his shame, the white smock imposed on his fathers by the fathers of his Muslim friends, became in this curious half-light a princely robe, the garment of a high mystery. It grieved me that I was not myself thus marked out. But I, at least, I too sat upon a throne. Whatever smoldering inferiority complexes my Jewish existence in a Gentile world had engendered in me were at that moment extinguished. "Make yourselves quite at home," I said, with gracious condescension.

Sidi Pinhas was, it was evident, happy to be entertaining us. His wife, he said, would shortly reappear from the well where the camel all day, at the end of a tether, made his sardonic rounds. She had gone with their first baby to draw water. In the meanwhile he drew forth a cruse of wine. He carefully poured away the layer of olive-oil with which it was protected from the air, even as the wine of the Romans two thousand years ago was protected and the wine of the Italians to this day. Then he passed a glass over to me and I made politely to pass it further to my friend, the Frenchman. Once more I heard the thud of the wings of taboo in the air.

"*Cashair!*" he exclaimed urgently, "*Cashair!*" I wondered in what language he spoke. But I perceived from my host that it was, in fact, I and not the others who was expected to drink that wine. "*Cashair!*" my host repeated. But upon his Jewish lips, although there was no demonstrable difference in his mode of pronouncing the word, I promptly understood it. *Kosher*, to be sure, the wine was *Kosher*. I saluted him and raised the wine to my lips, such a wine as I had never before tasted. A certain acidity there was about it, but an insidiousness which had once worked legendary woe. I was drinking the wine distilled from the lotus, incredibly after two or three thousand years denied the Gentiles and become the Jews' proud privilege—*Cashair*, forbidden! For that was the stress placed upon the word by the Frenchman. Till that time I had only known *Kosher* as a dietary mode or substance which all the world *might* partake of and the poor Jew *must*. It had now become a stuff of taboo. Only the proud Jew might, the poor Gentile must not.

Not that my friends were denied good cheer. To them Sidi Pinhas brought a flask of *boukkha*, the fiery distillation of peaches, which for some reason they might partake of what time the distilled lotus was denied them. To them he brought dried cakes; to me, in addition, the lotus itself preserved in spirit—*nebk*, he called it; and then for us all, out of the rug-recess, he brought a dish of still warm cooked meats, in the three-pronged clay shard in which it had lately been prepared. It was whilst we were engaged upon these foods and these liquors to wash them down, that his wife appeared, the loveliest lady, I think, I ever set eyes on.

I have seen in various lands ladies who were lovely in various modes. But the wife of Sidi Pinhas (and, to tell the truth, the greater part of these Jewesses from Djerba, though she was the loveliest) had a beauty I could not associate with any living race I had encountered. She was, of course, a long way removed from the cold creatures of the North, fair as they are. Under no grey skies were those eyes enkindled. But she was beautiful not in the way that, for instance, Spanish women are beautiful, or Italian women or the Turkish women whom Angora has permitted to walk forth unveiled. She recalled to me for a moment the Bedouin women of the mainland, but I was quick to see that that was because, like them, she wore great bangles over her elbows and above her brown feet, and the folds of her gown were held together by a large chased clasp. But she had not their nimbleness, their inquisitive chins, their ridged nose, their restless eyes. She wore a headdress of gold coins and seemed less like a living woman of the people, despite the child at her breast, than the queen of some race that has ceased to exist.

Or had I not seen somewhere certain women not unlike her, in their gravity, in their calm assurance? Where had I seen them then, if at all? Then of a sudden I remembered. In the uplands of Thessaly, in the smaller Ægean islands, where the Greek type still lingers. It was they who seemed her kinswomen, not the urgent and ardent Jewish women out of eastern Europe, not the tempered Jewish women of western Europe and America. She seemed, and all these Jewesses of Djerba seemed, not Jewish, not Semitic, but Greek. She seemed even earlier than Greek, as if she went back to the Greek beginnings in Crete and Mycenæ. There I had seen her precise image, I now at length realized, that same full chin, those long grave eyes, that unilinear brow and nose. I had seen her in the pattern of a Cretan vase treading an airy dance, or bearing an urn upon her head or distilling potions out of secret herbs. More recently, she had been distilling out of lotus the wine I held to my lips now.

What secret does that Jewess of Djerba hint at, who seemed so much more Greek than Jewish? What irrecoverable knowledge must first be recovered before it shall be divined? For seeing that it can not be disputed that she stands at the fountain-head of our race, that she presents our archetype unperverted by the strains of Khazar or Iberian or Teuton, shall we dare to believe that we were primordially creatures of the Mediterranean seacoasts and islands rather than sullen wanderers from the gaunt Arabian peninsula? The aspect of these or those do we perpetuate, these swift Greek creatures of sea and wind whom no creek in the ultimate antique seas did not harbor, or those swarthy submitters, the Arab Semites, those paragons of the principles of sterility?

Is it preposterous that the Jewess from Djerba should lead us so far away from all our ancient anchorages? Go with me so far as this, then. Admit the Jewess of Djerba and her kinsfolk in those proud ghettos to be not such dull Jews as you and I. Admit that when Odysseus brought back to their ships those of his sailors who had fed upon lotus, he could not find certain of them. For these had found sanctuary in the ghettos and had thereon taken to themselves Jewish maidens for wives; they it was who produced the race of the modern Lotophagi, whom you may visit for yourselves, those Hellenic Hebrews who read the Torah of Moses and feed upon the Lotus of Homer.

(—1926)

The Passing of the East Side

ZALMEN YOFFEH

I T IS high time a history of the East Side, of that period when it was a self-inflicted ghetto, be written. For the East Side, which played such an important part in the development of American Jewish life, the East Side in which, it is safe to assume, seventy-five percent of East European Jewry found their first American foothold, is fast disappearing. More and more the outlanders are overstepping the old border, the Bowery, and settling in what was Jewish land. One is just as likely to hear Italian, Polish or Chinese on its streets as Yiddish.

True, there are still many Jews on the East Side. But for the most part they are a young and assimilatory group, preaching, on the one hand, communism and internationalism, and practicing, on the other hand, Americanization. And if, in certain of the cafés on Second Avenue and Rivington Street, a form of Yiddish life still holds sway, the participants are mainly Yiddish actors and writers, desperately trying to stem the tide of Americanization that threatens to overwhelm them and leave them without a means of livelihood. So they make a point of living in the old section, speaking only Yiddish and endeavoring to create a "Yiddish" atmosphere.

But theirs is a hopeless task. The older folks continue on their way, distrustful of these heretics, these "epicureans." They attend sparsely filled synagogues and prepare themselves for the death which will take them away from this now unholy soil where shops keep open on the Sabbath and people eat on Yom Kippur. Their elder children have already moved to Flatbush or to the Concourse. The young are busy perfecting their imitations of Al Jolson or Eddie Cantor, looking forward to a day when they will be free from even the light hold the "old man" has on them. Then will the Italians and the Poles, the Chinese and the Hungarians, sweep down upon the once holy precincts. The synagogues will once more become churches, the cafés will become chop-suey joints, and the public library next to Seward Park, now the busiest branch in the city, will become a spot of peace and rest, a place of quiet contemplation. . . .

Already sentiment is creeping into this account. But by the very nature of things this will have to be a sentimental history. Removed from the scenes I describe by almost a score of years, I remember things hazily, yearningly. Man forgets and glosses over. No one man could have known all the East Side of those days. All any man can know is the immediate narrow circle he lived in.

Yet the only way to deal with the East Side is to be frankly auto-biographical. Telling of one's father, one may tell of thousands of fathers in the neighborhood. In describing one's mother one may be describing every mother on the East Side. And so on. To be sure, there is the possibility that my father and mother were not typical of the fathers and mothers about them. Indeed, my natural vanity cherishes the belief that they were not. But still I know that they and their children and the circle we moved in must have been typical to a great extent.

The East Side I knew was, I must say at once, not nearly so sensational as most popular accounts describe it. But it was strange enough. When I remember that I was thirteen when I first heard how babies came into being, and that my answer was, "Go on! My father and mother wouldn't do such a dirty thing," it seems clear to me that the more popular notion of the lurid East Side—the notion of extreme cunning and sophistication, even among the very young—cannot be very true. So I set myself to write my version, my impressions. I make no grandiose claims that the East Side was thus and so. I only claim that the East Side I knew, viewed from the sentimental distance, seemed thus and so.

The East Side of my boyhood was a completely Jewish world. The language of our home was Yiddish. The newspapers that came into our home were Yiddish. The store signs were all in Yiddish. The few Gentiles we dealt with spoke to us out of their smattering of Yiddish. Small wonder that after twenty years in America my mother could not speak a complete English sentence. Or that I, born in America, did not know a single English word until I was five years old!

The only holidays we observed were Jewish holidays. Our good clothing was not for Sunday but for Saturday. As Friday night approached, the pushcarts left the street, the stores began to close. Faces were washed and hair was fine-combed. Early Saturday morning found the streets deserted; everybody was in *shul*. In the afternoon the children played in the street, quiet games, not the boisterous games of the week, for one had to keep clothes clean. The restaurant across the street stayed open but served only food warmed over from the day before. The patrons came around in the evening and paid for their meals. After sundown everything would reopen.

The only Gentiles we knew were the janitor in the tenement, the barber around the corner, and the policeman on the beat. Gentiles, we understood, were a race of mental inferiors, fit only for the more menial tasks of life. All the world's wisdom was encompassed in the Jewish brain; when later I met intelligent Gentiles I was astounded. Not only astounded but also suspicious. Something was wrong; either there was some trick about their intelligence or else, very likely, they had Jewish blood in them.

Generally, we kept inside our world. When, occasionally, we left it, we did so with fear and trembling. Once on the other side of the Bowery, we were a marked race. Italian youths would swoop down on us, chase us, beat us, tear our clothing. It was rarely we went. Why take the risk when there was such a complete world right at hand? Let the Italians be physically superior. We readily granted it. We knew that in days to come we would be doctors and lawyers and professors, and they would come around to black our boots and clean our offices.

My father was a pushcart peddler. In the old country, educated beyond the comprehension of the village he lived in, he had found intellectual companionship only with the village priest. He knew Hebrew and the Torah, but could not even become a *melamed*. The Jews refused to trust their children to an *apikoros* who hobnobbed with priests and polished his boots on the Sabbath. So he came to the country of wider opportunity.

He drifted into the clothing shops. There he was very unhappy. Educated for higher things, when a beetle-browed foreman let out on him a string of abuse, my father would just walk out of the shop. This happened several times. Finally he hired a pushcart and became a fruit peddler. This he remained till the end of his life.

I remember him as slightly above middle height. His hair and beard

were black and curly. Most of his face was a deep brick red from
exposure to the elements, except that part of his forehead which the hat
covered. This was a startlingly pure white. His cheeks were sunken
and he had high cheek bones. His hands were long and thin and the
wrists were very delicate, almost a woman's wrists. Later I was to
see his physical counterparts in the Bedouins of Palestine. But I knew
nothing of Bedouins then. To me he looked like one of the red men
described in my history books. A red man with a black beard. The
thought used to tickle me.

We children rarely saw him during the week. He would rise at
five in the morning and come home after ten in the evening. Occasionally he sold out his complete stock early in the evening. Then we
would have a treat. A pocketful of pennies would cascade onto the
table and we would have the pleasure of counting them, and of putting
them in stacks of ten. My father would compute the amount and
deduct the money he had left with in the morning. There was rarely
more than a dollar profit left for the day's work. Occasionally there
was less.

His was a terribly lonely life. My mother, a wonderful woman in her
way, was no mate for him, never understood him. He was her husband
and as such warranted her loyalty and support, but, oh, dear God,
why could he not be like other husbands and make a decent living?
He had none but business relations with other peddlers, and never
exchanged a word with a neighbor. He had a few friends in the synagogue he attended, but even they were not close friends. He was the
Bal Keriyoh, the reader of the Torah, and they all conceded his piety
and learning, but "how could one warm up to an iceberg?" They would
have been shocked to learn that he wore no *arba kanfos,* that he did
not wind phylacteries, and that he never said his prayers except Saturdays and holidays in the synagogue. A member of the Socialist Labor
Party and an ardent revolutionist, he went to the synagogue because
that was the one place he knew where men put workaday thoughts
out of their minds and worshiped things of the spirit.

Poor man! Undeviating and strict, a despiser of sham and compromise, he saw early that his children were weak, diplomatic, inclined
to take the easier way always. He had hoped to see them attain the
intellectual heights denied him; when I was graduated from the elementary school with the highest honors he kissed me and cried, the
only display of emotion I ever saw in him. Yet he was doomed to see

his children, one by one, taken out of school to help supply the needs of the family. Everywhere frustration faced him and overwhelmed him. Even in such an insignificant matter as clothing. He was passionately fond of dressing well. His weekday clothes were always neat. But his Sabbath suit, though old and thread-bare, was scrupulously clean. More than an hour was consumed every Saturday morning in brushing, washing, shining and combing. The one thing he wanted more than anything else was a new suit of clothes. But it could never be managed. He always had to buy old clothes. In the early part of 1919 he finally bought himself a new suit of clothes. Two weeks later he suffered a stroke of paralysis. A week after that he died.

If I say that my mother was a Slavic type, I do not mean she was at all the high cheek-boned, sharp-nosed, splay-mouthed type that we usually think of as Slavic. I refer merely to her coloring which was pink and white; to her hair which was blond and had been flaxen; to the sturdy build of her body. I speak of the mother of my youth. She is getting old now. But old men of her town, when they seek a superlative, still say, "as pretty as Chaye Itte was in her youth."

What a glorious match was that between my father and mother. She came from a family of shopkeepers who owned just about everything in Yablonyi. So when her grandfather went to Byalistok and got my father, scion of a long line of rabbis and "learners," the entire district celebrated. Such learning and piety mated to such beauty and wealth. A perfect combination.

But alas, the wealth did not last. Much of it, invested in illegal dealings, was confiscated by the Czar's officers. When it came to making a living, my father was helpless. There was nothing he could do. And when, even in America, the "golden land," he could not earn enough to support a family decently, my mother suffered severely. How could she be expected to realize that it was just because he did no work and could do no work, that my father had been considered such a good match originally? She simply knew that children were coming one after the other, and that it was hard to raise them. Her brothers, when she first came to America, suggested a divorce. But this, too, was beyond her comprehension. Her husband, no matter what happened, was her husband, and to him and her children she must devote her life.

So with our one dollar a day she fed and clothed an ever-growing family. She took in boarders. Sometimes this helped; at other times it added to the burden of living. Boarders were often out of work and penniless; how could one turn a hungry man out? She made all our clothes. She walked blocks to reach a place where meat was a penny cheaper, where bread was a half-cent less. She collected boxes and old wood to burn in the stove instead of costly coal. Her hands became hardened and the lines so begrimed that for years she never had perfectly clean hands. One by one she lost her teeth—there was no money for dentists—and her cheeks caved in. Yet we children always had clean and whole clothing. There was always bread and butter in the house, and, wonder of wonders, there was usually a penny apiece for us to buy candy with. On a dollar and a quarter we would have lived in luxury.

She wanted to see us successful, *vee leiten*, as she expressed it. Of course it was a wonderful thing to become a doctor or a lawyer, but the main thing was to make a decent living. She was always pointing out to us so-and-so who went to work for two dollars a week and was now making ten or twelve. She was doomed to be disappointed too in her children. None of them has as yet made a fortune. But, feeling things less deeply than my father, her disappointment is not as keen as his would have been. She is slightly bewildered over the fact that her children do not seem to be as financially successful as other children. But she is beginning to accept their oft-repeated statements that they are "different" and "superior." Maybe they're right, she figures. Her own children would not lie to her. Anyway, so long as there is a piece of bread in the house she won't worry.

She is very religious. That is, she believes and practices everything her mother taught her. In the old days she never had time to go to *shul*. Now, thank God, the children are grown up and she has time to go. She is there every Saturday morning, the proud center of a circle. For her cronies cannot read Hebrew and so they follow her as she reads the prayers. During the High Holy Days she is absolutely indispensable to them. How else, except by following her, would they know when to start crying?

She has become a "society" woman. She belongs to a Ladies' Aid society and to a benevolent society and many more "societies." She has not much money to contribute to these but she expends a large amount of effort and work. She is getting old and sickness occasionally visits her, but her life is much easier than in the old days. Some of the lines seem to have left her face, her new teeth fill out her cheeks, and nowadays she is able to wash her hands perfectly clean.

I have told of my father's religion and my mother's religion. How, now, about our religion; mine, my sisters', the children about me? Brought up in such an atmosphere, were we not extremely Orthodox and pious? I am afraid not.

We accepted unreservedly the fact that there was a God; a Jewish God, reserved especially for us. But with us there was nothing like what I found later when I went out into the Gentile world: the belief in a personal god to whom one could pray for definite, personal needs, and who would give heed to such prayers. With us prayer was an exaltation of an infinite, superior being whom one had to placate, whose laws one observed.

The observance of religious laws was, with us, such a matter of routine, that we never considered their source. I remember at the age of twelve I was appointed to the staff of my school paper. All week long I racked my brain for ideas for an article. Then, on Saturday morning, seated in *shul*, it came to me. I muttered the prayers automatically. I hardly touched the meal that came later. The idea had possession of me and I could not forget it. My fingers itched for the feel of a pencil. All day Saturday I paced up and down the rooms, waiting for the Sabbath to end, so that I could sit down and write. I suffered acutely. Yet never once did the idea come to me that I might just sit down and write. And never once did I think of God. It was just a matter of doing the prescribed.

One of my sisters had real faith. More, she knew how to apply it practically. At night, on our way to our flat, we had to pass a doorway leading down to a cellar. The hall was always dimly lighted. (Landlords had a way of doctoring a gas-tip so that it gave only the merest light.) The open door of the cellar was the mouth of a horrible, black, evil-smelling chasm from which all sort of beings, human and otherwise, could spring at us. So we would hover about the entrance to the house, waiting for a grown-up under whose shelter we could negotiate the passage. Not so this sister of mine. She would walk bravely and alone up the long hallway and past the fearsome chasm. Her courage brought forth wonder and admiration from us. Later I learned that she would shut her eyes as she entered the hallway, and as she went along, her eyes tightly shut, she would say to herself, over and over, "God is with me. God is with me." When her feet touched the stairs she opened her eyes and flew.

But this was after she had had contact with the Gentile viewpoint, assimilated through books and her classes in school. I, too, became touched by it. Once, on a cold winter's day, when my ears were so cold that I was afraid they would drop off, I walked along the street praying, "Oh, God, please make my ears warm. Oh, God, please, please, do me a favor. I'll believe in you all the time." Suddenly relief came to me. The cold left my ears and the tears left my eyes. I was so wonderfully happy, I wanted to sing. My prayers had been answered. Here was actual proof of the existence and goodness of God.

But, alas, thus the way was paved for disbelief and adolescent atheism. The next time I asked God a personal favor it was not granted. I showed Him. I ceased to believe in Him.

For other children winter was a time of jollity. Warmly dressed, bubbling with energy in the brisk weather, they would run back and forth in the streets, shouting and playing. Not so with us. Winter was a time of fear and dread. When snow fell it was impossible to push a cart of fruit through the streets. When cold came the fruit froze. Housewives would not tarry in the cold, but did their shopping in warm stores. Then, too, we children needed heavier, more expensive clothing. In addition, there was the house to keep warm.

Coal cost ten cents a scuttel or fifty cents a sack. But often we could not spare even these trifling sums, and my mother and I would scour the streets for wood. I remember myself, cold and shivering, dragging large boxes, too heavy for me, while my ungloved hands became lumps of ice. Nor was that all. Such was my excessive pride, Lord knows where I got it, that I was ashamed to be seen at this task by my more prosperous schoolmates. So I often dragged my heavy loads blocks out of the way in order not to pass their houses.

Other children greeted the first flakes of snow with whoops of joy and rushed into the streets with their sleds. But snow meant that my father could not go out that day. It meant there would be no dollar for food at the end of the day. My father would stand at the window, stern-faced and silent, watching the flakes fall, occasionally looking up at the sky for signs of clearing. My mother would go about her household tasks with an ominous face, the tears threatening to come at any moment. In the strained, uncomfortable atmosphere of the house, we children would move about silently, unobtrusively, awed doubly by the sense of strain, and the unusual presence, in daylight hours, of our father. Occasionally, the silence would become too much for my mother and she would break out in a fit of temper, while we children cowered in corners, and my father stood as before, silent, aloof. Once, influenced by my readings (I had no personal, original ideas of beauty), I remarked on the beauty of the snow. I shall never forget the awful look my father gave me, or the tears of my mother. Beautiful, indeed! what did I know of beauty? what was beautiful about being penniless? I was hushed. Even today snow brings a sense of sorrow to me. I remember the poor and the unfortunate. I remember a thin, bearded figure with a slight stoop standing at a window, stern-faced and silent, watching the flakes fall.

The day was busy, not only for me but for all the children I knew. Generally I rose at about seven-thirty, washed and partly dressed. Then, being on the way to manhood, I rushed through some of the morning prayers. (My religious education had started at the age of five.) It was not until after breakfast that I finished dressing. One could not risk getting food on a clean white shirtwaist. I was generally in school by eight-thirty.

Teachers were strange, awesome beings to us. We knew they were not Jewish, most of them, but neither did they fit into our conception of Christians. Christians were dark, swarthy Italians, or clumsy, blond Poles, or huge, genial Irishmen. Besides, we knew, Christians were an ignorant lot. Yet these teachers were so clever, seemed to know everything. Many of them had a strange, fascinating odor about them, an odor which, I grew to know later, came from riding in stuffy elevated or subway trains. One always tipped one's hat to them and opened doors for them. They were of a superior world and this was due them, both the men and women. In addition one said "Yes, mam" and "No, mam" to them. A meaningless word to us, this "mam." We knew it only as something to use in school.

School kept until three. I would rush home, take off my white shirtwaist, and put on a colored shirt for the rest of the day—the white one being carefully put away until the next morning for another day of school. Munching a huge slice of buttered rye bread, I would rush off to *cheder*.

The *cheder* occupied half of a loft, the other half of which was used by a clothing factory. There were about twenty pupils seated at a long table with the *rebbe* at the head. He had a long whip which could reach to the end of the table and often did. We would recite in unison at the top of our voices, shouting to make ourselves heard above the din of the sewing machines. The prayerbook was our textbook, and we recited it over and over again. I became so proficient that I could recite it backwards, and I was often called upon to exhibit this precocity for the benefit of visitors to the *cheder*. But the teacher never dreamed of translating the prayers for my benefit or teaching me what they meant. He was paid twenty-five cents a week to teach me prayers.

By four-thirty I was usually out. I would go to my father's pushcart, which I would tend while he went to the wholesale market and chose his stock for the next day. At six or thereabouts I was released. After supper there was the street where I gathered with my cronies and played. When the games became violent, as they usually did, I would sneak away. I had neither the taste nor the physique for tests of physical skill and endurance. There was always a book in the house for me, and I would read until my mother chased me to bed.

Saturday was different. We all woke the same time as weekdays, but my father was with us. The girls would lie around in bed and chat while my father and I dressed. He would go off to *shul* first; I, being not yet a "man," was allowed to eat breakfast before I went. The synagogue was not a strict place. Only certain prayers required concentrated attention. For the rest I could move about and converse with my mates, silenced occasionally by a loud "shush-h" from the *shammes*. There were intermissions during which we children could run out and play. Every once in a while we had a bridegroom at the services or a Bar Mitzvah, which meant that afterwards there would be wine, brandy and cake. Of these I always managed to get my share. Then home and to dinner. After dinner my father would always take a nap. This time was always spent by me in a feverish poring over the portion for the week. After his nap my father would test me in my knowledge of it, and it was not well if I fell below his standard. (I generally did.) Later my father would take me and one or two of the girls, and off we would go for the afternoon.

He felt the responsibilities of fatherhood deeply, felt it his duty to give us as many advantages as possible. So he would take us on long walks, to the Aquarium at South Ferry, to the Museum of

Natural History in Central Park, to the bridges and places of interest all over the city. This meant a sacrifice of rest; more, it meant real danger.

We always, on those walks, went through Gentile neighborhoods. My father, with his beard and his derby, the picture of the Jews of the comic strips and the stage, was a marked man. Again and again he was beset. He was pushed and jostled, stones and decayed fruit were thrown at him, insulting names were called after him. He never resisted, he never answered back; he just went on, dignified and oblivious. And the next week and the week after, he was back, going through the same ordeal again. After a while, they grew to know him and, in a way, to respect him. That is, the hoodlums of the various neighborhoods would jeer after him, good-naturedly, but they did not molest him. When I grew older he often recalled those days as a proof of the futility of resistance. "Thus," he pointed out to me, "have we Jews been able to live through the ages. Always we have been out-numbered; had we attempted any open resistance, we must surely have been obliterated. So, outwardly, we bent our backs; our souls, however, were inviolate. And that is all that matters. The Gentiles can alter our outward observances; they cannot change our inner con-victions."

All that the holidays on the calendar—New Year's Day, Lincoln's and Washington's Birthdays, Memorial Day, Thanksgiving Day, Christ-mas—meant for us was a day or so off from school. Our real holidays were those of the Jewish calendar. Poor as we were, we always man-aged on them to put up a special show.

Rosh Hashanah, itself, did not mean much to us children. It was only two days of extra-long services and stricter observance. Yom Kippur, however, left its impress upon us. There was the day before, Erev Yom Kippur, with its strained, expectant air throughout the neighborhood. Everybody spoke in whispers; shops closed even earlier than on Fridays. The final meal before evening fell was a solemn affair; my father sat stern and silent, eating his food in an abstracted manner; my mother alternated between bursts of crying and loud urg-ings to us to eat more. Her bursts of crying turned to continual weeping by the end of the meal. She would kiss us all before she left for *shul*.

The *shul* itself was different, too. There were many more lights than usual, and it was much more crowded. All the men sat with shoeless feet; and nobody ever dreamed of opening a window. Everybody prayed with a feverish intensity. There was none of the lightness that was often present on the ordinary Sabbath. From the women's section came the sound of weeping and wailing. To me it was always a physical and emotional upheaval. Something big and overwhelming was happening to us, to all Israel. What was it all about? I would rush out of the synagogue when services ended.

By the next day the tension was somewhat relaxed. The synagogue was still crowded but the worshipers were more at ease. Many of the candles had burned down, daylight was streaming in, and a window was occasionally thrown open. The younger children would troop in and out of the synagogue, bearing bags of fruit and cake which they ate with open enjoyment, while the older children, those who had to fast, looked on in envy and despair. People chatted. Except for occasional prayers, the cantor went on in a dull monotone. Yom Kippur was not so bad.

Toward the late afternoon, however, the atmosphere changed again. A weariness settled over the congregation; younger men, mouths parched and throats dry, would slump down in their seats, heads buried in arms, too weak to move. Spirits of ammonia passed from hand to hand. People ceased to chat; they prayed concentratedly. Even the children were subdued and sat silent and weary. Thus the afternoon dragged on, till the moment or so just before nightfall. Then would come the blowing of the ram's horn, the single, long *tekiyoh*. The whole congregation arose. They would stand firm and upright on limbs that had buckled under them all day. From throats parched and cracked there came forth a lusty, resonant cry, *Leshono Haboh B'Yerusholayim;* the rest of the prayers were in the nature of an anticlimax. We would walk home through a newly-awakened world, a world that seemed brighter and fairer than it ever seemed before. And oh, how good the first taste of food seemed to us. Yom Kippur was over. Israel had served its penance and was itself again.

Then came Succoth with its feasting in the open; Simchath Torah with its merry-making in the synagogue and its glorification of the humble. In our synagogue there was a little shoemaker by the name of Chunni. He was unlearned and ignorant of the Law. Nobody paid much attention to him; he rarely was called to the reading of the Law. But the eve of Simchath Torah was different. Then he led the procession with the scrolls; he sang the appropriate prayers. I can still see him, laughing, singing, shouting, while the tears of joy streamed down his cheeks. He was a humble, ignorant man, but once a year, at least, he stood out in the sight of the Lord. With the heavy scrolls on his shoulders, he would leap high in the air for joy, and go cavorting and dancing about the synagogue. And we children followed, bearing aloft a paper flag and a lighted candle; our glorification came, too, when we were all herded under a prayer-robe and recited the blessing of the Law in unison. A vague, meaningless, yet highly enjoyable holiday.

On Hanukkah we children always fought for the privilege of lighting the candles. Purim gave us the opportunity to make as much noise as we wanted to in the synagogue; how we would rattle and boo and stamp every time the hated name of Haman was mentioned. Pesach always brought us new clothing, an immense quantity of nuts and much wine to drink. Shavuoth was a pleasant enough holiday, though of no special significance to us children.

I have said that my father was not a very religious man. How then did it come about that we celebrated all these holidays? But though not a pious man in the accepted sense of that day, my father loved the symbols and customs of Judaism and observed them all. They were to him a sign of a difference from the rest of the world, a difference he was proud of. So we went on in a northern country celebrating the harvest festivals of the south; in a Nordic country we exalted a Semitic language; in a Gentile world we stressed our Jewishness. That it was all a bit incongruous was never apparent to us. That the Gentiles about us might reasonably object never bothered us. Who, in those days, paid any attention to what the Gentiles thought?

And that there was nothing wrong with living as we lived, we never suspected. To live, a family of eight, in three rooms, seemed to us quite normal, as was being without a bathroom and sharing the toilet with three neighbors. Grass and trees were objects to be looked at when one went to a park. In winter all the windows were kept shut day and night, and in summer we slept on the roofs and on the fire-escapes. Nothing was wrong with that.

When I was nine years old my mother heard of a wonderful bargain in the then sparsely-populated Brownsville—four rooms with a private bathroom. We moved there. At the end of six months we moved back to the East Side.

What a horrible experience. Our nearest neighbor was over fifty yards away. At night the street was deserted and quiet. Gentiles lived across the way; one had to walk two and three blocks to reach a store. What self-respecting Jew could live in such a neighborhood?

We moved back to the East Side in mid-August. The street we moved to was filled with pushcarts. A continual roar arose from the occupants and it was with difficulty that one made his way through the crowds. Here and there were heaps of rotting fruit. The stench and heat, as I look back on it, were unendurable. Yet we were all happy to be back. Back on the East Side, back in a Jew's world. . . .

But eventually we followed the trail blazed by others; again we moved away from the East Side, this time permanently. A year passed, a second year, and I went back to the East Side for a visit. It all seemed so strange and unendurable. The streets were so narrow, so dirty, so unhealthy. The buildings crowded each other, the rooms were small and stifling. The people were coarse and vulgar and so very noisy. I stepped into the old synagogue and was appalled by its lack of dignity; was this a place for the worship of God, this tiny, ill-lighted, evil-smelling room?

I entered a restaurant. The tablecloths were dirty and there were no napkins. I resented the familiarity of the waiter. The food, I had to admit, was good. But there was no style. I went out and walked the streets again. I looked with disapproving eyes at the gangs of toughs on the corners. An overdressed woman winked at me as she passed by. How, thought I, was I ever able to live in this nasty, filthy section? In two short years I had been weaned away. I was no longer an East Sider.

The Ghetto, I have said, is fast disappearing. But it leaves its mark; it is not disappearing into nothingness. What is happening is that the Ghetto is spreading out, is taking in more territory, and becoming, in the process, diluted, weaker. But it has left its imprint upon New York at least. I do not only mean that Jews may now be found in every part of the town; the process of Ghettoizing New York has been much more subtle, has gone much deeper. It has given the very Gentiles a Jewish tinge. There was a time when one had to go to the East Side to get traditional Jewish food; now one can get it in the heart of Broadway. There was a time when the Jew who did not wish to fast on Yom Kippur was forced to compound sin and eat *trefe;* it is possible for him now to feast on "corn" bread, noodle soup and *kalbsbraten.* I verily believe he could even find a restaurant where he might be served *gefilte-fish* on that high holy day.

True, the Jew uses his hands less in talking; but his Gentile neighbor uses them more. The Jew has lost many of the Yiddishisms which were a part of his speech, but what he retains he shares with the *goyim*. More and more English creeps into the Yiddish dailies, but more and more Jewish news is found in the English papers.

The East Side, however, as an entity, seems definitely lost to the Jews. It can never again be the Jewish center it was. Those of us who are sentimental will mourn the loss. We will point with pride to the records of those it reared; doctors, jurists, actors, social workers, men of letters. And we will swear that never again can any one section be so blessed in the stalwarts it produced.

Others, however, will look upon the East Side's decline dry-eyed, even with satisfaction. They will remember the dirt and squalor, the poverty and bitter hunger. They will remind the sentimentalists of the gunmen and gangsters that were reared on the streets. And they will say, "We have lost the East Side, but we have gained the world—at least New York."

And the sentimentalist, not being versed in logic, and having been taught that dirt and poverty are terrible things, will be overwhelmed and say, "Yes, yes, but—." And when he is alone, and his thoughts turn that way, he will shed a sentimental tear for the old East Side. For he will feel that there was something fine in the life he lived there, something distinctive, individual, something worth keeping, though inexplicable. Still, if pressed too hard for a reason, he might admit that perhaps he weeps only because a sentimentalist must have something to cry over.

(—*1929*)

The Epic of the Warsaw Ghetto

CONSO

LUCY S. DAWIDOWICZ

MORE than six years have passed since the Battle of the Warsaw Ghetto.[1] This heroic chapter in modern history has become a symbol of Jewish resistance and fighting spirit.

Since not many survivors of the Warsaw ghetto are left, fewer still of the uprising, and only a handful of those who took an active part in the preparation and actual fighting, the experiences of each survivor have taken on extraordinary significance.

Warsaw ghetto history may be divided into three periods: from its establishment by the Nazis in 1940 to July 22, 1942, when the first large-scale deportations to the death factories began; the period of panic and preparation for struggle, to April 19, 1943; the period of the fighting which began on April 19 and lasted through the summer of 1943, until the razing of the ghetto in September.

Most of the literature in Yiddish deals with the second period. The first period apparently seemed idyllic in retrospect. Probably the fullest account of the earliest ghetto life is presented by Bernard Goldstein.[2] His book pictures this period most vividly in all its variety. He himself played a leading role in its affairs until the end of 1942 when he resumed his underground activity on the "Aryan" side of Warsaw until its liberation by the Russians. Subsequently he escaped to Czechoslovakia, stowed away in a plane to Belgium, and finally arrived in the United States in 1946, where he now lives.

Comrade Bernard, as he was known for over twenty years in Warsaw labor circles, occupied positions in the Bund of key importance as a

---

[1] For a detailed account, see "The Battle of the Warsaw Ghetto," by Shlomo Mendelsohn, in *The Menorah Journal* for Spring. 1944.—Ed.

[2] *Finf yor in varshever geto* (Five Years in the Warsaw Ghetto), by Bernard Goldstein (New York, 1947), Unser Tsait, 498 pages.

The Stars Bear Witness, translated into English by Leonard Shatzkin (New York, 1949), Viking Press, 295 pages.

union organizer and chief of the party's defense militia. Associated with the bakers, meat packers, and transport workers, his integrity and fearlessness gave him a unique authority among the most squalid, undisciplined, and roughhouse elements of Jewish workers. As head of the Bund militia, he was no novice in the use of arms; and his contacts with many Polish union leaders proved invaluable during the German occupation.

Always a fighting man though unimpressed by force, Goldstein writes little about himself. His role in the Bund underground never emerges clearly; he has subdued his own part almost to a shadow flitting under the nose of the Gestapo. Rather, he describes the children in the ghetto kindergartens playing amid the ruins of gutted buildings, begging on the streets, dying in the gutters. He writes of the idiot street-singer Rubinstein whose songs testified to the levelling in the ghetto—*ale glaykh* (all equal)—and to the supremacy of the bread coupon. He tells how the ghetto was established, the length and breadth of its walls, its division into parts, one large, one small, connected by a narrow wooden bridge. He pictures graphically the first movement into the ghetto and the later evacuation of the small ghetto; the confusion and wailing and dull-eyed despair; the dead and dying littering the streets; the black-market collaborators, policemen, and agents staggering home after drunken orgies in the ghetto night clubs. He describes the ingenuity of the people smuggling food into the ghetto; of a pipe passing over the ghetto wall through which milk was poured, and of a cow thrown over a wall. Of bribing the police; and about the children who crawled through holes in the ghetto wall to bring bread home to their parents.

Goldstein also describes the administration of underground public relief and the official ZTOS (Zydowski Towarzystwo Opieki Spolecznej —pronounced *jeétos*—Jewish Society for Social Welfare). He gives the programs of the Jewish parties in the fields of public welfare, education, political propaganda and activity. He tells about the house committees organized for internal relief, child care and recreation; the secret mobile libraries; the ghetto concerts and clandestine political rallies; the underground publications, their editors and printers; the forbidden schools where teachers risked their lives to teach children to read and write; and the community kitchens, the camouflaged center of most political activity—all portrayed against the background of an endless procession of jogging funeral carts taking the dead to the overcrowded cemetery.

Two important episodes in Goldstein's book are not found in any other account. One is his detailed story of the program of April 1940, before the official introduction of the ghetto. In Praga, a Warsaw suburb, a Jewish meatpacker had beaten up a Pole who was harassing a Chassidic Jew. A general fight ensued. The Germans arrested the meatpacker and shot him the next day. A few days later, bands of young Polish hoodlums began rioting in the Jewish section of Warsaw, looting shops, attacking Jews. For three days the rioters carried on unchecked, while the Germans came sightseeing with their cameras. On the fourth day the Bund militia was mobilized and fought back. Two days later Polish police broke up the fights, apparently on orders from the Germans. A good part of the Jewish population had opposed the Bund's resistance—though it was in the pre-war tradition—on the ground of possible reprisals. This incident is the first of any opposition, not against Germans but during their occupation.

The second episode concerns the establishment of the ghetto. The Germans had given the Judenrat (Jewish Council) instructions and orders to set it up. For some time the Judenrat had discussed the question, most of the members finding no alternative but to accede to the German "proposals." Szmuel Zygelbojm, known as "Arthur," was the Bund representative in the Judenrat. He had been one of the original twelve hostages demanded of the Warsaw City Council by the Germans upon their occupation to ensure order in the city. At one of the discussions concerning the proposed ghetto he submitted his resignation, declaring he could not lend a hand to any scheme which made the Judenrat an instrument of German policy. Shortly thereafter, his position having been made untenable by his resignation, Zygelbojm had to flee from Warsaw; but the Bund refused further to participate in the Judenrat. Zygelbojm, later the Bund delegate in the Polish Government-in-exile, finally committed suicide in London because of the unmitigated Jewish tragedy.[3]

In 1942 the Gestapo began looking for Goldstein. He hid in cellars and attics with rats as his only companions. Eventually he escaped to the "Aryan" side of Warsaw with the help of his party comrades, the bakers, the butchers, and drivers who knew him of old and risked their

[3] See text of his farewell letter in *The Menorah Journal* for Summer 1943—ED.

lives to save him. On the "Aryan" side he was in active contact with the Polish underground and aided in supplying the ghetto with arms. He writes little about the ghetto uprising, since his own experiences were those of a tortured observer on the "Aryan" side.

Bernard Goldstein's book is the first to reveal the ghetto in its day-to-day existence, its small joys and great sorrows. Nor does the heroism he writes of dwarf the reality of panic, fear, death and disintegration. A sprawling, overflowing documentary of ghetto life, his book is invaluable for any study of Warsaw under German occupation. In its English translation an introductory chapter has been added, briefly sketching the role of the Bund in pre-war Poland.

Quite different are Jonas Turkow's experiences.[4] His book, covering the period from the beginning of the war until Passover 1943, deals primarily with two aspects of ghetto life: his work in ZTOS and the theater in the ghetto.

Turkow and his wife, Diana Blumenfeld, were among the most gifted and prominent actors on the Yiddish stage in Poland. As in Goldstein's case, their survival was due in no small part to their immense popularity and fame. They escaped from the "Aryan" side of Warsaw to Hungary; and after the war performed in DP camps in Austria, Germany and Italy. They now live in the United States.

Turkow was employed in the housing section of ZTOS, and presents many details about its composition and program. Until the United States entered the war, the chief financial support for relief in the ghetto came from the American Jewish Joint Distribution Committee, which also provided food and clothing directly. It gave funds to such long-established agencies as CENTOS (child care), TOZ (medical care), ORT (vocational training). JDC also subventioned political parties which conducted their own welfare programs (community kitchens, children's homes), as well as ZTOS. When the Germans no longer recognized JDC because it was American, ZTOS had to assume all the greater responsibility for food, housing, clothing, financial aid, refugee care, health, and all the other needs of the stricken community.

In July 1942, the Nazis decided to liquidate "unproductive" elements in the ghetto. Labor cards became the symbol of survival. ZTOS, like other agencies of the Judenrat, retained the right to function and its

[4] *Azoi iz es geven* (How It Happened), by Jonas Turkow (Buenos Aires, 1948), Central Alliance of Polish Jews in Argentina, 529 pages.

employees the right to live. Its offices, like the factories (organized by the Germans for war production), were besieged by people who feared deportation, though few knew that deportation meant death. Turkow writes of executive meetings of ZTOS where two lines of reasoning conflicted. Some members opposed the issuance of additional labor cards, fearing it might jeopardize regular employees; others contended that every card issued meant a life saved. During the summer it turned out that even ZTOS was not immune; the organization suffered a collapse, some of its people being deported while others sought greater security. Turkow managed to find work in a factory.

Soon after the Germans had occupied Warsaw changes in economic and social position arose among the Jews as well as the Gentiles. New moneyed classes emerged from the black marketeers, the Jewish Gestapo agents, the Jewish advisers to the Germans on Jewish affairs, the Jewish police, and the aristocracy of the Judenrat. Many of the young people unaffiliated with idealistic movements began to follow the philosophy of *carpe diem*. Those with money and some measure of security resulting from service to the Germans made up the patronage of the numerous cafés and night clubs which mushroomed in the ghetto, thriving in the shadows of hunger, disease, and death.

Entertainers were in enormous demand. The cafés and cabarets provided a rich field of employment for destitute Jewish actors and singers. The demand was so great, in fact, that any attractive girl or good-looking boy who could muddle through a song or dance obtained work. The ensuing chaos in the profession led to the organization of a central management office, headed by Turkow, to manage the appearance of its affiliated actors and entertainers. Not only the demimonde was eager for the theater. The common people, marooned in their homes after 7 P.M. by the German curfew, clamored for entertainment in the mornings and afternoons. In Warsaw there was never any sensitiveness that a theater was inappropriate. (Vilna, the traditional center of Jewish culture, reacted otherwise when the same phenomenon of "night clubs" made its appearance. Bills were posted all over the Vilna ghetto streets: "The graveyard is no place for a theater.")

Turkow describes in great detail ghetto entertainment in its various forms—theater, revues, concerts—as well as other types of cultural recreation. This documentation alone, apart from his own experiences, makes the book valuable for the historian.

Viewed as a whole, Turkow's book takes on a peculiar proportion. Much space is devoted to the secret Jewish police, the various rival Jewish Gestapo agents and their conflicts for superior authority. Where Goldstein affirms the basic decency and humanity of the common people, Turkow tends to minimize their essential worth by overemphasizing the role of the scoundrels. It is common knowledge that no member of the Judenrat and no Jewish policeman in any ghetto ever had the confidence of the population. Leading members of both the Judenrat and the police were assimilated or converted Jews who in pre-war days had separated from their people. With no conception of Jewish problems or of Jewish strivings, most of them now acted out of ignorance as well as selfishness.

One possible exception, according to Turkow, was the first *Judenaelteste* of Warsaw—Engineer Adam Czerniakow. For three decades an important figure among organized Jewish artisans, Czerniakow accepted the chairmanship of the Jewish community organization in the absence of its leading members, deeming the offer an honor. When the *kehilla* became the Judenrat, with increased power, Czerniakow was reduced to appointing persons of dubious character. He himself was considered by all above reproach; but, as Turkow points out, Czerniakow was a bad judge of character, being himself weak and indecisive. When Turkow once taunted him about his subordinates, he answered defensively that the decent and honest people were not capable, whereas the others were efficient and useful. Suffering many indignities at the hands of the Germans, Czerniakow nevertheless believed that it was within his power to save most of the Jews. But on July 22, 1942, when the *Einsatz Reinhardt*, known throughout Poland as the "destruction commando," revealed the order for deportations, Czerniakow realized that he was no more than a pawn in German hands. He committed suicide.

Turkow describes his own work in a German factory making grinding instruments, and later as a guard forced to keep watch in the Werterfassung, the German organization for the systematic looting of Jewish property. His book closes just before the ghetto uprising. Though not a member of any group planning the resistance, he narrates some episodes showing his cooperation by providing arms through his own resources. Substantially, however, he offers no additional information to what we already know of this period. The book rests primarily on Turkow's picture of earlier ghetto life. Special mention should be made of the illustrations by Theophila Reich—moving into the ghetto, the funeral carts, a gallery of starving children (including one of the "snatchers," who used to snatch bread and other foods from passersby), smuggling, and so on.

The most important contribution so far to the history of the Warsaw ghetto, from the beginning of the deportation in July 1942 until its demolition, is the two-volume study by Meilech Neustadt.[5] Begun in 1944, it was published in Hebrew two years later. A considerably revised and enlarged second Hebrew edition, which appeared in the summer of 1947, has since been supplemented by the Yiddish publication, the most complete of the editions. Neustadt now lives in Israel.

Besides a summary of the deportations and the uprisings, with its intense preparations, the first volume consists of a collection of annotated reports and letters written by participants in the uprising, documents issued by both the Germans and the Jews, and eyewitness accounts of the deportations and the resistance. The Jewish documents are primarily underground reports of the Jewish National Committee (Zydowsi Komitet Narodowy), a coalition of Zionist-nationalist groups, and reports of individual Zionist organizations (Hehalutz, Poale-Zion, Left Poale-Zion, and others), sent to their representatives in England, Switzerland, and Palestine. In addition, Neustadt publishes, with certain omissions, two of the most important Bund reports. Because of the nature of the material, there is not much continuity of narrative; but the sources themselves, with the painstaking annotations, constitute an indispensable part of ghetto history. The first section contains the deportation order issued on July 22, 1942, by the Judenrat and the Jewish police, and an eyewitness account of the entire period through September 21.

The German order which the Judenrat issued through Engineer Mark Lichtenbaum, Czerniakow's successor, provided for the deportation to eastern areas of all the "non-productive" elements in the ghetto, that is, of all people not employed or employable in factories and work projects, in or out of the ghetto, contributing to the German war machine. During this period the control of the ghetto shifted from the Judenrat and its subsidiary agencies to the police, who compelled mem-

[5] *Khurbn un oifshtand fun di yidn in varshe* (Destruction and Rising of the Jews in Warsaw), by Meilech Neustadt (Tel Aviv, 1948), Executive Committee of the General Federation of Jewish Labor in Palestine and the Jewish National Workers' Alliance in U.S.A., 2 vols., 720 pages.

bers of the Judenrat to serve as auxiliary police during the "action" (any rounding up of people, with accompanying brutality). It was at this time that the ZTOS and other agencies dissolved because of the refusal of most of their members to participate in the "action."

The first phase of the deportations, according to the eyewitness report in Neustadt's book, lasted from July 22 until July 29, and was characterized by this procedure. Fifteen to twenty-five ghetto policemen would surround a house, or a block of houses, or even an entire quarter. The people inside the area were forced to submit to an inspection of documents. "Non-productive" elements were taken to the *Umschlagsplatz*, collecting-point for deportation, where cattle-cars were waiting on a siding. Between five to six thousand Jews were deported daily during this week.

The second phase, beginning July 29, marked the entrance of the German SS into the deportation procedure, subordinating the role of the Jewish police. For the first three days the Germans used food to ensnare the Jews. Everyone who reported voluntarily for deportation received three kilograms of bread and one kilogram of jam. Because of the acute starvation in the ghetto and the apparent hopelessness of the future, thousands appeared voluntarily at the *Umschlagsplatz*, believing they would be better off at hard labor in the eastern areas. The cordoning off of houses continued, with much more brutality and immediate killing. This "action" was carried out by ten to twelve SS men in cars or rickshaws (the predominant means of transportation in the ghetto), fifty to a hundred Ukrainians, Litts and Letts, and two hundred and fifty to three hundred Jewish policemen. Many small workshops were liquidated.

During the month of August, also, the ghetto population underwent forced transfer from one section to another, the workers billeted largely in the neighborhood of their factories. The "small ghetto," except for the Toebbens and Dehring factories, was liquidated. During this month, too, all children's institutions were liquidated.

Then, after a few days of comparative quiet, the third phase began on September 3, with renewed cordoning of houses. On the 6th, all the remaining Jews in the ghetto were ordered to report for "registration" within a circumscribed rectangle of a few streets, and to bring with them food and drink for two days. A major selection for life and death was made, the "productive" elements being given new registration cards. The Jews named this action the *kessl* (seething-pot). There was a pause in the deportations from September 13 to 20; on the 21st they were renewed, and among the deportees were many Jewish policemen, the total force having been drastically reduced by the Germans.

According to a table given by Neustadt, based on German sources, the total number of Jews deported from Warsaw between July 22 and September 21, 1942, was 266,156, of whom 11,580 were reported sent to *Durchgangslager* (transit camp), and apparently later assigned to labor camps. The rest were sent to Treblinka.

From the very start of the deportations most of the political parties knew the final goal of the cattle-cars. Previously a handful of individuals had escaped from Treblinka and lived to tell their horrible stories. Organizations had also sent couriers to discover the destination of the deported Jews. They knew that *Umsiedlung* meant, not transportation for work in the eastern areas, but extinction. All the parties, therefore, exhorted the population not to report voluntarily, to offer resistance, to hide. But hunger, despair, and (by tragic paradox) paralysis of will drove the people to *want* to believe in anything, even the German promises that they would be transferred for work.

The major part of Neustadt's first volume consists of reports bearing on the steps taken by the political parties for united action against the Germans, the establishment of the Jewish Coordinating Committee (Zydowski Komitet Koordynacyjny) and the Jewish Fighter Organization (Zydowska Organizacja Bojowa).

Most of the parties had suffered serious losses during the summer. But by the end of September 1942, when the deportations had ceased, it was again possible to engage in some form of organized activity. Negotiations begun in the spring were now resumed, and a united body of various Jewish political interests was formed—the Jewish Coordinating Committee. Its two elements were the Bund and the Jewish National Committee, which represented a consolidation of the various Zionist groups and the Jewish communists. Subject to the Coordinating Committee was the Jewish Fighter Organization. The previously existing party cells, usually organized in groups of five, and the party militias served as the basis for the Jewish Fighter Organization.

After the deportations the ghetto was split into four sections: the central ghetto, in which the Judenrat, police and other official organizations were located; the workshop area, including the major factories of Toebbens, Schulz, Miller and others; the brushmakers' area, comprising the tremendous factory and living quarters for its laborers; and the so-called small ghetto, where there was a large branch of the Toebbens factory. All the workers were quartered in the area in which they worked; the inter-areas comprised a no-man's-land from which Jews were prohibited. Generally, passes were required for movement from one area to another. It is estimated that from October 1942 until April 1943 there were about 30,000 Jews legally in the ghetto—that is, assigned to one of the factories or institutions—and about another 30,000 "illegals" living in bunkers, artfully contrived concealments.

It was under such conditions that the Coordinating Committee and the Fighter Organization prepared for resistance, knowing that the complete liquidation of the ghetto was inevitable.

The final section of Neustadt's first volume contains material on the ghetto uprising, most important of which are three eyewitness reports by members of the Fighter Organization: Shalom Grajek, Simcha Ratheizer, Tovye Boszikowski.

Neustadt's second volume contains the biographies of over three hundred and fifty leading figures who fell in the Warsaw ghetto. Included also are such men from other ghettos as Selig Kalmanovitch, the cultural leader of the Vilna ghetto; and Mordecai Tennenbojm, commandant of the Bialystok combat organization. Most of the biographies are of members of the Fighter Organization, young people in their teens or early twenties, without exception affiliated with one or another of the political movements. Reading these biographies and looking at the numerous photographs of these young unknowns, one is affected with a poignant sense of loss for the idealistic selfless devotion they offered the cause of Jewish resistance.

Of parallel interest to Neustadt's book is *In di yorn fun yidishn khurbn,* a collection of underground reports and eyewitness accounts bearing primarily on Warsaw, but including important material on Lodz, Vilna, Czestochowa, and other parts of Poland.[6] Sent to Bund representatives in the Polish Government-in-exile in London and to the Bund organization in New York, these reports summarize the program of the Bund during the ghetto period, the annihilation policy of the Germans, the ghetto uprising, and the problems thereafter of relief to small surviving groups of Jews scattered throughout Poland.

From these reports we see clearly the abatement of friction among

[6] *In di yorn fun yidishn khurbn: di shtim fun untererdishn bund* (In the Years of Jewish Destruction: the Voice of the Underground Bund), (New York, 1948), Unser Tsait, 342 pages.

the various political parties as the German threat grew, and the emergence of true solidarity in the Jewish Coordinating Committee. The reports tell of the excellent comradely relations, of the united and unpartisan approach to the problems they faced. An interesting detail concerns the funds of the Coordinating Committee, which did not maintain its own treasury. Its expenses were covered by both groups in mutual understanding. Originally, the Bund contributed forty percent; the Jewish National Committee sixty percent. Somewhat later, the Bund increased its grant to fifty percent.

These organization reports, together with the eyewitness accounts of Mark Edelman (published separately in English as *The Ghetto Fights*, New York, 1945), tell of the growth of the Jewish Fighter Organization from October 1942 until January 1943, and of its uncompromising attitude toward Jewish traitors, its retribution on leading Jewish police officers—execution of death sentences by verdict of the organization's tribunal.

At the end of December 1942 the Fighter Organization received its first transport of arms from the Polish Home Army. Though the shipment was small, containing old weapons, plans were made for an assault of the Jewish police on January 22. Events, however, took a different turn.

On January 18 the Germans surrounded the ghetto. It was clear that a repetition of the summer liquidation was about to begin. The Fighter Organization went into action. Only five combat groups took part; the disparity between them and the German forces was inordinate. Other groups could not be assembled in time to gain access to their arsenals. Four major engagements were fought. Jewish losses were great, but there were also German dead; and the Germans withdrew from the ghetto.

That January resistance marked the turning-point in ghetto history. The fact that Germans were killed and German plans were thwarted brought new prestige to the Jewish Fighter Organization, both within the ghetto and outside. The Polish underground began sending larger and better shipments of arms, and the ghetto population became permeated with the spirit of resistance. From January 18 until April 19, 1943, when the Germans again surrounded the ghetto, it was the Fighter Organization that ruled the ghetto; the Judenrat skulked in its shadow. To help maintain the Fighter Organization, to purchase arms and obtain food supplies, contributions were levied against the

Judenrat and everyone in the ghetto known to have money. Recalcitrant black marketeers subscribed under threat of force to the support of the Jewish Fighter Organization. An increasing number of death sentences was carried out against Jewish traitors.

The January resistance also provided a testing-ground for the later uprising. It was believed by some that the organization of barracked groups had not proved completely satisfactory, because they were insufficiently mobile and not readily adaptable to guerilla fighting, the least expendable method of combat for the ghetto.

This volume, of which less than 200 pages deal with Warsaw, contains almost no editorial comment. It is, in a sense, a counterpart of Neustadt's collection of reports. Together they provide the essential documentation of combined organizational activity in the Warsaw ghetto. Edelman's account, in all less than fifty pages, is a superb summary of ghetto history, one-third of it devoted to the major uprising in April.

Dr. Hillel Seidman's book covers the same period: from the beginning of the deportations until the liquidation of the ghetto,[7] Journalist and author, he early became a member of the archives staff of the Judenrat, working under Professor Meir Balaban, leading Jewish historian of Poland. There he stayed until he obtained papers as a Paraguayan citizen. Nevertheless, he was interned in the Pawiak prison in January 1943 for exchange with German nationals, a spurious device used by the Germans to entice Jews into the death camp of Bergen-Belsen. Eventually he escaped from the concentration camp, and now resides in the United States.

Most closely associated with the Orthodox and to a lesser extent with the Revisionists in the ghetto, Seidman writes almost exclusively of these two groups. He describes particularly the sufferings of the Orthodox and the role of their leaders in the ghetto. He writes about the Schulz factory, managed by a Chassidic Jew who once owned it, where dozens of Orthodox Jews obtained work. Here, repairing military boots, were rabbis, Chassidic leaders, talmudic scholars. Their work was extracting nails from the boots with pliers, done to the accompaniment of discussions on Maimonides, the Prophets, and the Talmud.

[7] *Togbukh fun varshever geto* (Diary of the Warsaw Ghetto), by Hillel Seidman (Buenos Aires, 1947), Central Alliance of Polish Jews in Argentina and the Federation of Polish Jews in America, 331 pages.

Seidman also gives us a picture of the intellectuals employed in the archives section of the Judenrat: Professor Balaban; Dr. Ignacy Shipper, a historian; Dr. Edmond Stein, a classicist; and others. He describes their discussions and the disputes between the optimists, who believed there was still some hope, and the pessimists, who were convinced that everything was lost.

Written in diary form, the book contains both lengthy and fragmentary entries. As he was interned in the Pawiak prison from January 1943 through the spring, Seidman obtained information subsequently about the ghetto uprising. His description of the resistance is also written in the diary form. The entries which he claims were written in the ghetto are not too convincing; days and dates are confused, and events within the space of a week do not tally.

We know not only from Seidman but also from other sources (especially Goldstein), that the Orthodox as a group suffered more than any other because of their identifiability. For another thing, when thousands of Jews, driven into the Warsaw ghetto from small outlying towns, sought a roof over their heads, the Orthodox among them tended to concentrate in small synagogues. In conditions of abominable overcrowding, starvation and sickness, disease spread rapidly through these places. They came to be known as "death points." They proved also to be excellent targets during the deportations.

The Orthodox had followed a policy of passive resistance. It was not until after the preliminary uprising of January 18, 1943, when the whole ghetto at last knew clearly the intent of the Germans, that the Orthodox leaders publicly urged support of the Jewish Coordinating Committee and its Fighter Organization. Nevertheless, many Orthodox Jews went to their death with the tranquil nobility that characterized the medieval Jews who died for *Kiddush ha-Shem*.

Seidman's book is the weakest in the present literature. It gives the least information, and its bias and embellishments tend to distort the real picture. But we cannot discard it because every detail added to the story is important.

Personal experiences for this same period are recorded in a completely different vein by Wladka Miedzyrzecki.[8] Born Feygele Peltel

[8] *Fun beyde zaytn geto-moyer* (On Both Sides of the Ghetto Wall), by Wladka Miedzyrzecki (New York, 1948), Educational Committee of the Workman's Circle, 358 pages.

of working-class parents, she was reared in the milieu of the Bund, attended Yiddish secular schools, and became a member of Skif and Zukunft, the child and youth organizations of the Bund. Seventeen years old when Warsaw was occupied, she took an active part in the ghetto program of the Zukunft, organizing children's groups within the house committees, working in the underground libraries and the like.

In this book, the best written of the memoir literature, Wladka writes of her experiences from the first day when notices were posted throughout the ghetto anonuncing the *Umsiedlung* (deportations). She and Turkow are, to date, the only persons who have written with first-hand knowledge about the ghetto workshops. Wladka's descriptions are more vivid and help us understand quite well the character of a ghetto factory, compared to which the sweatshop trades of the last century were a workers' paradise. With a wealth of detail, she transmits the nervous restlessness of the ghetto, the premonition of evil when the deportations began. She tells of the feverish attempts to get into a factory, of the hundreds and thousands waiting for hours at the factory gates, of those who lugged sewing machines and other tools with them to bribe their way into a factory. She takes us into one of the workshops under contract to the Toebbens factory to make uniforms for the *Wehrmacht*. Few of the people who had been hired could use a needle, much less a sewing machine. Those who could sew had to teach the others. In the beginning there was bitter competition for seats and machines because the Jewish factory managers, in their desire to save people by giving them labor cards, had hired more workers than there were facilities. Wladka describes the hum and roar of the machines when the German director was present, and the quiet desolation of the workers when they were alone.

She writes of a Bund meeting she attended in the fall of 1942, where plans were made for resistance and definite assignments given to all the members present. She alone was given no task, and felt humbled and neglected. But, on leaving, she was detained by Abrasha Blum, one of the young leaders of the Bund. The organization, he said, would like to send her to the "Aryan" side to help in the procurement of arms. Her non-Jewish appearance would be an asset. Thus, early in December, Feygele Peltel was transformed into Wladislawa Kowalska, or Wladka, a name which has since remained with her. She undertook the purchase of arms and smuggling them into the ghetto. These chapters are among the most exciting in the book, showing for the first time, step by step, in all its harrowing detail, how the ghetto was supplied with arms and how the underground apparatus functioned. Wladka tells of the sleepless nights of one comrade engrossed in chemistry books until he found the key to the manufacture of hand-grenades.

She writes movingly about the children saved from the ghetto for whom refuge had to be found, about the Poles who helped the Jewish underground, as well as about the Poles who blackmailed and threatened and, in many tragic instances, informed the police. Especially strong are the chapters dealing with her assignments from the Coordinating Committee as courier to the Jews in the labor camps at Radom and Czestochowa, and to partisan groups in outlying woods. She moved across Poland with the most dangerous contraband: money and underground literature. She left Warsaw at the end of the war and arrived in this country in 1946.

Her authenticity is unquestionable, the infinite detail convincing. She tends toward understatement and subtlety. The book is testimony to the many youthful underground workers whose idealism and heroism made possible the program in which Wladka took part.

The most comprehensive publication on the Warsaw ghetto is the book by B. Mark.[9] He was in the Soviet Union during the war, and returned to Warsaw following its liberation. On the basis of eyewitness reports, diaries, conversations with survivors, he has prepared a well-written history of the ghetto from its inception until its demolition. His style is lively and the description vivid, unencumbered by references or sources. This method makes possible the injection of numerous apocryphal incidents, part of the underlying pro-communist bias of the book. (Mark's legends of beautiful Jewish girls shooting German officers bear all the signs of a cloak-and-dagger series.)

The greater part of this volume is devoted to the political parties within the ghetto, their leadership and the rise of the Coordinating Committee, as well as to the uprising itself. Discussing Jewish politics within the ghetto, Mark constantly emphasizes the importance of the communists as an independent group, particularly in united-front activities. In passing he admits, nevertheless, that because the ghetto

[9] *Khurves dertseylin: dos bukh fun gvure* (Ruins Narrate: The Book of Heroism), by B. Mark (Lodz, 1947), Dos Naje Lebn, 394 pages.

was prejudiced against the communists for some reason (he does not mention the Hitler-Stalin pact of 1939), they resorted to the name of Lewica Zwiazkowa (left-wing trade unionists). But it is known from all other sources that the communists played a small role in the ghetto.

It is in regard to the actual fighting in the spring uprising that Mark has something to tell us. His description is more inclusive and easier to follow than any of the isolated reports, since he synthesizes the major reports of four members of the Fighter Organization (Edelman of the Bund, and the Zionists Grajek, Ratheizer, and Boszikowski) with other eyewitness accounts of people now in Poland.

He tells us about the composition of the Jewish Fighter Organization, its twenty-two units recruited exclusively from the Jewish parties. Each of these units was assigned to a specific area. The group of units within each of the four ghetto districts was responsible to a district commandant, appointed by the general staff. All of them were barracked, that is, they maintained food stocks and arsenals at one restricted point which served also as an observation post, local headquarters, and living quarters.

Besides these twenty-two units there were a number of others, loosely affiliated with individual parties. These groups were not organized under the central command because of the shortage of arms and their inability to barrack themselves. Factory workers, for example, were dependent for their daily bit of bread on the rations distributed in the factory; and their living quarters were restricted to factory grounds. However, the Bund recruited some combat groups from these workers, and there is some data to the effect that other parties did the same.

In addition to these groups there were also the so-called "wild" groups, completely unaffiliated and privately armed. These largely comprised people who were attracted to the idea of resistance but had no contact with the underground. Many obtained arms on their own initiative, sometimes even in larger quantities than the official groups. On the basis of the available information, it is impossible to determine the number of these loosely affiliated or unaffiliated combat units. But this is unimportant—as is the number of units in the Fighter Organization—because the few hundred fighters could not have achieved what they did if the resistance movement had not included the entire surviving population.

During the period from January to April 1943 it was a foregone conclusion that the Germans would eventually return to liquidate the last Jews in the ghetto. What was not known was that the Germans had brought to Warsaw one of their best army men, General Stroop, to take charge of the action. Stroop's report, submitted to his superiors in Berlin, on the battle of the Warsaw ghetto came to light at the Nuremberg War Crimes Trials; and Mark uses it for comparative purposes in his account of the fighting.

On April 19, 1943, the eve of Passover, the Germans surrounded the ghetto. But the Fighter Organization was not caught unprepared. Outermost observers gave the emergency alarm, and within fifteen minutes the combat units were at their stations.

The fighting did not abate in intensity until May 10, when the remnants of all but two of the official battle groups escaped through the sewage mains to the "Aryan" side. Sporadic fighting was continued by the survivors until some time in June. The Fighter Organization had various types of small arms, home-manufactured grenades and other kinds of explosives, and above all the unshakable will of its members not to be captured alive. The Germans had over two thousand men, artillery, tanks and planes. Their most effective weapon was gasoline with which they drenched the ghetto and sent it up in flames.

It is estimated that the Jews lost several thousand men and women in the fighting, the flames and the poison gas exploding in the bunkers. The surviving fifty thousand were taken away to the death camps at Treblinka, Trawniki, Poniatow, and elsewhere. The German losses were not insignificant. And all through the summer, when squads of forced laborers were sent into the ghetto to remove whatever property had not yet been destroyed, exhausted and emaciated survivors were still found.

These seven books tell us a great deal of the epic of the Warsaw ghetto. There has also been a considerable amount of periodical literature of uneven value. Collections of life-histories, such as those of the Yivo in New York and of the Central Historical Commissions in both Lodz and Munich, supplement the published material. Some day, perhaps, there will be enough for a complete history.

(—1950)

Beds for Bananas

ᑌᗩᑎᗩᑎᓿ

LAWRENCE KOHLBERG

W E WERE the eighth or ninth ship being sent across from America in May 1947 to take refugees to Palestine "illegally." The Hebrew name for this blockade-running was *Aliyah Beth*, the "Second Immigration." As the name indicates, it was not a matter of conspiracy. Everything had been done legally in America; and American dollars made it legal in Europe. As for keeping it secret from the British—well, we could always hope. But we'd be satisfied just to get the people out of Europe, even if it were only to Cyprus.

I took a launch out to the ship and, being the only passenger on the launch, I began talking to the man at the wheel.

"What ship are you on?" he asked.

"The *Paducah*."

"Does she fly the Panamanian flag?"

"Yes."

"She isn't running Jews to Palestine?"

"No. We're going to carry bananas."

What was there to give our ship away? The harbor pilot didn't notice it. He turned to our Jewish second mate with a puzzled look and said, "Christ, there are a lot of Jews on this ship."

The vessel was an ex-Navy training ship forty-five years old, speed 10 knots, tonnage 900. Even I couldn't believe she'd hold fifteen hundred passengers. More than the *Queen Mary*. If we ever got that far.

I used to wonder about that. You would, too, if you'd been aboard as we ploughed across the Atlantic. You might have gone down to the fireroom and found me looking up at the boiler gauge glass. No water in it.

The engineering regulations would be running through my head.

If the fireman loses the water, cut out the fires and secure the boiler. When the boiler is cool, have it inspected for burnt-out or sagging tubes.

"Cut out the fires, Len," I'd shout.

"Don't get so excited, Larry. The water will be coming up in a while."

I'd shrug my shoulders and walk back into the engine room.

Or, perhaps, you'd take a stroll on deck. The bos'n, an ex-Navy boy from Brownsville, New York City, would probably be looking for Buckshot. We called him Buckshot because he had such a load of lead in his tail. He had left college to make this trip, and he still retained the student's horn-rimmed glasses and four-syllable vocabulary. He was a Trotskyite and brought along huge stocks of literature to convert the crew and the refugees.

Buckshot had come with a college friend, "Eli"; and since they were inseparable, Eli suffered for the sins of his comrade. Collectively, they were "the Gold Dust Twins." To watch them when it was their turn to clean the heads was a privilege. Each had his own idea as to how it should be done, and they would spend an hour discussing the merits of their respective systems. Finally, Buckshot would say in a voice full of noble sacrifice, "All right, have it your way"; and then hand Eli the mop.

Eventually, we called a crew meeting where a motion was made to move the two of them into the galley where they'd really have to work. Thereupon, the Gold Dust Twins began a long filibuster proving that the fundamental rights of man were at stake and, in the end, they stayed on deck. I used to ask Buckshot if he got angry at his persecutors, but he'd answer, "It isn't the individual, it's the system that's at fault."

It was "Heavy," our three-hundred-pound Gentile third mate, who was their chief persecutor. He was one of our three crew members who had been on the notorious "League for a Free Palestine" ship, the *Ben Hecht*. After making one trip for the newspapers, these boys had decided to make one for the Jews. The explanation of Heavy's unpaid service seemed to be a soft heart, which he kept pretty well concealed from our volunteer sailors.

It was the policy of Haganah to hire a few regular merchant marine officers and depend upon them to teach the volunteer crew members how to be seamen. Most of these boys were not connected with any Zionist organization. They had read in the papers about the immigrant ships and hunted around until they found somebody who could tell them how to get in touch with Haganah.

Six days out, we reached Fayal, in the Azores, where our first hitch developed. We were supposed to get oil and water there, but the British had control of all the oil on the island and tied it up, and the agents demanded cash for the water and stores; so we were held up a week waiting for the money to come through.

Finally we left, bound for Lisbon where we were definitely supposed to get oil, and a few days later arrived and anchored in the Tagus River. While we were waiting there, the key man on our ship decided to quit. He was Max, our cook and steward, an old seaman hired from the union hall. Though half-Jewish he was a Catholic, the religion of his mother and of his wife in Alexandria, Egypt, whom he had married by telephone and hadn't seen at all. He was determined to get to Egypt by way of Palestine, but our independent-minded and educated galley hands were too much for him. The only way he could handle them was by getting drunk and throwing the meat cleavers around. However, sometimes even this didn't keep them in line, and he took more and more to drink. So, when we dropped anchor, he downed a couple of bottles and started packing his bags. He was quitting. Then, without calling a launch, he calmly went down the gangway into the river, bag in hand.

The second mate jumped in and fished him out and soon he was back in the galley fixing supper.

That evening the crew held a meeting where we decided not to go ashore so as not to get the ship into possible trouble with the authorities. Beer was then served as a consolation for our sacrifice; after which we all went ashore.

Again it was impossible to get oil; so we got orders to proceed to Bayonne, a small port on the Atlantic coast of France, near the Spanish border. By this time the chief engineer's report of the amount of oil left aboard was preceded by a minus sign; but, luckily, his calculations were wrong and we got into Bayonne under our own steam.

There we tied up next to another Haganah ship, the *Northland,* which was to accompany us until the end. Her crew was in such a confused state that we looked like a model of discipline beside hers. Their attitude was represented by Labal, a writer from Greenwich Village. It was claimed that he had come on the trip because he couldn't keep up the twelve-dollars-a-month rent on his apartment in the Village. Most of his writings were a little too obscure to have a wide popular appeal. However, a story had appeared in *Death Magazine*. This was a journal of which only the first number had appeared, edited by Labal. Shortly after its publication, he was forced to leave town to escape the printer, who was dunning him for the bill.

Along with most of the other boys on the *Northland,* Labal had not gotten along with the captain. So with an ultimatum that it was either himself or the captain, he left for Paris, where he continued to receive spending money from Haganah. Eventually, Labal was triumphant. The captain caused too much trouble and was sent back to the United States.

In the meantime, three Shu-Shus came aboard our ship. The Shu-Shus were Palestinian leaders of Haganah and our real bosses. John, in charge of the whole ship, was a tall, quiet, deliberate man in his early twenties. Chaim was a great talker, full of Yiddish gags, and an operator with the women; but, underneath, hard and calculating. He was to organize the people for distribution of food and work when they came aboard. Menachim, a small, quiet, genial man, with a wife and child in a collective settlement in Galilee, was to be our radio operator since he knew the Haganah code.

Haganah had a large organization in France, but they worked completely without ceremony. I was amazed later when I found the chief of the organization, who had negotiated with cabinet ministers and commanded ships, washing dishes in his collective settlement in Palestine. These Shu-Shus handled huge sums of money without any possibility of proper bookkeeping, but they lived just as we did, and none of us would have ever dreamed of doubting their complete honesty. They were driven by a seriousness of purpose which made them look upon us as playboys and adventurers.

French carpenters and ship-fitters started to take out all useless fittings and put in wooden bunks, three high, like shelves, while the crew was pretty much free. But we could always depend upon Max, the steward, to be on board at six o'clock every morning, even if he'd been heavy on the cognac the night before.

We were all badly shocked the evening we heard he had suddenly died. Our sorrow was somewhat mitigated, however, when we learned that he had died a true sailor's death. He had been found in the hotel bathtub, a cognac bottle clenched in his hand, and a girl in his room.

The next day we learned that Haganah had arranged to give him a
Catholic funeral with all the trimmings in the ancient Gothic cathedral
of Bayonne. No work was to be done on the *Northland* and the
Paducah during the day. And we heard that some of the ladies of the
town whom he had befriended and supported would attend.

The next morning forty-eight Jewish mourners marched into the
great cathedral and took their seats before the bier surrounded by
candles. Our Gentile first engineer was born a Catholic and, though
he had long since left the Church, we depended on him to show us
when to make the proper responses. But it was all very rusty in his
mind, and he too began to sneak looks toward the back of the church
to see what the other mourners, the ladies of the town, were doing.

Bayonne is one of the most attractive towns I've ever known. It
was an important city in the Middle Ages, and later a center for
pirates, but now it was only a town of 35,000 people, with quiet
streets, decaying battlements, and the beautiful old cathedral. At
9:30 at night the little Toonerville trolley which took us out to our
ship stopped, and we walked deserted streets. We never guessed how
crowded those streets would be a month later when a six-day fête
was held, with confetti-throwing, fireworks, bicycle races and dancing
on the cobbled pavement. The fête really centered around the bull-
fights, held in the stadium, for there were many Spaniards and Basques;
and *courses des vaches* were held, wherein cows were let loose in
the streets to be faced by the amateur matadors of the town.

The crew's pace was set by Lewis, our mate and now skipper of the
Northland. His first act on landing in Bayonne was to go to the police
station, introduce himself and describe his important position and connections, so that if he were brought around to be locked up he'd receive
good treatment. (He didn't have long to wait.)

Shortly afterward, we saw him in the square in front of the town
hall, where a United Nations celebration was being held. He was leading the parade of soldiers and giving commands, which they took
good-humoredly. Then the "Marseillaise" was played, which Lewis
sang lustily, getting the words however confused with "Hinkey,
Dinkey, Parlez-Vous." Later in the day he bought twenty dollars'
worth of candy, which he took out to the local orphan home and started
a riot among the children. That was when the gendarmes stepped
in. They didn't mind the riot; but when a man gives away twenty

dollar's worth of candy, the French know he should be locked up.

Our more spiritual side was represented by Buckshot, who managed to fall in love three times during our six-weeks' stay.

At first we seemed to be accepted as a cargo ship by the people of the town, but after a while our real purpose became known and French reporters and photographers began coming around.

They asked us what the wooden shelves were for, and we told them we were going to carry bananas on them. The next day the Bayonne paper was headlined *"Couchettes pour les Bananes"* (Beds for Bananas), with a story that we were going to run refugees to Palestine.

Of course, the French officials had known all along who we were. They now came out with a public statement that we were ordered not to load people aboard at Bayonne, which we never had any intention of doing. This was in July, just after the *Exodus* had been captured; the French officials "discovered" that it had left with faked visas and clearances from Sète. So they fined the shipping company which owned it $80,000. The *Northland* was owned by the same company, and it was to be held pending payment of the fine.

We were afraid they might decide to hold us too, so we worked feverishly to finish the new water tanks and put in the air vents and bunks. We left all our good clothes and passports and papers for Haganah to keep in France, and sailed at five one morning for a destination unknown to the crew.

As soon as we left the harbor we turned south, and the bets were it was to be the Black Sea behind the Iron Curtain. We were all tense as we approached the Straits of Gibraltar, since one ship destined to carry refugees had been seized there by the British. We timed it so as to arrive at night, and we hugged the North African Coast as far from the Rock as possible. We weren't challenged and we went to bed, exultant at slipping through the Lion's claws.

But the next morning, as I came off watch, I saw a British destroyer about a quarter of a mile behind us. There was no accident about it, she'd been trailing us since daylight. Soon she began to overtake us and began signaling. The bos'n started playing a record over the P.A. system, the popular song which goes "Welcome, welcome, we've waited and waited and now we're elated to welcome you home." The DE flashed over the question, "Where are you bound?" and we answered, "Leghorn, Italy." But she stayed alongside us while her crew lined the rail to look at us. A couple of our boys, in a playful mood, got out sheets and towels, dressed as Arabs and salaamed toward Mecca. We were so close we could hear a couple of the English sailors say, "Blimey, they've got bloody Arabs aboard." After a while she fell behind again and followed in our wake.

About this time we found our condensers were leaking, which meant that our water would never last until our destination; so we entered Bohn, in Algeria, to take on fresh water. Our British escort waited patiently outside the harbor, like a private detective in a divorce case, and took up the trail when we left the next day. By the time we reached the Greek coast, they seemed a little incredulous when we signaled Leghorn as our destination. We finally left them behind at the Dardanelles, where naval ships couldn't enter, and they flashed us, "Goodbye, see you again."

By this time the report of our oil supply was again on the minus side. There was only one tank which still held oil, and the fuel oil pump couldn't pick up suction on that. So the chief engineer ordered the whole crew to form a bucket brigade, passing buckets of oil from one tank to the next. Finally, our first engineer rigged up a portable pump and transferred enough oil to get us to our destination: Varna, Bulgaria.

As soon as we arrived a swarm of Shu-Shus came aboard, along with several Bulgarian secret policemen and government officials. It looked as if our path had been smoothed out there by Haganah, and a trainload of oil was supposed to be on its way from Rumania.

We weren't allowed to leave the ship. But if the Americans couldn't come to Varna, Varna would come to the Americans. We were the first American ship there since the war, and crowds of curious people came to look at us. Fulfilling the duties of hospitality, the bos'n played our latest jazz records over the loud-speaker, and we even gave a few impromptu radio shows, inoffensive since none of the people understood English.

Soon, however, our oil ran out, and without electricity or running water we awaited the promised oil train. Eventually the oil appeared, diminished from a train to a horse and wagon with a few barrels of Diesel oil. We started up the boilers and had electricity for a few hours until we ran out again and awaited the next load.

However, we forgot all about these little inconveniences when John, our Shu-Shu skipper, announced that he had gotten permission for us to go ashore. In a few minutes, the ship was practically deserted and we were all exploring life behind the Iron Curtain.

We were lucky to be in Varna, since it was the leading resort in Bulgaria, and there were many people who could speak French, German or even English. Although they were always whispering about the secret police and the militia, all of them seemed to feel free to gripe to us about the new regime. I think that, eventually, everybody in Varna who talked to us asked if we could smuggle him out on our ship. Even the movie queen of Bulgaria, whom the bos'n used to take around, said she'd give up her career to work as a housemaid in the States. Odd situations used to develop when Rudy, our captain, who was an old Communist Party member, began telling these Bulgarians how wonderful their new regime was and how decadent America really was.

But after the "scandal" everybody became cautious about being seen with us.

The "scandal" occurred after we'd spent the afternoon at a roadhouse in the country. The roadhouse consisted of a barn with benches and tables, where a farmer served up his home-brew vodka. Pigs wandered between our legs and chickens flapped around; still, in spite of these distractions, we managed to keep our attention on the vodka. Later we returned to a beer-garden on the main street of the town, where everything was fairly quiet until George decided to dance the hopak on the table. George, who was built like an ox, was normally the moral mainstay of the crew, but now he became really inspired, and there was soon a large crowd around us. Eventually he sat down, but then decided to do an encore, and when five of us tried to hold him down, he really cut loose, throwing tables and chairs in the air. Soon a bunch of Bulgarian soldiers and secret policemen appeared and rushed us all off to jail, until John the Shu-Shu came down and pulled us out.

There were quite a few Jews in Varna, but they didn't have much to do with us. Our passengers were going to come down from Rumania; no Bulgarian Jews were allowed to leave the country. Unlike the Jews in Rumania, these people are necessary in Bulgaria. They are descendants of Spanish Jews who came in during the Inquisition. There was never much anti-Semitism in Bulgaria; and during the war the Bulgarian Government, as an ally of Germany, was allowed control over its Jews. As a result, they escaped much more lightly than any of the other Jews within the German-dominated areas. Since most are well educated, they are useful in peasant Bulgaria.

The British had been putting pressure on the Government, through the Allied Control Commission, to make us get out. Finally we were ordered to leave Varna; so early Friday morning we left and landed again twenty miles down the coast at Burgos. The Allied Control Commission didn't meet over the weekend; the next week the Bulgarian peace treaty was signed and we were safe.

Soon we were joined by the *Northland,* which had finally gotten cleared in France, and we awaited the refugees together. Each day they were supposed to be on their way; but weeks passed before we received word that the freight trains loaded with people would definitely arrive that night.

The *Northland* was to be loaded first, as we still had to take on oil; but all of us were to go over to organize the loading, since it had to be finished before daybreak. It was D-Day for us, and we all shared the excitement of Davey, our fervently religious ex-Hebrew teacher.

Around midnight the train finally arrived and was shunted down to the dock. There were three thousand refugees, old people laden with huge packs containing all their worldly possessions, youth marching to the rhythm of militant Hebrew songs, orphan children, and at the end a woman with her child, born a few hours earlier in a box car.

Davey, who was supposed to direct the people, began embracing each one of them. Rudy, our skipper, burst into tears, even though it wasn't the Communist line. A soberer note was maintained by Charlie, our Gentile first engineer, who turned to me as the first refugee came up the gangplank, and said, "I'm not sure, but that guy looks like a Jew to me."

Soon we were all busy trying to squeeze one more mama or kid into those three-decker shelves. The people had expected to find Greek or Turkish sailors, so they were really surprised to find Jews, volunteer American Jews. John the Shu-Shu said he wished there were fifty more of us, not because we were any good as sailors but because we gave the people a lift.

It took us five hours to finish loading, and at six in the morning the *Northland* pulled out, with the people singing "Hatikvah," the Hebrew national anthem. She dropped anchor in the harbor to wait for us to load, but the people thought it was in order not to travel on the next day, which was Yom Kippur. The *Northland's* deck was thronged with people rocking in prayer, casting the sins of the year into the water. When their skipper, Lewis, appeared on deck with a skull-cap and a prayer shawl, rocking—although not because of religious ecstasy —they were sure their fate was in pious hands.

Meanwhile, the oil train finally arrived, and the next night we loaded our own fifteen hundred passengers and set out. The sea was calm and the people seemed happy. They got two hot meals a day as well as cigarettes and chocolate, and the ventilation wasn't too bad, even if sleeping conditions in the crowded wooden bunks were none too comfortable. Their main complaint was that they couldn't wash except with salt water.

There were plenty of doctors and nurses aboard, and we had a hospital set up. One of the boys even had his teeth drilled by a dentist who had brought along his equipment.

There were a couple of accordions, although there wasn't much room to dance, and everybody was very friendly. Soon Buckshot was in love again. But the most important social event of the cruise was a marriage, held on deck under a prayer shawl, and a reception in the galley afterward. Unfortunately, there was no stateroom for the young couple.

Most of the people were Rumanians, although many were survivors of the German camps and others had been in Russia during the war. We even had some ex-heroes of the Red Army with boxes full of medals. Their attitudes toward the Soviet ranged from lukewarm to cold. All of them complained about anti-Semitism in Russia, particularly in the Ukraine, although some said it wasn't the Government's fault. Most seemed to take the Russian methods of government for granted; ten years of suffering had made them a little hard-boiled. They could even joke about being sent to the soap factory. We didn't have any native-born Russian Jews. Apparently, it was impossible for them to get out.

Life took on a more serious note when we got through the Dardanelles, for there was the British destroyer waiting for us, soon joined by several other destroyers and a couple of light cruisers. As we passed between the Aegean Islands with the English behind us, they flashed us a message that the course we were taking would bring us dangerously close to mine fields. It was a terrible problem to the captain: should he take their word? To us it seemed incredible that they'd try to delude us; but the captain decided to continue on the old course, and we passed through safely.

All along we had been hoping to transfer our people to the *Northland* about a hundred miles off the Palestine shore, so that we could go back for another load. On the sixth night we got orders to stand by to make the shift; but when the crew of the *Northland* tried to move their people below decks to make room for our people, they found there wasn't enough room, so we had to prepare to be boarded.

The next morning the Hebrew flag, the blue star of David, flew from our mast, which the bos'n greased so the British wouldn't be able to get it down. A large sign was hung over our side with our new name, the Haganah ship *Geulah* ("Redemption"). The *Northland* also carried signs with her new name, *Medinah Yehudit* ("A Jewish State").

We had large stores of wooden clubs aboard and all the younger people seemed eager to fight off the boarding party, but we received a radio message from Palestine to offer no resistance. Around noon we made a broadcast to the Haganah radio station, which rebroadcast it through Palestine. Some of the people sang Hebrew songs; Chaim, our official orator, made a speech in Hebrew; and some of us got together and wrote a speech in English. Or rather, we let Lippy, our ex-social director of the Borough Park Jewish Veterans, write a three-thousand-word speech, which we got down to the required laconic three hundred words by cutting out some of the clichés.

By then we could see the coast of Palestine in the distance, and the British marines were lining up on the landing platforms built on the destroyers. Our crew, to disguise themselves, were all busy getting ragged clothes from the refugees, adopting babies and even complete families, and went around muttering Yiddish phrases to themselves. I noticed a young rabbi, complete with a beard, black coat and hat, prayer shawl and a Bible, which he was reading to a group of children. As I approached, without changing his intonation he broke into some profanity known only in Brooklyn. It was Lou the atheist, one of the boys who'd been on the *Ben Hecht* and been held by the British. Now I knew why he had nursed that beard all the way across.

The chief, Len the fireman, and myself were to be below when the British boarded the ship in order to put the pumps out of commission so she'd have to be towed in. Len and I were worried the British would find us below and try us as sailors with a possible four-year jail penalty. The chief said, "My only worry is Haganah will go broke"; he'd be getting paid in jail. But we were all relieved when they sent down twenty refugees to mix with us in the engine room.

About ten miles off the Palestine coast, south of Haifa, the British came alongside and told us to turn back. There was no answer to this, so they began throwing tear gas grenades and then boarded. Below, we felt a crash as the destroyer hit our sides. We sabotaged the plant, rushed up the emergency ladder and mixed with the people on deck. The British had gotten control of the wheelhouse without violence, and now they stood and looked at us, a little curious and a little worried.

John and Chaim distributed the remaining food and cigarettes to the people.

It was night by the time they towed us into Haifa harbor. Spotlights glared on us as we pulled in. Lou the "Rabbi," and myself were among the first to get off and go through the gauntlet of the search and D.D.T. job. The British were "Red Devils," First Airborne troops, mostly bored boys about my age. They directed us in English, and it was hard not to understand when a sergeant told Eli, "You look just like my stupid cousin." Another looked at Lou and asked, "What's that?" and the sergeant answered with an air of wisdom, "Oh, he's a very religious Jew." We were worried about Heavy, our three-hundred-pound mate; but we saw him climb onto the English ship with John the Shu-Shu, and we knew he was all right so far.

The boats used to take us to Cyprus were cargo ships with part of the deck caged off and a couple of large rooms with rows of benches. By some ironic twist they were called *Empire Rest* and *Empire Comfort*.

It was when we got aboard the *Empire Rest* that we first realized the gratitude our people felt toward us. As soon as we were past the British guards, a score of them ran around trying to make us comfortable, bringing us the crackers and tea the British gave out, making room for us to lie down on the benches, giving us their coats, and even apologizing for the shrew who sat across from us yelling at her husband and accusing him of making a scene whenever he opened his mouth to say "Yes, dear." I regretted then the harsh answers I'd given some of those people on the ship when they'd asked for favors, or when their manners weren't too good. It was nice being a hero and part of the legend of their ship, *Redemption.*

The British guards allowed us to go up for fifteen-minute stretches of air in the caged-off parts of the deck, women and children getting preference. As we waited at the door the English corporal said, "Don't look at me, it's that bastard up there who won't let you out," pointing to the sergeant at the top of the stairs.

As we left the ship at Famagusta, Cyprus, all the soldiers said good-bye to each of us and patted Lou on the back and said, "Take it easy, Pop."

When we got ashore a major asked in English for four volunteers to watch the baggage. As no one came forward, he picked them out of different parts of the crowd. Purely by chance he chose Lou, Eli, myself and our Spanish steward. He asked us if any of us spoke English and we all looked blank. Then he muttered something about "these Jews only speak English when they want a cigarette." Finally our Spanish cook said, "I spik a leetle Anglish." So we listened to the major's English and pretended to understand when the cook translated into Spanish.

We were loaded into trucks and taken to the other side of the island near Lanarca, where the refugee camps were. There we passed through an army and C.I.D. control which consisted of a search for arms, money which was deposited by the British, and valuables which were occasionally taken if the refugee was too frightened to complain.

As soon as Heavy entered there, a soldier said to him, "What the 'ell are you doing 'ere, Yank?" Heavy just looked aloof. But when he stripped and revealed the American eagles, anchors and mermaids tatooed on him from head to foot, they took him aside. All he would say was the Yiddish phrases we'd taught him, but they found a draft card he'd sewn in his pants, so he decided he might as well talk English. He was taken to the Major's office, where a girl from the camp was working. Later she told us that the Major had asked him what he was doing there. Heavy answered, "I'm going to Palestine."

"You're not Jewish, why do you want to go?"

"Everybody's going."

"Well, we'll let you go back to America if you tell us who the other crew members are."

"I'd like to be alone with you, Major"—the Major got up—"and I'd knock your block off."

They put him in the guardhouse overnight and he had another interview with the Major. The Major told him they were going to put him in the camp with the rest of the refugees to see how he'd like it for a couple of years.

He is still there, watched by the British. He has filled out deportation papers, but those things seem to go slowly. In the meantime, the refugees wait on him hand and foot, and Haganah gets a bottle of cognac to him every few days, but none of the other Americans can see him for fear of being identified.

Some of the other boys had close calls, for there was a Rumanian Jew in the control, a member of the British Army, who could speak all the European dialects. He seemed to have worked with the Nazis in Rumania, and the British themselves didn't have much use for him.

After the control, we were driven into the camp, issued a blanket, a plate, knife and fork, and left to our own devices. The British leave the organization of the camps entirely up to the refugees themselves, with the help of the Joint Distribution Committee and the Jewish Agency. We seldom saw any British soldiers except those guarding the barbed-wire fence and driving food trucks.

The camps themselves consist of tents and Quonset huts and a few shower huts.

After a refugee has been on the island for ten months he has usually acquired space in a Quonset hut and has probably made himself fairly comfortable. If he is with his wife, they can cook their own food, but must eat in the mess halls and share the kitchen duties. Food consists mainly of dehydrated potatoes and macaroni, with some meat, local vegetables, coffee and margarine. It isn't on a starvation level, but most people's health is fairly low. Most of us got dysentery and boils during our two months' stay. The starchy diet seems to have a peculiar effect on the women—they all become very well developed in the upper chest. In fact, there isn't a girl on Cyprus who doesn't put Lana Turner to shame.

The boys of the crew lived together in a Quonset hut, easily distinguished by its sloppy interior and the large wine barrel inside. Haganah bought us one hogshead of the local vintage each week, and the celebration we held when it arrived was our way of keeping track of the time. The refugees amused themselves more constructively, played soccer, practiced Haganah commando tactics, held amateur theatricals, or danced the Palestinian folk dances around a bonfire.

We had heard the British claim there were Soviet agents among the refugees. However, up to now, the British haven't revealed how they found this out. One thing is quite certain: they have not identified any Russian agents among the immigrants on the ships captured. They haven't even bothered to look.

The British C.I.D. and army "control" of the refugees going to Cyprus and entering Palestine was so inept that the thirty-eight American crew members of the Haganah ship *Redemption,* including myself, passed through it without being identified. Our attempts to disguise ourselves as refugees were definitely amateur. We were spotted as Americans by the people on Cyprus before we opened our mouths.

Did anyone know of any Soviet agents? The answer was "No."

There were many people who had been in Russia; but most shared the opinions of an American Jew, an ex-Wobbly who had jumped ship in Russia in the early 'thirties. Too independent-minded, he had been put away in Siberia to cool off. He'd been released to work during the war, and got across to Rumania where he'd joined the illegal immigration. He was only forty, but he was completely broken in health and spirit.

The people sympathetic toward Stalinism were members of a Zionist political party called Hashomer Hatzair, who numbered perhaps fifteen percent of the refugees. While we were on Cyprus they celebrated the anniversary of the Russian Revolution by marching around with pictures of Marx and Lenin. But most of the members I knew winked as they marched past me. They took its politics with a grain of salt. They had joined the organization in Rumania because its members were the quickest to leave Europe. The Communists prefer to have sympathizers leave rather than those openly disaffected. And in spite of its sympathy for Stalinism, Hashomer practices real and democratic communism on collective settlements in Palestine.

Most of the pro-Russians were young boys and girls who had spent their lives in the German prison camps until they were released by the Red Army. One boy told me that, after releasing him from a camp near Prague, the Red soldiers had set him down to the meal prepared for the S.S. officers. Compared to the Nazis, they were wonderful.

In any case, even these Hashomer sympathizers were as far from being Stalinist agents as the members of Hashomer here in America. They were Jews first and Socialists second. And the largest proportion of them came from the American zone, France and Italy.

A few days after we arrived, the crew of a previous ship, the *Despite*, left. It was a small landing craft which had sailed from Italy flying an Egyptian flag. They had been about fifty miles away from Palestine, still unsuspected by the British, when the captain noticed a light blinking in the aft part of the ship. A few hours later the *Despite* was boarded by the British. Then a girl, who was recognized as the one flashing the light, stepped forward and proceeded to identify the crew members. They were locked in the hold. However, in the mixup of unloading in Haifa, the crew broke out and mixed with the refugees and the British let it go at that. The girl went to England. Her half-sister, who was in Cyprus, said the traitoress' father was a British military *attaché* in Hungary and their mother was Jewish, but she had never suspected her sister was working with the British. Haganah was of course interested in finding her, although the red-haired young skipper of the *Despite* wouldn't say what would happen to her if they did.

The technique of getting us out of Cyprus was simple. The list of the seven hundred and fifty refugees who were allowed to leave each month was made up on the basis of priority of arrival. We were to assume the names of people on that list, who were therefore set back a month. The people who were supposed to leave had already waited about a year, but it was understood that the sailors should leave first.

Still there weren't enough places for all of us; so four boys volunteered to stay behind until the next quota. Labal, the Greenwich Village writer, was the first to volunteer. He was getting three square meals a day without working and was a hero to boot.

One of our Gentile volunteers, Dave Blake, also was for staying behind. Dave was a graduate chemist who wanted to live as a farm worker in a communal settlement in Palestine, where he felt life would be more natural and just than in America. He was always a little distant from the rest of us. We couldn't understand a man who studied Hebrew when he could go ashore in France and chase women. Nor could we understand it after we reached Palestine when Dave took the $100 Haganah gave each of us and went straight to a settlement and gave the money to the communal treasury. When we visited him there he was working hard in the fields and speaking a beautiful Hebrew. He seemed much happier than he'd ever been with us.

It was seven weeks after our arrival in Cyprus when we again went through the British control and boarded the ship chartered by the Jewish Agency to take us to Palestine. The other people were elated, but we were downcast at the thought of still another month in the British quarantine camp at Athlit, near Haifa. Of course, we could take heroic measures like John, our commander, who'd gone the month before. He had slipped over the side of the ship outside Haifa harbor, and stayed in the water nine hours before he found a place where he could land unobserved by Arabs or Englishmen.

Otherwise, it looked as if we'd be stuck, so I stuffed myself on the ship's biscuits, not knowing when I'd get my next meal.

As the ship pulled into the dock, we began looking around for methods of escape; but we all found ourselves on the buses going to Athlit. British tanks and motorcyclists were guarding us. There were no guards on the buses, and the drivers were Jewish.

We told the driver we were sailors and wanted to make a break. He nodded his head and soon all the buses stopped, one bumping into the next. The door opened and, as I later learned, sixteen of us streamed out. I was the first man out of our bus. I still don't know whether I jumped or was pushed by "Action Jackson" behind me. We walked straight across the street into an Arab garage where we asked for parts to a '38 Ford. When we saw the convoy had passed on, we walked down the street until a car stopped and asked us in Hebrew how to get to some street. Instead of answering, "I'm a stranger here myself," we climbed into the back seat and asked him to take us to an address in the city.

In a few more minutes we were safe in a room in the best hotel in Haifa. There we found eight of the boys. The others had been captured and sent on to Athlit. Everything was new and wonderful to us in the hotel—warm water, clean linen, beds, and finally a huge roast beef dinner.

Everybody turned to me, for I was swearing. I couldn't eat a thing. I was still stuffed with those damned biscuits.

(—1948)

The Agents of Ain Geb

❧

MEYER LEVIN

HERE on the rim of Palestine, on the far shore of the Sea of Galilee, there is a single, isolated Jewish settlement backed up against the hills of Transjordan. I saw this colony when it had just been founded, eight years ago, and it was only a stockade with a watch-tower. Now it has spread beautifully along the shore, with many white concrete houses and barns, and a boat-building shop where the comrades construct the fishing vessels they use on the Sea of Galilee.

The first *chalutzim* (pioneers) who settled Ain Geb were chosen for their particular qualities of bravery and steadiness, for when they came to this isolated spot they were considered to be almost on a suicide mission. Ain Geb stood completely naked and alone on the Transjordan side, and it was from Transjordan that Nazi-bought raiding gangs had for over two years made terror-attacks upon the Jewish settlements in Palestine. How could this outpost stand against them?

It stood, and grew, and spread, and served to impede the raiders. The men and women who went out to settle such a spot possessed a kind of nerve which was to be drawn upon for another purpose when the declared war broke out.

One of these men has returned from the war to tell the story of a unit whose exploits were secret until now. This young man of Ain Geb is today awaiting his berth on a ship to America, for he is being sent by the Jewish Agency as an emissary to American youth.

Reuben Dafni is one of the thirty-two Jewish Palestinian parachutists who served behind enemy lines during the war. Twelve were captured; seven were killed, among them two young women. Reuben was the leader of a section working out of Tito's territory in Yugoslavia. Before he came home to Ain Geb he found out what befell each of his comrades. One of them, who jumped with him, was the beautiful and gifted young Chanah Szenes whose name has already

(578)

become legendary in Palestine: her name was on the prow of the ship of illegal immigrants recently beached on the shore north of Haifa.

Since Jews had come to Palestine from all parts of Europe, individuals could be found who were completely familiar with the terrain and tongue of any area. If they could get back into their native lands they could work for the Allied cause. As early as 1940 the organization of such a unit was proposed to the British by Palestinian Jews, but it was 1943 before the plan was put into action.

Jews were to be dropped into enemy-occupied territory; they had two missions for the Allies; their third mission was for "the forgotten ally"—the Jewish people. The first mission of the parachutists was intelligence work—the collection and transmission of data on enemy military strength and movement. Their second mission was the organization of escape routes for British and American airmen and escaped prisoners of war. Their third mission was to contact the remnants of the Jewish population, organize underground resistance among them, and set up escape routes to Palestine. All three missions were brilliantly carried out, though at great cost.

The first Jewish parachutist was a radio operator named Perez Goldstein, 20, who jumped with the original British contacting party, to reach Tito in Yugoslavia in mid-1943. Through Perez radio communication with the outside was established. He remained for six months, then returned to base.

He accepted another assignment, to work his way into Hungary, and jumped again on June 18, 1944, together with Joel Lussbacher. They landed in the partisan-held zone of Yugoslavia, and made their way across the heavily guarded border into Hungary, reaching Budapest. But Gestapo agents had already burrowed into the underground organization which Goldstein and Lussbacher contacted. Both were arrested and tortured. From Perez the Nazis tried to get the radio code he had brought to Tito. They failed. Both boys were sentenced to death, and shipped off to Germany for execution. Joel Lussbacher leaped from the train and made his way back to Budapest where he worked successfully until liberation. Perez Goldstein is believed to have been executed in Oranienburg. In any case, since he has not appeared since liberation, he must be presumed dead.

Meanwhile other Jewish parachutists had been dropped to carry on

their work in Rumania, Hungary, Austria, Yugoslavia, and Italy. At
first they were dropped "blind" with the task of somehow making their
way to towns where they had the names of workers in the underground resistance.

The very first blind drop was ill-fated. Two men—Lyova and
Fishman—were dropped near Timsoara, in Rumania. The pilot mistakenly released them sixty miles from their target. One of them fell
directly into the yard of a police station. The other landed on a roof
and broke his leg. The Rumanian police handed them straight over
to the Gestapo. They were in uniform and had prepared stories in
case of being caught—they were supposed to be airmen who had
been ordered to bail out, and therefore would have to be treated as
prisoners. Luckily the radio equipment which had been dropped
separately was not found; the boys believe it fell into a river near
their landing place; by this accident their lives were saved.

Nevertheless, the Gestapo was suspicious. To keep up their pretense
of being British airmen they had to hide the fact they spoke Rumanian,
for this would have given them away as secret agents.

Arya Fishman was taken to Frankfort and tortured for six weeks.
The most dangerous torture, Fishman later related, was psychological
rather than physical. For the Gestapo put him into a cell with a
couple of Rumanians who told jokes, and good jokes, for hours on
end. If he had once laughed, he would have been lost. He got through
this ordeal, as well as through the physical ordeals which included
electric shock treatment in the nostrils and other sensitive parts of the
body. Finally he was returned to a prisoner-of-war camp in Rumania,
where he remained until the end of the war.

His partner Lyova, having broken his leg, was placed in a hospital
near Bucharest. There the doctors offered to operate since he would
otherwise be crippled for life, with one leg four inches shorter than
the other. However, he feared he might reveal the secrets of his mission while under anaesthesia, and therefore refused an operation.
During his long stay in the hospital Lyova won the close friendship
of a nurse who was able to carry out part of his mission for him,
contacting the underground, and sending out vital military information through a channel to Istanbul. After the war Lyova was returned
to Palestine, where a belated operation partially corrected the condition of his legs.

According to Reuben Dafni, a second "blind" drop also proved disastrous, as the second pair of Palestinian agents were also immediately apprehended. They were taken for airmen, however, and were sent to prison camp, where they remained until liberation.

After these disasters it was decided to try reception drops. The plan was to drop parties in Tito's territory; with Yugoslav partisan headquarters as their base, the agents would work their way through enemy lines into Hungary and Rumania.

Reuben Dafni and four others, among them Chanah Szenes, parachuted into Yugoslavia on the night of March 13, 1944. They fell eight miles from their reception party, but managed to slip through the woods and reach Tito's headquarters. They were well received, and given every aid to get into Hungary.

"We were 120 miles from the Hungarian border," Reuben recalls, "and the Nazis were putting on a counter-offensive. Tito sent a hundred partisans with us, and for ten days and nights we fought our way through enemy territory. Believe me, they had the roads watched! We had to cross two main roads, three railroads, and a river, the Sava river. They were on to us, and we were being chased. By the time we got to the river we had tanks after us. We had engagements every day, and moved by night. The partisans suffered many losses, but they protected us, and we got to the Sava safely. Then there was no boat. At last we found a rowboat, it could only take five people at a time. What an agony that night was! But a larger unit of partisans attacked the Nazis behind us, making a delaying action, and we got over safely."

But on March 18th the Germans had invaded Hungary. Originally the plan had been for Reuben's comrades to slip into Hungary; once there, they were to mix with the Jewish population and operate as Jews. All carried complete sets of identification papers, as Jews. Since the Germans were now in Hungary, it was of course suicidal to carry out any plan which identified them as Jews; a new plan had to be evolved. They tried to work through Croatia. The Hungarian-Yugoslav border was strung with high tension electrified wire, and Reuben's group had three months of narrow escapes, working along the border, trying to establish some sort of contact in Hungary. At last their break came. A party of eight people got out of Hungary into Yugoslavia: among them were four Jews, two communists, a Hungarian British agent, and a Frenchman who hoped to join de Gaulle.

Reuben's group took over the identification papers of some escaped Hungarians—three non-Jewish ones. Photographs were exchanged. The Frenchman and the two communists were persuaded that they could do more against the enemy inside Hungary than elsewhere, and they agreed to go back with the Palestinians. Reuben, meanwhile, was to remain as contact in Yugoslavia.

"The border, there, was the Drava river," he relates, "and it was filled with tiny islands. We fixed on one of those islands for a rendezvous; we had small rubber boats, dropped by parachute. We agreed to have a contact waiting every other day, to pick up messages, information they had to transmit, and also Jews whom they would send out for rescue. Chanah and the Frenchman and two communists went back as the first group: they were guided by professional smugglers. Chanah carried a small radio transmitter, and she knew the codes. Incidentally," Reuben smiles at one thing the Palestinians put over on the British, "do you know what the codes we gave them meant? In Hebrew they were *Aliyah Chofshith*, meaning 'Free Immigration,' *Medina Ivrith*, meaning 'Jewish State,' and *Am Yisrael Chai*, meaning 'The Jewish Nation Lives'!"

The party got safely into Hungary, and hid in an open field. On the second day, hungry and thirsty, the two communists ventured out on a scouting errand. They were picked up by local police and taken to the station. Reuben believes they might have gotten by, as they were probably only suspected of trying to cross the border, and were not thought to be secret agents. One of them, however, became panicky, and shot himself as they were taken into the station. As a result, the police became seriously suspicious, and conducted an intensive search throughout the entire area. They found Chanah and the radio set, as well as the rest of the party.

Chanah Szenes was a girl of twenty-three, daughter of a noted Hungarian writer, and herself extremely talented, as witnessed by a diary she left to be opened posthumously, with which were found several literary and dramatic works. She had come to Palestine as a young pioneer, and had been living in the commune of Caesaria, a Mediterranean outpost quite similar to Reuben Dafni's Ain Geb.

Reuben waited for her many days, at the tiny rendezvous island in the Drava river, and at last had to give her and her entire party up for lost. He could not rest until he found out what happened to them, but this came out only long afterward, through Joel Lussbacher, the agent who, as already related, escaped from a Nazi death train.

For Joel Lussbacher and Perez Goldstein, caught after working their way into Budapest, found themselves in the same jail with Chanah Szenes. The tortures to which the girl had been subjected were the legend of the prison. As she had been taken with a radio in her possession, the Gestapo felt certain she had memorized a code, and they wanted this code, in order to make false contact, pick up communications, and secure entry to the underground. But just as they had failed with Perez Goldstein, they failed with Chanah Szenes.

Her worst moment came when she was confronted with her mother. Somehow the Gestapo had discovered her true identity; her mother was still living in Budapest, and was brought to the girl's cell. The Nazis threatened to torture and kill Chanah's mother; nevertheless the girl kept her secret. The mother survived the ordeal, and is now in Palestine.

Chanah was tried and sentenced to death. Her comrades saw her before she died. The girl was scarcely recognizable. Her teeth had all been knocked out, and her face disfigured. Nevertheless, she found the strength to defy her tormentors during the trial, which was conducted by Hungarian quislings. The records of this trial were discovered, after the liberation of Budapest. When the prosecutor accused her of being a traitor, she flung the accusation back at him, crying "I came here to rescue my people. You are working for the enemy!" After the death sentence had been passed, Chanah was asked if she would appeal for mercy. "I don't want mercy from hangmen," she replied. On November 7, 1944, she was taken to the wall to be shot. She refused the blindfold.

All the efforts of the parachutists, however, were not in vain. Joel Lussbacher, Chanah's jailmate, who had made his way back to Budapest after escaping from his death-train, successfully contacted the Jewish underground, on his second attempt. Enspirited by the presence of this amazing Palestinian, they became more daring in their activities. Vital military information was sent out to the Allies. The Jewish resistance unit procured Hungarian uniforms, and arms. With faked orders, they presented themselves at the Budapest prison where seventy Zionist leaders were held; they pretended to be an execution squad with orders to take the seventy Jews out to be shot. They took

them out—to safety. Shortly afterward they repeated a similar ruse
at another jail, liberating forty-eight political resistance leaders, including many communists. Some of the forty-eight who were saved
by Lussbacher's troops are now high in the Hungarian Government: a
mayor and a member of the cabinet are among them. The underground
commandos also set up a false paper factory, which supplied thousands
of Jews with dummy Swiss passports and International Red Cross
passes; by these means their lives were saved.

In Rumania, too, the parachutists were successful.

Joshua Trachtenburg led a detail which arrived safely in Bucharest,
after being dropped blind near the town of Arad. In a blind drop,
obviously, the first attempted contact is the highest danger point; so
for two days and nights the parachutists lay in hiding, hoping for an
opportunity to get past the roadblocks into the town of Arad, where
they had a contact address. The checkpoint on the road was never
relaxed. Finally, hungry and desperate, they decided to try their
luck on the third morning. They had taken off their uniforms and put
on work-clothes. Mingling with the morning stream of workers entering Arad, they got by.

They didn't know the town, and couldn't find the street of their
contact address. But suddenly Trachtenburg espied a long-coated
Orthodox Jew, for the Jews of Rumania had not been arrested.
Trachtenburg approached, and asked his question in Yiddish. "What!
You're Jews?" the old man replied. "Come, we're just lacking two
men for our *minyan* (quorum) in the synagogue!" The secret agents
from Palestine burst into relieved laughter at this strangely easy outcome of their mission. Soon afterward they had organized a Jewish
underground railway which got over 3,000 people out of Rumania,
on their way to Palestine. Radio contact was established by this unit
with Cairo, and a constant stream of valuable military information
was transmitted to Allied headquarters.

Meanwhile, Reuben Dafni had not been idle in Yugoslavia. When
Chanah Szenes and her companions failed to return from their mission,
he concentrated on the non-Jewish aspects of his work, for there were
practically no Jews to rescue in all Yugoslavia—they had been eliminated in the earliest months of German occupation. "Of 75,000 Jews,"
Reuben says, "all but 3,000 were gone. I estimated at most 2,000 to be
alive with the partisans. I had brought money with which to help Jews,

but for the one time in my life I had plenty of funds I had no way to use them—I brought most of this money back to Palestine with me." He concentrated on his task of rescuing English and American airmen. During six months Reuben brought one hundred and forty fallen airmen, of whom one hundred and twenty were Americans, out of the No Man's Land between partisan and enemy-held territory in Yugoslavia. Plane crews whose missions took them over this territory were instructed to head for the forests in case they had to bail out, and small partisan units regularly patroled the forests to pick up Allied airmen.

"Once," Reuben recalls, "there was a dogfight between a Messerschmitt and a P-38, in plain sight of partisan headquarters. We all watched it, and both planes came down. We sent out a rescue party, and so did the Germans. Our boys came up against two German light tanks, but they got the American out of the plane. His name was Frederick Trafton, Jr. He had four bullet wounds, but we managed to take him on horseback to a partisan hospital where he stayed for six weeks. I made him a list of Croat words, with the English translation, so he could ask for everything he needed. After that we got him safely out of the country."

Another part of Reuben's job was to transmit map information to Allied headquarters in Italy, so that they were always accurately informed as to partisan-held territory—a most essential item of information for the briefing of airmen.

In the middle of September Reuben's work with Tito was completed, and he was flown to Bari where he prepared for a new assignment which would require his being dropped in Slovakia. While in Bari he learned the fate of Enzo Sereni.

Enzo Sereni, one of the best-loved men in Palestine, had come through on a parachute mission to German-held northern Italy. Sereni had insisted on this undertaking even though he was thirty-nine years old, which was considered beyond the age for such hazardous work. He had been dropped in May, and had not been heard from since. Later Sereni's wife managed to secure a place on an army welfare unit sent from Palestine; she used her club as headquarters for the organization of a search bureau, to find out what had become of her husband. Every soldier who got a cup of tea at the club was enlisted in the mission. And eventually one of them did trace the fate of Enzo Sereni. He had been captured through an unlucky first contact, and had been beaten and tortured and sent to Dachau, where he was burned.

Reuben Dafni checked up on the fate of other Palestinian parachutists too, while in Bari awaiting his second mission.

An ill-fated team of three men and a woman took off for Slovakia, his next area. They were dropped forty miles from their receiving party, but the pilot thought they had landed well because he saw many flashing lights after the drop, and took these lights as their agreed-upon flashlight signals. Instead, it was learned much later, these lights had been gun-flashes from a battle going on between Slovakian partisans and Germans. The parachutists had fallen straight into the battle, but managed to reach the partisans. They remained with them, organizing Jewish partisan units, and taking part in combat. They also set up their radio for transmitting information, and took part in the escape-aid for British and American fliers.

These Jewish resistance units were in almost constant contact with the enemy. Three of the four Palestinians were captured in battle and shot. They were Aviva Martinevic, a young woman of 30; Rafael Reis, 30, who was wounded when captured but nevertheless executed; and Zvi Ben Yaacov, 22. Their fourth comrade, Chaim Chermessi, escaped after capture, and managed to reach the Russian partisan lines. He lived for nearly two months in a hole in the snow, while fighting with a Russian unit. On the war's end he reached Odessa, and came home to Palestine to tell the fate of his companions.

After the departure of this Slovakian group, Reuben Dafni waited until October 28th, when he was to take off for the same area. But bad weather held up his plane; and on the next day it was learned that the place where he was to have been dropped had been captured by the enemy. The operation was called off. He learned meanwhile of the fate of another comrade, Aba Berditczev, 26, who, like Reuben, had completed a mission to Yugoslavia and come back to Bari. Aba Berditczev was then dropped in Slovakia, where he joined an Anglo-American unit trying to enter Hungary. All were caught and killed.

So Reuben Dafni came safely back to Palestine, and was released from the service. It is quite natural to ask him what the Palestinian parachutists brought with them into Europe, when they were dropped, beyond their radios and small arms and a little money. What could they do that the Jews of these areas could not have done for themselves? "Actually, nothing," says Reuben. "Any of them could have done what we did. Only, it was the idea of someone coming from Palestine. It was like a miracle to them. They had not been forgotten. It was just like the Frenchmen being dropped to contact the French underground, and the Norwegians in Norway—so we were to the Jews. We brought them only one message—if you are going to die, you might as well die fighting. And the mere presence of a Palestinian was enough. Their courage came back. They swarmed into the resistance movements. Jews became the toughest and the boldest of the partisans. All they needed was to know that we, in Palestine, remembered them."

He would like to stay home now, and live in Ain Geb, fishing in the sea of Galilee, and farming. But there is a new kind of mission for him, to the Jews of America who need a living link with Palestine. This is not so hazardous a mission, and that is perhaps why Reuben has his touch of reluctance in going. But it is necessary, and he'll go.

(—1946)

THE SPIRIT OF IRONY

The Adversary's Note-Book

MARVIN LOWENTHAL

"From going to and fro in the earth, and from walking up and down in it."
Job. I. 7.

You cannot define it, but you cannot deny an air of wildness in Lemberg, in Warsaw, and, I suppose, east of Vienna in general. I felt it first in Bratislava, so I know it is not exclusively Polish. It grew on me in Lemberg, which is only Polish by force of arms. Nothing explained it, yet almost everything helped to create or suggest it. I suppose the slatternly tilt of the roofs, the façades flayed of their plaster and long since estranged from paint, the streets sunk in mud, not dead quiet mud but mud stewed and boiled and spat and spun about by droshkies, Fords, and a dozen species of nondescript carts each and all driven by madmen, I suppose the filth and general decay helped most. Then the chambermaids in our hotel working about in bare legs, even though it was January, added a tone. I saw soldiers stumping through their marshy parade-ground barefoot, and that helped. A soldier in bare feet, wearing someone else's uniform—all Polish soldiers wear someone else's uniform—ceases to resemble that indispensable attribute of civilization, a soldier, and begins to look like a savage poorly disguised. Among the general population there was likewise too great a scarcity of clothing, and what there was showed too plainly of improvisation, like fantastic grace-notes in a gypsy dance. I must confess the very appearance of the Polish language helped. It is an admission of crass provincialism, but it is none the less true that a heavy dose of z's and w's and scki's argues a lapse of decorum to the western eye. A strange alphabet, such as Russian, is tolerable, but Polish (and Rumanian and

Originally published under the pseudonym "H. Ben-Shahar."

Magyar) looks too suspiciously like Latin plus vodka. Even the churches, or at least enough of them, were not quite tame. A Byzantine cupola is a cupola touched with derangement, a dome gone on the loose.

The general impression, whatever its origin, is unmistakable. You feel you are in a land where anything may happen and that beyond, vaguely, are lands where everything does happen. The air is raw, not with the rawness of a wilderness or of the virgin west, but because it has been breathed into by generations of raw men. It is loaded with violence, with the odor of Hulaga Khan and Chmielnicki.

It is not a land calculated to lower the tension of Jewish nerves.

The monotony of the Polish landscape, the dreariness of the winter sky, the universal squalor, and the petty shiftlessness of the people heighten the overtone of wildness by the force of contrast. There is nothing for the nerves to hit at. You are wound up, and then suddenly the works stop. You expect a Polish railway to plunge you malignantly or carelessly or for the fun of the thing into a ditch, and when it doesn't your wonder irritates you as much as your fear. It seems incredible that people hereabouts are sufficiently tame to run a train on time, clerk in a bank or sell postcards.

I took breakfast one morning in a sluttish café on the Legionärstrasse. People sat about much as they do in any café. An assay of their ambitions, occupations, habits, and prejudices would probably not reveal a perceptible difference from an assay made of any breakfast crowd in Childs' or Horn and Hardart's. Yet civilized and therefore commonplace as they seemed, you could not help but think that they were waiting for something more than their food—for something to begin. What? I do not know. On the far wall of the café I noticed a faded oil-painting of a Polish hunt; broad plains, exuberant horseman in furs and colors and wind-whistling beards, a rush of healthy barbarism. It seemed a pity one could not smash the filthy café and with it the ill-fitting sobriety and business airs of Lemberg, and liberate these dulled, fettered huntsmen, sitting about in soiled celluloid collars, drinking hot chicory-water.

Pick up your Dubnow. It may startle you at first to learn that Jewish persecutions in Poland begin with the dawn of modern culture and increase only as Poland becomes more civilized. Healthy barbarians must have their hunt.

The Legionärstrasse is a pitiful imitation of a Vienna "Ring" boulevard. It is too broad, the trees are too mangy, and the buildings are unimposing and decrepit. But despite the general dullness your attention is pricked by a strange figure met at every corner and a world away from the acknowledged type of *boulevardier*. He is invariably dressed in a long back shiny coat dropping to the ankles, he wears a hat as antiquated as a priest's and yet somehow unclerical. He walks at a swift steady pace, and glances furtively at every passer-by as though seeking for someone he knows. He always catches your eye and makes a motion to speak to you. Yet he remains silent. He does not even address his long-coated fellows. Jews, of course, but what Jews? I tell you, there is something in the air of Poland.

I enter a bank to cash two money orders. A long line stretches to the teller's window, and as I move slowly toward my turn, I find myself surrounded by long-coated Jews, brothers to these *boulevardiers*. One of them offers to exchange my dollars at a thousand marks each above the current rate. Another at two thousand, and still another raises the premium to a third thousand. I am now near the window and demand of the third long-coat what the current rate may be. "Ask the teller," he replies with generous honesty. The cashier tells me the rate, and before I can say a word the long-coat renews his offer, "three thousand marks more," and snatches me from under the very nose of the bank.

"Not here, not here," he whispers, and leads me out to the boulevard, then under an archway, down a cobbled passage, through a gate and into a dingy courtyard. I hear a waggoner pounding and hammering. There is a smell of stale food and blacksmithing. We withdraw to an obscure corner of the yard and hastily transfer our money. It is like buying synthetic gin. Only the money is good and the change exact.

A beastly traffic—for it was not printed paper but the bread of the needy we traded in—and these money-changers of Legionärstrasse, did they deserve the hate that the population was not shy of showing them? Not exactly. There are no morals for the hungry. The Jewish money speculator only did in retail what his masters and oppressors, the Polish bankers and the Polish government, did in wholesale. He robbed the crumbs and they the loaf. Today, now that the government printing presses have moderated their output (it was called coin-clipping in the old days and kings lost their thrones in the game), and speculation is no longer possible, I suppose my money-changer has gone back to his old trade of starving.

I asked him the way back to the hotel, whereupon he summoned a youth from across the road to act as my guide. The youth, his eyes shining, was eager to talk. I was from America? Did I know Jankel Schmiersky of Plainville, New Jersey? A pity I didn't, for if on my return I told Jankel I had met him, Jankel's wife's cousin, Jankel would send him two hundred dollars to come to America. *And*—the youth talked fast and low, his eyes on the ground—if he had two hundred dollars he could secure an option on a house he knew of *and* he could borrow so much more on the option *and* he could buy a piece of ground in the burnt-over district near the market *and* he could sell the ground at so much profit for Reb Malkus talked of building there *and* he could buy ten gross of hats from his uncle's brother-in-law in Vienna *and*—the details moved faster and lower—*and* in the end—the youth looked up at me, "I would be making twelve thousand marks a day and I wouldn't go to America at all."

"It's too bad," I said as I entered the hotel, "I do not know Jankel Schmiersky. But you are not going to America as it is."

Not every Jew in Lemberg does such a prosperous business. The market is a sprawling race of weary men and women whose chief stock in trade is their expectations and who have lived longer enough than Jankel's cousin not to expect anything. A fish-man with three salt herring; a fruiterer with a dozen apples and a side-line of a half-dozen candles; a dealer in general merchandise or whatever one would qualify a rusty button-hook, an alarm-clock minus the bell, and a bundle of old newspapers. These Jews are even deprived of that staple occupation of an indigent commerce, that is, of taking in each other's washing. No one washes.

An apple, a fish, a button-hook, is, however, something. In Warsaw one can meet Jews who live on the sale of nothing. Such was the first Jew I met. I wasn't out of the railway station before a youth of twenty-five took possession of me and insisted on escorting me to a *pension* he knew of. I shook him off, entered a droshky, and called out with some magnificence, "Hotel Bristol." I did not go unaccompanied, and standing on the running-board the youth explained to me the advantages of his *pension,* the chief of which I gathered to be the absence of accommodations elsewhere. The portier of the Bristol turned me down glassily, as did the portiers of eight or nine other hotels. My youth's eloquence increased; as he began to feel sure of me he took to pointing out the sights. Finally I yielded and we drove to the *pension*. It was full and had been so for the past week.

I now had a serious talk with the driver, who had no trouble in convincing me that I was a greenhorn, an American *greener* in Poland, and that every hotel was always full until the portier feels properly bribed. So the next portier we encountered pocketed twenty thousand marks, and gave me a room forthwith—at the rate of six thousand marks a day. "If I were the proprietor of this hotel," I told him, "I'd come to you and I'd say, I want you to be the proprietor and you let me be portier."

But I am forgetting my youth. This was more than he did, for he remained throughout on the running-board, demanding his pay. "Pay for what? Your *pension* was full." "Could I help that?' he answered, "I told you I knew of a *pension* and I did, and a good one, too." He ran the scale fluently from injured pride to indignant righteousness. "The *pension* was full," I repeat. "Your hard luck," he replies. It was like a responsive reading of the Psalms. Then he introduced a new theme. "Besides," he urged, "I showed you the city. I told you about the Russian church. I pointed out the cathedral."

Never mind how it ended; a Jew in Poland—as I set out to prove—is often compelled to make a living selling nothing.

It is unfair to leave Lemberg under the impression that it is exclusively a city of dirt, poverty, and barbarism. In the first place there are thousands of Lembergers unconscious of its dirt and other thousands who love it none the less. For Lemberg has its compensations. It has spiritual life and a history, the one naturally growing out of the other.

If you are seeking God I cannot advise you better than to go to Lemberg. Follow that caftan'd figure crossing behind the Rathaus and guiding a little boy by the hand. The boy wears a close-fitting cap and his two ritual ringlets curl down his round cheeks. They enter the courtyard of a synagogue, they disappear through the somber doorway of the Beth Hamidrash. Steal after them. The room is filled with somber figures, ringlets, dust, Polish tobacco smoke, and a raucous clatter of conversation. It is also filled with—and this is what you are seeking—the presence of God.

I do not know where else on earth this presence may be, doubtless in many places, but I know where it is not. I know scores of synagogues, temples, churches and Sunday schools where it is not; clean, comfortable, sunny, sanitary places, and in comparison beautiful. Why God shuns cleanliness, I do not know, perhaps because He is a jealous God. What say the Fathers? "He who has his mind on his fingernails has his mind away from Torah."

You may not enjoy this Beth Hamidrash in Lemberg, but then it is difficult at best to enjoy holiness. It is no holiday affair like beauty.

It is wise to go to Lemberg and learn your limitations.

The Jews were in Lemberg before the Germans and Poles. I am weary of finding the Jew everywhere before anyone else, but what can one do about history? In the early thirteenth century they were keeping their shops there along with the Ruthenians, Armenians, Tartars, and a doubtful people called "Saracens," who were likely Karaites and are now suspected of being a remnant of the Khazars. They continued to do most of the shopkeeping, even after the advent of the Poles and Germans, for in the sixteenth century, out of 3,700 merchants, 3,200 were Jews.

The first persecution took place in 1592. If you can recall the wandering historical notes scattered through these pages—more for my own delight, I admit, than yours—you will realize that this is a record. A century after the Spanish Expulsion before the first Jew is slaughtered! I can't put my finger on the facts but I suspect that 1592 dates the first efforts of the Jesuits to civilize the Poles of this region.

Behind the Rathaus, I have suggested, is a synagogue. It is the famous "Golden Rose," whose architecture is a monument to the stiff necks of the Jews. When it was built the Jews were forbidden to erect a building higher than the neighboring church. They were not content with the indifferent height of this church, they were determined at any cost to surpass it, and they decided that if they were forbidden to build up, nothing could prevent them from building down. And down they built, sinking a third of the synagogue into the ground.

Whereupon the Church authorities found a flaw in the title and confiscated the synagogue. Then the wife of the rabbi, golden Rose, pleaded in person before the archbishop and like another Esther won her suit through her loveliness. The simile is not mine; the Lemberg Jews were well aware of it and celebrated their golden *rebbetzin* in a special Purim hymn. I think the archbishop too deserves some honor for his sensitivity.

Warsaw at first sight is no different from Lemberg except that its greater size offers a greater expanse of dirt and Poles. You admire the Vistula, you admire the cathedral, you admire the mud, and you are ready to inquire about trains for Berlin.

Then a kind friend takes you to the Jewish quarter. A bored man you turn a corner, and before you catch breath the Nalewki is upon you. There is no gradation; in a trice it overruns you, drowns you, batters you, and grinds your fragments into an aching pulp. It is Israel wrestling with all the angels of the firmament.

For a length of time it is impossible to distinguish men, boys, beards, hand-carts, caftans, children, fur caps, women, butcher-shops, dogs, orange-peels. Beards, I think, emerge first. Very early I singled out a Zaddik, six feet of fur-lined coat and sable turban, striding with the majesty of Solomon, a *shammash* trotting at his heels. He was quickly lost behind a moving tower of hat boxes which permitted a glimpse of the porter buried pitifully beneath, before it dissolved into a pillar of silk goods and exploded in the cries of pickle-vendors.

I tried to look into the pigeonhole shops, peer up the dark passage-ways—dark with streaming men—and catch a black silk cap and its black beard and black eyes in a momentary glance, but the boiling hurry shattered every effort at attention.

My friend shouted explanations in my ear, and while I recall what he said I confess I remember nothing of what he described. I heard the Nalewki; I never saw it.

Luftmenschen, said my friend, these are *Luftmenschen.* Today a *Luftmensch* is a silk merchant, tomorrow he is a hatter, the next morning he is a shirtwaist dealer and in the afternoon a jeweler. But he does not deal in silks, hats, shirts, or jewels. He buys and sells information.

There is, you must know, a heavy tax on manufacturing and jobbing in Poland, consequently a great quantity of wares—especially that great quantity which is made and sold in small quantities—is produced and distributed surreptitiously. So if you have manufactured or laid up a stock of hats—in a back courtyard cellar bearing a sign over the low door "Umbrella Repairing"—you will experience considerable diffi-

culty in finding customers. If you advertise your wares, the tax collector will read your advertisement. And you can't depend upon the
people with broken umbrellas wanting hats. Moreover you must sell
your hats quickly, because you made or bought them with Reb
Fingelman's money, and you know Reb Fingelman. So you hurry up
and down the Nalewki until you meet a *Luftmensch* you know and
trust. Then the *Luftmensch* hurries up and down the Nalewki until
he meets another *Luftmensch* who by hurrying up and down the
Nalewski finds a *Luftmensch* who heard yesterday of a man who, by
hurrying, may be reached before he has bought the hats through
another *Luftmensch* who this very moment is hurrying up and down
the Nalewki in behalf of another hatmaker.

You know now what is a *Luftmensch.*

But still, I persist, why does *everyone* hurry? Business is conducted
elsewhere, much business, without this infernal and ubiquitous hurry.

That, said my friend, is a mystery. If you seize hold of the first man
who passes us, that little red beard whose legs are indistinguishable,
and ask him why he hurries, he would tell you he must reach his
destination as soon as he can. If you ask him where he is going,
he will tell you he does not know, but since everyone else is undoubtedly hurrying there—and a glance about you will convince you of
that—he must get there first.

The wares, continued my friend, are hurried about because they
may be too late for the sale, and the sale is hurried because the wares
may arrive too soon.

And everyone hurries, my friend concluded, because it is three
o'clock on Friday afternoon.

The club-rooms of the *Literaten Verein.* I flounder about in a welter
of introductions and debate almost as disconcerting as the elbows of
the Nalewki.

Zinger, the journalist and political writer, covers the law for me on
what is and what is not Jewish culture. I am just learning why
Bialik is in no sense a Hebraic writer, when Kipnes engages me with
his account of Jewish folk-songs; he has gathered and edited hundreds
of them. There is a vague movement toward the piano, but Massbaum
catches me in a side-eddy, rolls back his black hair, and tells me that
he is a "Belle-lettrist," that he spent six months in England, and that

Bernard Shaw was charmed with him. Weissenberg interrupts to explain that he too spent six months abroad, in America, in New York, that is, in the Bronx. He lectures now on America and appears to be impressed chiefly with the number of cats around 165th Street. I am fairly launched in a talk with Meif the violinist (adorned in a gorgeously colored scarf) when the eyes of his beautiful wife found me with a glance. She tried to enter the Polish movie world but found herself, as she put it, too "naive" to adopt herself to its morality; now she pins her hopes on America where, Weissenberg assures her, everyone is ghastly proper. If it had been anyone else but Greenberg I should have been talking with her still, but one cannot resist Greenberg, the futurist poet with red hair. In the first place his father is a *Wunderrabbiner,* and then on his own account Greenberg is sutaining two legal indictments for blasphemy relative to certain poetic fancies on the mother of God. The Polish government officials read every scrap of Yiddish literature; they should eventually become educated. Then Tunker, fat, jovial Tunker with shell-glasses, Tunker the humorist writer overwhelms me by insisting on speaking Russian to me. Despite my protests of ignorance, he eyes me sternly and suspiciously and persists. I presume it is an exercise in humor, but no, Tunker is convinced that all American Jews are Russians and when they deny it, liars. In my case he compromises by believing I do not know Russian but assures me that I am no Jew. I carom for a moment against Schwalbe, a gentleman journalist who writes political leaders and therefore wears a diplomatic air, fall into the hands of Brauner, who is a director of a Jewish marionette theatre and plans to carry his puppets, or have his puppets carry him, around the world; brush the sleeve of Broderson—poet, singer, painter, actor—who bears up under a gigantic gold ring, side-burns, and the pet name of "Indianer"; touch fingers with Warshowsky, the most widely read story-writer of Jewish Poland and the author of *Smugglers* who, despite his good looks, Mme. Meif complains is likewise "naive"; catch a word from Schapiro the bibliographer. . . .

Neumann, I tell my friend, let us go back to the Nalewki where there is peace.

A luncheon at the Hermitage with Dr. Schipper and Senator Ringel. Dr. Schipper is a Jewish member in the Polish Parliament, the editor of a Polish Jewish daily, *Nash Kourier,* teacher in a dramatic school,

professor of the History of Drama in a Yiddish normal school, author
of a two-volume work on the history of the Yiddish drama up to the
eighteenth century, and the wittiest man I met in Poland. He has
discovered that Shakespeare took part in a *Purimspiel*.

Senator Ringel, likewise of the Polish Parliament, is a petroleum
prince. Dr. Schipper is a socialist. This does not prevent their lunch-
ing together in the Hermitage.

In fact the necessities of Jewish politics create bedfellows which I
am sure Leviticus, if not Karl Marx, has long ago forbidden as unnatural manners. The richest Jew in Poland, Szereszfvsky, and the
rabbis with the longest beards can be found voting, any day, side by
side with the Jewish socialists. And the radical Pole votes with the
monarchists against the Jews.

I called on Reb Fishman, the son of a Jewish farmer, who is now
the patron of advanced art in Warsaw. He presented himself in a
dressing-gown like a plump bearded Franciscan, gave me the best cigar
I smoked since I left New York, and showed me, among his treasures,
the works of Marek Schwarcz, Bar Levi, Jankel Adler, other "Young
Yiddishists," and Antokolski's bust of Voltaire.

But Jewish art requires its own chapter. I do not propose to write
it until I know more about it than anyone else. This, I am free to admit,
is no difficult condition; for as yet no one is an authority on Jewish
art. No one has even recognized that it is desirable to become an
authority. I recommend that the Hebrew Union College or the Jewish Institute of Religion found a chair on the subject. If you found
a chair someone will eventually prepare himself to sit in it. And for
that lucky person there awaits a glory unrealized since Zunz.

The hour before taking my train, I spent in a busy café opposite
the Hotel Bristol.

I tried to compose my impressions of Poland; I recalled that some
had told me that of course Poland is uncivilized because if a man
becomes rich there either he lives like a pig or, if he is culturally inclined, departs for Danzig or Paris. But my impressions refused to
compose.

So I took to watching the faces around me. Here, I hazarded, in this
well-to-do café are the men who rule Poland. What are they? Among
the Poles I could discern only two types: cruel profiteers and genial

boors. Among the Jews: cunning *arrivistes* and flaming dreamers. Nowhere the stamina, reserve, self-control, and understanding to build
a modern state.

I had reached the ultimate in Europe. I had trailed the Jews from the
thin few in Chester through the ghettos and markets of England,
France, Italy, Germany, Austria, and Czechoslovakia to the headwaters
of Warsaw. I had sniffed up the trails of their history, inspected their
monuments, observed their gyrations in the multiplex guises of modern
life. I had dreamed over their tombs and prayed in their synagogues.
I had looked into their books, admired their paintings, and listened to
their debates. Everywhere I found them "prisoners of hope." Everywhere they stumbled at noon-day as in the night.

I shall go, I thought, to Gilead and see if the balm still be there.

(—*1925*)

Marginal Annotations

❦

ELLIOT E. COHEN

Purimspiel.—It was a quiet, sunshiny morning and the Elder was sitting quietly in his study, bothering nobody, very busy at his writing. To be sure, his white paper was no less white than it had been two hours before, and he had no more to show for his morning's labor than an enormous number of bright new yellow pencils sharpened to nice long needle-like points. Well, what can you expect with a bunch of robins yelling their heads off all morning in the chinaberry tree outside his window—it's high time those monsters started back up North where they belong. And a man can't write unless he has plenty of sharpened pencils, can he?

One thing or another, though, the Elder was not annoyed when there was a quiet knock on his study door, and Elsa, his daughter-in-law, put her head in.

"Busy?" she said.

"Well—" the Elder began, with dignity.

"No, come," she said, "don't you think with a little effort you might slip in a little time for the mother of your grandchildren?"

"If you put it that way—"

"Especially, since it's about your grandchildren, anyway."

"What is it?" said the Elder, assuming his sagest expression, "have they been thieving, not saying their prayers, cursing their mother?"

"Yes," said Elsa, "that is, no. No. It's about Purim!"

"Purim," said the Elder, astonished, "why only the other day it was Passover."

"Yes," said Elsa, "the other day last April. Well, anyway, it's next Tuesday. Purim."

"Who told you?" I said. "A German Jew should know of Purim, like a something-or-other knows of Wednesday—an old Lithuanian-Jewish folk saying."

"Yes, I've heard it, and it's nonsense. A German-Jewish girl shouldn't know of Purim? Didn't you ever hear of Purim balls. . . . Oh! those Purim balls of my girlhood. . . . Lord!"

"That's true," said the Elder.

"Anyway, it is Purim, and I thought maybe it might be nice for Dovid and Theodor to have some sort of a Purim celebration. Perhaps a little old-fashioned Purim Play with masks—goodness knows there are plenty of masks around the house from Mardi Gras—something light, not too hard to play—we could have a few people in from Bienville, Louise could make some kind of mild punch, and Mrs. Olinsky is going to send over some *Hamantaschen*—do you know of anything we might play?"

"I can't think of anything at the moment," I said. "Maybe something will occur to me. . . . But what's wrong with just doing the story of Purim?"

"I thought of that," said Elsa, "but somehow I can't say I warm up to the notion. For one thing, I don't like Esther much—Vashti, I always thought, has all the better of it, and Mordecai—I'm not sure he's good for the children. He's too crafty, too oily, too—"

"Go ahead and say it, you anti-Semite."

"All right, too Jewish. So hang me for it. Anyway, I'd like something new—something lively, light, something modern."

"Couldn't it have *any* Jews in it?"

"Have all Jews—I like Jews all right enough—only not good Jews, they're always so unreal and awful—I hate good Jews like Mordecai and Esther and Rebecca and Rachel and Daniel Deronda and Shylock and Mr. Lewisohn's Arthur Levy and Reb Moshe ha-Cohen."

"My goodness," I said. "Well," I said, "that's a pretty big order—something new, something light, lively, old-fashioned, modern. . . . As a matter of fact, though, I once wrote a sort of a little play myself. It's somewhere in my desk, I think—But, no, I don't think it would do—it's not a Purim Play at all—I never thought of it for Purim. But it does have masks, and it's modern, all right. . . . Maybe, it might do, at that. . . . No, I guess not."

"Well, there's no harm in looking at it," said Elsa. "Could children act it? Has it plenty of action? Do you think you could put your hands on it?"

"It's hard to say," I said. "Let me look." The Elder rummaged around for a few minutes in a bottom drawer, and finally brought out a large yellow envelope. "Yes, here it is." He leafed a few pages. "I'm afraid it's not very good," the Elder said dubiously, "you know, I never wrote any plays. . . . And I'm not sure it's practical. As a matter of fact, I'm not sure it's a play at all. It's more of a pantomime, sort of a ballet."

"Read it anyway," said Elsa.

"And it could stand a lot of polishing," said the Elder.

"Stop apologizing," said Elsa.

"Who's apologizing?" said the Elder. "All right, we'll read it. But best make yourself comfortable. And have a cigarette. But, first, you must remember—"

"All right," said Elsa, "I'll remember everything."

"All right," said the Elder, clearing his voice. "It is called 'Judentanz.' And it has a subtitle: 'A Little Jewish Comedy-Pantomime Ballet, for Child-Actors, with Masks, and a Few Speeches.'"

"Judentanz." A Little Jewish Comedy-Pantomime Ballet, for Child-Actors, With Masks, and a Few Speeches.

First Episode

It is night, and there is a heavy fog low on the ground, but at intervals the fog lifts and one sees a moon lying near the horizon and in the blue, damp hollow light a bare field. It is apparently an old farm, very badly taken care of, for the ground is deeply plowed-up, but so carelessly that one cannot make out any rows, and the barbed-wire fence that can be seen enclosing it, interweaving the five trees in the background, is strung very hastily and irregularly and broken in many places. The trees, standing black and flat against the sky, form a rough, widely-spaced semicircle: the trees are without foliage, as though locusts had stripped them bare, and most of their branches are broken away (except for an outflung arm here or there) as by a hurricane, so that an imaginative farm-hand might think of them as a row of crosses or gallows. At intervals the fog settles on the field, and lifts. It is quiet except for occasional rolls of thunder at some distance, and now and then there is a quick flash of light, like summer lightning.

There appears from between the trees on the far left A Figure of a Man, crawling on his hands and knees. He rises almost erect and tiptoes with slow, measured paces to the middle of the field, and looks carefully first to the left, then to the right. Then he turns slowly around, and looks again first to the left and then to the right. [This is the first figure of the ballet.] The man is slim and slight and young; he has a thin, sharp-nosed, sharp-chinned face and a small black mustache; he is very pale. He is costumed in a blue, close-fitting suit, cut military style, with tight jacket and narrow trousers; on his head he has what looks to be a trench helmet. He has a revolver in his right hand. There is a sudden crash of thunder, not very far away, and a flash of light. There is a strange whistling in the air. THE FIGURE OF A MAN *drops slowly to his knees. He begins to speak.*

THE FIRST FIGURE OF A MAN (*in a low, deliberate, almost sing-song voice, like a Sunday School boy reciting a well-learned piece. Now and then, however, his voice sinks to a mumble and the words cannot be heard at all*):

"This is my hour of glory and I must not prove unworthy. . . . My country, my beautiful country, that lies prostrate under the iron heel of the treacherous invader, your son offers his bare breast as a sacrifice on your altar. . . . My country, my poor beautiful country, as long as my heart beats, my breath. . . . The beasts, rapers of women, murderers of children, despoilers of cities. . . . Vandals and Visigoths . . . enemies of civilization, brute force incarnate, foes of all things of the spirit. . . . Only the sacred sword of France and her gallant allies stand between Europe and the abyss. . . . My country, my beautiful country, your poor lost provinces, how many years you have suffered . . . it shall not be blotted out, our pure culture, the beacon light of the West, our art, our music, our literature, our clear intellect, these must not fail the world. . . . My beautiful country, my beautiful Paris, father Seine, the rolling fertile fields of Champagne. . . . France must live. . . . Let me prove worthy . . . let me be true to the spirit of David and the Maccabees . . . let me be true to the spirit of the generations of France's heroic martyred soldiers who fought for my sake, who gave themselves that I might live in freedom and equality and liberty, who look down on me now . . . let me prove worthy. . . . Oh! God. . ."

There is a sudden roar on the right; a fog sweeps across the field. He rises slowly and walks back cautiously step by step, looking now to the right, now to the left, with his revolver in his outstretched hand, and is lost in the shadows. . . .

There is a short interval, and then there appears from between the trees at left-center A SECOND FIGURE OF A MAN. *He plods forward, his head low, his knees sagging as from fatigue; he limps slightly and at*

*intervals he stops and looks over one shoulder and then over the other.
[This is the second figure of the ballet.] The man is large, full-bodied
and young; he has a broad, open, round face and blond hair; his cheeks
are rosy. He is costumed in green-gray; on his head, a trench helmet.
He has a gun slung over his back and a grenade in his right hand.*

THE SECOND FIGURE OF A MAN *(in a low, deliberate, almost sing-song
voice, like a Sunday School boy reciting a well-learned piece. Now and
then, however, his voice sinks to a whisper, or the roaring about him
becomes so great that the words cannot be heard):*

"Oh! Fatherland, thy enemies surround thee in an iron ring, their
plots and machination and treacheries encompass thee about. But
thy strength is in thy right—and in thy sons. Dear Fatherland, trust
in thy sons, they will not forsake thee. . . . On the East the dark barbaric
hordes of the Slavic Bear thrust spears in thy side; in the West per-
fidious Albion and the greed of France claw at your flanks. . . . They
are envious of your strength, hungry to plunder the riches of your
science, your industry, your fertile lands. . . . Thy sons guard thee,
who hast the hope of civilization in thy keeping, who hast given the
world Schiller and Bach and Beethoven and Brahms and Wagner and
Kant, who art the fountainhead of culture for all mankind. . . . We
bring liberty in thy name to all the people of the East who suffer under
the oppressive yoke of the Tsar . . . our enemies cannot conquer us.
. . . I am proud to be thy soldier, of being young, of feeling brave
and full of life. I am proud of serving my country, of serving Germany: loyalty to the flag, love of my native land, respect for a spoken
pledge, a sense of honor, are not merely idle words; they resound in
my heart of eighteen like a clarion call; and it is for them that I shall
press forward, if it is necessary to the very limit of sacrifice." *(There
are a number of sharp reports nearby. The man flings his arms up to
the sky, whirls around and then quickly feels himself about the body.
His voice is hoarse with terror):* "Shema Yisrael Adonai Elohenu,
Adonai Echod." *But after an interval, as the fog returns, he crawls off
and disappears back into the woods. . . .*

*The fog rises, the moon is seen again very low on the horizon, and
from between the trees on the center there appears* A THIRD FIGURE OF
A MAN. *He strolls casually across the field as if he were walking across
a park, though a good deal slower; if he had his stick with him, one
feels, he would be chopping off the heads of daisies with it, if there
were daisies. But he seems a little nervous, like a man trying just a
little too much to appear at home in a strange drawing-room. There is*

a slight noise in back of him, and he jumps wildly aside in a sudden start, tearing his automatic from its holster. Then he laughs, as if embarrassed at something. [This is the third figure of the ballet.] He is a ruddy-faced, gangling, somewhat awkward chap; he is costumed in the uniform of the Nineteenth Royal Lancashires.

THE THIRD FIGURE OF A MAN *(in a low, deliberate, almost sing-song voice, like a Sunday School boy reciting a well-learned piece. But the increasing din breaks his speech into fragments, and much of it is heard only as a monotonous wordless chant):*

"Well, they asked for it, the bloody butchers . . . poor little Belgium . . . gallant little France, who'd have thought she had it in her . . . held them back, right enough, saved our necks, right enough . . . now it's our show . . . we're ready for them now. . . . And we'll make it the last. . . . A War to end War. . . . A War to make a new world. . . . A War to save human liberty from Prussianism and mailed fists and clanking swords, the whole evil nest of jingoism and paganism and armaments and bloody materialism and violence. . . . The madmen . . . the cowards . . . Belgium—a little country, that had done them no wrong . . . the atrocities in little Poland . . . the ancient Chivalry of England . . . the just strength of the British Empire that, here and across the seas, has always stood and struggled and fought for freer and better and ampler and nobler conditions of life for man, for the things of the spirit against the forces of matter, for civilization against the beast. Ah! England, this scepter'd isle . . . there is a spot in me forever England . . . oh! the downs of England. . . . Never fear, we'll carry on. . . . An Englishman knows his duty. . . ." *(The sky suddenly shows red with the light of a flare.)* "Oh! our Father, our King—"

He turns around and walks, slowly at first, then more quickly, into the woods. . . .

There is an interval. The moon begins to fade, the dark blue of the sky is now beginning to be a dull green gray. A little wind springs up. From between the trees left center there appears A FOURTH FIGURE OF A MAN. *He is short, stocky and young; his face is small-featured with high cheek-bones; his hair is very light. He is costumed in the infantry uniform of the Austrian Army. He crawls with snail-like slowness across the field on his hands and knees, stopping at every three steps to listen and look around, dragging his rifle behind him. [This is the fourth figure of the ballet.] He sits on his haunches, and puts his rifle down beside him.*

THE FOURTH FIGURE OF A MAN *(in a low, deliberate, almost sing-*

song voice, like a Sunday School boy reciting a well-learned piece. But the noises in the woods have become louder and more frequent and he can hardly be heard at all—only his upturned face may be seen and his lips continuously moving):

"Oh! Lord, everything so bleak, so withered. . . . It is spring now in Vienna. . . . But through this path of filth and blood and fire I must find strength to go for my soul's sake. . . . War must be for one thing, else it would be too horrible—to quicken and renew the soul of the world . . . out of this shall come an everlasting peace, this war by a miracle shall be the redemption of the world. . . . Evil shall not triumph, murderous plots and foul assassinations, the dark forces of the barbarous work shall not overtopple the civilization of our noble country, founded on justice and decency and order and peace. . . . The Tsar and his minions. . . . Oh! the foul enemies. . . . One feels oneself somehow very near to God. . . . I feel some very great thing is about to begin; and I feel comforted and able to do that which I must do for my country's sake. . . . I thank you, both my parents, for having brought me up as you have—to believe! that shall be your fulfillment. . . . Oh! mother, how in those trees blindly the birds fly to and fro and black shadows seize upon the earth. . . ." *(There is a quick succession of measured explosions off at the left. He begins to speak very rapidly, but few of the words are heard.)* "The great . . . mighty, the most high . . . bestoweth loving-kindness—" *There is a crash very near and he rises from his haunches and half-runs, half-stumbles into the woods. . . .*

The moon has gone down. The trees are very black and sharp. From the right center there appears A FIFTH FIGURE OF A MAN. *He runs across the field in a slow, graceful lope, but stumbles; he catches himself, and begins to run again, but he stumbles again; he stops and looks warily about him. [This is the fifth figure of the ballet.] He is tall, straight-shouldered, well-proportioned and young; he has the perfectly-modeled features of a street-car collar advertisement; he wears his costume, the khaki private's uniform of the United States Army, like a Brooks Brothers' suit. He has a rifle.*

THE FIFTH FIGURE OF A MAN *(in a low, deliberate, almost sing-song voice, like a Sunday School boy reciting a well-learned piece. But while he speaks, at regular intervals, with almost mathematical precision, there is a terrific roar from the left, so his voice is often completely drowned out):*

"To make the world safe for democracy . . . no selfish ends to serve . . . a war to end war . . . to make the world a better place to live in . . . no conquest, no dominion . . . no material compensation for the sacrifices we shall freely make . . . champions of the rights of mankind . . . fight without rancor . . . rules of right and fair play . . . succor poor Belgium . . . rescue gallant France . . . hold up the hands of noble Britain . . . protect our great country from the aggression of a barbaric foe . . . protect those shores that have been a refuge for all oppressed people fleeing the darkness and oppression of Europe . . . cause just and holy . . . hand of God is laid upon the nations . . . that idealism shall not perish from off the earth . . . the ultimate peace of the world . . . the liberation of all peoples, the German peoples, too, great or small . . . to prove our manhood in the greatest crucible in all history . . . that the United States may stand glorious and free and unashamed before the eyes of all the world. . . . Our country . . . land of our pilgrims' pride. . . . Land where my fathers died. . . ." *(There are three quick explosions, very near and very loud. The boy leaps with fright. He cries aloud):* "Hear, Oh! Israel, the Lord, Our God, the Lord is One. . . . Now I lay me—"

But all of a sudden there is a complete, deadly, unbroken silence which continues for some minutes. The boy listens with growing puzzlement and alarm. There is no sound. Suddenly he turns and dashes into the woods. . . .

SECOND EPISODE

The sky is perceptibly grayer. The earth and sky are split open by terrific colossal upheavals. There is an interval of silence. Then the sky is lighted by a succession of flares, red and green and orange, like fireworks at a children's Fourth of July party. In the wood somewhere a shrill siren screams, and off to the right a deep, hoarser siren bellows and bellows. There is the sharp tattoo of rifles and the steady patter of machine-gun fire. . . .

From the woods there burst out yelling and cursing FIVE FIGURES OF MEN. *There is a confused struggle, they throw themselves at each other, they wrestle with each other, they fling themselves about in all directions. They fire off their guns into each others' bodies, they club each other with the butts. Two separate from the mass and fight a little to one side with bayonets, screaming and cursing at one another.*

One with a sudden lunge transfixes the other, and tears him apart, but as he turns away he is shot down from behind by one of the others from the ground.

As the wood becomes lighter all five may be seen fallen on the field, most of them quite still, only one or two still writhing slightly. [This is the sixth figure of the ballet. It is, as may be seen, by far the most complicated, and requires the most careful rehearsal to do correctly. With intelligence and the proper preparedness, however, it may be performed with precision and dispatch, and is very effective.]

As the sun comes up, and the first red lights the wood and the sky, five bodies are seen lying loosely side by side, like drowned mariners cast up on the shore by the sea, a hand here and there flung carelessly over a fellow. In death their bodies seem different, smaller, darker and squatter. They look up into the sky and in the first rays of the sun their faces can be clearly seen.

Their masks have fallen off and lie beside them, and it can be seen that each has a nose with a certain curl, and dark hair a little curly, and a curious slight curl each at the side of his mouth.

They look almost as if they might be brothers.

THIRD EPISODE

Days pass and nights, and sun and rain and shell and sleet and storm have plucked at the five that lie in the bare field below the gaunt trees. Their costumes now, like the masks before, have been torn from them, except for a few rags.

So that if God would look down on them now, he could plainly see how they are all marked, each of them indubitably, with the Sign of His Covenant. But God does not appear to notice. Apparently the Lord God Jehovah is either asleep or deaf or absent-minded or walking in the garden or gone on a journey. In fact, God does not appear at all at any time during the ballet. [The author, it will be seen, has made every effort to keep the action true to life.]

FOURTH EPISODE

Days pass and nights, and weeks pass and months, and sun and rain and shell and sleet and storm have clawed at the five who lie in the field before the trees. Their faces, now, and their hair, with the certain curl, and the Sign of the Covenant, and their flesh even, as the masks and costumes before, have been torn off. What lies in the field before the trees, what a stranger would find walking in the field, are the white bones of a number of animals, but obviously of the same species, their skeletons are so very much alike.

Now, at any rate, it is undeniable that they who lie here are brothers.

FIFTH EPISODE

For the Fifth Episode, the stage, set as an immense semi-circle, is divided into five equal sections, like slices of a pie, with the wide side of the slice at the rear. The pantomime is played in one section at a time (beginning with the left), the other four remaining the while in darkness.

The curtain rises on a dark stage. Then studdenly the triangular section on the extreme left leaps out in brilliant illumination. The backs of a great concourse of people are seen sitting in rows on benches. They face an altar from which, further back and above, a row of marble steps leads to a curtained cabinet, before which hangs a red lamp burning feebly. On the left of the altar an improvised draped curtain covers a part of the wall: a rope hangs from the top of one edge of the curtain and there is a wreath on the curtain. By the two immense French flags that hang on both sides of the cabinet, and the two smaller French flags on standards on either side of the altar, one can tell it is a synagogue.

The people sit quietly. It is very hot. There is loud, shrill singing by a choir.

From one side of the platform comes a procession of men with silk hats and black frock coats. The people rise until the men have taken their seats. A MAN comes forward and spreads out his hands. The people rise. The MAN's voice is rhythmical and soothing and very elevated: Into thy keeping, O Lord, in this sacred hour, we commend the souls of our heroic dead, fallen on the field of honor for their country, in the Holy War, in thy blessed Name. He is speaking to God, so the people very courteously do not listen too closely and only stir about a little until he finishes and they can sit down again.

Then one of the men of the silk hats and the frock coats comes forward to the altar and moves his lips and makes gestures. It is a solemn occasion, the MAN is saying. We are met here to honor, he goes

*on. It is especially fitting, it is our very great privilege, it is an honor
I am sure we all appreciate, it is my very great privilege to welcome
him among us in your name, this great statesman, for decades labored
valiantly in the cause of our common fatherland, we value highly his
known and cherished friendship for our people, he continues. And I
am confident he knows, and I am sure that I speak for you all, that
as he has never had reason to doubt the loyalty of our people in the
past, he need never fear that in any future call that will come to us
we will prove wanting, he finishes.*

*He stands aside and points with one arm and there comes to the
altar another of the men of the silk hats and the frock coats. The people
rise and then sit down again. The* SECOND MAN *then sits down. The*
THIRD MAN *stands at the altar. He is a taller and bigger and much
more imposing man than the* SECOND MAN. *He has a great mane of hair
and he is very sure of himself as he begins to move his lips and make
his gestures. It is a solemn occasion, he is saying. We have met to
honor, to pay in some small measure our debt, to immortalize our
heroes, he goes on. It is a sad duty, a mournful duty, a heart-rending
duty, he continues. But there is solace, there is comfort, there is balm
to aching hearts, the knowledge of duty heroically done, our fatherland saved, our losses not in vain, the laurel wreath eternally enshrined
in our hearts, he continues. Nobly demonstrated your loyalty to our
Republic, industrious, God-fearing people, know that in any future
call your people will be among the first, no more respected citizens,
an asset to the State, he goes on. My privilege now, help dedicate, in
everlasting memorial, the heroic dead, he finishes.*

The MAN *walks to the left of the altar and the people rise. He pulls
at a rope and the curtain and the wreath fall away and a brass tablet is
revealed with a roll of names.*

He begins to read:

> ANDRÉ MARTIN
> GEORGES BLOCH
> MAURICE MARECHAL
> ARTUR LEVI . . .

There is subdued sobbing from the benches, but the SECOND MAN
*of the silk hat and the frock coat looks down sternly and the unseemly
noise ceases.*

The THIRD MAN *continues to read as the lights go down, and his
voice can be heard as the second section suddenly lights up, and it is*

still heard in the darkness throughout the whole time the scene in the second section is being played. . . .

As the second section leaps out in brilliant illumination, the backs of a great concourse of people are seen sitting in rows on benches. They face an altar from which, further back and above, a row of marble steps leads to a curtained cabinet, before which hangs a red lamp burning feebly. On the left of the altar an improvised draped curtain covers a part of the wall: a rope hangs from the top of one edge of the curtain and there is a wreath on the curtain. By the two immense German flags that hang on both sides of the cabinet, and the two smaller German flags on standards on either side of the altar, one can tell it is a synagogue.

The people sit quietly. It is very hot. There is a loud, shrill singing by a choir.

From one side of the platform comes a procession of men with silk hats and black frock coats. The people rise until the men have taken their seats. A MAN *comes forward and spreads out his hands. The people rise. The* MAN's *voice is rhythmical and soothing and very elevated: Into thy keeping, O Lord, in this sacred hour, we commend the souls of our heroic dead, fallen on the field of honor for their country, in the Holy War, in thy blessed Name.*

Then one of the men of the silk hats and the frock coats comes forward to the altar and moves his lips and makes gestures. It is a solemn occasion, the MAN *is saying. We are met here to honor, he goes on. It is especially fitting, it is our very great privilege, it is an honor I am sure we all appreciate, it is my very great privilege to welcome him among us in your name, this great statesman, for decades labored valiantly in the cause of our common fatherland, we value highly his known and cherished friendship for our people, he continues. And I am confident he knows, and I am sure that I speak for you all, that as he has never had reason to doubt the loyalty of our people in the past, he need never fear that in any future call that will come to us our people will prove wanting, he finishes.*

He stands aside and points with one arm and there comes to the altar another of the men of the silk hats and the frock coats. The people rise and then sit down again. The SECOND MAN *then sits down. The* THIRD MAN *stands at the altar. He is a taller and bigger and much more imposing man than the* SECOND MAN. *He has a great mane of hair and he is very sure of himself as he begins to move his lips and make*

*his gestures. It is a solemn occasion, he is saying. We have met to
honor, to pay in some small measure our debt, to immortalize our
heroes, he goes on. It is a sad duty, a mournful duty, a heart-rending
duty, he continues. But there is solace, there is comfort, there is balm
to aching hearts, the knowledge of duty heroically done, our fatherland saved, our losses not in vain, the laurel wreath eternally enshrined
in our hearts, he continues. Nobly demonstrated your loyalty to our
Republic, industrious, God-fearing people, no more respected citizens,
an asset to the State, know that in any future call your people will be
among the first, he goes on. My privilege now, help dedicate, in everlasting memorial, the heroic dead, he finishes.*

The MAN *walks to the left of the altar and the people rise. He pulls
at a rope and the curtain and the wreath fall away and a brass tablet
is revealed with a roll of names.*

He begins to read:

   HANS POLLACK
   FRANZ LEVY
   WALTHER GEBHARDT
   WILHELM ROTHMAN . . .

There is subdued sobbing from the benches—

Epilogue.—I felt a hand on my sleeve.

 "All right! I get the idea," said Elsa, a little sharply, I thought.

 "Well, how about it?" I said, tentatively.

 Elsa didn't say anything.

 "Well?" I repeated. No answer.

 "You mean it won't do?" I said.

 "No, I wouldn't say that," said Elsa, "but . . ."

 "Yes," said the Elder, "I can see where it wouldn't do—after all,
there's only Theodor and Dovid, and possibly you and Saul, and I
guess you'd need more people. . . ."

 "That's true," said Elsa.

 "Yes, I guess that's right," said the Elder, "it does need a lot of
people. . . . Well, that's too bad, in a way. You know, Elsa, really I
think it doesn't make such a bad Purim play after all."

 "Possibly," said Elsa.

 "Maybe," said the Elder enthusiastically, "we might get the Bienville
Temple to put it on. . . . They have plenty of kids. I'll call up Rabbi
Hardman."

"No," said Elsa, hastily, "I wouldn't do that. I think Miss Betty Goldsmith told me—I'm sure—they've already organized their Purim exercises."

"That's really too bad," said the Elder, "you know, now that I think about it, why isn't it the ideal sort of a Purim Play for a Reform Sunday School?"

"You think so?" said Elsa. She sounded somewhat skeptical.

"Why not?" the Elder said. "It's a Jewish play, isn't it? Aren't practically all the characters Jewish? And the words are simple, but not too simple, and there are some good long speeches that the Sunday School boys can use their elocution on. And you can't deny there's plenty of action—"

"Yes, I know," said Elsa.

"And, besides, some of the things they have to do in the last part may come in handy some time. It will be good training for them."

"Yes?" said Elsa.

"And," said the Elder, "there are nice bright costumes, aren't there, and masks? After all, the main thing about a Purim Play is, it should have masks—"

"Yes," said Elsa, "I know."

"And the subject matter, you really don't think there's any difficulty there, do you, Elsa? It's timely enough, isn't it? And after all, it's about peace; you got it, Elsa, that it was in a manner of speaking about peace—"

"Yes," said Elsa, "I *almost* got it."

"And they'd certainly like that in a Reform Sunday School, wouldn't they—why they're always talking about peace in the Temples: it'll be just the thing for them."

"Yes," said Elsa, "I can see that."

"I'll have copies made. I'll tell you what I'll do—I'll send a copy to Rabbi Stephen S. Wise for his Sunday School. Surely he'd like a Jewish play about peace for his Sunday School. He's always talking about peace— Why, he's one of the biggest men in the whole United States for peace."

"Oh! he's for peace, is he?" said Elsa.

"Now, Elsa," I said, "you don't mean to sit there and tell me that Rabbi Wise is not—"

"Why, if he was for peace, how come in the last war he got himself and his young son up in overalls and got himself snapshotted in the shipyards—if he was for peace, how come he made those rip-roaring four-minute speeches whooping the boys overseas for Democracy—"

"Oh! Elsa, aren't you a little harsh? How was he to know about secret treaties and the ins-and-outs of Allied diplomacy and intrigue. Why, Dr. Wise is a rabbi, and what does a rabbi know about politics?"

"Well, then, why does he talk about them?"

"Now, Elsa, be fair. Was he the only one? Why, what rabbi in the whole United States didn't do the same as he did? Is it fair to single him out? . . . And then, maybe, Rabbi Wise knows by now he did wrong. Maybe he's sorry. A man can make a mistake—"

"Has he ever said he was wrong? Has he ever said he was sorry? Has he ever promised he won't do the same thing again next time? I read the papers and you read the papers. Perhaps, you saw something —I didn't—"

"Elsa," said the Elder, "please be fair. After all, we don't see all the papers. Isn't it possible that we both could miss just the edition—"

"All right," said Elsa, "send him the play."

"Besides," said the Elder, "does a man have to have the same idea all of the time? It would get monotonous. New things happen in the world, some years are different from other years. You wouldn't have a man go on year after year, no matter what is happening, saying the same old thing over and over again: Peace, Peace, Peace, Peace. A man doesn't wear the same clothes all the time, does he? No, everything in its season. When it's winter you wear winter clothes and when it gets to be summer, do you go on wearing winter clothes? What sensible man would? And Dr. Wise is a sensible man. What's wrong in that?"

"All right," said Elsa, "I *said* send him the play. After all, as you say, it *is* peace season now—this year . . ."

"Yes," said the Elder, enthusiastically, "I think Rabbi Wise will like it. And whom else shall I send it to? There are so many of the rabbis that are always speaking for peace, I hardly know where to begin. There's Rabbi Louis I. Newman of New York, and Rabbi Edward L. Israel of Baltimore, and Rabbi H. G. Enelow of New York and Rabbi Louis Mann of Chicago and Rabbi Harry W. Ettelson of Memphis and Rabbi Philipson of Cincinnati—"

"Pardon me," said Elsa, "do you happen to know of any nice small country entirely surrounded by impassable mountain ranges, say, about ten thousand miles away from the United States and Europe—"

"Well, there's, I don't know—Peru," the Elder said, somewhat confused, "or Tib—what's that got to do with it?"

"Oh! I just happened to know of a woman with two young sons who, say, in case of a certain emergency, would like to know some place good and far away to run away to—"

"Well, she might make them rabbis—"

"And save their own wretched necks by getting other people's sons killed—"

"Be serious, Elsa," the Elder said.

"Serious!" said Elsa. "God damn it, what are we going to do! Must we stay here and wait like rats in a trap! . . . But I'm being impolite. I'm interrupting. You'll excuse me."

"Not at all," said the Elder courteously. "And there's Rabbi Ephraim Frisch of San Antonio, Texas, and Rabbi Jacob Weinstein of San Francisco, and Rabbi Abba Hillel Silver of Cleveland, and Rabbi Barnett Brickner of Cleveland, and—"

"You certainly stand to make a lot of money in royalties," said Elsa.

"Royalties!" said the Elder. "You don't think I'm going to ask for royalties! It's in a good cause, and, after all, I'd like to see the thing put on, and besides, in a year like this with money so scarce that might be an incentive. So I'm going to let them have it scot free."

"Yes," said Elsa, "that ought to be quite an inducement."

"And then," the Elder went on, very excited, "there's Rabbi Abram Simon of Washington and Rabbi Wolsey of Philadelphia and Rabbi Fineshriber of Philadelphia and Rabbi Bernstein of Rochester and Rabbi Krass of New York and Rabbi Goldenson of Pittsburgh—how many copies, Elsa, do you think I ought to have made?"

"I'm sure I can't say," said Elsa. "Why don't you just make plenty?"

She rose and walked across the room. "Well, anyway, lunch in about an hour. . . . So long and thanks."

"Don't mention it," said the Elder.

She stopped at the door. "And be sure and tell me how you make out—"

(—1931)

"I Believe—"

ᴄᴡᴀᴏ

YOSSEF GAER

1. I BELIEVE, *with an unshakable belief, that I had a grandmother.*

IN HER younger days, we were told by those who still remembered, she was a pretty woman with a gracious bearing. But to us, her grandchildren, she presented a shrivelled, wrinkled, toothless being with eyes half-blinded by translucent films, and fleshless hands—mere bones covered by a mesh of hardened veins held together by a parched skin; a silent being who rarely spoke and rarely left the house, except on Saturdays and Holidays, when mother accompanied her to synagogue. Forbidden and spared the slightest effort, she moved about like a wandering shade ever puzzling the members of the family by her constant search amongst the drawers and the cupboards. As if it were her past she was searching. When through with the linen closets and the silverware in the sitting-room buffet and dressers, she would betake herself to the kitchen and rummage through the boxes of useless keys, old locks, nails, and such trifles as accumulate in a household through five generations. And through the evening she would sit in silence upon the sofa in the dining-room, swinging her dangling feet rhythmically, keeping time with the burdened pendulum of the clock upon the wall. She wished she would not do that, she said. She wished she would not keep on knitting stockings for the Devil. But she could not control herself, she said. And it troubled her.

2. I BELIEVE, *and I am justified in my belief, that my grandmother was a pious and God-fearing woman.*

She had never left the village of her birth. And before she knew the wonder of life and living she had been given in marriage to a stranger. Without question or understanding she sought to please her Master who was in Heaven, and him whom God had chosen, she was told,

(618)

as her consort through life. Grandfather was a student of the Holy Law before marriage and continued his studies at synagogue throughout his life—leaving grandmother to provide for their worldly needs, even though in twenty years she gave birth to nine children, all of whom survived and prospered in later years. The few ritualistic laws given the Jewish woman to observe formed the soul of her religion, and she adhered to them with unrelenting severity. Even in her old age she superintended *kashruth* in our home with the stolid rigidity of final conviction. There was a life hereafter to be thought of, and God's laws to women were their only salvation.

3. I BELIEVE, *and am certain, that my grandmother died.*

For months she languished in her bed, her blind eyes pitifully expressing the hope for a quicker end. Yet through the early winter months she confided to mother her longing to survive until the month of *Nissan*, when the pious and those whom God forgives their earthly sins reach the end of their days. But she died in midwinter when snow and frost and wind convulsed outside, and the house was filled with gloom. Mother's eyes were red with weeping, and father paced the room with folded arms seeking consolation in the web of movement. Grandmother rested on the floor of her bedroom with candles burning at her head—yellow weak-eyed candles that wept ivory tears when doors were opened and closed. Strange women came in bringing lumps of snow upon their shoes. Then we children were ordered from the house. And when we returned late in the afternoon mother was seated on the floor in her stocking-feet poring over a large volume in her hands, reading in a voice pinched by sorrow. And in the corner of the window-sill the soul's light flickered.

4. I BELIEVE, *and I have seen it with my own eyes, that grand-mother was buried.*

Deep in a cold grave they laid her. Snow was falling over the graveyard on the slope of the hill. And the wind was cold. Far away the village seemed unreal with its naked trees and white heavy roofs. A dog kept barking in a distant yard. Around grandmother's grave a number of men clad in black murmured hasty prayers, whilst two Fellows of Holiness, whose living was encouraged by the burial of the dead, filled it with shovelfuls of lumpy, heavy dirt. Then it was all over.

The mound of black earth was covered with snow before the prayers were at an end.

5. I Believe *that grandmother is in Heaven now.*

For it is written that unto the pious this life on earth is likened only to a hallway to the Palace of Peace. And where else could a soul such as she find rest as compensation for a life such as hers on earth?

6. I Believe *there are no bureau drawers in Heaven.*

Is it not said that the Lord our Lord rests in Holiness and His abode is full of song and praise? Song and praise, and not bureau drawers for grandmother to search. Instead she can chat with Sarah, Rebecca, Rachel and Leah about days and ways other than were hers; or she can listen to the Heavenly Chorus whose chants, undoubtedly, surpass the best of cantors.

7. I Believe, *also, that the day will come when the Messiah will appear to emancipate the Jews from Exile.*

Our great prophets have foretold that there shall come an Emancipator to Zion and to the repenters in Jacob. And though the sins of Israel may delay his arrival, yet in the end he shall come. Why shouldn't he come?

8. I Believe *implicitly in the resurrection of the dead.*

Is it not expressly said that they who have followed the Ways of the Lord and observed His Laws shall not have come and gone as the winds and snows, forever to be forgotten; but they shall rise to life again when the Messiah appears?

9. I Believe, *therefore, that the pious dead are assembling in readiness for the day when the Messiah's trumpet shall be heard.*

The bones of the pious, so it has been prophesied, wherever they may have been interred, keep rolling underground to Jerusalem. And

when the trumpet call is heard the dead shall rise to praise the
Creator who performs miracles.

10. I BELIEVE *that when the Messiah comes all Jews, and we
among them, shall return to Jerusalem.*

With black fire on white fire it has been promised that He shall
lead us in peace from the four corners of the earth and bring us
triumphant into our Holy Land. They who know not the Lord and
understand Him not will seek the safety of iron bridges and mechanical
devices in crossing the oceans and depths leading to salvation. Their
bridges shall collapse and they shall perish with their folly. But we
Jews, with the wisdom that has long been ours, shall seek our safety
on a bridge of paper, and reach unhurt our Promised Land.

11. I BELIEVE *that when we shall have reached the Land of
Israel we shall witness a miraculous reunion with those dear
to us long departed.*

For it is recorded that when God celebrates our return to Zion we
shall be as dreamers of dreams. Then our mouths shall be filled with
laughter and our tongues with song. And we shall rejoice in His
miracles. And we shall rejoice in the return to those who had left
before us on the long journey.

12. AND I BELIEVE *grandmother will be there.*

Among the pious she shall have risen. And she shall return to us
just as she was. She shall join us in our rejoicing. And if there should
be no bureau drawers in our new home in Jerusalem for her to ran-
sack, she can watch us planting the olive tree, and harvesting the
grape.

13. ALL *the foregoing I believe wholeheartedly and with an unshakable belief. But this last article of Faith puzzles me:*

*I do not know whether grandmother will come to life again when the
Messiah arrives, or whether the Messiah will arrive when my grandmother will come to life again.*

(—1925)

AI Harei Catskill

❧❧❧

MAURICE SAMUEL

My uncle (father's side), a remnant dealer,
Was wont to say: "Of all that deal in remnants
The God of Israel was the first, for He,
(His name be blessed) looking on our despair
And knowing, too, the bitterness of exile
(Is it not written *Schinta begalutha?*)
Found comfort for Himself and us in this:
'A remnant of my people shall return!'"

This was the proper style of the Creator
Since first He made a covenant with us:
He took a remnant and He made a people.
He took a remnant of the seed of Terach
And in the land of Goshen wrought a people.
He drew a remnant from Mizraim forth
And in Judea made Himself a people,
A Law, a Temple and a Prophecy.
A handful left the plains of Babylon,
Its bursting fields, its markets and its glory,
The envy of the nations and their prize:
A remnant turned again to make a people—
A land of armories and synagogues,
Of bearded warriors of intemperate will,
Of saints and sages gentler than the dove—
The Maccabean fury and the love
That wakened in the wise old eyes of Hillel,
Akiba's sweetness and Bar Kochba's rage.

My great-grandfather was a honey-gatherer,
And he had thirteen sons and all are dead.

His birthplace is unknown; his resting place,
A family legend tells, is Palestine.
His name, his occupation and his grave
Is all that's left to rumor and record.
One son, my father's father, lived and died
In Glodorlui, which if ten living Jews
On this side the Atlantic know the name,
It's nine more than I'd dare to take an oath on.
My uncles, father's cousins, second cousins,
By pairs and handfuls cover the world.
Some peddle socks in the Nalewki; some
Sell diamonds on the *Faubourg Cracovie.*
The former sing their Yiddish with an *Iy,*
The latter condescend to German only.
I've met a sprinkling of the stock in Paris
(*"Mon fils unique est mort pour la patrie."*)
A minor tribe has England for its home
But mingles badly with the lost ten tribes;
Some live beside the Golden Gate, and some
Beside the *Brandenburger;* some, I hear,
Are Talmud students in the Gaon's city,
Vilna the old—and some are "Harvard men,"
While I, who live in Babylon the New,
Preach the Return to startled Jews, and spend
This summer in the Catskill Mountains here.

The honey-gatherer, who sent his seed
To inherit graves a thousand miles apart,
Had never heard of Catskill: for the rest,
Paris and London, Warsaw and New York,
Were one to him. His straight geography
Knew only of two worlds—Golus and Zion.
He did his duty to the former—thirteen sons
After some generations do their share
Toward filling earth; and with his duty done
He packed his portion in a bundle, took
The wanderer's staff (that's how I pictured him)
And sought the latter out to die in peace.

My grandfather, his son (the one who lived
In Glodorlui, of old Wallachia)
Was likest to have followed in his steps.
He, while the fresh wind of a western world
Troubled his brothers and inclined their steps
In quick succession toward the setting sun
(Some, disillusioned, sought the east again
And came by stolen frontiers into Poland)
Alone inherited the father's dream
Which made of all his life a pilgrimage
Between his birthplace and his grave in Zion.
But something in his actions and his ways—
Perhaps the passion for antiquity,
Perhaps his oriental inclinations,
Perhaps his nose—displeased his peasant neighbors.
Moishe the Jew (I got my name from him—
'Twas given me in the hope that I would prove
A zaddik, or a martyr, for his sake)
Became impossible; and thus, one night,
A band of them, with murder in their hands,
Broke in on him while he, by candlelight,
Was deep in Babylonian mysteries.

Something, a *soupçon* of the Talmud chant
My sainted grand-dad loved, rings in my ears.
It comes from younger lips. Judea's daughters
(Modern edition, but as like as peas
To those intolerant Isaiah once
Cursed with such detail anatomical)
Accompanying the lilting phonograph:

> *O Katerina, O Katerina,*
> *Please—get leaner . . .*
> *Bettina, my Bettina,*
> *I can't eat my farina,*
> *Ta-ram-ta-ra-ra-ra-ra,*
> *Ta-ram-ta-ra-ra-ra-ra.*

The crowded porch is hidden from my view
While here I scribble in a nest of pines,

But I can see them: hips and shoulders jolly,
The body subtle-swaying, eyes half-closed,
And soft waves galloping from top to toe
Like waves of shadow through a field unshorn.
Is it romantic fancy that invests
Their twanging melodies with shadow tones
Strayed from the pages of my grand-dad's *Schass?*

My Paris uncle, mourning for his son
(*"Mon fils unique est mort pour la patrie"*)
Speaks of his fatherland with tears of pride.
"La France quand-même. Is there in all the world
The peer of her? Mother of liberty,
Gay with immortal youth! Alone she solves
The double mysteries of faith and joy.
She worships life with laughter. From of old
The nations laboring dourly at the task
Of merely living, turn to her for breath,
And catch from her a moment's merriment.
Yet she is strong. Behind her laughing eyes
Lurks steel—a rapier in a dazzling sheath.
Greatness and grace! Tradition in a jest
And wit the soul of wisdom! *C'est la France!"*
In faultless French delivered: but the flame
That flushed his temples had a somber hue,
A something deadly, something too intense.
My grand-dad's curse! If I had never known
The martyrdom of Glodorlui, or if
They had not told me why I bore my name
I would not look for the exotic east
In uncle's patriotic sentiments,
Or hear the echo of the arghool's drone
In voices chanting to the ukulele.
And yet—and yet—why do the heathen rage?

The singing on the porch dies quick. A stir,
A mighty shout goes up—I can't resist.
"I held four aces, with the joker out!
Four aces with the joker out and lost!"

"Suppose you held four aces? What of that?
Four of a kind was held before and lost."
"I held four aces with the joker out!
Four aces and no joker!" "Did you see?
A straight flush from the nine! He bought the Jack!
An inside straight!" "I held four iron aces!
I held four aces and the joker out!
Four aces!" *By the streams of Babylon.*

I turn back to my shelter, through a field
Of sunlit grass; with every onward step
A bursting cloud of grasshoppers goes up,
And patters down again. A squirrel sits
And flicks his armpit with a rapid leg.
He sees me, starts, outstares me for an instant,
And passes in a flash. I dream again.

My cousin by the *Brandenburger Tor*
Is scientific-international.
Last night an intellectual youth was here
Put me in mind of him. "I mix with Jews
By accident of contiguity.
That's all, my friend. Don't look for deeper cause,
Traditions, missions, and the rest of it.
This is an age of science. What's a Jew?
What cranial index has a Chosen People?
What's the description of a Race of Priests
That answers to laboratory tests?
The *Jew* is an illusion: Jewishness
A dying system of transmitted dreams.
That settles it."
That might have settled it,
But all unwary and unwitting he,
Enfranchised of transmitted dreams, broke forth
In unprovoked apocalyptic terms:
"Behold, the brotherhood of man draws nigh,
The night of error and delusion passes.
The light of reason dawns on all the earth,
And war shall die."

Isaiah, Chapter Two,
Has something to the same effect, I thought,
Though rather better phrased. But what's the sense
Of polemizing with an obstinate Jew?
The way of faith is hard—and just as hard
The way of unfaith, both by checkered loops,
Twist within twist, each tinier than the last,
Lead back to wonderment and weariness.
"The Jew is an illusion!" Is not life,
All life, self-watching, an illusion too?
"There's no belief!" But thinking is believing,
And merely living is an act of faith.
Since living and believing are the same,
The Jew, believing most, the longest lives.
That's pretty! Let's see what the Jew believes.

My Paris uncle, he who lost his son,
Believes that France illumines all the world.
My cousin in Berlin, the Ph. D.,
Believes that science will redeem mankind.
My second cousin, in the *Vilner Kleisel,*
Believes whatever's written in the *Schass.*
My Harvard relatives believe the Jew
Must suffer till he learns how to behave—
To wit: To talk discreetly, take to sport,
And temper his uncivilized *élan*
Either in argument or eating soup.
Another, by the Golden Gate, believes
We have a mission, which, in brief, is this:
To teach the world that God is only One,
That peace is good and war is bad: that men
Are all of them the children of One Father.
But all our teaching must be done politely,
Without insistence or obstreperousness—
So gently that the world will not perceive
That we are different from the rest of it.

And here in Catskill what do Jews believe?
In *Kosher,* certainly; in *Shabbas,* less,

(But somewhat, for they smoke in secret then.)
In *Rosh Hashanah* and in *Yom Kippur,*
In charity and in America.
But most of all in Pinochle and Poker,
In dancing and in jazz, in risqué stories,
And everything that's smart and up-to-date.
("Milton, thou shouldst be living at this hour,"
To hear the Catskills ringing with thy name.)

Is that what Jews believe? Give up the ghost then!
You've lived with shadows, not with living men.
If this were all, how simple were the story!
There's something else! "A remnant shall return . . ."
Define that something else! Pluck out the secret,
And lay it on the table for dissection.
Yes, if creation were a formula
And life a scientific incantation.
But here's a something that no man can read
Or ever will: the book before *Bereischith!*

                                                     (—1925)

The Flying Litvak

ᕙᕗ

LOUIS BERG

Zu vos hot er es gedarft? Issac Levine

Social note: Mr. Charles A. Levine, prominent businessman of 150
Beach 135th Street, Belle Harbor, Rockaway Beach, well known in
his community for his interest in Jewish charities, has returned home
after a six months' tour of Central Europe. He was greeted by fellow members of the Brooklyn Chamber of Commerce, and a banquet
was held in his honor. During his trip Mr. Levine visited many of the
principal capitals, such as Berlin, Vienna, Warsaw, Paris, Rome and
London. Mr. Levine made most of the journey by airplane. . . .

Of course, there was more to it than that, Charles Levine being
the same who with Clarence Chamberlin broke the transoceanic flight
record by flying from New York to Eisleben, Germany, a distance
of 3,825 miles. No mere businessman of the Rockaways, however
successful, can expect to hear sirens screaming deafeningly—at intervals—and tugs in the river tooting—every now and then—as his
liner steams into New York Harbor. Nor expect to find the official
welcoming tug *Macom* waiting to transfer him to the Battery for a
triumphal march to City Hall. True, the resplendent uniforms of the
National Guard were missing; there was a lamentable shortage of
ticker tape streamers and telephone book confetti when the parade
passed up lower Broadway; also it rained miserably, and the enthusiasm of the populace, for this or other reasons, seemed considerably
dampened.

But otherwise the welcome accorded Mr. Charles Levine was not
markedly different from those given the other victorious flyers. He
was hailed from the steps of City Hall by the dapper Mayor of New
York City, given an embossed set of resolutions, and his name was

officially inscribed with those of Lindbergh, Byrd, Acosta, Maitland, and by this time too many others.

Yet how different is Mr. Levine from all these worthy heroes! How disconcertingly different!

But how else? These are veritable lions of the North. And Mr. Levine . . . Mr. Levine, let us speak freely, is a Jew. More—to tell all!—not only a Jew, but a Litvak.

His father, Mr. Isaac Levine, was born on the Rudnitzky Gasse, in Vilna, from which city come all of the really precious Jews who do not come from Kovno. The elder Levine studied in the Katzina Clois. His father had the rabbinate in view, but Isaac rebelled, and fled to America, to open a junk business in North Adams, Mass. Isaac's father had been a pious Jew who travelled about in Lithuania exhibiting a model of Solomon's Temple. His grandfather was the learned and pious Rabbi Moishe Levine (*a Yid a lamdan*) who could discourse most eloquently upon the Talmud, and who spent his last days in Jerusalem, going there to die.

This is the lineage of Mr. Charles Levine. From his paternal great-grandfather he no doubt inherited a love for argument; from his grandfather, a desire for travel; from his father an obstinate and adventurous spirit and a shrewd eye for business. And from the land of his fathers—who would think otherwise who knows it and its sons? —that subtle virus in the blood which made him the prosaic-poetic, idealistic-realistic, ambitious, stubborn, quarrelsome, cantankerous, yet quite admirable sort of hero he is. Litvaks—everybody knows— are like that.

No wonder the Gentile press and public failed to understand. No wonder they were from the very beginning bewildered—and annoyed —by the unaccountable conduct of this new aviator-hero. In the annals of aviation there was simply no precedent for this mixture of Don Quixote and Sancho Panza. which Lithuania and the tribe of Levine had contributed to the greater glory of God, the U. S. A., and transoceanic flying. Besides, when a Jew and a Litvak departs from the business of making money, he is apt to be as obnoxious as when he sticks to it.

To be sure, in the very beginning, Levine, as backer of the proposed Bertaud-Chamberlin flight, had cut no prepossessing figure. The war had made him a millionaire. The press had it that he had been a dealer in junk, although his father Isaac indignantly denied this allegation, insisting that Charlie dealt only in the newest of steel pipes and plumbing fixtures. He made his money by reclaiming shells and other munitions abandoned by the War Department; and although the Government shared in the profits, certain officials were so far from being satisfied with their distribution as to threaten suit against him for a sum ranging from $500,000 to $1,000,000.

No background, this, for a hero, for a modern Daedalus. Nor as a backer of the proposed aeronautical excursion to Paris did he behave according to American ideas of sportsmanship. He quarrelled with Bertaud, and he quarrelled with Bellanca, designer of the plane. There were constant bickerings and dissensions in the Levine camp, nor was the atmosphere improved when the young *goy* Lindbergh stole a march on the whole lot, and speeded across the Atlantic to a fame that has already endured seven months.

For regardless of where the fault lay in the quarrels between Levine and the ill-fated Lloyd Bertaud, which culminated in the resignation of the latter, the fact remains that the quarrel was over money, and the finger of suspicion was quick to point to the squat and none too heroic figure of the Jew. Comparisons were ready: the daring of the aviators on the one hand, the mercenary attitude of the man of business on the other. Clearly Levine's interest in aviation was the money to be made of it through the heroism of others.

For a frenzied week, Lindbergh, having arrived pajama-less in Paris, occupied nearly the entire front page of the newspapers and a good deal of the remaining space. Levine had been forgotten when the announcement appeared that Chamberlin was preparing the "Columbia" for another attempt to fly the Atlantic. The name of the flyer who was to take the place of Bertaud was not given.

Recall that solemn Viking Lindbergh, gripping his friend's hand that misty dawn on Roosevelt Field. As he mounted his plane, he pronounced for an anxious world and posterity these portentous words: "When I climb into that cockpit, it's just like a man going into the death chamber. But when I land in Paris, it will be just like getting my pardon from the Governor." Then, with a swirl of the propeller, away the lone eagle flew, to glory and a world-wide acclaim.

Look now upon this picture. A small mob of skeptical reporters and photographers summoned for the steenth time to witness the take-off of a flight that somehow never materialized. The Bellanca and Chamberlin are finally going. Yes, they are. Like hell! Who's taking Bertaud's place? Into the empty seat in the cockpit quite casually stepped Levine. Just going for a trial spin, he told his wife and friends, Going on a record-shattering flight around Mineola, L. I., said the cynical reporters to each other. But the plane, after swerving, rather foolishly, to avoid running down a motorcycle cop who blundered into the path, lifted into the air, and to the consternation of newspaper reporters and photographers, friends, mechanics and curiosity seekers, winged straight ahead for Europe.

By a simple act of daring Levine had completely dumbfounded his calumniators, who were many. Dressed in the plain business suit he wore every day to the office, Levine had set out to achieve the impossible. It was as if a rooster had flapped his wings, and flown.

His wife behaved that morning as no hero's wife should; but then she had been given no time to rehearse her part. How was she to know her husband was a hero? She had married a cocky and self-assured business man, whom she had known from the time they went to high school together, and later when she went to work in his office as stenographer. It is true they eloped to Baltimore to be married, but after that Levine had settled down to be a good husband and father, and, to say the least, an excellent provider. And now all of a sudden he had turned eagle. Mrs. Levine shrieked and fainted.

Nor was the behavior of Levine's father any better, if the news reports are to be credited. He showed an utter lack of sympathy for this latest crack-brained exploit of his son, who had always been hard to manage. For when Levine was a boy, we learn, he wished to become a jockey, and had been restrained with difficulty. Then, with quite unnecessary recklessness he had insisted on personally helping remove the powder from the shells abandoned by the Government. Later he had fancied being an aviator, and again his father had wrestled with him. This time Levine had consulted no one.

As a Yiddish paper reported him, the elder Levine was plainly annoyed. *Zu vos hot er es gedarft?* he is quoted as saying, and in this remark lies a complete Lithuanian-Jewish philosophy. "Now what did he have to do that for?"

Do it he did, however, to the confusion of a Christian world. He landed in Eisleben, Germany, some 46½ hours and 3,825 miles later. The press was not incoherent in his praise. For him no double-columned leaded editorials, later to be engraved on silver plaques. For him lifted eyebrows and little condescending paragraphs. Indeed, he was hailed rapturously only in a letter to the papers from a man who signed himself suspiciously L. Mortimer Fortesque, Chairman Husbands Union Committee of Welcome to Charles A. Levine, who brevetted him for his high courage and reckless daring—for making the trip without consulting his wife.

But it must be remembered that Lindbergh was the idol of the period, and Levine's exploit had tended somewhat to cast a shadow upon that hero's earlier deed. The populace would not have been very pleased, even in the olden times, if after the line of march celebrating the latest triumph of St. George, there had followed some country bumpkin unconcernedly dragging a second dragon. The presumptuous varlet—stone him!

It must be admitted, however, that Levine's conduct toward friend and foe was not what might be called conciliatory. Tact was never his prime virtue.

"Lindbergh had all the luck," he told the first reporters in Germany, and some have seen something less than the perfect tribute of one sportsman to another in the fact that he named his dog "We." For a little man he was uncommonly militant, bristling at the least touch. In his quarrel with Bertaud he was utterly uncompromising, and his remark on closing the discussion was not of the sort usually issued for publication.

"So far as Bertaud's ability as navigator is concerned, I congratulate him on his prowess to land with such glowing success in the newspapers," he said. And in answer to the news that the Government might effect a compromise of $300,000 in its suit against him: "I intend to bring suit against the Government for twice that amount."

He had two fist fights in Paris because his courage was questioned, and invited reporters to his rooms to give testimony that if anyone bore the marks of the encounters it was not he. "I used to be a boxer," he exclaimed proudly.

Even the Yiddish press grew uneasy as reports began to filter into this country of his quarrels and adventures in Europe. Not even to members of his own race did he make concessions, and it must be admitted they began to regard him with suspicion. What sort of a Jew is this? In Warsaw he declined to meet the Jewish pressmen or mingle with any Jews. (Just the same the Polish press had to be warned by the

Government not to abuse him as a Jew—was he not an American?) Even his own people began to be rather dubious as to whether his exploits reflected entirely to the credit of the Jewish people.

There was some haste, therefore, on the part of the American press to explain that, while Levine might approach Lindbergh in daring (and Levine was something of an amateur in the hero business), yet he was far deficient in certain moral qualities, and certainly a less outstanding personality.

As a matter of fact, it is perhaps in the last that Levine chiefly outshines his Nordic rival. For some tastes, let it be whispered, Lindbergh is too much the glorified Boy Scout, which is to say he is loyal, brave, trustworthy, dignified and public-spirited, if not always cheerful. Levine, on the other hand, is a true individualist, who gives not a rap for his foes and critics, who drives hell-bent ahead, and leaves his friends to do the explaining behind. What if he is vainglorious and boastful? Who will not say with Bill Nye: "I luv a rooster becaws he crows and becaws he has claws to back up his crow with"?

Those who love him cherish particularly that rotogravure photograph of all the eighteen or more transatlantic flyers, taken beside the Nation's Chief before the White House. On this picture Levine sticks out, as the common expression goes, like a boil. While all the other seventeen or more flyers are gazing obediently at President Coolidge, Levine is perversely staring in the opposite direction. He is the shortest person present, counting even Ruth Elder, and it looks suspiciously as if he were standing on his toes.

But enough of weary comparisons; enough of apologia and analysis. Let the exploits of this remarkable young man—why is one surprised to find that he is not middle-aged but thirty?—speak for themselves. Let us turn back to the files of the newspapers where they are enduringly inscribed.

Even to the story of the flight itself as Chamberlin tells it for the *New York Herald Tribune*. Scene: mid-air; the cockpit of the "Columbia." Characters: Clarence Chamberlin, pilot; Charles Levine, passenger. To look at them you would think the one is a peppery business man taking a ride in a taxi, of which the other is the driver. So it is no surprise to discover them arguing.

There is plenty to argue about. Chamberlin has announced that the gasoline supply will not last; Levine has discovered that the oars for the collapsible rubber boat had been left behind. Moreover, the indicator to the electric compass has broken. All of which Chamberlin considers more than ample reasons for turning back. "What," Chamberlin asks Levine, "do you wish to do about it?" "I'd rather be buried in Davy Jones' locker than face that newspaper gang in New York," Levine says with vehemence.

And all the way over Levine worries because he has the payroll of his company in his pocket, having absentmindedly forgotten to leave it behind. "It would be a shame to drop into the Atlantic with all that money in my pocket," he observes.

Even more exquisite is the "real inside" story of how they missed Berlin.

For miss it they did. Not theirs the swift unerring flight of Lindbergh, who landed in Paris as if drawn to the spot by some magnetic influence. In somewhat less precise fashion did Chamberlin and Levine reach their goal—or rather one of their goals, for when they left New York they were rather vague as to whether their destination was Berlin, Paris or Rome.

"When we got over Essen," says Chamberlin, "I thought we were over that town, but Charlie thought we were over Bremen. He said he had been there. I had never been to Essen. When Charlie was resting, I would fly in the direction I thought Berlin lay from Essen, but when he relieved me as pilot, he would fly in the direction he thought Berlin lay from Bremen."

They landed first in Eisleben, 105 miles west of Berlin. As a bit of aerial navigation, their trip left something to be desired: but they broke the record for the trans-Atlantic flight. It was inevitable that Levine, missing one mark, should hit one as great. He is a Litvak.

Leaving Eisleben for Berlin, they blundered again, were lost in fog, and suffered a forced landing in a marshy field at Klinge, 70 miles southeast of Berlin, where a good crowd of citizens waited to welcome them, grew tired and went home cursing the Jews. . . .

Despite their little difficulties on this crazy voyage and later, the good-natured Chamberlin seems to have been the only man to properly appreciate Levine. To this day they appear on excellent terms with each other, and they were both more or less in high good humor while they toured Germany. Not until they reached Paris did they sever relations, and Chamberlin, in addition to establishing the world's long distance flight record, also has the more rare distinction of being the only pilot hired by Levine who was able to complete the contract. To the very end Chamberlin insisted loyally that the only point of difference between them was that, "I want to go back by boat; he wants to go back by plane. I am going back by boat; he is going back by plane. So everybody is happy."

A slight unpleasantness did arise, however, from Levine's unhappy challenge to Commander Byrd, who had by this time reached Paris. Failing to appreciate the serious scientific and diplomatic purposes underlying all transatlantic flights, Levine suggested that they race back home. Ignorant Litvak that he was, he thought flying was some sort of a game, which he had just discovered he played as well as any.

Dismayed at this breach in the ethics of transoceanic flying, Chamberlin hastily denied all responsibility for the cable that contained the challenge. Levine had, as a matter of fact, signed for both. Levine, snubbed again, said little or nothing.

In Paris, after the restraining hand of Chamberlin was removed, Levine, with the best intentions, committed an even more serious breach of etiquette. He had learned his lesson that flying was not sport, but statesmanship. Why, then, could he not become an ambassador of good will, like Lindbergh? It must have appeared to him a particularly tactful gesture to suggest that a French pilot take him back home. He chose the Frenchman Drouhin.

But, incomprehensibly, the French chose to become incensed. The reasons assigned were that Drouhin was the only French aviator whose preparations for an Atlantic flight were so far advanced as to justify the hope a start might be made that year. And if Drouhin were to fly with an American, and in an American plane, the glory of the achievement would not be 100 percent French.

Somehow Levine received a greater share of the abuse than did the Frenchman who had consented to the arrangement. Amiably Levine offered to make the flight in a French plane, which offer was rejected. Bewildered as he must have been at the sudden storm, as usual he gave no apologies, and proceeded stubbornly with the work of preparing for the flight.

Before long, however, he was in serious quarrel with Drouhin over the terms of their contract. In characteristic fashion, Levine began making overtures to English pilots. Drouhin got wind of the scheme to supplant him, and there ensued, as the *Herald Tribune* put it, "an argument as stormy as one between two persons not speaking the same language could be." Drouhin threatened an injunction, and Levine retorted by attempting to remove the motors from his plane. The Frenchman countered by placing his friends on guard. It was a merry warfare, and on one occasion blows were passed between Levine and the English-speaking interpreter-friend of Drouhin, a man who towered a foot above the testy little Jewish business man.

Apparently some sort of reconciliation was effected. The public was assured through the papers that the difficulty had arisen through the inability of the two men to communicate with each other except through the means of officious interpreters. Levine capitulated, and signed a new contract, and having yielded—a strange act for him—was all eagerness to be off.

Weather and engine trouble, however, intervened, and Levine became entirely unmanageable. He began to fuss around the equally nervous Frenchman, and was only silenced when the Frenchman dramatically offered his revolver as a better means of committing suicide than the proposed flight to New York. Levine could not be contained for long, however. Soon he was negotiating with English pilots for a second time, making several flying trips to London, and conferring with Captain Courtney, Hinchliffe and others. The canny Drouhin again stationed his friends to guard the plane.

On August 29, after a month of such tactics, Levine engineered the coup for which he should be remembered long after his flight to Germany is forgotten. He stole his plane from under the noses of the guards at Le Bourget airdrome; and, making his first solo flight, crossed the channel to land in Croydon, England. And in bringing the plane to earth on his first attempt as pilot, he gave the veteran pilots and officials of the British flying field, said the *New York Times*, "an exhibition of flying they never saw equalled for craziness."

The officials had been warned of his coming, read the dispatch, and knowing he was an amateur flyer, they had summoned all emergency apparatus to be in readiness.

"Every attaché of the great commercial flying area rushed to the field when the siren hooted that the American had been sighted. It was a busy hour, passenger planes arriving, and others departing over Europe's numerous air routes, and the whole place was fidgeting."

Levine was flying low and the officials watched breathlessly. "He had a runway about a half a mile across the airdrome, but was coming so fast he did not approach the ground until he had traversed almost half the distance towards the field's northern end. The officials groaned. An ambulance and a fire engine, which were held in readiness at the edge of the field, started to move slowly towards the north center, where they were expecting the wild pilot to crash, and the plane to crumple and burst into flames.

"No such thing happened. Levine suddenly seemed to realize that a landing was not likely to be gentle at such a rate, and started skyward like a rocket. There was where the miracle came in. Levine, ignoring all the first rules of piloting and practically at the point of losing all his flying speed, tried to make a climbing turn manouver which has caused more deaths than almost any other from loss of flying headway when near the ground.

"One wing of the machine dropped until it seemed certain it would hit the ground. Then somehow or other the machine started upward.

"A veteran Channel pilot swore softly. 'It takes a jolly good pilot to do that,' he added.

" 'It's the engine, the engine,' muttered another at his side.

"Whatever it was, good luck or good engine [or God taking care of one of his Chosen], it carried Levine at a crazy angle almost to the roof of an outbuilding, which he unbelievably cleared, and then upward and away from the spectators. . . .

"Down to the southern end of the field he turned, and tried it again, but again too fast, and at too steep an angle. Ambulance and fire engines were now rushing madly back, but Levine was away again.

"Pilot Smith of a local air taxi company then leaped into the breach. He took up a small Avro plane to show Levine how the landing was done. Levine says he didn't see the Avro. But as soon as the latter landed, Levine, following at a distance, tried again. The Avro, rolling on the ground, turned out of his path, and scuttled off sideways towards the distant hangers like a scared rabbit scooting for shelter before a pouncing hawk. Levine's plane pounced, but was not flying so fast as before and was going flatter. It bounded, according to witnesses, between twenty and thirty feet in the air, fluttered, wobbled, hit the ground and bounced again, but not so high, and finally rolled a short distance bumpingly and stopped.

"The officials, from being scared, turned wrathful, though relieved. They rushed forward only to meet a hatless civilian-clad pilot who was the least shaken man in the airdrome.

" 'Oh, hello,' said Levine as they congratulated him on his landing. He was rubbing his chin and grinning. 'You know I think I need a shave. I didn't really know I was coming until I almost started.' "

So ends the account in the *Times* of this unparalleled flight. Levine was rushed to the quarters of the Air Ministry where, after the excitement had somewhat cooled, the officials began to enumerate the various rules, regulations, codes, enactments, ordinances and laws of the two countries that Levine had broken.

"By leaving France without proper clearance papers, he had broken the customs laws of both England and France.

"He had not observed the flying rules of Britain, which say that no plane shall be flown more than three miles from any airdrome by other than a licensed pilot. He had not made the proper circlings in the airfield."

There were other violations. What were rules and regulations to a man like Levine? "When a Litvak takes to flying" . . . there ought to be a proverb.

In England, Levine began to materialize his plans, and engaged Hinchliffe as his pilot. When the transatlantic flight was given up because of the unfavorable weather reports, Levine conceived the idea of a non-stop flight to India instead. And engaged in a quarrel with his latest pilot.

This time he came off rather the worse. The flight had been postponed for several days because of rain, and when the anxious Hinchliffe finally summoned Levine to make ready to leave, the latter's ardor had apparently cooled. He sent back word that he did not consider the weather yet favorable. Hinchliffe, however, was of a different mettle from Levine's other pilots. In Hinchliffe, indeed, Levine finally met his match.

The angry pilot strode up to Levine's rooms and was for dragging him bodily to the field. Under the single and venomous eye of the one-eyed pilot Hinchliffe, Levine seems to have quailed. The Jewish Ulysses could do no more with this Cyclops than to explain, which he seems to have done satisfactorily, by admitting that it was the press of important business and not the weather that prevented him from flying that day. A week later they started, without the fuss and commotion that usually attended Levine's activities. The journey ended in Vienna, where because of a broken feed-pump they were forced to descend.

Here end Levine's adventures—except for one. He flew to Italy, and there he had an audience with the Pope.

Two appointments did that august personage make with the former dealer in steel pipes and plumbing fixtures. On the first occasion, Levine was delayed so long at the papal gates by people seeking autographs that the appointed time passed, and the gates clanged to. His Eminence was reported to be extremely angry, but diplomatic friends arranged another appointment, which Levine came within a half second of missing. He was just able to rush through the gates, clad in his plain business suit, as they were closing.

As the papal major-domo escorted him to the door of the little throne room, and as he walked past the gravely saluting Swiss Guards, his uneasiness increased; and when he was finally ushered into the presence of the Pope, he was completely overawed.

"I was so impressed," said Levine afterwards, "that I couldn't say a single word. I felt as if I were in another world. I felt more celestial in the Vatican than when flying across the Atlantic, so high in the air."

Where was the gaunt astral shade of his paternal great-grandfather, the learned and pious Reb Moishe Levine of Vilna, as that world famous great-grandson of his dropped to his knee and kissed the Pope's ring? Surely Charles was not wearing the *talith* which the Polish Jews had presented him as a talisman for his flight back when he kneeled and pressed his Jewish lips to the papal seal, and received the papal blessing for the safety of his future flights.

The next day the plane in which he and Hinchliffe were flying crashed to the ground.

(—*1928*)

The Quest of a Jewish Intellectual

ᥫ᭝

ADOLPH S. OKO

THERE is, in this land, such a human animal as the Jewish Intellectual—that groper for clarity and excellence, that recluse in matters religious. Born into Judaism, he is yet outside of the Temple: an established institution with established interpretations. His beliefs are not those of the average member of the average congregation in Israel, nor his mode of thought and expression that of the contemporary Interpreters of the Torah and the Learned in the Law. What is offered there as Jewish religious thought he finds wholly inadequate to his modern consciousness. Nor does he accept past authority uncritically or tradition unanalyzed. And yet he refuses to consider himself outside of the pale of Judaism—even as he struggles against being a Jew by memory only.

This somewhat snobbish word, Intellectual, is used without snobbish intention. A Jewish Intellectual, like his non-Jewish counterpart, can be simple and human. His business, indeed, is not to shock grandmothers. He need not be a "foreigner," either. And he may be a philosopher, a poet, or a saint. In view of certain current notions, it is perhaps not unnecessary to say that "intellectual" is not synonymous with "college graduate" or with "professional"—such as lawyers, dentists, veterinaries, college professors, or, for that matter, journalists. The intellectual man is characterized by a certain quality and temper of the mind. It is not intellectual power as such but a certain quality of the "soul" that determines its *niveau*, that gives it an altitude and a direction. In other words, it is a manner rather than a method of thinking —the soul rather than the substance of thought. It is something for which one has what physicians call a "disposition," and not a thing that one casually acquires. We only have to watch how a mind disports itself in order to determine the particular quality of soul. If the intellectual man perseveres, he becomes a philosopher—by which is

(641)

not meant a professor who teaches a safe and sane, separate, closed, and teachable discipline, but a man with a philosophic and vital attitude towards knowledge. If he happens to have secured a higher academic degree, he will leave his diploma in the closet, unframed. As an undergraduate he will mark out his own problems and set about by himself to seek for their solutions. In short, he is always autodidact and, therefore, an educated person. As a citizen, the Intellectual may be a "practical" human being, and even make a "career" for himself. But practical considerations play no part in the shaping of his attitude towards knowledge, and his success, if any, in business or profession is only an incident. Lastly I may remark that I am not, in this essay, indulging in an overdeveloped autobiographical instinct. Neither am I the Boswell of a "synthetic" Johnson. I have in utter honesty of purpose selected a case which I know to be a typical one, human and modern. However, the whole of the truth is that we can never get outside ourselves. In a certain sense, observes Schnitzler, we all speak and write autobiography. That is one of our greatest misfortunes, intellectually speaking.

One of his grandfathers was the poorest rich (or the richest poor) man—like so many of his Jewish contemporaries in Russia, in Poland, in Lithuania, and even in Germany, in the first half of the nineteenth century. He was, undoubtedly, "Orthodox." Everybody was. According to a family tradition, his grandfather's Orthodoxy was the outer form of an inner reality. He was a man of great piety, resigned to the Will of God. And he was learned in the Law. It is surmised that the grandfather's will-to-believe was transformed in the grandson into a will-to-think, to search for truth. So much for antecedents.

He is now in his early forties, and a father of grown-up children. The cultivation of the things of the mind not being a trade by which a man can support himself and his family, he has chosen (or maybe has drifted into) the profession of—but never mind. He is not a college professor. It just so happens.

It also happens that he is not quite a first-class brain—as far as intellectual power, as such, goes; and judged by the standards of the intellectual man. In his calling he does with sweat and toil what a man with a lesser sense of personal value (otherwise called responsibility) would leave undone. He often has to flog his brain: he is using it, and thinking is not easy. He is not really striving for something be-

yond his attainment, professionally. In fact, he is wholly without ambition. Being over forty, his brain is already forced into certain grooves,
and formed. Its power of sudden expansion is, naturally, diminishing.
But in a world of perpetual change, defeat, and imperfection, he is
glad to remain an unfinished product. To be sure, he is what is commonly called mature; and he is reflective, and rather sensitive, and
more or less bookish. No—he is not a pedant. But he loves exactitude.
He has almost a genius for it. As a critical observer of human affairs,
and as a student of social institutions, he distrusts missions—Jewish,
Christian, Mohammedan, and even French and Japanese—and district visiting. He does not "study" the poor or the scapegoats of society:
a noble and beautiful woman has taught him to understand their original language. He is not disinclined to accept her philosophy of life:
"Nothing else really matters but goodness—goodness of heart." She
was "a true daughter of the Jewish Prophets" who were always at war
with the Jewish kings. All of which goes to say that he is not, strictly
speaking, a member of the Republican Party, and that he did not
take courses in idealism at the Y.M.C.A. or in the I.O.B.B. But though
a radical of the pigment of America's aborigines, more or less, he never
grinds a sociological axe.

His "moral" temperature is generally quite normal. But he never
sticks his private moral thermometer into the mouths of others. The
natural man, he knows, is inspirited to live and strive in hope of his
illusions by Hunger, Love, and Vanity, the three imps that stand at
the cradle of all human action. Why, then, nag at the man or woman
who seeks virtue by way of happiness in preference to the philosopher's
path which is supposed to lead the other way 'round? Though an American citizen, and holding a job in a country where "the standards of
living are high," and where a banal optimism is the general standard
of right thinking and the special equipment of Presidential candidates, he looks upon life with profound distrust. But only once, and
in an especially sad frame of mind, did he use the expression "that
spider, Life." For in his ultimate view he is a follower of Spinoza
rather than a disciple of Schopenhauer or Leopardi. "A life without
sorrow would probably be as bare as a life without happiness." Or,
in the language of philosophy, a thing is not evil merely because it
displeases you; and *vice versa*. He is ever learning not to view life
and the world in their personal perspectives, teleologically.

In fact, teleology and theology are to him synonymous terms. The difference being that whereas both man and animal are teleological, it is only man that is theological. Theological opinion, he maintains, no matter how liberal, however equipped with learning, lacks a certain faculty, a certain realness. (I cannot describe it more accurately.) The most accomplished speakers, in his opinion, are found among practicing theologians; to say nothing, but say it so well, is an accomplishment indeed. Whenever encountered by them—which is rather often—he tries to speak first, or else change the conversation. Not that he lacks in frankness, or that he is particularly fearful and greedy, but because he has a strong distaste for debates. But he is a student of history and he knows that religions are historically interesting, and that they may be socially important. Come to think of it: no—he is not hostile to religion, which has been well defined as poetry mistaking itself for science. That religion is "man-made" does not matter. Art, science, and philosophy are also man-made. Religion is the philosophy of the believer, as philosophy may be the religion of the unbeliever. At any rate, as regards religion in the Hebraic sense—religion as a life, and not as an opinion—prejudice against it, he intimates, should have but little place in modern learning. Thus—and for illustration—he agrees with the Spinozist philosopher Morris R. Cohen about God; but he does not share his (reported) opinion about Jewish monotheism being immoral. The *Ehad*, says he, is no immoral concept. And this not for the reason that so much blood has been shed over it. The idea of the *Ehad*, he holds, is interwoven and shot through by a thousand threads with the moral grandeur of Israel's prophets and sages (who silently or noisily abandoned the original tribal view of Yaveh), with the Messianic hope—that beautiful Dreamthorpe—of the Jewish people, and, above all, with their yearning for *Ge'ulah* (Redemption) —the Jew's Dream of the Ideal, and, perhaps, Judaism's grandest thought. It is true, there is more of the sense of the *joie de vivre* in the nature religions of antiquity; and the pluralized Godhead of Christianity may be more gracious or elegant. . . . Still, severe monotheism, in ancient times and during the Middle Ages, if not in modern times, had a fascination for the philosopher, the lonely thinker, as well as for the exalted religious temperament. Dr. Cohen (whom—and this parenthetically—he considers the nimblest intelligence among American philosophers) is here mistaken—even as was his great master, Ernest Renan, who taught that Jewish monotheism was solely due to Israel's wandering through the Desert, evidently confounding monotheism with monotony. Philosophers, too, may err. It is their natural right. He only regrets that they err so frequently where Judaism and Jews are concerned. However, he is not really "shocked" by Dr. Cohen's opinion, and he does not consider him or Renan an "anti-Semite." Nor is he making propaganda for Jewish monotheism, ethical and spiritual though it be. Civilized people, he suggests, with different modes of thought, should give up, with mutual respect, the attempt to convert each other.

Needless to say, he is uncompromisingly modern; without, however, claiming to be modernism's last word. The fact that Jewish traditional dogma teaches that God is personal, and that Judaism's official theological doctrine is the *creatio ex nihilo,* does not disturb him in the least. "What of it?" says he. We shall be very wrong if we suppose that he was busy writing a book on the reconciliation of Jewish theology with modern thought. He simply finds no difficulty in rejecting these things wholesalely. Pharisaic or Rabbinic Judaism, claims he, abandoned many a biblical doctrine, sometimes silently but more often learnedly by proving the abandonment to be in accordance with the authority of Scripture: in the almost identical manner and by the almost identical method of learned jurists. In modern times, he points out, Reform Judaism accepted that "comfortable word" evolution— the very antithesis to the view of creation—with or without the intellectual labor of reconciling it with the Book of Genesis. He has heard of a number of enlightened rabbis who, despite Genesis, are no more disturbed by their disbelief that sun and stars, animal and plant, man and morals, came into existence by a "direct and willful" act of Almighty God, than Protestant clergymen are troubled over the evidence for the antiquity of man, the geological record, the place of the earth in cosmogony, or bishops lose their sleep over such ancient difficulties as the Flood, Jonah and the whale, and the stopping of the sun to decide the outcome of a fight. But I am digressing.

Our Jewish Intellectual is also a skeptic, both by disposition and conviction. Are not Jews supposed to be born skeptics?

Early in life, in his *Sturm und Drang* period, he was driven from the naive Eden of warm religious convictions (which included a belief in immortality) into the cold climate of Reason. There he pitched his tent. The tent he rented: he is not a tent-maker. In that region every new tenant begins where countless tenants have begun before

him, where countless tenants will begin after him. Death removes the
tent-makers who act as guides, and each apprentice must repair the
holes himself and find his way to the water springs alone. The years
roll by, and many are the changes that take place both inside and
outside the tents. The wintry landscape, too, changes somewhat. Only
the interrogation point on the blackboard in each tent remains un-
changed; it is unchangeable. Those tenants who are quick to realize
this tragic fact, and feel it in their heart of hearts, become spare and
haggard of body and weary in soul—"noia" is the name given to their
illness. The remedies against it are but few in number: to die by one's
own hand, passionate love, fervent friendship, true religion, and philosophical mysticism—five prescriptions, all told. (Social service is not
a strong enough medicine for ardent temperaments; Faust, he points
out, chose it as a last remedy, and only when he was with one foot
in the grave.) But the majority of the patients grow pale, wipe their
foreheads, and die. They die of broken spirits. The more robust among
them, when exhausted, take a *siesta:* they call it "a system of thought."
For the human mind, like the human eye, needs a zenith in the horizon: it cannot pursue its course into eternity and infinity. The thinker
grows tired thinking, and his need for rest gives him the illusion that
his human system of thought is a true system of the universe.

In this wise, without prolonged dialectic, he became convinced that
metaphysics is a mere diversion of the spirit, and that we can have no
knowledge of Reality or the *Ding-an-sich,* for the very terms describing
it are but the dim shadows ("ghosts" is his favorite expression) from
the urgent or practical world of sense; and that we can no more reach
an objective standpoint in ethics than we can in art. But while there
can be no valid system of thought, and no one "true" philosophy, there
are great thinkers and deep philosophers—that is, wise persons whose
manner and temper of thinking and knowing makes them philosophers.
And Plato, Spinoza—not to give a catalogue—do not lose their claim
to the presidency or vice presidency of the Immortals because their
systems are not valid: their thinking has remained vital.

He is not unaware that skepticism is not the predominant life-conception of the modern intellectual man. He would be likely to contend
that there is today no predominant life-conception. Besides, skepticism,
he advances, may be an expression of spiritual energy and the satisfaction of a real spiritual need. Nor is the skeptic altogether homeless. For he may have both, the aching sense of relativity and unrest,

as well as the love of the eternal illusion which envelops us all. He may (intellectually) renounce the world and (psychologically) continue to live in it with a smile, with a mystic doubt, with—a hope. The world may not be "real"; and life may be a dance of atoms in the void. Still there is much beauty in it—enough for a free man's worship. There is music, and roses, and jade, and noble and beautiful women to fill the emptiness of life. And there is philosophy—in the older sense, at any rate, which meant the supreme human effort towards knowledge, and whose last thought is mysticism. Not the Jewish Kabbalah and Christian Theosophy, those heaps of ugliness, but the poetic mysticism of a Plato and the less poetic but even more illumined mysticism of a Spinoza, or of his contemporary Angelus Silesius, or of the Dominican Meister Eckhart (fourteenth century)—the mysticism, in short, that comes at the end of philosophic thinking, the very soul of philosophic thought. Hence (or is he emulating the great Spinoza?), his reverence for religion as a matter of sentiment. He clearly conceives the close relationship between naive piety (the will-to-believe) and the philosopher's search for truth (the will-to-think).

It is quite likely that he does what so many others have done before him—rationalizes his "values." Perhaps. This thought, however, no longer frightens him.

He accepts the universe, despite the apparent hostility of the cosmic process to the ideals of man. And, like Whitman, he accepts himself. Not that he is in love with himself. He accepts the fate that made him Jewish—despite the "stigma," and though he is not so cocksure about the specific Jewish virtues. He does not merely accept his nose: he accepts his Jewishness inwardly. He has no desire to escape it. On the contrary. He would, if he knew how, cultivate those racially colored modes and moods of his—not alone for the sake of loyalty (which he, somehow, considers a virtue) but even more so for the sake of liberty: for the sake of inner harmony. For the Jew has never been happy in the dark Egypt. In plain, he wants to be free. "*Auch ich bin in Arkadien geboren,*" says he. He, too, despite the "Jewish complexion" of his views, is a man of his time, a modern, a good European—he snapped back at H. L. Mencken, some ten years ago, across a table in a Baltimore restaurant (and, of course, over a stein of the nearest beer). I was present. Nietzsche and Veblen, Judaism and the Catholic Church, I recall, were the subjects of discussion. He was defending Veblen's scholarship against Mencken's animadversions, or, maybe, he was emphasizing the poet and thinker in Nietzsche against Mencken who was stressing the controversialist, the author of *The Antichrist*. At any rate, I was quite impressed by the fact that the Jewish Intellectual was so alive to European traditions and so full of European memories, notwithstanding his hereditary strain and his consciousness of his Jewish self. Mencken, the howling or whirling dervish of the American critical fraternity, seemed by comparison no more modern than the average Humist or Kantian "professor." But I may have been mistaken.

To resume. Many cultures have contributed their share to produce that complex entity, the Jewish mind. Hence the unique problem that Jewish culture (and there is such a thing, he believes) will always present to the historian and thinker. Jewish culture, throughout history, has stood under the sign of "symbiosis." From the Exodus to the Balfour Declaration, the cultural development of the Jewish people has not been determined by its own formative power alone; in addition to the creative impulse from within there is always discernible an extraneous *agens* at work, molding and shaping it, giving it dress or style. Every other nation of antiquity has lived its individual life, and, when this was no longer possible, was doomed to perish or to be completely absorbed into a foreign nation. Only the Jewish nation was able to live and develop its own life amidst foreign and often hostile surroundings and at the same time participate in the culture of these surroundings. And so, he concludes (or assumes?), dependent as Jewish thought has always been on environment and the particular *Zeitgeist*, it is also independent. As with culture, so with freedom. At the cradle of their history, freedom came to the Jews as a gift from heaven. Later as a present received from kings and potentates (Cyrus, for instance), and through revolution and parliament in modern times. But the source for it, he thinks, should be looked for in the impulses and cravings of the race itself: it has a genius for it.

Now, he does not claim to have a "complete" Jewish philosophy; for Judaism itself is not something complete, dead. Nor are Jewish ideals something crystallized, sterile. Ideals shift from age to age, from generation to generation. Immutable goals are set by theology; they are not visible in history. At least, they are not open to view. Jewish history (with which he claims to have more than a bowing acquaintance) has taught him that Jewish beliefs and desires have changed since the close of the Canon, and since the redaction of the Mishnah or the completion of the Talmud. The Jews, he knows, have traveled far from the Middle Ages—"too far," it may be—when Jewish thought and action were dominated completely by "Rabbinic" teaching. I may remark in this connection that he is a close student of the writings of Leopold Zunz and so has an almost boundless enthusiasm (or is it bias?) for the strong and exalted moral convictions of medieval Jewries, especially of France and Germany, felt and expressed by them so fervently in their religious poetry, embodied as laws in their codes, and recorded as performance in their *Responsa*. Our modern teachers, it is his conviction, are not finer examples of civilization than, say, the medieval Rabbi Judah the Pious, for the simple reason that they can be heard thousands of miles by radio. And it was not exactly easy to be a Jew, or to be a man of virtue, in the Middle Ages. Nor, for the matter of that, is it in modern times. He would grant that much, I am sure. But, he insists, it is wiser to sink under the weight of a great enigma than to solve it falsely or ignobly. It is not a matter of taste or opinion. It is to him a question of wisdom—a moral question of first magnitude.

Being a skeptic, he would never put it in the axiomatic form but would say that it is *perhaps* easier to "believe" in Judaism than to define it. Of course, he does not know the whole of Judaism. Not even Maimonides, in his opinion, knew the whole of it. And he does not regret the fact that there is no adding machine that could sum up his Judaism. Hillel's famous extract, he is certain, was a clever ruse to get rid of a bore and a nuisance—an interviewer or reporter—who insisted on being told the whole of Torah in one minute and a half, *standem uno pede*. Only social workers, speech manufacturers, and other spiritual patent-medicine men still advertise it. He also rejects the proposed notion of a "minimum of Judaism" by the gentle Hillelite (Prof. M. M. Kaplan); it smacks somewhat of the Minimum Wage. Not that he is willing to swallow the whole of the so-called 613 *Mizwot*. He claims the right to pick and choose, indeed. But the old Covenant, he thinks, is still valid for all such intents and purposes, and thus there is no need of a new contract. Considerations of minima and maxima are in place with regard to the breviary and the missal, but not as concerns Judaism.

His idea namely is that Judaism is not a school for the study of the Bible, or the Talmud, or the *Posekim*—or all of these together—and that it is not the name of a religious sect embracing the faithful, and

nothing more or nothing else. The concept "Judaism" is not synonymous with "Jewish religion." The religion of the Jews—he would hesitate to say: the religions of the Jews—is the frame of the picture which
consists of Judaism or the three-thousand-year old quest of the Jewish
people, including its makers and framers, the Jews. An unfinished
painting, to be sure; as unfinished as its background which is the world
itself. But art is long; and the artists are still busy at it. So are the
frame-makers, who, artists in a way of their own, endeavor to produce a right sort of frame. In olden times, the frame formed an
integral part of the picture it enclosed, protected, and, in certain
periods of history, even enhanced: the Jews lived their religion. Proof
of his contention, he argues, is the fact that there exists no history
of the Jewish religion as apart from that of the Jewish people and
Jewish literature. It simply cannot be written. For you exhibit a picture, framed, to be sure; but you do not exhibit a frame. A shopkeeper
may: for purposes of sale. But no artist would, unless the picture has
been lost. . . . Hence, too, the reason why the Jews do not maintain missions for proselytizing, though Judaism has proclaimed that it
had a Mission: an ethical and spiritual message for the martyred spirit
of man. (Parenthetically, this "mission" has but little in common with
the tribal view of a "chosen people," that dangerous notion of the
"Semite" of yore, the modern "Nordic," and, for that matter, his contemporary Jewish counterpart.)

Nor is Judaism synonymous with Zionism. He maintains that one
may be loyal to Judaism and at the same time transcend the bounds
of nationality, instancing the Babylonian Isaiah. (A rather rare example, I admit.)

Is Judaism the truth? To the skeptic there is no such thing as *the*
truth. But there may be a great many truths—human truths: poetic,
philosophic, livable—without a single one of these truths being the
only, the real, the true Truth. In fact, his skepticism is rational rather
than metaphysical. Freedom of the mind is to him all important. It is
the very essence of the being and thought of the intellectual man. A
life without Reason would be no better than the animal's existence or
the actions of the automaton. Without freedom of mind there can be
no clearness of vision, no peace, no happiness of wisdom—the things
that are most excellent.

With the Santayanas—the skeptics with healthy animal faith—he

loves the Cross, the mystic contemplation of sorrow; and he loves the
Botree with the Fritz Mauthners and Anatole Frances. But his eternal
home is among the Cedars of Lebanon: evergreen and shady, strong
and high and indestructible. There is also the home of *Ge'ulah,* of
beatific freedom.

He is not seeking a happy hunting ground. He is not grasping for
solids. He is schooling himself in renunciation. It is freedom and quiet
and peace that he is craving. It is this skeptic's certitude that there,
among the Cedars of Lebanon, he can find all this. There is a clear
atmosphere; you can breathe. There, too, is not vulgar truth but a
grand *Stimmung:* not apathetic, but serene.

In terms of "actual" living, and not in those of contemplation,
Judaism affords him a Life in Reason, by which he understands something bigger than logic, something more simple than logic, and also
something more true than logic. Accordingly, he would urge those
who have a fancy for saving the world, not to attempt it with
mysticism or Nirvana, but with Intellect. Intellect alone will free
man from past authority and current superstition. The problem that
confronts Judaism, as well as humanity at large, "at the present junc-
ture," is not: To be—or not to be? To think—or not to think?—that
is the question.

(—1926)

Nudnick

❧

CHARLES REZNIKOFF

To BEGIN WITH, I insulted him. The Slavonic room in the New York Public Library is, as you probably know, next to the Jewish room —on the same corridor. I was reading in the Slavonic room when I heard someone outside the door talking away in Yiddish at the top of his voice. I thought, he can't keep it up much longer, he will become tired. The other readers in the room—patient Slavs—looked up and went on reading. My heart was like Jericho besieged, and I rushed out. There, talking away to someone who could only nod, stopping only to chuckle, was a man of about sixty, drowning someone's opinion in a torrent of speech.

"Pardon me," I said, "but do you know that what you are doing is— technically—polluting the name of the Lord: there are non-Jews in that room who are trying to read."

"Are you a rabbi or a prophet?" he asked angrily, but became silent and went away. I was somewhat sorry for what I had said, because he was older than I and, in fact, the non-Jews did not seem to have minded much.

Later in the day I was introduced to him. Someone I knew was listening to him on the steps of the Library and called me over as I passed. He recognized me, of course, but was polite—in a stilted way with my-dear-sir's and pray-pardon-me's. Gleefully he was upon a demonstration of the superiority of the Jews, as compared with the English, as shown by how much oftener the word *heart* is used in the Bible than in Shakespeare. I suggested that *heart* was merely idiomatic in Hebrew where the English use other words. This was a fillip to his gaily trotting tongue, a blow that made the waters of his speech gush. I did not like to go away for fear of hurting him again; so I listened and nodded, and watched the pigeons strutting about until they went to roost.

Next day, as I went up the steps of the Library, I saw him, brief-case in hand, running towards me. "My good sir," he said, "will you do something for me—a great favor? I will appreciate it, I assure you." And he held out his arms, smiling beneficently. "My dear sir," he went on, when I had come to an unwilling stop, "I have written a novel. Do me the favor, sir, to read just the last chapter, or, if you are too busy, the last page—the last few sentences. Here, begin here." And he had his brief-case open, the manuscript in his hands. "The novel is about Moses, the leper. Ah, that is new to you! We are told, are we not, that Moses' sister was stricken with leprosy and he him-self, after he had been in the presence of the Deity, wore a veil to hide his face, because its radiance was unbearable—was it not rather to hide his leprosy?" And he smiled in triumph. "You have never thought of that, have you? And then, finally, his burial-place is to be unknown. Why? That he may not be worshiped, we are told. Rather that his leprosy may not be discovered. In the last chapter, I have depicted the scene between Moses and Joshua before Moses goes away to die. Read it, sir; please to tell me what you think of it; I assure you, sir, you will not regret the few minutes."

I ran over it. "It has some good things in it," I said weakly. "But you must excuse me: I have work to do."

"Ah," he said, "so you like it. A publisher wants to take it. It is wonderful, wonderful, he tells me. But he wants me to add a little— to the beginning; it is too brief. He suggests to me that I describe the childhood of Moses, Aaron and their sister Miriam. But I have never been a child. I was only a little Jew. At the age of three I could read, at the age of eight I could interpret. So you see, dear sir, I do not know how children play. I have already written this addition. It took me no more than an hour. Will you read it, sir, and give me your opinion of it?" I remembered the story of Sindbad, who gave an old man a lift and then could not get him off his back. I looked at my old man of the sea unkindly, but he smiled and held before me the yellow pages on which he had written the addition. "Read only a few sen-tences," he said, and added, as if to himself, "I have never been a child."

Weakly, I took the sheets, their yellow as ugly to me at that mo-ment as the yellow of sulphur. "There are some good things in it," I said gently, as I gladly handed them back. "But—" I added, and stopped too late.

"But what?" he said eagerly.

"It is a little rough in spots. Of course, I understand that this is only a draft—and such things are trivial."

"Rough in spots? That is nothing."

"Certainly; so I said."

"This is only the first pen."

"Of course, of course, I understand."

"One moment, sir. The publisher is in a hurry for this, my friends are out of town, and I myself—it is so hot, sir, I cannot work in this weather. I am sick. Ah, I am growing old; I have never felt the heat as much. Besides, I am a foreigner. Please, my dear young man, do this for an old man: make these little corrections for me. I will pay you for your time. I will pay you well."

My thoughts were in a jumble: poor old man, I thought; and what publisher would take this? It would only need an hour or so to make the worst places better; how I hate to waste the time, and I don't want his money. "If I do it," I said, thinking aloud, "I won't charge for it—even if what I do is worth charging for."

"Please to do it, sir. But if you will take no payment, at least you must have dinner with me. You will have dinner as my guest, and, afterwards, you will make the corrections." I don't want any dinner, I thought. I have eaten too much today; I have eaten too much for fifteen years. "I will take you to a place," he went on, "where they have the best coffee in the world and the best pastry. Whatever you will eat there is good, but you have never eaten such pastry." Oh, sly old man, I thought, I am in your power. "Come," he said.

He led me to a place which I knew well enough, for I had been there a hundred times. Its pastry was good, but not the best in the world. But it was too late, and I went inside. "Have soup, fish, meat— a good dinner," he said. "Everything here is good; have whatever your heart desires!" When the waiter had taken my order and turned to my host, he motioned away the pad in the waiter's hand. "You will excuse me," he said to me, "but it is too hot for me to eat. I can have nothing now; perhaps later."

I ate sadly, wiping the sweat from my face; nothing was good, perhaps because the food had spoiled somewhat in the heat, perhaps because I was not hungry, perhaps because of my conscience. You are going to help an old man, I thought, throwing it a bone.

"Before I give you the pages that you have so kindly offered to correct, permit me, my dear sir, to show you—others. These are to be inserted at places indicated; glance at them, if you please." And he put about twenty closely-written sheets on the table.

"I can spare no more than this evening," I said desperately, and, pencil in hand, set to work.

For a while my host was silent, content with drumming his fingers on the cloth, humming now and then, sucking his teeth, and scratching himself. But then he began to talk. At first only now and then, asking me how I liked this or that choice bit of his writing. But, more cheerful as the evening wore on, he told anecdotes—until he was always talking. I did not listen, bent over the work I tried to do, struggling against the web of talk.

The waiter came over a number of times and stared at us moodily. A new waiter took his place. My host was not abashed: he merely called for another glass of water. At last the waiter avoided us. But this stirred up my host to demand his meed of tumblers, to rap and quarrel for his water until he got it. He would stop talking for a moment to drink, and, cheerful and refreshed, would begin again. Whenever I looked up I could see the teeth in his open mouth, as in the new motion pictures from Russia.

I was through—after a fashion—at last. I looked at my watch: it was almost midnight. "Thank you, how can I thank you," and my host, lifting his palms, began an oration. I saw myself taking the heavy tumbler and striking him in the face with it. If I stay another moment, I'll do it, I thought, and left him in the middle of a sentence, his hands reaching out towards me, his cheated mouth still talking.

Later, that night, as I came back on a walk, I saw him in the light of a store window. I stopped, and stole away. He was counting the coins in the palm of his hand, looking worried. He is hard up, I thought. That is why he went without dinner tonight. I looked back at the man as one might into a brown pool, on the bottom of which many leaves are rotting.

(—1929)

O Spirit of Our Times!

❧

HENRY M. ROSENTHAL

IN THE first day of the month, in the seventh month, in the year of the Atomic III, the year of Bikini II, the year of the betrothal of the Princess Elizabeth I, an angel of the Lord lifted me up and carried me aloft, out of the city, and over the state of Pennsylvania, in the corner of the state, near to where it joins with the state of Ohio, near the fair city of Zanesville. And he said unto me, "Son of man, what seest thou?"

And I said unto the angel, "I see a pipeline."

Then the angel said unto me, "What seest thou in the pipeline?"

And behold, the pipeline was pierced with light so that I could see within; and I said unto the angel, "I see oil. It flows like blood in a man's vein."

Then the angel of the Lord carried me yet further aloft, until the states commingled, the continents touched, my vision failed and my heart swam for blackness; and the angel of the Lord said unto me, "Son of man, what seest thou?"

I lifted up mine eyes, and behold, the whole earth covered with pipelines like veins in the body of a man; and the pipelines were pierced with light and I saw the oil flowing; the oil of the Mexics, the oil of California and its shoals, the Lone Star oil, and the oil of Oklahoma; yet farther, and the oil of Mongolia, the oil of Thailand, and the oil of Baku; the oil of Afghan, and the oil of Romagna; the oil of Thrace, and the oil of Sahara; the oil of Polonia, and the oil of Ethiop; the oil of the Icecaps, polar and anti-polar, the oil of Ararat, the oil of Iran, the oil of Iraq, of Saudi Arabia, and the oil of New York. And behold, a great commotion.

And the angel of the Lord said unto me, "Son of man, what seest thou?"

Then I looked, and behold the pipelines that covered the earth heaved like the veins of a man when the skin is flayed and the secret flesh is laid bare, and I was filled with dread. I looked further and beheld that the pipelines lifted out of the earth like the eightfold arms of the cuttlefish of the sea and waved to and fro, strickenly; and the oil was jetted forth from the stricken limbs like the black blood of the great squid, and the earth was sprayed and drenched with water of death, and a great moaning arose.

Then said I to the angel of the Lord, "The earth has veins, and the veins bleed; but where is the heart?"

Then a great wind roared from the east and bore me yet farther aloft and turned me, so that my eyes looked toward the sun, and behold, the shining sea. And upon the middle of the eastern shore of the great middle sea, upon the sands of the shore, the likeness of a land, in the likeness of a heart: auricle and ventricle, and all fitting chambers. And the name of the auricle was Mosul, and the name of the ventricle was Haifa.

I looked, and behold, as the veins flow to the heart so the pipelines flowed to the heartland.

Then I cried to the angel of the Lord, "What is the meaning of these signs?"

And the angel of the Lord said unto me: "Thus is the word fulfilled that Israel shall be the heart of the nations. Thus is Zion enthroned above the nations, and the Lord upon His holy hill."

Then I looked yet further, and behold, the heartland sought to tear itself free from its veins, but it could not. So that the heartland was in great commotion, and was lifted up in anguish like the lifting up of the woman that giveth birth before she beareth down. And I cried aloud, "Behold, the pangs of Messiah!" But the angel of the Lord answered not. And the land was lifted up like the heart when it knocketh at the door of a man's life. And the heartland beat forth blood and beat forth oil; and the blood and the oil were mingled together so that their stench rose. Then dread assailed me, and I cried yet again to the angel of the Lord, "What is the meaning of these signs?"

Then the angel of the Lord said unto me: "The heart of flesh that was put in the heart of man has been taken away, and he has been given a heart of shale.* And when he beats upon his breast to

* Cf. Ezekiel 11.19

humble his heart in contrition, forasmuch as the Lord dwelleth with him that is broken-hearted, he beats with the fist of a hypocrite; for he beats to strike oil. The heart of the nations is turned to shale, and it pumpeth oil!"

Then the wind which had borne me aloft blew yet farther; it roared to the uttermost corners of the earth and returned; and there returned with it, when it returned from its roaring, four great winged beasts: one had the feet of a lion, and one had the feet of a bear, and one had the feet of an eagle, and the last had the feet of a vulture bird, but its face was hidden.

Then the four great beasts soared aloft and circled the heart that lay upon the shore seven times; but the fourth beast circled apart. And the three beasts, and the fourth beast, swooped upon the heart and seized it with their claws and beak and rent it, and smote one another for its possession; for they were athirst for oil; and the heavens were filled with the sound of their fury, and the beat of their wings rained oil and darkness upon the face of the earth, like the darkness of Egypt. And the commotion and wailing of the earth deafened the seat of the Most High. Then the three beasts, and the fourth beast, rent one another tooth and claw; until one beast only remained. And behold, it was the beast with the feet of a vulture and the face that was hidden, that circled apart.

Then in my dread I cried out yet again to the angel of the Lord, "What is the meaning of these signs?"

And the angel of the Lord said unto me: "The three beasts, and the fourth beast, are three kingdoms: the Lion, the Bear, and the Eagle. And when they turn to rending one another, the fourth beast will prevail. He is the kingdom of Carrion. His face cannot be seen."

Then the angel of the Lord said yet again unto me: "Go speak to the nations and say unto them:

Because ye looked upon death and shrugged, therefore death will twitch his shoulder at you, and you will be the scab upon his shoulder that he will scratch with his pitiless nail.

Because ye played the Solomon and said, "Rend the child, rend it, and let the two mothers divide the child, they are both harlots"; and because thou didst rend it, from navel to crown, and from pudendum to bridge of the nose didst rend it, and the reins, and the liver, and the fat parts didst pluck for thyself; forasmuch as it was commanded to Noah and to his sons, Shem, and Ham, and Japhet, "thou shalt not rend the living limb from the living body to eat it,"

Therefore, shall you be rent as a shirt is torn to bind up a wound; you will be divided against yourself; and you will hop like the fowl that is flung from the slaughtering knife; but there will be none to save.

Forasmuch as you were the stick in the hand of the Lord, yet you raised up your thick end to strike the Lord, saying, "Mine is the power and the glory, and I will beat the Lord about His face, for I am the stick that dealeth blows."

Therefore you will be broken in pieces and flung upon the fire.

"And to the Lion, and the Bear, and the Eagle, say:

Treat not for your hostages, and dangle not your hostages before My face, lest ye be given over to dangle; for ye are all hostages in my hand; saith the Lord.

Thou roarest, O swimming Lion, but none feareth thy roar when the waters are dried up, and thou liest panting upon a far shore; wounded unto death; thou crushest with thine embrace, O Bear, but the bees will swarm over thine head when thou puttest thine hairy paw into the honeycomb that is not for thee, and they will put out thine eyes, and sting thee to death; thou fliest, O Eagle, but time is swifter than thee!"

Then there was a blackness in mine eyes, and a great roaring, and the vision ceased, and I knew no more.

But on the second day, in the seventh month, in the year of the Atomic III, the year of Bikini II, and the year of Princess Elizabeth's Betrothal and Espousals I, the angel of the Lord lifted me up and carried me aloft. And I saw the Island beneath me and the Great Atlantic and the Harlem Canal. The angel of the Lord set me down in a meadow that the Lord had pulled up from the sea, so that the smell of life was in it, and the beauty of the moss on the bottom stones when thou goest down to the sea. Beguiling to the eye was the meadow, with the breezes of the sea upon it; and I said to the angel of the Lord, "What is this place?"

Then the angel of the Lord said unto me, "This is Flushing Meadows, and this is Lake Success. Here are the Prisoners of Hope."*

Then the angel of the Lord lifted me up and bore me aloft to the upper heavens, so that all was disclosed before me, and he caused me to rest upon the Great Highway of the Constellations, and he planted my feet upon the Scales. And the angel of the Lord said unto me, "Son of man, where art thou?"

Then said I with joy to the angel of the Lord, "My feet are on the Heavenly Scales, but I stand within the Sign of the Scorpion and I look toward the Heavenly Archer, and all is disclosed before me."

And the angel of the Lord said unto me, "Son of man, look farther, and say what thou seest."

Then I looked upon the Heavenly Way, and in my joy I trod upon the heels of the Archer, and I said to the angel of the Lord, "I see the He-goat prancing." But the angel of the Lord said unto me, "Son of man, look farther." Then I looked even farther as he bade me, and I beheld the Sign of Aquarius, and I said to the angel of the Lord, "I see the Water-Carrier upon both shoulders." And my heart was filled with joy to see the spectacle of the Great Heavens. But the angel of the Lord said unto me, "Son of man, look yet farther."

Then I looked as he bade me to the farthest end, where the very heavens do stand before the wheel of the Ancient of Days that maketh the winds to return, and the rain to fall, and the dead to rise in season; and I looked toward the Sign of the Fish.

And the Fish started from his place.

And the Fish was huge, to fill the very heavens. And it opened its great mouth to send forth fire and flame. And the ecliptic was rent, and the Great Zodiac was buckled, and a rosy cloud came forth and consumed, like the cloud of the sun for fierceness and for dread, and the Dipper and the Bear swung from their courses, and fled for terror. And the Fish closed its mouth and sealed its eyes and made its dread snout to be smooth and blind, and it became the likeness of the great engine of death, even the iron fish with the blind snout, that raineth death and destruction from the sky.

And upon the back of the Great Fish, the likeness of a Rider, even like unto the likeness of the Ancient of Days, Lord of the hosts of heaven.

And at the sight thereof, I fell down upon my face for dread.

* Zechariah 9.12

A stillness was over the heavens and over the earth.
Then the voice of the Ancient of Days spoke, saying:

"Canst thou draw out Leviathan with a fish-hook? Or press down his tongue with a cord? Will he make many supplications unto thee, or will he speak soft words unto thee? Will he make a covenant with thee, that thou shouldst take him for a servant forever? Wilt thou play with him as with a bird? Behold, round about his teeth is terror, his sneezings flash forth light, his eyes are like the eyelids of the morning, out of his mouth go burning torches, and sparks of fire leap forth; strength in his neck abideth, and before him danceth dismay; when he raiseth himself up, the mighty are fearful; they are beside themselves with despair!"*

And the voice of the Ancient of Days spoke further, saying:

"Thou hast found thee thy pitchblende, and bespoken thine isotopes, and divided the nucleus from the nucleus, and thou stretchest the neck of thy cyclotron, and thou settest the Clock of thy Counters, and thou tetherest thy goats and thy bullocks; and thou sayest in thine heart that thine is the greatness and the power and the glory and the victory and the majesty; and though ye say, but a little while longer of our frenzy and defilement and we will make it well, upon the right hand and the left hand we will make it well; yet in thy secret heart thou thinkest that thou are god; therefore with an outstretched arm and with poured-out fury will I be king over you, and you shall know that I am the Lord."

On the tenth day, in the seventh month, in the year of the Atomic III, the Year of the Nuremberg Trials.
Rabbi Akiba said: "but the collectors regularly make their daily round, and exact payment from man whether he be content or not."
Concerning, then, my father's kid:
My father had an only kid that he bought him for money; he brought it to the house, and the kid did gambol. And in my father's house was a cat; and the cat killed the kid. Then in my father's house was a dog that killed the cat. And my brother that loved the cat did pick up a stick that was in my father's house and did break

* Job 60.25–29; 61.6–14

the dog's neck that used to run howling; and my brother did cast the stick upon the fire, that burnt the stick, for my brother was afraid for the stick with which he had beaten my father's beloved dog. But the stick was a great stick and a dry one, and the flame that licked at it did lick at my father's hearth, and leaped up to burn. And my father did run to the trough wherein our fine ox did drink and my father took water to quench him the fire that licked at my father's house; and the ox followed my father, his master, and did lick at the water that my father would cast upon the flame. Then my father's rage rose high, and he called to the Slaughterer that he should come to slaughter the ox that pulled my father's plough.

Then the Slaughterer did slaughter our ox; and my young brother did weep for his cat; and for the fire that burnt. Then the Holy One Blessed be He in His wisdom did send the angel of death to do what he did with the Slaughterer.

And my father that was watching found it more than he bargained for; so he did rend his garment from seam to seam, and said, "Blessed be the true Judge." And my brother, the apple of my father's eye, did answer, Amen. And the Holy One Blessed be He then slew the angel of death; and my father said to my brother, "Now death has lost his victory; and thou, O grave, thy sting."

Then was my father's yard filled with unbearable knowledge of the Lord, so that my father and my brother turned to go; but as they did so, they heard the voice of the Lord God in my father's yard, Who called unto my father, saying, "Whither goest thou?"

And my father stayed his step and did answer the Lord God: "Thou knowest, O Lord; to the quicklime."

And my brother added to my father's words: "That it may all be forgotten, O Lord."

"But the Ledger lies open," said the Lord God.*

Now come let us reason together about my father's only kid; whether our sins be red as scarlet, or white as the driven snow.

For my Friend, blessed be His holy Name, had a vineyard; and my father had a kid.

In the seventh month on the fifteenth day, in the Year of the Atomic III, the Great Year of the Candidates.

Hearken unto me, O people of the valley; and give ear, O isles afar off.

* Abot 3.20

O, my Friend had a flock, and he tended them well, until the rams had great horns and could mind the ewes and the lambs, and knew the wind and the lie of the pasture, and the flock was well watered and come of discretion. And my Friend had burred them and had combed their fleece and had taught them knowledge, the knowledge of mating and of giving the udder and of cutting the cord when the young came forth and of uttering calls. And the flock thrived exceedingly; it lambed in season; and it stood off the wolves with well-lowered horns, the lambs and the ewes in the center; and the flock found room for strays; lovely was the flock of my Friend; and it waxed very fat.

Then said my Friend to his flock: "Ye are come of discretion and shall choose your shepherd."

And my Friend caused shepherds to be sent for the flock of his fondness; to be chosen of them for their shepherding.

O, woe unto the sheep, and woe, woe, unto the shepherds; for the flock of my Friend is perished!

There was a shepherd that prophesied, "Lie down with the wolves," for, said he, "the wolf and the lamb shall feed together; and a little child like me shall lead them." But he prophesied not unto the wolves; he prophesied unto the sheep! and the flock of my Friend chose him to be their shepherd.

And there came to them a shepherd of silence saying, "I am a shepherd of utter discretion; I talk of the side of my mouth; am odorless to leeward and windward; and have a way with dogs." Then he clapped his hand to his mouth to close up his wind, and was chosen of the flock for their shepherd. O woe to the flock of my Friend.

And they chose them merchants and traffickers to be their shepherds, merry with laughter and cold in the eye and fat for the love of mutton: all ready men that would stop at nothing. These did say they were at home with sheep, and knew their handling better than any, and what was good for their fattening and dressing. They were merchants of wool, and merchants of gut, and merchants of parchment; and they said to the sheep, "Entrust us your wool and your hides and your gut, for we serve your Final Cause." And the flock of my Friend did choose them to be their shepherds.

And there was one that loved sheep as a man loveth woman, and he was worthy of death by the Law. He bullied the sheep and blandished them and dragged them to their defilement; and they trampled and betrayed one another to be near to his sneezings;

and they said, "He loveth us sheep; behold his strength and mastery; our soul panteth after him as the hart for the watercourse." And they chose him to be their shepherd. Woe to the flock that is worthy of death by the Law.

Then a great evil arose between the flock and their shepherds; and the wolves crept upon the fold.

And now hear ye and judge, O peoples, between my Friend and His flock and their shepherds! If the sheep be forsworn shall the shepherds be faithless?

And on a day toward the end of that Era, in the year of the Atomic III, the year of Bikini II, the year of the Betrothal and Espousals I, the Year of Nuremberg, and the Year of the Candidates, there came to me a man in the prime of his life and declared himself saying:

"I am the Spirit of the Times and the Child of my World. I have tried me the ways of all flesh to see wherein it shall profit a man under the sun. I got me the learning and the cunning that are current, and repute for the same even more. I have tried goodwill, the sense of beauty, psychoanalysis and real estate. I have joined me a movement, more than one; and in the kingdom of letterheads have roamed far and wide. I have looked on the Right and considered the Left, and have said in my heart, I will try them both together, and perchance yoke them together; for 'if two lie together, then they have warmth; but how can one be warm alone?' And I would be warm among them. Then I did try them both; for both gave luncheons. I shall not say where I made the better connections.

"I have maneuvered for office, judicial, liturgical, conciliar, academic, civic, fraternal, and communal; have been both head to the foxes and tail to the lions; and this too was much profit. I denounced the black market and have taken my hire.

"But I have also known this great pain and tearing of the heart: that profits have to be shared. But then my record for service is second to none.

"I have known also great vexation of spirit that people bowed not down to me more than to three or four others. Needing more room, then, I made of the Law a spade to dig with. If some stumbled in the pit that I left here and there, I was not unprepared to see men weep; and I did.

"My sharing friends bespoke my testimonial, and I heard my praise to my face. Yet, the rankling fact remains that others have been praised too.

"Then I arranged for myself a distant journey on a suitable mission conformable to my station in life. My considered decision was to be a prophet.

"I took measures to promote the book that I was soon to write; and gave appropriate instructions to my man-secretary and my woman-secretary and to public relations. . . ."

Then I rose from my place and passed my hand before the face of the Spirit of the Times and the Child of this World, and I saw that he was blind; and I spoke into his ear, and I saw that he was deaf. Then, while he was yet speaking, I did leave and I went down into the City.

There I looked, and behold, the Spirit of the Times had spoken truly, for I saw that all the peoples of the Lord, from the Sunset Boulevard of the Whore of Babylon on the West to NBC and CBS of Nineveh on the East, were prophets of the Lord; they had found the spirit of the Lord, and had haltered it, and yoked it, and spanned it, and held forth fodder before its nose; the Klieg lights blistered like horns of light from the head of Moses; and the spirit of the Lord sang for its supper. I looked, and behold, the Generals too were Philosopher Kings; and the poets were bought to make music while the secret thing in the laboratory churned.

Then I saw that this was the City of Destruction. Then I said in my heart, I will flee the City of Destruction, nor even stay to listen to the beautiful tolling of the bells the while the Prophet Toynbee soundeth Doxology Interminable to the Church Well-Established, and I will get me upon the way that leadeth to the Heavenly City while yet there is time. And as I issued from the City of Destruction to set foot upon the way, behold, despair! My heart fainted within me and my knees faltered and my tongue swelled for dryness. For the way out of the City of Destruction was a broad highway that was trod by hosts upon hosts; and there blazoned over it in letters of Gold and letters of Fire the legends of the way that some had placed there, "This is the Way to the Delectable Mountains, This is the Stairway to Heaven"; and I saw that the signs were neon, and that the way to the Heavenly City had been let to hucksters; and that the bookmakers had set up their booths to take bets on the time of Destruction.

Then said I in my heart, to every thing there is a season, and a time to every purpose under the sun; a time to flee, and a time to stay, and who knoweth but this is a time to stay; a time to speak, and a time to keep silence, and who knoweth but some must be silenced that others may speak; lest bad money drive out good; a time for war and a time for peace, and who knoweth but the time cometh that is beyond war and beyond peace: a time to fear God and keep His commandments and be man wholly.

(—1947)

POET'S LEGACY

August 1914

ISAAC ROSENBERG

What in our lives is burnt
In the fire of this?
The heart's dear granary?
The much we shall miss?

Three lives hath one life—
Iron, honey, gold.
The gold, the honey gone,
Left is the hard and cold.

Iron are our lives,
Molten right through our youth;
—A burnt space through ripe fields.
—A fair mouth's broken tooth.

If Only Daniel Were Come

EDWIN SEAVER

Come all you wise men, you sorcerers, tell me the meaning of these
    dreams:

In the darkness I saw a man gnawing the heart out of his own breast.
In the shadows I saw a man drinking the bitter gall of his own tears.
And when I asked him why, he said:
I am hungry.

And I saw another man groping among a multitude of machines.
And he had no eyes with which to see, wherefore he bumped his silly
    head at every turn.
What are you seeking, I asked him, and he groaned:
I am looking for God.

And I saw another man scratching figures on a tombstone.
One third for labor, he muttered, that I may snooze comfortably an-
    other third and have something with which to fill my belly part of
    the remainder . . .
But that still leaves a fraction of time to kill.
Then when do you live? I ventured to ask.
But he only waved me away with his paw, and growled:
Go away, fool. Do I look like a dead one?

Jezebel

SIEGFRIED SASSOON

*"And the carcase of Jezebel shall be as dung upon the face
of the field in the portion of Jezreel"* (II KINGS 9. 37).

How lived this lump, round which lame beggars spat
And cur-dogs sniffed today,—this filth for midden?
This was the Queen that as a queen had ridden
Contemptuous of the proletariat.
Proud in her house the royal harlot sat:
By painted dyes the hag's pouched face well-hidden:
Yet she, who slaked with captains, unforbidden,
Is now the meat of many a scampering rat.

She loved to watch the Ballet from a box;
And ran a hospital for handsome youths
The Philistines had wounded,—not too badly.
But when Elisha came she got some shocks
*(He was the Labor leader whose home truths
Caused her career to finish somewhat sadly.)*

Roast Leviathan

❧

LOUIS UNTERMEYER

(Editors' Note: The readers of the following poem will be greatly interested in the explanation which accompanied it, in the form of a letter from the poet, which we take the liberty of quoting:

"I am enclosing," writes Mr. Untermeyer, "my latest and what, in many ways, I consider my best poem. The germs of it (its basic 'plot,' certain images and figures) I discovered in Talmudic-Midrashic literature—mostly *via* Ginzberg's *Legends of the Jews,* but the super-structure is altogether original.

"So many of us have been expressing, in one form or another, the traditional Hebraic strain of rapture and prophecy—what, for lack of a more specific phrase, I might call the Isaiah-Messianic note—and neglecting other Judaic qualities. There has been, particularly in poetry, little of that blend of racy humor and Oriental fancy that is as native to us as the more exalted (and more exploited) vein. 'Roast Leviathan' is an effort to capture some of the Eastern humor as well as the wild fantasy inherent in our post-biblical treasures.

"Technically, the poem may also interest you. It is an experiment in a form which I have been working at for about a year. I call it 'contrapuntal verse'—the counterpoint being furnished by an elaborate system of rhyme-patterns (external, interior and hidden rhyme) woven through the regular design of what seems to be perfectly formal verse. This poem marks my furthest development of the form."

"Old Jews!" Well, David, aren't we?
What news is that to make you see so red.
To swear and almost tear your beard in half.
Jeered at? Well, let them laugh.
You can laugh longer when you're dead.

What? Are you still too blind to see?
Have you forgot your Midrash! . . . They were right,
The little *goyim,* with their angry stones.

You should be buried in the desert out of sight
And not a dog should howl miscarried moans
Over your foul bones. . . .
Have you forgotten what is promised us,
Because of all our stinking days and rotten nights?
Eternal feasting, drinking, blazing lights
With endless leisure, periods of play!
The thousand pleasures, myriads of gay
Discussions; great debates with prophet-kings
And rings of riddling scholars all surrounding
God, who sits in the very middle, expounding
The Torah. . . . *Now* your dull eyes glisten!
Listen:

It is the final Day.
A blast of Gabriel's horn has torn away
The last haze from our eyes, and we can see
Past the three hundred skies and gaze upon
The Ineffable Name engraved deep in the sun.
Now one by one, the pious and the just
Are seated by us, radiantly risen
From their dull prison in the dust.
And then the festival begins!
A sudden music spins great webs of sound
Spanning the ground, the stars and their companions;
While from the cliffs and canons of blue air
Prayers of all colors, cries of exultation,
Rise into choruses of singing gold.
And at the height of this bright consecration,
The whole Creation's rolled before us.
The seven burning heavens unfold. . . .
We see the first (the only one we knew)
Dispersed and, shining through,
The other six declining: Those that hold
The stars and moons, together with all those
Containing rain and fire and sullen weather;
Cellars of dew-fall higher than the brim;
Huge arsenals with centuries of snows;
Infinite rows of storms and swarms of seraphim. . . .

Divided now are winds and waters. Sea and land,
Tohu and Bohu, light and darkness, stand
Upright on either hand.
And down this terrible aisle,
While heaven's ranges roar aghast,
Pours a vast file of strange and hidden things:
Forbidden monsters; crocodiles with wings
And perfumed flesh that sings and glows
With more fresh colors than the rainbow knows;
The *reëm*, those great beasts with eighteen horns,
Who mate but once in seventy years and die
In their own tears which flow ten stadia high;
The *shamir*, made by God on the sixth morn,
No longer than a grain of barley corn
But stronger than the bull of Bashan and so hard
That it can cut through diamonds. Ringed and starred
With precious stones, there struts the towering *ziz*.
Now see, with overpowering savagery,
Those banded tribes go by: the *Zamzummi*,
Six-handed giants who hurled defiance at death;
Nephilim, whose black breath could scorch the world.
Haters of men, *'Nakim*, come scraping low,
Though they could blow down mountains and each one
Could reach the sun and pull the skies asunder. . . .
For thrice three hundred years the full parade
Files by, a cavalcade of fear and wonder.
And then the vast aisle clears.

Now comes our constantly increased reward.
The Lord commands that monstrous beast,
Leviathan, to be our feast.
What cheers ascend from horde on ravenous horde!
One hears the towering creature rend the seas,
Frustrated, cowering, and his pleas ignored.
In vain his great, belated tears are poured—
For this he was created, kept and nursed.
Cries burst from all the millions that attend:
"Ascend, Leviathan, it is the end!

We hunger and we thirst! Ascend!" . . .
Observe him first, my friend.

God's deathless plaything rolls an eye
Five hundred thousand cubits high
The smallest scale upon his tail
Could hide six dolphins and a whale.
His nostrils breathe—and on the spot
The churning waves turn seething hot.
If he be hungry, one huge fin
Drives seven thousand fishes in;
And when he drinks what he may need,
The rivers of the earth recede.
Yet he is more than huge and strong—
Twelve brilliant colors play along
His sides until, compared to him,
The naked, burning sun seems dim.
New scintillating rays extend
Through endless singing space and rise
Beyond the skies . . . and swell the cries:
"Ascend, Leviathan, ascend!"

God now commands the multi-colored bands
Of angels to intrude and slay the beast
That His good sons may have a feast of food.
But as they come, Leviathan sneezes twice . . .
And, numb with sudden pangs, each arms hangs slack.
Black terror seizes them; blood freezes into ice
And every angel flees from the attack.
God, with a look that spells eternal law,
Compels them back.
But, though they fight and smite him tail and jaw,
Nothing avails; upon his scales their swords
Break like frayed cords, or, no more aid than straw,
Bend towards the hilt and wilt like faded grass.
Defeat and fresh retreat. . . . But once again
God's murmurs pass among them and they mass
With firmer steps upon the crowded plain.
Vast clouds of spears and stones rise from the ground,

But every dart flies past, and rocks rebound
To the disheartened angels falling 'round.

A pause.
The angel host withdraws
With empty boasts throughout its sullen files.
Suddenly God smiles.
On the walls of heaven a shining wonder falls;
Low thunder rumbles like an afterthought,
And God's slow laughter calls:
"Behemot!"

Behemot, sweating blood,
Uses for his daily food
All the fodder, flesh and juice
Of what twelve mountains can produce.

Jordan, flooded to the brim,
Is a single gulp to him;
Two great streams from Paradise
Cool his lips and scarce suffice.

When he shifts from side to side
Earthquakes gape and open wide;
When a nightmare makes him snore
All the dead volcanoes roar.

In the space between each toe,
Kingdoms rise and saviours go;
Epochs fall and causes die
In the lifting of his eye.

Wars of justice, love and death,
These are but his wasted breath;
Chews a planet for his cud—
Behemot, sweating blood.

Roused from his unconcern,
Behemot burns with anger.

Dripping sleep and languor from his heavy haunches,
He turns from deep disdain and launches
Himself upon the thickening air,
And with weird cries of sickening despair,
Flies at Leviathan.
None can surmise the struggle that ensues—
The eyes lose sight of it and words refuse
To tell the story in its gory might.
Night passes after night,
And still the fight continues, still the sparks
Fly from the iron sinews . . . till the marks
Of fire and belching thunder fill the dark
And, almost torn asunder, one falls stark,
Hammering upon the other! . . .
What clamor now is born, what crashings rise!
Hot lightnings lash the skies and frightened cries
Clash with the hymns of saints and seraphim.
The bloody limbs thrash through a ruddy dusk
Till one great tusk of Behemot has gored
Leviathan, restored to his full strength,
Who, dealing fiercer blows in those last throes,
Closes on reeling Behemot at length
And pierces him with his steel-pointed claws—
Straight through the jaws to his disjointed head.
And both lie dead.

Then come the angels!
With hoists and levers, joists and poles,
With knives and cleavers, ropes and saws,
Down the long slopes to the gaping maws,
The angels hasten; hacking and carving,
So nought will be lacking for the starving
Chosen of God who, in frozen wonderment,
Realize now what the terrible thunder meant.
How their mouths water while they are looking
At these miles of slaughter and sniffing the cooking!
Whiffs of delectable fragrance swim by,
Spice-laden vagrants that float and entice,
Tickling the throat and brimming the eye.

Ah! What rejoicing and crackling and roasting!
Ah! How the boys sing as, cackling and boasting,
The angels' old wives and their nervous assistants
Run in to serve us. . . .
And while we are toasting
The fairest of all, they call from the distance—
The fair ones of Time, they share our enjoyment,
Their only employment to bear jars of wine
And shine like the stars in a circle of glory.
Here sways Rebekah accompanied by Zilpah;
Miriam plays to the singing of Bilhah;
Hagar tells tales for us, Judith her story;
Esther exhales bright romances and musk.
There, in the dusky light, Salome dances.
Sara and Rachel and Leah and Ruth,
Fairer than ever and all in their youth,
Come at our call and go by our leave.
And, from her bower of beauty, walks Eve,
While, to the strings of her lute, she sings
Of Eden, young earth and the birth of all things. . . .

Peace without end.
Peace will descend on us, discord will cease;
And we, now so wretched, will lie stretched out
Free of all doubt, on our cushions of ease.
And, like a canopy over our bed,
The skin of Leviathan, tail-tip to head,
Soon will be spread till it covers the skies.
Light will still rise from it; millions of bright
Facets of brilliance, shaming the white
Glass of the moon, inflaming the night.

So Time shall pass and rest and pass again,
Burn with an endless zest and then return,
Walk at our side and tide us to new joys;
God's voice to guide us, Beauty as our staff.
Thus shall Life be when Death has disappeared. . . .

Jeered at? Well, let them laugh.

An Old Song

❧

YEHOASH

In the Blossom-land Japan
   Somewhere thus an old song ran:

Said a warrior to a smith,
"Hammer me a sword forthwith.
Make the blade
Light as wind on water laid.
Make it long,
As the wheat at harvest-song,
Supple, swift
As a snake. Without a rift
Full of lightnings, thousand-eyed!
Smooth as silken cloth and thin,
As the web that spiders spin.
And merciless as pain, and cold!"

"On the hilt what shall be told?"

"On the sword's hilt, my good man,"
Said the warrior of Japan,
"Trace for me
A running lake, a flock of sheep
A cottage with a cherry-tree
And one who sings her child to sleep."
      Translated from the Yiddish by Marie Syrkin

Amos

CHAIM NACHMAN BIALIK

. . . Seer, go flee (Amos 7. 12)

"Go flee?"—No man like to me flees!
Slow to plod have I learned from my herds;
And my tongue does not know speech with ease—
I hammerlike smash down my words.

If futile my power—mine no fault.
'Tis your sin and bear ye the bale!
On no anvil is my hammer caught.
In rotting wood did my pick fail.

'Tis nought! With my lot let me stay;
Vessels to girdle I tie,
And, an hired man without my day's pay,
Slow as I came—back do I hie.

To my dwelling I go in its dale,
With the wood-sycamores long to sway.
And rot here and perish—the gale
Tomorrow shall bear you away.

                    Translated from the Hebrew by I. M. Lask

Before The Statue Of Apollo

❦

SAUL TCHERNICHOWSKY

To thee I come, O long-abandoned god
Of early moons and unremembered days,
To thee whose reign was in a greener world
Among a race of men divine with youth,
Strong generations of the sons of earth:
To thee, whose right arm broke the bound of heaven
To set on thrones therein thy strongest sons,
Whose proud brows with victorious bays were crowned.
Amongst the gods of old thou wert a god,
Bringing for increase to the mighty earth
A race of demi-gods, instinct with life,
Strange to the children of the house of pain.
A boy-god, passionate and beautiful,
Whose mastery was over the bright sun
And over the dark mysteries of life,
The golden shadow-treasuries of song,
The music of innumerable seas—
A god of joyousness and fresh delight,
Of vigor and the ecstasy of life.

I am the Jew. Dost thou remember me?
Between us there is enmity forever!
Not all the multitudes of ocean's waters,
Storm-linking continent with continent,
Could fill the dark abyss between us yawning.
The heavens and the boundless wilderness
Were short to bridge the wideness set between
My fathers' children and thy worshippers.
And yet behold me! I have wandered far,

(681)

By crooked ways, from those that were before me,
And others after me shall know this path.
But amongst those that will return to thee
I was the first to free my soul that groaned
Beneath the agony of generations;
For a day came I would endure no more,
And on that day my spirit burst its chains
And turned again towards the living earth.

The people and its God have aged together!
Passions which strengthlessness had laid to sleep
Start into sudden life again, and break
Their prison of a hundred generations.
The light of God, the light of God is mine!
My blood is clamorous with desire of life.
My limbs, my nerves, my veins, triumphant shout
For life and sunlight.
                              And I come to thee,
And here before thy pedestal I kneel
Because thy symbol is the burning sun.
I kneel to thee, the noble and the true,
Whose strength is in the fullness of the earth,
Whose will is in the fullness of creation,
Whose throne is on the secret founts of being.
I kneel to life, to beauty and to strength,
I kneel to all the passionate desires
Which they, the dead-in-life, the bloodless ones,
The sick, have stifled in the living God,
The God of wonders of the wilderness,
The God of gods, Who took Canaan with storm
Before they bound Him in phylacteries.
                    Translated from the Hebrew by Maurice Samuel

The Frogs

❦

JACOB CAHAN

Quark, quark, quark, quark . . . Listen to the joyous croaking
Of the Frogs,
Of the cold Frogs, the sleek, cold Frogs.
How goodly are they in their own eyes,
Hopping and dancing in their bed of ooze,
Fat with delight of mud, drunk with the smell of mud,
Chanting, great-hearted and full-voiced, chanting
The righteousness of the Frogs, the wisdom of the Frogs.

If you do not know the Frog-folk,
Then listen, I will tell you of them.
Though in form and color they be diverse,
By these signs, the signs of the Frog-folk,
May they all be known:
Narrow head and mighty paunch,
And great glass eyes,
Eyes bulging with greed,
And, in their eyes, treachery and terror.

And do you know their dwelling-place,
The dwelling-place of the Frogs?
Do you think that they inhabit the deep heart of ocean,
That they stir and rouse to anger the heart of ocean,
Like the children of Leviathan? Oh no!
But yonder they dwell, on the edges of the ponds and marshes,
Yonder, where for water there is noisome stagnation,
Where the ooze at its deepest comes up to the hips,
Where sunlight is changed into treacherous twilight,
Where malodorous vapors, vapors of sickness, bubble up;

There the Frog-folk swarm and spawn.
The foul waters of the ditches are living waters to them,
Darkness is light; a delight and an ecstasy
Is the slime of the depths, the odor of filth.
Multitudes, countless multitudes, wander in the darkness,
In quest of booty—the booty of mudworms.
And for the sake of booty Frog quarrels with Frog,
And for the sake of booty there is love between them.

And do you know the righteousness of the Frogs?
He that hunts the mudworm most,
He that puffs himself up most,
He is righteous.
Him the congregation holds in honor,
And his praises are sung by the sons of mud.

And do you know the wisdom of the Frogs?
He that is best at singing the song of the Frogs—
He is the wisest.
And if you, my brother, know not the song of the Frogs,
I know it.
Oh many a long day did God condemn me
To dwell among the marshes,
Many a long day have I stood there, silent, listening,
Listening to the song of the Frogs and learning it.
And this is the song of the Frogs.

Quark, quark, quark, quark!
Life is smooth and cool and dark!
Leave fantastic dreams alone
And mind no business but your own.
For wisdom's aim, the wise one knows,
Is obedience—and repose.
Quark, quark, quark, quark!

For what will be, has been.
Nothing the wisdom of old surpasses;
Our fathers were wise, their children are asses.

Eternal their laws, beyond question or doubt;
Our business is only to carry them out.
And what has been, will be.

How goodly is our lot!
What could be better than this our dance
Which is our ancient inheritance?
'Tis full of logic, of common sense,
And wisdom and experience.
How goodly is our lot!

Long live the world of mud!
What pleasure or temptation lies
In deserts, or seas, or open skies?
But bless the mud that shelters one
From tempests and the burning sun.
Long live the world of mud!

Quark, quark, quark, quark!
Life is smooth, and cool, and dark!

This is the song of the Frogs, but wait a little, brother,
I will reveal to you the soul of the Frogs.
Not in the likeness of fire is their soul, of a flame
Lifting arms towards the sun.
Its likeness is the aftermath of fire,
A handful of ashes, smoke and sparks . . .
And the sparks glow in the ashes,
Ascend in the smoke,
And whirl and wander and fall, and are swiftly extinguished.

Wait a little longer, and I will tell you,
O knowledge-hungry one,
What lies in the heart of the Frog.
Do you think that they search the deeps of the golden heavens,
That they wander free under the golden heavens
In the greatness of love, in utter devotion,
Like the children of eagles? Oh, no!
One cubit, two cubits

They hop at times from the edge of the swamp
Into the green couch by the shadow of rushes;
There for a brief hour they doze in the sunlight,
Dreaming
(Who knows what crazy sun-dreams
Are born then in the tiny reptiles?)
There they taste in stealth
The joy of the forbidden . . .
Till a sunbeam by chance scorches them,
Or till a light sound startles them,
The sound of a bird's wing, footstep of man or beast—
Oh then! Repenting bitterly of their indiscretion,
Hop! hop! back into the marsh!
Ho, ho, how good it is
To see them in the terror of that moment,
To see the sickness and confusion in their hearts!
Ho, ho! How good, how good it is
To mark and consider this unhappy race,
To consider its ways, its lusts, its wanderings and movements,
To hear the noises of its idiot multitudes,
And to laugh! Out of the wells of the free and living heart,
      to laugh!

What? . . . Is this a thing for laughter?
Nay, it is a thing to SMITE!
For hear my words, O House of the Free,
And ye Children of the Light, hearken to my prophecy!
A day approaches, and it is near at hand, a day of visitation,
And the Lord will send the Frogs upon us!
Then all the marshes will spawn Frogs,
And they will come up from the marshes and into our houses,
And into our eating and our drinking.
And the croaking of them will deafen our ears,
Till a man will not hear the words of his brother.
And the odor of slime will spread about the earth
Till the air will be a stink in our nostrils.
And this plague of the Frogs will be
Of all the plagues the greatest that has smitten earth
Since the day when the first man and woman did eat

Of the tree of knowledge of good and evil . . .
Let us arm today! Let us fight the Frogs with light!
We will draw the sun out from his course
And with his burning beams dry up the marshes,
And the Frogs will die.

And if it be that God denies His mercy to no living thing,
And He has appointed for every living thing a place
In the order of His mighty kingdom,
Yea, and even for the Frogs has taken thought
That their memory and their remnant shall not be cut off,
Then let the Frogs remain in their appointed place!
But our boundary, which is boundary of the sun,
They shall not cross, and from all our land
They shall be wiped away, and hunted into the rivers,
And only in the rivers shall they dwell.

Translated from the Hebrew by Maurice Samuel

Two Poems

❦

ZALMAN SCHNEOUR

I

I Weep Not For the Life...

I weep not for the life that I must leave,
A single tear were too much to lament it,
For the far future and its mysteries,
Which even the words which I have written here
Perhaps shall never look upon, I weep. . .

For I will die—and after me my words
Will still behold the changing of the world:
Death and rebirth, and wars that storm and die;
And drunk with living blood, the ancient Goddess
Will rise and take the earth again with green.

Then the eternal iron will return
And lay the blossoms low, and in their place
Shall prison-houses greet the rolling heavens.
In these will man take refuge from creation
To guard the gold extorted from the earth.

Until the gold shall be a pain and burden
Unto his spirit, and its chilly lustre
Shall be a weariness unbearable.
Then will he leave his gold and issue forth
To find again the founts of life and light. . .

And then new marvels will adorn the earth,
The labor of great hearts; and one great tower,
Stone upon stone, shall rise into the heavens;
And still shall stone be added unto stone,
Until the tower will tremble and dissolve.

And he that raised it shall a second time
Be dashed again to earth, and wounded lie
Amid the ruins of his sanctuary:
And in the chaos he shall yet desire
The shattered glory to uplift again.

Then dreams of life and riddles of creation
Shall be declared in an exalted tongue,
And one man from the dead shall suck the blood
And in his brother nourish like therewith,
And race with race shall mingle and be lost.

And to one generation, slave-like bound
With visions as with shackles, shall succeed
A generation young, with wings untried;
And with its fathers' shields lay a triumphant road,
And sing the pæan which its fathers sang. . .

So will the magic colors of the world
For ever and for ever change—and I—
I shall not see, I shall not see these things,
Except in prophecy, as one, thirst-withered,
May look on water in a crystal locked.

Bitter oppressive, bitter to despair,
Intolerably bitter is this thought—
That I and all life shall not cease together,
That after I am dead, in earth dissolved,
Their wild dance will go on above my grave.

How good, how good it were to live for ever,
Calm and exalted, sundered from the life
Which brings up foulness from the nether seas—

Alone upon the top of some wild mountain,
And like the mountain savage and alone.

Naked as at my birth, to wander free,
To sleep in the clefts of the rocks, my couch to be
The skin of some wild animal, my food
And drink, the dews and berries of the field,
And with the sun to rise and lay me down.

Invisible, I should behold the world,
And mark the tempest breaking at my feet,
And I should sing with pæan and lament
The triumphs and disasters which revolve
For ever and for ever and for ever.

And when the final agony shall shake
The earth below, I would intone a dirge
Which not the heavens nor the earth have heard.
And when I fall in death, above my body,
The echoes of the hills shall still lament.

II

And There Are Times...

And there are times when dreams are vanities.
Shadows of beauty, altars unto love,
And, in the heart, the longings that arise—
All, all are beautiful—and all are lies.

For wind is not a comfort unto hunger,
Nor gold a snare to immortality.
I cry then: "For the bitter truth I long,
Though grim like iron, yet like iron strong!"

I cry then: "Weary is my soul of dreams,
False prophecies, and golden visions false;
For, blinded with their vacant light, I gave
My strength to beauty, an eternal slave."

Though all are trapped, must I with them be trapped?
I shall be first to tear the treacherous net,
And thunder, as the golden strands I sever,
"Down, down with gold: Let iron live for ever!"
            Translated from the Hebrew by Maurice Samuel

Maariv

∞

BABETTE DEUTSCH

He faced the darkening window as he stood
to say the evening prayer.
And those who moved about him there,
the strangers, who were all his own,
giving him neither scorn nor care,
left him the more alone.
His old eyes
echoed the dimming skies. His fingers
fluttered, as tho' he sought
to catch the faded fringes of his thought,
the while he warmed his aching bones
with words of praise
that lit like sunset the cold end of days.
And as he prayed,
a feeble patriarch in a thin old coat,
drawing about him like a sacred shawl
the comfort of his ancient ritual,
the room grew wide, and wavered. . . .
Thru the dusk,—
on velvet paws, inscrutable-eyed, remote,
the desert rose.
Out of the east, licking the dunes like flame,
tawny and purple, came the climbing caravans,
whose colors died among the hilly sands,
and flared again
against the sands.
And still flowed forward, travelling to find
some gold oasis bright with sudden fruit,
but might not ever leave
the oblivious sands behind.

And at the desert's edge,
creeping between the heavens and the sand,
carrying households on their restless road,
driving their flocks, themselves beneath the goad,
striking their tents at dawn and wandering on:
the chosen seed,
the eternal aliens pass.
They know the feebleness of desert streams,
the indurate darkness of the grave they know,
the thoroughfares of war,
the burning feet that can go forth no longer, and must go,
the burning eyes that look to withered grass
and green, untrampled dreams.
Have they not made their covenant with One
stronger than desert sun?
One who surrounds them like encompassing wind,
who is above them like the night, and under
their feet like patient earth, and in their ears
a low terrible thunder.
How might they else
bear the long burden of this dusty heat,
the long strange way
among strange people always,
the long day of labor that is seasoned with slow tears
and by the rapid thieving years is snatched
too soon away.
How might they bear
to see their children eat the broken bread
of homely custom, staled,
now they are fed not by their own.
How might they bear
to hear their fathers in defeat
muttering the evening prayer,
when every dusk comes down on a new loss,
and seems familiar since it, too, will pass.
They keep an ancient covenant; they have heard
the desert's heart beat with a sacred Word
credited and unknown.

They do not fear
stars in their cruel courses, which are shewn to be
His handiwork; they do not dread
men, strangely made
in His unthinkable image.
Their tented bed
is safe beneath His hand,
who are His pride. . . .
The sand
vanished. The darkness changed,
as the old man, from the security of his solitude,
turned to the world, and sighed.

Two Poems

ANDRÉ SPIRE

To France

O exquisite country,
You who have swallowed up so many races,
Do you want to take me too?
Your language shapes my soul;
You make me think clear thoughts;
You force my mouth to smile . . .
All your sweeping plains so dearly tended,
Your woods so finely pruned, so civilized,
The flowing curve of your landscape,
Your sleeping streams, your cities, your vineyards . . .
Have more than half swallowed me already!

But must I love your tournaments of words,
Your gorgeous gewgaws and your finery,
Your café-concerts and your theaters,
Your button-hole ribbons and your drawing-rooms?
Must I become cock-sure?
Must I become methodical
Like your carefully laid-out vegetable farms?
Or drawn out and lifeless
Like the stalks of your formal hedgerows?
Must I sprawl out on the ground
Like your docile apple-trees?
And some day must I count out little verses
For genteel ladies in lace?

(695)

Ceremony, you want to make me too insipid!
Humbug, you want to squeeze my soul!
O warmth, sorrow, passion, madness,
Invincible genii to whom I have been vowed,
What shall become of me without you?
—Come, defend me against the dry reasonableness of
        this happy land!

The Ancient Law

She appeared before me last night, the vanquished one, eyes bandaged,
  neck bent forward, head bowed in defeat.
She appeared before me last night looking just as I had seen her on
  the pillar of the cathedral, leaning her rose sandstone hand on
  the broken staff of her standard; she, the cursed one, with over-
  turned book, young body, the straight folds of her chaste tunic.
She appeared before me last night, the desolate one.

"You will strive in vain," she told me. "You will never really love their
  theaters, their museums, their palaces, their playthings;
Your forehead leaned too early toward grief and sadness.
Beauty will seem to you a luxury, luxury an abomination, your dis-
  tractions a theft.
You will think you love your neighbors and your friends . . .
But open your eyes to yourself! When does your heart awaken?
Only when you hear hoarse voices, when you see hands a little
  feverish, eyes close-set;
When the mouth which begs your aid cries: you owe it me
For only such a one is your brother, has a soul like yours, and he
  claims you as an equal.

You will want to make songs of daring and of power;
But you will love only dreamers unarmed against life.
You will try to listen to the joyous song of peasants, to the brutal foot-
  steps of soldiers, to the pretty roundelays of little girls . . .
Your ears are made only for hearing the lamentations which rise from
  the four corners of the earth."

Translated from the French by Stanley Burnshaw

With All My Heart, O Truth

(Jehuda Halevi)

For Mezzo or Baritone Solo, Mixed Voices and Piano

E R W I N   J O S P E

❦

1948 Award of the Musarts Club of Chicago

Copyright 1948 by Erwin Jospe

Judah Goldin's translation of "With All My Heart, O Truth" appeared in *The Menorah Journal* for Autumn 1945.

Translated by Judah Goldin

With All My Heart, O Truth

Translated from the Hebrew of Jehuda Halevy
by Judah Goldin

Erwin Jospe

WITH ALL MY HEART, O TRUTH

WITH ALL MY HEART, O TRUTH

WITH ALL MY HEART, O TRUTH

WITH ALL MY HEART, O TRUTH

WITH ALL MY HEART, O TRUTH

WITH ALL MY HEART, O TRUTH

A Compassionate People

(For the Thirtieth Year of *The Menorah Journal*)

CHARLES REZNIKOFF

Where is that mountain of which we read in the Bible—
Sinai—on which the Torah was given to Israel?
Perhaps it is in Egypt
where the wild Israelites left the little idols
of the sons of Jacob, the little idols
which stood in the corners of the tents
and rode with the rider
under the saddle-cloth; perhaps it is in Egypt—
a land of such affliction
three thousand years or so afterwards
we speak of it to this day.
Blessed are You, Lord, God of the Universe,
Who has kept us alive.

Where is that mountain of which we read in the Bible—
Sinai—on which the Torah was given to Israel?
Perhaps it is in Palestine;
for Sinai was built out of the skeletons
of much suffering,
in which the lives of the Israelites
were like the sands—
that become in the centuries rock, ledges of rock,
a mountain, and at last
the Law,
cut into tables of stone.
Blessed are You, God, King of the Universe,
Who has kept Israel alive.

Where was the Bible written?
Some of it in Babylon
where the Jews wept when they remembered Zion;
exiles among the hosts of Persia,
to be given away by a nod of a drunken king
to a Haman for slaughter,
or, in another whim of the king,
to be saved by an Esther and a Mordecai.
Yes, they sang the songs of Zion
in a strange land,
even in the land of their captivity.
Blessed are You, Lord, God of the Universe,
Who has kept Israel alive.

Where was the Mishnah written?
In Palestine
where bands of Jews had fought against the legions
until Jewish slaves were so many
a Jewish slave was not worth as much as a horse
and no Jew might enter the city
where Jerusalem had been
except by stealth to weep there
on the day of its fall;
and the Torah might not be taught,
and the houses of study were darkened,
and the scholars and their disciples
were hunted down and crucified
or flayed alive
or wrapped in a scroll of the Torah and burned to death.
But still the Jews at dawn
before binding the grain into sheaves,
before the women turned to their spinning,
or the dealers set out the wares in the market-place,
and the porters lifted their burdens,
turned towards the hills of Jerusalem and the God of their fathers.
Blessed are You, God of the Universe,
Who has kept Israel alive.

As when a great tree, bright with blossoms and heavy with fruit,
is cut down and its seeds are carried far

by the winds of the sky and the waves of the streams and seas,
and it grows again on distant slopes and shores
in many places at once,
still blossoming and bearing fruit a hundred and a thousandfold,
so, at the destruction of the Temple
and the murder of its priests, ten thousand synagogues
took root and flourished
in Palestine and in Babylonia and along the Mediterranean;
so the tides carried from Spain and Portugal
a Spinoza to Holland
and a Disraeli to England.
God, delighting in life,
You have remembered us for life.

One man
escapes from the ghetto of Warsaw
where thousands have been killed
or led away in tens of thousands, hundreds of thousands,
to die in concentration camps,
to be put to death in trucks, in railway cars,
    in gullies of the woods,
in gas chambers,
and yet he who escapes—
of all that multitude—
in his heart the word *Jew* burning
as it burned once in Jeremiah
when he saw the remnant of Judah
led captive to Babylon
or fugitives in Egypt,
from that man
shall spring again a people
as the sands of the sea for number,
as the stars of the sky.
Blessed are You, God of the Universe,
delighting in life.

Out of the strong, sweetness;
and out of the dead body of the lion of Judah,
the prophecies and the psalms;

out of the slaves in Egypt,
out of the wandering tribesmen of the deserts
and the peasants of Palestine,
out of the slaves of Babylon and Rome,
out of the ghettos of Spain and Portugal, Germany and Poland,
the Torah and the prophecies,
the Talmud and the sacred studies, the hymns and songs of the Jews;
and out of the Jewish dead
of Belgium and Holland, of Rumania, Hungary, and Bulgaria,
of France and Italy and Yugoslavia,
of Lithuania and Latvia, White Russia and Ukrainia,
of Czechoslovakia and Austria,
Poland and Germany,
out of the greatly wronged
a people teaching and doing justice;
out of the plundered
a generous people;
out of the wounded a people of physicians;
and out of those who met only with hate,
a people of love, a compassionate people.

The Patriarchs

MORTON SEIF

For Allen Tate

When we left the garden with our prize of bone
A towering wall of onyx stone
Rushing to the firmament's unseen
Was raised where the ravished tree had been.

Where the four black rivers went no creature lived
But the winged fowl and fruitful beasts.
By thorns and thistles on the bruised land we strived
In the fields and with green herbs made three feasts.

One each time a son was born: the first came
Tilling his mother's strength in the dark night,
The second at noon conceived more tame,
And the last at dawn to redeem the seed's blight.

Where the others dwelled no king, no queen ruled
But a patient voice lashed their dry deeds
(They had become as one of us and lulled
To death good flowers with their evil weeds).

Who survived in the small gopher-wood ship
Shored on fugitive new coasts incanting pacts
As a Hasid enthused in the grip
Of wine under the eucalyptus acts.

Now Baal-Shem-Tov, you know the humble source
Of rainbow spirit and informal joy,

Bialik, gentle singer, the living force
With which your sleeping dead stormed Troy.

For it will always be a tale to tell:
The stolen queen and banished bands of men
Fleeing from guilty settlements that fell
Through the vengeance of their God, as when

A blind man wrote on the Aegean sands

Ancestral Portraits

A Sonnet Sequence

SAMUEL YELLEN

I

I see no bearded Hebrew patriarch
In some illuminated manuscript,
Clad in gold breastplate, ephod, mitre—mark
Of Aaron's sons—with somber face tight-lipped,
Aglow with sacred destiny; whose dim
Forefather spoke with the Lord of Creation
On Sinai's hill, and was ordained by Him
A kingdom of priests and a holy nation.
I see no broidered robe, no precious stones,
But this spat-upon Jewish gabardine
Cloaking a frail cowering skin-and-bones
In a Polish ghetto, dark and unclean.
I read in this sick countenance's gray
The harsh dichotomy of We and They.

Denied both pride of place and pride of name,
He wears for treasured heirloom, boast of birth,
A malignant gem, an old badge of shame.
Thy seed shall be as the dust of the earth,
Promised the Lord.—Yes, as dust blindly tossed
Into the whirlwind. This grim irony
Could best be savored by one who had lost
In the Diaspora his ancestry.
Fury-driven, scattered through evil-eyed
Proud alien peoples, everywhere he knew
A hate more ancient than their foolish pride.

Thus was he Chosen and thus made a Jew,
Not by crazed myths of race or blood or creed,
But bitter suffering and dire need.

To this cold Northland, far from fig and palm,
His fleeing forebears came. I hear them weep,
Each night crying the cry of David's psalm:
I will both lay me down in peace, and sleep.
Around the edges of the Euxine Sea,
From Morocco into the Spanish trap,
Through the crooked alleys of Germany,
I trace their wanderings on this mute map.
Had this map but a tongue, what might it tell
Of hopeless staggering from place to place,
Of desperate means and aching farewell,
Of all the tortured seepage of a race?
Who said 'a rootless people' said in vain;
They sank their roots deep in the soil of pain.

Thou preparedst a table before him,
Oh Lord, in the presence of his enemies,
Heaped with dust and sour ashes to the rim.
His heart, cramped by ceaseless anxieties,
Quivers to the oblique glance, the slight,
The sneer—dread portents of shattered quiet,
Savage curse, bestial howl in the tiger night
Aflame with the pogrom's frenzied riot.
How the mere word can hatch maggots that teem
Within the guilty lesion of the soul,
Veiled fears bodied as in the purging dream,
Foul creatures creeping from the mind's bunghole!—
Phantoms? Vain conjurings?—Once you have heard
'Jew!' hissed, then doubt the power of the word!

Perhaps you find this portrait incomplete.
Where are the hands? you ask. The mouth and hair?—
Obliterated by time's winding-sheet
Long since.—Is he tall or short? Dark or fair?
Does he have this one's forehead? That one's nose?—

Dead silence.—This much can be said: the print
Of grief, the morbid uncertainty shows
In the fringes of the eye.—One more hint:
This portrait should be done in Rembrandt's style—
Faint lights, swart shadows, sober coloring;
The skull's flesh-and-blood, lightened by no smile,
Like an apparition; while menacing
In the background, fitful brute figures lurk,
Half-extinguished by the glimmering murk.

                                II

Even as a child, her dark and grave eyes —
Not the child's mirrors easy to divert—
Wear the light of sunset, not of sunrise,
The long anxious brooding on some deep hurt.
The careless laughter of a tender age
In her is underscored by something sad;
In all her girlish play lurks something sage,
She has a heart not readily made glad.
Through a cloud of years I see this ghetto maid
Tread the twisted lane of a medieval hive.
Her skin is fresh, her hair coiled in a braid;
Northern girls ripen late, but she soon grows,
Biding the single duty of her life,
From folded bud to Sharon's full-blown rose.

One day she wed.—Here, in an alien tongue,
I tell once more the tale of Rachel, told
Long ago; once more sing Solomon's song.
For this, I plunder that treasure of gold
Minted by crabbed scholars in James's day.—
Oh, like jewels are the joints of her thighs!
Rise up, Oh love, Oh fair one, and come away!
Yes, a garden enclosed is she!—He lies
All night betwixt her breasts, and his left hand
Under her head, his right embracing her.
He kisses her with the kisses of his mouth.
He is come into his garden. The drouth

Is ended. Her hands drop with sweet-smelling myrrh,
And the voice of the turtle is heard in the land.

Behold then her fierce resolve to annul
Her proud maiden beauty! She shaves the bright
Prized tresses from her head and bares the skull,
As the humbling wont of the Israelite
Prescribes. Thus self-abased, she meekly wears
The ordained coif to hide the naked bone.
Can we now grasp what this cruel act declares?—
She cleaves to one man, and one man alone.
Not like the tight-choking vine does she cleave,
But leans on him and lets him lean on her,
His comforter and sweet idolater.
His love is breath itself: her sole desire,
That all their living moments interweave,
And then their dust fuse in the grave's slow fire.

Were this a novel, each particular
Might be recorded in fine rhetoric—
The wretched progress of her calendar,
The births, the deaths, the nursing of the sick;
The close-knit web of smell and sight and sound,
The day-to-day events, the cares, the brief
Fading interludes of joy quickly drowned
In the consuming gloom of man's common grief.
Man's common grief, and more! She dwells apart
On an island hard beset by danger,
And living as the Jew must live, withdrawn,
Always the pariah, the loathed stranger.
Her hours are measured by her troubled heart—
And soon the days, the weeks, the years are gone.

Unheralded, a widowed crone in black
Appears one day where once a shy girl stood,
With a thick host of phantoms at her back.
But yesterday she shed her maidenhood;
But yesterday that joyous sacrifice
Of her first-born son at the circumcision.

She now knows the extorted bleeding price
Paid for time's smallest fugitive division.—
What perverse spell brought this transformation?
From what tissue did these gnarled hands emerge?
Whence came this wrinkled skin and infirm flesh?—
Her children scattered in humiliation,
Her ear echoing with her husband's dirge,
She awaits the hound straining at the leash.

Poems

❦

ITZIK MANGER

Parted

We walked together in the field,
And over the grass so green.
You gave me a golden ring,
And a blue scarf, my Queen.

The ring is made of the purest gold.
And the scarf is silk right through.
But you, my Queen, my own true love,
How far away are you!

You went away on the train.
And by ship across the sea.
At my window now I stand,
And wait for your letter to me.

Notte's Lullaby

I sing to myself a lullaby:
"Sleep, you lonely man.
Fate has buried you far away
In Uzbekistan.

"The wind quietly rocks your grave.
Sleep, Notte, rest.
When one's eyes are shut like yours,
Then sleep is best.

"Hear the rustling of the grass,
And of the wild flowers, too.
Be not angry that your grave
Hides the stars from you.

"The stars, those silvered lying thieves
Have cheated a million men,
Who with believing eyes have looked
For the Messiah in vain.

"Hear the cry of the sparrow-hawk,
Who flies across the land.
His sharp beak is stained with blood.
Him nothing can withstand.

"Then thank the earth that has hidden you
In her honest lap, deep, close.
She has raised a monument over you,
A sunflower and a rose.

"The monument will bloom and fade,
And will bloom another day.

October will extinguish it,
To be relighted by May.

One day your brother in his wanderings
May come wandering along,
And lay upon your grave your dream,
An everlasting song."
Maybe.—Meanwhile the clouds pursue
Their old eternal way—
Figures, plants, chimeras,
Till the end of the last day.

I sing to myself a lullaby:
"Sleep, you lonely man.
Fate has buried you far away
In Uzbekistan."

The Ruins of Poland

Under the ruins of Poland
There is a blond head—you.
Both the head and the ruins,
Both, my dear, are true.
Dearest, oh my dearest.

The little Polish lady
For her sins has died.
She will from her sleep, no doubt,
Arise purified.
Dearest, oh my dearest.

Over the ruins of Poland
Falls the falling snow.
The blond head of my dearest
Makes me die of woe.
Dearest, oh my dearest.

My woe sits at my writing desk,
And writes a letter to you.
The tear in my eye, my dearest,
Is deep as it is true.
Dearest, oh my dearest.

Over the ruins of Poland
A bird flies about,
A big bird of sorrow,
With wings devout.
Dearest, oh my dearest.

The big bird of sorrow,
Is myself, my dear.
It bears on its wings this song for you.
Under the ruins can you hear?
Dearest, oh my dearest.

By the Wayside Stands a Tree

By the wayside stands a tree,
Bent and bowed, alone.
All the birds from that tree
Long ago have flown.

Three to the east, three to the west,
South the others went.
And they left the tree alone,
Storm-tossed and bent.

"Mother, dear," I said to her,
"Please don't hinder me,
And no sooner said than done,
A little bird I'll be.

"I shall sit upon the tree,
And all the winter long
I will hush and comfort it
With a lovely song."

"Don't, my child," my mother said,
Weeping bitterly,
"You'll be frozen, God forbid,
Sitting on the tree."

"Don't spoil your lovely eyes," I said,
"Please mother, dear, don't cry."
And no sooner said than done,
A little bird am I.

My mother weeps: "Itzik, dear,
I fear you'll catch a chill.
Take your scarf or, God forbid,
I shall have you ill.

"Take your heavy boots with you.
The frost will be severe.
And your winter overcoat.
Please, Itzik dear.

"Put on your winter vest, you fool,
Your fur cap on your head,
Unless you want to sleep tonight
Together with the dead."

I lift my wings. How heavy are
All these things I wear.
My mother put on me much more
Than a little bird can bear

I look into my mother's eyes
So regretfully.
Her love made it impossible
That I a bird should be.

I Shall Take Off My Shoes

ᕙᕗ

I shall take off my shoes and my sadness,
And I will come back to you.
I will come as I am, a loser,
And stand up for you to view.

My God, my Lord, my Creator,
Purify me in your light.
I lie on a cloud before you.
Rock me to sleep in the night.

And speak to me words of kindness.
"My child, my child," to me say.
And with a kiss, from my forehead
Take the signs of my sins away.

For I have fulfilled your mission,
And have carried your holy song.
Is it my fault, if it happens
That "song" rhymes with "wrong"?

Is it my fault, if it happens
That "tone" rhymes with "moan,"
And that longing, true longing
Wanders always alone?

Is it my fault, Enlightener,
That I am now weary and sad,
And that this weary poem
At your feet is laid?

My God, my Lord, my Creator,
Purify me in your light.
I lie on a cloud before you.
Rock me to sleep in the night.

Auld Lang Syne

We sing together Auld Lang Syne.
I hold your hand in mine.
The wine in the glasses sparkles red.
The lights in the mirror shine.

I sing with you for Auld Lang Syne,
My eyes with weeping red.
I sing with you, and I hold the hands
Of my six million dead.

Epitaph

Here lies the sorry weary singing-bird
For the first time in his own bed,
The tailor-lad, the vagabond-poet,
From whom more songs will not be heard.

Don't pluck the weeds that grow over this house.
And in winter sweep not away the snow.
Nothing will now hurt him who sleeps below.
He lives at peace with the worm and the mouse.

Scatter no flowers upon this mound.
Put back nothing the storm hurls to the ground.
And do not drive the owl from the tombstone.

Let the wasp and the bee undisturbed hum.
Let the sexton's goat to these pastures come.
And leave me lying here alone.

Translated from the Yiddish by Joseph Leftwich

Portraits of a Minyan

❧

ABRAHAM M. KLEIN

1. *Landlord*

He is a learned man, adept
  At softening the rigid.
Purblind, he scans the Rashiscript,
  His very nose is digit. . . .
He justifies his point of view
  With verses pedagogic;
His thumb is double-jointed through
  Stressing a doubtful logic.
He quotes the Commentaries, yea,
  To Tau from Aleph,
But none the less, his tenants pay,
  Or meet the bailiff.

2. *Pintele Yid*

Agnostic, he would never tire
To cauterize the orthodox,
But he is here, by paradox,
To say the Kaddish for his sire. . . .

3. *Reb Abraham*

Reb Abraham, the jolly,
Avowed the gloomy face
Unpardonable folly,
Unworthy of his race.

When God is served in revel
By all his joyous Jews,
He says the surly devil
Stands gloomy at the news. . . .

Reb Abraham loved Torah,
If followed by a feast:
A Milah-banquet, or a
Schnapps to drink, at least.

On Sabbath-nights, declaring
God's praises, who did cram
The onion and the herring?
Fat-cheeked Reb Abraham.

On Ninth of Ab, who aided
The youngsters in their game
Of throwing burrs, as they did,
In wailing beards? The same.

And who on Purim came in
To help the urchins, when
They rattled at foul Haman?
Reb Abraham again.

On all Feasts of Rejoicing
Reb Abraham's thick soles
Stamped pious metres, voicing
Laudation of the scrolls.

Averring that in heaven
One more Jew had been crowned,
Reb Abraham drank even
On cemetery-ground.

(733)

And when Messiah greeting,
Reb Abraham's set plan
Is to make goodly eating
With roast leviathan.

When God is served in revel
By all His joyous Jews,
He says the surly devil
Stands gloomy at the news. . . .

4. *Shadchan*

Cupid in a caftan
    Slowly scrutinizes
Virgins and rich widows,
    And other lesser prizes.

Cupid strokes his chin, and
    Values legs as so much,
So much for straight noses;
    What if wives don't know much!

What's a squinted eye, or
    What's a halting stutter,
When her father offers
    More than bread and butter? . . .

Cupid whets his arrows—
    Golden, golden rocket. . . .
Aims not at the bosom,
    Aims them at the pocket.

Cupid in a caftan
    Disregards the flowery
Speech of moon-mad lovers.
    Cupid talks of dowry.

5. *Sophist*

When will there be another such brain?
Never; unless he rise again,
Unless Reb Simcha rise once more
To juggle syllogistic lore. . . .

One placed a pin upon a page
Of Talmud print, whereat the sage
Declared what holy word was writ
Two hundred pages under it!

That skull replete with pilpul tricks
Has long returned to its matrix,
Where worms split hair, where Death
    confutes
The hope the all-too-hopeful moots.

But I think that in Paradise
Reb Simcha with his twinkling eyes
Interprets, in some song-spared nook,
To God the meaning of His book. . . .

6. *Reader of the Scroll*

Divinely he sang the scriptured note;
He twisted sound, intoned the symbol,
Made music sally, slow or nimble,
From out his heart and through his
    throat. . . .

For in a single breath to hiss
The ten outrageous names of those
Who on the Persian gallows rose—
Oh, this was pleasure, joyance this! . . .

7. *Sweet Singer*

O What would David say,
Young David in the fields,
Singing in Bethlehem,
Were he to hear this day
Old Mendel slowly hum
His sweetest songs,
Old Mendel, who being poor
Cannot through charity
Atone his wrongs,
And being ignorant
Cannot in learned wise
Win Paradise,

Old Mendel who begs Heaven as his
    alms
By iterating and re-iterating psalms? . . .

8. *Junk-dealer*

All week his figure mottles
    The city lanes,
Hawking his rags and bottles
    In quaint refrains. . . .

But on the High, the Holy
    Days, he is lord,
And being lord, earth wholly
    Gladly is abhorred. . . .

While litanies are clamored,
    His loud voice brags
A Hebrew most ungrammared.
    He sells God rags.

9. *His Was an Open Heart*

His was an open heart, a lavish hand,
His table ever set for any guest;
A rabbi passing from a foreign land,
A holy man, a beggar, all found rest
Beneath his roof; even a Gentile saw
A welcome at the door, a face that
    smiled;

The chillest heart beneath his warmth
    would thaw.
And for these deeds, God blessed him
    that he saw
The cradle never emptied of its
    child. . . .

10. *And the Man Moses Was Meek*

This little Jew
Homunculus
Found four ells too
Capacious. . . .

He never spoke,
Save in his prayer;
He bore his yoke
As it were air. . . .

He knew not sin.
He even blessed
The spider in
His corner-nest.

The meek may trust
That in his tomb
He will turn dust
To save some room. . . .

Coming Deluge

⚜

EMANUEL LITVINOFF

We shall not know the dawn's apocalypse,
nor stride beyond the midnight's edge of terror:
no cocks, no bells, no trumpeting of flowers
invade us in our sleep. Our tide
creeps up too far, our islands shrink
and lose to flood the commonwealth of earth—
now is the mind's last cave besieged
by water. Dark time is near its end.
We shall not hear the carillons of Spring,
the bud's explosion in the chiming heart,
nor will the green renewal of our tree
surprise the iris of our fire-quenched eyes.
Dark time is near its end and now for us
only the dark air's silence and the muffled bell
tolling the sea's cathedral.

Some will launch forth the little ships of life,
the flood-defying arks bearing the seeds
of some strange fruit of sorrow: but not of us.
The interval of death will pass away.
White doves will scan the bitter waste of sea
but not discover us, nor branch, nor leaf—
only the tide's recession, the resurrected valley;
only the new-born gleaming pinnacles of Ararat.

Man in Space: 1961

(For Henry Hurwitz, in Abiding Appreciation)

❧

CORNEL LENGYEL

Behold what comes forth out of mud to cast
his moving shadow across a web of stars:
a question-mark from the darkest pit of time
that spirals from ameba toward the moon.
In fear and trembling at first but now more boldly
he crawls from the ooze of his puddles and rises to soar,
girdles the globe in ninety weightless minutes,
surveying his tomb while planets await his call.

Confounder of reason, compounded of paradox:
In love of his fellows he burns himself for fuel,
In fear of his fellows he forges his end-earth weapon;
himself the arrow in flight, the target in place.
A thinking atom: the riddle in the rocket
composed of elements old as the oldest star.

The New Babel

LIBBY BENEDICT

What use the mounting dream,
If tongues are still asunder?
What use the flowered paths?
Plain ones suffice for blunder.

This was not evil scheme
To pierce device celestial,
But humble manifest
To subjugate the bestial.

Nor was it heaven's wit
That cleft our speech and broke it,
Until the very sense
Is lost to him who spoke it.

The sword within our hearts
That struggles from its sheathing,
Has bedlamized our words,
And stirred our thoughts to seething.

Suspicion's bitter fumes
Drive us to buried hovel,
Where we had hoped to climb,
We will but crawl and grovel.

The towers rise and rise,
Our hands are skilled at dreaming;
Is left to them alone
The ultimate redeeming?

Tomorrow Is in Danger

A Recitative

⸎

ALLEN KANFER

Tomorrow is in danger: therefore, stand
On guard against the fallen spirit saying:
"Be born again? the end is come when the end
        is come, and the bitter corruptible
        puts on the sweet
Incorruptible of death, disintegration, worms, atoms
        and oblivion.
Wherefore should dust be tortured into breath
        for nothing but a metaphor
        of poignancy?
This the weary question, the weary answer,
        the tearful supplication for the glory
        long denied: flesh into essence, man into seraph,
        sin into sanctity, groans into carols,
        weariness of the bones into peace everlasting,
        vale of tears into Abraham's bosom."

Now is the bitterest of times: the midnight of humanity:
        no nightingale sings requiems
        while the listener in transport longs for death:
        but death comes now
Without poetic straining or a bird's enchantment: comes
        noisily, comes flying, comes murderously,
        publicly, in the name of the living terror
        to the house of the meek, the bed of the innocent,
        in the name of death's humiliation,
        yea, in the name of the oppressor's howl:
        death is degenerate.
        Now for fascists

To die is to die: to leave no heritage: to be done
                with living: to shake off the terror:
                to cancel living nothingness with nothing's death.
Something within this living vanished: when?
                when men too brutish for a melting love
                broke men too fragile for a brutish rage,
                froze all freedom in an edict, made
                mockery of precious things the only mirth
                permissible,
                praised anonymity, wedded men to state and
                maids to kitchens, elevated the bloody base,
                forbade one's sleeping
On a poet's lips: and regimented children and their wonder
                to diurnal certainty
Of vaudeville dogs in a staged routine.

Be born again! Somewhere this echo has a ring
                familiar to historical remembrances:
                who will bear me again, knowing
                the horror? who will, beginning life,
                begin the abhorred recital?
Be born, you unborn! now, now in the midst
                of men, burdened with wish for loving.
Tomorrow there is hope, there is promise, ships
                will sail again, bearing furs and iron,
                pomegranates, olives, beef and toys, and
                no fear of the sea or the pirates' preying:
                travel is the balm, and all earth Gilead, the
                open sesame to that tomorrow,
                tomorrow when you, unborn, will be born,
                will marry or part: will drink in peace,
                will search for runes or build a bridge:
                will sit in the sun and call it goal enough:
                will write a verse and leave all fame
                to a naked emperor in a fairy tale.
Meanwhile tomorrow is in danger:
                meanwhile the living committed to live
                cannot deny you: cannot, dare not, forbid:
                will not shut out you to be born: in whom

we that lamented will be reborn singing:
in whom our legacy to be entrusted is to
praise life: share it: renascence unending.
Now the query is not to be reborn:
it is the duty to be born: to live
to usher in tomorrow: when other sons
of joy to these sons will be born.

MAN THE CREATOR

The Dybbuk

❧⳾❧

MAURICE SAMUEL

Der Rebbele, der Gabbele, der Shammesel, der Bederel,
Dos ganz klei-koidesh gehen tanzen. . . .
Singktsche chassidimlach mit'n ganzen koyach—
Der Rebbe allein geht doch tanzen. . . .

The little Rabbi, the little President, the little Sexton,
   the little Bath-keeper,
All the holy vessels are going a-dancing. . . .
Sing then, all ye little pious ones, with all your might—
The Rabbi himself is going a-dancing. . . .

What it sounds like in English

EVERYBODY knows the story of *The Dybbuk*. It is so simple that in itself it is the least important part of the play. It is a peg, an excuse, nothing more. But not everybody knows the particular life and culture which Ansky took as his instrument of expression. Hence there will always be at least two opinions about any Dybbuk production: the opinion of those who look at the effectiveness of the fable, and the opinion of those who know something about the world that Ansky was portraying.

Now the fundamentals of the play are universal. The story concerns a man and a woman who, for one reason or another, were destined for each other from before their birth. You may call it *zivug* in Hebrew, or *Wahlverwandschaft* in German, or *elective affinity* in English, and everyone will know what you mean. By a trick of circumstance the young lovers are kept apart, and the father of the girl arranges for her a marriage with an innocent intruder. The predestined lover learns of this and dies. His soul, wandering between heaven and hell, being ready for neither because it has not fulfilled its earthly destiny, returns to earth, and on the eve of the marriage invests the body of the bride, so that the marriage cannot be consummated. Efforts are then made to expel the demon from the body of the possessed woman, and they are sufficiently successful to expel both the intruder and the tenant proper: in other words, the woman dies.

These fundamentals are, I repeat, universal. The play itself might be done in any style, in any place and any time. The mood might be coldly realistic, or crepuscularly romantic, or angularly cubistic. It might be medieval Europe, or voodoo Africa, or one of Maeterlinck's never-never lands. No treatment, no place, has the advantage over any other. But what must be borne in mind is this: that not the fable constitutes the play, but the particular world, the particular culture, civilization, style of life, in which the fable is set. So that if a company promises to produce Ansky's *Dybbuk*, and nobody else's, some regard must be given to the world that Ansky dealt in.

Three Dybbuk productions have possessed New York: Maurice Schwartz's (the Yiddish Art Theatre) in Yiddish, David Vardi's (the Neighborhood Playhouse) in English, and Vachtangow's (the Moscow Habima) in Hebrew. These are three organizations which must be taken seriously. Nothing bad can come from any one of them, so if I speak of the comparative failure of two of them I must be heard to the end.

Maurice Schwartz had the obvious advantage of producing the play in the language of that particular world which Ansky was portraying. It was a Yiddish-speaking world, a Chassidic village in Russia, say seventy-five or a hundred years ago, with its ancient *shul*, its ghetto, its thick atmosphere of piety, snobbery, mysticism, poverty, purse-pride, superstitution, learning, and dirt—a world intensely real, in which the miraculous and the commonplace, the esoteric and the respectable, were woven into a pattern unknown to anyone but the East-European Jew. It is impossible to translate this life into West-European (or perhaps any other) terms. It is not as though a play written round the slums and west end of Berlin were being produced in London and New York. There the difference is, in comparison, negligible. Between Yiddish and German there is a wider gulf than between English and French. For it is not the etymological similarity that matters: it is the tone and temper of the world which utters itself in the language. Those ghettos and villages of Eastern Europe were an incredible mixture: the romance and filthiness and glamour and exaltation of the Orient, with its fantastic symbolism and its unabashed literalness, mingling with the economic ferocity of the Occident. The whole is indescribably intimate and affectionate for one who has known it; the task of transmitting its flavor to an alien world is hopeless, almost blasphemous. It is *sui generis* in the sense that one cannot explain it— it must be a direct experience, *unmittelbar*. It needs a lifetime of preparation.

Does this mean that either the Habima (which spoke a magnificent goyish Hebrew) and the Neighborhood Playhouse (which spoke a magnificent Oxford English) failed, artistically speaking? By no means. They produced *Dybbuks,* good ones, thrilling ones (for those who were not startled by the absurdity of the parody), in clever settings, as good a job as anyone could make, I imagine. But it was not *the Dybbuk.*

The English Chanan (the *yeshivah bocher* who later becomes the possessive *dybbuk*) resembled a Galahad rather than a *mathmid* or *ilui.* There was no down upon his cheeks (how can Anglo-Saxon heroes wear whiskers or a beard?), his caftan was immaculate, his collar unrumpled, his steps graceful, his speech modulated. *This* a *yeshivah bocher?* Had this young fellow actually learned five hundred pages of the Talmud by heart? Was this the mingled realist-mysticist who swallows the whole of *Nidah* without blinking—because his soul is really pure and the actual cannot be unclean? A Galahad is one who knows not that ladies have legs. A *yeshivah bocher* is too sensible for that kind of thing. He typifies the Jewish blend of hardheadedness, exasperating commonsense, and supreme mysticism. A Nordic romantic shudders at a reality: a single page of *Nidah* would kill him. And yet the English Chanan did his decent best. His colleagues in the *shul* backed him heroically. They "boom-boomed" (though I believe they should have "bom-bommed") and "Iy-iyed" skilfully, and at times— as, for instance, when they rose by degrees to dance with Reb Sender —they were impressive even to me. But I cannot bear to hear *shul-batlonim, minyan-yidden* speaking a rich, throaty, cultural English. If they had only de-Oxfordized the English a little: if they had found a sort of ghetto pronunciation which might give a hint of the homeliness of Yiddish without being a comic-journal parody! But in this I must say that most highbrow actors in arty theaters are at fault: through all their characterizations they insist on letting the audience know that they are culchahed.

Not the speech alone, but the training of a lifetime balked the

English Chanan. He took steps toward his beloved and stopped abruptly, he raised his arms and dropped them despairingly to his side, he crushed to his bosom the embroidered altar-cloth she had touched, he lifted his eyes yearningly, he clutched his heart, he did everything which the Occidental stage hero is supposed to do to indicate that he is in love. Whether or not this kind of behavior corresponds to behavior off the stage does not matter in this connection: this is the Occidental stage business of being in love. Now a *yeshivah bocher* hasn't all this technique at his finger ends. He is shy, dumb, awkward, impotent, ridiculous, pathetic. He does his yearning quite undramatically. I do not insist on realism in the *Dybbuk*—but at least we should get a plausible or reminiscent sort of symbolism.

This criticism of the English Chanan is the key to my criticism of the whole production. It was not Jewish—not because the speech was English, but because the entire atmosphere, all the shadings of it, the lesser rhythms and movements, were not Jewish. The *meshulach* was quite a dignified fellow, and would have served his purpose anywhere else. But he looked very simple and had a small blond beard, and the *meshulach* should be dark, bitter, and shrewd. Here again it is a difference between the Occidental and the Jewish idea of romance: in non-Jewish romance, commonsense is out of place: it does not interfere with Jewish romance.

The second act falls into two parts, the dance of the beggars, and the movement which leads toward the tremendous moment when the *meshulach* declares that a *dybbuk* has entered the bride. There is no doubt that Ansky, with his revolutionary background, had meant no good to the *verdammte kapitalistische Ordnung* when he laid the second act among the beggars. But see what happened with this intent in the English and the Hebrew productions. In the former, the irresistible Lewisohn penchant for folkloristic dances turned the incident into a dancefest. There was much too much of it. In both the Hebrew and the English the beggars were dehumanized—particularly in the Hebrew, where they became not beggars, but goblins, hideous figures hopping about in an unreal light, and lifting the unreal faces of animals to a bewildered audience. The last moment of the act, when the *meshulach* says: "Into the bride there has entered a *dybbuk*," cannot fail to strike. And yet both the English and the Hebrew were disappointing after the Yiddish. For again, they turned either into romance or style that which in utter simplicity is overwhelming. The English failed because of its wording; "Into the bride there has entered a *dybbuk*" is an uncomfortable sentence, twisted in order to keep the word *dybbuk* for the end, as climax. The Hebrew translation gave up this effect and went *"Dybbuk nichnas bekallah,"* but it was uttered in an affected staccato. Only in the Yiddish version was the effect real and full.

It is the second act which gives the key to the faults of the Hebrew production—and I need choose only one incident. When the *meshulach* utters the dread sentence, a certain horror is supposed to clutch the audiences on the stage and in the theater. But in the Hebrew production the beggars, who form an arched background for the chief protagonists, stand up on the chairs and benches and pointing their fingers at Reb Sender and his daughter emit three times a long-drawn "Aha!" of infinite malevolence. Now this is not Jewish. It may be Russian and Bolshevistic, to which I have no objection in principle; but I find it a ridiculous, propagandistic distortion of the play. Ansky's dislike of the purse-proud Senderel was enough: one did not have to add this utterly un-Jewish touch of venom. The Russian theme runs unerringly through the Hebrew production. Reb Sender looks like a burly boyar. The *meshulach* is vaguely suggestive of a wandering hedge priest, and the great Rabbi himself, Azrael, made me think of Peter the Hermit. But this is no worse than the English production.

Another, more general fault marred the Hebrew production for me. It was not the strain of getting used to beggars speaking *bahavarah sephardi*: again this was no worse than the Oxford English of the Neighborhood theater. It was the fact that, in spite of the strong Russian coloring of the make-up and decorations, this particular *Dybbuk* was in four dimensions—out of time and out of space. Abstracting the inevitable Russian intrusion, it did not belong anywhere at all. The effects were remarkable in their power. The *meshulach* sitting with his head twisted to meet the full glare of the lamp, the set face white-streaked, staring, immobile; Reb Azrael, whiter still, thin, ascetic; the beggars, demonaic, incredibly tattered; the spare scenery, rectangular, black and white; all of it was monstrous and powerful, but not Jewish. And, this apart, there was much too much self-consciousness; at every opportunity the grouping was effected with an eye to the photographer; bodies, faces, hands, all jumping into place to provide a cubistic, futuristic, expressionistic, whatnotistic picture. And yet it was powerful.

Were I not an East-European Jew myself, my enjoyment would have been almost unmarred even by the obvious self-consciousness of the actors and the director.

The last act is the most powerful. Here the play ceases to be artificial, and becomes a reproduction of the ritual proper to the expulsion of a *dybbuk* with *shofar*, book and candle. But the effect of the English and the Hebrew would have been much more powerful if the last act, unreal in its realism, had been thrown against the background of a more matter-of-fact opening. Here again Schwartz's Yiddish production had the advantage. The first two acts were simple and appealing, and their charm was that of intimacy. Hence the crushing effect of the third act, when, in the presence of a *minyan* of Jews, the saintly Asreal wrestles with the obstinate *dybbuk*, and drags him forth *bal korcho*. As I watched I felt that thus, or about thus, the thing must happen; the rationalistic explanation found room for itself in the very emotions of terror which the ritual inspired. But the English and the Hebrew versions again tried to paint the lily, by adding unnecessary effects of their own. In the Hebrew we hear, instead of the *shofar*, with its dread associations, a whole orchestra. In the English we hear a mellow cornet. Musically, the effect is improved. But the *shofar* is not, properly speaking, a musical instrument.

To those who are not acquainted at first hand with East-European Jewish life, both the English and the Hebrew productions may be recommended as sincere, clever and effective work. As for me, I am waiting for the reappearance of Schwartz's Yiddish production to wash out of my mind the disturbing memory of the others.

(—1927)

Jacob Epstein • *Samuel Alexander*

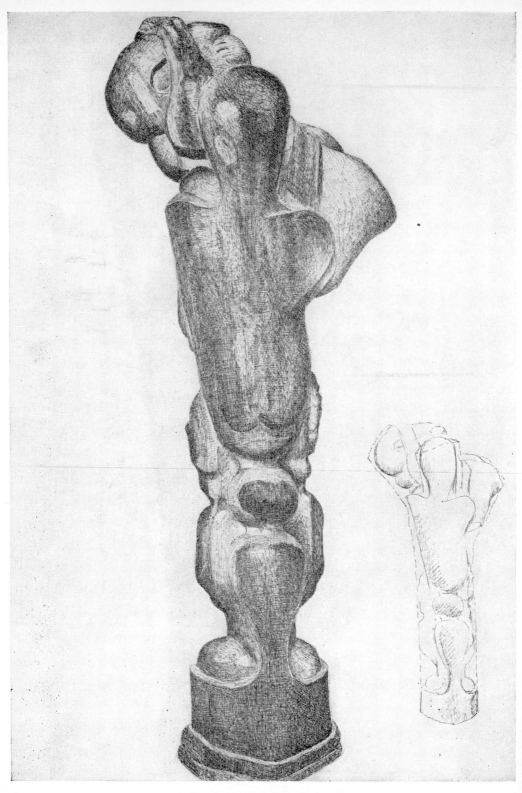

Peter Krasnow • *Figure with Small Drawing*

Max Weber • *Sabbath*

Mané-Katz · *Two Disciples*

Camille Pissarro • *The Hay-Makers*

Max Untermayer-Raymer • *Interior of the Synagogue at Kirchheim*

Arthur Szyk • *David Triumphant*

Jules Pascin • *Immigrants on Deck*

Numa Patlagean   •   *Mrs. Lewis Chanler*

S. Simkovitch • *The Festive Dance*

Louis Lozowick • *Coney Island*

Reproduction from The Prague Haggadah (1526)

Chaim Gross • *Jazz*

Chana Orloff • *Mrs. Mendelson Bronze*

Leopold Gottlieb • *Harvest*

The Liebermann Saga

⌘

MAX OSBORN

WHEN Max Liebermann died in Berlin on February 8, 1935, at the age of eighty-seven, the remaining Jews in Germany felt as if they had been deprived of their spiritual leader. This great artist had focused on himself all the fame of modern German painting and had enjoyed to the fullest whatever honors the outside world had to bestow. To his coreligionists he appeared as the embodiment and noblest expression of their own aspirations and happiest achievement, a symbol of comfort and consolation in a time of bitter suffering.

Up to the moment when Hitlerism began to race over the globe, Berliners generally considered Liebermann one of the most distinguished personalities of their city. For almost half a century they would point to the little glass cupola of a noble old house on the Pariser Platz, Berlin's beautiful entrance hall, and say to a stranger (or even to each other), with a respect mounting to reverence: "Up there Max Liebermann is working!"

The house stood on the north side of the Brandenburger Tor. Its two rows of windows overlooked the famous Unter Den Linden on the left and the Tiergarten on the right. What more typically "Berlinish" kind of residence could one imagine? His parents had bought it, and after their death he continued to live there. The master loved the old-fashioned building, which had been erected in the 1840's. It was a walk-up, and even at an advanced age he used to climb the winding staircase to his apartment on the third floor.

He was proud of his family, which for generations had been among the wealthiest and most highly respected members of Berlin society. With particular affection he used to speak of his grandfather, a merchant and industrialist, who had once boasted to King Friedrich Wilhelm III: "Your Majesty, *I am the man who swept the English from the Continent*—as far as printed cotton is concerned." Liebermann's brother Felix was an outstanding historian. A cousin was the chemist Professor Carl Liebermann, who laid the groundwork for the manufacture of aniline colors. Another cousin, Emil Rathenau, founder of the A. E. G. (Allgemeine Elektrizitaets-Gesellschaft), was the father of Walter Rathenau, the German Foreign Minister after World War I, who was one of the earliest victims of Nazi barbarism.

The visitor who walked up that winding staircase in Liebermann's residence had a foretaste of all those treasures which were to overwhelm him in the apartment. In that stair-well were hung some of the beautiful drawings of Adolph Menzel, a painter of Old Berlin whom Liebermann considered his artistic ancestor. But that was only an earnest of what was to come: a collection of exquisite paintings and drawings, particularly delicious specimens of French impressionism, and again and again Menzel. Many a visitor was astonished that among all that wealth hardly any work of the host himself could be found (except an early portrait of his wife in a garden chair). When somebody once broke out in amazement, "But—there are no Liebermanns here?" the master whispered into his ear with a sly smile, *"I can't afford them!"*

Witty remarks fill the pages of the Liebermann saga. They took on when uttered the additional flavor (which, unfortunately, cannot be preserved in translation) of the Berlin dialect, that unique lingo of the man in the street which Liebermann learned in his early youth. He used it purposely because, as he often told me, he believed it would protect him from bathos and sentimentality. That sharp, typically North German city argot flavored every sentence of his with a dry, mocking quality, a self-irony which made solemnity impossible. Liebermann became so accustomed to using it that he could hardly talk in any other way, in polite society as well as in everyday conversation. It was a fascinating experience to listen to him propound the most spiritual statements, the most ingenious aphorisms, in the slang phrases of Berlin dialect. He always seemed to be putting up warning signals, both for the listener and for himself. Be natural! Be simple! None of your highbrow blah-blah!

Then what pleasure it was to climb the steep narrow stairs which led from the patrician elegance of the apartment to the modest studio with the round glass ceiling, and to "disturb" the master for a while. What unforgettable hours! The conversation would turn swiftly from the most trivial topics of the day to the profoundest problems of art and life, to the ultimate questions that occupied the artist's mind. Striking judgments, interesting formulations, and furious invective against his adversaries would assail the visitor.

All the while Liebermann would keep right on working, bent over one particular spot on the canvas. Suddenly he would step back, put his hand to his forehead to make an eye-shade, dab his brush on the palette, mix his colors, rush back to the picture, insert a few strokes, retouch a bit here and there. His talk ran from the Old Masters and beloved contemporary colleagues to politics and society, from literature and philosophy to public events and private experiences. The words spurted from his mouth as his eyes sparkled. One day we discussed Dutch painting. "You know," he said, and this time he even stopped working, "when I see a Frans Hals, I feel like painting—but when I look at a Rembrandt, I feel like giving it up for good!" Another time we talked about an exhibition of English eighteenth-century portraitists then current in Berlin which had come in for a good deal of sharp criticism. Liebermann remarked: "That's all so much poppycock! I like to be invited to rich people's houses."

I always regretted, when sitting up there in his studio and listening to him, that I didn't know shorthand. There were days when almost every sentence he uttered deserved to be put on record. What a boon if he had had such a faithful chronicler as Goethe had in Eckermann, who jotted down his conversations with the poet.

The theme which inspired the painter to his most amusing remarks was the eternal one of the fair ladies. Liebermann belonged to the most fervent admirers of female beauty. His attitude was rather naively sensuous: the loveliness of a young face, the tender shape of a hand, the lines of a slender figure enchanted him; and whether or not the owner of such attractions was blessed with the gift of clever words, he didn't care at all. Hence his delightful maxim, which made the rounds all over Berlin: "If a woman is pretty, that's very pleasant. But if she is stupid on top of it—then she is irresistible!"

He also liked, when occasion offered, to give his repartee a slightly naughty tinge. Once a lady visiting his studio thanked him with a rather exaggerated enthusiasm for the charming reception he had given her. "Ach, Herr Professor," she said, "this was the loveliest hour of my life!" Whereupon Liebermann replied: "I hope not!"

However, it was by no means as a painter of women that Liebermann created his most alluring works. An essential and very conscious quality of his art was to avoid whatever might be called "sweet" or "pleasing." He was a penetrating analyst. In every object of his painting, in every human being, in every face and landscape, he searched for a deeper meaning which he attempted to reveal. His portraits of women give you the impression that he was literally afraid to meet the taste of the general public. He jealously refused to be seduced by mere prettiness, by a picture-postcard ideal of beauty. That was a sign of strong character, a trait that honored him; but it became a drawback too. This stubbornness prevented him from celebrating genuine beauty even when he met it. It was as if his joy in the blessings of the outer world were offset and absorbed by his talent for penetrating and recreating it in accord with his own very personal concept.

An episode in the last years of his life throws a revealing light on this attitude. He had been painting a very attractive young woman, by whom he was so charmed that, after he had discharged himself dutifully of the ordered portrait, he asked her again and again to return for another sitting. There exist at least five pictures of her, not counting the sketches. One day, taking her courage in both hands, she said: "Look here, professor, you have painted me now a great many times, and I don't have to tell you how flattered I am about that. But there is one thing I must ask you. People have often told me I am a pretty woman—well, it is not for me to say whether they are right—but one thing I can say: the way I look in your pictures, nobody would ever think of calling me pretty. How do you account for that?"

The old man was embarrassed; he scratched his forehead and growled: "No—really? Do you really mean that? Well, maybe you aren't so far wrong, either. But that's just too bad—that's the way it is."

If he thought he would get off so lightly he was quite mistaken; the young lady had made up her mind to know, and she was persistent. "I should like to ask you one more question," she continued, "but you must promise not to get angry with me. I cannot help feeling, forgive me for saying it, there is a certain deficiency in your personality—a lack of something . . . how shall I put it? There you are, a great artist, a famous man—and yet, all your life you have been a law-abiding bourgeois, a faithful husband—how little room

there must have been in your life as well as in your art for women, for
the 'feminine' in general!"

Liebermann gave a start: this time she had touched on a problem
he was very sensitive about. "That's where you are quite wrong! I
know you aren't one of those stupid girls; but the way you figure things
out for yourself in that pretty head of yours just isn't the way things
happen! What do you know of how often, in this very studio here,
a holy passion overcomes me to take one of these handsome young
women into my arms and kiss her . . . but then, damn it, the lighting
is just so beautiful I'd rather paint her!"

Things were quite different in the case of a male sitter; those pictures belong to Liebermann's greatest achievements in the realm of
portraiture. Where he was not expected to transform the canvas into
a piece of pure delight for the eye he saw his opportunity, and seized
it with enthusiasm, to probe the deepest layers of a man's character.
Often he developed his theory for me: that the painter was not only
entitled but even bound to conjure up, out of the factual appearance
of a model, the deeper meaning of his being; to recreate, as it were,
the head of his sitter in the way the Divine Creator may have conceived it; Who, however, fettered by the unwieldy clay which was
His material, had to abandon His plan. Hence Liebermann's reply to
a man he had painted who could not quite persuade himself he really
looked the way the master had made him out on his portrait: "That's
the way you *should* look!"

No, those male portraits were not paragons of beauty. Anyone who
expects a portrait to give his eyes the treat of a cheap idealization
will find no satisfaction in them. The master went over faces as with
a plow over a field in order to lay bare the deeper hidden strata. He
used broad and juicy dabs of color, and the strokes of his brush did
not glide one into the other with a polished smoothness; rather, the
surface was roughened and broken open, so as to lure the glance
beneath and beyond that surface into the innermost secrets of a
human being.

To the simple-minded and inexperienced onlooker this style, especially on the painter's earlier works, appeared as inharmonious,
rugged, lacking in "appeal." Liebermann himself liked to tell a little
story on this point.

After he had painted the portrait of a big industrialist, the subject's daughter brought her little girl to the studio for a "preview" (to which they had not been invited). For some minutes the child stood in front of the portrait and was silent. Then she asked: "Is it going to get a frame?" The artist replied: "Why certainly, my child." There was a pause, then the dialogue continued: "And it is going to be sent to grandpa's house?" "Yes, my dear." Silence. "And will it hang there on the wall?" "I guess so, my child." "In the big drawing-room?" "Probably." Another, longer silence. "And will it then be beautiful too?"

Liebermann felt not at all comfortable during this trial. In the end he did not answer any more but smiled and stroked the little girl's head. When he told the story to a circle of intimate friends, one had the impression there was a bitter taste in his mouth. Why is it, he seemed to ask himself, that a work which I consider well done does not seem attractive to a naive, unbiased young child, and even rather the reverse? And he kept on pondering over the enigma hidden there.

As the years went on, however, all those innumerable persons who had him paint their portraits were well pleased to put up with his very individual manner. They all liked to climb up the steep staircase, the prominent personalties of science and business, of diplomacy and politics, of literature and art, of finance and society, of high officialdom and even of the army. From the 1890's up to shortly before his death, the master's portraits comprised the cultural life of an entire epoch.

The portrait of the Berlin surgeon Ferdinand Sauerbruch, painted in the spring of 1932, a few months before Liebermann's eighty-fifth birthday, may perhaps be called the most splendid masterpiece of the whole long series. This work was also the occasion for another amusing story. The painter, not satisfied with one particular detail, asked the famous physician (his neighbor during the summer months in the suburb of Wannsee, where both had country homes) again and again to come in for a short sitting so that he might correct that sore spot. Finally Sauerbruch, who was a very busy man, became impatient and said: "My dear professor, you are really too conscientious. I think you are taking too much trouble." To which Liebermann replied: "It's easy for you to talk. When you make a mistake, it is soon covered with green grass. But when I make a mistake, it hangs on the wall and stares at me—all the time."

That was more than a witty remark. It illustrated Liebermann's inexorable conscience. From early youth he had been his own hard task-master, never allowing himself to take it easy, to overlook trifling mistakes, to be satisfied with approximations. If, in spite of all that self-discipline, once in a while a work did not turn out to be quite as perfect as he wanted it, he used to console himself with the witticism: "After all—what are historians for? Come to think of it, the only function of the art critic and historian is to declare our flops to be forgeries!"

I soon had occasion to learn how right he was. I had given a lecture in the small town of Cottbus, not far from Berlin, and was afterwards invited for tea at the house of an amiable gentleman who was both a jurist and an art lover. "I have just recently bought a picture," he said, "a Liebermann. Wouldn't you like to have a look at it?" And in he brought the most godawful thing: a beach scene with figures in pastel, but insufficiently focused and hence blurred and distorted; on the whole, it was obvious it had been handled very carelessly. In short, a quite unpleasant piece. I tried to express that opinion without hurting the owner's feelings too much. "I am sorry, my dear Herr Justizrat," I began, "that I have to disappoint you. But it seems to me that this is a forgery, and a pretty clumsy one at that." The would-be art collector was simply flabbergasted and, naturally, very much depressed over this discovery.

A few days later his son came to Berlin and brought the horrible thing along. I consulted a colleague who was also intimately familiar with Liebermann's work; he just had a look at the picture and burst into scornful laughter. The art dealer who sold the pastel to the jurist in Cottbus was summoned, and at him he shouted: "How dare you foist a dud like that on an innocent provincial?"

The art dealer was completely floored. "You must know, gentlemen," he said, "the picture came to me from a highly reliable source; everything about it seemed entirely on the level. And so I sold it; at a cheap price, of course, on account of the bad condition it was in. I must admit, however, that now when you draw my attention to some of the very doubtful details, I can see your point: maybe your objections are justified, after all. But," he continued, and a sound of hope crept into his voice, "Liebermann is still alive. Let's ask him!"

So, the day after, the four of us betook ourselves to the Pariser Platz and submitted the *corpus delicti* to the master himself. Liebermann took a good look at the picture; his glance went over it from

top to bottom, and then again from bottom to top; he held it close to
his eyes, he sniffed it, made a serious face. Finally, he grinned and
said: "That's an outrage! A nightmare! A hideous thing! But I did it
all right!"

Tableau! The art dealer and the Herr Justizrat's son were so over-
joyed they all but started dancing. My colleague and I were slightly
less happy. "I can't help it," the old man smiled at us, "I am the one
who made it!" And then he went to work over it, corrected, retouched,
until finally the pastel looked like a different piece altogether. He wrote
the whole funny story on a slip of paper which he pasted on the
back of the picture. The jurist and art lover in Cottbus was more than
pleased.

From the very beginning of his career Liebermann had to counter
the reproach that he had no "feeling for beauty." When, in the 1870's,
he came out with his early pictures, "Women Plucking Geese" and
"Women Working in a Canning Factory," which combined superb
original brush-work with an entirely fresh social attitude, he was
immediately tagged as "a painter of ugliness." How on earth could
anybody choose a group of unpleasant old women for the subject of
a large canvas!

This criticism left Liebermann dumbfounded. He was searching
for nature, for unadulterated reality; and nature knows of no such
notions as beauty or ugliness. His maxims for life and for art were
deeply rooted in the soil of reality. At first, he may have been quite
unaware of following those maxims—driven, as he liked to quote from
Goethe's orphic words, "by that same law which hither sped thy feet."
But as he progressed he adopted them consciously, to erect on them
the proud edifice of his whole life.

Liebermann's painting as well as thinking always took the throbbing
outer world for springboard. Truth remained forever his guiding star,
his hand never tired to reveal it, nor did his mind. Berlin rationalism
was too deeply ingrained in his spiritual makeup for him ever to lose
belief in the absolute validity of reality. If that explains the immense
power of his life work, it also accounts for its limitations. He wouldn't
know the artistic problems of today. For Liebermann "imagination in
painting" (as he once called an essay of his in the *Neue Rundschau*)
was not concerned with the subject, the "topic," the invention of the
picture. It had to do rather with the interpretation of the theme and

its expression in colors, according to the personal concept of the artist. Hence his saying: "A well-painted turnip is worth more than a badly painted Madonna."

Again and again he stated this as his credo. Among the many letters I received from him during almost a half century (some of which I have, miraculously, salvaged even through these recent years of wandering and flight), I find one of April 1909 which makes that point very clear. I had sent him galley proofs of an article of mine on Johann Gottfried Schadow, the Berlin sculptor and forerunner of Menzel, whose life span (1747-1833) comprised about the same years as Goethe's. His most famous work was the bronze Victoria with the quadriga for the crest of the Brandenburger Tor, which Napoleon carried off to Paris in 1806, and which was brought back to Berlin in 1813 without ever having been unpacked!

After thanking me for sending him the article, Liebermann wrote: "I am sure you know that I am an enthusiastic admirer of Schadow; what half-way sensible person would not be! I see in him also the artist to whom the Berliners should turn for inspiration; his clear and simple conception of nature should be the basis for a free and great art. Any renaissance in art—and I do indeed believe that we are living through such a renaissance now—must needs be based on naturalism; in reverting to Schadow, we are preparing the ground for the development of a future genius. I hope this genius will now soon appear; I should like to be still here to see him. If not, I shall have to be content, like Moses, to have descried the promised land from afar!"

True enough, reverence before nature alone will not suffice. It has to be complemented by the "personal concept of the artist." And this concept embraces not only the "imagination" of the painter but also his "ideality," a point Liebermann stressed time and again, especially in those famous speeches he made every year at the opening ceremonies of the exhibitions of the Berliner Sezession.

These speeches contained treasures of art wisdom, some of which appeared in print. For instance, in the Spring 1906 address (the manuscript of which lies before me), he said: "The most efficient way of furthering art consists in giving the artist the possibility to realize *his* ideal. There is no such thing as an absolute ideal; there are as many ideals as there are true artists. For what does an ideal mean but the eternally renewed attempt of the creative mind to reach out for the sublime? From which it follows that every artist swears by his own, and only by his own, ideal. Let us not be misled by that hazy notion of a 'general ideal'; there are no two persons who mean the same thing when they use that word which, in the last analysis, is nothing but an empty phrase."

This was intended as a sortie against the adversaries of the then modern movement of "naturalism," who made life miserable for the Sezession, an association of painters Liebermann had founded in 1899. Very powerful and influential adversaries they were! Behind their banner marched not only the Prussian Art Academy, the large and wealthy Verein Berliner Kuenstler, the majority of the critics and of the "cultured public," but also, in the front rank, the Kaiser himself, who expressed his displeasure freely and vociferously.

At that time, however, even in Germany freedom of opinion prevailed. The tenets of the leader of the Reich himself were publicly discussed and challenged! While Wilhelm II stormed against "modern art," the mayor of Charlottenburg, the borough of Greater Berlin where the little house of the Sezession was located, attended the openings of its exhibitions, wearing the golden chain of his office over his frockcoat, and replied to Liebermann's addresses. Once, two weeks after a speech in which the Kaiser spoke flippantly of the "gutter art" of revolutionary innovators, the new Fall exhibition of the Sezession was advertised all over Berlin with a poster that Th. Th. Heine, the witty cartoonist of the Munich comic magazine *Simplicissimus*, produced at Liebermann's suggestion. In the delicate but unmistakable lines of a drawing in Japanese style there was to be seen a gutter out of which blossomed a bouquet of the loveliest flowers.

Within his basic concept of "naturalism" Liebermann's *oeuvre* is, of course, a succession of different styles, phases of development and modes of expression. The first period was that of a grave, uncompromising resolution to depict the surrounding reality. A definite social bias is plainly visible. While he was studying at the Art School in Weimar, the idea struck him one day, with the suddenness of lightning, to paint simple folk at their work. It was at that time that he painted the "Women Plucking Geese." Liebermann told me once that the old man in the picture carrying the geese, a favorite model in Weimar, had in his youth been Goethe's coachman, and Liebermann bought from him an old greatcoat the poet had given him as a present.

This style—continued and deepened during his stay in Holland under the influence of Josef Israëls—reached an unexpected peak in the 1880's. Now the figures grew out of their everyday appearance into monumental postures, as if they were monuments of a whole caste. The greatest triumph of that group of paintings was "Women Mending Nets" that belonged to the Kunsthalle in Hamburg. (Under the Nazis the Liebermann rooms of that museum were closed to the public and locked up.)

There followed a third, rather extended period during which the master leaned on the French, on Manet and the Impressionists, without however forgetting Holland. With a fourth period, that had the country house in Wannsee for its background, the circle was rounded.

Visits to that villa in Wannsee always followed a definite procedure. First, we would climb to the studio of the beautiful summer house which had been built shortly before 1914; and there we would talk and argue on art and time, people and events, and especially about the young rising generation of painters who called themselves "expressionists." Then Liebermann would reach for his enormous Panama hat and step down into the garden. He was very fond of that straw hat; it turned up in a number of those self-portraits which have preserved the artist's appearance through many years of his life.

Liebermann was not a "handsome man"; his features by no means came up to the requirements of classical symmetry. In fact, judging by normal standards, he was rather homely. But his face had that sharpness of character which more than made up for such shortcomings. "When I start painting myself," he once confessed to me, "and I first look into the mirror, I feel sick to my stomach! When I put the brush to the canvas, I feel better already. And in the end, I must say, I rather like myself!" He was proud of the Jewish type he represented in a pure form.

It was logical enough for Liebermann to step down into his garden after we had sat upstairs for hours. This beautiful bit of land, which the master tended with love and care, was but an extension of the studio. The garden stretched down to the waters of the lake, and there the old man sat, day after day, during the warm months of the year, and painted those luscious flower-bed pieces, which were to be the last chord in the symphony of his work, in a way similar to the water lily pictures in Claude Monet's.

At seventy, at eighty, Liebermann reached in these garden pieces the climax of his powers as a colorist. In the shining voluptuous glow of those colors with all their endless shadings, the master revealed to our delight that part of his artistic being which was concerned with the "art of pure painting." Now he had become free in his outlook on the beauty of the outer world, free in the relation of a visual hedonism to his own creative principles.

During those last years of his life there was but one subject for our talks under the old rustling trees in his garden—the fate of the Jews; the things that were happening in Germany (only in Germany, at that time). Liebermann was a very typical representative of the class of Jews who advocated assimilation; but, at the same time, he confessed passionately to his origins, to his race. One day, during the weeks when he was painting Prince Lichnowsky, the German Ambassador at London before 1914, I found him quite excited. "Can you beat it!" said Liebermann. "I told the prince that the somewhat strange shape of his skull reminded me of the pictures of Jewish prisoners on an old Assyrian relief. Did he get furious! 'If you please,' he remarked, 'I happen to belong to the oldest Polish German nobility!' So I shouted at him: 'If *you* please . . . I belong to a still older nobility!' And out he strode, raving mad. Now what do you say to that?"

Liebermann was an inexorable critic of his fellow-Jews. He expected them to be continuously aware of their responsibility to the entire Jewish community. But should an outsider permit himself to look down on the Jews, to talk about them with the usual malicious and nonsensical generalizations, what a terrific beating he let himself in for!

The new "trend" which the Nazis dictated in 1933 shook Liebermann to the depths of his being. The garden in Wannsee reverberated with the open expressions of his disgust, his contempt. It was there that he uttered to a visitor the afterwards famous *mot*—or rather, on account of his increasing deafness, he shouted it: "I can't eat as much as I would like to vomit!"

One day, at the entrance of the villa in Wannsee, I met the painter X, a non-Jew, who continued calling on the master and thus distinguished himself from the great mass of weaklings who could not adopt the Nazi slogans quickly enough. It is better not to print his name; otherwise the hounds of the Gestapo might yet get after him

and call him to account for his crime of paying visits to a Jew!* Anyhow, I asked this decent man I met at the garden door: "Well, how
are things upstairs?" Good old X raised his hands in a gesture of
warning; for Liebermann, by the frankness of his talk, exposed all his
visitors as well as himself to the direst perils, should ever a spy overhear them. "Don't go up! Today there is danger for your life!"

The events of those unhappy years aroused in Liebermann an
awareness of belonging to the community of Jews and of the problems
of that community which formerly he had not possessed with such
clarity. When, in 1933, the Hebrew poet Bialik and Mayor Dizengoff
of Tel Aviv wrote him that they had named one of the rooms in the
Museum of Tel Aviv "Liebermann Hall," he was deeply moved. In
his reply he added that he too would like to emigrate to Palestine
were it not for the fact that "you can't transplant an old tree."

Thus the end of his long life lay under the black shadow of bitter
grief. Artistically, too, his last years were under a cloud of breaking
storm: young radicals were raising new banners; forswearing naturalism, they considered the great old master "passé." All his life he had
found his enemies on the "Right"; and now, of a sudden, he was attacked from the "Left"! However, he was not dismayed. He persisted
in his artistic principles: he kept faith with himself.

And soon it became evident that, however changed the times, however vicious the Nazis might be in their efforts to erase his name from
the record, the greatness and power of his work could be neither re-
viled nor belittled. Calmly and serenely it shines through the darkness.
Its place in the history of German art is assured.

Max Liebermann is like a solid rock at the seashore. The waves
assail it, throw their scum around it, once in a while even sweep over
it so that it seems to have disappeared. But then the waters flow back
—and there it stands, proud and unconquerable in its dignity. This
great Jewish painter of Berlin belongs to that rather small group of
European masters to whom Art, whenever it has drifted up into all
too airy altitudes, will revert in order to set foot on solid ground
again.

(—1947)

* This was written in 1944.—ED.

Meetings with Franz Kafka

❧

JOHANNES URZIDIL

Fully to understand Franz Kafka's personality it is not enough to try to reconstruct it, to try to re-establish his characteristic traits from his works. One must have known him personally. For instance, in his works hardly any special significance is given to nature as scenery, except in his fragment of a novel, *Amerika,* where an imaginary landscape is depicted with all the appropriate urgency of an "exact fantasy." Nevertheless, Kafka was a true lover of nature in its reality. He liked to roam through the country; in that respect he might be compared to Thoreau. Kafka also loved every simple, straightforward expression of life. In conversation he was clear and simple. Indeed, the simpler his remarks, the more they seemed to open up depths. His habit of always starting out from facts, from realities, recalls Goethe and Stifter, both of whom he held in unbounded veneration. His road to the most abstract came from the most everydaylike.

Kafka was twelve years older than I, and not at all famous when, at the age of twenty, I had the good fortune to become acquainted with him. The city of Prague possessed a remarkable intellectual atmosphere which brought people together and stimulated them, especially the natives. Czechs, Germans, Jews, and the supra-national Austrian aristocracy had, in the course of centuries, created in Prague a world full of explosive creative force. Seldom have so many men of significance flourished in such a comparatively small area as in Prague between 1912 and 1924. Though Rilke no longer lived in his native city, there were still Kafka, Werfel, Karel Capek, Max Brod and many others, each of whom contributed to the development of modern European literature.

The meeting-place of the *"Hommes des Lettres"* was the Café Arco. At one period Werfel came there almost every day, and Kafka was there very often. German and Czech writers got on well together in those days.

I myself was then a young man and full of enthusiasm for humanitarian ideas. I was editing a monthly called *Der Mensch*, sponsored by a businessman, Leo Reiss, who loved literature. The First World War was on, and in every issue I stressed the slogan "Humanity!" Thus I endeavored to contribute my humble mite to the idea of the reconciliation of the nations. *Der Mensch* published contributions by modern authors of different nations side by side, especially by German and Czech writers.

Among the Prague German writers of this group was a young poet named Karl Brand. Only a very few people might remember his name today. He was marked for death early by an incurable disease. Yet, with his constant fever, he sat regularly at our table, listening with ecstasy to Werfel as he read one of his newest poems, or gazing raptly at Kafka who, though he spoke little, always with his few words opened up endless vistas of thought. We all loved Karl Brand, and treated him with a kind of shy solicitude, feeling we were in the presence of something otherworldly, which evoked an attitude of awe from us. Though Brand was no genius, he showed cotyledonian signs of a talent that nature, alas, allowed no time for development. His works existed only in manuscript.

Kafka always watched Brand attentively and spoke to him with anxious considerateness. He seemed to be singularly attracted to this young man, who had death written on his forehead.

Kafka's story, "The Metamorphosis," describes a man, a family, and conditions of life very similar to Brand's. Brand lived with his parents and sister in a gloomy old baroque house, where the family's attitude to his slow physical disintegration was like that of the Samsa family to the dying Gregor in "The Metamorphosis." Werfel and I, who often went to see Brand, told Kafka of our visits. "The Metamorphosis" was written long before Brand died in 1918, but to Kafka the case of Brand appeared to be a live re-enactment of his own tale, which later became so famous.

Werfel and I had visited Brand on his deathbed; I was present at his death; and to me he entrusted his last wish to have his small literary legacy published. I made a selection, and asked Werfel, who was then in Vienna, to write a foreword. The book, *Karl Brand: The Bequest of a Young Man,* appeared in 1921, published by Eduard Strache of Vienna-Prague-Leipzig. It has probably disappeared by now, except for a few rare copies. I would like to quote from Werfel's foreword which describes his attitude to Brand, both because of Kafka who gave his opinion of it afterwards, and because there are things said in the foreword which have again a certain significance in these days. (Of course it is translated from the original German.)

Proper consideration discloses that the seemingly rounded and complete works of the foregoing—of the men whose ripening does not fall within the epoch of the War, its causes and consequences—were to come about only through a lie due to the conditions of the time. People who no longer had any ground under their feet persuaded themselves, with an Olympian attitude, that they were standing on firm earth. These men—I am not speaking of the very few who knew what was going on—produced but semblances of perfection, vainglorious soap-bubbles that reflected long-vanished landscapes and then burst completely, one after the other. The force of the young generation that came into existence under this unlucky star was their realization that they were shipwrecked. It was their obsessed, unconditional leap into the sea. These people did not create "lasting" values, nor anything which might be called accomplishment. But the swimmer fighting for his life is glad when he grabs at a plank, and he does not think of building a house.

Our good modest Brand had disquieting eyes, and many of the twenty and thirty year-olds have similar disquieting, relentless eyes; they are incorruptible to the point of cynicism, and they are so tormented by the lie that they must sacrifice beauty. They all know that they are denied immortality which beckons only to serene minds, and love that is harvested only by him who blissfully rests in his own personality, and happiness which is gained only by those who joyfully surrender to or profess illusions—that is, by the believers. They have given up. They have been sacrificed. Solitary, on the high seas with no lifebelts, lonely Columbuses, they set out on a hopeless *Conquista* in search of a truth by which they could live. They were the target not only of the earthly guns. They are the cannon-fodder of the world-spirit, the victims of an incomprehensible evolution. One of these many men, one who belonged to them, was Karl Brand.

When the book appeared I sent a copy to Kafka. I knew it would shake him more than all other readers to the inmost depths. These are the words (translated from the original German) he wrote me at that time, when he too was beginning to draw near to death:

The book reminded me very much in essence, but also in structure, of "Ivan Ilyitch." First, Werfel's very simple and terrible truth (true too of the weird ones who "joyfully surrender to or profess illusions"); then the death of this young man, the three-days-and-nights-cry—one really heard no sound of it, and had it been made audible one would have gone a few rooms further away, there is no other "way out" than this; and, finally, your manly and consoling epilogue, to which of course one would prefer to turn had it not come, as is natural with consolation, too late—after the execution. It is no different with "Ivan Ilyitch"; only here in *The Bequest* it is more distinct, because each stage personifies itself specifically.

Kafka readers will not fail to find this private note* a remarkable piece of typical Kafka prose in both style and content. But one who knew him personally hears also the sound of his voice—a voice which, without emphasis but self-accusingly, says: ". . . the death of this young man, the three-days-and-nights-cry—one really heard no sound of it, and had it been made audible one would have gone a few rooms further away, there is no other 'way out' than this."

The hint at Tolstoy's "The Death of Ivan Ilyitch" closes the ring between the life and death of Karl Brand and the life and death of Gregor Samsa in "The Metamorphosis."

I have another note from Kafka. It belongs to the year 1913. Here in America it lies before me, for it is addressed to a young girl who later became my wife. Kafka used to go with her to the opera. And Kafka's favorite opera was Bizet's *Carmen*. He loved in that opera the utterances of elementary passion, the sensual splendor, all that he himself kept hidden. Perhaps too he loved *Carmen* especially because Prosper Merimée's story had always fascinated him.

This time I can't go to *Carmen*. I am on afternoon duty. I had forgotten it in front of the telephone, as I always forget everything in front of the machine. . . . Incidentally, do you think it economical to obliterate the memory of a good performance with the memory of what might probably be a faulty one?

So the date for *Carmen* was not kept that time. But Kafka turned up a little later, to give the young girl a copy of his first book, *Betrachtung*, which had appeared shortly before. That book also lies

---

* The original note is reproduced in facsimile, together with a photograph of Kafka, as part of Mr. Urzidil's article—"Franz Kafka: Novelist and Mystic"—in the Autumn of 1943 issue of *The Menorah Journal*.

before me; on the flyleaf there is this characteristic Kafka inscription (of course in German):

To Miss Trude Thieberger with cordial greetings and a suggestion: this book has not yet taken heed of the proverb, "No fly gets into a mouth that is kept closed" [final sentence of Merimée's *Carmen*]. That is why it is full of flies. Best of all, keep it always closed.

Well, that girl, as I have said, was then very young, little more than a child. And when Kafka gave her the book, which was printed in excessively large type, he said: "Look at it. It's like a primer. A children's book."

Kafka's own death recalls the death of Ivan Ilyitch, and perhaps also poor Karl Brand's. Not only because all death is so much alike essentially, but also because of the slowness, the awareness of it, the quiet adjustment of oneself to *the other*, the unknown.

When Kafka was buried in Prague on the afternoon of June 3rd, 1924, I stood among the group of his bereaved friends. Strange chances had acquainted me from earliest childhood with dying and death. That may, alas, be nothing unusual for our present generation. It was not so for people whose youthful development belonged to the days before the First World War. Later I had to witness many more partings forever. But I can still feel today, as on that afternoon of his burial, what the parting with Kafka meant.

At the memorial meeting in the Prague "Little Theatre," it fell to me to say a few words in behalf of the young writers. I spoke as in a trance. The speech was published in a periodical which I no longer possess. But I do remember that there was in that speech a presentiment of Kafka's later world-wide significance, of which but few people at that time had any idea.

(—1952)

Ernest Bloch and Modern Music

《◦◦◦》

JOHN HASTINGS

"**P**ERHAPS modern music," says Schopenhauer, in Professor Irwin Edman's reincarnation of him in *Philosopher's Quest*, "does peculiarly catch the note of reality. Its discords and dissonances, its broken melodies, its shattered harmonies—these are the very nature of the essence of things, the blind frustrations of the reasonless desire, the futile reiterations of the will always doomed to futility. Perhaps the music of your day is something like the music I have been waiting for. But, from the little I have heard of it, there is something missing: the touching quality of song, the poignance of feeling. It is the geometry of tragedy rather than the heartbreak of it that these cerebral young composers have caught. But if ever the great musician comes, he will have caught the very tone of world sorrow itself, and of human fatality, and in listening we will become one with it and our own little tragedies will find their fulfillment in transfigured union with the tragedy of all things."

If anybody knows what Schopenhauer would say to our time it should be Professor Edman. But I have a notion that the philosopher, relieved of the Edman ventriloquism, would be at least as thorough as he was clear. And chances are that, while continuing to deplore the existing geometry of tragedy, he would balance the books with the discovery of the great musician Professor Edman has him looking for without finding. In fact, it is almost uncanny that so accurate a description could be written of that musician when the author, to all appearances, does not know him at all. Certainly no musical Missing Persons Bureau, handed the word-picture of the composer sought, could fail for long to identify him as Ernest Bloch.

To be sure, Bloch can no longer claim the youthfulness that Professor Edman associates with "modernism"; yet he belongs to the "music of our day" more meaningfully than some have been able to discern. In contrast to the "cerebral young composers," there is not lacking in him "the touching quality of song, the poignance of feeling." And almost alone, he has stood out against the geometry of tragedy with scores that have, like no one else's in our time, caught the very tone of world sorrow and of human fatality.

That Professor Edman could overlook even so major a master is not hard to understand. For the music of Bloch has too often been bypassed for the novel, the spectacular and the chic. Unlike those who have strained to be up-to-date more than to be artistically communicative, Bloch never succumbed to the esthetic gangrene of his time. He had no interest in fashions, cults, isms, formulas or systems. And he had no use for the sensationalism that was the crutch of many a precarious celebrity. For these reasons his music, while it has steadily consolidated its grip upon a growing audience, has never been the vogue; and therefore it has often been snubbed by that sector of the critical fraternity that follows every mode like a housemaid with a dustpan after a shedding dog.

Bloch believes that the artistic representation of a world can be true only if it comes from the honest response of the native instinct to reality—not if it is hatched, like an algebraic theorem, from an intellectual preconception of that reality. He has refused to acknowledge that any man can be a spokesman for an age whose public neither responds to what he has to offer, agrees with his basic premises, nor can ever bear to listen to him more than once. His music has shown the spontaneous forthrightness that, in most of his contemporaries, arbitrary theorizing has strangled in its bassinet. His, indeed, is the miracle of whole genius which, occurring so seldom in any generation, transcends the cocoon of "conditioning factors," of which it is never essentially a part.

Bloch's example proves that if a man has genius to begin with, the sickness of his age is no excuse for the infection of his art. Its special lesson is that many of the others who failed where he succeeded, often greatly gifted men, were only half-geniuses or imperfect geniuses who voluntarily surrendered to the spiritual damage of their world. The contrast of such a man against such a background provides an illuminating commentary upon a whole epoch.

Seen in the spectrum of its cultural expression, that epoch of two decades between wars can only impress us with its overpowering spiritual atrophy. We could, in fact, undoubtedly reconstruct the civic bankruptcy of the Twenties and Thirties from the esthetic bankruptcy alone that equally pervaded them. For it would take scant argument to prove that the paralysis of the creative mind which brought us the "Vertigralists" and the twelve-tone scale was the exact counterpart of the paralysis of the political mind that brought us to Munich and Pearl Harbor. There was no reason we shouldn't have detected the same sickroom odor in the art gallery we would have sniffed in the Senate if our noses had been in adequate sniffing order. The germ the patient was dying from in both wards was the same: the germ of moral dry-rot. The tragedy is that the patient's decline seems now to have been more voluntary than our determinism would allow us to admit, and the death-rattle he uttered instead of music was only a refusal to rally to the challenge.

The setting, then, against which Bloch composed the major part of his output was a dolefully barren *mise-en-scène*. All the trick gadgetry that must be called on when the wells run dry, rattletrap and ramshackle alike, was noisily there: the mechanistic apparatus of atonalism which, backed up by pretentious and essentially bogus because meaningless scholarship, was actually a kind of musical lockjaw; the theory of "music for use," like a Bendix washer; the faddism of music-for-the-eye which, like Victorian children, was intended (with ample justification) to be seen and not heard; dissonant neo-classicism whose formalistic decorum and "correctness" claimed critical immunity for its pointlessness and cacophony; "horizontalism" with its insistence that harmony ride not upsydaisy but sidesaddle; experiments in orchestration involving wind-machines, fire sirens, steamboat whistles, outboard motors, cement-mixers, sandblasters and, in all probability, the kitchen sink (if the pump could be wired for sound); "new" scales like the latest labor-saving can-opener; the rash of "tone-clusters" for the production of which a piano was not fingered but struck with a blunt object like a thug—a fist, say, or an elbow, or, if nothing else was handy, the piano stool; and, last but not least, the philosophy that music is only another expression of the "class struggle," according to which diminished sevenths are spokesmen of the proletariat, whereas Neapolitan sixths are only capitalist propaganda of the most bourgeois, reactionary stripe.

This was the era of wonderful nonsense, when any composer more intent on getting his name in the papers than on serious creative activity could promote anything from a back-to-Bach movement to a new school for "schematic thematic chromatics." One headline-snatcher even came up with the howler that some day all music, instead of being played, would be read like a book, which was like saying that the housing shortage could be solved not by building houses but by distributing architectural blue-prints. No fantasy was too crackbrained to get a hearing.

What it all added up to was that a mask had come over the face of music, completing a Mardi Gras costume that was, in all, exhibitionist, a defense mechanism, a comfortable hideout, and the accomplishment of that ilk of vandals that sticks figleaves on Michelangelos. The purpose of the mask was to conceal a gaping hollowness and poverty within. Obviously, a very real loss of faith was at the bottom of the cave-in. But it is not with the loss of faith that we have our quarrel. It is with the moral stupefaction and intellectual immaturity with which that loss was met, and which were used as a shield to advance a decadence that, because it was as synthetic as its sponsorship, was fundamentally not a decadence at all. It would not require a psychoanalyst to diagnose so neurotic a psychological climate as schizoid—and schizoid beyond that measure of detachment which the schizophrenic so often finds useful to him as an artist. For here was a living organism that had turned against itself, using the very means of its own promotion as the weapon of suicide. Such din, in fact, came forth from music's determined self-destruction that a common question in the concert hall in those days, reversing the cliché, was "It's ugly, but is it art?"

With such conscientious paranoia Bloch has had simply nothing to do. Instead, he has gone his own way, consistently alone, and often, by the people who "matter" most, unhonored and unsung. What has set him apart has been his whimsical idea that music is a whole spiritual expression involving on the part of both composer and listener not the use of the microscope and the seismograph, but the exercise of the mind undivorced from the heart and the activation of the spirit unalienated from the pulse. He is one of the few present-day composers to whom being different at all costs is an undignified motive and who has been able to distinguish between originality and the eccentricity that, calling itself by that name, is actually—like the man who can think up nothing better to stand out from the crowd than to walk down the street on his hands instead of his feet—only the humdrum in reverse. Yet Bloch's music, dismissed by the shock-troops of the chic because it fits no known category of orthodox unorthodoxy, is as fresh, as personal, as much his own and no other's as any that has been composed since Debussy.

The reason is not hard to find: Bloch wrote out of himself. In so doing, he made capital sport of those who wrote only out of an over-preoccupation with their materials and their concussion effect on the loges and who, therefore, producing works that already sound dated today, best exemplify Wilde's observation that "nothing is so dangerous as being too modern; one is apt to grow old-fashioned quite suddenly."

If Bloch is "old-fashioned" at all, it is in the sense that he belongs, as Ernest Newman has pointed out, to the tradition of Beethoven rather than to the tradition of Arnold Schoenberg. This is a tradition of release rather than a tradition of repression, a tradition of expansion as opposed to contraction, a tradition of the ear as against the eye, a tradition of emotional leverage in contrast to one of intellectual legislation, a warmly human tradition in contradistinction to a coldly mechanical one. He has been concerned with the technology of his craft only as a means to an imaginative end, whereas, with Schoenberg, the tail wags the dog. To Bloch all systems like the twelve-tone theory are, musically, a kind of hardening of the arteries and represent, "ideologically," an esthetic-scientific totalitarianism, a musicological Marxism, a dialectical materialism of counterpoint according to which tones are ordered quite as "inevitably" and literal-mindedly as economic determinism claims the subjects of the state are "conditioned." And to him they are a horror, most particularly when they sprain a work of such poignant imagination as the Alban Berg "Wozzeck," whose romantic psychological impressionism, though set forth as an example of a chromatic scheme, succeeds (perhaps because it is closer to Debussy than to Schoenberg) not because of but in spite of the formula.

Indeed, both as philosopher and musician, Bloch is opposed to almost everything that has come to be termed "modernist." And where he is the spiritual brother of Moussorgsky and the Hindemith of "Mathis der Maler," he is also the spiritual antithesis of the Hindemith of the "Gebrauchsmusik" phase. If he has looked upon music as experience rather than recipe, he has also looked upon it as expression rather than convenience.

Amid the prevailing sterility of his cultural world, Bloch has truly been a voice crying in the wilderness. And yet, perhaps the most remarkable aspect of his music is that, for all its position of the outsider to contemporary mainstreams, it comes through as an extraordinarily probing portrait of our times, which the essential timelessness of its character does nothing to dissipate. Such a portrait becomes all the more incredible when one realizes that he has evoked the chaos and hysteria of our epoch without, in any measure, stooping to the dissolution that was their principal by-product. For, while he has utilized the whole arsenal of the modern composer's artillery, from dissonance to atonality, he has maintained the classic rather than the contemporary attitude toward its usage: he has been the master of the machinery; he has never allowed the machinery to master him. The effect has been that of a prophet from the Old Testament transplanted into the present with all its ferment and complexity, and moving about amid the toppling masonry without forfeiting either his understanding or his majesty.

The lofty stature arising from this link with the great past is such as has not been heard, perhaps, since Mahler. It is doubtful, indeed, if any musically knowledgeable person could listen to Bloch's "Piano Quintet" or the "Violin and Piano Sonata" or the "Viola Suite" without realizing that they stand as close in structural grandeur and moral and emotional passion to the eighteenth and nineteenth centuries as they do, in psychological sophistication, to the twentieth. Here, unmistakably, are the utterances of a wide-ranged spirit which combine the nobility of a former age with the disillusion of the present, fusing the two into a whole statement of our spiritual condition which, while not forgetting its disorder and confusion, is able to dignify it with the reminder that the past is of our destiny.

Bloch's has been the voice of faith in a cynical era. But a faith without glibness or automatism: a faith that has passed through the bitterest sufferings of our time and has emerged, not unscathed, but mindful of the eminence that lies behind us and looking with some measure of hope into the future. In his music, he has seen life piercingly and seen it whole. The world Bloch has created is a whole world, as filled as the one we call real with tumult and shouting, with longing and despair, with savagery and frustration, and with tenderness and loveliness and enchantment. He has not blinked at tragedy; but he has not stopped with it, either. And against all the howlings of the negative voices, he seems to beckon us toward the possibility of something better.

This positive element—which is not contradicted by the predominantly tragic cast of all his works—consists less in facile optimism than in the deeply religious nature that pervades everything Bloch has composed. The fact, indeed, that the creation of music is a kind of sacrament to Bloch is the particular attribute that sets him apart from most of his contemporaries. And yet, while that religious essence may have expressed itself most eloquently in the more notably Hebraic works, like the "Sacred Service," "Schelomo," the "Israel Symphony" and the "Three Jewish Poems," it is really beyond all ecclesiastical connotation in a dimension that has nothing to do with the synagogue. Actually it lies within the very fabric of the music itself, in the simple maintenance of a traditional tonality. For all the *ersatz* organology often substituted in its place, nothing could be more anarchic than the abandonment of such tonality. Composition that does not return to a basic *do* is like a deacon who does not believe in God: each is pretending to serve a cause while declaring that cause to be mythical.

The total desertion of atonalism by composers who have matured since it was modish is surely evidence enough for the prosecution. The adherence, meanwhile, of Ernest Bloch to the traditional inner framework of musical architecture is the most eloquent testimony he could have made of his persevering trust in the essential edifice of the cosmos as the great minds of the past have always seen it. The elegiac note so characteristic of his music should not put us off. Perhaps a man never believes so truly as when lamenting his disbelief, because in that lamentation is dramatized the clamorous need to believe— and the need to believe is often the same as to believe.

How much of the virtual sacerdotalism of Bloch's music lies outside the composer's consecration to his art and inside the temple of the Hebrew religion itself perhaps no one not of that faith can properly speak. It may be that Bloch is a "Jewish composer" in the same sense that Debussy used to like to call himself *musicien français*—a sense, that is, characterizing his derivations and identifying the indigenous nature of his work, but not necessarily limiting his significance or appeal to geographical or, as in Bloch's case, religious boundaries.

To be sure, Bloch has spoken in no uncertain terms of his concern with the Hebrew spirit, but the emphasis is revealing: "It is not my purpose, not my desire," he has said, "to attempt a 'reconstitution' of Jewish music, or to base my work on melodies more or less authentic. I am not an archaeologist. I hold it of first importance to write good, genuine music. It is the Jewish soul that interests me, the complex, glowing, agitated soul that I feel vibrating throughout the Bible . . . the freshness and naiveté of the Patriarchs; the violence of the Prophetic Books; the Jew's savage love of justice; the despair of the Ecclesiastes; the sorrow and the immensity of the Book of Job; the sensuality of the Song of Songs."

Notice that Bloch is not occupied with exploiting any hypothetical traits that might be said to set apart "the Jewish character"; rather he is inspired by the profoundest qualities in human nature itself as they may be colored and illumined in the people he loves and of whom he is one. Neither freshness, naiveté, violence nor love of justice, despair and sensuality, are features exclusive with any ethnic or religious group. And the power of his music to move Jew and non-Jew alike is the final repudiation of any such arbitrary lines of demarcation which, to each, is to "draw the circle that shuts him out" from some vital part of the whole human family.

Bloch's is a far more universal mind than can be arrested at the borders of meaningless dichotomies. To call the reflections of Solomon, as voiced in "Schelomo," an address merely to the Jewish people would be like calling the Sermon on the Mount a picturesque example of foreign lore. Put into effect, the hypothesis would annihilate not only Christianity but all religion. Bloch speaks rather of the human soul entire; more precisely, he speaks to it.

Undoubtedly, the metaphysics Bloch studied and lectured on in Switzerland show through the interstices of his scores, and explain not only much of his universality but how it was that, when religion went out of music and sociology and psychiatry came in, he was incapable of following the crowd. His art simply was too vast to be contained in the capsules that misuse had made of the social sciences. Many of the most burning questions of the day had, for him, no meaning, obviated as they were by a higher perspective: for the diseases of society were the frontier beyond which he had set himself to penetrate.

One of those questions still plagues the more rationalistic of our self-conscious composers: What is the function of art? Is it to provide a solace for the human heart or is it an impersonal transcript of civilization's general cardiac condition? Is it, in short, a sedative or a stethoscope?

To Bloch it is both and neither. For the question is badly off center, by seeking to limit the esthetic prerogative to one or the other two factors: both are piecework of the artist's office, neither taxing its cabinet of instruments nor representing its principal service. It's like asking: What is an apple? Is it round or is it red? When it may be both and still elude description.

The work of Bloch is all-encompassing: it is all things to all men. The paradox is that, despite his enormous range of vision, no scrutiny of man's living has been more intimate than Bloch's and no orientation emotionally more articulate. In the music that has ensued, the cosmic and the microcosmic join together into a perfect union. From it the ear catches the most particularized detail, housed though that detail may be in a construction of the most imposing scope: there is nuance within magnitude. The mind responsible for what we have heard is as clear about the whole as it is thorough about the parts. We never question either that Bloch has observed the material condition or that he has related that condition to the infinite. What has come from that relation in his music is no glacial abstractionism but a sympathetic human warmth based on a complete idea, in which is embodied a brotherhood as explicit as it is universal, and for a counterpart of whose magnificence one must go back to the Beethoven of the "Ode to Joy."

For only, perhaps, in Beethoven do we find a spirit with which Bloch's, in its sense of struggle and conflict and aspiration, may be compared. Indeed, the life work of each bears a striking spiritual resemblance to the other, for the center of both is a compassionate preoccupation with the human predicament. Because, moreover, Bloch's greatness, like that of the composer of the "Eroica" and the "Missa Solemnis," goes beyond purely musical boundaries into a mystical and philosophic realm, no one acquainted with both was surprised when Ernest Newman remarked their singular affinity. Referring to

Bloch's "Second String Quartet"* as "the finest work of our time in this genre," the perhaps foremost music critic of our time declared it "worthy to stand beside the last quartets of Beethoven." Certainly the comparison is more than fortuitous. Perhaps Beethoven alone, of all the composers we know, would be capable of the intense dynamic relationships that distinguish this among so many other of Bloch's achievements. Even as the "Ninth Symphony" expresses a love of man that in no way depends on the inspiring words of Schiller, so the music of Bloch expresses the most passionate democracy that needs no program notes to his "America Rhapsody" to become communicable. For the music, from Bloch as from Beethoven, belongs to a grandly humanist tradition.

That humanism, in fact, is the moral and emotional backbone of everything Bloch has composed. Difficult and complex as his "Second Quartet" may be, it is the animating force of that masterpiece quite as much as it is the fiery core of "Schelomo." For, while he has never written a more "radical" work, harmonically, than this Quartet —the frequent dissonance of its voice-writing, in fact carries it close to certain works in the same form from Bartok's middle phase without, however, forfeiting its grip upon the springs of common feeling —Bloch has also, perhaps, never achieved a more perfect balance between the affective and the intellectual, whose discipline, far from restricting his emotional compass, only sets it off to better advantage.

The very breadth of the passacaglia theme which dominates the "Quartet" fairly proclaims its composer's assurance of human dignity. The workmanship, the skill with which a most compound† organism has been constructed, is eloquent testimony to Bloch's belief in what he has often referred to as "hierarchy": the concept of the formal structure of things as proof of a plan of high human destiny. And yet the loneliness and disillusion of the opening movement with its arabesque-like motif, its wistful, introspective poetry of dream, amply indicate that, for all the affirmation of his faith, he has not forgotten the searing doubts, the "tone of world sorrow and human fatality," with which our age is afflicted. The rhythmic vigor of the second

---

* The work which, played with consummate musicianship by the Grillers in February 1947, was awarded the chamber music prize for the season by the New York Music Critics' Circle.

† A little too compound, apparently, for one of our leading newspaper critics who, even after having seen the score of what is one of Bloch's most prodigiously architectural works, wrote of the "Second Quartet" that "it follows no pattern"!

movement seems to imply a resurgence born even of desperation of that dogged invincibility which lies at the heart of human survival, and, which only the passing hopelessness and resignation of the third can even temporarily contradict. As for the fourth movement, it is a world in itself, a vivid energetic human world full of dazzling contrasts. The cumulative excitement of the great passacaglia, prefaced by a pizzicato passage of the most electric effect and followed by the extraordinary fugue and the extended coda of the "Epilogue," testifies to the vitality and depth of Bloch's response to the sensational world.

The entire "Quartet," indeed, is so remarkable a blending of voices, with each heard canonically like the members of a courtly debating team; so deft a weaving together of themes, with the sad arabesque-like motif running throughout the piece to its last mournful recollection in the final measure; so fabulous a reconnaissance into terrains of sound combinations and tone values too rarefied to be accessible to any but the most phenomenally sensitive ear—that a hearing of its performance is like eavesdropping on a sorcerer's magic. By the time the work comes to a close it is impossible not to feel that we have been granted an experience comparable to little, if anything, we have known before.

For the cultural historian it may be that the "Second Quartet" will be to the "Viola Suite" (and its period) what *Meistersinger,* say, is to *Tristan:* a work of the final maturity of creative perspective in contrast to one of the burgeoning maturity of a creative prime. For the awe and astonishment and admiration we feel for the "Second Quartet" do not, for all its genius, persuade us to forget such masterful works as the "Viola Suite" that were its logical forerunners. Already, I suspect, the "Suite" (1918–19) has become a kind of classic, regarded by most musicians as one of the few great works of all time written for that instrument. The soaring lyricism of its melodic line against the often savage bitterness of its underlying thought makes it a provocative and deeply moving imaginative exploration.

Similar qualities are evident in Bloch's "Sonata for Violin and Piano" from the same period, a composition of elemental force and often a brooding, psychological, even Dostoievskian pallor. The subsequent "Piano Quintet" (1921-23) was a product of his early years of acclimatization to this country, during which he was Director of the Cleveland Institute of Music. No work we have from him is more majestic in sweep, richer or more sensuous in its tonal tapestry or more poignantly affecting. In it we hear the tragic suffering, the piteous outcry, the sense of terror and sinister foreboding that are so typical of Bloch; and the canvas, for a chamber work, is almost symphonic.

Also belonging to this general period are the enormously powerful "Schelomo" ("Rhapsodie Hebraïque") for cello and orchestra (1916), a masterpiece too familiar to require comment; the "First Quartet" (1916), a model of "romantic" pathos and dramatic fire within a panoply of the most "classical" precision and control; the "Concerto Grosso" for string orchestra and piano obbligato (1924-25), written for his students as an example of the Handelian form in contemporary mode and characterized by exceptional rhythmic vivacity, a plaintive melodic strain, and the distinction of a lively fugue of great color and variety; and the "America Rhapsody," which won the *Musical America* award for an orchestral work in 1927. With remarkable impressionist evocation of American history, from the days of the earliest settlers through the Revolution and the Civil War to the "machine age," this Rhapsody is Bloch's passionate embrace of the democracy of Whitman.

If the "Second Quartet" is to the "Viola Suite" what *Meistersinger* is to *Tristan,* the "Viola Suite" is to Bloch's "C♯ Minor Symphony" what *Tristan* is to *Lohengrin.* This *Symphony* was written when the composer was but twenty, just at the turn of the century. Antedating the recognition of Mahler, it is not only prophetic but seriously preempts much of the originality attributed to Mahler and other composers since influenced by his work, like Shostakovitch. Its soaring spirit recalls even more the Beethoven (again!) of the "Pastoral"—the sunlit meadows and the sweep of skies are in it; beyond that, man's endless spiritual struggle and redemption. Bloch calls the "Symphony" his "optimistic" work, casting a wry reflection on the frequently acid bitterness of much of his subsequent music. It is true: despite the monumental conflict embodied in this work, there hovers above it a surpassing serenity, a promise of benediction which we know the climax cannot fail to fulfill.

The work is incredible for a number of reasons: for none more than the age at which the composer created it. Mozart, the free introspective prodigy, we take, mistakenly or not, as a phenomenon of nature. But to conceive that a boy scarcely out of his teens could fashion the searching, psychologically expository music in the "C♯ Minor

Symphony" amounts almost to a profession of belief in necromancy. At the time of its first performance, Romain Rolland, the author of *Jean-Christophe,* wrote: "Your Symphony is one of the most important works of the modern school. I do not know any work in which a richer, more vigorous, more passionate temperament makes itself felt. . . . From the very first measures to the end of such music one feels at home in it. It has a life of its own; it is not a composition coming from the brain before it was felt."

His one opera, *Macbeth,* was also composed early in Bloch's career and received a resoundingly successful première in Paris at the Opéra-Comique in 1910. Although there is some basis of comparison with *Pelléas,* Bloch's is decidedly less evanescent than the Debussy opera and far more vigorously dramatic. It is a matter of record that Bloch spared no pains to give Shakespeare's drama, from which the libretto of Edmond Fleg was faithfully fashioned, a musical setting ideally appropriate to its psychological and theatrical character.

Other early works include the "Israel Symphony" for great orchestra and two sopranos, two altos and bass (1912-16), an expansive expression of intensely religious cast from which the lamentation "Adonai, Elohim," is especially familiar; his two symphonic poems, customarily played together, "Hiver" and "Printemps" (1905), with their luminous atmospheric impressionism; and the "Three Jewish Poems: Danse, Rite and Cortège Funèbre" (1913), notable for their austere melancholy and driving climactic fervor.

Outstanding among Bloch's compositions that seem to fit no particular period or stylistic phase are the "Piano Sonata" (1935), the "Violin Concerto" (1937-38), the "Evocations" (1938), the "Symphonic Suite" (1933–34); as well as the "Sacred Service," "The Voice in the Wilderness," "Four Episodes" for chamber orchestra, and "Helvétia," all four of which are from the late Twenties and early Thirties.

The "Piano Sonata," all too seldom played, is a rhapsodic work remarkable even from Bloch for an intensity of poetic ardor, often couched in the harshest terms, that almost bursts the dynamic resources of the piano. Composed in the "grand manner," it requires the ministrations of a pianist with an emotional gamut as large as his technical equipment. Like certain piano works of Prokofieff, it reminds us what the soft, dreamy, delicate music of the impressionists bade us forget: that the piano is a percussion instrument—despite the fact that in the second movement we are treated to a pastorale as shadowy, as finespun, as iridescent as anything the impressionist school has left. Certainly the Sonata makes the fullest possible use of the whole range of the piano's tonal and expressive potentialities, opening with a richly declamatory and even songful *maestoso ed energico* and closing with an *alla marcia* of almost brutal violence. But however dissonant and rhythmically spasmodic, the work never entirely abandons either the basic diatonic key-relationships or the melodic cantilena. Here is a composition which, because of its infrequent performance and no recording, is a challenge to the true musicians among today's more enterprising pianists.

As for the "Violin Concerto," that is a work of the most affecting melodiousness and of vibrant, almost primeval power. Utilizing both American Indian and Oriental themes, it expresses the throbbing atavism characteristic of so much of Bloch's music. Its wide latitude extends from a contemplation of a tribal day to an acerb, tumultuous celebration of the mechanistic complexities of our own age. It impresses one as a kind of allegory of man's pilgrimage from primitive simplicity to the sophisticated confusions of the present, and seems to call for a rebirth of man's essential unity. It is distinguished by one of the most hauntingly beautiful slow movements in all musical literature.

The "Evocations" is a tone-poem of lustrously Oriental configuration and coloring that takes full advantage of the timbre scale of the orchestral medium. The "Symphonic Suite" embraces something of the neo-classicism of the "Concerto Grosso" while maintaining a contemporary modality. Composed of an Overture (*maestoso*), a passacaglia with twenty-two variations, and a finale that Bloch calls, "a kind of *moto perpetuo*" that is "*un peu grotesque*," it affects this writer in much the same way as might a Brandenburg Concerto written for full orchestra and given overtones half tragic and half nostalgic. Actually, though, in emotional roundness and impact if not in form, it is closer to Handel than to Bach.

The "Avodath Hakodesh," a religious service of most exalted character, marks something of a departure for Bloch from many of the features of his usual style. "The Voice in the Wilderness" is a brooding symphonic poem for cello and orchestra which has also provided Bloch with the material (abbreviated) for his piano suite, "Vision et Prophéties." The "Four Episodes" compose a group of tone-poems whose moods, descriptive fancy and psychological incandescence seem to come from the palette of a visionary but none the less puckish and robust painter. "The Helvétia" is an orchestral score reminiscent of Bloch's native Switzerland.

In addition, Bloch has also written the "Baal Shem Suite" for violin and piano, from which the "Niggun" has already become one of the classic staples in the repertoire of the present-day violinist; vocal settings of Psalms 22, 114 and 137, as well as of a variety of French poems, including Beatrix Rodès' *Poèmes d'Automne;* a number of quartet pieces; and such piano works as the tenuously suggestive "Five Sketches in Sepia," "the Poems of the Sea," "In the Night" and "Nirvana."

If asked to describe the style that is peculiarly Bloch's and no other composer's I should emphasize one attribute that stands out above all others. It is, I think, his spiritual reach, that intense quality so peculiarly intrinsic to his music: the quality of aspiration.

In the world of Bloch's imagination the voices seem forever striving to go beyond traditional limitations: to mount not into the treble but the stratosphere; to descend not into the bass but the Stygian depths; to expand the proportions of form; to burst the very seams of dimension itself. It may be risky to put a psychological and spiritual interpretation on something that to many seems merely technological. But to one observer no more lucid demonstration could be made of what is actually the central motivation not only of creative art but of human life as well; the theme of the quest. When Bloch's tonal interlocutors soar to loftier climes than the compact group they belong to is accustomed to engage, we have in notational as well as instrumental terms, but no less in terms of human longing and hunger and desperation, a dazzling instance of man's ceaseless search beyond the perimeters of what he knows. The search, if carried to its logical extremity, must penetrate into those vast spaces whose silence used to terrify Pascal.

In the basic musical lexicon, Bloch is a mystic, a seer. The signal of his restlessness, his impatience with boundaries, his seeking to invade uncharted wilds—this is something neither programmatic nor superimposed; it lies within the very warp and woof of his music. If his instrumental voices are explorers in range and tonality, he is no less an explorer in creative thought. Such is the limitless province of music: it is an atlas of both reality and dreams; it shows what we are and what we desire, what we think and what we pretend, how high we can hope, how low we can despair.

For a composer, in the final analysis, deals with essences, not facts; with meaning at its source rather than with the appearances of meaning. Music is not so much a comment on life as a form of living itself. It takes more than consciousness or logic to encompass it, and for that reason alone it defies all effectual censorship. It would be as impossible to censor a flame: you must either let it burn or put it out. When we realize how full an expression is Bloch's music of the elevation of his mind and heart and spirit, we realize the truth of Buffon's *"Le style, c'est l'homme."*

Against the general musical sterility of the epoch in which he has lived, Bloch's position until now has been rather equivocal. Of course, he is inaccessible to those whose tastes have not developed beyond the juke-box perversions of Tchaikovsky and Rachmaninoff. For them his music cuts a little close to the bone; it probes too deep into what we feel, into our underlying sorrows and losses and frustrations; and their rejection illustrates a peculiarly American psychosis: the dread of inward understanding. By the various cliques of futurism he is dismissed as a "romantic"—a synonym, presumably, for outmoded. Since, however, such stock labels as "classical" and "romantic" no longer have any semantically fixed meanings, it may be doubted that the epithet has found its mark. The fact is that today we are seeking a return to the free, spontaneous emotionalism of what used to be called romanticism, with composers as dissimilar as Honegger and Hindemith and even Bartok (just before he died) recoiling from their previous scorn of common melodic feeling to write more simply, more naturally, more humanly. Bloch, perhaps alone of all the composers of his time, has never had to shift his policy because he has never lost sight of its goal. That goal was not the sponsoring of fashions, movements or ideologisms but the perfecting of a true musical language through which to communicate with the world. Because his life work has steadily moved in that straight line, it has constantly increased in stature for the honest core of intelligent music-lovers.

Bloch is one of those composers—like Brahms, in particular, but Beethoven and even Bach as well—whom each succeeding generation sees in a different light, now "classical," now "romantic," now something else. Just as we used to think of Brahms as a stuffy traditionalist

Evening Service for Sholosh R'golim

Prelude I for Organ
Invocation
By Ernest Bloch

(*Written for the Cantorial Anthology*)

SHOLOSH R'GOLIM

Nov. 9th, 1946

(786)

where now we discern the songful lyricism in his music; just as we used to see more of Mozart than of the soul-shaken stormy petrel in Beethoven; just as we used to consider Bach a dry intellectual rather than as the dramatic Vulcan of the tumultuous organ toccatas and the mighty turbulence of the "St. Matthew Passion," the dreamy poet of the twenty-fifth Goldberg variation—so we shall in time come to recognize the wholeness of Bloch as a creative artist, his equal eminence in the spheres of the intellect and of spontaneous feeling. Perhaps what has most militated against his full acclaim is that he was born into a time that had grown self-conscious about the "heart," and rightly too, since so much hypocritical use had been made of it; and that he refused to be swept along with the main current of that self-consciousness whose net and synthetic effect was what C. S. Lewis wryly describes as "the horror of The Same Old Thing."

But Bloch has a deeper understanding of man. He knows that, where the new cannot warm him against the cold, it is precisely "The Same Old Thing" he truly craves: the ageless flame of human love. And, in having fought the "geometry of tragedy" with an art that brought man into "transfigured union with the tragedy of all things," Bloch has asserted a spiritual integrity that places him with the masters.

(—1948)

Guglielmo Ebreo and the Ballet

❧⚬᷅⚬

WALTER SORELL

WHEN the curtain came slowly down on the Middle Ages European man felt reborn, as if a divine power had given him the strength to rediscover his own being through mind and body, and he leaped into a life of joy and passion which was marked for greatness. It was indeed an aura of greatness, however indefinable, that then surrounded European man, an atmosphere in which he could not help but become creative. For us today art is, on the one hand, a means of "self-expression," and on the other hand a pleasant addition to life, one of the many ways of mental relaxation. But in ancient Athens or in the Florence of the fifteenth and sixteenth century art belonged to the functions of man and was as vital to him as the air he breathed, the food he ate.

The power and purposefulness of the individual and all his talents were more decisive than any laws and customs. It was the time when *condottieres* became dukes, when bankers founded dynasties in which their sons were anointed popes, whose sons in turn rose to the title of princes. Illegitimate children were nothing unusual, nothing one had to hide. On the contrary, how many of those illegitimate children became the most redoubtable dukes! Their ability—often enough, their ruthlessness—counted more than the cleanest pedigree. Aeneas Sylvius spoke of Italy as of a country "that loves the change, in which nothing is solidified and where no rulers of long standing exist. Small wonder, then, that it is easy for servants to become kings!"

Even Jews, who had just come through the trial of the Inquisition and who lived huddled together in ghettos, or wandered from country to country, from fair to fair as entertainers, since this profession bought them some freedom—even Jews were not only tolerated; they began to be esteemed, in an otherwise still hostile world, when their talents proved the worth of their personalities.

In no other time, and in no other part of the world but Northern Italy of that time, could we have found the roots of our modern theatrical dancing.

The ordinary people who shared little in the great achievements of the artist and men of letters, who stood awestruck outside the palaces and inside the churches, had their own little joys, their games, their fairs and carnivals and, at all of these, their rustic dances. Everyone felt something contagious in the air, everyone was seized by that inexplicable feeling of something great happening around him. Was there any better way of becoming one with the spirit of beauty, of rejoicing over the liberation of one's soul, than by expressing it through one's body? The dance was no longer considered evil. It graduated to one of the creative manifestations of man.

The lively rustic dance was not becoming to the ladies and gentlemen at the courts. Their dresses of rich heavy brocades would have been in utter contrast to their movements. But not only their dresses. Their moods, their thoughts and conversations as well, the halls and gardens in which the dances took place.

The dance too, then, must needs be perfected. It had to become an art, to be studied and performed with dignity and grace. The air of greatness that had permeated everything certainly could not halt before the dance.

For the creation of a dance art there were needed a vocabulary of steps and a choreographic pattern or design. To achieve both, dance teachers were essential, dancing masters. With them was laid the foundation of a dance theory. Spontaneity, natural inclination, the learning from mere observation, all that was left to the masses. The dancing master ruled all that out. For him dance was a matter of restraint and refinement. He was very aware that he worked for people of taste and culture. The dance he composed had therefore to consist of steps striving toward elegant movements. There was no longer anything folkloristic in it: it was theatrical dancing created for certain stage effects, though the stage was the ballroom floor of princely courts. For the first time a clear distinction was made between folk dancing and this complicated refined art of movement pattern.

We might easily get a wrong conception of the Renaissance dance as the groundwork for the modern ballet. Those dances were, undoubtedly, closer to today's social than artistic dancing. But their systematic attempt to achieve coordinated steps within the frame of a pattern, the training and rehearsing of steps and figures, the establishment of a dancing profession and the arrangement of dances for groups watched by the other courtiers—all this became the first step toward our own theatrical dancing.

The few records and fragmentary choreographic literature of that time make it clear that the interest of the dance recorders was concentrated on the court dances which often turned into elaborate spectacles. The dances of the common people find no mention anywhere. Only some painters of the period help us out. For instance, in Mantegna's picture "Parnassus" and in Giulio Romano's "Apollo Dances with the Muses" we can see the lively large movements of the peasants whose wide steps are in utter contrast to the restrained, regulated and strictly defined movements and gestures of the court dancers.

What did the people of that era dance? They had slow and fast dances; but, though they already possessed their set vocabulary of steps, one dance could easily be performed like another. And, in fact, it was often a strange mixture. Lively rhythms would suddenly interrupt what had started as something stately and ceremonial. This may have been a kind of holdover from the Middle Ages. Or was it brought about by the temperament of the people?

In the main, three dances existed. The favorite one of the time, particularly at the courts, was the *basse danse,* or *bassa danza,* the "queen of all dances," as it was known. The entire fifteenth and a greater part of the sixteenth century can be called "the age of the *basse danse,*" as we speak of the beginning nineteenth century as "the age of the waltz," or the early twentieth century as "the age of jazz."

The word *basse* means low. This dance was essentially without jumps or any other lively movements. The dancers were supposed to move slowly and solemnly, their toes somewhat lifted from the ground, but their feet hardly ever leaving it. Dignity must be preserved. The exultant joy of life and the erotic element—however uppermost in everybody's mind—must be kept hidden, or only slightly hinted at. But not for the entire duration of the dance. Suddenly the *saltarello* rhythms would liven up the tune and dance.

The *saltarello* was a vigorous three-beat dance supposed to be done with leaps or jumps—probably a milder, more urbane edition of the maniacally danced *tarantella.* Curt Sachs, linking the *tarantella* with the Roman *saltarello* or the Tuscan *tresca,* gives this description of its modern but true traditional form:

. . . the dancer, kneeling, adores his female partner and then, as though sated, speedily forsakes her again. How with a thousand turns and tricks he now holds aloof and now rushes upon her! His gambols and capers are grotesque and yet charmingly light and tender. His bearing is now proud and resolute, now querulous and elaborate. Legs and arms, even the fingers strumming on the tambourine, and above all the glance, ardent, languishing, suddenly bold and shameless, reinforce the expression of the posture. The girl comes out of her corner, now wayward, now willing. Her smile is eloquent, her eyes are drunken. She swings her skirt; she picks up the corner of it as if she were going to gather things in it; or she raises her arm so that the hand hangs down loosely over her head as though from a hook, while the other hand presses against her heart. Now she is the axis around which the male dancer rotates.

"What a dance!" once exclaimed Rainer Maria Rilke—"as though invented by nymphs and satyrs, old yet rediscovered and rising up anew, wrapped in primeval memories—cunning and wildness and wine, men with goat's hooves again and girls from the train of Artemis." Of all this "cunning and wildness and wine" we find, at the Renaissance courts, little more than a gay and light dance with an occasional leap and graceful smile. But the *saltarello* was no doubt a welcome interruption of the ceremonial, gliding *bassa danza.*

The third dance fashionable at this time was the so-called *piva,* a dance of double steps to a rapid tempo. But whatever dance was chosen, the movements were hardly ever the same; they were constantly combined into new and various versions. These versions had the fanciest names: Bel Fiore, Anello, Venus, Cupido, Mignotta, Zaura, Piatosa, Lioncello, and so on. The names and, above all, the combinations of steps were left to the imagination of the dancing masters.

Up till then the professional dancer didn't exist. There were only wandering mimes, the jesters and jugglers who entertained the people at the fairs, often with dances too—familiar figures throughout the Middle Ages. The greater artists among them, those who specialized in the dance, settled down as dance teachers. A surprisingly large number were Jews, and one of the greatest was a certain Guglielmo Ebreo of Pesaro—"William the Hebrew of Pesaro"—about whom it was said that he "excelled all men in the dance." Not only did contemporary poets write flattering verses to his agility as a dancer but also to his skill as a musician. The esteem of his contemporaries is substantiated by the fact that his work on dancing was used in several places at the same time. (The extant manuscripts of the work are now in the Bibliothèque Nationale in Paris and in the Libraries of Siena and Florence.)

We are unable to say where he originally came from, but he shared the fate of many of his Jewish contemporaries. With economic conditions in the medieval ghetto as poor as they were, many a talented Jew took to the road. The wandering Jew as entertainer can be found almost everywhere in Europe until the end of the eighteenth century. The parents of more than one great Jewish artist of the nineteenth century belonged to these itinerant entertainers. We only have to think of the French tragedienne Rachel (*née* Élisa Félix, 1820-1858), whose parents belonged to such a group of wandering Jewish dancers and acrobats. The musical genius Jacques Offenbach was descended from *letzim* (vaudevillians); his father, the *Schutzjude* ("Protected Jew"), Isaac Juda Eberst, came from the ghetto of Offenbach.

The importance of the *Tanzhaus* in the ghettos can be judged by its effects at the beginning of the Renaissance. It created a consciousness for music and the dance in Jewish families. The teaching of these two subjects had, at that time, become an integral part of the education of the Jewish child. In fact, particularly among the Jews in Italy and Spain, it was considered the duty of a Hebrew teacher, however learned he might be, to be well versed also in music and dancing. This is why we find so many professional musicians and dancing masters among the Jews at that time—professions as characteristically Jewish as those of pawnbroking and medicine.

The supremacy of the Jews in these professions is clearly attested to by the reactions of their Christian competitors, such as the pressure from clerical and governmental circles that from time to time expressed their disapproval. In 1443, for instance, the authorities in Venice ordered schools of music, singing and dancing run by Jews to be closed, and "they should be stopped from teaching these subjects under pain of imprisonment and fine." Nevertheless, this provision had to be frequently re-enacted.

Indeed, Jewish dancing masters with a large Christian clientele were nothing unusual. It even went so far that, in the year 1313, Rabbi Hacen ben Salomo taught the Christians to perform a choral dance around the altar in the Church of St. Bartholomew at Tauste in the Spanish province of Zaragoza. We also know that in Parma many of the noble ladies took lessons in dancing from Jewish women, who were later expelled from the city. But in certain instances the authorities, both the secular and clerical princes, could not help acknowledging the superiority of the Jewish dancing masters. As late as 1775 the Pope gave special permission to two Jews in Ancona, Grescion Azziz and Rabbi Emanuel de Jalomacis, to teach dancing and singing. Earlier, Sieur Isaac d'Orleans must have played a great role at the French Court about 1700. The English poet Jenyns wrote of him:

> And Isaac's Rigadoon shall live as long
> As Raphael's painting, or as Virgil's song.

During the Renaissance many Jewish loan-bankers, who formed an aristocracy of their own, emulated princes and popes and maintained a great number of Jewish artists, dancing masters among them. And we may be sure that many more of the Italian and Spanish dance teachers than the records show were Jewish. For not everyone could withstand the outside pressure and face the danger of persecution as well as the envy of his baptized competitors. It is understandable that only those among them who achieved incontestable mastership added proudly to their name: *Ebreo*.

Guglielmo Ebreo of Pesaro was one of the first to write on the dance. He was born about 1440, possibly somewhat earlier. Neither the date of his birth nor of his death is quite certain; but he appears to have been active during the second half of the fifteenth century. And he must have traveled extensively, for he was known to have visited many places of the Italian peninsula. Of the importance of his work—"*De praticha seu arte tripudii vulghare opusculum*"—we cannot doubt. It must have been used as a text-book by many of the dance masters of the period. Thus his contribution is one of the earliest few on which the huge pyramid of theatrical dancing rests.

Pesaro—a smallish place on the eastern coast of Italy, on the Adriatic Sea—was not far from Rimini, better known both as a modern seaside resort and for the tragic love story of Francesca da Rimini which has haunted world literature. But it was Pesaro that gave the dance world one of its first creative spirits. Pesaro also gave to the political world the great name of the Sforza. There were two brothers Sforza. Francesco, the most daring and scheming freebooter and *condottiere* of the fifteenth century, "worked" his way up until he became Duke of Milan, a rich and powerful man. His brother Alessandro Sforza, Duke of Pesaro, was far more modest and limited in scope. With little to rule over, he was dependent on his brother, a stronger personality, and on the great Federigo of Urbino, whose father-in-law he managed to become.

Guglielmo's parents had probably come the long way from Spain, escaping the Inquisition there. But in Pesaro not many possibilities were open to them. At a rather early period of his youth it must have become obvious to his parents that Guglielmo had a particular talent for the dance.

A certain Domenico, or Domenechino, who lived in Piacenza on the river Po, had made a great name for himself as a dancing teacher in the first half of the century. Guglielmo wandered northward, into the Duchy of Milan, to become Domenico's pupil. He was accepted and served his apprenticeship, not always easy in those days, involving sacrifices and many menial chores. In his own work—one of the most complete as well as earliest works on the art of dancing—Guglielmo refers to himself as the *"divotissimo disciepolo e fervente imitatore del diguissimo cavaliere, Messer Domenico da Ferrara, nell' arte del virtuoso et onesto danzare dottissimo,"* and many of Domenico's dance compositions can be found in Guglielmo's compilation.

Of course he was not the only pupil in Piacenza. Antonio Cornazano, a famous dancing teacher and poet who was a contemporary of Guglielmo, also wrote a book on the dance, with the simpler title *Libro dell'arte del danzare,* which bears a similar dedication to Domenico whom they both adored and to whom they owed so much. How difficult it is to write on an art as visual and fleeting as the dance was already recognized by Antonio Cornazano when, after trying to make a dance clear to his readers, he fled into the statement: "This cannot be well explained unless you are present to make you do it." Although both Guglielmo and Antonio tried their best to give in detail a choreographic technique, their explanations and some expressions they used remain rather obscure in places. (They could not surmise, of course, that it would take the dance teachers another five hundred years before Rudolf Laban would perfect a workable dance notation.) How hard it was to keep the many variations of the three main dance forms in mind becomes evident through Guglielmo's stress on *memoria* as one of the essential prerequisites of the dancer. But Antonio bragged in his book that he needed only to have a dance shown to him once to be able to repeat it without the slightest mistake.

We know that Domenico became the dancing master at the house of Sforza in Milan. Whether Guglielmo followed him there, for a time at least, is not known. But when he left his master he soon established himself as the person who "excelled all men in the dance." His must have been a strong and proud character. He never considered conversion to Christianity in order to make life easier for himself. Nor did he ever try to conceal his faith. He wanted to be known by the name of "Guglielmo Ebreo of Pesaro." What might have begun as a childish challenge to the world, defying a stigma, turned in his case into a *forte*. To be known as *Ebreo* certainly did not harm his career. He spent some time in Bologna; that is quite certain since one of his dance compositions reads: "*Alis nominata Caterva*" *composta in Bologna*. Another entry shows that he had access to members of the most powerful Roman family, the Colonna, though we cannot be sure he was ever called to Rome. But his famous dance "Colonnese" was composed for Madonna Suena di Casa Colonna, a relative of the most celebrated woman of Italy, Vittoria Colonna.

At a time when passion ruled without restraint, when the noblest was attributed to the strongest, in a country of so many rakes and brutal cynics, we find time and again that precisely those men lost themselves in utter adoration of *l'amor divino*. The heavenly, the platonic love became idealized in the persons of a few women: among them Guilia Gonzaga, Veronica da Corregio and, above all, Vittoria Colonna. Ruthlessness and power needed a counterpoint, sought symbols and idols beyond their own limitations. The recovery of antiquity, the realization of the creative spirit through the building of palaces and domes, through painting and writing, all this did not suffice. Personal purity, sublime love was thought to be one of the antidotes to their own lives.

Guglielmo could not have done better than compose one of his dances for Madonna Suena. And how clever to have the dance carry the name of one of the greatest women of all Italy—a name belonging also to some of the most cold-blooded and cunning men of history. The dance, for so long in disrepute and defamed as carnal stimulation, had to fight hard against so much prejudice piled up against it through the centuries. Dance and purity must now become synonymous! So he felt. And Guglielmo appears to have been an ardent fighter for raising the dance to an incontestable esthetic level. How else could we understand these words in his treatise?

The art of dancing is for generous hearts that love it and for gentle spirits that have a heaven-sent inclination for it rather than an accidental disposition—a most amiable [*amicissima*] matter, entirely different from and mortally inimical to the vicious and artless common people [*meccaniche plebei*] who frequently, with corrupt spirits and depraved minds, turn it from a liberal art and virtuous science into a vile adulterous affair, and who more often in their dishonest concupiscence under the guise of modesty make the dance a procuress, through whom they are able to arrive stealthily at the satisfaction of their desires.

We still hear through these words the bitter voices of the Christian priests. It becomes clear that Guglielmo tried to free the dance from one of its primordial, most innate impulses, the love and sex motive. He endeavored to elevate it to an artistic display of pure beauty, grace and enchantment.

During one of his short sojourns in his home town of Pesaro, where his exceptional ability was of little use to Alessandro Sforza, Guglielmo was very likely recommended by Alessandro to his son-in-law, the great Federigo, Duke of Urbino. Alessandro could dispatch a note to the Duke, saying: ". . . and since there is no better man in the whole of Italy today who could outdo Guglielmo Ebreo of our town in the dance, and since there is no court more illustrious than yours, I think that you would do a great service to Guglielmo Ebreo and yourself by adding the very same to the galaxy of the many noted and renowned men at your court. . . ."

It may have been due to Alessandro Sforza's recommendation, or to Guglielmo's own reputation having grown to such an extent that several courts vied with each other to have him in their employ. Perhaps Guglielmo could decide for himself and choose the court closest to his home town. However it was, we find him in the service of Federigo of Urbino, where he probably remained until death overcame the Duke in 1482.

Urbino is situated on the eastern slopes of the Mighty Apennines, not far from Pesaro. On its left, when you face north, is Monte Cutria, crowned by the Convent of San Albertino, 5600 feet above the sea, and Monte del Cavallo, a beautiful peak in the Apennine chain. To the north lies the massive Monte Carpegna which terminates with the triple peak of San Marino, that rugged independent mountain island with which everyone who collects stamps is familiar. Thus Urbino has an ideal geographical position, ideal not from a scenic point of view only, but from the viewpoint of any military-minded man. In whatever glorious colors Federigo may be painted, it cannot be denied that he began his career as a *condottiere* and, at least in the beginning of his reign, was fighting so many feuds and little wars that he was rarely at home where it fell to his wife, Countess Battista Sforza, to see to it that everything went right.

It may be interesting to have a look at the Duke. We can find no portraits of him which do not show his left profile, since he had lost his right eye in a tournament. At that time tournaments were still fashionable among the *nouveaux riches* and new aristocrats although, in essence, they belonged to the past, to the world of medieval knights. It was only two decades later that Cervantes wrote his great satire on chivalry and knights errant—*Don Quixote.*

Federigo's mother had had a frightening dream the night before. Federigo, like most of his great contemporaries, was a strong believer in astrology and the interpretation of dreams. Nevertheless he dared his fate and fought in the tournament against Guidangelo de' Ranieri, a gentleman of Urbino, who had just returned from Florence where his skill with the lance had triumphed. The news of his victories for Urbino had reached the palace. Federigo received him with all due honors and challenged him. Result: his right eye was knocked out, his nose broken. But Federigo remained cheerful, dismissing this mishap as lightly as his mother's dream.

Indeed, Federigo was probably the most perfect representative of the Renaissance and of the self-styled aristocrats of his time. He had the political morality of the *condottiere* (or it may be better to say the Machiavellian amorality) as far as his "foreign policy" was concerned; and yet, at the end, he ran the most accomplished court in Italy. No other ruler of his time was so much beloved by his people, and it is said that he even dared to walk around among his people unprotected. He kept an efficient household in which everyone had his tasks and everyone felt secure. His concern for the welfare of his people was so great (and so modern in conception) that he commissioned persons who were called "revisors" to travel about his dukedom for no other purpose than to find out the condition in which his people lived, what desires they voiced, and what improvements were necessary. He was well known for eating frugally, for listening to his readers and poets (he was fondest of Livy, the greatest prose writer of the Augustan age), for conversing on holy topics with the Mother Superior of the nearby cloister of the nuns of St. Clare. He himself directed the physical exercises of the Urbinian youth. In fact, he took interest in everything that went on in his state. When he walked through the streets his subjects would kneel down and say: *"Dio ti mantenga, Signore!"*—the Renaissance version of "God Save the King!"

His palace, though not the most luxurious in Italy, was strictly classical in structure. Federigo prided himself most on his library. To speak of Urbino and not to mention its library was like speaking of Rome without thinking of the Pope. There were two wings. One contained the famous collection of manuscripts, the other printed books. In 1465 the first book was printed in Italy, and it was during the last ten years of his life that Federigo's library gained its reputation. He employed no less than thirty-four transcribers who worked throughout Italy and even went to France to complement his collection of manuscripts. As for his books, the Duke made it a rule that every volume must be bound in crimson, ornamented with silver.

All told, Federigo had between 350 and 500 people on his payroll. One of the lists, as they have been preserved, mentioned among others:

Counts of the Duchy	45
Knights of the Golden Spur	5
Gentlemen	17
Judges and councillors	7
Ambassadors and secretaries	7
Secretaries of State	5
Teachers of grammar, logic and philosophy	4
Architects and engineers	5
Readers during meals	5
Chaplains	2
Singing boys	5
Organists	2
Fencing masters	2
Dancing masters	2

One of the two dancing masters was Guglielmo Ebreo of Pesaro. Among the teachers of grammar, logic and philosophy was a certain Giovanni Mario Filelfo, poet laureate at the court. A very long poem of his was written in honor and praise of Guglielmo. He called it *"Canzon morale di Mario Philelfo ad honore et laude di Maestro Guglielmo hebreo."* He praised not only Guglielmo's agility as a dancer but his skill as a musician. Here are a few lines of it:

> *Tanto é soave e angelica harmonia*
> * Nel dolce suon di Guglielmo hebreo,*
> * Tanto è nel bel danzar la lizadria,*
> *L'arme faria riporre al Machabeo,*
> * A Salamon il senno, e al re Davit,*
> * Humiliare il crudel Heuristeo.*

> So gentle and angelic is the harmony
>   In the sweet music of Guglielmo, the Hebrew,
>   So much grace is in his beautiful dancing
> That Maccabeus would lay down his arms,
>   Solomon forget all his wisdom as would king David,
>   And he would make cruel Eurystheus feel ashamed of himself.

Filelfo ought to have known since he was, so to speak, visiting professor of literature in several cities of Italy where he had occasion to observe other dancing masters at work. He could not help comparing them with Guglielmo, and he came to the conclusion that Guglielmo "excelled all men in the dance."

When Duke Federigo died, in 1482, Guglielmo very likely left Urbino and may have come to Florence. He must also have been in touch with Lorenzo de Medici, because two of Lorenzo's dances, which he called Venus and Zauro, were incorporated in Guglielmo's work. The Florentines were fond of the pageants, of the festivals and processions, arranged by Lorenzo, and for all these not only musicians were needed; the dancing masters played a great part. Their sphere extended far beyond the mere teaching of dance steps and the composing of dance variations. Today they would also be called masters of etiquette. This can be seen from a paragraph in Guglielmo's manuscript in which he is concerned with carriage and the general deportment of the dancers. He advised the young ladies how to conduct themselves:

Her glance should not be proud nor wayward, gazing here and there as many do. Let her, for the most part, keep her eyes, with decency, on the ground; not however, as some do, with her head sunk on her bosom, but straight up, corresponding to the body, as nature teaches almost of herself. . . . And then at the end of the dance, when her partner leaves her, let her, facing him squarely, with a sweet regard, make a decent and respectful curtsy in answer to his.

Guglielmo's writings on the dance were not lightly undertaken, nor did he see their final aim in a mere compilation of dances and their instruction. Guglielmo tries to cover as much ground as possible; above all, he attempts to explain the fundamentals of dancing.

Dancing is an action, showing outwardly the spiritual movements which must agree with those measures and perfect concords of harmony which, through our hearing and with earthly joy, descend into one's intellect, there to produce sweet movements which, being thus imprisoned, as it were, in defiance of nature, endeavor to escape and reveal themselves through movement. Which movement of this sweetness and melody, shown outwardly (when we dance) with our person, proves itself to be united and in accord with the singing and with that harmony which proceeds from the sweet and harmonious song or from the measured sound we are listening to.

He thought a great deal of the relation of the dance to music. At that time music for the dance was based on four *voci principali* which—like many other things of the time, as for instance the human temperament—were linked with the four elements of earth, air, fire and water. Properly balanced, Guglielmo says, the four voices of the music fill the ears of the hearers with a most gentle sweetness,

so that they often stand still and listen. For they are constrained by this sweetness and melody to make some bodily movement, some external demonstration that shows what they feel within. The dance is derived from this melody, as an act demonstrative of its own nature. Without the harmony and consonance the art of dancing would *be* nothing and could *do* nothing.

The teaching of the dances proper was not always as simple as we may imagine. Through generations people had been used to dancing spontaneously, with steps more or less dictated by the mood of the moment. But now for the first time the dancing teachers aimed at precision, striving for elegance of movement and the memorization of a well defined vocabulary of steps. Any dance thus performed on a stage, instead of on one of the courtly ballroom floors, would have contained all the elements of theatrical dancing.

Guglielmo took the teaching very seriously. He must have given much thought to coordinating music and dancing, to making the dancer more aware of what he heard and how to translate the imageless music into dance figures. He says, for instance:

Let the dancer try a measure or two against the musical time. If he carries it through, it will afford him much pleasure, will sharpen his intellect, and make him attentive to the music . . . for everything is known and better understood by its contrary.

There were still other, though similar, tests. Particularly to test the beginner, have the dancer start against the time, Guglielmo suggests, and let the musician try to bring him into time. The skilled, of course, will not be confused. Likewise, one who knows how to dance will keep time, even though the musicians do their best to put him out by every known device. All these tests will show whether or not the dancer has grasped the principles of *misuro*, that is, the ability to keep time.

To cite a classical example of one of those early Renaissance dances, we may choose a *bassa danza* by Guglielmo. His *piatosa* belonged to those dances most widely known and done all over Italy at the time. His explanations are not always too clear, but they do give us a fair notion of the dance's conception.

The *piastosa* begins with two simple steps and one double step, commencing with the left foot. Then the dancers make a *ripresa* [a stepping backward, not quite clearly explained] on the right foot, while the man makes two *continenze*. [A *continenza* is a kind of leave-taking from the lady wherein he bows before her, then takes her by the hand and leads her back to where the dance began.] During the time of the *continenza* the lady goes from the hand of the man with two simple steps, beginning with the left foot again. Then the couple join hands and make two *riprese*, one on the left foot, the other on the right, and they follow it up with two *continenze*. Then they repeat all they have done so far and the gentleman returns to his place. The next step is a curtsy on the left foot, whereupon the gliding *bassa danza* is interrupted by two bars of the livelier *saltarello* followed by a curtsy of the man on the left foot. During the time of his curtsy the lady makes a half turn, then they go contrariwise, one to the other with two double steps, again beginning with the left foot. After a half turn on the right foot and two *riprese*, one on the right, the other on the left foot, they curtsy on the left. Now they go towards each other and, taking hands, make a *ripresa* on the left foot and then a full turn with two simple steps, commencing with the right foot this time, and a *ripresa* on the right followed by a curtsy on the left. And when all is done, it is repeated once more.

Whatever we may think of such dances today, they were revolutionary for the fifteenth century. A new style was created, the foundation laid for our ballet. The word itself derives from *balletti*, a diminu-
tive for *balli* which, in turn, was a technical term for all livelier dances
in contrast to the low, the *bassa*, dances.

In the beginning, the term *balletti* carried no theatrical meaning, it
simply referred to dance figures. However, after the Medici had
brought the Italian art of dancing to France, where it was destined to
reach undreamt-of perfection, the term *balletti*—or, in French, *ballet*
—gained dramatic significance.

Guglielmo wrote a great many *balli*, among them the famous "Colonnese," mentioned before. But he was more concerned with the basic
needs of the dancer than with anything else. He outlined six prerequisites for all dancers:

(1) *Misuro*: the dancer's ability to keep time according to the
    musical rhythm;
(2) *Memoria*: the ability to recollect the steps in correct sequence
    of the dance;
(3) *Partire del terreno*: the ability to judge the physical limits of
    the dance floor: briefly, the ability to do the right move-
    ment in space;
(4) *Aiere*: a somewhat obscure term which seems to denote a
    "certain swaying and upward movement of the body with
    the corresponding settling down";
(5) *Maniera*: descriptive of a certain movement in the style and
    manner of that time: "when one performs a single or a
    double step he should turn his body, so long as the move-
    ment lasts, towards the same side as the foot which performs
    the step, and the act should be adorned and shaded with
    the movement called *maniera*";
(6) *Movemento corporeo*: most likely meaning the ability to move
    gracefully.

Guglielmo Ebreo was probably unaware that he was outlining the
basic necessities for the artistic dancer of all times. All *he* intended
was to compose dances for courtly balls.

(—1954)

André Spire

❧〜♨〜☙

BABETTE DEUTSCH

AMERICAN poets of Jewish antecedents are not race-conscious to any great degree. It is true that James Oppenheim writes in the long rhythms of the Psalms, in the beautiful idiom of the Old Testament. Louis Untermeyer pleads for race-consciousness and enjoys playing on talmudic themes; but his vigor and passion express themselves most readily elsewhere. Perhaps the most significant poem about Jewry published here is *The Ghetto*, by Lola Ridge, herself an Australian Gentile. These States seem to offer conditions under which the process of assimilation is less painful. No David extends his withered right hand toward a forgotten Jerusalem.

In Europe the problem is older and infinitely more complicated. With all her other legends, the Continent has preserved that of the wandering Jew, the man without a country, the scapegoat and the accuser of the nations. The European Jew is more intensely aware of his isolation from established cultures, more sensible of his difference from those who suffer him to dwell among them. His assimilation is less easily perfected; he does not sell his ancient heritage with the same cheerful insouciance.

This difference between the American and the European Jew is vividly illustrated by the work of André Spire. Spire is a Frenchman. Race-conscious Franco-Jewish poets are few, and if I have chosen Spire rather than Eugène Manuel or Catulle Mendès, it is because he presents more clearly than either of these the peculiarities of the group to which they belong. The stream of Manuel's poetry ran humbly *"et fait peu de bruit."* His work as one of the founders of the Alliance Française is probably more important than the verse for which his friend Victor Hugo gave him a leaf from those golden laurels with which Paris crowned her hero. It is true that Manuel helped to carve out the path for an objective poetry, dealing with the works and days of simple unromantic people. But his Muse is stricken with moralism, and the preacher and the pedagogue do not easily mount Pegasus. As for Mendès, the "protean poet" and "prince of critics," who has also been placed in the first rank of French prose writers, he was so thoroughly assimilated that he cannot be seriously considered as a contributor to Jewish literature. Spire is neither so orthodox as Manuel nor yet so French as Mendès.

There is no doubt but that the country of Spire's adoption is full of profound associations for him. He has made a definite place for himself in French literature. He is admired by such close students of that literature as Richard Aldington, and he writes about the war with all the patriotic fervor and sincere sentimentality of a Frenchman. Even his technique is reminiscent of French rather than Hebrew poetry. And yet it is not only in his *Poèmes Juifs* (is there, in the United States, a poet who so frankly acknowledges his racial background?), not only in his multifarious quotations from the prophets and the propagandists for his people, that one finds Spire's deeper allegiance.

It is a bromidiom that the chief marks of the Jewish spirit are sensuousness and irony. From Isaiah to Heinrich Heine, and beyond, the tradition is sustained. In spite of a puritanical dislike of representation and ornament, one finds repeatedly the richness of Oriental imagery, the insistence upon the gratifications of the flesh, the appeal to the nostril and the palate, as well as to the ear and the eye. There are few poems in any literature that compare in this respect with the Song of Songs or even with the reproaches of a Jeremiah or the admonitions of a didactic Ecclesiasticus. It is the latter who declares:

> As a signet of carbuncle
> In a setting of gold,
> So is a concert of music in a banquet of wine.
> As a signet of emerald
> In a work of gold
> So is a strain of music with pleasant wine.

And withal, there is the note of rigorous simplicity and savage sarcasm. Death overshadowing all splendors. The bitter humor of the oppressed, who laugh that they may not weep. The denunciatory thunders of the spirit, ashamed of the flesh that is as grass. These qualities, so inseparable both from Jewish poetry and the poetry of Jews, are in a sense the elements of all great poetry.

Curiously enough, it is not because Spire's verse shows forth these essential qualities that one recognizes him as a Jew. He is not primarily a poet. He does not, his admirable admirers notwithstanding, communicate that rapture, that intensity, be it of the body or of the mind, which makes poetry a well of living waters. Reading these yellow-backed volumes, one wonders frequently how a man dares offer these fly-blown platitudes, this cloying stock-in-trade, this forensic bombast. A sophisticated age can have but little patience with these disappointing clichés, these stale and withered variations upon pointless themes. At first blush, Spire reminds one of Whitman, cataloguing with hospitable inclusiveness the details of those pageants which he witnesses or imagines, all the more as he employs Whitman's unrhymed cadences. To the Frenchman, however, he is more apt to suggest Victor Hugo, with his near-sighted romanticism, his astigmatic sentimentality. This is peculiarly true of Spire's more recent work. He writes with fatal facility about birth and death, about war and peace, about profiteers and the League of Nations. He watches the procession on the boulevards, and the fashionable ladies knitting for soldiers, with an equal eye. He thunders against the bourgeois, he delights duly in children and pigeons, with the same apparent indifference to his subject. And he infringes upon the canons of taste with appalling regularity in his insistent refrain regarding the "poet's" view of the universe. In a way, he is an artist killed by eclecticism, always a dangerous treasure to the Jew, as witness his tirelessly flaunted quotations, from Shakespeare, from D'Annunzio, from Goethe, from Renan, from street songs and from Pirke Aboth.

And yet even in his latest feeble murmurings there are clashes of proud timbrels. Spire's poetry is intensely real, even if it is seldom intensely realized. He lacks the inspired image. He fails of the enchanting music. But he has, after all, the divided soul of the Jew, the awareness of his isolation, of his difference. He bears within him the unhealed wound of secret battles: the scars of a chosen people. The finest example of this is in the poem addressed to "La Nation Juive," in honor of Balfour's declaration that Palestine would become once more the homeland of the Jewish people. This is in sharp contrast to the poem called "Exode," celebrating the hope of that event, which was written

over a dozen years earlier. "Exode" is composed in the spirit of jubila-
tion, with a fine disregard for the stern actualities of life rebuilt in
what is, after all, a strange land. "A La Nation Juive," though it opens
with pipes and cymbals, strikes an unresolved chord. *"Est-ce la fin de
l'exil,"* the poet demands, *"ou son commencement?"*

This ironic questioning, typical of some of the best in Jewish literature, seldom intrudes upon Spire's late observations. There are good
things here. "Insomnie" has a certain cerebral quality not to be ignored. "Nativité," a poem surprisingly woven around a litter of kittens,
has a charm. "Volupté," with its strong sense of kinship with the earth,
its bitter awareness of life, whose work is *"doucement refaire de votre
être une chose,"* is better than most of the verses with which it is
bound. The emphasized distrust of the gods and gauds of Parisian
civilization echoes the plaint of the prophet. But Spire, recalling to
Paris the downfall of Babylon, is not arresting. He becomes the
wandering Jew, lost in the mazes of the Bon Marché, and the position
is not sufficiently dignified to be tragic. The poet is pretentious rather
than precise. One returns, after all, to Spire's earlier work to find
that sad self-consciousness, those rough adjurations and solid realities
which are the substance of racial art.

Naturally enough, these are to be found primarily in his *Poèmes
Juifs.* But also in *Et Vous Riez,* marked by angry propaganda for the
oppressed of all nations, one comes upon lines of peculiarly Jewish
emotion. One of the first poems in this group, for example, "Un
Militant," concludes on a note characteristic of the *Poèmes Juifs:*

> Chante-moi, hurle-moi les hymnes fanatiques
> Des plèbes sans espoir!
> Ferme mes yeux, ferme mon coeur.
> Fais sonner à mes tempes
> Un jet obscur de sang boueux.
> Cache-moi tous les fruits et les fleurs de la terre;
> Arme-moi d'ignorance;
> Casque-moi de tristesse;
> Et pour sauver, un jour,
> Ces immenses troupeaux d'innocents qui périssent,
> Fais de moi, malgré moi,
> Une bouche qui crie et des bras qui se tendent.

"Casque-moi de tristesse": that is the ancient, reiterant cry of the Jew,
armored in the courage of despair. There is here, too, a curious poem

about Mary, the mother of God, which, while not necessarily Jewish in
its conception, exhibits an exotic irony. It begins:

> Ils te nomment Marie;
> Mais moi, je le sais, ton vrai nom.

An opening suggestive of the primitive reluctance to name the Unnam-
able One. And then, mid-way in the poem, the poet suddenly an-
nounces: "Injustice, je sais ton nom." It is injustice, then, whose womb
is ripe with the sacred fruit:

> Ils t'empoignent. Ils te détrônent.
> Ils te dévoilent . . . Tu es nue!
>
> Mais tu oins ton corps toujours jeune
> De l'huile subtile de tes pleurs.
>
> Tu ne te défends pas; tu glisses;
> Tu coules à travers leurs doigts.
>
> Et tu fuis, montrant ton gros ventre.
> Magicienne! Tu es enceinte! . .

Injustice and tragedy, poverty and unrest are the Jewish inheritance.
Spire, the agitator, hammers on these themes in the verse addressed
to the pariahs whom he loved, because they are "le seul prolétariat
en qui je puisse encore espérer." There is an interesting dialogue
toward the beginning of this volume, in which over and above the siren
voices there sounds the recurrent cry of the deserted and oppressed.
"Laissez-moi les aimer ces choses passagères," pleads the one. "—O mes
frères, ô mes égaux, ô mes amis," cries the other:

> "Peuple sans droits, peuple sans terre;
> Nation, à qui les coups de toutes les nations
> Tinrent lieu de patrie,
> Nulle retraite ne peut me défendre de vous."
>
> "Écoute, de nouveau leurs lamentations
> Jusqu'ici montent."

It is the strong sense of social justice on the one hand, and the desire
for ephemeral beauty, on the other—that beauty which social revolution must destroy before it can create—which makes the conflict this
poem expresses. And it is this conflict, tacit or explicit, which is Spire's
true strength. Especially noteworthy is the poem addressed to France,
for here the struggle becomes personal, and we see the poet, wounded
in his most intimate relations, seeking a vain reconciliation between

the country which is his home, the country which gave him the medium of his art, and the miserable race of pariahs who are his brothers in more than blood. The conflict is between the rationality and joviality of France and the Oriental mysticism and sense of tragedy which belongs to the Jewish tradition.

> Politesse, moi aussi tu voudrais m'affadir!
> Blague, tu voudrais jouer à rétrécir mon âme!
> O châleur, ô tristesse, ô violence, ô folie,
> Invincible génies à qui je suis voué,
> Que serais-je sans vous? Venez donc me défendre
> Contre la raison sèche de cette terre heureuse.

The division is re-emphasized in "Tu Es Content," with its quotation from Renan: "Israël aspire à deux choses contradictoires; il veut être comme tout le monde et être à part." Someone has spoken of a man carrying his ego in a sling. It might be said of Spire that he does the same with his Judaism. His nature is not whole: a limb of his soul is in splints, and he cannot help a certain human pleasure in the conspicuity of his wound. When he dines with a Christian, he must bear the broken member carefully, lest the furniture of the household jar it. When he goes into the streets and sees the poor and the sick and the mourners, he must look at his sling and remember that he too has suffered. He likes to repeat the ancient law, to insist on an indifference to gilded calves and precious ointments, things of the fugitive present, which distinguish the Jew from his Gentile neighbors. He quotes Zangwill on the Jewish pysche, with its disregard of form, its carelessness of art, its total immersion in reality, forgetting that art, philosophically considered, is also real. And, of course, he is most powerful where he yields to art most graciously, as in "Écoute Israël." Aside from the gratuitous beauty of the borrowed opening, the poem is significant for its original vision of the outstretched hand of God, a vision tinged with Job's melancholy rebellion:

> "Regarde donc sa main qui traîne sous les nues.
> Est-ce une main pour l'action?
> Est-ce une main d'ouvrier?
> Pas une ampules, pas une ride, pas une écorchure, pas un cal."

If anything were needed to clarify the eternal struggle in Spire between the Jew Solomon and the Jew Isaiah, or between the French poet and the Jewish prophet, one has only to glance at the first and last poem in this special group. The first puts away the theatres and the galleries, the toys and palaces of Paris for the lamentations of Israel:

Tu auras beau faire, me dit-elle, jamais tu n'aimeras vraiment leurs théâtres, leurs musées, leurs palais, leurs amusettes.
. . . Mets-toi en face de toi-même. Qu'est-ce fait battre ton cœur?
C'est, quand tu entends des voix un peu rauques; quand tu vois des mains un peu fievreuses, des yeux un peu serrés.
Quand la bouche qui demande ton aide te crie; tu me la dois. Car celui-la est ton frère, qui a ton âme; qui se declare ton égal.

Tu voudras chanter la force, l'audace;
Tu n'aimeras que les rêveurs désarmés contre la vie.

The last, "la fin des tristes poèmes," celebrates the burgeoning of the lilacs, the blossoming of the violets, the crowing cocks, the laughing girls: "Tout est clair, tout vibre, tout chante. . . .

"O Soleil, qu'ils soient durs ou justes,
Comme ça m'est égal, ce matin!"

It is hardly necessary to emphasize that if Spire is most a poet when he is least acquiescent, he makes our hearts beat faster when we are aware, with him, of his divided allegiance.

(—1922)

Letters from Pissarro

Introduction by JOHN REWALD

IN 1883 the twenty-year-old Lucien Pissarro left for England from the village near Paris where his parents lived. His father wrote many letters to the young artist, his oldest son: this correspondence continued until the master's death in 1903, at the age of seventy-three.

Camille Pissarro was concerned not only to advise his son about his career but to communicate his own deeply held convictions. The fact is that Pissarro had varied interests; literature and politics were almost as important to him as art, and he had a way of bringing to bear on whatever problem he approached a characteristic kindliness and wisdom.

In the following selections of letters, now published for the first time,* the painter expresses certain of his political and artistic views. Revealing a man without any pose, Pissarro's letters give us a precise account of his situation in life, his artistic development, and the part he played among his friends from the time the Impressionist movement finally broke up—the time at which this correspondence begins.

This is the period in which the old comrades who had fought together for so long, but had by no means won their fight, wavered and became irresolute; wanting to progress, each one strove to renew his art independently of the others. Doubt and discouragement seem to have seized hold of these audacious innovators. Some, like Cézanne, sought refuge in total solitude; others, like Renoir and Monet, abandoning their comrades, tried to exhibit at the official Salon; others still, like Gauguin, hoped to find new inspiration in far-off countries; while Pissarro turned to the new generation, wanting to guide it, and accept-

---

* These letters were translated from the original French by John Rewald and Lionel Abel. See the article on the life and works of Pissarro, by John Rewald (with reproductions of four of Pissarro's paintings), in *The Menorah Journal* for Winter 1939—ED.

ing in exchange a share of its ideas. To this new generation belonged his oldest son; and it was through his father that Lucien Pissarro came to be associated with Vincent van Gogh, Seurat, Signac, and other painters.

Lucien Pissarro, adopting Neo-Impressionism with his father, was closely linked with the originators of the movement. He worked at his father's side and was the first of Camille Pissarro's sons to exhibit with him. When Lucien finally settled in London and set up the press with which he published superb works illustrated with his own woodcuts or with engravings of his father's drawings, he called it the "Eragny Press" in honor of the village where his parents lived. Eragny was for him a symbol of sincere and careful workmanship. Thus Lucien went his own way, painting, drawing, working on his books in close collaboration with his wife, introducing in his turn his only child to the delights of art.

Uninterruptedly went the letters with their freight of ideas between father and son. It is clear, on reading this correspondence, that even in London Lucien was closer to Camille Pissarro than any other of his children.

I will calmly tread the path I have taken . . .

PARIS, May 4th, 1883

Duret left today for London. He promised to look you up; he will tell you about my exhibition. It goes without saying that I received not a few compliments. The ones I value most came from Degas who said he was happy to see my work becoming more and more pure. The etcher Bacquemond, a pupil of Ingres, said—possibly he meant what he said—that my work shows increasing strength. I will calmly tread the path I have taken, and try to do my best. At bottom, I have only a vague sense of its rightness or wrongness. I am much disturbed by my unpolished and rough execution; I should like to develop a smoother technique which, while retaining the old fierceness, would be rid of those jarring notes which make it difficult to see my can-

vases clearly except when the light falls in front. There lies the difficulty—not to speak of drawing.

An artist should have only his ideal in mind . . .

ROUEN, October 31st, 1883

M* finally left. The poor boy kept deferring his trip. However, I never
let him see how bored I was with his absurd conceptions, which if not
wholly wrong are certainly depressing. I did not want to hurt him, but
such reasonings could never lead to anything strong. He was fated by
his very logic to get nowhere.

"Why make studies from nature? Nobody appreciates them. I
dropped that, I made myself a jack-of-all-trades, I used every trick. . . ."

"And," I replied, "you are a success?"

"You see they didn't want good work; very well, I'll give them something for their money. . . ."

Ideas stemming from impotence, for an artist should have only his
ideal in mind. He lives poorly, yes; but in his misery one hope sustains
him, the hope of finding someone who can understand him; in three
out of four cases he finds this man. I know perfectly well that
tricksters, tricksters with real energy, heap up fortunes; but either
they pass by like clouds, or they know they are inferior, and feel
degraded. Of course, this is a question of temperament.

When you put all your soul into a work . . .

ROUEN, November 20th, 1883

You tell me that if I have a show in London I should send my best
works. That sounds simple enough; but when I reflect and ask myself
which are my best things, I am in all honesty greatly perplexed.

* A young painter whom Pissarro met in Rouen and advised.

Didn't I send to London my "Peasant Girl Taking Her Coffee" and my "Peasant Girl with Branch"? Alas, I shall never do more careful, more finished work; however, these paintings were regarded as uncouth in London. So it is not improper selection which explains why my works offend English taste. Remember that I have the temperament of a peasant; I am melancholy, harsh and savage in my works; it is only in the long run that I can expect to please, and then only those who have a grain of indulgence; but the eye of the passerby is too hasty and sees only the surface. Whoever is in a hurry will not stop for me. As for the young misses—touched, alas, with the modern neuroticism—they are even worse, the romantics were much less ferocious! If they looked into the past they would see to how slight a degree the old masters were—how shall I say?—precious, for they were indeed elegant, in the artistic sense of the word.

I have just concluded my series of paintings, I look at them constantly. I who made them often find them horrible. I understand them only at rare moments, when I have forgotten all about them, on days when I feel kindly disposed and indulgent to their poor maker. Sometimes I am horribly afraid to turn round canvases which I have piled against the wall; I am constantly afraid of finding monsters where I believed there were precious gems! . . . Thus it does not astonish me that the critics in London relegate me to the lowest rank. Alas! I fear that they are only too justified! However, at times I come across works of mine which are soundly done and really in my style, and at such moments I find great solace. But no more of that. Painting, art in general, enchants me. It is my life. What else matters? When you put all your soul into a work, all that is noble in you, you cannot fail to find a kindred soul who understands you, and you do not need a host of them. Isn't that all an artist should wish for?

From now on the novel must be critical . . .

Osny, December 28th, 1883
I am sending you *Les Fleurs du Mal* and the book of Verlaine. I do not believe these works can be appreciated by anyone who comes to

them with the prejudices of English or, what is more, bourgeois traditions. Not that I am completely in favor of the contents of these books; I am no more for them than for Zola, whom I find a bit too photographic; but I recognize their superiority as works of art; and from the standpoint of certain ideas of modern criticism, they have value to me. Besides, it is clear that from now on the novel must be critical; sentiment, or rather sentimentality, cannot be tolerated without danger in a rotten society ready to fall apart.

One must arm oneself at the start . . .

OSNY, January 14th, 1884

I had a long conversation with Alice; we talked of you. I told her to remind you to go to the academy, and seriously devote yourself to drawing the nude. To draw the figure you have to know anatomy. You need four or five months of work at the academy as a start; the thing to do is to discontinue when the weather gets better and then go back in the winter. If you could go just in the morning, that wouldn't be bad. When I went, I went only at night, so that I could paint during the day. But that is too much to expect of young Englishmen who go out in the evening, isn't it? But calculate that you have little time ahead. Soon you will have to support yourself, and then, beset by other needs, you will have to neglect certain studies. And besides, one must arm oneself at the start with everything necessary for the future fight.

Better to follow the great concepts of Justice . . .

OSNY, January 22nd, 1884

I keenly regret the bad turn Esther* has taken; it is a pity for she has intelligence. . . . Once at a concert we were admiring the splendid

* Camille Pissarro's English-born niece.

unity of the Lamoureux orchestra; she said to me, and with deep conviction: just as an orchestra needs a conductor, humanity needs a leader, a chief. I only had time to make this reply: but not without the consent of his collaborators, for otherwise everything would go to pot; thus there is a kind of contract between the musicians of an orchestra and its conductor, who is there simply because he is best able to direct the artists, but is not free to do whatever he pleases—from this it is a long way to authoritarianism! . . . She would have done better to follow the great concepts of Justice instead of withdrawing into a stupid, absurd, and narrow pietism.

The sweep of a great artist . . .

Osny, February 17th, 1884

In Rouen I bought a copy of Champfleury's *Histoire de la caricature,* an invaluable book with illustrations by Daumier. In it the whole story of Daumier is told. Looking through this book you see at once that Daumier was the man his drawings show him to be, a convinced, a true republican. And you feel in his drawings the sweep of a great artist who marched towards his goal but did not cease to be an artist in the most profound sense, so that even without legends and explanations his drawings are beautiful.

France is sick—she may die . . .

Paris, January 1886

On every side I hear the bourgeois, the professors, the artists and the merchants saying that France is finished, decadent, that Germany holds the field, that artistic France must succumb to mathematics, that the future belongs to the mechanics and engineers, to the big German and American bankers. As if we could foresee all the surprising things to come! Damn it, yes, France *is* sick, but what is the cause of her sickness? that's the question! She is sick from constant change; she may die, that is true; her fate depends on the other countries of Europe. If they are moving, even if ever so little, in the same direction, we shall see something new. Evidently things cannot remain as they are!

I am forced to beg people to buy . . .

ERAGNY, February 25th, 1887

This epoch is certainly full of stupidities. One has a reputation gained by many years of effort; one has drudged, despite your mother's constant remarks to the contrary; one has done the work of four to attain a true and proper renown, the kind won in fair fight. Bah! It is as if one had been singing to himself all the time; your bourgeois, when it is a question of rewarding such efforts, turns his back on you. Even people like Nunès,* to whom I have made concessions, seem to take me for an old idiot! . . . As a final humiliation, I am forced to beg people to buy one poor picture which cost me so much in toil. . . . It is all very discouraging.

I would much rather be a worker . . .

ERAGNY, May 31st, 1887

The fact that I can't sell my own works does not at all prove that I would have been a successful businessman; damn it all, I know how I would have made out: I would have gone bankrupt two or three times; in this I would even have been blameless; bankruptcy would have resulted, perhaps, from too great trust in my dear competitors, and hence be come by honestly. Into the bargain, I would not even have had the satisfaction of living by my ideas; what regrets! Besides,

* A distant relative of Pissarro.

it was not possible. I would much rather be a worker than a business-man who is actually nothing but a middleman or intermediary, and should properly conduct his business for the worker's profit. It is simply for being my agent that he takes the lion's share of the returns for my work! No, it is too idiotic.

Aren't we all under the influence of the milieu . . .

PARIS, May 7th, 1891

I sent you with the etchings an issue of the *Hommes d'Aujourd'hui,* which has a portrait of Cézanne by me and a critical note by Bernard. This ignorant fool claims that Cézanne for a time was under the influence of Monet. That is the limit, no? However, Gauguin knows all about the Cézanne studies done in Auvers, Pontoise and elsewhere! Zola himself noted—and, as I see it, correctly noted—by whom Cézanne was influenced.*

But I was wrong to speak of Bernard's ignorance; it is just sharp practice *à la* Gauguin. Bah! What's the point of this? Aren't we all, including the great Gauguin himself, under the influence of the milieu?

People have such peculiar ideas about me . . .

PARIS, December 8th, 1891

I lunched with Rodin yesterday. He has real charm. During our conversation he asked if I would like to see the Goncourt collection;

---

* Pissarro here alludes to the incontestable fact that it was he himself who had influenced Cézanne when the latter worked near him at Pontoise and Auvers-sur-Oise from 1871 to 1874. It was in this period that Cézanne purified his palette and changed his hitherto fiery execution for one based on impressionistic touches of color. Cézanne always openly admitted what he owed to Pissarro, and in 1904, after the death of his friend, even described himself as "Pissarro's pupil." It seems that the symbolists grouped around Gauguin and Emile Bernard, all ardent admirers of Cézanne, wanted to ignore the fact of his indebtedness in order to magnify him.

he promised to write me a note of introduction to the eminent novelist. Shall I go? . . . People have such peculiar ideas about me.

A march in a new direction . . .

ROUEN, September 30th, 1896

I am sending you an issue of *La Société Nouvelle;* read the article on "The Semitic God and the Aryan God," it is the last of a series. You will see that scientists clearly foresee a march in a new direction which will be neither neo-Christian nor Jewish.

The Dreyfus case is agitating public opinion . . .

ERAGNY, Sunday, November 14th, 1897

I am sending you a batch of newspapers which will bring you up to date on the Dreyfus case which is so agitating public opinion. You will realize that the man may well be innocent, at any rate there are honorable people in high positions who assert that he is innocent. The new brochure of Bernard Lazare which has just appeared proves that the document the General gave the press is a forgery. Lazare's contention is supported by twelve scientists of different nationalities. Isn't it dreadful?

The Third Empire has indeed been pernicious . . .

ERAGNY, January 13th, 1898

The Dreyfus case is causing many horrible things to be said here. I shall send you *L'Aurore* in which there are the very fine pieces of

Clemenceau and Zola. Today Zola accuses the General Staff. Ajalbert has published a very courageous article in the *Droits de l'Homme*, but the bulk of the public is against Dreyfus, despite the bad faith shown in the Esterhazy affair. I heard Guillaumin say that if Dreyfus had been shot at once, people would have been spared all this commotion! He is not the only one of this opinion! At Durand-Ruel's everyone took this view except for the door-man, and I heard many others speak that way too. Alas for a people so great in '93 and '48! The Third Empire has indeed been pernicious in its effects.

We are threatened with a clerical dictatorship . . .

PARIS, Hotel du Louvre, January 21st, 1898

I repeat that you should not worry; the anti-Semitic ruffians are much less noisy and aggressive since the beating they received at Tivoli Vauxhall, where they had organized an anti-Semitic demonstration. No, it is becoming clear now that what we are threatened with is a clerical dictatorship, a union of the generals with the sprayers of holy water. Will this succeed? I think not. Indignation against the General Staff seems to be growing here in the provinces, the socialists are active, it is possible that the clouds will lift. But will the review of the trial take place? No one knows. I hope it will not interfere with my work, for I am in high fettle.

One cannot with impunity conceal the truth . . .

PARIS, January 28th, 1898

Things are beginning to calm down around here; at least the demonstrators are keeping quiet. The trial of Zola is awaited impatiently; evidently he will be found guilty, for everybody declares that the Government is in the right and that Zola should have minded his own business. . . . There speaks prejudice, you see; but one cannot with impunity conceal the truth, sooner or later it will out.

England where you can expect a little more justice . . .

PARIS, February 10th, 1898

Things have hardly improved. You can read the account of Zola's trial in the *Daily News*. It is favorable to Zola since it was written by Duret. You will notice that all the witnesses for the prosecution were unwilling to answer the questions of Zola's attorney; nevertheless, the truth emerges, breaks through. Zola will be condemned just the same, the mob is against him, he will be condemned even against the evidence! No, the people want a tyrant, they unanimously assert the infallibility of the army. Poor France! Who could have imagined this nation, after so many revolutions, enslaved by the clergy like Spain! The slope is slippery.

And now I see that you are right to stay in England where you can expect a little more justice and common sense. Here I fear the end has come.

Anti-Semitism is now condemned even in the Chamber of Deputies . . .

PARIS, February 22nd, 1898

Don't worry any more about the Zola case. No new anti-Semitic outbursts. Anti-Semitism is now condemned even in the Chamber of Deputies: it is propagated only by immature idiots who do not even shout any longer. The Government is mighty sick of the whole affair, but does not know how to dispose of it; people are beginning to reflect. Grave, whom I saw yesterday, says it is all over, it will be hushed up soon like the Panama Canal scandal!

In the end free men will have the upper hand . . .

PARIS, Hotel du Louvre, November 19th, 1898

You need not worry about my safety here. For the moment we have
to deal with nothing more than a few Catholic ruffians from the Latin
Quarter who are favored by the Government. They shout "Down with
the Jews!" but all they do is shout. The healthy majority has come to
its senses and understands that the object of the shouting is to overturn
the Republic, or rather to make the Jesuits absolute rulers. I believe
and hope that in the end free men will have the upper hand. Yesterday,
at about five o'clock, while on my way to Durand-Ruel, I found myself
in the middle of a gang of young scamps seconded by ruffians. They
shouted "Death to the Jews! Down with Zola!" I calmly passed through
them and reached the rue Laffitte. . . . They had not even taken me
for a Jew. . . . Protests against the verdict in the Zola case abound
everywhere. All the intellectuals protest, and there are the socialists
who organize meetings; the day before yesterday the socialists and
the anarchists made a terrible row about the meeting of Rochefort and
the Jesuits. Who could have imagined such behavior from Rochefort?
The idiot, he lost his bearings this time. France is really sick, will she
recover? We shall see after Zola's trial. I wrote him a few lines to express my wholehearted admiration. Yesterday I received a card from
Mirbeau asking me to sign the protest with Monet and various others.
Despite the grave turn of affairs in Paris, despite all these anxieties,
I must work at my window as if nothing had happened. Let us hope
it will end happily.

Things change so quickly in France . . .

ERAGNY, December 28th, 1898

You should not worry so much about the events in Paris. Nothing
has appeared in the papers; people await impatiently the decision of
the highest court of appeal; it is difficult to know what is going on. . . .

Everything is so muddled, and the Jesuits are so strongly supported by the bourgeoisie, the nobles, and the Government itself. . . . But things change so quickly in France! And while the people are coming to their senses, nothing seems to be happening at this moment!!!

The Anti-Semites are beginning to be ridiculous . . .

PARIS, January 22nd, 1899

The Drefyus case is not progressing too quickly, but it is not going too badly either. The Chamber of Deputies voted against the reactionaries by big majorities several times in a row; the latter will certainly have a hard time going against the current. The anti-Semites and Esterhazyites are already beginning to be ridiculous, and that is always fatal!

Zola is dead—a terrible loss to France . . .

ERAGNY, October 3rd, 1902

You have heard that Zola is dead. It is a terrible loss to France! And coming after the Dreyfus case, it is, as you can see, a grave event. I sent my condolences to his widow, but I do not believe, considering my age, that I can attend the funeral. I would not dare follow the procession. . . .

(—*1943*)

THE PROMISE OF AMERICA

The Pilgrims and the Hebrew Spirit

❦

OSCAR S. STRAUS

OUR COUNTRY is fortunate in that the beginnings of its history
are not enveloped in clouds of tradition and superstition, as
is true of the older nations of Europe and Asia. Our history is an open
and legible book, and on anniversaries like this of the Pilgrim Tercentenary we can turn back to its earliest pages for guidance and
inspiration.

Three hundred years ago a little group of English Protestants from
among those who had twelve years before gone to Holland to escape
persecution, to find liberty and to follow the religious convictions
which had been denied them at home, embarked in a little ship for
the new world. Like the band of Gideon, they were reduced by elimination to one hundred and one souls, men, women, and children. They
were a plain, working folk, none of them, except William Brewster,
having had the advantages of a university training, and he only in
part; but their souls throbbed with determined purpose and noble
ideal, to worship God according to the dictates of their consciences.
Besides being intensely religious, they were a brave and determined
group of men and women, though ill prepared except in spirit to
endure the hardships and privations necessary to establish a home
and a civil community in a new world which was verily a savage land.
Their pilgrimage, in the light of developments, is the most epochal
event in the history of democracy and religious liberty. The ship that
brought this little group, the *Mayflower*, has acquired a fame beside
which the great leviathans of our day sink into insignificance. The fact
is, so large a number of our population lay claim to *Mayflower* ancestry,
that in order not to offend their pride we should in all politeness permit ourselves to believe that the *Mayflower* was indeed a leviathan.

"THE MODERN PEOPLE OF THE BOOK"

Their pilgrimage was determined by persecution in conflict with a sublime religious idealism. Together with the Puritan groups who began to come eight years later, they had such an intense and literal devotion to the Scriptures that they regarded themselves as the modern People of the Book. They drew their inspiration chiefly from the Hebrew Scriptures. It is a significant fact that the ancient People of the Book were destined to find liberty for the first time to worship God under the guarantee of equal laws, in the Commonwealth whose foundations were laid by "the modern People of the Book." It is eminently fitting, not only as Americans, but as American Jews that we should with an emphasized sense of patriotism unite in this historical celebration. It was only thirty-four years after the arrival of the *Mayflower* that the first group of Jewish immigrants who had settled in Barbados and in Brazil (when the latter country was again conquered by Portugal), in order to escape from the agents of the Inquisition came in their Mayflower, the ship *Santa Catarina*, to Manhattan.

The relationship between the Jewish refugees from Spain and Portugal and the Brownists and other English Separatists who were refugees in Amsterdam, began in Holland in the decade preceding the departure of the Pilgrims from Delft Haven. Leonard Busher in his book written under the influences of these exiles, entitled *Religious Peace or a Plea for Liberty of Conscience*, published in 1614, made a plea for the extension of religious liberty to Jews.[1] Amsterdam was at that time the seat of a flourishing Jewish community, some of whose members, according to Lucien Wolf, came into contact with the philo-Jewish refugees. At the very beginning of the Civil War in England, the Royalist spies in Holland reported that the Jews sympathized with the Republic, and even alleged that they had offered the rebels "considerable sums of money to carry on their designs."[2]

The great heroes of the Old Testament with the fear of God in their hearts, and the Judges of Israel, freeing the oppressed people from foreign domination, were the favorite characters of the Puritan warriors. In the Books of Joshua, Judges, Samuel and Kings, they

[1] *Menasseh Ben Israel's Mission to Oliver Cromwell*, by Lucien Wolf, XVIII, Tracts of Liberty & Conscience—1614–1661 (Hanserd Knowllys Society).
[2] Hist. MSS. Com. Rep. VII MSS. of Sir F. Graham, 401–405.

saw their own condition portrayed. Oliver Cromwell compared himself to Gideon the Judge. He said, "Great is my sympathy with this poor people, whom God chose and to whom He gave His law."

THE HEBREW COMMONWEALTH AS A PURITAN PATTERN

The politics of Puritanism was developed from its theology, and that politics, which was derived from the Hebrew Commonwealth, was opposed to monarchy. The King of kings was enough for them. Their formula was: "No bishop, no king." The Puritans were undertaking to found and organize a State. The Christian Scriptures contained nothing direct and specific for aiding this object. As Ellis, one of the leading authorities on the Puritan Age, says: "It was the Old Testament that furnished the Puritan pattern." He maintained that if the Colonies of Massachusetts had been Episcopalian there might have been no American Revolution.[3]

We need not, however, depend upon speculation. The evidence as to the influence of the Hebrew spirit and political structure of the Hebrew Commonwealth upon the origin of American democracy is definite and direct. The Hebrew Commonwealth was explained and held up as an example in the sermons and writings of the Separatists in Amsterdam and among the Fifth Monarchy Men and by the Levellers or ultra Republicans in England. Some of the latter even called themselves Jews and were formally received into the Amsterdam synagogue. As is well known, the New England Puritans, with the Old Testament as a model, established as their first form of government a "Theocracy," in which the Church brethren usurped the powers of the God of Israel. In this they followed the letter rather than the spirit of their biblical model, failing to make allowance for differences of opinion in time, conditions and circumstances. Growing out of the intensity of their religious spirit, they became as narrow as the Established Church and even more intolerant of differences of opinion. Their aim during this period was not to establish democracy but theocracy; but the logic of events is so often more potent than policy, that the example they held up as their guide, the Hebrew Commonwealth, developed on lines of a democracy. They based their theocracy and claim for uniformity upon the Ten Commandments, and here is where they struck their first rock. The Moses who

[3] *The Puritan Age in Massachusetts,* by George E. Ellis, pp. 139 and 174.

caused the pure waters of religious liberty and democracy to flow from that rock was Roger Williams.

The Commandments were divided into "Two Tables." The first table concerns the duties which man owes to God, as those of religion. The second table defines the duties which men owe to one another. Roger Williams took his determined stand that the civil power had no jurisdiction over the matters contained in the first table. Because of his advocacy of this doctrine he was banished. He founded his little commonwealth upon that principle which he characterized as Soul Liberty—the separation of Church and State. Verily, the stone the builders rejected became the cornerstone of our American system—a free Church in a free State.

THE SCRIPTURAL ARGUMENT FOR DEMOCRACY

The Rhode Island experiment which throughout New England it was predicted and hoped would be a failure, served as a grateful place of refuge from intolerance and persecution in Massachusetts and in other American colonies, and under the guiding direction and spirit of Roger Williams became a success. The success of the Rhode Island experiment served as a concrete proof, contrary to the opinion of the Christian world, that an orderly State could be developed with Church and State separated and with full liberty in religious matters.

The contention that democracy as evidenced by the Hebrew Commonwealth and not monarchy was the God-given government, was carried forward in all of the New England colonies by the leading ministers from 1633 until the adoption of the Constitution of the United States. In the year 1633 each of the Governors and Assistants in the New England colonies appointed ministers to preach sermons immediately following the election. These sermons, known as "Election Sermons," were of a political religious nature. In them the arguments were stressed against the claim of Parliament and King to bind the colonies in all cases. Political and theological arguments were united. It was urged, says John Adams, that if Parliament could tax the colonies, it could, by the same token, establish the Church of England and prohibit all other churches.[4]

Time does not permit me to refer in detail to the many sermons

[4] *Works of John Adams,* x–87.

that were preached by the leading divines during the period I have mentioned, all holding up the Hebrew Commonwealth as a model for American democracy. I will instance only a few. Jonathan Mayhew, no less a statesman than a divine, who first suggested the idea of a Committee of Correspondence between the colonies, in his sermon on the "Repeal of the Stamp Act," developed in fullest detail the Scriptural argument that the Hebrew Commonwealth was the God-given government, that He gave Israel a king in His anger because they had not sense and virtue enough to continue God as their King.

AMERICAN STATESMEN AND THE "REPUBLIC OF ISRAEL"

Similar arguments were advanced by Samuel Langdon, D.D., the president of Harvard College, who was afterwards a member of the New Hampshire Convention for the adoption of the Constitution. In his election sermon in May, 1775, he maintained that the Hebrew Commonwealth according to its original constitution was divinely established and was a perfect Republic. A later sermon delivered at Concord in 1788 he entitled: "The Republic of the Israelites an Example to the American States." Sermons upon similar texts were delivered before the representatives of the New England colonies by Dr. Stiles, president of Yale College, Rev. George Duffield, Samuel West, Simeon Howard, and many others. This argument, putting forward the Hebrew Commonwealth in support of a democratic form of government as the God-given, and as opposed to a monarchy, was advanced with great force and effect by Thomas Paine in his *Common Sense*, which was so highly praised by Washington. As Dr. Rush phrased it, its effect "has rarely been produced by types and paper in any age or country." The former part of this book is devoted to the subject of "Monarchy and Hereditary Succession." The argument is drawn entirely from the Hebrew Commonwealth and he instances the refusal by Gideon to accept the offer to make him king. He quotes in full Samuel's warning, and concludes with these words: "These portions of the Scriptures are direct and positive; they admit of no equivocal construction. That the Almighty hath here entered his protest against monarchical government is true, or the Scriptures are false."

The Scriptural argument for democracy based upon the Hebrew Commonwealth was advanced in the conventions of many of the States before which the Constitution came for adoption. In New York, reference was made to it by Chancellor Livingston and more fully by John Lansing and John Smith.

As a remarkable evidence of how thoroughly the history of Israel influenced the thoughts of the leading statesmen who framed and adopted the Declaration of Independence, the following circumstance is impressive. On the same day that the Declaration was adopted, a committee was appointed to prepare a device for a seal of the United States. The committee consisted of Franklin, Adams, and Jefferson. The device they proposed was with the reverse representing Moses standing on the shore extending his hand over the sea causing it to overwhelm Pharaoh, and around it the legend: "Rebellion to tyrants is obedience to God."

The new England Puritans took up the age-long conflict between obedience enjoined as a divine right and the freedom claimed as a human right. In the beginning they endeavored to misappropriate that freedom in support of religious uniformity. They failed as they deserved to fail. The different sects dominant in the several colonies, and the differences among the Puritans themselves, militated against uniformity and therefore against the establishment of religion in any form. This fortunate divergence in matters of religion made possible in the first instance the union of the colonies and thereafter the United States of America.

THE TRIUMPH OF RELIGIOUS FREEDOM

The statesmen who framed our government were well versed in the history of nations and fully recognized that the union of Church and State had contributed more than all other causes to redden the Christian centuries with blood. America was the first among the nations of the world not to *accord toleration* but to *guarantee liberty* in matters of religion, without discrimination or restriction. The influence of the American system throughout the world cannot be measured. Charles Sumner, in his "Prophetic Voices Concerning America," says: "The national example will be more puissant than the Army and Navy for the conquest of the world."

On anniversaries like this, how wholesome it is to cast our eyes backward so that we may look forward with more clearness and with renewed confidence in the principles of our democracy, and with that confidence be ever watchful that "the Republic shall receive no harm." Whatever political theories and panaceas the oppression in other lands has given rise to, they have no place in our system, a system which has stood the test of time as best adapted to conserve and advance the principles of democracy and the rights of man under organized government, in accord with his needs and justified demands in our progressive age.

(—1920)

What Do We Owe to Peter Stuyvesant?

I. M. RUBINOW

RECENTLY there was widespread criticism in the American Jewish community because in a certain large city a group of Gentiles addressed an appeal to the Gentile population to come to the financial assistance of the local Federation of Jewish Charities. Said *Every Friday,* energetic paper of the energetic Cincinnati community: "In 1652, Peter Stuyvesant, Governor of New Amsterdam, now New York, received the promise from the Jews who came to settle there that the Jews would care for their own poor. Ever since then the Jews of this country have prided themselves that this sacred promise which the first Jewish settlers in America made has never been broken."

This curious quotation is interesting, not only in reference to the local and temporary issue which called it forth, but also for its revelation of the basic theory underlying Jewish philanthropy in America. Indeed, in these sentences there is expressed the fundamental philosophy which has ruled the economic and social relationship of the four million American Jews to the country as a whole.

For the paragraph quoted above is not exceptional. In some form or another, the same statement has been made and repeated a thousand or a thousand thousand times, from the platform, in popular articles, even in serious books. In fact, time was when no discussion of Jewish philanthropy in America could begin without reference to our promise to Peter Stuyvesant. In the only comprehensive work on Jewish philanthropy in America, the late Dr. Boris D. Bogen said: "The Jews did not forget the promise given two and a half centuries previously to Governor Stuyvesant ever to care for their poor in such a manner as they should never become a burden upon the community. American Jews have fulfilled their pledge."

Now, the historic accuracy of the statement is, of course, a problem primarily for specialists. But whether the views expressed represent

sound social ethics and good social work, whether it ought to continue serving as the basis of our communal life, is a problem for all
of us. I propose, therefore, to examine somewhat critically the above
statements and the underlying theory.

Is the promise to Peter Stuyvesant a pledge that still remains binding upon the Jewish community?

Has American Jewry in fact kept the pledge so sacredly?

Can American Jewry continue carrying the entire responsibility for
"their own poor"?

Does the exercise of such communal responsibility offer a satisfactory basis for meeting the problem of poverty and distress?

Is the effect of this tradition under present economic and social
conditions productive of good or harm?

This is primarily, therefore, a socio-economic study and not a historical one. To be quite candid, the historic accuracy of this legend
is a matter of minor importance. But having once made the historic
allusion, one might as well dwell upon the point for a moment.

Is it good history? If we made the promise, just what kind of a
promise did we make?

Here is a somewhat more comprehensive and let us hope more
accurate statement of what happened two and a half centuries ago
than the customary one. I realize that from the point of view of a
professional historian, *Justice to the Jew,* by Rev. Madison C. Peters,
may not appear a very learned or reliable source, but the account
it gives is at least somewhat more detailed and substantial than the
broad statements quoted earlier, and from the point of view of the
general reader it may suffice.

"At this time the Governor was Peter Stuyvesant, a stern, unbend-
ing, narrow-minded bigot, whose veins had been inoculated with the
virus of Calvinism and to whom all other sects were insufferable, especially the Jews. Therefore, with characteristic alacrity, despite his
wooden leg, he began preparation to have the Jews banished from
the community. He petitioned his employers, the Dutch West Indies
Company, for permission to drive them beyond the pale of the New
Netherlands, but the worthy directors were more tolerant than their
representative, to whom they replied, saying that this request was
inconsistent with reason and justice. To further show their disappro-
bation of Stuyvesant's bigotry, they passed an Act permitting the

Jews to reside and trade in New Netherlands, stipulating that they, the Jews, would care for their own poor, to which they willingly acquiesced."

If this is the famous promise, it should not be too difficult to defend the Jews against any action against them in any court of public opinion for its breach. Obviously, this promise, if it was a promise, was obtained under duress, under the threat of expulsion. Besides, isn't a promise, if it was a promise, given by the handful of Portuguese Jews *ultra vires* as far as the German, Russian, Polish, Rumanian and other Jews are concerned? And, after all, the promise, if it was a promise, was made to the Dutch West Indies Company and New Netherlands, and the Dutch West Indies Company and New Netherlands are no more. And one doesn't have to be very clever to think up many more equally good arguments, serious or otherwise.

If the fear of the threat of compulsion was responsible for Jews acquiescing to the condition or making the promise, it is a similar fear of discrimination, of national and religious antagonism, that has been largely responsible for American Jews keeping the promise or pretending to do so. Around this fear has crystallized a curious mixture of holy tradition, race pride, and a typical Jewish sense of group guilt which has definitely colored the theory and practice of Jewish philanthropy and social work, and much of the social philosophy of the American Jewish community. Until finally, necessity, or what seemed to be necessity, has been made into a virtue.

Just why did the appeal in Boston from non-Jews to non-Jews on behalf of Jewish poor stir up American Jewry? Was it because we found it damaging to our pride, discrediting to our economic status or reputation for charity? Was it because we instinctively felt it to be a revelation of an unpleasant truth? Was it because we still live in a ghetto and are afraid to disclose our sores to the enemy?

If it was pride, is the pride justified? Have we, as a matter of fact, always taken care of our own poor in this country? If we have made the promise, can we really claim to have kept it?

Far be it from me to deny the well-known generosity of Jewish philanthropy in this country as judged by comparison with non-Jewish groups. Figures available indicate the average family supported by Jewish relief philanthropic agencies receives about twice as much in relief as non-Jewish families from non-sectarian agencies. I believe that in every city where Jewish philanthropic federations exist side by side with the non-sectarian Community Chests, the per capita contribution for the Jewish population is considerably higher than for the general population. In many cities (though there are some sad exceptions) where all-embracing Community Chests exist, it is again a matter of pride with leading Jews that the Jewish contribution to the Community Chest should be greater than the amount required by Jewish agencies. It hardly seems necessary to overburden the reader with much statistical evidence to establish what is so generally conceded.

And of these things we Jews are proud, perhaps justly so. I say "perhaps" deliberately. For even in this respect there is considerable room for discussion, since it has not yet been established with equal degree of statistical accuracy that the Jewish voluntary contribution to general civic and social needs is in excess of what would be its fair proportion, according to Jewish population and economic resources. It is, for instance, claimed that the total amount expended for such purposes, including colleges, universities, libraries, museums, hospitals, churches and similar institutions, reaches some three billion dollars per annum. The four million Jews constitute approximately six percent of the urban population of the United States, and it has not yet been established that the Jews contribute the 200 million dollars per annum which is their proportionate share. It is true that within the last few years Jewish contributions to many of these cultural purposes have been increasing. It is significant, for instance, that individual Jewish contributions ranging from five to ten million dollars have been made during the very year when the problem of insufficient funds for Jewish philanthropy has arisen.

However, the consideration of this problem is really somewhat beyond the scope of this discussion. After all, no one has said that the Jews promised the one-legged gentleman to build University Stadiums, Airports or Halls of Fame. In Peter Stuyvesant's time, luckily for us, these somewhat fancy things had not even been foreseen.

We did, however, promise, or at least we were forced to promise, to support all our poor. Have we done that?

Let us, therefore, come somewhat more closely to the specific problems of poverty and relief.

Injured Jewish workmen receive large amounts through compensation legislation. Jewish widows are in the lists of most widows' and mothers' pension funds. Presumably among the 50,000 men and women over 70 years of age that will have been put on the roster of the New York Old Age Security scheme, there will be no dearth of Jewish names.

The plain, unadorned truth, therefore, is that the Jews have not singly and entirely supported their own poor. They haven't kept their promise.

But the Jews have not yet been expelled from the country for their failure to keep their promise. Nor are they likely to be. For times have changed.

Such a promise as the Jews made—to accept the responsibility for "their own"—may have been not only diplomatic but fair and just in its own day and generation. It was based upon a certain definite social philosophy which, like all other social philosophies, derived its strength from a certain social structure. Two hundred and fifty years ago, and perhaps even fifty years ago, poverty may have been primarily a result of individual factors, or, at most, group or racial factors. The shrewd business people who signed that blank check 250 years ago accepted this theory of responsibility; and probably they felt they had good reasons to believe that the amount to be written in need never become a very heavy burden.

But conditions today are different. Vastly so! Instead of the quarter of a million of Jews of scarcely a generation ago, we have four million and a quarter. Instead of a country of small individual enterprise, America has become the greatest industrial country in all the world and in all history. Instead of simple society to which strong but simple minds could escape from the perplexities of European civilization, America has become the most complex organization in the world.

In this America of today, no individual, or race or group, can live alone. An excited rumor within one square block near Wall Street destroys fortunes of thousands of people scattered over hundreds of thousands of square miles. A change in an automobile model may throw hundreds of thousands of men and women out of work. Even though there be a great deal of racial, national or religious concentration in economic activity, we are nevertheless all bound together in our economic life, the 125 million of us. It may not be accurate to say that we always all stand and fall together; but in this mad rush which we call American life no one may be responsible for his own fall, or be particularly proud of having escaped it.

Why, then, under these conditions of our modern American life this somewhat naive, antiquated emphasis upon Jewish isolation in philanthropic work aimed at dealing with the problems of economic distress?

Of course, it may be argued with a good deal of conviction that the veneration of this historic tradition, even though it be based upon very poor history and very poor sociology, has served a useful purpose. It has encouraged giving; it has helped to hold Jewish communities together; and it has met the problem of the Jewish poor. So, judging principles, conventions and theories by their pragmatic use rather than their abstract scientific truth, it has been a good thing.

Perhaps it has been a good thing—with the emphasis upon the "has." But if it should appear that in our day and generation it has ceased to be a constructive force, that its destructive implications are much more powerful, then it may be found necessary to abandon the rather pretty social myth.

To begin with, we are not even altogether certain that even in the past, the recent past of large Jewish immigration, the past that really matters, it has been quite as successful as we often imply it was in meeting the problem of the Jewish "poor." We are aware of the rise of thousands of conspicuous individual Jewish fortunes. We are also aware of the general improvement in the life of the Jewish working masses during the last fifty years. But as to the squalor and misery and want and disease that accompanied these individual successes and this general improvement during the self-same fifty years, as to that there are no figures. The science of social statistics, the quest for accurate data concerning social conditions, has not developed in this country until very recently indeed. Not an inconsiderable proportion of Jewish immigrants since 1881 have already died. And, except for picturesque literary reminiscences, we have little accurate information on record as to the amount and degree of economic suffering of the Jewish masses of America during the last thirty or forty years.

After all, did the country which admitted them so freely do so fairly by these immigrants? Did the older Jewish community, which so definitely expressed their own responsibility, really meet it at the time? The scientific material for such a study has by this time been hopelessly lost; and individual memories are not very trustworthy. It is safest not to be too proud of the way American Jewry actually met the problem of "their own poor" in the past.

However, it is the present and the future that presents a much more important responsibility.

Business cycles—the mad zigzag of periods of economic prosperity and depression—are not new things in American history. Yet apparently in times of prosperity our memories somehow never go back to the leaner years; otherwise, it might be reasonable to assume, we would have by this time discovered some method of preventing or at least relieving the frightful suffering of depressions and periods of unemployment. Or failing in that, we might at least have learned to expect them.

Yet we let the recent period of prosperity lull us into a feeling of complete social security. Social workers and contributors alike began to feel so safe, indeed, that numerous community enterprises were advocated, not primarily because of their intrinsic necessity, great as that may have been, but in order to find an outlet for the social, the communal and the philanthropic motive in the heart of the large giver, which in a completely and permanently prosperous America no longer found its customary objective. Weren't we just five years ago definitely assured that the volume of Jewish dependency has been decreasing rapidly? "It is now half that of fifteen years ago. Within the next three years, the problem will again be halved. . . . We must look forward to a radical revision of program, to a redirection of released energies."[1]

And then came the jolt. I hope no one will suspect me of any malice in reminding the reader of an old controversy begun at a meeting of the National Conference of the Jewish Social Service in Denver, in 1925, continued at the meeting of the same Conference in Cleveland, in 1926, and concluded (though not finally disposed of) in the hospitable pages of *The Menorah Journal*.[2] There is little joy and surely no reward in being a Jeremiah, nor can I make any particular claim to wisdom because a quarter of a century of statistical training and experience had taught me some healthy skepticism in regard to the permanency of temporary fluctuations.

Certainly the present economic situation and the present state of Jewish philanthropy make it amply clear that any expectation the Jewish community cherished of the disappearance of the need for Jewish relief was quite groundless. There is evidence enough now to indicate that while so short a time ago we were talking of the complete liqui-

[1] Hyman Kaplan, "Visible Effects of the Present Immigration Policy in the Work of Jewish Family Welfare Agencies," Proceedings of National Conference of Jewish Social Service (Denver, Colorado, 1925), pp. 116–17.

[2] See "The Future of Local Charities," by I. M. Rubinow, in the August, 1927, issue; and "The Passing of Poverty," by Hyman Kaplan, in the January, 1928 issue of *The Menorah Journal*.

dation of the Jewish poor, we were all sitting on a powder magazine, or, to change the simile, living in a Fool's Paradise. The blow has fallen. The cycle has turned. What do we see? In almost every Jewish community, exactly as in non-Jewish communities, the demand for relief has increased by leaps and bounds. The statistics of Dr. Samuel H. Goldsmith for the Jewish community, and those of Dr. Ralph Hurlin of the Russell Sage Foundation for the general community, tell the story beyond any shadow of doubt. In every Jewish community the available resources for relief have been strained to the utmost. And if the crisis is felt in some communities more than in others, the differences are most often due to differences in degree of communal aid available than to the need present.

It still remains true that Jewish relief agencies have shown a greater sensitiveness, a greater anxiety to meet the situation than many Catholic or Protestant agencies. We do not need any statistical evidence of the effect of the sight of need and suffering on the generous Jewish heart. Long before the catastrophic aggravation of the unemployment situation had stirred all agencies, governmental, semi-public or private to feverish activity, Jewish organized philanthropy had reacted to the problems of mass distress. But, what does not appear in the figures, what is much more difficult to establish statistically, is the extent to which private relief, whether Jewish or non-Jewish, has failed.

Immediately after the November collapse a leading Jewish social worker of the country, Dr. Solomon Lowenstein, in a brave article in the *Survey*, on the basis of results of campaigns then held, endeavored to demonstrate that, in face of this collapse, both Jews and non-Jews were bent on following the slogan, "Charity as usual." The figures appeared convincing, yet I confess that I, for one, could not avoid a feeling of apprehension. This attitude was too much of a piece with the whole unsound social psychology of the American propertied classes immediately after the business collapse. There could be no break in American prosperity. There could be no economic defeat. It was all a horrible nightmare from which we were bound to awaken. It was all psychological, anyway. We will refuse to get panicky. We will not reduce our standard of living and spending. We will prove to each other and to ourselves that prosperity is here to stay. If necessary, we shall even prove it by large subscriptions to charities.

However praiseworthy as an attitude, it simply couldn't stand up. And that it didn't stand up was clearly and rapidly shown by the campaigns and drives which followed. In face of much greater effort on the part of both lay leadership and professional direction, comparative failures of campaigns both for general local philanthropic needs, as well as for various national causes, and especially for foreign relief, have been reported from dozens of cities, many of which (like Philadelphia or Cincinnati) had for many years been justly proud of their record for philanthropic generosity. Campaigns are being postponed. Collections of old subscriptions have fallen off. Many subscriptions are being repudiated. Economy and retrenchment have become the slogan. Activities are being eliminated, and the profession of social work is in a state of panic, both for its own future and for the preservation of high (and therefore expensive) standards of work.

And now that we have sobered up and counted up our losses and begun to estimate our prospects for the future, we have had to come to these conclusions: first, that even Jewish philanthropy is subject to inexorable law, that its resources must become more restricted as the result of the very forces which make for an increasing demand; and, second, that *voluntary* group responsibility is bound to be found inadequate in meeting the serious social problem of mass distress.

What shall be the answer of the Jewish social worker to this very real and very serious social problem—this very real and very serious impasse of rising need and falling resources? Shall he simply exercise more energetically the old methods of persuasion? Shall he beg and cajole and exhort even more than he has done in the past in the hope that he may thus achieve the needed increase in the flow of philanthropic contributions? That, of course, is the easiest way theoretically, though certainly not the line of least resistance, considering what the resistance on the part of the public is likely to be, particularly in view of the ever-growing competition among the numberless appeals. But it is the straight path—when wider perspectives are carefully eliminated by blinders; and, as a matter of fact, it still remains the most popular answer to the problems so far presented. Perhaps it is even a noble gesture. "We are bound to pay our debt to Peter Stuyvesant." But it is an answer which doesn't disclose any constructive social thinking on the part of the professional social worker.

Shall we appeal to the Gentiles? But that, too, has already been tried and perhaps more frequently than is generally known. The outburst of virtuous indignation because of such appeals is interesting, but not impressive. Non-Jewish contributions to Jewish drives and campaigns are not at all as rare as this indignation would seem to imply. Such contributions have been gratefully received in the open, and it seems to be a justifiable assumption that they have been diplomatically solicited on the inside. Nor can one at all believe that the Jewish community has lost its virtue through such appeals. If it be true that the Jewish community finds itself in distress, and if the outside world has available funds, then such appeals appear quite justified.

There are, however, much more potent arguments against dependence upon relief from the non-Jewish part of the community than that of Jewish pride or Jewish responsibility. There is absolutely no evidence to support the theory that, in times which are hard for Jewish philanthropic activities, the remainder of the community has an available surplus. In fact, all the evidence points to quite the contrary conclusion. For, of course, it is not only the Jewish poor who have felt the pressure of the recent economic changes. The gruesome picture which any careful reader of newspapers could garner during the last six months, including soup kitchens, bread lines, overcrowded lodging houses, flop houses, increased begging, and increased suicide and general mortality rate—this picture has no racial or religious traits.

The method of appealing to the non-Jewish community for help to meet the need of the Jewish poor is indeed an immoral one, but for a more fundamental reason than the one more commonly given. Its immorality lies not so much in the breaking away from the "sacred tradition that the Jews must take care of their own" but in the silent implication that problems of poverty and distress can be met in no other way except through appeal to voluntary generosity—to a narrow group generosity if sufficient, and to the broader but still voluntary generosity of the larger community if absolutely necessary; the implication that no other more effective methods exist.

It is in this direction that the Jewish community may be committing a serious error. And insofar as the Jewish social workers are depended upon to shape the social policies of their communities, they may be carrying a serious responsibility. They are supposed, if not to lead, at least to point the way. The over-emphasis of Jewish communal responsibility for "their own poor" in total disregard of what is known in Europe as *"Soziale Fuersorge"* or *"prévoyance sociale"* has been harmful even in prosperous days. It may become dangerous in days such as these.

In one of the largest Jewish communities the private relief agency almost discourages widowed families from claiming the widows' pension that is theirs by right by offering them a more generous rate of assistance. In another large Jewish community a few years ago, when the question of a municipal appropriation for relief of unemployed had arisen, Jewish leadership remained inactive on the plea that "we Jews will be able to meet the situation." Not only did this attitude deprive the Jewish dependent of a certain amount of aid that might be made available, but the entire movement to a very large extent remained without Jewish participation, and to that extent was weakened. Illustrations of this character could be multiplied.

Group pride thus may easily become a definite reactionary force. Consider the wider implications of this attitude. Much of the progressive social and labor legislation in this country dealing with wages, accident, compensation, housing reform, public recreation, etc. has been to a very large extent influenced by efforts of American social workers. Hull House, the A. I. C. P. (Association for the Improvement of the Condition of the Poor), the larger schools of social service, the National Conference of Social Workers—these have been the powerhouses from which came to a large extent the moving force for development of broad social programs. How few and far between have been the Jewish social workers active in the movement! How many programs of social reform have been advocated or even discussed at the National Conference of Jewish Social Service? Insofar as this Conference was dealing with problems of interest to the Jewish minority group alone, such reticence is perhaps understandable. It is, one may say, consistent with the Peter Stuyvesant philosophy. It represents the obverse side of the same social attitude. The Jews must take care of their own. By the same token they must not meddle too much in the corresponding problems of the country as a whole. As a result, and to the extent to which the fundamental problems of American economic life have been kept within the narrow limits of group philanthropic interest, the Jewish profession has kept outside of the progressive current of American life.

The majority of Jews in America, even the leading Jews, both the generous contributors as well as the professional social workers, have

either themselves come from Europe or are only one generation removed from it. May not the question be asked whether in the praiseworthy anxiety to adapt themselves to the new environment they have
not too quickly and too completely embraced the prevailing individualistic American philosophy, that what in Europe constitutes a proper
domain of social policy must in America remain and can be better
achieved as an enterprise in private philanthropy? So anxious have we
been to adopt this prevailing philosophy that many of us have failed
to notice the powerful critical reaction against it among American
leaders of social thought who had no foreign dust to shake from their
shoes.

Workmen's compensation, mothers' pensions, old age security, and
in the future the possibility of health and unemployment insurance,
these movements—except for the interval occasioned by the post-
War reaction—have been growing for over two decades. In their
achievement we have played almost an insignificant part—surely a
very much less significant part than Jews have played in the development of similar policies throughout Europe. If the cause of such inertia
was due to the fact, if it be a fact, that up to now we have been able
to meet the problem of poverty in this voluntary way (though there
is a good deal of evidence to the contrary), even then the result of
group pride must be described as a harmful one insofar as our participation in the civic growth of the country is concerned. May we not
have deliberately kept ourselves in a social and economic ghetto?

Surely the pragmatic bent of our thinking, on which we Jews so
pride ourselves, should have convinced us by this time, if we but
give due consideration to American economic problems, that for all
of the publicity given to or purchased by private philanthropy in this
country, it is but a very impotent method of meeting the problems
which it claims to meet. But for the fear of over-burdening the reader
with statistical figures, comparisons could be made between the total
sums available for relief of distress in poor England and rich America
which would hardly be complimentary to our country. But even limiting ourselves to American conditions, how pitiful, how tragically pitiful
are the figures of private philanthropy and relief as compared with
public resources already made available.

A year or two ago the *Jewish Social Service Quarterly* announced,
with a great beating of drums and sounding of trumpets, that Com-

munity Chest were collecting the fabulous sum of some sixty to sixty-five million dollars per annum. How much "scientific" publicity, at what cost, was necessary to obtain this amount? How much flattery was poured out before the generous givers? But how many social workers were aware that at the same time, for the relief of only one group of cases, namely, industrial accidents, a comparatively minor cause of poverty and distress in the experience of social agencies— for that group of cases alone, 250 million dollars are paid out each year through the instrumentality of Workmen's Compensation laws, and the amount is annually rising. Some fifteen years ago, when the Mothers' Pension movement first came up for discussion, the leaders of our profession fought against it on the ground that private philanthropy was amply able to handle the situation and could do it in a more scientific way. But already some 50 million dollars a year are distributed in mothers' pensions for public funds. In little England some hundreds of millions of dollars annually are spent for unemployment insurance, while we in America, when confronted with the situation of perhaps three or four times as many unemployed as in England, have been forced to rely upon soup kitchens and bread lines and sentimental *Zukunftsmusik* about stabilization of industry. Do we want to get at least an inkling of the problems which the present era of unemployment has created and which have remained uncorrected? Then look what has happened in just one city of this country, Detroit, which has perhaps the most comprehensive system of public outdoor relief. Within less than two years the amount of public relief distributed in that one city, with a population about one-half of the city of Philadelphia, increased from some $50,000 a month to over $600,000 a month. What Jewish Federation or Community Chest has shown an ability to expand to an equal extent?

If we recognize the purpose and duty of organized society to eliminate suffering and distress while undertaking the arduous task of preventing its causes, then private philanthropy has never done it and never can do it, while public relief combined with the policy of compensation and social insurance can and must. Space will not permit me, nor is it necessary to repeat here at great length, the argument I have made elsewhere in defense of this thesis.[3] And, in any case, here my purpose is a more circumscribed one. Here I am dealing primarily with the problems confronting Jewish philanthropy and Jewish social

[3] "Can Private Philanthropy Do It?" *Social Service Review,* September, 1929.

service, the problems which, in a very personal way, concern both the Jewish giver and the professional Jewish social worker.

The soundest approach to the problem of Jewish philanthropy might perhaps be best summed up in the following statements.

Jewish poverty is not a result of conditions confined to the group. It is a part and parcel of the whole economic and social problem of wealth production and wealth accumulation of the country as a whole.

The expectation that the problem of Jewish poverty can be met individually, or can be eliminated irrespective of those general economic forces, is a naive expression of group pride uncontrolled by scientific research and thinking.

The assumption of independent group responsibility becomes a definite anti-social force if it destroys Jewish interest and Jewish participation in progressive social movements.

But I do not wish to be misunderstood. Having been a staunch defender of Jewish social service and philanthropic work, I have not suddenly committed a *volte face*. Not for a moment would I want to be understood as advocating the abrogation of Jewish relief work in face of the existing catastrophic situation. Nor do I advocate its merging either immediately or in the near future with the so-called non-sectarian field.

Jewish social service has not been an artificial growth forced upon the community by a few energetic propagandists. It has largely grown for at least the following three reasons:

(1) To perform functions which otherwise would have been left undone.

(2) To give expression to the needs and desires of communal co-operation.

(3) To enable the Jewish minority to make its contribution to the development of ethical and social values and concepts in the community in which it lives.

We have made that contribution by introducing and popularizing a higher standard of relief than the community would have been ready to accept without the benefit of our example. We have made that contribution by emphasizing the sense of group responsibility to an extent which sometimes seems to have shocked non-Jewish philanthropic agencies, always fearful of the "demoralizing" effect of excessive generosity. We needed a philanthropic effort throughout all these years for the purpose of holding the Jewish community together when the passion for individual success and the equally strong passion for internal dissension might have torn the communities asunder. And last but not least there were many group needs, group functions which none but ourselves could perform, which we have no right to expect that politically organized society will take any concern in, and which we would not want politically organized society to interfere with.

All these things we have done. They were necessary and their value should not be minimized. But perhaps the time has come to realize that even a larger contribution is possible and may be expected from the Jew in America. Everywhere throughout Europe Jewish thought, energy and action have been with the advance guard of general economic and social reform. Shall the influence of Jewish thought and energy and action in America be limited to the Jewish community alone?

Nor is the suggestion an entirely revolutionary one. I venture to say that the Billikopf who succeeded in organizing public opinion in the State of Pennsylvania to such effect that appropriations for Mothers' Pensions were increased by a round million dollars annually has done more in one stroke for the relief of the poor, both Jewish and non-Jewish, than that other Billikopf who abstracts such large contributions from Jewish pockets. I venture to think that Abraham Epstein, who would not be known as one of the Jewish social workers except for his name, in contributing so largely to the passage of the Old Age Security Law in New York State, has done more in the field of relief than perhaps a dozen executives of Jewish philanthropic Federations.

What they and a few others have done is only an indication of the potentialities. At least there is the hope that in this direction permanent results can be achieved, and that functioning in the wider field is not only a privilege but a duty of Jewish social service.

And there is this further vital consideration. With these permanent results achieved, with the oppressive problem of relief of distress and starvation lifted from our shoulders, we then may have a little more energy left for the development of a healthy Jewish life in America. We can make a much greater contribution to the creation of Jewish values—to Jewish education and culture—if this tremendous problem of poverty and relief is shifted upon the responsibility of the organized State where it properly belongs. And this shift will not have taken place at the expense of the Jewish poor. There should be no competition between the interests of Jewish culture and the immediate interests of Jewish masses. The present situation which has created a competitive attitude between Jewish body and Jewish soul is an unhealthy one. There may be (we all assume) specific Jewish cultural needs. There are, we hope, no specific needs of the Jewish stomach. Only when proper provision is made for the economic need will we be in a position to devote the necessary effort to the need spiritual.

In order to achieve both these important aims—the elimination of Jewish poverty, and the building up of a sound Jewish cultural life— we must have the courage to repudiate the alleged debt to Peter Stuyvesant.

(—1931)

Toward a Transnational America

◦◦◦◦

RANDOLPH S. BOURNE

B EFORE the American people at the present time there are two
ideals of American nationalism, sharply focussed and emphasized
by the war. One is that of the traditional melting-pot, the other is
that of a co-operation of cultures. The first is congenial to the ruling
class, the nativist element of our population; the second appeals, however vaguely, to the leaders of the various self-conscious European
national groups which have settled here. The idealism of the melting-
pot would assimilate all Europeans, as they are received into the
American social and economic scheme, to a very definite type, that of
the prevailing Anglo-Saxon. For however much this desire may be
obscured, what the Anglicized American prophets of the melting-pot
really mean shall happen to the immigrant is that he shall acquire,
along with the new common English language, the whole stock of English political and social ideals. When they attempt to judge how far
any group has been Americanized, it is by this standard that they
judge them.

The effect of the melting-pot ideal is either to influence this
Anglicizing, or to obliterate the distinctive racial and cultural qualities, and work the American population into a colorless, tasteless,
homogeneous mass. With large masses of our foreign-born of the second
generation this latter process is far advanced, and the result is that
cultural pointlessness and vacuity which our critics of American life
are never weary of deploring. Both effects of the melting-pot idealism,
I believe, are highly undesirable. Both make in the long run for
exactly that terrible unity of pride, chauvinism, and ambition that has
furnished the popular fuel in the armed clash of nationalism in Europe.
To preach a pure and undiluted Americanism with the spectacle of
suicidal Europe before us is to invite disaster and destruction. American idealism is face to face with a crucial dilemma. Cultural self-

consciousness, concentrated, inspiring vigor of intellectual and personal qualities such as the French possess, for instance, is the most
precious heritage a nation can have. Yet apparently this intense national feeling leads straight into chauvinistic self-assertion, into conflict with other nationalisms, into a belligerency which drags the
world down in mutual ruin. Who can doubt that, if we ever obtained
this homogeneous Americanism that our Rooseveltian prophets desire,
the latent imperialism of our ruling class would flame forth and
America would follow the other States in their plunge to perdition?
America's only hope is in the development of a democratic and pacific
way of life. We have an opportunity at last to try to make good that old
boast of our being a model to the nations. We can at least make the
effort to show that a democratic civilization founded on peace is a
possibility in this portentous twentieth century.

WHEREIN THE "HYPHENATE" HAS BEEN A BLESSING

I feel so strongly on this subject that I am willing to believe that the
so-called "hyphenate," by keeping us from being swept into a premature and nebulous cohesion, has actually been our salvation. I believe
that almost anything that keeps us from being welded together into a
terrible national engine which powerful political or financial interests
may wield at will, flinging the entire nation's strength in a moment to
any cause or movement that seems to advance their will or their private
class-sense of honor or justice—I say that anything that keeps us from
being thus used is a salvation. I do not say that division and confusion
are good for long. I do not say that we do not need a unity of purpose
and sympathy. But I do say that any confusion which results in giving time for the weak democratic, radical and pacific forces in this
country to struggle to their feet and become strong is a beneficent
confusion. Such, I believe, is our present confusion, which even that
present evil genius of the American people,———* has been unable
to dispel. We want no national unity that is not based on democratic
and socialized and international goals.

That is why I am almost fanatically against the current programs of
Americanism, with their preparedness, conscription, imperialism, integration issues, their slavish imitation of the European nationalisms
which are slaying each other before our eyes. The current war is the

* Who shall be nameless here—THE EDITORS.

terrible price which European nationalism has had to pay for its hard, bright, inspiring integrity. By welding themselves into a spiritual and patriotic cohesion, these peoples have handed themselves over to their rulers as single, compact, all-powerful weapons for those rulers to wield. America is still an industrial oligarchy. Were America to get that cohesion which is urged upon us before democratic forces developed, would it not be wielded in exactly the same way? In defense of so-called "rights," what could prevent our own rulers from brandishing our strength and using the nation as a hammer to wage a needless war? Nothing will save us but the firmest insistence on a different kind of Americanism. We must somehow acquire this intensity and vigor of cultural self-consciousness without paying the price of terrible like-mindedness.

SHALL THE IMMIGRANT GIVE UP HIS CULTURAL ALLEGIANCE?

Now it is exactly this gradual solution of the dilemma which I look to the ideal of co-operative Americanism to achieve. If America is to be nationalistic without being chauvinistic, we need new conceptions of the state, of nationality, of citizenship, of allegiance. The war, to my mind, has proved the utter obsolescence of the old conceptions. Even without the war the old conceptions would have been obsolete. For the development of backward countries, the growth of population in Europe, the demand for labor and colonists in all parts of the globe, the ease and cheapness of travel, have set in motion vast currents of immigration which render impossible the old tight geographical groupings of nationality. The political ideas of the future will have to be adjusted to a shifting world-population, to the mobility of labor, to all kinds of new temporary mixings of widely diverse peoples, as well as to their permanent mixings.

The Jews have lost their distinction of being a peculiar people. Dispersion is now the lot of every race. The Jewish ghetto in America is matched by the Italian, by the Slovak ghetto. The war will intensify this setting in motion of wandering peoples. The age-long problems of Jewish nationalism have become the burning problems of other dispersed nationalities. America has become a vast reservoir of dispersions. The adjustment which the Jew has had to make throughout the ages is a pattern of what other nationals have to make to-day. From their point of view, the same dilemmas of assimilation and absorption, of cultural and racial allegiance, beset them. In the new country they have often the same alternatives of disintegration or sub-national life. To the intelligent and enthusiastic emigré from the Teuton or Slavic or Latin lands, it seems no more desirable that his cultural soul should be washed out of him than it seems to the Jew. America puts to him the same problem of becoming assimilated to New World life, of meeting his new political freedom and vague expansion of economic opportunity, without becoming a mere colorless unit in a gray mass. And the immigrant puts to America the problem of finding a place for him to make his peculiar and whole-hearted contribution to the upbuilding of the America which is still in process of creation. The problem of the Jew in the modern world is identical. As a Jew has said, "The modern world sets the Jew the problem of maintaining some sort of distinctive existence without external props of territorial sovereignty and a political machine; the Jew sets the modern world the problem of finding for him a place in its social structure which shall enable him to live as a human being without demanding that he cease to be a Jew."

HOW JEWISH IDEALISM SOLVES THE PROBLEM

If then this co-operative Americanism is an ideal which meets at once the demands of a native American like myself who wishes to see America kept from militarization and feudalization, and also the demands of the foreign immigré who wishes freedom to preserve his heritage at the same time that he co-operates loyally with all other nationals in the building-up of America, I believe we shall find in the current Jewish ideal of Zionism the purest pattern and the most inspiring conceptions of transnationalism. I used to think, as many Americans still do, that Zionism was incompatible with Americanism, that if your enthusiasm and energy went into creating a Jewish nation in the Orient, you could not give yourself to building up the State in which you lived. I have since learned that however flawless such a logical antithesis would be, nothing could be falser than this idea. This dilemma of dual allegiance must be solved in America, it must be solved by the world, and it is in the fertile implications of Zionism that I veritably believe the solution will be found.

To the Orthodox Jew, I presume the ideas clustering about the founding of Zion will seem only the realization of age-long Jewish

hopes. To me they represent an international idealism almost peril-
ously new. They furnish just those new conceptions that I said this
new American idealism would need. Indeed my own mind was set
working on the whole idea of American national ideals by the remarkable articles of Dr. Kallen in *The Nation* last year, and the very phrase,
"transnationalism," I stole from a Jewish college mate of mine who, I
suspect, is now a member of your Menorah Society here.* The idea
is a Jewish idea, and the great contribution of Jewish intelligence
in America I conceive to be to clarify and spread these new conceptions.

It may be daring of me to assume that the Jew, with his traditional
segregation, his intense fusion of racial and religious egoism, will contribute hopefully to the foundations of a new spiritual internationalism.
But has it not always been the anomaly of the Jew that he was at once
the most self-conscious of beings—feels himself, that is, religiously,
culturally, racially, a being peculiar in his lot and signally blessed—
and yet has proven himself perhaps the most assimilable of all races
to other and quite alien cultures? Which is cause and which is effect? Is
he assimilable because he has had no national center, no geographical
and political basis for his religion and his mode of life, or has he not
had his Jewish nation because he has been so readily assimilated?
Is it not just this in the Jewish personality that has piqued and irritated and attracted other peoples, that it is at once so congenial and so
alien? And can we not connect the so very recent flowering of the
hopes of Jewish nationalism with the fact that Zionistic ideals now
for the first time seem to be making towards internationalism? They
move in line with the world's best hope. For as I understand it, the
Jewish State which Zionists are building is a non-military, a non-
chauvinistic State. Palestine is to be built as a Jewish center on purely
religious and cultural foundations. It is not to be the home of all the
Jewish people. Zionism does not propose to prevent Jews from
living in full citizenship in other countries. The Zionist does not believe that there is a necessary conflict between a cultural allegiance
to the Jewish center and political allegiance to a State.

A DUAL CITIZENSHIP—A SPIRITUAL INTERNATIONALISM

This distinction between State and nationality is a very modern conception. The successful State to-day is a federation of autonomous

* This was spoken before the Harvard Menorah Society on November 8, 1916.

units, or a federation of different peoples living in justice and amity. The State becomes more and more a coalition of people for the realization of common social ends. It is becoming more and more difficult to identify State and nationality. The modern world, with its mixings and shiftings of peoples, its differences of potential between large and small national groups, simply will not fit into these terms. Cultural allegiance will not necessarily coincide with political allegiance. A sort of dual citizenship becomes possible and desirable, if fullest expression is to be given to those feelings of racial sympathy, similar traditions, cultural distinction, which make peoples cling so fiercely together and sacrifice so much for political unity. The world has thought that it must have its culture and its political unity coincide. Witness the strivings of Italy for Italia Irredenta, of Greece for its Islands and Asiatic shore, of Serbia for the greater Serbia. But suppose these unreclaimed nationalities autonomous and unoppressed within their larger Empire. Does not the example of transnational Belgium and Switzerland imply that in such peaceful and just States these irredentist problems would disappear, and is it not oppression that causes the egotism of small nationalities to swell unwholesomely? The Zionist philosophy, I take it, assumes that with a national center for the Jewish race in Palestine to which the oppressed might flee, and to which, as the place where the type of life corresponding to the character and ideals of the Jewish people, the eyes of all Jews might turn, cultural allegiance and political allegiance might automatically strike a balance and a Jew might remain a complete Jew and at the same time be a complete citizen of any modern political State where he happened to live and where his work and interests lay.

If this interpretation of mine is correct, then the modern world, and above all America, needs these Zionist conceptions. What I mean by co-operative Americanism—that is, an ideal of a freely mingling society of peoples of very different racial and cultural antecedents, with a common political allegiance and common social ends but with free and distinctive cultural allegiances which may be placed anywhere in the world that they like—is simply a generalization of the practical effect of the Zionist ideal. I see no other way by which international sympathy may be created and the best human expressivenesses and distinctive attitudes and traits preserved. And if the Jews have been the first international race, I look to America to be the first international nation.

TWO REAL DANGERS OF MISDIRECTED TRANSNATIONALISM

Groups of identical culture must find some way of leading a national life that is neither belligerently egotistic like the hectic nationalism of Europe nor sub-national like that of the Jews of the Russian Pale. The American ideal must make possible such an ideal national life within our own country if the peoples who came here are to be enriched and enriching.

My argument for Transnational America* has seemed to be vitiated by two considerations. One is that this transnationalism of the foreign national groups in America is too often colored by political as well as cultural allegiance to the homeland. Deutschtum is not only a movement for the keeping alive of a noble German tongue and literature, which is desirable, but it has become at times suspiciously like a Kaisertum, which is wholly undesirable. Another dangerous corollary to transnationalism is that the national groups, if this patriotic and cultural emphasis are too great, if their Deutschtum and their Kaisertum become too intensified, might tend to become actual political groups of racial rivalry within the American nation. This is a consummation even more sinister. I do not argue for an artificial stimulation of transnational feeling. I only argue for its freedom, believing that when it is free it will fertilize and enhance the common American life. But even when it is free, there is another danger. The Kultur that an expatriated group of nationals cultivate may be one that has already been superseded at home. This has happened repeatedly in America. The contemporary official German-American element, for instance, seems to reproduce a fussy, transitory stage of German bourgeoisie of the seventies and eighties, and very little the peculiar Nietzschean flair of the present-day Germany. The English South is still mid-Victorian, though English culture has been revolutionized. The official Irish-American is rather wierdly different from his expressive Irish brother. These groups, transplanted to America, are victims of arrested development, in spite of their fierce transnational cultural patriotism. They fondly imagine that they are keeping the faith. But in merely not changing, these expatriated groups have not really kept the faith. This faith is a certain way of facing the world, of accepting experience. It is a spirit and not any particular forms. A

* In the *Atlantic Monthly,* July, 1916.

genuine transnationalism would be modern, reflecting not only the peculiar gifts and temperament of the people, but reflecting it in its contemporary form. America runs a very real danger of becoming not the modern cosmopolitan grouping that we desire, but a queer conglomeration of the prejudices of past generations, miraculously preserved here, after they have mercifully perished at home.

BUT THE JEWISH ASPIRATION IS WHOLESOME

Jewish transnationalism, on the other hand, seems to me just to avoid these very pitfalls. The Zionist's lack of chauvinistic and dynastic aims for his new nation removes the fear of Jewish political groupings in this country. And the fact that the Jewish national life is in the future avoids that danger of the petrifying of outworn expressions of the national idea. The Zionist's outlook is intensely modern. The nation that he is building in Palestine is clearly designed to work out the Jewish mode of life on the most scientific modern lines. Scientific agriculture, the protection of health, education, equitable taxation, economic justice between individuals—all this indicates a union between the noble old Law and the most enlightened spirit of modern social welfare. As I read of the admirable features of the suburban settlement at Jaffa, or of some of the other colonies, I realize that the transnational Jew will have a nation to look to which he can really adore as no other transnational, forced to look at vexing compromises between the medieval and the new, will be able to adore. An ancient spirit of justice and sobriety, expressed with all the technique of modern science and sense of social welfare—what could more perfectly symbolize the nationalism which will keep our old earth rich, sweet and varied?

If I take this Zionism, which seems to me to contain the best current Jewish idealism, as a pattern for American transnationalism, I may unwittingly be doing it injustice. It will seem to you that I have ignored the religious aspect, and I have perhaps unknowingly caricatured its political conceptions. But I am looking at Zionism from the outside and not from within. My interest is in the question how far do Jewish ideals contribute to that larger internationalism of which America might be the exponent? There is very real danger that a reactionary idealism may force a fatally narrow patriotic spirit upon us. In new conceptions, such as those which this Jewish idealism seems to contribute, I see our salvation. The Jew in America is proving every day the possibility of this dual life. To clinch one's argument one would need no other evidence than the figure of Justice Brandeis, at once an ardent Zionist and at the same time an incomparable American leader in economic and social reconstruction. And what shall we say of the younger generation of Jewish intellectuals, which includes such men as Felix Frankfurter, Horace M. Kallen, Morris R. Cohen, Walter Lippmann? The intellectual service which such writers are doing us with their clarity of expression, their radical philosophy, their masterly fibre of thought, can hardly be over-valued. Their contribution is so incomparably greater than that of any other American group of foreign cultural affiliations that one can scarcely get one's perspective. A large majority of this younger generation is, I understand, Zionist in its sympathy. Yet that Jewish idealism has not in the least vitiated their peculiarly intimate insight into American problems, their gift of picking a way through the tangled social and economic maze. In their light we all see light. They are my last proof of the practicability of the co-operative American ideal. And they suggest that an ardent Zionism involves the responsibility for an equally ardent effort for that progressive democratic reconstruction in America which is the ideal of all true Americans, no matter what their heritage or transnationality.

(—1916)

A Search for the True Community

LEWIS MUMFORD

AMONG modern people the belief in the principle of nationalism is
almost as sacred as the belief in witches was in Western Europe
during the seventeenth century. In the present article we are going to
inquire whether nationalism has any more reality, any more humane
efficacy, than the lamented superstition of witchcraft; and in particular
we are going to find out, if possible, whether nationalism in its present
apotheosis has any particular significance to the life of the Jewish
community, or holds any promise for its development. In other words,
I shall try to show the relation of nationalism to Jewish culture and
civilization, and to suggest the terms upon which Jewish culture
and civilization will probably flourish.

If in an age that has made nationalism a fetish it is a heresy to
suggest that nationalism is not a fact—in the sense that Jerusalem is a
fact or a congregation in a synagogue is a fact—I willingly plead guilty,
with the innocence of the little boy in Hans Andersen's fairy tale,
who insisted that the king was naked when everybody else was prais-
ing his elegant clothes.

THE RECENT ORIGIN OF NATIONALISM

When one examines the literature of nationalism that has grown up
in the past century, from Mazzini onward, one is confronted by a
curious fact: there is no agreement as to what nationalism means, no
clear concept as to what a nation is, and no means of deciding when
a nation is entitled to possess certain mystical rights which groups
that are not nations do not possess. The statesmen who talk glibly
about the rights and prerogatives of nationalities, about self-determination and the need for national unity, are not disconcerted by this
vagueness; but any one who has had the slightest training in science

cannot help being suspicious of this pervasive ambiguity. The endless differences as to the attributes of nationality remind one of the wrangles about the characteristics of the seraphim in which Catholic scholasticism delighted during the Middle Ages; and one is inclined to believe that the "reality" with which political philosophers are dealing exists chiefly in their minds, and differs in many important respects from the realities which a scientific investigation would bring to light.

Our initial suspicion deepens when one recalls that a belief in nationalism is a product of the last four or five hundred years, and that it is closely associated with the rise of a hitherto unknown institution—the national State. Let me at the outset, then, attempt to define the difference between the scientific aspect of nationality and the mythical aspect; between nationalism as a fact and nationalism as a belief. In order to remove confusion we shall then be able to give the fact of nationalism a new name, which will relieve it of some of its pretensions and impertinences.

HISTORIC NATIONALITY, OR CULTURISM

As a fact, nationality was known to the ancient world: and it was, I suggest, of precisely the same order in Palestine as it was in Hellas. The qualities which characterized the nation were the possession of a body of literature in a common tongue, and the respect for certain shrines and holy places. The idea of a definite territory, which crept into Jewish nationalism at the beginning, or of political unity under a single sovereign, had nothing to do with the two fundamental conditions of nationality. So traders from other regions who visited Athens or Jerusalem carried their "nationalism" with them, even as the Hanseatic merchants did in the Middle Ages; only under exceptional conditions were they assimilated, and this "assimilation" had nothing to do with the mere act of residence in a particular territory.

In other words, in the ancient world nationality meant the acquisition and maintenance of a common body of observances, habits, and ideals. In so far as these ideals and observances lapsed you became one of the heathen, even though you remained on the old soil; in so far as they were maintained you were one of the chosen people—a Greek as distinguished from a Barbarian, a Jew as distinguished from a Philistine —no matter how far away you might wander in Orbis Terrarum.

The important thing to bear in mind is that ancient peoples did not "believe" in nationality: they believed in the cultural heritage which gave them their distinction as a nationality. National unity did not mean an arbitrary political unity, or an equally arbitrary territorial unity. If nationality grew up in a certain soil, and showed the effects of regional influences, it could nevertheless adapt itself to other environments. Like the man whose home is wherever he can lay his hat, nationality in the ancient world existed wherever a community could plant its cultural institutions. Such unity as existed was that of a small city-region. When the Roman Empire made the Mediterranean world a single political area, it did little violence to the cultural attributes of nationality.

During the Middle Ages, up to the fourteenth century, the situation in Europe was not much different. The hardships suffered by the Jews in that era were due not so much to their separateness as a community as to the difficulty of finding a place for them under a system of feudal land tenure and under a dispensation in which the Roman Catholic Church encouraged the same attitude towards the "heathen" as the national State exhibits today towards "foreigners." Political unity in the Middle Ages had nothing to do with nationality. Nationality as a fact was recognized: hence the division of the great universities into "nations"; nationality as a mythic unity between people in a certain territory under a single system of government could scarcely have been understood, I believe, by a contemporary of Dante.

If these facts are true—and anyone may verify them—the conclusions that may be drawn for the Jewish community are obvious. The Jewish community has always possessed the reality of national existence, even during the most dismal periods of the Diaspora, and the absence of a political domain has in no wise dissipated this reality. In order to make the reality clear and distinct, let us call it *culturism*—that is, the belief in a system of common values, and the effort on the part of the community to work these values out in its daily life. The confusion of culturism with its bastard offspring, nationalism, has been, I believe, one of the main misdemeanors that have been committed by modern thought.

HOW CULTURALISM FARES IN THE POLITICAL STATE

As opposed to culturism, nationalism, in the modern sense, is a creature of the political State. Historically, nationalism has been devel-

oped in order to make the political States which were founded in
Europe, from the fourteenth century onwards, unified territories from
which tribute might be extracted without difficulty. Anyone who will
take the trouble to examine Dr. Franz Oppenheimer's *The State,* will
scarcely be prepared to quarrel with this interpretation. It is a commonplace of political theory. In *The State and the Nation,* Professor Edward Jenks, a fairly conservative student, does not hesitate to look
these facts in the face, and to admit the primacy of military conquest
and tribute in the foundation of the modern national state. What we
have still to take account of is the stupendous sleight-of-hand by which
the State was able to transform the plain citizen into a willing taxpayer
and a loyal soldier, and, under the increasing influence of "popular
government," make an institution whose capital functions are odious
seem the repository of all the community's hopes, aspirations, and
virtues. The main twist in this little feat of legerdemain was, I suggest,
the utilization of culturism as an agent of the State. The growth of
nationalist sentiment and the aggrandizement of the State go hand
in hand.

Let us examine this political magic a little more closely. In any
area as large as the contemporary national State there are necessarily
a number of culturisms. Even in a country as small as Belgium there
are two distinct elements, the Flemish and the Walloon, with different literatures and different outlooks on life. What is called "nationalism" or "national culture" is that particular culturism which
dominates the region around the capital city—the Paris basin and
the London basin, for example. By propaganda, by education, and at
times even by law and military coercion, the capital city inflicts its
local culturism upon the other regions that make up the country.
Nationalism, as opposed to culturism, is an entity molded, if not
created, by the State, and consciously or unconsciously subservient to
the ends for which the State exists.

Now the unity which is promoted by "nationalism" is a highly artificial condition; that is to say, it runs against the natural grain of local
interests and local activities. Hence, this unity can be purchased only
by the extirpation of rival culturisms. Looking for examples of this extirpation we turn perhaps too readily to the ruthlessness with which the
Germans rooted out the French language in Alsace-Lorraine in 1871, or
the similar manner in which the French, by all accounts, have lately
attempted to wipe out the German language in that territory. There

is no need, however, to go so far afield or to take such drastic instances; the process is much more widely spread and much more subtle. It is paralleled, for instance, by the attitude of disapproval which the inspectors from the Ministry of Education in Great Britain exhibit towards, let us say, the Yorkshire dialect. The notion behind this behavior, in spite of the fact that York has never been separated from England and never been a foreign territory, is that a Yorkshireman is less likely to be willing to pay taxes and go to war at the behest of the central government if he feels that he is a Yorkshireman first and an "Englishman" a long way behind. This disapproval becomes something like wary respect in relation to such a distinct culturism as Scotland's, and with Ireland, as is notorious, it has only recently retired from a position of open combat.

If there is any doubt remaining as to the enmity between nationalism and culturism, I need quote only a final example—the attitude of the oppressed nationalities that have been made into States, in relation to culturisms that remain within their borders. The same motives of state-building are operative; and the oppressed nationality uses its new-found powers to oppress minor nationalities, in the interests of "political unity." Perhaps the situation may be best summed up by saying that nationalism is the predatory phase of culturism: it is culturism "on the make." Nationalism is accordingly another instance of the ancient heresy, that of the "spiritual power," in Auguste Comte's phrase, seeking temporal dominion; and nowhere has it proved more true that he who takes up the sword shall perish by the sword. The flowers of culture, propagated for "reasons of state" degenerate into stinking weeds; and political nationalism becomes the base thing that the great historian, Lord Acton, declared it to be.

THE TWO REACTIONS AGAINST STATE NATIONALISM

It is not at all surprising that genuine culturism reacted to the growth of the national State during the nineteenth century by attempting to turn every separate cultural area or people into a sovereign political territory. Where culturism made a critical mistake, however, was in believing that territorial unity had any value to a culture except for the purpose of getting rid of a foreign political yoke, such as that which had been imposed upon Italy. They failed to see, these disciples of culturism, that a unity which was necessary to war, and which could be promoted only by war, was useless except for the duration of war. The development of a so-called national culture, if it meant the concentration of power, prestige, wealth, and ability in the national capitals of Paris, London, Rome, or Berlin, meant at the same time the increasing destitution of culturism in the provinces. Regional culturism, deprived of its own vitality, lived on transfusions of blood from the capital city.

Aside from the demand of each culturism for a separate national State, and the speedy obliteration of these several demands in the States that actually were founded, the reaction against nationalism expressed itself in another fashion. If the first reaction resulted in the growth of new national States, the second emphasized the necessity for diminishing the scope and power of the national State. The name of this second reaction is regionalism, and its home is Provence. Regionalism emphasizes the corporate unity and the independence of the local community, focussed in its local capitals, as opposed to the unity which is supposed to exist within the frequently imaginary boundaries of the State.

Where has the Jewish community stood in the midst of these two reactions? The Jewish community, under the ægis of Zionism, has followed—as Dr. Kallen points out in his admirable survey of Zionism and world politics*—in the footsteps of Mazzini; that is to say, it has pinned its hopes for Jewish culturism upon the ultimate foundation of a separate national State, an aspiration which it has shared with the Czecho-Slovaks, the Croats, and a score of other peoples. If our analysis has established any point, however, it has shown that there are grave reasons for distrusting the claims and powers of nationalism, as developed originally in England and France, and copied in other regions. It now remains to point out that nationalism threatens to undermine the basis of Jewish culturism in particular, and that the very triumph of Jewish nationality in Palestine may prove abortive to its dearest hopes. Jewish culturism stands to lose more from nationalism at large, it would seem, than it is likely to gain from the establishment of Jewish nationalism. If this statement holds, the time has come for a new departure. Jewish culturism must, I believe, use other tactics than those which were suggested in the nineteenth century by the growth of national States during the past three hundred years.

* *Zionism and World Politics*, by HORACE M. KALLEN (New York, 1921, Doubleday, Page & Co.).

ASSIMILATION OR ZIONISM: IS IT A REAL DILEMMA?

The keyword of modern nationality is assimilation; and by assimilation we mean nothing other than the assimilation of diverse culturisms, and their final extinction. The country in which this process has been carried farthest, perhaps, is the United States; but we must not suppose that the process is confined to this area: every State has its melting pot and the chief difference between the United States and France, for instance, is that the culturisms of Brittany and Provence have long been rooted in the soil, and have probably a greater chance of surviving than the national State itself, whereas the culturisms that have been transplanted to America are like cut flowers, and even though they have been stuck in the soil here and there, they are only too ready to wither.

If nationalism, as manifested in the current Americanization program, continues to flourish in every region, it does not take a very acute observer to foresee that Jewish culturism is doomed, and the Jewish community, or that part of it which remains conscious of its racial stock, will simply be a collection of individuals without a common set of values other than the secular values—the belief in reform and optimism and Mary Pickford and acting like one's neighbor—which are the common denominator of New York and Keokuk and New Orleans and Los Angeles. For a mordant picture of the modern Diaspora one has only to follow almost any Jewish family that has been bred in the Ghetto of New York, as it achieves prosperity, sends the younger generation to the public schools, and moves up into a "select neighborhood" in the upper west side. This is not merely a dispersion of people; it is a dissolution of values. In the modern metropolis at large there is scarcely any civic or community consciousness worthy the name; and in leaving the warm intimacy of the Ghetto, with all its poverty and ugliness, the Jew abandons such values as have made his life beautiful and rich; and the improvement in pavements and plumbing which accompanies this change is scarcely a compensation.

Culturism, let us observe, is rooted in the integrity of the local community. In its common *shul*, its common meeting places, its common literature, its common leaders and intellectuals, culturism develops its own organs of expression. Without these shared possessions culturism must languish, and the mechanical formulae of nationalism take its place. It is folly, I believe, to think that the Jew can maintain his cultural integrity whilst the demands of nationalism transgress upon every activity from the moment he goes to school to the time when he is conscripted to serve in war. Unless the Jew values culturism more than nationalism, unless in fact he values culturism even more than Jewish nationalism, his whole set of spiritual standards and disciplines is likely to disintegrate in the modern world. A remnant may be saved in Palestine; but the Jew in America cannot live vicariously on the triumphs and glories of the homeland in Asia Minor; and if he is not able to develop freely the institution of his culturism on the soil where he is established, he is destined either to be a stranger in a strange land, or a 100 percent patriot in an even stranger land.

Must either horn of this dilemma be grasped? I do not think so. If nationalism, apart from its uses for military *realpolitik,* is a superstitious conception, like witchcraft, there is also the consolation that it may vanish as swiftly as witchcraft. Before leaving the subject, therefore, let us examine the prospects of culturism in the modern community. The maintenance of Jewish culturism is, as I have tried to indicate, but a fragment of a much larger and more difficult problem.

THE TRUE COMMUNITY

The ideal of a modern national State is that of a city in a siege. It is an ideal that cannot be kept up without the aid of an enormous amount of deliberate lying and obstruction—called national education and national self-preservation—except during wartime, or the period in which war is being actively prepared, in which case the community becomes almost automatically immune to reality. In war, a modern State achieves something like its legal pretensions. It maintains an arbitrary physical unity by closing the frontiers and supervising with repulsive strictness the entry of goods and people. (In order to produce this effect in "peace time," the State creates tariffs and immigration barriers.) Since intercourse with the outside world is severely regulated the inhabitants must devote themselves to "business of national importance," or at least make believe that their business is of this character. Any scientific research which does not contribute, directly or remotely, to the business of warfare, and any art that does not by suggestion or avowal deliberately inflame the populace against its enemies, is all but prohibited; if not by law, at any rate by custom and social disapproval. Every man is potential cannon-fodder, and every woman the potential breeder of cannon-fodder. There are no values, there are no interests, except those which pertain to military aggression. The ideal of the national State has been admirably satirized by Lucian (Mr. John A. Hobson) in a neglected pamphlet called "1920," and the reader may turn to that little picture of a nation at war in order to fill in this hasty sketch.

The national State at peace differs from that at war only by its emphasis: its outlines are the same. Beneath the national State at peace, however, one can detect, like the colors of a mural decoration struggling beneath a coat of whitewash, the real communities, the real interests, the real activities which the State at war ruthlessly extirpates, and which the State at peace endeavors with more or less success either to hide or to harness to its own chariot.

Now, the real communities that underlie the national State are much differently constituted from the fake community called a nation. Instead of uniformity, there is diversity; instead of a single aim there are a multitude of aims; instead of a rigid order there is a flexible adjustment. Contrary to the formless unity of thought and action which the State attempts to promote by setting up definite boundaries, there is a specific unity in diverse groups for the sake of accomplishing concrete aims of one sort or another. We have seen that the chief aim of the national State is aggression; and that other activities are promoted or tolerated only with a view to their eventual service towards this aim. When the interests of people as individuals and as members of groups are regarded, however, we discover that they polarize naturally about particular, concrete, locally-embodied institutions—the school, the synagogue, the market, the business corporation, the trade union, the city, and in the absence of national boundaries these institutions tend to flow naturally across frontiers and to link up, one with another, in an increasingly complex pattern.

But for the gratuitous interference of the national State, these communities, groups, and societies would tend to form loose federations. They would be united in so far as there were common interests to promote, and independent in so far as they could satisfy their own requirements by their own efforts. In no case would the local group attempt to fulfill its needs by shunting its actions through the national State— getting something for nothing at the cost of having its every activity defined, planned, financed, inspected and carried out by a remote central authority. The conditions of transport and communication in the modern world have made this federalism genuinely possible; and were it not for the existence of national barriers, groups with common interests would tend to draw together—as the co-operative wholesale societies did before the war—without regard to the fact that they were located in different regions of the world.

On such an economic, political, and social basis as I have just briefly outlined, culturism would, I believe, flourish abundantly. There would be a rich local life; and each region, each local community, would contribute in decent measure to the spiritual heritage of humanity at large; an achievement which culturism, so long as it keeps within national boundaries and gets the sanction for its activities from the policeman, the soldier, and the bureaucrat, cannot come within miles of reaching.

THE HOPE OF CULTURALISM

What, then, is the upshot of this survey? The answer can be put quite simply. Jewish culturism depends for its existence upon the activities of the local communities. Hence the triumph of the nationalist mythus—with its assiduous extirpation of rival culturisms within the national boundaries—is a menace to Jewish culturism, and will remain a menace even if the Jewish community in Palestine should, at no distant date, attain the status of an independent national State.

The hope for Jewish culturism, and this is also the hope for every culturism except those which have been nationalized in the service of the State, lies in a decrease of State activity, in decentralization (regionalism), in the reduction of the sovereign political State to a convenient administrative area (when it actually is that), and in the total abandonment, in consequence, of warlike activity and combat. Before the Great War this hope was a tangible one. At the present moment, I confess, it is a little removed; for the "coldest of cold monsters" was never more alive and never more repressive in its activities.

But in spite of the ugly posture of affairs, we must not forget that nationalism rests upon a very narrow basis in fact, and that its united front is a real one only in the presence of an active enemy. The way to remove that basis and destroy that front is to act as if it did not exist. It is fatal to attack the national State; for at each attack it obtains a new lease of power; and it is no less fatal to seek to capture it. The way to decrease the activities of the national State is to ignore it. This is the gospel according to Thoreau, and Mr. Gandhi, who is a follower of Thoreau, has put it into practice with tolerably effective results. In the meanwhile, wherever two or three people are gathered together, thinking creatively, there is the germ of a new society; and the aims of Jewish culturism will be fulfilled when the local Jewish communities throughout the world have the courage to follow the advice that Thomas Carlyle gave to the emigrant Irish, which one may paraphrase as: "Here or nowhere is your Jerusalem."

(—1922)

Our Richest Inheritance

❦

LOUIS D. BRANDEIS

WHILE I was in Cleveland a few weeks ago, a young man who has won distinction on the bench told me this incident from his early life. He was born in a little village of Western Russia where the opportunities for schooling were meager. When he was thirteen his parents sent him to the nearest city in search of an education. There —in Bialystok—were good secondary schools and good high schools; but the Russian law, which limits the percentage of Jewish pupils in any school, barred his admission. The boy's parents lacked the means to pay for private tuition. He had neither relative nor friend in the city. But soon three men were found who volunteered to give him instruction. None of them was a teacher by profession. One was a newspaper man; another was a chemist; the third, I believe, was a tradesman; all were educated men. And throughout five long years these three men took from their leisure the time necessary to give a stranger an education.

The three men of Bialystok realized that education was not a thing of one's own to do with as one pleases—not a personal privilege to be merely enjoyed by the possessor—but a precious treasure transmitted upon a sacred trust to be held, used and enjoyed, and if possible strengthened—then passed on to others upon the same trust. Yet the treasure which these three men held and the boy received in trust was much more than an education. It included that combination of qualities which enabled and impelled these three men to give and the boy to seek and to acquire an education. These qualities embrace: first, *intellectual capacity;* second, *an appreciation of the value of education;* third, *indomitable will;* fourth, *capacity for hard work.* It was these qualities which enabled the lad not only to acquire but to so utilize an education that, coming to America, ignorant of our language and of our institutions, he attained in comparatively few years the important office he has so honorably filled.

Now whence comes this combination of qualities of mind, body and character? These are qualities with which every one is familiar, singly and in combination; which you find in friends and relatives, and which others doubtless discover in you. They are qualities possessed by most Jews who have attained distinction or other success; and in combination they may properly be called Jewish qualities. For they have not come to us by accident; they were developed by three thousand years of civilization, and nearly two thousand years of persecution; developed through our religion and spiritual life; through our traditions; and through the social and political conditions under which our ancestors lived. They are, in short, the product of Jewish life.

THE FRUIT OF THREE THOUSAND YEARS OF CIVILIZATION

Our intellectual capacity was developed by the almost continuous training of the mind throughout twenty-five centuries. The Torah led the "People of the Book" to intellectual pursuits at times when most of the Ayran peoples were illiterate. And religion imposed the use of the mind upon the Jews, indirectly as well as directly, and demanded of the Jew not merely the love, but the understanding of God. This necessarily involved a study of the Laws. And the conditions under which the Jews were compelled to live during the last two thousand years also promoted study in a people among whom there was already considerable intellectual attainment. Throughout the centuries of persecution practically the only life open to the Jew which could give satisfaction was the intellectual and spiritual life. Other fields of activity and of distinction which divert men from intellectual pursuits were closed to the Jews. Thus they were protected by their privations from the temptations of material things and worldly ambitions. Driven by circumstances to intellectual pursuits, their mental capacity gradually developed. And as men delight in that which they do well, there was an ever widening appreciation of things intellectual.

Is not the Jews' indomitable will—the power which enables them to resist temptation and, fully utilizing their mental capacity, to overcome obstacles—is not that quality also the result of the conditions under which they lived so long? To live as a Jew during the centuries of persecution was to lead a constant struggle for existence. That struggle was so severe that only the fittest could survive. Survival was not possible except where there was a strong will—a will both to live and to live a Jew. The weaker ones passed either out of Judaism or out of existence.

And finally, the Jewish capacity for hard work is also the product of Jewish life—a life characterized by temperate, moral living continued throughout the ages, and protected by those marvellous sanitary regulations which were enforced through the religious sanctions. Remember, too, that amidst the hardship to which our ancestors were exposed it was only those with endurance who survived.

So let us not imagine that what we call our achievements are wholly or even largely our own. The phrase "self-made man" is most misleading. We have power to mar; but we alone cannot make. The relatively large success achieved by Jews wherever the door of opportunity is opened to them is due, in the main, to this product of Jewish life—to this treasure which we have acquired by inheritance —and which we are in duty bound to transmit unimpaired, if not augmented, to coming generations.

But our inheritance comprises far more than this combination of qualities making for effectiveness. These are but means by which man may earn a living or achieve other success. Our Jewish trust comprises also that which makes the living worthy and success of value. It brings us that body of moral and intellectual perceptions, the point of view and the ideals, which are expressed in the term Jewish spirit; and therein lies our richest inheritance.

THE KINSHIP OF JEWISH AND AMERICAN IDEALS

Is it not a striking fact that a people coming from Russia, the most autocratic of countries, to America, the most democratic of countries, comes here, not as to a strange land, but as to a home? The ability of the Russian Jew to adjust himself to America's essentially democratic conditions is not to be explained by Jewish adaptability. The explanation lies mainly in the fact that the twentieth-century ideals of America have been the ideals of the Jew for more than twenty centuries. We have inherited these ideals of democracy and of social justice as we have the qualities of mind, body and character to which I referred. We have inherited also that fundamental longing for truth on which all science—and so largely the civilization of the twentieth century—

rests; although the servility incident to persistent oppression has in some countries obscured its manifestation.

Among the Jews democracy was not an ideal merely. It was a practice—a practice made possible by the existence among them of certain conditions essential to successful democracy, namely:

First: *An all-pervading sense of the duty in the citizen.* Democratic ideals cannot be attained through emphasis merely upon the rights of man. Even a recognition that every right has a correlative duty will not meet the needs of democracy. Duty must be accepted as the dominant conception in life. Such were the conditions in the early days of the colonies and states of New England, when American democracy reached there its fullest expression; for the Puritans were trained in implicit obedience to stern duty by constant study of the Prophets.

Second: *Relatively high intellectual attainments.* Democratic ideals cannot be attained by the mentally undeveloped. In a government where everyone is part sovereign, everyone should be competent, if not to govern, at least to understand the problems of government; and to this end education is an essential. The early New Englanders appreciated fully that education is an essential of potential equality. The founding of their common school system was coincident with the founding of the colonies; and even the establishment of institutions for higher education did not lag far behind. Harvard College was founded but six years after the first settlement of Boston.

Third: *Submission to leadership as distinguished from authority.* Democratic ideals can be attained only where those who govern exercise their power not by alleged divine right or inheritance, but by force of character and intelligence. Such a condition implies the attainment by citizens generally of relatively high moral and intellectual standards; and such a condition actually existed among the Jews. These men who were habitually denied rights, and whose province it has been for centuries "to suffer and to think," learned not only to sympathize with their fellows (which is the essence of democracy and social justice), but also to accept voluntarily the leadership of those highly endorsed morally and intellectually.

Fourth: *A developed community sense.* The sense of duty to which I have referred was particularly effective in promoting democratic ideals among the Jews, because of their deep-seated community feeling. To describe the Jew as an individualist is to state a most misleading half-truth. He has to a rare degree merged his individuality and his interests in the community of which he forms a part. This is evidenced among other things by his attitude toward immortality. Nearly every other people has reconciled this world of suffering with the idea of a beneficent providence by conceiving of immortality for the individual. The individual sufferer bore present ills by regarding this world as merely the preparation for another, in which those living righteously here would find individual reward hereafter. Of all the nations, Israel "takes precedence in suffering"; but, despite our national tragedy, the doctrine of individual immortality found relatively slight lodgment among us. As Ahad Ha-'Am so beautifully said:

Judaism did not turn heavenward and create in Heaven an eternal habitation of souls. It found 'eternal life' on earth, by strengthening the social feeling in the individual; by making him regard himself not as an isolated being with an existence bounded by birth and death, but as part of a larger whole, as a limb of the social body. This conception shifts the center of gravity not from the flesh to the spirit, but from the individual to the community; and concurrently with this shifting, the problem of life becomes a problem not of individual, but of social life. I live for the sake of the perpetuation and happiness of the community of which I am a member: I die to make room for new individuals, who will mould the community afresh and not allow it to stagnate and remain forever in one position. When the individual thus values the community as his own life, and strives after its happiness as though it were his individual well-being, he finds satisfaction, and no longer feels so keenly the bitterness of his individual existence, because he sees the end for which he lives and suffers.

Is not that the very essence of the truly triumphant twentieth-century democracy?

THE TWO-FOLD COMMAND OF NOBLESSE OBLIGE

Such is our inheritance; such the estate which we hold in trust. And what are the terms of that trust; what the obligations imposed? The short answer is *noblesse oblige;* and its command is two-fold. It imposes duties upon us in respect to our own conduct as individuals; it imposes no less important duties upon us as part of the Jewish community or race. Self-respect demands that each of us lead individually a life worthy of our great inheritance and of the glorious traditions of the race. But this is demanded also by respect for the rights of others. The Jews have not only been ever known as a "peculiar people"; they were and remain a distinctive and minority people. Now it is one of the necessary incidents of a distinctive and minority people that the act of any one is in some degree attributed to the whole group. A single though inconspicuous instance of dishonorable conduct on the part of a Jew in any trade or profession has far-reaching evil effects extending to the many innocent members of the race. Large as this country is, no Jew can behave badly without injuring each of us in the end. Thus the Rosenthal and the white-slave traffic cases, though local to New York, did incalculable harm to the standing of the Jews throughout the country. The prejudice created may be most unjust, but we may not disregard the fact that such is the result. Since the act of each becomes thus the concern of all, we must exact even from the lowliest the avoidance of things dishonorable; and we may properly brand the guilty as traitor to the race.

But from the educated Jew far more should be exacted. In view of our inheritance and our present opportunities, self-respect demands that we live not only honorably but worthily; and worthily implies nobly. The educated descendants of a people which in its infancy cast aside the Golden Calf and put its faith in the invisible God cannot worthily in its maturity worship wordly distinction and things material. "Two men he honors and no third," says Carlyle—"the toil-worn crafts-man who conquers the earth and him who is seen toiling for the spiritually indispensable."

And yet, though the Jew make his individual life the loftiest, that alone will not fulfill the obligations of his trust. We are bound not only to use worthily our great inheritance, but to preserve and, if possible, augment it; and then transmit it to coming generations. The fruit of three thousand years of civilization and a hundred generations of suffering may not be sacrificed by us. It will be sacrificed if dissipated. Assimilation is national suicide. And assimilation can be prevented only by preserving national characteristics and life as other peoples, large and small, are preserving and developing their national life. Shall we with our inheritance do less than the Irish, the Serbians, or the Bulgars? And must we not, like them, have a land where the Jewish life may be naturally led, the Hebrew language spoken, and the Jewish spirit prevail? Surely we must, and that land is our fathers' land: it is Palestine.

A LAND WHERE THE JEWISH SPIRIT MAY PREVAIL

The undying longing for Zion is a fact of deepest significance—a manifestation in the struggle for existence. Zionism is, of course, not a movement to remove all the Jews of the world compulsorily to Palestine. In the first place, there are in the world about 14,000,000 Jews, and Palestine would not accommodate more than one-fifth of that number. In the second place, this is not a movement to compel anyone to go to Palestine. It is essentially a movement to give to the Jew more, not less, freedom—a movement to enable Jews to exercise the same right now exercised by practically every other people in the world— to live at their option either in the land of their fathers or in some other country; a right which members of small nations as well as of large—which Irish, Greek, Bulgarian, Serbian or Belgian, as well as German or English—may now exercise.

Furthermore, Zionism is not a movement to wrest from the Turk the sovereignty of Palestine. Zionism seeks merely to establish in Palestine for such Jews as choose to go and remain there, and for their descendants, a legally secured home, where they may live together and lead a Jewish life; where they may expect ultimately to constitute a majority of the population, and may look forward to what we should call home rule.

The establishment of the legally secured Jewish home is no longer a dream. For more than a generation brave pioneers have been building the foundations of our new old home. It remains for us to build the superstructure. The ghetto walls are now falling, Jewish life cannot be preserved and developed, assimilation cannot be averted, unless there be re-established in the fatherland a center from which the Jewish spirit may radiate and give to the Jews scattered throughout the world that inspiration which springs from the memories of a great past and the hope of a great future. To accomplish this it is not necessary that the Jewish population of Palestine be large as compared with the whole number of Jews in the world. Throughout centuries when the Jewish influence was great, and it was working out its own, and in large part the world's destiny during the Persian, the Greek, and the Roman Empires, only a relatively small part of the Jews lived in Palestine; and only a small part of the Jews returned from Babylon when the Temple was rebuilt.

The glorious past can really live only if it becomes the mirror of a glorious future; and to this end the Jewish home in Palestine is essential. We Jews of prosperous America above all need its inspiration. And the Menorah men should be its builders.   (—1915)

Democracy's Religious Root

⌒∞⌒

EMANUEL RACKMAN

IF THE STUDY, analysis, and synthesis of immediate self-verifying experiences are "musts" for the theologian, they are no less so for the political philosopher who would uphold the democratic faith. The extent to which the ideas and institutions of religion have impeded or advanced the development of democratic government is not the issue. The more fundamental problem is whether it is possible to validate the doctrines that are both explicit and implicit in our conception of democracy without relying upon our self-verifying experiences which prompt us to believe in God and the reality of a moral order in the Universe.

The fact is that every great thinker and writer on democracy has made assumptions which are based upon the reality of a moral order in the Universe. Yet many of them would resent the imputation that their thought is theological. Nonetheless, their ultimate rationale involves the validity of self-verifying experiences which underlie so much of modern theology; and it is intellectually dishonest to assume the existence of certain moral and esthetic values on the ground of self-verifying experiences while, at the same time, rejecting religious values which are validated by the same capacity of the human soul.

Bertrand Russell's admiration for democracy, for example, is based on his reverence for the life of the individual and its fulfillment. The highest value is placed thereon. He deems the totalitarian state most objectionable because it makes the welfare of the state, not the welfare of the individual, the end to be sought.

This is the essential difference between the Liberal outlook and that of the totalitarian State, that the former regards the welfare of the State as residing ultimately in the welfare of the individual, while the latter regards the State as the end and individuals merely as indispensable ingredients, whose welfare must be subordinated to a

(875)

mystical totality which is a cloak for the interest of the rulers. . . .
Liberalism, in valuing the individual, is carrying on the Christian
tradition; its opponents are reviving certain pre-Christian doctrines.
(*Power*, pages 302–303.)

Mr. Russell acknowledges that the religious tradition has heightened,
accentuated the value placed upon the individual human being. But
on what basis shall this value become a conviction? Mr. Russell graciously applauds the saints and sages of the religious tradition. Yet he
fails to see that they were able to achieve the idealism he cherishes
because they felt it to be part of a divine order of things.

Nor can a utilitarian philosophy preserve that idealism when all
values become only functions of the general happiness. From the point
of view of most men's happiness, a state that guarantees the majority
food and shelter and some amusement, and relieves them of the burden
of intelligent participation in government, is by far more desirable—
even if some minorities and some freedoms are sacrificed upon its
altars—than a state which imposes governmental responsibilities upon
every citizen, and makes all citizens co-partners in the onerous task
of self-government. Every fibre of Mr. Russell's free being would
rebel against the former. Yet, according to the doctrines of utilitarianism, the craving for security and the necessities of life that pre-
possesses the vast majority is the criterion of good.

Should Mr. Russell argue further that, while the majority may prefer
security now, in the future more men will come to resemble him and
entertain his wishes, and therefore we should promote the cause of
democracy in behalf of the future, then one can only ask why men
should sacrifice their essential desires now for a hypothetical general
happiness of unborn generations.

And, while we struggle to preserve democratic institutions, it would
be the sheerest folly to believe that our adversaries have no "general
happiness" which *they* want to conserve. The enemies of democracy
derive very certain pleasure from the magnification of their states.
That is the thing they seek. They cherish the thought of dying for
their fatherland on the field of battle. To be sure, their success and
happiness would not contribute to the happiness of other peoples over
the globe: far from it! There would not be universal happiness. But
if they are firm in their faith that for a thousand years they can
dominate the world, what makes their point of view wrong and ours

right? If victory were theirs, their own happiness might have been unparalleled. If sixty million Germans could live on the slave labor of six hundred millions, what a paradise they would have wrought for themselves!

The truth is that the basis for our faith in democracy is not that its achievement will make us happy. It is rather a self-verifying moral experience with regard to the sanctity of human life. We would rather lose our lives than violate the mandate of this moral experience. By our own intuition we sense the rightness or wrongness of a viewpoint regarding rights that inhere in man; and so strong do our convictions become that, for them, we do not hesitate to call upon our sons to make the supreme sacrifice.

It is interesting that Tom Paine, in his classic *Rights of Man,* uses biblical texts to predicate his most unscientific assumption that all men are equal. You cannot establish human equality by sense perception. No visual or auditory tests will help you. From the point of view of the chemist, an obese man has greater chemical content than a thin man. From the point of view of the economist, men with different talents have different economic worth. Even our legal system recognizes that. Kill a pauper by automobile accidentally, and his next of kin will recover a mere pittance compared to what the next of kin of a banker would receive. So Tom Paine must needs resort to biblical authority for his assumption.

Today we reach the same conclusion through man's self-verifying moral and religious experience. But to posit man's equality merely as a useful assumption does not do justice to human experience. For we regard man's equality as a real fact, even if that equality leads us to a course of conduct which may not be immediately advantageous to us. We prefer the democratic form of government, even when inefficient, to the most efficient and benevolent tyranny. To say that we exercise such preference because we have the future in mind—the mortality of the despot and the possibility that he may be succeeded by one less benevolent—is to evade the fact that we abhor the paternalism of even the benevolent dictator, because it comes from one who would ignore his basic equality with all other men.

Professor E. M. Sait, in his book *Democracy* (New York, 1929), discusses many of the criticisms that have been leveled in recent years against the democratic state. His concluding defense of "government by the many" is a theological one, though very similar to Bertrand

Russell's in tone. For he too finds the ultimate reason for preferring democracy in "the dignity of human personality."

What, then, makes this item called "human personality" so important that we attribute to it dignity and sanctity? If our faith in democracy, and its *raison d'être*, must derive validity from a conception of man as a sacred being, are we not relying upon a self-verifying moral experience no different in essence from the religious experience? The moral experience vests man with an ineffable sacred character, while the religious experience vests all the earth therewith.

Now to deem moral and religious experiences real because they are "powerful in action," and yet not to deem the objects of these experiences as real, is to deny reality to a basic element in all of such experiences. Be the object God, or the Oneness of the Universe, or the Oneness of Humanity, these objects are real—as real as the experience itself. And if one regards the objects of sense experience as real—the sun, the moon, a chair and a table—because the predication of reality to these things is a natural process of thought, so too must one predicate reality to the objects of our moral and religious experience—God, the soul, humanity, and the totality of the Universe.

Professor A. C. Knudson writes:

> . . . there is a psychological "immediacy" in objective experience that carries conviction with it. This immediacy cannot be explained away as illusory in the case of religious experience and accepted as valid in the case of sense experience. If it has epistemological value in the latter case, there is no necessary reason why it should not have it in the former. Suggestion and expectation, it is true, play a larger part in religious than in sense experience; but they do not create the objective reference of religious experience. At the most they determine to some extent the particular psychological forms that the experience takes. The objective reference is as original and immediate in religious as in sense experience. And the assurance that the apparent immediacy of the religious object carries with it has the right to be treated in the same way as the corresponding assurance in sense experience. (*The Validity of Religious Experience*, pages 99–100.)

This type of naturalism in religion, it may be added, does away with the ancient dichotomies of naturalism and supernaturalism, relativism and absolutism.

In moral and religious experiences, supernatural objects and absolutes are the things experienced. But, insofar as they are a part of man's natural experiences, they too are natural. If man believes in the reality of the world he experiences, and its intelligibility to his natural self, then he must accept the reality of those absolutes of which he catches but a glimpse. And man's capacity for moral and religious experience is part of the permanent texture of nature, not an illusory or transitory phase of his existence. With this capacity he comes to know God and the moral law. With it he grasps the infinite and eternal values.

Furthermore, such an approach makes not only for the reality of good in our conception of the Universe but also for the reality of its purpose, because our capacity for religious and moral experience involves the use of certain categories of thought. In sense experience the categories are space and time. In religious and moral experience the categories are value and purpose. They are just as real as the spatio-temporal categories by which we behold and interpret the objects of sense experience.

These spatio-temporal categories have received the attention of many philosophers in recent years. But what requires more reiteration is the pre-eminence of the *a priori* in both religious and moral experience. As Dr. Jacob B. Agus puts it, "There is indeed vouchsafed to man, albeit admittedly at rare moments only, an intuition of the eternal validity and of the extra-human source of ethical values." The values, however, are not ethical alone. They involve a perspective with regard to all that constitutes the realm of nature.

Thus one arrives at certain ideas that are fundamental in Judaism's philosophy of religion.

The first conviction is that the idea of God does not grow of itself in the human mind, "owing nothing to God's self-disclosing action." God is real and reveals Himself in the religious experience. Israel's teachers have differed in their interpretation of the account of revelation in the Bible. But all are agreed that there is direct communication between God and man.

Second, the coincidence of moral and religious experiences has always been the rule in Jewish tradition, rather than the exception. The prophets enjoyed self-verifying experiences not only of God but also of His will. His commands and exhortations of justice, peace and human brotherhood were as certain as His reality. Not all Christian philosophers would deem morality and religion inseparable; but Rudolph Otto, in his book *The Idea of the Holy*, asserts an *a priori* relation between the two. That is unequivocally the Jewish point of view.

Third, the conviction that God exists and constantly reveals Himself to man in religious experiences, which are almost invariably moral experiences also, makes Judaism a religious tradition with very few dogmas and with a primarily this-worldly emphasis. Since man's capacity for religious experience and his interpretation thereof vary constantly, Judaism makes no attempt to formulate for all times its basic beliefs. Nor does it attempt to visualize the world beyond, a world beyond physical experience, while it does seek to alter the present world through our moral experience.

Orthodox, Conservative and Reform Judaism all subscribe to these premises.

And it is by our insistence upon the validity of man's experience of God, and the simultaneity of religious and moral experiences, that we establish the validity of those aims and ideals which prompt us to preserve our democratic institutions.

(—1951)

Judaism and the Pursuit of Happiness

MILTON R. KONVITZ

"I DO NOT like the United States at all, and I am going home." These words, from an open letter which appeared in one of our leading newspapers, were written by a native of Java who had spent six years in this country as a university student. "You are so rich and so powerful," he addresses the American people, "that you have lost your sense of moral and ethical values. Perhaps that is what over-abundance does to you. You have not developed a sensitivity of conscience and an integration of spirit that come through suffering and a life of tight poverty and tears and sweat . . . Your materialism is very obvious . . . You are a country of what your writer Sinclair Lewis calls Babbits. Clothes, houses, automobiles, appearances are what matter. The spirit starves and in the end dries out . . ." And the letter closes with the words, "I am going home, therefore, to my people and [shall] tell them to cultivate our own ways and try to avoid the contamination of yours. This is better for me and for them."

As coming from one who has lived among us a good many years these words are not to be brushed aside lightly. The student from Java is expressing a view of the United States which is shared by millions of men and women who know us only by hearsay or who judge us by the libelous propaganda of the U.S.S.R. To these people we are a nation of materialists, devoted to nothing but money and gadgets. It is shouted at us from across the oceans that man does not live by bread alone. We are pelted with epithets, "barbarian" being the favorite. "They come here, these barbarians," says an Italian educator, "to teach *us* architecture—we, who are the sons of Michelangelo."

What are we to say to our disappointed visitor from Java? Or to the millions like him throughout the world who think of us as materialists preoccupied with bath tubs, dishwashers, automobiles, and central heating? I shall argue* that the indictment is not only of the American people, but of Judaism as well, and that the answer to it lies in Judaism itself.

We may heartily agree that man does not live by bread alone. It is what the Bible tells us. Man lives by everything that proceeds out of the mouth of the Lord. But where does the Lord say that bread is unimportant?

In India a child at birth has a life expectancy of forty-two years; in Egypt an expectancy of thirty-eight. India and Egypt are ancient civilizations. In the young United States, a child can be expected to reach the age of seventy—that is twenty-eight years more than in India and thirty-two years more than in Egypt. Precisely because of the American concentration on material things it has become possible, since 1900, to increase life expectancy in this country by over twenty years, to achieve the biblical life-span of three score and ten. While the population of the United States has doubled since 1900, the population of people sixty-five years of age and over has quadrupled. Our problem is not how to save the infant, but what to do with the aged. Slowly but surely gerontology has become as important to us as pediatrics.

Have such facts no spiritual import, no religious value? The Mishnah tells us that "Only one single man was created in the world, to teach that, if any man has caused a single soul to perish, Scripture imputes it to him as though he had caused a whole world to perish; and if any man saves alive a single soul, Scripture imputes it to him as though he had saved a whole world." For in the biblical view, as we know from the story of Adam and Eve, and again from the story of Noah and the flood, God needs only one man and one woman for the creation of mankind; and so, causing one man to perish is like causing the whole world to perish, and saving one life is like saving the whole world.

In 1953 the national income per capita in the United States was $1,650, the highest per capita income in the world. At the bottom of the list were China with $27 and Indonesia with $25. The figure for Saudi Arabia was $40, for Syria $100, and for Egypt $112. Our per capita income was probably five times the average for the world as a whole. Is our friend from Java prepared to say that these figures

* This essay is an adaptation of the sixth annual Horace M. Kallen Lecture given at the New School for Social Research.

have only a material significance; that they have nothing to do with a country's cultural level, with its soul, in fact?

Whether because of a lack of income or because of ignorance, some Americans fail to provide themselves with a proper diet. But few suffer from constant hunger. It is a ghastly fact that the major portion of the world's population—some two billion persons—are sick with constant hunger. "Two-thirds of the world will go to bed hungry tonight," it was reported in the *New York Times* recently. "Most of the hungry," the writer continued, "are in areas that have always been desperately poor. They very rarely see meat, milk, cheese, or eggs." The children "don't want to work or play; they are very sick and tired little people."

Again we put it to our friend from Java: Is it not sheer insensitiveness, even heartlessness, to ignore the spiritual or religious significance of these facts? The Prophets of our religion have taught us that the Lord demands that we feed the hungry. If it were not for our concern with what our critics so callously call "gadgets"—our tractors, our refrigerators, our storage bins, our trucks, our contemptible yet indispensable tin cans—we, too, would have millions of hungry men, women and children. Will the hungry continue to be fed with words or will the effort be made, even at the risk of incurring the charge of materialism, to raise their standard of living? What sense does it make to a hungry man to say to him: "Not by bread alone, but by everything that proceedeth out of the mouth of the Lord doth man live"? While you speak to him of his soul, he imagines a dish of savory food. "Bread for myself is a material question," said Nicholas Berdyaev, "bread for my neighbor is a spiritual question." But the fact is that whether it is my neighbor or myself, bread is a spiritual as well as a material question. The two questions are inseparable. With Rabbi Eleazar ben Azariah, we know that where there is no bread, there is no Torah, and where there is no Torah, there is no bread.

And we Americans work much less for our abundance than others do for their scarcity. An American works only four minutes for the money he needs to buy a pound of wheat flour, while a person in Paris works five times as long for the same thing. An American works one-half hour for a pound of beef, while a Parisian works two hours. We say nothing of the countries in which the head of the family averages no more than $100 income per year.

Today in the United States a person employed in manufacturing works about forty hours a week. A hundred years ago it was seventy hours. It is not only that the American worker himself does things more efficiently, for we have made even our barnyard animals work more efficiently. In the last twenty years the yield of milk from our cows has increased by twenty-four percent, and our hens lay forty-two percent more eggs. In 1957 we had the smallest number of cows in many years—20,500,000—yet their milk output was the largest in our history. In the last ten years we have raised our agricultural labor productivity by eighty-four per cent. The government spends over a million dollars a day for storage of our surplus wheat.

We would ask our critic from Java as we would ask other critics of American civilization: Is it more spiritual to compel a man to work seventy hours per week than to work only forty hours? Is it immoral for an American worker today to produce nearly six times as much in an hour of work as did his great-grandfather in 1850?

In the ancient land of Egypt, called the cradle of civilization, one-half of one percent of the population owns 36 percent of the cultivable land. As a consequence, fifty percent of the national income goes to 1.5 percent of the population; an agricultural worker—and sixty percent of the employed are agricultural workers—earns on the average about $64 per year. A recent Rockefeller Foundation study showed that the standard of living in Egyptian villages was the lowest in the civilized world. In Iran—ancient Persia—300 families own eighty percent of the land; and the annual per capita average income in Iran is $85. In the United States sixty percent of urban homes and seventy-five percent of the farms are occupied by their owners; and both these figures are moving up with the passage of years.

The prophet Isaiah cried out against the land-robbers of ancient Israel.

> Woe to those who join house to house,
>   who add field to field,
> Until there is no more room,
>   and you are made to dwell alone
>   in the midst of the land.

Land robbery, says the prophet, carries with it retribution upon the community which tolerates it: for then ten acres of vineyard will yield but one measure, and a homer of seed but one measure.

All these things, and much more, we could say to our student from Java as well as to the other critics of America, who see only our cars, tractors, telephones, bathtubs, but who fail or refuse to see their meaning as spiritual facts. I recall not long ago telling a Cornell student from India that in our kitchen we have an electric refrigerator, an electric stove, a washing machine, a dishwasher, a freezer, and a miscellany of smaller appliances. Mention of the dishwasher amused him. Why, he asked, could not my wife wash dishes? Was she an invalid? Then it was my turn to ask questions: Why should my wife stand over the sink to wash dishes if this drudgery could be done for her by a machine? The women of India, I reminded him, go down to the river or to the street ditch to wash the clothes. We graduated from that stage a long time ago when we piped water into our houses, and then our women stood over the wash tubs and did the laundry by hand. Now we have a machine in the house that does this work, and even a mechanical drier. It is not against our religion to lighten women's lot. Our Bible tells us that when we see an animal that is loaded down with too heavy a burden, even if the animal belongs to an enemy, it is our duty to relieve the beast. Should we not show at least equal consideration for our own wives? Is not such consideration a *religious* duty?

And I told him, too, that the woman who comes to our house to help with the cleaning drives up in a new automobile. We do not think that this is strange or wrong. Such things are taken for granted among Americans.

Today in the United States muscle power as a source of industrial production has been almost entirely eliminated, for inanimate energy accounts for nearly ninety-nine percent of our work output.

I see in these facts an inextricable union of matter and spirit. They are facts which demonstrate the conquest of matter by spirit in the interests of life-enhancing values. Whatever tends to lengthen the life of men, to reduce pain and suffering and drudgery is not mere matter; it is also mind and spirit. In the successful war on our problems, I see mind, spirit, conquering matter; but mind or spirit that uses matter in a war on matter. There is no running away from matter, and no subjection to matter. There is only its creative use. It is like Jacob struggling with the angel and not letting him go until he has blessed him.

Our visitor from Java says that we "have not developed a sensitivity of conscience and an integration of spirit that come through suffering and a life of tight poverty and tears and sweat." In other words he idealizes suffering and poverty. And he does this because for thousands of years most religions and philosophies have done precisely the same thing. They have set up self-denial, poverty, indifference to nature and the social environment as guiding ideals. The class structure of society was accepted as God given, as was the fact that the masses of people, especially women, were born slaves, untouchable and degraded, a condition from which only death could deliver them. Since life was short, brutish, and nasty, it was a virtue to deny life. Since the world that confronted the senses brought only pain and humiliation, it was wisdom to deny its reality, to think of it as illusory, and to look elsewhere—to the infinite or the hereafter—for the true and the real. Only when man withdraws from a life of action, only when he ceases to be concerned with what is relative and longs for the Absolute, does he establish some relation with Brahma or with the Absolute Reality or with God. The ideal was the solitary soul, without wife or children, without property, without personal attachments or private ambitions.

Nor was this ideal of renunciation of the world confined to peoples of the Far East. Christianity, too, preached that happiness could be found only within the soul or in heaven. The good man was not to take thought of pleasure or food or drink or clothing. The flesh was to be mortified. Men were taught that the body and the world and life itself—especially the body of woman—were nothing but corruption and gateways to hell. A. L. Goodhart, of Oxford, relates that some years ago when he called on a distinguished Oxford philosopher, he heard him say in a worried voice to one of his pupils: "I am not at all happy about pleasure." Christianity has never been happy about pleasure.

Traditionally the Christian view of life emphasized the duality of matter and spirit, body and soul, the here and the hereafter, and identified the vital and virtuous with spirit or soul alone. As long as these views ruled the minds and lives of people, there was no thought for the emancipation of slaves and women, no chance for the ideals of equality and freedom, no opportunity for universal education. People failed to see that they were in fact living not a spiritual but a materialistic life, subject as they were to matter—to plagues and epidemics, to hunger, to discomfort, to pain and suffering, to cold, to ignorance, to the brutal facts of a brutish existence.

It was only two hundred years ago that men, in revolt against the ideal of other-worldliness, began to question the premises which led to the dismissal of this world. They began to speak of happiness, and of its possibility and virtue. The thinkers of the eighteenth century launched a full-scale attack on the religion of their day and its other-worldly ideas. It was man's duty and right to plant his feet firmly on the solid ground of the visible and give up striving after the blissful state of angels or the disembodied condition of ghosts. Let us, they said, look at the near rather than the distant, at the useful rather than the use-less, the tangible rather than the speculative, the relative rather than the absolute, this life rather than the next, the earth rather than heaven. These thinkers questioned the goodness of a God who demanded of men that they purchase a happy life in the hereafter at the cost of a miser-able life in the here and now. They and their followers started a revolu-tion in the minds of men. The right to the pursuit of happiness was the first article of faith that they wrote into their religious, moral and constitutional codes.

The ideas of the eighteenth-century rationalists and humanists had in them an explosive quality, and they were let loose in full force in 1776 and in 1789. Things have not been the same since. The ground was laid for a friendly reception of science and technology. Labor-saving devices were welcomed as blessings to mankind. Utilitarianism, democracy, and humanitarianism found in the new machines means for actualizing their ideals. The new gospel of happiness was spread, not by societies for the propagation of a religious faith, but by the steam engine. The Industrial Revolution was hitched to the American and French revolutions to wipe out poverty, ignorance, slavery, class consciousness, and misery.

Today, in one way or another, people everywhere seek to make the gospel of happiness their own. Our student from Java and others who attack Americans as materialists dare not tell their own people that sickness is better than health, poverty better than wealth, scarcity better than plenty, illiteracy better than knowledge, slavery better than freedom, suffering better than pleasure. The leaders of peoples every-where clamor for American "know-how" and technical assistance. They are beginning to see that the effort to conquer nature, to make matter the servant, rather than allow it to be the master, of man's interests is a spiritual, not a materialistic effort. They see that by con-quering, assimilating matter, man transcends himself as well as matter. They are coming to realize that the modern saint is not the man who withdraws from the world, but rather a man like Albert Schweitzer who tries to spread knowledge of hygiene, medicine, and health.

Yet even today churchmen use the word "matter" or "materialism" as if it were a dirty word. Not long ago a statement signed by the heads of the Roman Catholic Church in the United States attacked materialism as "the real enemy at home as well as abroad." "The way of matter and of the flesh is the way of death," they said. They attacked "materialism" as "atheistic," and spoke of our era as "the new paganism." Thus it is that Roman Catholic and Protestant clergymen and laymen under their influence unconsciously echo the charges made by the student from Java and other critics of our country.

While Christianity is undergoing a crisis in its attempt to meet the challenge of the new philosophy of happiness, which finds no virtue in miseries that human intelligence can prevent, Judaism is not faced with a similar crisis. For Judaism has never preached that the body is evil, that the earth is profane, that poverty is a blessing, that scarcity is better than plenty. Renunciation as a way of meeting life's problems is no part of Judaism, which has always affirmed life. Judaism has never put an abyss between good and evil, saint and sinner, the saved and the damned, the selfish virtues and the social virtues, body and soul, earth and heaven, the city of God and the city of man, revelation and intelligence, time and eternity, man and woman, religion and culture. Not escape from life but involvement in and the betterment of life has been the Jewish ideal. In so far as the peoples of the world now accept this view, they accept at least part of the teaching that has come out of Zion.

Take, first of all, the plain fact of longevity. Throughout the Old Testament we find a persistent emphasis on the desirability of a long span of years. Abraham "died in a good old age." I cannot recall a single Old Testament hero who died young. For an event of this sort we have to turn to the New Testament. Jesus was only in his early thirties when he died; and he was the first Jew whose *death* was celebrated. In the Old Testament the emphasis is always on life, not death. The essence of this biblical affirmation of life is stated in Psalm 115: "May the Lord increase you, you and you, children . . . The heavens are the heavens of the Lord; but the earth hath he given to the children of men. The dead praise not the Lord, neither any that go down into silence; but we [the living] will bless the Lord from this time forth and for evermore."

The body, whether of a man or a woman, is not, in Judaism, the creation of Satan. It is the creation of God, as Genesis teaches. The body is the gateway of life and a source of joy. Abraham is quoted as saying to Sarah: "I know that you are a woman beautiful to behold"; and Isaac knew that Rebecca his wife "was fair to look upon." The patriarchs did not close their eyes to the beauty of God's creatures. And there is the story of Jacob's long wooing of Rachel, not the *idea* of Rachel, but the real woman. Not to the scale of angels are the patriarchs drawn but as men of flesh and bone and spirit—whole persons as God made them.

"And thou shalt love the Lord thy God with all thy heart, and with all thy soul, and with all thy might." To the rabbis "with all thy heart" meant "with all thy desires, including the *yetzer hara*, the evil inclination." The Jew must make even his passions and ambitions contribute to the service of God. The "evil inclination" is not to be rooted out; it is to be made the servant, rather than the master, of the whole person.

Everywhere in the Old Testament "freedom from want," an economy of abundance is held up as a divine ideal for man. The Promised Land which the Lord conjures up for the Israelites is "a good land, a land of brooks of water, of fountains and depths, springing forth in valleys and hills; a land of wheat and barley, and vines and fig-trees and pomegranates; a land of olive trees and honey; a land wherein thou shalt eat bread without scarceness, thou shalt not lack anything in it . . . And thou shalt eat and be satisfied." Job, the man of Uz who "was blameless and upright, one who feared God, and turned away from evil," had a wife and ten children, seven thousand sheep, three thousand camels, five hundred yoke of oxen, five hundred she-asses, and very many servants. He was a rich man, yet there is no intimation that Job could no more enter heaven than a camel could go through the eye of a needle.

The genius of Judaism resides not in reducing the sacred to the profane or secular, but in raising the secular to the sacred, the material to the spiritual. Just as Judaism raised the seventh day to the Sabbath, so it seeks to raise every weekday to the Sabbath; so that in the end the distinction would be not between the sacred and the secular, but between the sacred and the sacred—*ben kodesh le-kodesh.*

The ideal of Judaism is a kingdom of heaven on this earth in which every man will live under his own vine and his own fig tree, enjoying God's bounty, free from want and fear, in a social order based on justice, freedom and righteousness: an order of society which combines God's bounty with God's law—man walking in the way which the Lord commanded him, and God prolonging man's days, and blessing the fruit of his body and the fruit of his land, a nation constituting a kingdom of priests, a holy people. Man is given dominion over nature, over the works of God's hands; all things have been put under his feet, "all sheep and oxen, and also the beasts of the field, the birds of the air and the fish of the sea, whatever passes along the paths of the sea." This is what it means to have been made "little less than God," and to have been crowned with glory and honor.

"The ant is knowing and wise, but he doesn't know enough to take a vacation," Clarence Day said. "The worshiper of energy is too physically energetic to see that he cannot explore certain higher fields until he is still." But Judaism, with its emphasis on righteousness, with its institution of the Sabbath day, and with the importance it attaches to study as a form of worship, has taught the Jew to avoid imitation of the ant. The Jew has been taught to stand still. But a vacation is important only if one customarily works, and to stand still is important only if one is ordinarily in motion. Judaism tries to be true to a healthy rhythm of life. Built into it, therefore, is a principle of asceticism which is not that of total resignation or renunciation, but of acceptance of the vital needs of the whole human being, the needs of getting and spending, of work and rest, of affirmation and denial. Man must be engaged and yet suspended, involved and yet withdrawn. Judaism teaches self-denial for the sake of a greater affirmation. Jewish asceticism is, thus, one of the poles of a natural organic rhythm; it is an asceticism that affirms life and serves the self in its quest for fulfillment. It is not stagnation, not resignation, not renunciation, but the sabbatical pause, the sabbatical rest, the sabbatical withdrawal that is itself an enjoyment as man lets his soul loaf and looks for reconciliation with all that is beautiful and lovely and holy.

Some Christian theologians have begun to turn against the traditional Christian perversion of the Jewish attitude to life. Tillich, Reinhold Niebuhr, and Cherbonnier are among the leaders in this effort to reinterpret Christianity. For example, Cherbonnier's reinterpretation of the doctrine of sin in the light of Old Testament teaching leads him to affirm the *goodness* of creation, and the radical freedom of man, and to call the doctrine of original sin and belief in predestination Christian misconceptions. In reaching this conclusion he finds it necessary to challenge Augustine, Aquinas, Luther, and Calvin, in the name of and for the sake of biblical religion. In so far, he says, as Christianity manifests "a negative view of the world in general and a repressive attitude toward the flesh in particular," it has been infiltrated by "pagan value judgments." When Aquinas placed matter in the lower half of his scale of realities he bifurcated human nature into mind and matter, and thereby sacrificed the Bible to Aristotle. And Cherbonnier goes on to say that the God of the Bible wants "not the annihilation of unruly passions, but their conversion, for the greatest power of evil may also be transformed into even greater forces for good." The Bible does not demand *"disuse* but redemption," and the "joyous affirmation of the goodness of the present life" is an essential biblical outlook.

Writing in 1870 Emerson formulated a number of tests of civilization. First, he said, civilization depends upon man utilizing effectively the aid of nature, letting the elements do his hard work. That, he said,

is the wisdom of man, in every instance of his labor, to hitch his wagon to a star, and see his chore done by the gods themselves. That is the way we are strong, by borrowing the might of the elements.

Secondly, man, in his effort to become civilized, must lean on principles, for they are the most powerful of all supports. "Gibraltar may be strong," said Emerson, "but ideas are impregnable." Again, "Work . . . for those interests which the divinities honor and promote —justice, life, freedom, knowledge, utility."

Thirdly, by working with the energies of the universe and the commandments of God, "we can harness also evil agents, the powers of darkness, and force them to serve against their will the ends of wisdom and virtue." The power "to combine antagonisms and utilize evil" is an index to civilization.

In all this, Emerson, I submit, is describing not only civilization, but the genius of Judaism. He is giving expression to the hope that underlies the American dream: Hitch your wagon to a star, so that you may harness the star's energies to turn your wheels, so that the stars may do the work of innumerable human hands. Hitch your wagon to a star, so that you may raise your sights to the vision of celestial principles, which alone can make gods of men—ideas like justice, truth, equality, freedom, goodness, beauty, happiness. Hitch your wagon to a star, so that you may harness the energies even of your "evil inclination" and let it, too, serve God.

This, as I know it, is the teaching of Judaism. It is also the sense of that glorious phrase of the Declaration of Independence: "life, liberty, and the pursuit of happiness."

True, the biblical injunction is not: "Happiness, happiness shalt thou pursue." Israel was told: "Justice, justice shalt thou pursue." But as long as body and soul are conjoined, as long as man is a complex of matter and spirit, there can be no pursuit of justice without the pursuit of happiness. Humanity—since the eighteenth-century revolutions— has at last begun to accept this "word of the Lord out of Jerusalem."

(*—1962*)

Ends and Means of Jewish Life in America

ｃＡＮｏ

JACOB B. AGUS

W E HAVE all become used to—and perhaps spoiled by—the suave and tolerant expositions of those who glibly solve the matter of Jewish status in America by the artful strategy of blurring the concepts of nationality and religion, so that each one may behold in the resultant harmonious formula the image of "whatsoever his heart lusteth after." It has become fashionable in recent years to declare that the categories of nationality and religion are "alien" to the Jewish mind; that the pattern of values in Judaism is a "unique" combination of these two loyalties, which have been supposedly separated in the Christian world through a process of degradation; that, in consequence, Jewish loyalty and Jewish status are neither religious nor national, but partake somehow of both conceptions in something altogether new that is *sui generis*—something that is currently being denominated as "peoplehood."

This strategy is being employed even by writers whose position is really very close to ours, who are nevertheless constrained from holding it explicitly by considerations weightier by far than those of semantics.

Let us examine the strategy.

First, it is naive to declare that the concepts of nationality and religion are borrowed from the "alien" Christian world and that these concepts are incommensurate with the categories of the "Jewish mind." Much else in this modern world would thus be strange to the "Jewish mind," including the extreme solicitude of ultra-modernists for the authentic brand of pre-modern nationalism. In this proposition the term "Jewish mind" is taken to be the mind of the pre-modern Jew of biblical, talmudic or medieval times. But we know that religion and nationality were intimately related also in the ancient pagan world, as well as among the Jews. And in Christian Europe the ties between nationality and religion were severed only by degrees and at the sacrifice of many valiant lives.

To view our own situation in the proper perspective it is well for us to recall the observation of the great historian Ranke: "In most periods of world history nations were held together by religious ties alone." We tend to forget that at the dawn of the modern era the emergent nations of Europe were still closely bound to their established churches, and that it was the separation of church and state, violent or peaceful, that ushered in the era of democracy and made possible the emancipation of the Jew.

If the spirit of modern democracy is rooted in Judaism, how can the very essence of democratic society be "alien" to it?

Furthermore, as modern Jews of Western civilization, we operate necessarily and inescapably with the concepts of the Western world, "alien" as they may or may not have been to the mind of the ancient Jews. Can it be honestly maintained that the modern Jew is incapable of recognizing the difference between national and religious values? Is not our problem due precisely to the acute awareness of this distinction, on the part of both Jews and Gentiles?

The claims of "uniqueness" and "difference" for Jewish nationalism must be exploded before the complex situation of American Jewry can be placed in the perspective of history. If the term "mission" is merely a euphonious designation for the culture of a nation or the religion of a group, then it is entirely meaningless. If, however, it is offered as a means of raising national loyalty out of its proper sphere and elevating it to a supreme end in life, then we may adduce ample evidence from history to prove its inherent menace. For the history of modern times shows nothing so clearly as the beguiling hypnotic lure of romantic messianic nationalism claiming the quality of "uniqueness" and "difference," and the inevitable moral ruin of all such movements.

WHAT DO WE MEAN BY JUDAISM?

Ever since the opening of the modern era there have been among us those who favored the expurgation from the Jewish religion of all national elements, as well as those who championed the contrary thesis of a Jewish nationalism completely independent of religion. By their very existence the movements of both classical Reform and

secular nationalism demonstrated the theoretic possibility of abstracting the religion of Israel from the nationalist aspirations of Jewish
people. But neither of these extremes is capable of serving today as
the vital nucleus of a philosophy of Jewish life—the one austere and
abstract, the other unable to offer a livable alternative to the seemingly inevitable choice it propounds between evacuation from the
West and assimilation into it.

For the majority of American Jews the real choice is not between
those two extreme interpretations of Jewish loyalty, as they were
formulated in the nineteenth century. It is rather between a conception of Judaism that includes the healthy earth-bound and fructifying
elements of loyalty to the people of Israel, and a conception of nationalism that includes religious life and expression within its pattern of
values. This issue between the two sets of hierarchical values, though
they contain for the most part the same elements, is of extreme
urgency and pith in molding the mentality of the American Jew. While
it may seem to be only a matter of relative emphasis, and therefore
of interest only to professional theologians and pedantic theorists, in
actual fact it indicates the inner struggle for the soul of the Jew that
is even now taking place on the American scene.

To understand why we feel bound to repudiate the philosophies
which interpret nationalist loyalty as being the heart of Judaism,
even though they condescend to employ religious symbols and practices, we shall do well to remove the cloak of "uniqueness" from this
combination and see it as it actually functioned in other nations.
For, as a matter of fact, modern nationalism, especially in its romantic
reactionary phases, did not at all scruple to employ, and thereby
subvert for its own purposes, the sentiments and principles of religion.

Thus Fichte, the prophet of modern German nationalism, urged
the adoption of a modified Lutheranism as a new national religion, an
ambition which attained its climax in Bismarck's *Kultur-Kampf*. The
most popular slogan in the German War of Liberation in the first
decade of the nineteenth century was "German freedom, a German
God, German faith without a scoff." Nor was Italian nationalism
essentially different in its professions. As formulated by Mazzini,
nations are "prophets of the Lord," the "social instruments through
which a divine mission is fulfilled." "We cannot have Rome," he
declared, "without initiating a new religious epoch." He looked forward
to the time when "religion would be the soul, the thought of the new

state." And in this respect the Russian spokesmen of black reaction spoke the same language as the quasi-socialist Mazzini. Dostoevsky, probing the mysteries of the so-called "Slavic soul," was led to preach reaction and Orthodox Christianity. The arch-reactionary and arch-anti-Semite Pobiedonostzev regarded Orthodoxy as Russia's national religion, inasmuch as it had been completely suffused with "our Russian soul." "A Russian feels chilled in a Protestant Church," he declared. Hence he felt justified in persecuting all sectarians and in seeking to coalesce pan-Slavism with Russian Orthodoxy as the expression of Slavonic mysticism. That curious and, let it not be forgotten, dangerous conjunction of ideas is clearly if inconsistently expressed in this passage quoted by Professor Salo W. Baron (*Modern Nationalism and Religion,* page 195): ". . . sacred idea of Slavdom, which is based not upon the quest of power, but on the idea of the equality of all humanity. We fight for freedom, the Orthodox cross and civilization. Behind us is Russia."

These examples of nationalist religious thought should suffice to arouse our suspicion that Hitler's pseudo-religious brand of nationalism was not the product of just a personal aberration but, in large part, the final fruition of the evil seeds planted by those who thought of God as the junior partner of the nation.

Achad Ha'am, who frankly construed the Jewish religion as the "exilic garments" which the national soul in the past created for itself in order to ward off the inroads of assimilation, was honest and spiritually sensitive enough to repudiate such a servile role for religion in the spiritual makeup of his own generation and the future. For he came to recognize that religion, as the highest expression of the human spirit, can function only as the supreme end in life; hence religion must not be subverted into an instrument for national purposes. In any synthesis of national sentiments with religious values it is the latter that must be raised to the supreme level of importance; the former may be allowed but a subsidiary role, and encouraged only so long as they remain in accord with the standards and ideals of ethics and religion.

Accordingly, in our conception of Judaism the ethical-spiritual values of personal piety constitute the luminous core and substance; while around it, shading off into a penumbra, there cluster the instruments and methods of collective expression, the national sentiments and values in all their variety, concern with the fate of Jews the world over, intimate spiritual identification with the life of the people in the Land of Israel, the love of Hebrew and of all the creative achievements of the Hebraic renaissance. Whatever is creative in Jewish life is dear to us, but not all expressions equally, for they are subject to evaluation and continuous remolding in terms of universal spiritual standards. We regard all activities as falling into a hierarchial pattern of relative value, a ladder of Jacob standing on the ground and reaching up to the heavens.

NATIONALISM AS A CREATIVE FORCE

The reasons for the hard fact that nationalism, whether frankly secular or dressed up in dubious religious garb, cannot serve as a goal for Jewish life in America. As an independent motive, sheer nationalism —especially as "normalized" since the establishment of the State of Israel—can only lead either in the direction of headlong assimilation or toward the status of a racist minority.

The enhancement of Jewish pride through the military victories of the Israelis does not at all serve to counter the assimilationist trend. On the contrary, assimilation works most effectively when the minority group is not obsessed by inferiority complexes. History provides abundant illustrations for the thesis that a minority is difficult to assimilate if it is oppressed and humiliated. Thus the emotional boost to Jewish pride, administered by the nascent State of Israel, merely underscores the important truth that the national impulse, as such, is not capable of functioning in America as a goal for Jewish living.

But when subordinated to higher considerations Jewish nationalism may continue to be a powerful creative force, serving the ends of Jewish religion, as it did in the past, by bringing to the aid of piety additional motivation, and by supplying foci of sentimental loyalty within the Jewish community.

For, as we have learned from the study of Judaism and other faiths, religion is not merely an abstract set of dogmas but an organic pattern of values, sentiments and practices, in which a variety of social impulses are utilized, guided and interpreted so as to form a dynamic whole. This truth, which was not realized by the builders of classical Reform, calls for the establishment of a set of values in the spiritual realm and a pattern of organization in the social realm within which national feelings and aspirations may play a healthy productive role.

When, however, the nationalist ideal is elevated to the status of a supreme goal, it begins by leading our people into an emotional *cul-de-sac*, since it cannot offer a worthy *raison d'être* for American Jewish life; and it ends, through the surge of its blind momentum, by relegating Jewry to the status of a self-segregating racist minority, since it deliberately rejects the goal of assimilation which is the natural end of other immigrant nationalists in America.

TOWARDS THE CLARIFICATION OF JEWISH BEING

The need for clarifying the status and pattern of loyalties of American Jewry is made imperative by factors which, though once overstressed, are now utterly ignored. As we have maintained, the Jewish situation in America is not essentially unique. But it has been overlaid—in the old European pattern—with a cloud of misrepresentations and hazy notions, which cannot now be overlooked. The barrier—compounded of theological devilries, romantic delusions and reactionary guile—for ages interposed between Jews and Gentiles, was rendered the more formidable by Hitlerite propaganda and strategy. The whole point of our analysis is that this barrier, representing Jewry as invincibly "unique," is an accumulated medley of old notions which are without foundation in present realities. They can be dissipated by clear vision and ruthless logic.

Current discussion of the evolving Jewish status in this country still continues to formulate the question in the Napoleonic manner: Are the Jews a nation or a religion? The several arguments, smoothed out into bland clichés, have been bandied about backwards and forwards so many times that the underlying volcanic force which first propelled this question to the surface is forgotten.

After the triumph of Zionism in our day is it any longer necessary to belabor the point that neither the category of nationalism nor the category of religion is capable of containing and expressing the full measure of Jewish loyalty? But it is not yet realized that these two much-overworked categories, even when taken jointly, do not adequately reflect the character of Jewish being. It is the elusive quality which escapes both categories that is precisely the essence of the problem.

For in addition to his religious convictions and his sense of kinship with the scattered remnants of his people, the Jew in the past felt himself set apart from other nations in yet a deeper sense. He did not simply belong to another nation, nor did he simply hold on to another faith; he belonged to a group that was "set apart" and that "dwells alone"—an *am segullah*. So that between his people and the other peoples of the world there yawned a gulf deeper by far than the other boundary lines which divide humanity. As the Midrash put it, Abraham was called the "Hebrew" (literally "from across") "for the whole world is ranged on one side and Abraham and his children on the other side."

Echoes of this awareness are found in the doctrines of "the holy seed," the "uncleanness" of other lands and other peoples, the kabbalist and pre-kabbalist beliefs in a special Jewish soul, and in the entire complex of sentiments and valuations and aspirations clustering around the concepts of *Galut* and the Messiah. Even in our own day it is easy to cite instances of psychological self-isolation in proof of the fact that the awareness of being Jewish is not exhausted either by religious conviction or national loyalty, nor by both types of allegiance taken together. Do not even non-Zionists and non-religionists regard with dismay the prospect of their children marrying out of the faith?

To facilitate our analysis we are forced to coin a new term—the "meta-myth."

The meta-myth designates that indeterminate but all-too-real *plus* in the consciousness of Jewish difference, as it is reflected in the minds of both Jews and Gentiles.

THE META-MYTH AMONG GENTILES

On the part of Gentiles the meta-myth is echoed in the verbal contrast of Gentile and Jew. The Jew is different in some mysterious manner. In the imagination of the untutored he may appear to be now partaking of divine qualities, now bordering on the diabolical, now superhuman in his tenacity, now subhuman in his spiteful determination to survive; but always, in some dim sense, the traditional stereotype of the Jew held by the Gentiles includes the apprehension of deep cosmic distinction from the rest of humanity.

This feeling has been reflected in the mythological substructure of anti-Semitism from its very origins. In the Roman world the Jews were popularly baited as "misanthropes," who stubbornly insisted on

their separation from the rest of humanity, a stereotype which under-
lay the accusation then made for the first time that in the Holy
Temple the blood of a Greek was used for some mysterious ceremonies.
In the Christian religion the meta-myth was elaborated into an all-
embracing cosmic design, where the Jew figured as the earthly embodiment and symbol of those who reject and are rejected, the son
of the Anti-Christ. From earliest childhood the Christian is still inculcated with the image of the Jew as a dark figure, semi-mythological
and semi-diabolical in character, living in this world and yet not of
this world, arrayed against mankind in some occult fashion—a hateful,
embittered, self-isolating Shylock in the mundane realm; a perennial
Satanic mystery in the theological realm. This meta-myth constitutes
the apperceptive base for the *Protocols of the Elders of Zion,* the
bizarre reasoning of which, we must not forget, is so seductive in its
appeal to the Christian mind that so sober and critical a newspaper as
the *London Times* at one time printed it as a possibly authentic
document.

It remained, however, for the neo-pagans Chamberlain, Rosenberg
and Hitler to seize and develop the floating meta-myth into a systematic and all-embracing "Myth of the Twentieth Century," and to
use it as the cornerstone for their entire superstructure of propaganda.
In the course of time they were driven by the very logic of their
mythology to murder the six million Jews in "proof" of the viciousness
of the mythological figure of the "non-Aryan."

The meta-myth has not been a cause of anti-Semitism in the conventional understanding of causality, as it never functioned alone
and in the full light of day in the minds of either Jews or Gentiles. But,
from its roots in the subconscious, it has lent plausibility and force
to any and all causes. It constitutes even today the mystical and
emotional miasma which, like tar, clings to the image of the Jew in
the public mind, making it possible for the vile feathers of malice,
thrown out by professional anti-Semites, to stick.

It would take us too far afield to search for all the roots of the
meta-myth. Suffice it to say that for the last two thousand years it
has formed part of a vicious circle of cause and effect, in which the
meta-myth provoked persecution which, in turn, served as "proof"
of the meta-myth to the subconscious mind, thereby strengthening it
the more and setting the stage for a fresh series of persecutions. The
tragic history of the Jew in all lands made it appear that never could

the Jew find peace among the nations, and that in some mysterious manner this fate was inescapable and inexorable.

The debates in the Emancipation period concerning the either-national-or-religious character of Jewish loyalty were not motivated by a zeal for semantics or a flair for verbal jugglery. The emergent nations of Europe were, even then, not ethnically "pure" nationalities; so that the fact of deriving from a different national origin need not have stood in the way of Jewish emancipation. Did Englishmen attempt to circumscribe the civil rights of Welshmen or Scotsmen? Did the Prussians impose a special tax on the movement of Slavs or on their rights of residence, as they imposed special taxes upon Jews? Why, then, should the conception of Jewish nationhood have appeared to the Jesuits and reactionaries to be a valid reason for repudiation of the Emancipation? And why did even the liberal statesmen of Germany, Austria and Russia feel that only through secular education would the Jews "improve" morally so far as to deserve equality of rights, at a time when their own nations were still largely illiterate?

The answer is to be sought in the dim recesses of the European mind, where the meta-myth ruled with undiminished sway even when the power of the Church was broken. The category of a separate nation echoed the meta-myth in interposing the barrier of alienism between Jew and Gentile. It called attention not so much to the ethnic origin of the Jew as to his persistent refusal to follow the normal course of assimilation pursued naturally by other scattered groups. It compelled the interpretation of this extraordinary Jewish tenacity as being due, on the one hand, to perverse pride, nurtured by centuries of enforced segregation and voluntary self-isolation, hammered out by an endless series of pogroms; and, on the other hand, to the indoctrination of self-worship as the "Chosen People."

The Napoleonic insistence on the clear formulation of the religious nature of Judaism had as its purpose the allaying of the meta-myth, so that the Jew could become part and parcel of Western society without external limitations or inner reservations. But the hovering specter of the sinister, strangely powerful myth continued to be reflected in all the discussions of the Jewish problem through the nineteenth century and down to our own day. It has received a new lease on life through the rise and growth of romantic-religious nationalism, which saw in the Jew the image at once of its fulfillment and negation—fulfillment in the doctrine of the "Chosen People" and negation in the attempt of assimilationist and liberal Jews to become part of the nations.

THE META-MYTH AND ZIONISM

The rise of Zionism was directly occasioned by the growing menace of the meta-myth.

The conception of World Jewry as a national entity need not, in itself, have resulted in the movement to re-establish a homeland and regain independent political status. A scattered ethnic group normally solves its problems by gradual dissolution and assimilation. Actually, it was the ominous thundercloud of the meta-myth that convinced Herzl and the Western European Zionists that the greater part of European Jewry would have to be evacuated into a re-established homeland while the remainder would be completely assimilated.

Herzl's whimsical suggestion, in his pre-Zionist days, that all Austrian Jewry be converted *en masse*, was not really abandoned by him after he beheld the prophetic vision of a reborn Land of Israel; for the alternative to evacuation, in his message to the Jews of Europe, was still absolute and total assimilation. In his correspondence with the leaders of German and French Jewish assimilationists he argued, with some plausibility, that the Zionist program would make the path of assimilation that much easier. As Dr. Emanuel Neumann recently put it, in his address to the Zionist Organization of America's Convention on "Reorienting Zionist Education Today": "Many people, thousands and perhaps hundreds of thousands, who till now have felt that they could not desert a beleaguered people, will no longer be constrained, but will feel able to depart without those qualms of conscience which have deterred them in the past." In any case, Dr. Herzl felt that a vital and secure type of Jewish life was impossible in the lands of the Diaspora.

East-European Zionists, however, did not envisage their movement as the means of liquidating the Diaspora. On the contrary, they looked upon it as the only way of exploding the meta-myth, and thereby rendering Jewish group-life possible in the form of a minority nationality, in all the lands of the dispersion. Dr. Leo Pinsker diagnosed the meta-myth as a mass psychosis, resulting from the bodyless "ghostly" character of the Jewish nation. He was certain that this psychosis would be cleared up as soon as the Jewish position in the world was "normalized" by the establishment of a territorial center. World Jewry would then be removed from the category of the mysterious and the unique, and classed along with other ethnic minorities in the various lands of the Diaspora.

WHAT STATUS NOW FOR AMERICAN JEWS?

The establishment of the State of Israel can affect the meta-myth in both directions at once.

On the one side, it might serve to the American public as proof positive of the meta-myth—if it is presented as the means of "redemption" for World Jewry and the solution of the "Jewish problem" in all countries, including our own. The tremendous fanfare of publicity which attended the formation of the State of Israel might then have cumulatively the effect of evoking the image of American Israel as a people in flight, unable or unwilling to follow the course of the other immigrant nationalities which are even now steadily on the way to becoming part and parcel of the emergent American nation. It would serve as "Exhibit A" of the meta-myth—to wit, that the gulf between Jew and Gentile is absolute and unbridgeable, that there can be no peace for the Jew in the Christian world, that he must remain forever unabsorbed and alien, paying willingly indeed the price of patriotism in blood and treasure, as he pays for all else, but remaining inwardly foreign, bound by the indissoluble ties of a uniquely tempered tribalism.

But, on the other side, the birth of the State of Israel might also serve as the means of shattering the meta-myth once and for all, as Leo Pinsker had hoped, by demonstrating the sameness in quality and aspiration of Jewish and non-Jewish national loyalties. This effect will result if it is made sun-clear that the intention in establishing the homeland was not at all the evacuation of American Jewry either in whole or in part, but the founding of a haven of refuge for the persecuted Jews in other lands, and the creation of a cultural-religious center for World Jewry. In that case the emergence of a new type of "productive" and fighting Jew will help to banish the time-worn Jewish stereotype from the minds of Christians, and at the same time aid the American Jew to accept his Jewish origin with pride and his religious heritage with ease and naturalness, as all other Americans accept their origins and religions. To this end the theses of Herzlian Zionism must be repudiated insofar as American Jewry is concerned.

Thus the choice of permanently validating or dissipating the meta-myth depends today upon the judgment and insight of American Jewish leadership. The organization of Jewish life in America on a nationalist basis, quite apart from the presence or absence of concrete political ties with the State of Israel, would serve as an invitation for the awakening of the meta-myth in the minds of Jews and Gentiles alike. When Herzlian Jewish nationalism is put forward as the cause and purpose of Jewish survival, then the inherent ideology of the movement cannot be aught else but a confession of the inevitable triumph of the meta-myth. The incorporation of this fear-born conviction into the organizational structure of Jewish life is bound to affect powerfully the minds of Jews and Gentiles alike, helping to create a climate of opinion favorable to the malignant growth of the meta-myth.

Though the academic theory of Jewish nationalism is in itself innocuous and neutral, an intense survivalist nationalism—being by its very nature unique on the American scene, where other immigrant nationalists commingle naturally to produce the emergent American nation—will of necessity be fitted into the mold of the meta-myth. Thus, while nationalism in general is spelled out in the psychological terms of alienism, erecting the barrier of "mine" and "thine" in the battle for the world's goods, American Jewish nationalism in particular would suffer from the additional burden of association with the distorting and soul-smothering nightmare of the meta-myth.

We are led irresistibly, then, to emphasize the religious purpose of Jewish group survival in this country. Now let us see some of the implications of this position.

COROLLARIES OF THE RELIGIOUS STATUS

The achievement of a religious status for American Jewry cannot be effected by the mere say-so of spokesmen. It is a great and complex task, requiring a many-sided effort in various directions. For the actual living philosophy of a group is expressed but partly and superficially in verbal pronunciamentos. It is expressed largely and deeply in its organizational structure. The implications of an avowed acceptance of religious status may be outlined under three headings: (1) public education; (2) communal structure; and (3) relationship to the State of Israel.

Our field of public education is far wider than the limited sphere usually denoted by the term "Jewish education." It includes, in addition, the message delivered from pulpit and platform, and the tremendous oratorical marathons that are associated with the fund-raising efforts for the United Jewish Appeal. To all these activities the following corollaries of a religious conception apply:

(a) *The preaching of fear to American Jews must cease.*

If we are to sink our roots into this soil, we cannot do it half-heartedly and without faith. In the long run, whipped-up mass hysteria is bound to set in motion a train of events culminating in the very horrors conjured up by the purveyors of fear. One hears so frequently the argument for Jewish insecurity in America: the ultimate catastrophe happened before in Spain where the Jews for a time enjoyed a Golden Age and then suffered the tortures of the Inquisition and the expulsion; it happened before in Poland, once "the Paradise of the Jews," but where ghetto benches and economic exclusion prevailed even before the Nazi subjugation; it happened before in Germany, where assimilation seemed to have prospered most but whence nevertheless the deluge of devastation burst forth upon the Jews of Europe. Why, then, not expect a similar fate for American Jewry?

This popular cadence of calamities, abstracted from the bi-millennial history of Diaspora Jewry, lends itself beautifully to the meretricious art of the orator and is particularly beloved by professional fund-raisers. This type of argumentation, drawing as it does a sharp line of distinction between the fate of Jews and that of the other immigrant nationalities that are steadily coalescing to form the American nation, is in reality an appeal to the psychical neurosis of the meta-myth, as previously described. For it lumps all nations together in the one suspicion-laden, pogrom-reeking, hostile category of "goyim"; and it assumes that the gulf between Jew and Gentile will never permanently be bridged by sympathetic understanding.

The sober fact is, of course, that vast differences obtain between any past situation elsewhere and the position of Jews today in America— differences which need not be enumerated here. But one thing should be underscored. *Those who have no faith in America obviously cannot be trusted with the task of building the future of Jewry in America.*

(b) *Diaspora Jewish existence must not be depicted as unworthy and shameful.*

In the flush of enthusiasm over the establishment of the State of Israel the derogatory references to exilic life, current in neo-Hebraic literature, were seized upon with avidity, as if Jews had no right to be decently proud of their people prior to the passing of the Partition Resolution. Characteristic of this self-induced mood was the frequently heard expression, "I am not a *damned* Jew any longer! I got a country of my own." As if the Jew was deservedly damned before the State of Israel was called into being!

In the merited adulation of the pioneering type, the *chalutz,* one often hears echoes of the philosophy of Israel Chaim Brenner, prophet of *chalutziuth,* whose bitter denunciations of Jewish life in the Diaspora formed part of the ideology of the Zionist Labor movement. Brenner held that the Jews in the Diaspora lived "the life of gypsies who attach themselves to the natives for their pleasure, the life of dogs who flatter and serve their masters." The whole millennial travail of World Israel he envisaged as "a bitter mistake, bloated pride, falsehood and delusion." He described the whole exile as a thing of shame, and the Jews who have chosen it as "non-human people, called Jews—wounded dogs." Such is the Brennerian mentality which is so frequently invoked these days as self-evident truth.

Listen to a sentence in the clarion call to teachers of a prominent Jewish educator in America: "The proud, but true, boast of the *Yishuv* is that within one generation the shame and desolation was removed from our land, and the shame of exile and ghetto from our souls." Exile and the ghetto may indeed be construed as calamities; but what is that "shame on our souls"? Why should the oppressed feel ashamed? According to Judaism it is the oppressor who bears shame on his soul, not his victim, "for the Lord seeks the pursued." Are we, in a moment of triumph, to throw overboard our standards of true spiritual dignity? How much wiser were the Rabbis when they upheld the contrary extreme, knowing that between it and human nature the proper balance would be struck. Thus they said: "Those who are insulted, but do not insult, who bear their humiliation and do not reply in kind, of them the sacred verse speaks when it says, 'And those who love Him are even as the sun in its might.'"

(c) *We must be on our guard against the cultivation of a sense of alienism from the American nation.*

Too many of our young people have been taught to ridicule the formula of being "American by nation and Jewish by religion." Even some of our tribunes committed to a religious status for American Jews continue the traditional pastime of satirizing the designation "Americans of the Jewish faith," though it echoes their avowed conception. In the rush of climbing on the secular nationalist bandwagon they seem to have forgotten the redoubtable fact that the totality of national feelings contains barriers of exclusion as well as bonds of inclusion. If nationalism in all its implications is given free rein in the Jewish schools and public life, it will eventually induce a state of mind most congenial to the meta-myth.

The sense of alienism is not to be confused with the popularly discussed fear of "double loyalty," for it functions in the realm of the spirit, not in the domain of politics and patriotism. It is concerned with the inner sense of self-identification which may or may not find expression in overt acts. When this sense of self-identification is not directed into spiritual channels, thus serving as additional motivation for the good life, but is allowed to develop its inherent logic and acquire its own momentum, it cannot but eventuate into a self-induced mood of alienism.

It should also be noted that the line of division on this issue cuts clear across the ranks of organized Zionists, as was demonstrated at the recent conference on "Reorienting Zionist Education Today." In the years ahead the rift between Zionists and non-Zionists will likely disappear; instead, a deep gulf will be revealed between those who regard American Jewish life as viable and worthy in itself, and those who think of it merely as a temporary financial and spiritual colony of the Israeli mother-country, slated for eventual liquidation.

Since the mentality of the latter group is rarely brought into the open, it may be well for us to observe its operation in the writings of one of its best exponents.

THE MENTALITY OF COLONIALS OF ISRAEL

The late Dr. Jacob Klatzkin, noted Hebrew philosopher, formulated the logic of secular nationalism in words that capture its full dynamic impetus. They can therefore serve as a clear warning to all of us who wish to raise a generation of Jews who will feel perfectly at home on the American scene.

The following quotations are taken from Dr. Klatzkin's Hebrew book, *T'chumim*, which has been used as a basic text of Zionism in at least one American Hebrew Teachers College.

Know that so long as the nations of the world battle against us, it is a good sign for us. It indicates that our national form is not yet rubbed out and that our alienism is still felt. The ending of the war, or its weakening, would testify to the erasing of our identity and the softening of our alienism. We shall not attain equality of rights anywhere, save in reward for an implied or expressed confession that we are not a national body in itself, but parts of the body of the people of the land—or at the price of complete assimilation.

Who are our enemies and how do they present the case for the prosecution? They look upon us as a separate national group and complain against Israel: one people it is that does not mingle with the nations. One people it is, though scattered and dispersed; and if Jews declare themselves to be good Germans, good Frenchmen, good Russians, don't believe them: Jews they are, nonetheless. . . .

Who are our friends and how do they present the case for our defense? They see us as the remnants of a dead people and they advocate our cause by saying: "He is already dead and passed out of this world and only the bare name is left. The Jews of our time become progressively bone of our bone and flesh of our flesh; they speak our language and learn our literature and the sancta of our civilization, love the country of their birth, and admire the great of the land and strive mightily for the welfare of the nation. Already their share in the nation's cultural wealth is very great; and if their assimilation into our midst is still not completed and there is left in them some of their ancient alienism, who is to blame for the postponement of the consummation if not the anti-Semitism of the nationalist reactionaries, which erects boundaries between us and them, preventing a proper amalgamation? Therefore, it is our duty to accord them complete equality, to act towards them as to children of our nation and to treat them as faithful brothers."

And the defendant himself, the Hebrew people, what do we say? If we desire to live a national life in exile, we should tell our defender: "We desire neither your honey nor your sting! The prosecution is right. An alien people we are and we desire to continue in our alienism. We admit the propriety of your being concerned over your national character and your desire to maintain separation between us and yourselves, but we protest against the vulgar forms of this separation."

Thus, instead of forming societies to defend us against anti-Semites, who seek to limit our rights, we should establish societies to defend us from our friends who fight on our side, as it were. [Pages 70, 71]

Also many of our nationalist Jews, when they demand civil rights, say to the nations: "Citizens, we are like you; we are patriotic and prepared to offer the supreme sacrifice; and we demand one law for us and for you without any kind of distinction or discrimination." It has already become a common cliché in the mouths of our nationalist spokesmen: We are loyal Jews and loyal Germans, loyal Jews and loyal Frenchmen," and so on . . .

But if the power of our ancestors' endurance and if the qualities of truthfulness and national dignity had prevailed among us above the rush for full equality of rights, we should not have hesitated rather to say to the people of the land: "You are strangers to us and we are strangers to you. Your culture is alien to us, as well as your language, your customs, your holidays and the sancta of your life. Your joy is not our joy. Your mourning is not our mourning. Your aspirations and hopes are not our aspirations and hopes. Strangers we are; and insofar as it lies within our power we shall safeguard our alienism and the barriers between us. We do not at all wish you to behave equally toward us and toward the children of your own nation; and we do not aim to share equally with you in the prerogatives of the nation, for complete equality might injure many of your own national rights and humiliate our national personality." [Page 72]

Even if we should assume that exilic life is viable and that, after the bankruptcy of religion in our time, complete assimilation is not inevitable, we should still have to insist that exilic Judaism is not worthy of existence. [Page 76]

What, then, should be done with the Diaspora? Should it be permitted to degenerate more and more?

It should be regarded as the passageway to the redemption of the people in its own land. For many generations to come the land of Israel will require aid from the Diaspora. Israel will draw elements of strength from the Diaspora, exploiting little by little the doomed community and through this very exploitation save it. [Page 81]

We should guard exilic Judaism insofar as we can. We should develop within it a national culture, set up in the teeth of reality and the inevitable lines of development. We should multiply fences and prohibitions calculated to protect our particularity and uniqueness. We should erect barriers upon barriers between us and the nations among whom we are steadily being assimilated . . .

There is a purpose to this temporary survival, because it is only a stage of transition. [Page 82]

Nevertheless, we should save the ruins of our religion—not religion itself or its spiritual essence, but its national wealth, its laws. We should save the laws, fences and prohibitions, which have the effect of erecting a ghetto for us among the nations. [Page 83]

This is the basic principle of our national work in the lands of the Diaspora: *the exile is dough for the land of Israel.* And such is the character of this contemporary work: *impudence toward reality.* [Page 85]

It might be objected that the views of Dr. Klatzkin are not representative, since he was an avowed "negator of the Diaspora." But the negation of any long future for Diaspora Jewry, and the determination meanwhile to exploit (*nitzul*) all its human and financial resources for the *Yishuv*, are of the very essence of the Herzlian Zionist ideal, as originally propounded. The moment a future is allowed for the Jews of any country the message of secular Zionism, insofar as that country is concerned, is no longer Zionism but pro-Palestinian refugeeism. As Dr. Robert Gordis has put it: "A secularist who is a Zionist must, if he is logically consistent, become a '*sholel Hagolah*,' a negator of a Jewish future in the Diaspora."

BUT WHAT OF THE IRRELIGIOUS?

The most telling objection raised against the conception of a religious status for American Jewry is the indubitable fact of its limited inclusiveness. Where does this conception leave the masses of those who are religiously indifferent?

In a formal way, to be sure, this question is easily answered.

First, we might point out that no worthy conception of Judaism is possible that would confer automatically, in blanket fashion, the status of "Jewishness in good standing" upon all and sundry people called Jews. If any such all-inclusive conception were proposed, it would have to confer essential meaning and worth either internally, upon Jewish blood or, externally, upon anti-Jewish animus, since these are the only common ineluctable factors. But racism, whether biological and mystical or spiteful and puerile, is unacceptable in scientific honesty, in moral conscience, or even in sheer expediency.

Remaining on the formal level, we might point out, in the second place, that a truly nationalist conception of Jewish status, which is the only alternative to a religious status, would require personal participation in the life of Israel. Hence, genuinely nationalist Jews in America are as much in the minority as religious Jews are supposed to be. Wendell Willkie and Franklin Roosevelt, though of German and Dutch descent, were in no sense members of the German and Dutch nationalities. If, as Ernest Renan put it, "nationality is a plebiscite repeated daily," then the vote of individuals even belonging to it by birth may be altered from day to day. Indeed, on the basis of a national criterion, the process of linguistic assimilation which American Jewry is at present undergoing is of decisive significance.

However, on both sides, the religious and nationalist, there is a broad swath of marginal loyalties, which are shared by the vast majority of American Jews.

We might then take our cue from the Talmud, which offers two complementary definitions of what it takes to belong to the Congregation of Israel. One would exclude all who knowingly transgress any *mitzvah* (commandment) three times. The other would embrace within the fold all who reject the idolatry of other nations. As these two definitions delimit the boundaries of those who belong to the nuclear and to the protoplasmic sections of the living cell of Israel, so might our conception of religious status offer a similar standard of graded belonging, that is bounded by the inexorable hairline of conversion.

But all these replies, correct as they may be on a formal level, do not really capture the essence of the problem. There are among us many spiritually sensitive people unaffiliated with the Synagogue, yet whose entire being is profoundly stirred by Jewish associations and problems. How can they be termed "marginal" without a perversion of Jewish values? Then, on the other side, we have masses of indifferent materialists, included through one avenue or another in the organizational complex of the Jewish community, but not susceptible to any kind of spiritual message or orientation, left cold and unmoved by any appeal to spiritual values.

We must recognize that for several generations Jewish national loyalties were being steadily substituted for religious loyalties. The change has been so all-pervasive and continuous that few of our "best" Jews are now capable of realizing the extent of inner transmutation that has taken place, let alone retrace their steps. The successive calamities that have befallen our people weakened their faith in both God and Man, while strengthening their grim reliance on their own collective powers. This new spirit of militant defiance has been subtly molding the residual Jewish loyalties in its own shape and pattern.

The moral task before us, then, is to transmute deep ethnic consciousness into reawakened dedication to the ideals and values of the Jewish spirit. We must chart a path from the sense of being part of an embattled camp to the sense of being a partner of the Lord in the creation of a world patterned after His Word.

This task of psychic alchemy may appear to present insuperable difficulties. Hasn't the course of development in modern times proceeded in the opposite direction, from ethical humanism and religious liberalism to glorified nationalism and romanticized racism, from Kant to Hitler? What, then, leads us to think that the process may be reversed?

Indeed, much can be said by those who despair of so arduous a task. Yet this transformation was effected by the great of our people time and again, when they achieved a universal faith out of the tears and tribulations of their sorely harassed brethren. It is precisely this achievement that constitutes the greatest contribution of Israel on the altar of humanity. Do not the historic parellels indicate that our task is not utterly hopeless?

THE CREATIVE GENIUS OF JEWISH HISTORY

If we schematize the fundamental factors in the rise of Judaism, we note a steady repetition of the three elements: (a) sorrowful circumstances; (b) an ideal interpretation; and (c) the attainment of a new height of dedication to the life of the spirit.

Enslavement in Egypt was interpreted by Moses and his prophetic school as a purifying cauldron for those selected by God to become "a people of priests and a holy nation"; and it was followed by the dedication of the whole people to the ideals of loving the stranger, respecting the slave, honoring the Sabbath Day as an inviolate rest day for servants and masters alike, and *the prohibition of despising Egyptians, their former oppressors.* Thus the so-called normal or human reaction, in which hate breeds hate and all its ugly brood, was transcended. The intense consciousness of persecution was made to yield the glorious fruits of the spirit.

The same scheme was followed by the great prophets of the Babylonian exile. The bitter national catastrophe of defeat, devastation and exile was interpreted as divine punishment by the Lord of heaven and earth for ethical and religious backsliding, and as evidence of the uncompromising justice of Providence. As a result of this prophetic interpretation, the Babylonian exile raised the level of the Jewish religion from the particularist stage, denoted by scholars as the religion of Israel, to the universalist faith of Judaism.

The genius of Israel effected a similar leap into the realm of the spirit when the Second Temple was destroyed "for the sin of causeless hatred," as the Rabbis put it. The four ells of *Halakhah* (the Law) came to take the place of the altar of the priests as the abode of the "Sh'kinah" (God's Presence).

All through the later dark centuries of persecution, calamities became the stepping stones for spiritual progress.

As Edmond Fleg put it:

The Jew has suffered so much, he has endured so many injustices, experienced so completely the misery of life, that pity for the poor and humiliated has become second nature to him. And in his agonized wanderings he has seen at close range so many men of all races and of all countries, different everywhere and everywhere alike, that he has understood, he has felt in the flesh of his flesh, that Man is one as God is one. Thus was formed a race which, though it have the same vices and the same virtues as other races, is yet without doubt the most *human* of all races.

And thus has been charted for us, by the creative genius of Jewish history, the logical path from the Jewish situation in the lands of the Diaspora to the values of the spiritual life.

CHALLENGE TO THE AMERICAN JEW

American Jewish experience is richly productive of spiritual enlightenment. It can provide an inspiring way of life to those who identify themselves with it and grow in maturity through it.

Our keen awareness of the perversion of fact through prejudice should lead us to devote ourselves all the more to the love of truth, to the accompanying discipline of objective thinking, and to the esteem of learning as a high end in itself. The deep gulf that yawns between ideals avowed verbally and their sadly limited application we should interpret as a universal human failing to be remedied through the willingness of ever greater numbers to impose the disciplines of good breeding and noble aims upon themselves. Our awareness of the evils resulting from the atavistic sentiments of tribalism and clannishness should lead us to greater efforts in behalf of all causes that strengthen the cementing bonds of humanity. Our consciousness of the ugliness and drabness of provincialism and babbitry should quicken us to appreciate the universal standards of ethical and esthetic beauty, so that we may help to create that unitary realm of the spirit essential for the ultimate emergence of the unitary society of man. Above all, our ready observation of the vices of others we should construe as a challenge for the ruthless examination of our own shortcomings, in the spirit of the true prophets, repudiating the easy excuses and self-flattering clichés purveyed by our publicly acclaimed pseudo-prophets.

Thus our exposed situation in the Diaspora is fertile soil for the creation of spiritually minded men and women.

Granted that this pathway is difficult enough to follow. There are two human reactions to hostility. One is to escape its brunt by hiding under a protective covering of one kind or another and ultimately joining the hostile camp itself. The other is to close ranks defiantly and reply with hate for hate. Both policies are spiritually poisonous, and it is a toss-up which one is ultimately the most ruinous. The true Jewish way is to rise above the hatred by recognizing it as a universal evil, found in ourselves as well as in others, and to labor for its cure both within ourselves and in the total society of which we are a part.

By cleaving to the spiritual interpretation of Jewish experience we provide a means for the non-religious among us to progress in the realm of the spirit through their Jewish identification. To be sure, we have not shown how the gulf in many men's minds between adherence to spiritual values and the convictions of religion may be bridged. There is in fact a plus of conviction in religious faith, with regard to the roots in eternity of spiritual values, which cannot be obtained by the cultivation of a humanist attitude alone. Spiritually minded people will still find congregational life the best means of continuing their own spiritual progress, through self-identification with Jewish experience in the religious interpretation, and by promoting its values in the social grouping of which they are a part.

WHAT LEADERSHIP FOR AMERICAN JEWRY?

If the spiritually sensitive should fail to take or build their place in the leadership ranks of American Jewry, we may almost be certain that World Jewry will fail to acquit itself honorably in these days of unprecedented challenge. It will rather drift along one or both "human" directions—of militancy *à la* Ben Hecht and mammonism *à la* Sammy Glick.

So long, then, as an intellectual does not accept Lenin's dictum that "religion is opium for the people," he must not fail to see in the modern congregational setup, with all its present failings, his best available means of promoting spiritual values in the concrete social situation wherein he finds himself.

I would emphasize that all who are genuinely concerned with the advancement of spiritual values among our people will find the institutions and disciplines of religion most suited for their purpose, even if they do not accept *in toto* the ideological basis of the modern synagogue.

As to our materialists and mammonists who—whether affiliated with the synagogue or not—subscribe neither to its convictions nor to its spiritual program and implications, the problem is of universal scope; though among us it is aggravated by the prevalence of so many pseudo-philosophies which shed an aura of respectability over any and all types of Jewish identification. However, the more the status of American Jewry is clarified, the easier it should be to bring the straying and groping marginal groups within the historical influence of the synagogue; and the more truly representative and spiritual should become the leadership of American Jewry.

(—*1949*)

Towards a Noble Community

༄

HENRY HURWITZ

A TRUE community must have a spiritual cohesion, a central core of purpose and direction. A deep-felt philosophy of collective life. What is that sanction for the Jews of America?

The establishment of the State of Israel in Palestine will make our true position in America more explicit. We should have the courage to analyze our present situation with the most rigorous honesty, regardless of powerful partisanships and entrenched interests. Old clichés no longer do. We have to rise above old issues and isms and even, when possible, the very vocabulary of former days. Perspectives must be realigned; we should not hesitate to propose new forms of communal organization that the times require.

What positions are now past holding?

One is the notion of "Diaspora nationalism." It had its heyday in eastern Europe before World War I, and its twilight with "national minorities" during the truce till the Second. Among the Yiddish-speaking it still burns with a sort of vestigial flame; but it has little meaning for their Americanized children. For most descendants of the immigrants—from eastern and western Europe alike—"Jewishness" became clannishness, bereft of the former nationalist as well as religious inspiration.

Then Zionism, galvanized by the brutal enemy Nazism, won over millions of Jews in the free countries whose hearts were wrung by the fate of their brethren in Germany and eastern Europe. Now it has eventuated in the State of Israel. How does that affect our position in America?

There are some extreme Zionists who look upon American Jews as "expendable." Though domiciled here, they neither see nor desire any future for Judaism in America. In their view, the only use of American Jews is to provide the financial resources to Israel—through the United Jewish Appeal, through loans and investments—and to exercise all possible political pressure upon the United States Govern-

(916)

ment, upon Congressmen and voters, in behalf of Israel. As soon as Israel is strong enough to dispense with American funds and political influence, according to this belief, American Jews will no longer be necessary and need not survive. Such Zionists are, in effect, colonials of Israel.

Most Zionists are far from taking this view. However, if the utterances of their political leaders and intellectuals are a true indication, they propose not to liquidate American Jewry but to make it a permanent cultural dependency of Israel. What else can be the meaning of their talk about "Zionizing" American Judaism, directing all Jewish education in America, and seizing control of the whole community, its agencies, organizations, institutions?

From this program too, when its full implications are realized, the vast majority of American Jews will recoil. The vast majority include not only the anti-Zionists, many of whom are now giving their support to Israel for humanitarian motives. They include also most of the Zionists themselves who, however ardent their love for Zion and their desire to help Israel grow and flourish, will reject any move by Israel's Government and the World Zionist leaders to control or improperly influence American Jewish life.

At the moment the threat comes not from Tel Aviv but from New York. It is true that the many envoys and messengers of Israel now in the United States, both official and unofficial, are encouraged by their enthusiastic receptions to make demands as though they were talking to colonials and children of a mother country. But the boldest assertion of authority issues from the entrenched leaders of the Zionist Organization. The World Zionist Organization and the Jewish Agency for Palestine seem now to be interchangeable. The American Section of both, with headquarters in New York, is in command; and, through control of the American United Jewish Appeal, controls to a large extent the Provisional Government of Israel itself. For that Government could not exist without the millions from America.

Many thoughtful Zionists have begun to ask themselves soberly whither this can lead. They are asking whether, after all, the establishment of the State does not call for new agencies of relationships with American Jews: whether the very success in achieving their purpose does not make both the Jewish Agency and the Zionist Organization obsolete. Surely the people of Israel will be too proud to subsist indefinitely on *chalukah de luxe*. And, with greater maturity, the Israeli Government and its representatives will without doubt perceive the dangers of treating American Jews as if the whole purpose of their existence was to give everything to the "homeland" without regard to the needs of Judaism in America itself.

At all events, this kind of sacrificial devotion cannot last. Level-headed Zionists who are concerned for their children's future in America—who in fact are first and last Americans, however fervid their hopes for the success of Israel—will realize that the center of their Jewish life must be, not in any land overseas however dear, but in America itself. They will realize that the preponderant emphasis in the Jewish education of their children, if they wish them to continue Judaism in America, must be on those universal religious and ethical traditions and concepts which make Judaism at home in every free land—which are now indeed the only true sanction of any distinctive Jewish life in the Western world.

Is it too much to hope that—when the present emotional urgencies are past and it is more clearly seen that the only acceptable stance for permanent and congenial Jewish life on American soil is Judaism—the former quarrel between Zionists and anti-Zionists will be transcended into a higher synthesis? What generous-hearted Jew, however anti-Zionist before, does not wish the State of Israel well, and does not wish to help it give a home at last to thousands and thousands of weary DP's? What intelligent Zionist will not in time perceive that, with the consummation once again of the millennial love affair between Israel and Zion, the situation is radically changed? The old feud between Zionists and anti-Zionists is senseless to continue. A status either of Diaspora nationalism or Israeli colonialism in America is unacceptable. Hence it is the religious sanction of Jewish life which is paramount; that is the common cause of all of us who want Judaism to flourish in America.

Well, then, our action must suit our faith.

✦   ✦   ✦

This way lies the true Jewish future in America—that all of us throughout the country who regard religion, broadly conceived in the comprehensive classic Jewish sense, as the sole justification of *organized* Jewish life in America should now withdraw from the secular bodies and concentrate on a religious reorientation and reorganization of all legitimate Jewish interests. This can be done only on the basis of the Synagogue. The Synagogue is at once our historic enduring institution in the world and the Jewish institution most congenial to the spirit of American democracy.

But the Synagogue door is wider by far than a church door. Within the broad ambit of the Synagogue the Jewish head as well as Jewish heart has found its home in the past, and can do so again in the future. All our legitimate Jewish interests and endeavors—philanthropic and protective, intellectual and cultural, as well as the purely devotional —can be attached again to the Synagogue, as of yore. Tradition creatively interwoven with modernity can, we believe, once more bring forth fresh fruit, for the enrichment of American spiritual life as a whole.

Such a reaffirmation of the Synagogue as the seat, center and incentive of Jewish life in America calls for a basic change in the thinking of many of us. It means more than annual synagogue worship on the High Holy Days, or perfunctory attendance on Sabbaths or Sundays. It involves a regathering of the Jewish laity around the Synagogue *revitalized*. It involves, no less, a rededication of the rabbinate to a more dominant and constructive role than it plays at present.

Singly, a rabbi can perhaps do little in this respect. But if a goodly number of rabbis come together and determine that at whatever risk to themselves they will set their faces against the galloping vulgarization of Jewish life in America, and not only set their faces and kindle their tongues but *take action*, they will be joined by hosts of laymen. By laymen who, though members of synagogues and temples, are today indifferent, cynical, helpless. But they are not all. Many now unaffiliated men and women, not the least intellectual and spiritual of our people—whom rabbis have some reason to regard, not indeed as renegades from Judaism, but as aloof or outside critics— will rally enthusiastically to their side when they display a stout unmistakable determination to set the Jewish house in order, on truly spiritual terms.

Mere appeals to laymen to put aside secularism and embrace religion won't do at all. Lip-eloquence comes easy and costs nothing; besides, the state of our communal life today is beyond curing by rhetorical poultices. There must be action.

✦ ✦ ✦

In venturing to present a proposal for a new representative body to meet our needs at this time, I would emphasize first of all its tentative character. It is the spirit that must count. No matter how imperfect or halting a plan may be at the outset, if the right spirit and well-tempered men are there to take hold, it can become something good and fair. Our plan will no doubt seem utopian to many; but theory to start with is as important in social organization as in nuclear physics or biochemistry. At all events, the rough sketch offered here may at least serve as a basis for discussion, towards a more adequate and detailed blueprint.

It is proposed, then, to establish what might perhaps be called the Jewish Assembly of Representatives in America—JARA.

This assembly of representatives will not presume to speak for all the Jews in America, still less for the Jews of the world. But it will endeavor by all fair means of persuasion to win over the great majority of American Jews to its way of thinking and organization. And thus in as short a time as possible come to be recognized as truly representing all American Jews who consider themselves as differing from their fellow-Americans only in religion.

JARA can be initiated informally through a meeting of rabbis and laymen from, say, a hundred congregations. If sufficiently representative of all sections of the country, and of the various theological viewpoints, they should make a good enough constituent session to set up the framework of the Assembly and tentatively formulate its procedures and operations. These tentative formulations should be submitted to all congregations of the country, to Jewish institutions of learning and societies of Jewish scholars, and to, say, a thousand individuals, for their constructive criticisms and differing proposals. The cream of such criticisms and proposals should be published and then duly taken up at the second session of the Assembly, not later than three months after the first. At this second session—with, it may be hoped, representatives from many more congregations—the permanent organization of JARA could be effected.

The spirit and scope of JARA will become more explicit as we consider a possible *modus operandi*. Of course, checks and balances must be worked out to prevent JARA from being seized by any one group to serve its own interests rather than the whole community's.

Two modes now operating in Jewish affairs must be definitely avoided. One is government by bureaucracy; the other is government by mass meeting resolutions.

JARA should be sharply differentiated in methods as well as in spirit from all national Jewish bodies now existing and presuming to represent the community. Unlike Jewish Congress or Committee or Conference, it is designed as a responsible communal assembly, deliberating and deciding on programs and petitions and budgets in the open, with the services of experts. These experts will not constitute a permanent bureaucracy which acts for a nominal constituency of paper members. Nor is JARA to be a mass meeting occasionally summoned, nor an annual meeting of a corporation or a benevolent institution.

It is not suggested, of course, that JARA sit in session for extended periods of time. The contemplated members of JARA—not only rabbis but professional and business men, teachers, journalists, laborers, housewives—cannot be away for long periods from home. But during the intervals between sessions they must still be actively occupied with the business of JARA—with the study of reports, recommendations, motions, petitions, bills, budgets to be taken up at the periodical and (when need be) extraordinary sessions.

Commissions of experts are to provide the impartial scientific information that is indispensable for intelligent action. It is now too notably absent from Jewish public and even private deliberations, where emotions and prejudices and propaganda take the place of carefully gathered, impartially analyzed facts which, to repeat, are indispensable to efficient action and farsighted policy.

JARA's experts will not be bureaucrats with power to speak and act for JARA: rather, trained men and women, specialists, engaged to procure the essential information and provide their expert advice on specific questions and proposals. Nor, on the other hand, will these experts or technicians be subservient to JARA: they must be independent scholars and consultants, paid for their work like any other professional men retained by a corporation or public body for special services within their trained competence and experience. The full responsibility for utilizing their services must rest solely with the members of JARA, who must be responsible in turn to their synagogues and to the community.

Thus in all matters likely to come up before JARA for action—matters of education, communal regulations, philanthropies and foreign relief, defense against anti-Semitism, and so on—the decisions are not to be come by through oratory, half-knowledge, prejudice, emotional evacuation; but, so far as humanly possible, on the basis of facts, analysis, recommendations from commissions of experts both scientifically and spiritually equipped to inform and advise for the communal good.

Here an attractive prospect opens for the greater employment than ever before of trained intelligence for Jewish life in America— men who hitherto have been mostly aloof from Jewish service for lack of the right opportunity and acceptable auspices. Certainly we need the "communal leader" type, men and women of both ambition and capacity to serve Judaism in forensic and civic ways; the best of them, it is hoped, will be members of JARA. What we have lacked so far, at least to an adequate extent, is the participation of men with particular skills and professional experiences, who are accustomed to approach all problems with objectivity and scientific exactingness. Propaganda and political organizations generally have no use for such minds. Nor need their objective approach and *expertise* by any means dry up the warmth of their personal loyalties to principles and causes in Jewish as well as the general life.

But the Commissions are by no means to be limited to Jewish specialists and researchers, since in some fields (especially those of Jewish-Christian relations) the knowledge, experience and judgment of Christian minds are not only desirable but indispensable. In general, the more collaboration of Jewish and Christian minds we can promote in all matters affecting mutual relations and common concern as Americans, the better.

✦ ✦ ✦

Now to a few concrete items of agenda. They are not meant to be exhaustive, to cover all matters that should come under JARA's purview and jurisdiction. Only several broad fields for study and action are here suggested.

Commission of Higher Learning and Letters

It is fitting that JARA's first and foremost concern should be the intellectual state of Judaism in our country. A great deal has been said about the transfer of the Jewish center of gravity from Europe to America, and our consequent duty to take over the intellectual and spiritual torch from the all-but-destroyed European Jewries. This sacred duty we must surely fulfill. Ours is the most numerous and wealthiest Jewry that has ever lived on earth; last year it contributed some 350 million dollars for Jewish purposes at home and overseas, to say nothing of the countless millions given by Jewish citizens to Christian and general American philanthropic, cultural and educational causes. American Jews, then, can well afford to take adequate care of all desirable institutions and activities for our spiritual life. For example, our institutions of learning should not be forced to go abegging—this necessity inevitably affecting their programs to a degree. The Presidents of The Dropsie College, Hebrew Union College, the Jewish Theological Seminary and Yeshiva University, the heads of Learned Societies such as the American Academy of Jewish Research, the American Jewish Historical Society, the Menorah Faculty Council, and individual scholars and artists, all should be invited to submit their needs and proposals for the advancement of Jewish learning, letters and art in this country. *A veritable renaissance can be brought about.* For our resources of intellect and spirit are happily abundant; though at present far too much unencouraged and unexercised. The cost in money will be incredibly small in the total Jewish communal budget—and in comparison with the wasted and misused millions of our present secular agencies, as will be presently shown.

Commission on Colleges and Universities

Not merely to see to it that full collegiate and professional school opportunities are open to every Jewish boy and girl able to profit by them. That is not a specifically Jewish interest at all, it is a general American interest; and the only proper way to handle that matter is for all higher educational and civic forces to join together for the solution—not only for Jewish but for all American youth.

What does require our special care are two matters. One is the furtherance of Jewish studies, in a purely scientific spirit, in the regular curricula and research seminars of our colleges and universities throughout the country, as well as in our seminaries themselves. Not the least important aspect of this completer "naturalization" of Jewish learning in our general academic institutions will be an increased number of positions open to Jewish scholars and also to Christian scholars specializing in these fields.

The other matter involved is the extracurricular Jewish influence upon the tens of thousands of Jewish students in the colleges and universities. This concern is to be distinguished sharply from the provision of social facilities for the students—a distinction not generally borne in mind. Without enough support and guidance for the educational and intellectual concerns, they are apt to be put in the shade by the social, as has been amply demonstrated in the past decades. This whole matter, of very first importance for the tone and substance of the future of Judaism in America, is crying for thorough re-examination and fresh action.

The sponsorship for student activities is most important, setting their whole tone and emphasis. No secular organization, however well-intentioned, can properly handle it; by insisting on domination and even a monopoly, secular organizations only render harm to Judaism in America. They render harm by wrong emphasis and an inadequate approach to our intellectual youth, from whom must come the temper and leadership of the morrow.

This problem should be in the van of JARA's agenda. It is a matter that lends itself perfectly to impartial study. On a long view, the consequent action by JARA can well be among its most significant contributions for our intellectual and spiritual life.

Commission on Foreign Relief and Rehabilitation

The American Jewish Joint Distribution Committee has done a magnificent job over the last thirty years and more—a job unparalleled for scope and beneficent results in the whole history of private philanthropy, either domestic or foreign. Though technically a private organization, JDC is one of the greatest public agencies even in this land of gargantuan enterprises. Since its formation in 1914, JDC has distributed close on $300,000,000.

A time comes when the faithful stewards and directors of such a vast communal enterprise may well call for an outside impartial survey and appraisal of their work. Not for applause, though there is ample cause for that. Rather for cool expert examination, by trained and sympathetic Christian as well as Jewish minds—with the emphasis on what still remains to be done, and what methods will be best for doing it. It can scarcely be held that the improvisations and techniques developed through the cataract of successive emergencies abroad, and the unremitting pressing needs of raising ever more and more funds on this side, are adequate for the present purpose.

No doubt, good use can be made of many more hundreds of millions of dollars. There is a limit, however, to what American Jews—and friendly Christians too—will be inclined or able to contribute in the future.

And have not the relations between JDC and the Jewish Agency been radically changed by the establishment of the State of Israel? In a sense, the Jewish Agency is now an anachronism, having achieved the objective for which it was formed. But since it is against nature for any Jewish organization to dissolve of its own accord, what are to be the relations henceforth between JDC and the Jewish Agency?

Nor should we minimize the needs of our coreligionists who are remaining in Europe, in the countries of their birth or adoption. Even if they wished it, they could not all be accommodated in Israel. But some prefer to remain in European countries, or to migrate to South America, if they cannot be admitted into the United States or Canada. In any event, the talk of total Jewish evacuation of Europe is as unrealistic as it is intolerable. We must resist the enormous propaganda pressures; we must endeavor to see the picture as a whole, and help Jews get on their feet everywhere they can find opportunity.

It is only human for people who believe they have the sole answer to a problem to insist that nothing else matters: everything must be staked on their particular solution. It is human, but may not be wise either now or in the long run. There must be many American Jews willing to make an effort, regardless of their personal predilections, to review Jewish questions today from every angle.

It is hard to see how any good cause can be harmed by dispassionate re-examination through fresh competent minds in the light of past experience and new conditions. Especially do new conditions like the present call for new insights and a willingness to face new situations, even if they might require changed actions. We have cheerfully undertaken obligations to our fellow-Jews in Europe and Palestine; and we owe it to them, as well as to ourselves, to carry through with the utmost effectiveness.

There are thus plenty of questions for the JARA Commission to study, on which to give the public all the facts and independent analysis, free of the pressures of special propagandas and techniques of fund-raising.

These are indeed great times for us, with extraordinary opportunities for reconstruction, thanks to the will and long-suffering endurance of our brethren in Europe, to the industry and tenacity and heroism of our brethren in Palestine. They all deserve, not noisy old-fashioned charity any more, but the most constructive and far-reaching cooperation we can calmly work out with them; and we shall expect *quid pro quo* in their reborn happiness, in their sustainment of Judaism abroad, and in the contributions they may make to our spiritual life in our own country.

Let JARA's Commission, then, give us impartially all the facts and fresh thought; let our public discussions, in consequence, be lifted to the height of our historic time.

Commission on Inter-Faith Relations

In the *New York Times* of July 1, 1948, there appeared this alarming headline: "ANTI-SEMITISM IN U. S. HELD UNPRECEDENTED." Under it was a United Press dispatch from Montreux, Switzerland, where the World Jewish Congress was holding its sessions. The secretary-general of the Congress, Dr. Alex Easterman, a Briton, is reported to have declared that "democracy in the United States is at present being swept by unprecedented currents of anti-Semitism." And he continued, according to this dispatch: "It is significant that every great American Jewish organization, including the American Jewish Congress, is obliged to spend a vast amount of energy and millions of dollars to combat the growth of anti-Semitism."

That isn't all. The United Press correspondent went on to report: "Dr. Easterman, who recently toured Eastern Europe, said that greater freedom for Jews from anti-Semitism existed there now than in many parts of the world, including Britain."

This calculated hysteria over "unprecedented currents of anti-Semitism" in the United States, combined with "greater freedom from anti-Semitism" in Eastern Europe, is of a well-known pattern of propaganda. The report of decreased anti-Semitism in Eastern Europe, true or not, is a curtsy towards a certain power in that part of the world.

Now on this side of the water anti-Semitism is exploited for a different purpose. It provides the "scare-power" without which the "defense agencies" could not demand their ever-increasing budgets from the communities.

We are fortunate to have the uniquely informative and illustrated *Reporter* published by the American Jewish Committee. In its issue for July-August 1948 it reports: "New campaign strategy to bolster the 1948 effort of the Joint Defense Appeal was drawn up at a recent emergency meeting of the executive committee of the national council . . . held in New York." It continued: "After reviewing the progress of the campaign, the meeting formulated a program for action, detailing new methods for obtaining full JDA quotas from welfare fund communities."

We may be certain that the demands of all "defense agencies," whatever their politics, will continue to be insatiable, ever more ravenous, regardless of the actual state of anti-Semitism here or in other parts of the world. In 1945 the Joint Defense Appeal of the American Jewish Committee and the B'nai B'rith Anti-Defamation League reported receiving $3,017,993; in 1946, $3,696,067; in 1947 ("Actual 10 months, estimated 2 months") $4,410,000. And for 1948 the goal is $6,104,540. The stakes of the leaders and managers in ever-increasing funds for their disposal are too obvious to detain us. As for the public justifications: (1) if there is a lull in anti-Semitism, we have to prepare for its recrudescence; (2) if there is an upflare of anti-Semitism, we have to fight it more vigorously than ever. These are the perennial arguments used by the fund-raisers for the "education" of American Jews.

Regarding the methods of waging that fight, what is precisely done with those millions, how far the activities are effective, to what extent harmful, it has been impossible to get detailed information for the general public. It all appears to be considered a kind of *mystique,* a "dark and riddling thing," to be controlled by a priesthood not responsible to the vulgar. The reports and budgets issued to the local Jewish Welfare Funds have been so vague, evasive and deliberately confusing or inept as to be worthless.

One would reasonably suppose that for their own protection— let alone the public interest which is primarily involved—the men responsible for raising and spending the millions would not only welcome but actually seek disinterested review and checking. That is the accepted way of all public-service agencies in a democracy, whether maintained through taxation or through voluntary support.

In the American Jewish Committee's budget for 1948 there is indeed an item called "Scientific Research and Program Evaluation—$287,-503." This figure is grotesque, unless it is deliberately meant to mislead or to cover up something, as was the case with the Committee's "Library of Jewish Information," which in its 1947 budget was put up at $374,996 and in its 1948 budget (as a result of *The Menorah Journal* Inquiry) was put down at $164,418. The figure of $287,503 is in any case grotesque for "Program Evaluation" (even if added to vague "Scientific Research"), because for one-tenth of that sum a reputable firm of public-relations counsel could be engaged to evaluate the Committee's work scientifically and to make recommendations for more effective as well as more economical administration and operations.

The observations just presented are the barest indication of the imperative need of reordering our whole "defense program." The present setup is dangerously and incurably wrong, for these reasons:

First, there are several mutually competing agencies, each with its own extravagant overhead and duplicating activities. From the point of view of communal welfare this is simply an insane "defense" strategy.

Second, each agency, to enhance its own prestige, enlarge its organization, and justify ever-increasing demands for funds, is continually thinking up new grandiose ways to beguile the, in their minds, yankelry. Thus, the American Jewish Committee took on the championship of human rights for all human beings all over the globe; though the Anti-Defamation League more modestly proposed for itself only the fight for democracy in America.

Third, the agencies are irresponsible to the public, claiming the necessity of secret activities and influences. This is a terribly dangerous tactic for any group of Jewish citizens to employ even privately, let alone with public tax-exempt funds.

Fourth, by artificially separating "defense" from the whole context of Jewish life in America, and exploiting it far out of proportion to our affirmative interests as a whole, they are distorting and debasing Jewish life in America.

Fifth, and most important of all, the segregation by Jews themselves of anti-Semitism from other discriminations and bigotries that have to be fought by right-minded Americans together, irrespective of race or creed—this *voluntary ghettoizing* of what should be a general non-sectarian American effort—the constant needling of the public on the subject of anti-Semitism—not only exaggerates the very evil to be fought; it tends also to perpetuate division between Jewish and Christian Americans on an utterly wrong basis.

Well might our self-appointed philosopher-protectors ponder a pregnant maxim of the dean of American sociologists, Professor W. I. Thomas: *"If men define situations as real, they are real in their consequences."*

The situation for us to define as real is not, negatively, segregation between Christian and Jew. The situation to be defined as real in American democracy is, affirmatively, that all Americans strive *together*, mutually respectful of each other's religious faith, within a common Judeo-Christian civilization—as President Conant of Harvard reminds us. Strive together to protect the human rights of every individual and remove injustice against any. That is the only statesmanlike program for American Jews to pursue.

Accordingly, JARA must repudiate all the present "defense agencies": must repudiate the very notion of a separate Jewish agency "to fight anti-Semitism." JARA should consider the entire situation afresh. The JARA approach is to be characteristically American—regarding the problem as essentially a matter of interfaith relations and interfaith responsibility.

Hence a JARA Commission: a body of independent experts with no organizational axe to grind, no past policies and actions to vindicate, no vested positions to maintain, no commitments for the future to discharge, but concerned only with the over-all best interests of American Jews, and therefore of America. A body of Jewish and Christian social scientists and social-relations experts working together to explore the whole field afresh as objectively as possible, by the most scientific methods available.

It will no doubt be astonishing to many to propose the abolition of our so-called "defense agencies." But there is nothing sacrosanct or rooted about them. In point of fact, they are a very recent growth. Of course this in itself does not argue against them. New conditions, as we ourselves contend, call for new methods, new organizations. They must, however, show reasonably satisfactory results, which could not be obtained at less cost to the community. Their theories and operations must be soundly in the public interest. They should not, in any case, give rise to new undesirable practices in Jewish life, and raise dangers that were non-existent before.

There is a devastating sentence in Dr. Cecil Roth's *Short History of the Jewish People,* where he describes the effects of the European ghetto in its decadent stages upon Jewish character. The Ghetto Jew, Roth says, "had become timorous and in many cases neurotic . . . His sense of solidarity with his fellow-Jews had become fantastically exaggerated, and was accompanied in most cases by a perpetual sense of grievance against the Gentile who was responsible for his lot."

How ironic that such a psychosis should now be deliberately implanted or stimulated among our people in a country where, when all's told and balanced, we have never before—but *never*—enjoyed so much freedom, opportunity, prosperity and happiness!

An excellent way of endangering it all is to continue our "defense agencies." Their supporters throughout the country do not realize where they are actually being led by this "new profession" of "protectors."

We have indicated four areas for fresh study and action by the proposed representative body, JARA. There are of course other fields too. In all it is the spirit that is of first importance—devotion to the intrinsic Jewish interests as a whole, not to the competing power and prestige of this or that organization or individual.

If, again, the charge of utopianism is brought, it can only be replied, hearkening to old wisdom, that without vision great causes perish; without active pursuit of the ideal—a full harmony of all our legitimate interests—Jewish communal life in America becomes raucous, banal, and not worthwhile.

✦ ✦ ✦

"See, I have set before you this day life and good, or death and bane." These somberly eloquent words of the Deuteronomist have quickened the pulse of Judaism through the ages. In this spirit the Prophets preached. To permit Jewish life today in America to be ruled through secular power-organizations, seeking their own aggrandizement above the communal good as a whole, is a modern backsliding to idolatry against which true leaders of Judaism must stand up.

If the forces of secularism and materialism are too strong to overcome—if the spiritual and intellectual sources of Judaism in the Prophetic-Zakkaian tradition are too weak to assert authority—then many an American Jew will decline to affiliate with a Jewish community at all. He is under no compulsion to do so. He may, with good conscience, reject as irrelevant in our circumstances the old rabbinic injunction *Al tifrosh min hazzibur*—"Do not separate yourself from the collectivity." In other times and countries one had no choice but to be part of the Jewish community, or else be treated as a pariah, excluded from Christian as well as Jewish society. In other times and countries the Jewish community was an organism with a system of morals and education, a distinctive regimen of life which included the power to enforce order and discipline within its ranks.

In America there is no such power, nor should there be—nor, we trust, will there ever be.

One of the glories of our American freedom is that Jewish association here is purely voluntary. This gives every one of us, all the more, a superb opportunity to realize the highest peak of religion enunciated by our Prophets: "What does the Lord seek of you but to do justice, love mercy, and walk humbly with your God."

Only in this spirit can a noble Jewish community in America be fashioned, along the lines I have sketched or along better lines. In such a way the corporate life and activities of Judaism may be continued in full accord with its ethical and spiritual character. Will American Jews, rising in their freedom to the height of their religion, carry its spirit and principles into all their communal life?

(—*1948*)

The Bold Experiment of Freedom

ᶜᴗᴧᴧᴗ

FELIX FRANKFURTER

B Y ITS FOUNDERS this nation was committed to democracy, in which
we all profess our faith. Even its enemies pay democracy the
tribute of appropriating its name. For democracy is the only form
of social arrangement which fully respects the richness of human
society and, by respecting it, helps to unfold it. Democracy is thus
the only adequate response to the deepest human needs and justified
as such by the long course of history. All the devices of political
machinery—parties and platforms and votes—are merely instruments
for enabling men to live together under conditions that bring forth
the maximum gifts of each for the fullest enjoyment of all. Democracy
furnishes the political framework within which reason can thrive most
generously and imaginatively on the widest scale—least hampered,
that is, by the accident of personal antecedents and most regardful
of the intrinsic qualities in men.

Not only the experience to which history testifies, but nature herself vindicates democracy. For nature plants gifts and graces where
least expected, and under circumstances that defy all the little artifices
of man. To meet nature's disregard of distinctions that are not intrinsic, but merely man-made, we need political and economic institutions which allow these mysterious natural bounties their fullest outlet.

Thus we Americans are enlisted in a common enterprise, whatever
our antecedents, whatever the creed we may avow or reject—the bold
experiment of freedom. It is bold because it cannot be realized without the most difficult and persistent collaborative effort. It demands
the continuous exercise of reason, and self-discipline of the highest

Address delivered at Aaronsburg, Pennsylvania, on October 23, 1949, on the
occasion of the 150th anniversary of Salem Evangelical Lutheran Church, built
on land given by Aaron Levy, a merchant of Revolutionary days, who founded
the town.

order. This is so because it places ultimate faith for attaining the common good in the responsibility of the individual.

We are thus engaged in the most difficult of all arts—the art of living together in a free society. It is comfortable, even if slothful, to live without responsibility. Responsibility is exacting and painful. Democracy involves hardship—the hardship of the unceasing responsibility of every citizen. Where the entire people do not take a continuous and considered part in public life, there can be no democracy in any meaningful sense of the term.

Democracy is always a beckoning goal, not a safe harbor. For freedom is an unremitting endeavor, never a final achievement. That is why no office in the land is more important than that of being a citizen.

And we can say with all humility that the United States has a special destiny because its moral cohesion derives from a unique circumstance.

No other nation has been composed of such heterogeneous elements. We represent a confluence of peoples whose bond of union is their common instrinsic human qualities. From its very beginning this country has bestowed upon those born under other skies the great boon of participation in its fellowship, with a single exception that created a moral lesion in the nation, requiring the healing forces of a civil war and its aftermath.

The saga of our republic is the story of the most significant racial and religious admixture in history. The fifty-six signers of the Declaration of Independence were men of varying religious outlook and eighteen of them of non-English stock. It cannot be too often recalled that when the Continental Congress chose John Adams, Franklin and Jefferson as a committee to devise the national emblem, they recommended a seal containing the national emblems of England, Scotland, Ireland, France, Germany, and Holland, as representing "the countries from which these States have been peopled."

The event that the Commonwealth of Pennsylvania is so worthily commemorating today makes the reminder especially pertinent. Our cultural history—the sciences and the arts—reflects the genius and labors of men and women who came to these shores from all corners of the world. If a single faith can be said to unite a great people, surely the ideal which holds us together beyond any other is our belief in the worth of the individual, whatever his race or religion. In this faith America was founded; to this faith have her poets and seers and statesmen and the unknown millions, generation after generation, devoted their lives.

The opportunity which America has afforded implies the deepest obligations. What have those who have come here, beckoned by America's hospitality, made of this opportunity? Franklin Roosevelt gave the final answer. What he said on the occasion of the fiftieth anniversary of the Statue of Liberty was true of the stream of immigrants that came here, like Aaron Levy, before the Revolution; it is no less true of those who made their discovery of America more recently:

I like to think of the men and women who, with the break of dawn off Sandy Hook, have strained their eyes to the West for the first glimpse of the New World.

They came to us speaking many tongues—but a single language, the universal language of human aspiration.

How well their hopes were justified is proved by the record of what they achieved. They not only found freedom in the New World, but by their effort and devotion they made the New World's freedom safer, richer, more far-reaching, more capable of growth.

I shall not call the roll of the foreign-born and those who have been treated like aliens who, since this nation was founded, have performed distinguished service on the field of battle, in legislative halls, in executive offices, on our judiciary. For the ultimate heroes are always the unknown—the unnumbered, obscure people who have brought and today bring the dreams of America nearer to living truths.

This is our heritage. In confidence that their successors will maintain it the founders built this nation. That heritage is always endangered by inertia and complacency, by timidity and reluctance to keep abreast of the needs of a progressive society. This is a graver challenge than any from without. With active devotion to the ideals we profess it would be unworthy of our whole past to fear challenge by any rival system.

Love of country, like romantic love, is too intimate an emotion to be expressed publicly except through poetry. Happily one of the statesmen of the Wilsonian era, Franklin K. Lane, himself a naturalized citizen, was possessed of a poetic vein which made the flag, for him, express the meaning of America:

I am not the flag, not at all. I am but its shadow.

I am whatever you make me, nothing more.

I am your belief in yourself, your dream of what a people may become.

I am all that you hope to be, and have the courage to try for.

I am song and fear, struggle and panic, and ennobling hope.

I am the day's work of the weakest man, and the largest dream of the most daring.

I am the Constitution and the Courts, statutes and the statute makers, soldier and dreadnaught, drayman and street sweep, cook, counselor, and clerk.

I am the battle of yesterday, and the mistake of tomorrow.

I am no more than what you believe me to be and I am all that you believe I can be.

I am all that you make me, nothing more.

I swing before your eyes as a bright gleam of color, a symbol of yourself, the pictured suggestion of that big thing which makes this nation. My stars and my stripes are your dream and your labors. They are bright with cheer, brilliant with courage, firm with faith, because you have made them so out of your hearts. For you are the makers of the flag and it is well that you glory in the making.

The upheavals of the war let loose forces from which hardly a corner of the world is immune. Over vast areas the very foundations of society have been shaken. Great events are in process, and great events must be met by greatly daring. The ultimate task of the statesmanship of today is to translate edifying precepts about the dignity of man into their progressive fulfillment.

Here in Aaronsburg, at the very birth of the Republic, a handful of men, of whom Aaron Levy was only one, well realizing that faith without works is sterile, proved by deed their belief in the common humanity. Thereby they stored this very spot with electric example. Thus it has fallen to the honor of this tiny village to charge the conscience of this nation and to invigorate its endeavors.

You and I are heirs of a noble past. But . . . *what's past is prologue; what to come, is yours and my discharge.*

(—1950)

EPILOGUE

We Cannot Bid Farewell

ALLEN KANFER

We cannot bid farewell to destiny
Or heritage where earth
Spins on eternal axes—love and truth—
Linking the past and present;
We cannot bid farewell to ancient proof
Of the imperishable
Humane, wherewith our vigilance is armored
Against abstractions—icebergs
Of treachery, one-seventh visible.

When Rome and Greece and Babylon decayed,
They boasted myriad slaves
And pyramids and subterranean tombs:
Splendor and sham-frounced flicker, all farewell!
Farewell, holy fakirs:
And present dynasties illusory,
Sacred and secular,
Preserved in blood and so destroyed, farewell!

Now royal science wears the purple toga
And tosses golden discs,
Pellets of powdered lead, and measured loaves
To slaves of poisoned slogans.
Hail the nuptials! Science has been wedded,
The bridegroom death is merry.
Anointed science wears a crown of ions,
And bakes synthetic bread
(Mocking a parable of loaves and fishes)
For distant days of tragic emptiness,

Juggling motors, testing
Its doom, and piling arms in pyramids.

2

O Self-loving nations,
O little blind states,
hugging your vanity
and feeding on shadows
conjured from blood,
beware! beware! beware!
Know you a land where tombstones grow?
There we are purified,
and there lie in solitude:
when you crouch on the river bank
and bark at your shadow
and leap to embrace it,
beware! beware! drowning's there!

Beware the self-inflicted blindness
to shut out the image of the past,
the indestructible verity:
forgetting is calamity—
you cannot say farewell to time
who looks eternally, not in,
but far beyond the mirror
where narcissus strikes a nation's pose
and dreams of truculent beatitudes,
of legislating his divinity,
and meanwhile weaves a myth of destiny
and purgation through the blood
and the death of the innocent:

but truth, the priest, will purify
and time, the warder, pacify
with requiems for lullabies,
where history's invective falls:

know you a land where tombstones grow?

3

We cannot bid farewell,
pluck out the rooted what-will-live.
Repudiated jungle ways
of mystical loons
and bloody jugglers,
abhorrent ancestry
of swastika swallowers—
not to these, never to these
can we not say farewell.
We cannot bid farewell
to snow-bearded winters
brooding on the dream posterity
of green prophetic spring:
we cannot bid farewell
to the voice in Rama weeping,
Rachel weeping for her children;
to Mann hewing at the shackles
where fettered truth lies groaning;
to Montaigne's skeptical humanity
and tender chiding of philosophy
for barren whoredom;
to ancient canticles of love;
we cannot bid farewell
to Christ ironical with sand
and parables of coins and heaven's kingdom;
to light-bearers surviving vultures;
to meek Hosea inheritor of the earth;
to lovers and freemen, preaching
mine is thine, comfort ye,
and I scorn not thy countenance,
only tell me is my brother well:
we cannot bid farewell to these,
nor to them who loved and cried
unheeded in the wilderness.

4

Beware the prophet in Caesar:
believe in me, counsels Caesar,
machines and dynamos,
sacrifice and warrior's death,
the holy mysteries;
who dies for me believes in me
and he shall live in Valhalla.
Beware Caesar—he hath the falling sickness,
and he shall fall
no lower than the earth,
for death knows neither Caesar
nor his promised lies.

5

We cannot say farewell to what remains
Of faith in beauty beauty mirroring;
In mercy that proscribes all human anguish:
In freedom that no esoteric rites
Will bide; in diuturnity of peace
And intercourse among inquiring men
Of love; in valiance born of tenderness.
We cannot say farewell to love and time
Destroying, roots and all, sword's vanity
And horror, stony hearts, and walls of hate,
Their venomed builders, villainy and villains:
We cannot say farewell to voices crying
Courage: we cannot bid farewell to them
Whose memory shines upon our dark dejection,
And strengthens us whose last defense is our
Conviction that we cannot say farewell
To valiant men that for disclosing truth
Were brought to bitter martyrdom:

Never farewell to those who went their ways
Still armed with love: proud hearts, their bold emprise
Asked neither pardon nor consent: wherefore,
To man's victorious return to earth
Shall we be faithful, never bid farewell.

Biographical Notes

The issues of The Menorah Journal *in which the selections in this book appeared are identified at the end of each of the following notes.*

JACOB BERNARD AGUS was born in Poland in 1911 and came to America in 1927. Educated at Yeshiva College and Harvard University, he has distinguished himself as both rabbi and scholar. He now serves as rabbi of Beth El Congregation, Baltimore, Maryland. Among his books are *Banner of Jerusalem* and *The Evolution of Jewish Thought*. XXXVII, 1 (Winter, 1949), 10-36.

CHARLES ANGOFF was brought to Boston from Minsk, Russia, in 1908 at the age of six. After graduation from Harvard College in 1923, he became a newspaperman and then an editor of the *American Mercury, The Nation,* and the *North American Review*. He is a member of the faculty of New York University and Fairleigh Dickinson University. *Summer Storm,* the sixth of a projected series of ten novels, was published in 1963. XLIX, 1 & 2 (Autumn-Winter, 1962), 136-147.

ISAAK BABEL (1894-1941), the son of a Jewish tradesman, was born and educated in Odessa and moved to St. Petersburg at the age of twenty-one. He served with the Cossacks in their campaign against the Whites and the Poles. His work was first published by Gorky, and his two books, *Odessa Tales* and *Red Cavalry* have won him an international reputation. He disappeared in a concentration camp during one of the Stalin purges. XVI, 1 (January, 1929), 70-77.

BERTHA BADT-STRAUSS, born in Breslau, Germany, in 1903, came to America in 1939. She was educated at London University College and received her Ph.D. from Breslau. Among her works are *Rahel und ihre Zeit* and *Moses Mendelssohn, der Mann und das Werk*. XXXIX, 1 (Spring, 1951), 90-100.

SALO WITTMAYER BARON was born in Tarnow, Austria, in 1895 and was educated at the Jewish Theological Seminary in Vienna and the University of Vienna. He served as Professor of History at the Jewish Institute of Religion in New York from 1926 to 1930 and occupied the chair of Jewish History, Literature, and Institutions on the Miller Foundation at Columbia University from 1931 to 1963. His major work is *A Social and Religious History of the Jews* of which eight volumes have appeared. XIV, 6 (June, 1928), 515-526.

M.Y. BEN GAVRIEL (born Eugen Hoeflich) was born in Vienna in 1894.

Educated at the University of Vienna, he became the editor of *Das Zelt,* a literary monthly, and wrote several books (*Feuer im Osten, Der Rote Mond,* and *Der Weg in Das Land*) devoted to a theory of Pan-Asian unity. He became a resident of Palestine in 1926 and adopted a Hebrew name. XI, 2 (April, 1925), 184-185.

YITZHAK BEN-ZWI (born Isaac Simselevitz, 1884-1963) was born in Poltava, Russia. Educated at the University of Kiev, he was a founder of the Poalei-Zion and emigrated to Palestine where he became a labor leader and the second President of the State of Israel. He wrote on labor and historical subjects. XVIII, 3 (March, 1930), 262-266.

LIBBY BENEDICT (née Goldberg) was born in Kansas City, Missouri, and studied at New York University. She traveled abroad as a free-lance journalist and wrote articles, verse, literary criticism, and a novel, *The Refugees.* XXXVI, 1 (Winter, 1948), 52.

LOUIS BERG was born in Kovno, Russia, in 1900 and grew up in Portsmouth, Virginia. Most of his fiction was published in *The Menorah Journal* in the twenties. He wrote a column on Hollywood for many years in *This Week.* XIV, 1 (January, 1928), 85-93.

CHAIM NACHMAN BIALIK (1873-1934) was born in Radi, Russia. He became a major figure in the Hebrew revival and made his home in Palestine. He excelled as poet, printer, translator, and editor. An annual prize for Hebrew Literature has been established in his name. Much of his verse and a number of his books have been translated into English. XIX, 2 (November-December, 1930), 183-184; XX, 1 (Spring 1932), 20.

RANDOLPH SILLIMAN BOURNE (1856-1918) was born in Bloomfield, New Jersey, and was educated in Europe and Columbia University. He wrote on educational and sociological topics in many of the leading journals, including *The New Republic* and the *Atlantic Monthly.* II, 4 (October, 1916), 277-284.

LOUIS DEMBITZ BRANDEIS (1856-1941) was born in Louisville, Kentucky, and was educated at Harvard. One of the finest legal minds of his time, he was appointed as Associate Justice of the Supreme Court in 1916. He played an important role in the Zionist movement during and after World War I. I, 1 (January, 1915), 13-19.

MARTIN BUBER was born in Vienna in 1878. Educated at several German universities, he won an international reputation for his rendering of Hasidic legends into German and his espousal of cultural Zionism. He made his home in Palestine and was a member of the faculty of the Hebrew University. He has written numerous books on biblical, religious and philosophical themes, many of which have been translated into English and have won great vogue. XXIV, 3 (October-December, 1936), 272-275.

JACOB CAHAN was born in Slutsk, Russia, in 1881 and was educated at the University of Berne. Poet, editor, and scholar, he has played an important role in the renascence of Hebrew literature. VIII, 6 (December, 1922), 347-352.

ELLIOT ETTELSON COHEN (1899-1959) was born in Des Moines, Iowa, and educated at Yale University. He served as an editor of *The Menorah Journal* in the twenties and later was the first editor of *Commentary*. XIX, 3 (March, 1931), 308-318.

MORRIS RAPHAEL COHEN (1880-1947) was born in Minsk, Russia, and came to the United States in 1892. Educated at the College of the City of New York and Harvard University, he taught mathematics and philosophy at many institutions of higher learning and wrote influential works on philosophy and the history of ideas. XI, 4 (August, 1925), 332-341.

LUCY SHILKRET DAVIDOWICZ was born in New York City in 1915 and studied at Hunter College, Columbia University, and the Yiddish Scientific Institute in Vilna, Lithuania. She serves on the staff of the Institute of Human Relations of the American Jewish Committee and has written on social and political subjects. XXXVIII, 1 (Winter, 1950), 88-103.

BABETTE DEUTSCH was born in New York City in 1895 and educated at Barnard College. She has excelled as poet, literary critic, novelist, and translator, and is the author of a score of books. VIII, 2 (April, 1922), 79-80.

IRWIN EDMAN (1896-1954) was born in New York City and educated at Columbia University. Long a professor of philosophy at Columbia, he wrote verse, fiction, and works on psychological and philosophical themes. X, 5 (November-December, 1924), 421-427.

IRVING FINEMAN was born in New York City in 1893 and was educated at Harvard University and the Massachusetts Institute of Technology. He taught engineering and literature at various colleges and later was a script writer in Hollywood. Of his novels, *Hear Ye Sons* and *Ruth* are memorable. XVI, 2 (February, 1929), 169-179.

JOSEF FRAENKEL was born in Warsaw, Poland, in 1903 and studied at the University of Vienna. A lawyer and journalist, he has written a standard biography of Theodor Herzl. He lives in London. XXXVI, 1 (Winter, 1948), 140-144.

FELIX FRANKFURTER was born in Vienna in 1882 and was educated at the College of the City of New York and Harvard University. He was associated with Brandeis in the Zionist movement. He was a Professor of Law at Harvard until 1939 when he was appointed by President Franklin D. Roosevelt to the United States Supreme Court. He is the author of many works, including *Mr. Justice Holmes and the Supreme Court* and *Felix Frankfurter Reminisces*. XXXVIII, 1 (Winter, 1950), 1-5.

ESTI DRUCKER FREUD was born in Vienna in 1901 and was educated at the University of Vienna. She is a speech and voice therapist at the Cornell

Medical School and several New York hospitals. XXXVI, 1 (Winter, 1948), 126-130.

YOSSEF GAER was born in a Bessarabian village in 1896 and attended schools and college in Canada and the United States. He has published works on the Bible, religion and legendry. He is the founder and director of the Jewish Heritage Foundation in Los Angeles. XI, 6 (December, 1925), 627-629.

LOUIS GINZBERG (1873-1953) was born in Kovno, Russia, and came to America in 1899. Educated at the Universities of Berlin, Strassburg and Heidelberg, he was one of the leading talmudic scholars of his time. He served for a generation as Professor of Talmud and Rabbinics at the Jewish Theological Seminary, New York, and was honored with a citation at the Harvard Tercentenary in 1936. His erudite works number more than 500, but he is known to the general reader by his seven-volume collection of *The Legends of the Jews*. VII, 2 (June, 1921), 93-102.

LOUIS GOLDING (1895-1958) was born in Manchester, England, and was educated at the Manchester Grammar School and at Oxford University. Novelist, poet, essayist, and traveler, he wrote numerous books and was considered the literary heir of Israel Zangwill. XII, 5 (October-November, 1926) 459-470.

ROBERT GORDIS was born in Brooklyn, New York, in 1908 and was educated at the College of the City of New York, The Dropsie College of Philadelphia and the Jewish Theological Seminary, New York. A leading rabbi and Bible scholar, he is Professor of Bible at the Jewish Theological Seminary, New York, and has taught at many other institutions of higher learning. He is the author of numerous books and articles on biblical and religious themes. XXV, 1 (January-March, 1937), 20-32.

BERNARD GORIN (real name Isaac Goido, 1868-1925) was born in Lida, Lithuania, and after a life of great literary activity died in New York City. He wrote many stories and articles in Yiddish, but his chief work is *A History of the Jewish Stage for Two Thousand Years*. XIII, 2 (April, 1927), 205-208.

MORDECAI GROSSMAN was born in Minsk, Russia, in 1897 and came to America in 1911. He is a Doctor of Philosophy of Columbia University and wrote occasional articles on Jewish and philosophical themes as well as *The Philosophy of Helvetius*. XVI, 2 (February, 1929), 97-111.

FRANCIS HACKETT was born in Kilkenny, Ireland, in 1883 and attended Clongowes Wood College, Kildare, Ireland. He came to America in 1900 and distinguished himself as author, editor, and critic. Among his numerous works are two volumes of literary criticism, *Horizons* and *The Invisible Center*. X, 4 (August-September, 1924), 403-404.

MOSES HADAS was born in Atlanta, Georgia, in 1900 and was educated at Emory University, Columbia University, and the Jewish Theological Seminary of America. One of the most distinguished classical scholars, he has served for many years as Jay Professor of Greek at Columbia University. He is the author of many learned books and articles and the translator of Greek and Hebrew classics. XLVII, 1 & 2 (Autumn-Winter, 1959), 61-67.

JUDAH HALEVI (*circa* 1085-1142) was born in Toledo, Spain, and probably died in Palestine. He was both physician and poet-philosopher. Among his writings available in English are his philosophical work, *Book of the Khazars* and *Selected Poems* translated by Nina Salaman. XXXIII, 2 (October-December, 1945), 196.

ALBERT HALPER was born in Chicago, Illinois, in 1904 and studied at Northwestern University. The author of numerous novels and short stories, he is regarded as one of the significant American writers. XIX, 2 (November-December, 1930), 142-157.

JOHN HASTINGS was born in New York City in 1912 and studied at Ohio Wesleyan University, Harvard, and the Sorbonne in Paris. Musician, playwright and novelist, he is a well-known critic and interpreter of the seven arts. XXXVI, 2 (Spring, 1948), 196-215.

HENRY HURWITZ (1886-1961) was born in a Lithuanian village and grew up in Gloucester, Massachusetts. Educated at Harvard University, he was a founder of the Harvard Menorah Society, a leader of the Menorah Movement, and served as editor of *The Menorah Journal* from 1915 to 1961. A Valedictory Issue of the Journal (vol. XLIX) was published in his memory. XXXVI, 4 (Autumn, 1948), 281-299.

RUTH SAPIN HURWITZ (1888-1961) was born in New Albany, Indiana, and was educated at Wellesley College. She wrote short stories and articles on educational and welfare topics, and collaborated with her husband, Henry Hurwitz, in Menorah activities. A volume of her writings and unpublished manuscripts is being prepared for publication. XXXV, 1 (January-March, 1947), 111-126.

CHARLES EDWARD ISRAEL was born in Evansville, Indiana, in 1920, and studied at the University of Cincinnati, the Hebrew Union College and the University of North Carolina. He served in the U.S. Merchant Marine in World War II and as a welfare aide in postwar Germany. After writing dramas and documentaries in Hollywood and Canada, he has devoted himself to fiction. His novels, *The Mark* and *Rizpah*, have been made into films. XXXVII, 4 (Autumn, 1949), 311-327.

HORACE MEYER KALLEN was born in Silesia, Germany, in 1882, and brought to America at the age of five. Educated at Harvard, Oxford and Paris, he has taught in many institutions of higher learning and written hundreds of essays and books on education, esthetics, politics, philosophy, and religion. His eightieth year was widely celebrated, and he continues to teach at The New School in New York City. XXXIX, 2 (Autumn, 1951), 109-143.

ALLEN KANFER was born in St. Louis, Missouri, and studied at Washington

University and New York University. He teaches English at the Grover
Cleveland High School of Queens, New York, and has published verse in
the quality magazines. XXXI, 1 (January-March, 1943), 15; XXVI, 1
(January-March, 1938), 45-49.

MORDECAI MENAHEM KAPLAN was born in Swenziany, Lithuania, in 1881
and came to America in 1889. He was educated at the College of the City
of New York, Columbia University, and the Jewish Theological Seminary
of America where he is Professor Emeritus of Homiletics. The founder and
leader of the Reconstructionist movement, his statement of the religious
philosophy of Judaism first appeared in *The Menorah Journal.* He has
written numerous articles and papers as well as a score of books. XXI, 1
(April-June, 1933), 33-52.

ABRAHAM MOSES KLEIN was born in Montreal in 1909 and was educated
at the Montreal Yeshivah and McGill University. He has been lawyer,
editor, and publicist. An outstanding poet, he has published a considerable
body of verse and *The Second Scroll,* a highly acclaimed novel. XVII, 1
(October, 1929), 86-88.

LAWRENCE KOHLBERG was born in Bronxville, New York, in 1927 and was
educated at the University of Chicago. During 1947-48 he worked as
engineer on crews, bringing Haganah ships to Mediterranean ports. XXXVI,
4 (Autumn, 1948), 385-399.

MILTON RIDVAS KONVITZ was born in Safad, Palestine, in 1908 and came
to America in 1915. He was educated at New York University and Cornell
University where he has been Professor of Industrial and Labor Relations
and of Law since 1946. He has published many articles and books on
social, economic, religious, and legal subjects, and has received several
honorary degrees. XLIX (Autumn-Winter, 1962), 120-129.

ISRAEL MEIR LASK was born in London, England, in 1905 and settled in
Palestine in 1930. His verse, criticism, and translations from the Hebrew
were introduced to American readers in *The Menorah Journal.* He has
Englished most of the modern Hebrew poets and the major Hebrew novel-
ists. XLIX, 1 & 2 (Autumn-Winter, 1962), 130-135.

MARGHANITA LASKI was born in London, England, and studied at Oxford
University. She is the daughter of Neville Laski and granddaughter of the
late Haham Moses Gaster. She has written a number of novels, a work of
literary criticism, and is a frequent contributor to magazines. XXXV, 2
(April-June, 1947), 212-215.

CORNEL LENGYEL was born in Fairfield, Connecticut, in 1915. Dramatist,
historian, poet, and lecturer, he has received numerous awards for poetry
and literature. His verse was recorded at the Library of Congress in 1961.
XLIX, 1 & 2 (Autumn-Winter, 1962), 32.

WILLIAM ELLERY LEONARD (1876-1944) was born in Plainfield, New Jersey.
He served for many years as Professor of English at the University of Wis-

consin and was one of the leading American poets of his generation. I, 1 (January, 1915), 20-22.

MEYER LEVIN was born in Chicago in 1905 and studied at the University of Chicago. He has excelled as reporter, columnist, dramatist, and novelist. He now lives in Israel. Many of his books, including *The Search, Compulsion,* and *The Fanatic,* have won international recognition. XXXIV, 1 (April-June, 1946), 122-132.

EMANUEL LITVINOFF was born in London, England, in 1915, and was educated at the public schools. He served as an officer in the British Army for six years in World War II. His poetry was introduced to the American public in *The Menorah Journal.* XXXIX, 2 (Autumn, 1951), 162.

MARVIN LOWENTHAL was born in Bradford, Pennsylvania, in 1890, and was educated at the University of Wisconsin and Harvard University. Critic, historian, translator, and expert on Montaigne, he has been a lifelong exponent of Zionism and Jewish humanism. An editor of *The Menorah Journal,* he was a major contributor to its pages. Among his notable books are *A World Passed By* and *A History of the Jews in Germany.* XI, 2 (April, 1925), 190-196; XI, 2 (April, 1925), 190-196.

ITZIK MANGER was born in Berlin in 1900 and grew up in Rumania. A wanderer since youth, he is a foremost Yiddish balladist and poet. In 1952 he was honored by the Yiddish literary world with the publication of a 450-page volume of his selected poems and ballads. XL, 1 (Spring, 1952), 67-80.

MAX LEOPOLD MARGOLIS (1866-1932) was born in Merecz, Russia, and studied in several European universities and at Columbia University. He held professorships in Bible and Semitics at a number of institutions of higher learning and was the author of numerous learned papers and books in his field. He served as Editor-in-Chief of the English translation of the Bible published by the Jewish Publication Society in 1917. I, 1 (January, 1915), 33-38.

FRITZ MAUTHNER (1850-1923) was born in Horspitz, Bohemia, and studied at several Czech and German universities. He was a free-lance journalist and philosopher and the author of many works of criticism and philosophy. X, 1 (February, 1924), 1-14.

GEORGE FOOT MOORE (1851-1931) was born in West Chester, Pennsylvania, and studied at Yale University, the Union Theological Seminary, and European universities. He served as Frothingham Professor of Religion at Harvard and crowned a career of great scholarly achievement with a three-volume work, *Judaism in the First Centuries of the Christian Era.* VIII, 1 (February, 1922), 1-14.

LEWIS MUMFORD was born in Flushing, New York, in 1895, studied at the College of the City of New York, and was a United States Navy radio operator during World War I. An outstanding American intellectual, he is the author of many books and articles, among them the notable series, *Technics and Civilization, The Culture of Cities,* and *The Condition of Man.* VIII, 3 (June, 1922), 129-138.

ADOLPH SOLOMON OKO (1883-1944) was born in Shavel, Lithuania, and studied at several European universities. He was an expert on Spinoza and served as an editor of *The Menorah Journal.* For many years he was Librarian of the Hebrew Union College in Cincinnati. XII, 5 (October-November, 1926), 449-458.

MAX OSBORN (1847-1946) was born in Berlin and before he came to New York City in 1940 he was a leading art critic and historian in Germany. He wrote a history of art and a number of monographs on individual modern painters. XXXV, 3 (October-December, 1947), 284-298.

ISAAC LOEB PERETZ (1851-1915) was born in Zamascz, Poland, and became one of the masters of modern Yiddish literature. His genius found expression in drama, poetry, journalism, and short shories. He was also an ardent advocate of social reform, espousing the cause of working people in Poland. XXV, 2 (April-June, 1937), 172-177.

JAKOB PICARD was born in Wangen, Germany, in 1883 and studied at the Universities of Munich, Berlin and Heidelberg. Before coming to America in 1940, he practiced law in Germany and Switzerland and wrote poetry, criticism and short stories which appeared in English translation in *The Marked One and Other Stories.* XXX, 2 (July-September, 1942), 220-225.

LUIGI PIRANDELLO (1867-1936) was born in Girengti, Italy, and studied at the universities at Palermo, Rome and Bonn. One of the major modern playwrights, he also published volumes of criticism, poetry and stories. X, 1 (February, 1924), 15-20.

EMANUEL RACKMAN was born in Albany, New York, in 1910 and was educated at Columbia University and Yeshiva University. He has distinguished himself as rabbi, teacher and writer, and published articles and books on legal and religious subjects. XXXIX, 2 (Autumn, 1951), 163-168.

JOHN REWALD was born in Berlin, Germany, in 1912 and studied at the Sorbonne in Paris. Before coming to America in 1941, he was an established art critic and was awarded the Prix Charles Blanc of the Académie Française for a work on Cézanne. XXXI, 2 (July-September, 1943), 137-146.

CHARLES REZNIKOFF was born in Brooklyn, New York, in 1894 and was educated at the University of Missouri and New York University (LL.B.). He contributed verse, drama, and fiction to *The Menorah Journal* for over thirty years and served as a Contributing Editor. He has published numerous volumes of verse, fiction, history and biography, and now serves as editor of the *Jewish Frontier.* XVII, 2 (November, 1929); XXXII, 1 (April-June, 1944), 1-4.

BERNARD GERSON RICHARDS was born in Keidan, Lithuania, and came to

America in 1886. He was a founder of the American Jewish Congress in 1915 and was Secretary of the American Jewish Delegation to the Peace Conference in Paris in 1919. He has contributed to English and Yiddish periodicals, and is now Director of the Jewish Information Bureau in New York City. XXXVIII, 1 (Winter, 1950), 80-87.

MOISHE RIVLIN was born in Jerusalem, Palestine, in 1896. He came to America in 1916, and returned to Palestine two years later as a member of the Jewish Legion. A graduate of the School of Journalism at New York University, he served for many years on the staff of the New York Jewish Morning Journal. XIV, 5 (May, 1928), 491-496.

ISAAC ROSENBERG (1890-1918) was born in Bristol, England. He was one of a number of gifted young poets who were killed in action in World War I. A collected volume of his verse, Poems, was published posthumously. XIX, 4 (June, 1931), 372.

HENRY MOSES ROSENTHAL was born in Louisville, Kentucky, in 1906 and was educated at the Jewish Theological Seminary and Columbia University. He contributed essays and sketches to The Menorah Journal and is the author of several books on philosophical subjects. He is Professor of Philosophy at Hunter College in New York City. XXXV, 3 (October-December, 1947), 241-252.

CECIL ROTH was born in London, England, and was educated at Oxford University where he has served for many years as Reader in Jewish Studies. He has published numerous historical articles and essays and over thirty volumes, and is one of the leading contemporary Jewish historians. He settled in Jerusalem, Israel, in 1964. XVII, 3 (December, 1929), 219-233.

ABRAHAM ROTHBERG was born in New York City in 1922 and attended Brooklyn College, the University of Iowa, and Columbia University. He teaches English at Hofstra College, Long Island, New York, and has contributed fiction and criticism to the quality magazines. XXXVI, 2 (Spring, 1948), 184-195.

ISAAC MAX RUBINOW (1875-1936) was born in Grodno, Russia, and came to America in 1893. Educated at Columbia University and New York University, he first served the U.S. Government as an economic expert and then became a leader in social welfare. He organized and administered the American Zionist Medical Unit in Palestine (1918-1922). He was the author of hundreds of studies on economic, social and political subjects. XIX, 3 (March, 1931), 209-222.

EDWIN HERBERT SAMUEL, son of Lord Samuel, was born in London, England, in 1898 and educated at Westminster School and Balliol College, Oxford. He settled in Palestine and has served as government official in both the Mandatory and Israel regimes. He contributed articles and sketches to The Menorah Journal over many years. He is Principal of the Institute of

Public Administration in Israel. XLIV, 1 & 2 (Spring-Summer, 1956), 115-119.

MAURICE SAMUEL was born in Macin, Rumania, in 1895 and came to America in 1914. He studied at the High School in Manchester, England, and at Manchester University. He has been a lifetime advocate of Zionism and an influential lecturer on Jewish themes. Essayist, novelist, critic and translator, his numerous articles, books, reviews and translations have won him international note. His book, *The World of Sholem Aleichem*, is considered a masterpiece. IX, 6 (December, 1925), 602-606; IX, 3 (August, 1923), 215; IX, 2 (June, 1923), 83-87; IX, I (February, 1923), 20-22; XIII, 1 (February, 1927), 63-67.

VISCOUNT SAMUEL (1870-1963), born Herbert Samuel in Liverpool, England, and educated at Balliol College, Oxford, was made a Viscount by King George VI on the occasion of his coronation. He was the leader of the British Liberal Party, held many Cabinet posts and was the first High Commissioner to Palestine (1920-25). The author of many books on philosophy, he was awarded the Order of Merit by Queen Elizabeth II for "meritorious service toward the advancement of Art, Literature, and Science." XLVIII, 1 & 2 (Autumn-Winter, 1960), 9-30.

SIEGFRIED SASSOON was born in Sussex, England, in 1886 and educated at Cambridge University. He fought as an infantryman both in France and Palestine in World War 1, with an interval of rebellious pacifism when he was declared "temporarily insane" by British military authorities. He published a number of volumes of poetry and two volumes of memoirs which won international recognition. XX, 1 (April-June, 1932), 74.

WILLIAM SCHACK was born in Brooklyn, New York, in 1898 and studied at Cornell University. Journalist, editor, and drama and art critic, he contributed frequently to *The Menorah Journal*. XXV, 3 (October-December, 1937), 333-339.

ZALMAN SCHNEOUR (1887-1959) was born in Shklov, Russia, and lived in Odessa and Vilna before sojourning in the capitals of western Europe. A Yiddish and Hebrew writer, he became a major figure in modern Hebrew poetry. Aside from the translation of his novel *Noah Pandre* and some of his verse in anthologies, there is an English version of selected writings in *Restless Spirit* by Moshe Spiegel. In 1951 he was awarded the Louis LaMed Prize in New York and the Bialik Prize in Tel Aviv. He died in Israel. IX, 2 (June, 1923), 83-87.

EDWIN SEAVER was born in Washington, D. C., in 1900 and was educated at the Worcester Academy and Harvard College. He contributed poetry, criticism and fiction to the quality magazines and is the author of a number of novels. VIII, 5 (October, 1922), 324.

MORTON SEIF was born in New York City in 1928 and studied at the University of North Carolina. He has contributed criticism and poetry to literary journals. XLI, 1 (Spring, 1953), 62.

ISAAC BASHEVIS SINGER was born in Radzymun, Poland, in 1904, of a family of notable writers and rabbis, and came to America in 1935. A member of the staff of the *Jewish Daily Forward,* he has written numerous short stories and novels, many of which have been translated into English. He is recognized as the most distinguished living Yiddish novelist. XLIX, 1 & 2 (Autumn-Winter, 1962), 71-76.

WALTER SORELL was born in Vienna in 1905 and was educated at the University of Vienna. Before coming to America, he was editor of *Die Literarischen Monatshefte* and is now a contributing editor of *Dance Magazine* in New York. XLII, 1 & 2 (Spring-Summer, 1954), 79-95.

ANDRÉ SPIRE was born in Nancy, France, in 1868 and was educated at the Sorbonne in Paris. A high governmental official for many years, he is a pre-eminent man of letters in France and although a nonegenarian, is still an active writer. He has published many volumes of poetry and criticism, including distinguished works on Jewish themes. XLIV, 1 & 2 (Spring-Summer, 1956), 67-85; XV, 2 (August, 1928), 117-118.

MOSES STAVSKY was born in Onterpol, Russia, in 1884 and settled in Palestine in 1911. He is the owner of a dairy farm on the outskirts of Tel Aviv, and has written stories in both Yiddish and Hebrew. XVIII, 4 (April 1930), 316-322.

MILTON STEINBERG (1903-1952) was born in Rochester, New York, and studied at the College of the City of New York, the Jewish Theological Seminary, and Columbia University. He was a noted rabbi and a leader of the Reconstructionist Movement. His books on Jewish history and problems had great vogue, and his historical novel, *As a Driven Leaf,* is noteworthy. XXXVII, 2 (Spring, 1949), 163-180.

OSCAR SOLOMON STRAUS (1850-1926) was born in Otterberg, Germany, and educated at Columbia University. His services as statesman and peace advocate are recorded in the pages of American history. He was the author of several volumes dealing with the origin of the republican form of government and the development of religious liberty, in the United States. VI, 6 (December, 1920), 305-310.

SAUL TCHERNICHOWSKY (1875-1943) was born in the Crimea, Russia, and settled in Palestine in 1924. He was one of the pre-eminent Hebrew poets of his time and the translator of Homer, Plato, and Longfellow into Hebrew. His collected works were published in ten volumes. IX, 1 (February, 1923), 20-22.

LOUIS UNTERMEYER was born in New York City in 1885 and, after working in the jewelry business until 1923, he devoted himself entirely to a literary career. He has been recognized as critic, editor, poet and translator of the highest excellence, and written and edited numerous books. VII, 1 (February, 1921), 22-27.

JOHANNES URZIDIL was born in Prague, Czechoslovakia, in 1896 and educated at the University of Prague. He came to the United States in 1941, and is the author of volumes of art criticism, biography, and poetry, XL, 1 (Spring, 1952), 112-116.

JOSEPH WECHSBERG was born in Prague, Czechoslovakia, in 1907 and attended the Universities of Vienna, Paris, and Prague. He was an officer in the Czech army, Secretary of the Jewish Party in the Czech Parliament, and editor of the Prague *Tageblatt* and the Jewish weekly *Selbstwehr*. A contributor to numerous magazines, he is now writing in Hollywood, California. XXX, 3 (Autumn, 1942), 313-315.

YEHOASH (real name Solomon Bloomgarden, 1870-1927) was born in Wierzbolowo, Lithuania, and came to America in 1895. An outstanding man of letters of his generation, his collected works consist of twelve volumes of verse and prose. He also published a Lexicon of the Hebrew Elements in Yiddish and a Yiddish translation of the Hebrew Bible. X, 3 (June-July, 1924), 245.

SAMUEL YELLEN was born in Vilna, Lithuania, in 1906 and brought to America a year later. He studied at Western Reserve University and Oberlin College, and now teaches English at Indiana University. His stories and poems have appeared in numerous periodicals. XXXVII, 2 (Spring, 1949), 181-185.

ZALMEN YOFFEH was born in 1898 in New York City where he was educated in the public schools. He was editor of *Every Friday* and contributed articles to magazines until the thirties when he abandoned literary work for a career in public relations. XVII, 3 (December, 1929), 265-275.

ISRAEL ZANGWILL (1864-1926) was born in London and attended the Jews' Free School and London University. He was the most distinguished of Anglo-Jewish authors, excelling in fiction, drama, criticism. He also played a notable role as a champion of the downtrodden and persecuted. The hundredth anniversary of his birth was commemorated throughout the world. VIII, 6 (December, 1922), 338-346.

INDEX OF AUTHORS

INDEX OF TITLES

(959)

INDEX OF TRANSLATORS

THE JACOB R. SCHIFF LIBRARY
OF JEWISH CONTRIBUTIONS TO AMERICAN CIVILIZATION

1. Jacob R. Marcus
   EARLY AMERICAN JEWRY (2 Volumes)
2. Jeanette W. Rosenbaum
   MYER MYERS, GOLDSMITH
3. Robert D. Abrahams
   THE COMMODORE
4. Norman Bentwich
   FOR ZION'S SAKE
5. S. N. Carvalho (Bertram W. Korn, editor)
   INCIDENTS OF TRAVEL AND ADVENTURE IN THE FAR WEST
6. Bernard Postal and Lionel Koppman
   A JEWISH TOURIST'S GUIDE TO THE UNITED STATES
7. Jacob R. Marcus
   MEMOIRS OF AMERICAN JEWS (3 Volumes)
8. Benjamin II (Charles Reznikoff, translator)
   THREE YEARS IN AMERICA (2 Volumes)
9. Rachel Wischnitzer
   SYNAGOGUE ARCHITECTURE IN THE UNITED STATES
10. Edwin Wolf, 2nd, and Maxwell Whiteman
    THE HISTORY OF THE JEWS OF PHILADELPHIA
11. Charles Reznikoff (editor)
    LOUIS MARSHALL (2 Volumes)
12. Alexandra Lee Levin
    THE SZOLDS OF LOMBARD STREET
13. Selig Adler and Thomas E. Connolly
    FROM ARARAT TO SUBURBIA
14. Harry L. Lurie
    A HERITAGE AFFIRMED
15. Moshe Davis
    THE EMERGENCE OF CONSERVATIVE JUDAISM
16. Louis J. Swichkow and Lloyd P. Gartner
    THE HISTORY OF THE JEWS OF MILWAUKEE
17.-19. Joseph L. Blau and Salo W. Baron
    THE JEWS OF THE UNITED STATES 1790-1840
20. Irving Malin and Irwin Stark (editors)
    BREAKTHROUGH
21. Alexandra Lee Levin
    VISION: A BIOGRAPHY OF HARRY FRIEDENWALD
22. Oscar I. Janowsky (editor)
    THE AMERICAN JEW: A REAPPRAISAL
23. Leo W. Schwarz (editor)
    THE MENORAH TREASURY